A Dictionary of

First
Names

SECOND EDITION

PATRICK HANKS,
KATE HARDCASTLE, *and*
FLAVIA HODGES

OXFORD
UNIVERSITY PRESS

OXFORD
UNIVERSITY PRESS

Great Clarendon Street, Oxford OX2 6DP

Oxford University Press is a department of the University of Oxford.
It furthers the University's objective of excellence in research, scholarship,
and education by publishing worldwide in

Oxford New York

Auckland Cape Town Dar es Salaam Hong Kong Karachi
Kuala Lumpur Madrid Melbourne Mexico City Nairobi
New Delhi Shanghai Taipei Toronto

With offices in

Argentina Austria Brazil Chile Czech Republic France Greece
Guatemala Hungary Italy Japan Poland Portugal Singapore
South Korea Switzerland Thailand Turkey Ukraine Vietnam

Oxford is a registered trade mark of Oxford University Press
in the UK and in certain other countries

Published in the United States
by Oxford University Press Inc., New York

British Library Cataloguing in Publication Data

Data available

Library of Congress Cataloging in Publication Data

Data available

Typeset by SPI Publisher Services, Pondicherry, India
Printed in Great Britain by
Clays Ltd., Bungay, Suffolk

ISBN 978-0-19-861060-1

5

HANKS, P and HARDCASTLE, K and HODGES

Contents

Introduction to the Second Edition

It is over fifteen years since the first edition of this standard reference work was published. In that time, fashions in naming have changed. Traditional names such as *John* and *Mary* are in decline, while new coinages such as *Kai* and *Tia* are in favour. Throughout the English-speaking world it is becoming increasingly fashionable to name children with words and coinages that have never been used as names before. Nevertheless, an overwhelming proportion of the English-speaking population still choose familiar traditional names. These are names whose history goes back for thousands of years. They ebb and flow in popularity over time like the sea, and occasionally some of them fall completely out of use—as has happened to Old Testament names that were once popular, especially among Baptists and Methodists: *Ahab*, *Jabez*, and *Zillah*, for example. Perhaps, like the seeds of desert plants, these splendid Old Testament names are waiting patiently for revival, should the rainfall of fashionability come their way again.

Creating new names is now the rage, so it makes sense to start with a brief overview of the ways in which new names are coined.

Coining a New Name

Simply because they are one-off creations, newly coined names are not included in this dictionary. However, some new names that were coined two to four decades ago have now become almost conventional, used by increasing numbers of parents—in which case a dictionary entry is appropriate. Examples include *Jayden*, *Keira*, *Luella*, *Tyrese*. Such a name is particularly likely to come into use if a bearer of it grows up to become famous, as has happened for example in the case of *La Toya* Jackson.

There are five main sources of newly coined names, of which the first is by far the most important, linguistically speaking:

1. The most dramatic name-creating process is one that has been described by one journalist as "throwing the Scrabble tiles at the wall"—creating a name that consists of a string of letters or syllables that have never been used before, either as a word or as a name, in any language. The idea that such names are simply random combinations of letters is amusing but of course not strictly true. There are principles governing the invention of names, just as there are principles for all other kinds of language use. However, these have not yet been systematically studied. Nevertheless, some general principles may be observed. The phonological pattern and spelling-to-speech rules of the language are almost invariably adhered to by parents creating a new name, even though most parents could almost certainly not tell you what the rules are. Language rules such as these exist in the subconscious mind and cannot easily be articulated explicitly. Thus, if coining names from raw phonology were common practice in Polish, it would be possible to make up a name such as *Zbaczdjiew*. Even though this is actually a meaningless string of letters, which (as far as I know) has never been used as a word, a name, or anything else in Polish, its spelling pattern is recognizably Polish and it invites realization according to Polish spelling-to-speech rules—not those of (say) Czech, German, or English. While such coinages are uncommon in the Slavic languages, French, German, and Scandinavian languages—some countries still have laws or regulations that discourage the coinage of new names, often reinforced by the Church—they are increasingly common in English, where it is, of course, the normal rules of English spelling and speech sounds that prevail. Not only is the basic phonology of English observed in these coinages, but certain combinations of syllables and endings are more common than others in name-creation, while some first syllables and last syllables are distinctively male or female. Thus, the first elements *La-* and *Sha-* are regularly used in coining girls' names, and the ending *-a* almost always signals a girl's name. On the other hand, a consonant ending, especially a plosive such as /d/ or /t/, is more often used for boys' names. Name inventors sometimes (by design or accident) invent a name that is actually a rare or obsolete vocabulary word, or a word in another language. This is one reason why caution in name creation is advisable. No one wants to give their child a name that means something unpleasant in Shakespearean English or in another language.

Coinages from raw phonology are particularly favoured in the African American community, where perhaps the most famous example is *Condoleezza*, closely followed by *Oprah*. *Condoleezza* Rice's name is a coinage from first principles, said to have been inspired by the Italian musical direction *con dolcezza*, meaning 'with sweetness'. *Oprah* Winfrey is said to have got her name as the result of a spelling mistake on her birth certificate. Her parents' original intention was to use the biblical name *Orpah*. *Shequoyia*, the middle name of the hiphop artist Ashanti (whose full name is Ashanti Shequoyia Douglas) appears to have been inspired by a species of tree (*sequoia*), blended with the feminine pronoun *she*, with the letter *y* thrown in for luck. (Her first name, *Ashanti*, comes from the name of a West African people.)

The creation of new names which may never have been borne by anyone else before is now common in many communities throughout the English-speaking world. These new names are more common for girls than boys, though they are used for both sexes. Other examples that can be mentioned include *Shanella*, *Shantara*, *Lamazia*, and *Laronia* (for girls); *Feralion*, *Cardrant*, and *Wyrand* (for boys).

2. Another common source of newly coined names is suffixation. Again this is much more common for girls' names than for boys'. An existing name (male or female) is used as the base and a diminutive suffix is added. The suffix is usually a conventional feminine ending, for example *-ina*, *-etta*, *-ella*, and *-linda*. Occasionally the suffixes *-son* and *-man* are used to coin a boy's name. It comes as no surprise to learn that *Patson* is the son of someone called Patrick or that *Geoffson* is the son of Geoffrey. Such coinages often overlap with conventional surnames (which may also be used as male given names), e.g. *Johnson* and *Jefferson*. Female diminutive names such as *Georgina* and *Georgette*, *Marietta*, and *Jacquetta* have been in common use for centuries, but now the suffixes are more productive than ever and coinages such as *Rachelina*, *Jacquella*, and *Margalinda* are commonplace. The name *Waynetta* was invented or adopted by the English comedian Harry Enfield in a spirit of parody of the trend for such coinages, but, like all good parodies, there is more than a grain of truth in it. A glance at the Internet will show that *Waynetta* really is used in the United States. In fact, coinages such as these have been created since at least the 19th century, but what was previously a trickle has become a flood.

3. Blends of existing name elements are another source of coinages, for example *Diandrea*, a blend of *Diana* and *Andrea*. This trend is an extension of the practice, particularly common in the southern U.S., of using two first names as if they were a single given name, as in *Mary Sue*, *Billy Bob*, *Willie Mae*. In such names, it is usually the second element that determines the gender (unlike in French, where *Jean Marie* is a male name rather than female). Compound names are also common in Scandinavia, for example *Maj-Britt*.

4. Respellings of traditional names have been common for many years, and represent a more cautious way of individualizing a traditional given name than some of the types of coinage mentioned above. Examples are *Danyal* (for *Daniel*), *Deidre* (for *Deirdre*), *Deniece* (for *Denise*).

5. Use of vocabulary words as given names. This practice is as old as the 16th century in English, if not older. In some other cultures, for example Chinese and most African languages, it has always been traditional to use vocabulary words to name children. It was favoured by the Puritans in the 17th century, who created names such as *Hope* and *Unity* which became conventional and are still in use today. Other Puritan vocabulary-word names have fared less well: *Comfort*, *Repentence*, *Silence*, and *Temperance*, for instance. The Pilgrim Father William Brewster named his two sons *Wrestling* and *Love* and one of his daughters *Patience*. Of these, only the female name continues in use. The given name *Wrestling*, however, was traditional in the Brewster family of Massachusetts throughout the 17th and 18th centuries. It is probably a reference to the puzzling but evocative story of Jacob wrestling all night with an angel (Genesis 32), or to the notion of the need for a good Christian to be constantly wrestling against sin.

Puritan names derived from vocabulary words almost always had a religious connotation and were generally derived from nouns denoting abstract qualities. In the 19th century the stock of female names was augmented by two other classes of vocabulary words: flower names such as *Marigold* and *Daisy* and gemstone names such as *Ruby* and *Beryl*. Nearly a century later, in the 1960s and 70s—the flower power era—names taken from words denoting natural phenomena became fashionable. *Storm* was already established as a given name by this time, but now it was followed by *Rain, Leaf, River, Ocean*, and many other words, used as names for both boys and girls.

Among the more bizarre names taken from vocabulary words and bestowed on their children by celebrities in recent years are *Banjo, Denim, Audio Science*, and *Pilot Inspektor*. Such names may be bearable for the children of rock stars (has anybody ever asked them how they feel about their names?), but they are definitely not to be recommended outside the glitzy world of show business. Slightly less eccentrically, the Texan film director Robert Rodriguez and his wife Elizabeth Avellan named their children *Rebel, Racer, Rocket*, and *Rogue*. By these standards, names such as *Story, Sonnet*, and *Saffron Sahara* (the latter being the name bestowed on the daughter of Simon Le Bon of Duran Duran) seem positively conservative.

The practice of using vocabulary words as names continues to thrive, and parents in search of an unconventional name for a child could do worse than to search a general English dictionary for inspiration, in place of a traditional names dictionary such as the present volume.

Borrowing Names from Other Languages

Another very noticeable trend in the naming of children in recent years is the increasing use of names from other languages and cultures. Names are borrowed both from living languages and from culturally important languages of the past, even by people who do not speak those languages. It has long been acceptable for people with Irish connections to use traditional Irish names (or Anglicized forms of them) and for people with Welsh ancestry or connections to use traditional Welsh names, for example names taken from the haunting stories of the Mabinogi. Now, the names of characters from Welsh and Irish legend are freely bestowed on children, even in families which have no ethnic connections with Wales or Ireland and even (as in the case of *Sean* and *Siobhan*) when the spelling-to-speech rules of Irish are at variance with those of English.

Names are selected from all the languages of the world, as long as they 'sound right'. The Canadian singer *Shania* Twain, for example, whose beloved step-father was a full-blooded Ojibwa, claims that her adopted first name is from an Ojibwa word meaning 'I'm on my way'. The actor *Keanu* Reeve's first name is from a Hawaiian word meaning 'cool mountain breeze'.

Names from continental European languages were always used in North America among descendants of immigrants from the regions where those languages were spoken, even after these families had ceased to speak the language of the source country. Now, such names are used in the wider English-speaking world, even by people with no ethnic connection with those countries. Spanish and Italian names such as *Antonio, Carlos, Diego, Orlando, Paolo, Romeo*, and *Vincenzo* are well established, as are French *André, René, Renée*, and *Thierry*; and German *Anton, Kai, Karl, Kurt*, and *Steffan*, for example. The stock of Russian names popularized in the English-speaking world in the late 19th century continues to expand with the addition of names such as *Maxim* and *Nikita* (the latter used primarily in the English-speaking world as a girl's name, though exclusively masculine in Russian).

In recognition of the relentless expansion of the 'global village', and the consequent growth of the pool of names available to parents, this edition of the *Oxford Dictionary of First Names* contains thirteen appendices on the most common names in some of the non-English cultures that will be of greatest interest to English-speakers. The integration of some of these sources into the general name bank is at present still in its infancy. The use of Arabic names, in particular, remains more or less discrete, but the trickle has begun; names like *Yasmin*, for example, are to be found among those without connections with the Arab or Muslim world, and in a decade or two the name bank will no doubt be further enriched by the addition of these and an increasingly diverse selection of names from other cultures.

Other Trends and Developments

An interesting feature of recent naming practice is the regular use of names which for centuries were avoided as names for children because some bearer in literature or legend had a bad character or came to a bad end. Examples of such names include *Antigone* (who kills herself after being sentenced to be buried alive), *Cain* (the biblical character who killed his brother, Abel), *Cassandra* (the Trojan prophetess of doom, to whom nobody would listen), *Desdemona* (the innocent wife whose husband, Othello, smothers her wilh a pillow in a fit of blind jealousy), and *Jocasta* (the mother of Oedipus, with whom she inadvertently contracts an incestuous marriage). Apparently, people are less superstitious than they once were, or perhaps the link between a name and its origin and history is taken less seriously now than it was in former times.

The use of surnames as given names is by no means new. All that needs to be said about it was already said in the introduction to the First Edition (see below). A subtle development of this practice, however, is the direct use of place names as first names, as, for example *Brooklyn*, *Chelsea*, and *India*. The choice of such names often seems to arise from a sentimental or romantic attachment of the parents to the place in question. The name *Paris*, for instance, was originally a boy's name taken from Greek legend, but in recent times, it has been used, especially as a girl's name, almost certainly with reference to the French capital rather than to the Trojan prince who abducted Helen of Troy.

PWH
March 2006

Acknowledgements

We would like to record our grateful thanks to the following for their contributions to this second edition of the *Oxford Dictionary of First Names* and the appendices:
Mona Baker (Arabic names), Malcolm Watson (Chinese names), Robin Sawers (German names), Ramesh Krishnamurthy (Indian names), the late Tomas de Bhaldraithe (Irish names), Flavia Hodges (Russian names), Olav Veka (Scandinavian names), Ronald Black (Scottish names), Dieter Kremer (Spanish names), Gwynedd Pierce (Welsh names).

Introduction to the First Edition

Scope of the Work

What is a 'first name'? Strictly, it is the first of a sequence of one or more given names borne by an individual. A given name is one that is bestowed on a child by its parents or guardians at birth, as opposed to an inherited surname. More loosely, the term is used with much the same significance as 'given name'. All the names listed in this book can, of course, be used both as first names and as second or subsequent given names. But the range of names used as second, third, or fourth given names is somewhat wider. Typically, for example, a mother's maiden surname, or an unusual personal name with some special family significance, may be found used in this way. In many cases, this has been a first stage in the transfer of a surname to use as a common conventional given name. Those names that have clearly completed the transfer, for example *Douglas* and *Dudley*, are included in this dictionary. Other, less usual secondary given names are not included here.

A person's given name is a badge of cultural identity. Cultural identity is closely allied to religious identity: religious affiliation and native language are often key factors, overtly or subliminally, in the choice of an appropriate name for a new member of a family. Even agnostics and atheists typically choose names for their children that are common among the sect or religion which they may have rejected but in whose midst they live, rather than totally alien or invented names.

It is difficult to imagine a human culture without personal names. The names that people bear are determined in large part by the culture that they belong to. A woman called *Niamh* can be presumed to be Irish; at the very least, her parents, in choosing this name for her, were announcing some sort of cultural identification with Ireland and Irish culture.

Even the commonest names are to some extent culture-specific in form. *John* is one of the commonest first names in Europe, but it is still a reasonable guess that a man called *John* is English-speaking. If he is German, we expect him to be called *Johann* or *Hans*: the choice of the form *John* for a German is unusual and suggestive of Anglophilia. At the very least, it invites comment or explanation. Names such as *Maria*, which are shared in the same form by several languages, are the exception rather than the rule in Europe, despite the shared cultural history and the cross-fertilization that are characteristic of Europe and that have played such an important part in determining choices of names.

For underlying the differences are deeper unities, connecting naming practices across linguistic boundaries. *John*, *Seán*, *Ia(i)n*, *Giovanni*, *Johann*, *Jean*, *Jan*, *Ivan*, and so on are in one sense all variants of the same name, with the same 'meaning'. A description that is relevant to one will be in large part relevant to another.

The purpose of this dictionary is to record and explain these similarities and differences in the names of Europe and the English-speaking world, giving the forms, linguistic origins, cultural peculiarities, and cognate relationships of each. Where a name that is essentially 'the same name' is found in many different forms in the different languages of Europe, the main entry is placed under the usual English spelling. There are cross-references where differences in spelling mean that two names are more than a few entries apart.

Also included are two supplements on naming traditions that up to now have been largely independent of the European tradition, but that are of increasing interest among English speakers and others. The first of these describes the most frequent given names in the Arab world. These are important not only in their own right, but also because they are the source of the most common Islamic names in every part of the globe where Islam is practised. They provide a striking parallel to the Judaeo-Christian tradition. The other supplement records and explains the most common Indian names. The ancient religions and culture of India have long attracted interest in the West, and the need for summary information on the names from this rich and varied culture is reinforced now by immigration.

The Set of Conventional Given Names

Conventional given names constitute quite a small set of items (compared, say, with surnames or vocabulary words). In each of the main European languages, only a few hundred male names, and even fewer female names, form the inventory from which children's names are ordinarily chosen. This set of common conventional names is supplemented in various ways, for example by the use of surnames and vocabulary words as given names. Some of these new coinages in turn achieve conventional status.

In most European languages, over half of the common conventional names (in some cases, almost all of them) owe their importance to Christian tradition. These common Christian names usually have numerous cognates in the other European languages. In some countries, for example post-revolutionary France and pre-revolutionary Russia, there were official sanctions against straying outside the set of names sanctioned by the Church or the State. Christian names taken from the Old Testament overlap to a large extent with Jewish names of biblical origin, although there are often distinct Jewish forms, either representing the ancient Hebrew more closely or existing in a specific Yiddish, Judezmo, or other form.

This small, central set of Christian and Judaeo-Christian names is usually augmented by a much more language-specific set of survivals of very ancient names from a pre-Christian past. Many of these owe their long-continuing popularity to having been borne by royalty or by members of the aristocracy. In English, for example, such names as *William* and *Richard* are of Germanic origin, while *Malcolm* and *Brian* are from Gaelic. In Scandinavia many ancient Norse names (e.g. *Sigurd*, *Gunnar*, and *Torsten*) can be found in modern use. In Poland the names *Stanisław*, *Kazimierz*, and *Wojciech* represent survivals of a pre-Christian tradition. Polish names of this type very often have Czech cognates, while some Old Slavonic names have survived in Czech but not in Polish. In Russia, on the other hand, the use of such pre-Christian names was forbidden by the Orthodox Church; on the whole, those that are now in use are recent reintroductions from a pre-Christian past, often borrowed under the influence of some other Slavonic language. Conventional Russian names are typically of Byzantine Greek origin, being those bestowed in honour of saints venerated by the Orthodox Church.

The set of conventional Christian, Judaeo-Christian, and pre-Christian Germanic and Celtic names is further augmented in other ways. Typically, vocabulary words, surnames, topographic terms, and place names may be found pressed into service as given names. Some of these are so rare that they have no place in a dictionary. Others are found over the centuries mainly in just one family, and a few of these (for example *Fulk* and *Kenelm*) are recorded here. Finally, we must mention the class of 'made-up' names, usually blends of parts of other names, such as *Charlene* and *Raelene*. A few of these have become used conventionally and are recorded here.

Given Names in Use over the Centuries

In some cultures, the relationship between names and vocabulary words is generally transparent: that is, the names are just special uses of ordinary words. In such cultures, a name can be chosen on account of its meaning, as well as on grounds of its historical or religious associations or euphony. This is not the case with English, nor with most of the languages of Western Europe. English names are mostly opaque: that is, the 'meaning' of almost all of them is to be sought in languages other than modern English, often ancient languages no longer spoken and only studied by specialists.

Because of this, among English speakers (and indeed among speakers of French, German, Spanish, and so on) there can rarely be any question of choosing a name for a child on the basis of its meaning. A name is chosen either on ornamental grounds—'because it sounds nice'—or in honour of some close relative. These are private reasons for choice, which cannot be recorded in a dictionary.

There are, however, other, more public reasons for choosing one name rather than another, and these have clearly affected the continued popularity of certain names over the centuries. There are definite vogues for given names; they come into fashion and go out again for reasons that can sometimes be recorded: for example, a name may experience a sudden increase in use after it has been used for a character in a popular book, film, or television series. More seriously (but less noticeably), a particular set of names may be associated with a religious sect or cult, which will affect the popularity of those names. In other cases, the popularity of certain names seems to ebb and flow with the generations, so that (for example) some of the names that came into vogue in the seventies can be expected to go out again during the nineties. Some have already gone. Leslie Dunkling has carried out a most interesting partial survey of the rise and fall in the popularity of English names.

Not all names undergo significant fluctuations in popularity. Some, such as *John* and *Mary*, are so widespread that any factor that might diminish their popularity for one reason is offset by other factors increasing their popularity. These are the hardy perennials of nomenclature.

Biblical Names

The most widespread of all given names are those taken from a biblical original. Names derived from the major characters whose story is told in the Old Testament (and indeed many of the minor ones) are borne by Jews and Christians alike in every country of Europe, in the United States, Canada, Australia, New Zealand, the West Indies, South Africa, and elsewhere. This dictionary records the various forms in which such names appear in the major vernacular languages of Europe: names such as *Adam* and *Eve*; *Benjamin*, *Joseph*, and *Jacob*; *David*; *Sarah*, *Deborah*, *Rebecca*, and *Ruth*.

Some of these Old Testament names are rare now. Among non-Jews, names such as *Reuben*, *Seth*, *Hezekiah* and *Caleb*, *Bathsheba*, *Zillah*, and *Beulah* are associated particularly with Nonconformist sects of the 17th century. *Adam* was a popular name among such groups, but *Eve* was shunned, on the grounds that the biblical Eve brought sin into the world.

Many of these Old Testament biblical names were revived among Christian fundamentalists of the 19th century. A few, especially female names such as *Abigail*, have survived or been revived in modern use, but others have once again dropped out of fashion. Some of them, for example *Moses*, *Solomon*, and *Zipporah*, are now found almost exclusively among Jews.

David is one of the most common names among English speakers of all creeds. It is borne by Christians and Jews alike. As well as being the name of the greatest of all the biblical kings of Israel, it was also borne by the patron saint of Wales and by two kings of Scotland. These are among the reasons why *David* is freely used as a Gentile name in the English-speaking world. In other countries, however, there is no such tradition of Gentile use, and the name is regarded as characteristically Jewish. In general, Old Testament names are found among both Jews and Protestants, but are uncommon among Roman Catholics.

New Testament names are shared by Christians of all sects and persuasions, and their overwhelming frequency in all the countries of Europe, as well as in North and South America, Australasia, and elsewhere, bears witness to the pervasive influence of Christianity over the past two millennia. It is only in the Islamic world and the Far East that New Testament names are rare or not used.

The most important names in the New Testament are those of the four evangelists, *Matthew*, *Mark*, *Luke*, and *John*, and the apostles, principally *Peter*, *James*, *Andrew*, *Thomas*,

Philip, Bartholomew, John, Matthew, and *Simon.* The gospels agree that there were twelve apostles (twelve was a number with symbolic significance in Judaic tradition, as witness the twelve tribes of Israel). However, they do not agree on the precise identity of the twelve names. The picture is further complicated by the fact that in at least one case (*James*) the same name was shared by two different apostles, and by the fact that St Paul is generally regarded as an apostle, and indeed refers to himself in his letters as 'an apostle, not of men, neither by men, but by Jesus Christ, and God the Father, who raised him from the dead' (Galatians I: 1). There is no evidence that St Paul knew Christ personally before the Crucifixion, so he was not one of the original twelve.

John is trebly important as a Christian name based on the New Testament: it was borne by an apostle (the son of Zebedee), by the author of the fourth gospel, and by the forerunner of Christ, John the Baptist. In France, Italy, and elsewhere, compound names such as *Jean-Baptiste* and *Giambattista* distinguish the Baptist from the apostle and the evangelist. The frequency of forms of *John* among early Christians ensured that it would be borne by some early saints, which further reinforced its conventional status.

With the exception of Mary, the mother of Jesus, very few women play a major role in the gospels. This helps to explain why the set of conventional female Christian names is even smaller than that for males, and why *Mary* has been so enormously popular.

In Roman Catholic countries the Virgin Mary is the subject of a religious cult of great importance and influence. In Spain, in particular, a set of female names has grown up associated with different aspects of this cult: names such as *Dolores, Mercedes, Concepción, Presentación,* and *Candelaria.* In some cases, for example *Pilar* and *Rosario,* these are used as female names even though the vocabulary word from which each is derived is masculine.

The name *Mary* is borne by others in the New Testament—principally Mary Magdalene, a woman who 'had been healed of evil spirits and infirmities' (Luke 8), and who was identified in Christian tradition with the repentant sinner of Luke 7. The French name *Madeleine* was coined with reference to this particular Mary, although in fact *Magdalene* in the New Testament is not a personal name, but refers to a place name. Other important New Testament female names from the gospels are *Martha* and *Elizabeth.* The latter was borne by the mother of John the Baptist (Luke 1: 5), although the name of his father, *Zacharias,* never achieved similar popularity.

Some equally popular Christian names are derived from Christian folk tradition rather than from the Bible itself. For example, *Anne* was, according to an ancient tradition, borne by the mother of the Virgin Mary. There is, however, no support for this story in the New Testament itself.

The stock of Christian names, especially female names, was augmented from the early centuries AD onwards by use of names found in the Acts of the Apostles and St Paul's Epistles. One of the best known is *Timothy,* the name of St Paul's companion, but even the names of characters who are no more than mentioned in passing were picked up eagerly in the Christian naming tradition. Among female names so transmitted are *Berenice, Chloe, Dorcas, Drusilla, Julia, Lois, Lydia, Priscilla,* and *Rhoda.* A few male names also fall into this category, notably *Felix* and *Jason.* However, it will readily be seen that names borne by minor characters in the Acts and the Epistles have achieved only a fraction of the popularity of the names of the apostles and other principal characters of the gospels.

Saints' Names

A very large number of European names owe their importance to the fact that they were borne by early, famous, or canonized Christians. These include an extraordinarily wide variety of different personalities, ranging from learned Church fathers (*Athanasius, Basil, Ambrose, Jerome, Augustine,* and *Gregory*) through innumerable martyrs (*Agatha, Agnes, Anastasia, Lucilla, Lucia; Lucian, Laurence, Sebastian*), mystics, ascetics, and visionaries (*Anthony, Simeon, Francis, Teresa*), founders of religious orders (*Benedict, Bernard, Dominic*), to the simple 19th-century French peasant girl (*Bernadette*), whose visions of the Virgin Mary led to the foundation of a healing shrine at Lourdes.

What they all have in common is that at some time during the past two millennia a cult grew up around them. In some cases (*Christopher, George, Blaise*) the legends of the cult have obscured any basis of historical fact that may once have existed. In other cases the facts about the lives and doings of the early saints are well known and well documented.

Names of Classical Antiquity

Christian sainthood is almost the only channel by which old Roman names have been transmitted to present-day use as given names. In spite of the pervasive use of Latin during most of the Christian era, Roman names that were not borne by early saints have almost entirely dropped out of use. This is because, officially at any rate, the early Church made repeated attempts to suppress classical literature and to obliterate all memory of pagan classical history. The role of Latin before the Reformation was as a liturgical language and lingua franca, not as the language of pagan civilization and literature. In the Christian era, therefore, there has been almost no tradition of naming children in honour of the great and admired figures of classical antiquity. Where a Roman name such as *Antonius, Claudius, Julius,* or *Marcus* has yielded modern derivatives, we may look with confidence for an early saint or martyr somewhere along the road.

The same is even more true of ancient Greek names, although since modern Greece took up and won the struggle for independence from Turkey, ancient Greek names such as *Sophocles, Socrates, Aristotle,* and *Thucydides* have become commonplace in Greece itself. They also now occur occasionally, rather surprisingly, in South America, so that combinations such as *Epaminondas López* may be found. However, these are still the exceptions rather than the rule. Insofar as they are not common and conventional at the present time outside Greece, classical Greek names have not been included in this book.

Local Cults and Patron Saints

In many places in Europe, the name of a local saint is regularly used within a small community, but has not spread far beyond it. St Leocadia of Toledo, St Godleva of Flanders, St Pons of Cimiez, and St Brizio of Spoleto are examples of saints whose cults are highly localized, and with them their names.

In other cases a local saint's name has become much more widespread. Because of the cultural importance of Paris, the names of its patron saints, *Denis* and *Geneviève*, have become popular far beyond the French capital, and indeed beyond the boundaries of France itself. *Didier* is widespread in France, having been borne by at least four different early saints and bishops, in Langres, Auxerre, Cahors, and Vienne. Similarly, *Gennaro*, the name of the patron saint of Naples, is found mainly in the south of Italy, but has certainly spread beyond Naples itself.

Status as a national patron saint is even more influential, as can be seen in the cases of St George of England, St Andrew of Scotland, St David of Wales, St Patrick of Ireland, and St Birgit of Sweden. This explains why *Beat* is still found in use as a Swiss male given name: St Beatus is venerated as the apostle of Switzerland, although he is a shadowy figure—even his dates are uncertain.

Saints can also function as patrons of particular occupations, and we find cases where this, too, influences the choice of a name. It is not unusual for the daughter of music-loving parents to be named after St Cecilia, the patron saint of music. A more mundane example is the choice of *Baldomero* as a name for the son of a Spanish locksmith, after St Baldomar, the patron of locksmiths in Provence and Iberia.

Names Associated with Particular Religious Denominations

A number of given names are associated with particular Christian groups: *Calvin, Luther,* and *Wesley* are the main examples borne by Protestants. Among Mormons, *Brigham* is sometimes used in honour of their early leader Brigham Young. By contrast, certain names are found exclusively or almost exclusively among Roman Catholics: examples are *Aloysius*, *Xavier*, and *Ignatius*.

Royal and Aristocratic Names

A name that is borne by a member of a royal family, especially a successful and much-admired monarch, invariably rapidly increases its currency among his or her subjects. Thus, the popularity of the New Testament name *Elizabeth* was enormously enhanced by the fact that it was borne by the enlightened and skilful queen of England who reigned 1558–1603. It has remained popular, partly because of that association, ever since. Its popularity increased again in the 20th century, after it became clear in 1936 that the then Princess Elizabeth would become queen, as Elizabeth II.

Elizabeth, like *James* and *John*, is a biblical name, firmly rooted in the Christian tradition. However, the majority of English, and indeed European, royal names derive from a pre-Christian, pagan tradition. English speakers are sometimes surprised to discover that ordinary, everyday names such as *William*, *Henry*, *Richard*, and *Robert*, not to mention *Charles*, have their origin in a distant, pre-Christian Germanic past in continental Europe. Moreover, these names have not even been transmitted to us through Old English. With the exception of *Edward*, most names of Old English derivation, even royal names, went out of use some time after the Norman Conquest. *Edward* survived, mainly because King Edward the Confessor was venerated by Normans and Saxons alike. Other names derived from Old English, such as *Alfred* and *Edwin*, *Audrey* and *Elfreda*, were revived in the Victorian period. Many of them now once again seem somewhat old-fashioned.

A few modern English first names reflect Old Norse personal names established in England before the Norman Conquest, such as *Harold*. However, the Normans themselves had abandoned their Norse language and pagan culture when they settled in northern France in the 10th century. Even more surprisingly, they abandoned their traditional Norse names. Within a few decades, they adopted the Christian religion, the French language, and French names. It so happens that although the French language is mainly derived from Latin, many French names are derived from Germanic. These are survivals of the ancient names that were used in the Germanic languages once spoken in France, in particular Frankish, the vernacular of the court of Charlemagne. Thus, *William* is from *wil* meaning 'will' plus *helm* meaning 'helmet'. Its cognates, French *Guillaume* and German *Wilhelm*, are from the same source. Germanic names are normally 'dithematic': that is, they consist of two vocabulary elements. These names are often extremely ancient, the elements reflecting qualities that were prized in prehistoric Germanic society: they have meanings such as 'war', 'strife', 'battle'; 'protection', 'rule', 'counsel'; 'raven', 'wolf', and 'bear'.

Many, but not all, of the most common male names of Germanic origin that are used in Britain today owe their importance to having been royal names: they were borne by one or more kings of England (or, as in the case of *Robert*, Scotland). But some, such as *Gerald*, *Hugh*, and *Roger*, were borne by members of the aristocracy rather than royalty.

Rather fewer Germanic female names, such as *Alice*, *Emma*, and *Matilda*, have survived into modern English. Generally, they are no less warlike in meaning than their male counterparts. The origins of these Germanic names owe nothing to Christianity, although in some cases, for example *Bernard*, their survival does: many such names were borne by people who became Christian saints, after whom children were named in succeeding generations.

Elsewhere in Europe the story is similar. *Louis*, *Charles*, and *Henri* became well established as French given names because from an early period they were borne by kings of France. *Hugues* is an ancient royal and aristocratic name, which was borne by Hugues Capet, founder of the Capetian dynasty.

In the German kingdoms and principalities the most popular names, alongside those of Christian origin, were those borne by royalty and princes: *Otto*, *Ludwig*, *Friedrich*, *Albrecht*, and *Wilhelm*, for example. In the Austro-Hungarian Empire we find extensive use of names favoured by the Habsburgs, such as *Rudolf*, *Franz*, and *Josef*. When a name of Spanish origin, *Ferdinand*, was brought by marriage into the imperial family, it soon came into use among their subjects as well.

Likewise in Eastern Europe, the traditional names once borne by famous kings are firmly established and continue to enjoy great popularity. Examples are *Kazimierz* and *Władysław* in Poland and *László* in Hungary.

The Celtic Tradition

After Christianity and Germanic royalty, the greatest influence on the stock of names in the English-speaking world has been the Celtic tradition. Its influence has sometimes been underestimated. Many names are now used throughout the world by people who may be only vaguely aware, if at all, of their derivation from Irish or Scottish Gaelic, or from Welsh. Examples are *Barry, Brian, Bridget, Donald, Duncan, Ian, Kenneth, Kevin, Neil*, and *Sheila* from Irish and Scottish Gaelic, and *Gareth, Gladys, Gwendolen*, and *Trevor* from Welsh. These are all Anglicizations of Celtic names. Other Celtic names exist in an Anglicized form, but are still used mainly by people conscious of their Celtic ancestry. Examples are *Brendan, Connor, Cormac, Declan*, and *Rory* from Gaelic and *Branwen, Dylan, Dilys, Gwyneth, Olwen*, and *Wyn* from Welsh.

In Ireland, Gaelic names such as *Aodh, Conchúr, Meadhbh*, and *Naoise* have survived in Gaelic-speaking areas from generation to generation among a rural community who were normally illiterate in Irish, English being the only language permitted for education. Increasingly now, it is fashionable, especially in Ireland, even among city-dwellers, to revive such names in their original form, unscrambling the garblings due to Anglicization. It is also fashionable to bestow Gaelic names such as *Fiona* on children, and this has led not only to revivals but also to new coinages based on Gaelic, widely used by the Irish and by Highland Scots, including those who no longer speak the ancient language of their forebears.

The phonology of Gaelic is very different from that of English, and the spelling system of the Gaelic languages has its own logic. The medieval Gaelic spelling system is largely preserved, so that etymological connections can normally be perceived, which would not be apparent if a purely phonetic modern orthography were adopted. Gaelic names can therefore look very different from English names, even when they are quite closely equivalent. For example, the Irish Gaelic form of *George* is *Seoirse*. Irish *Séamas* and Scottish *Seumas* are the Gaelic equivalents of English *James*. The vocative case of the latter, *Sheumais*, has been re-Anglicized as *Hamish*. The Irish name *Siobhán* (Scottish Gaelic *Siubhan*), related to English *Jane*, has in recent years been Anglicized as *Shevaun* and *Chevonne*; its cognate *Sine* is found in the Anglicized form *Sheena*.

Thanks to the generous help of two leading Gaelic scholars, Professor Tomás de Bhaldraithe and Mr Ronald Black, this dictionary has attempted to unravel some of the complexities of Gaelic personal names, showing both the Gaelic versions of common European names and the unique contribution of the Gaelic tradition. We have also recorded new coinages where we have encountered them. In 1981 an excellent small book on *Gaelic Personal Names*, by Donnchadh Ó Corráin and Fidelma Maguire, was published in Dublin; this has a strong orientation towards Irish history. An equivalent work on Scottish Gaelic names is still wanting: until such time as a specialist study can be undertaken, Mr Black's contribution to the present work will, it is hoped, help to go some way towards supplying the deficiency.

A striking feature of the Gaelic naming tradition is the antiquity of its independence and folklore. It predates the royal names of English by a millennium and more. *Meadhbh* (*Maeve*) recalls a 1st-century queen of Connacht, leader of 'the Cattle Raid of Cooley'. The name *Deirdre* recalls the tragic story of a beautiful girl betrothed against her will to Conchobhar (*Connor*) and her elopement with her beloved Naoise, who is eventually caught and killed by Conchobhar. The historical events on which this famous story is based probably took place at around the time of Christ.

Other names recall pre-Christian beliefs that vanished some fourteen hundred years ago. *Aodh* (the Anglicized form of which is *Hugh*) is the name of a Celtic sun god. *Niamh* is the daughter of the sea god, who falls in love with the hero Oisín, son of Finn MacCool, and carries him off to her kingdom beyond the sea. Several Irish and Scottish Gaelic names currently in use are associated with ancient myths such as these.

The influence of Christianity has been as profound on Irish names as on any naming tradition in Europe. The names of St Patrick (*Pádraig*) and St Bridget (*Bríghid*) are characteristically Irish names bestowed in honour of the Christian saints who bore them. The Irish saint who brought Christianity to Scotland in the 6th century is commemorated both in the name *Calum* and in *Malcolm* ('servant of Calum'). The name, which is traditionally given as *Columba* 'dove' in Latin, reminds us of the influence of Latin on early Christian names in Ireland. *Patrick* itself is derived via Irish *Pádraig* from Latin *Patricius* 'nobleman'.

During the Dark Ages, Christianity was as firmly established in Ireland as it was in Rome, and Irishmen were appointed to bishoprics in every part of Europe. Many of them set out as missionaries to pagan areas, and this explains, for example, why the Irish name *Colmán* (*Columbanus*, *Kálmán*) is popular in Hungary, and *Gall* (*Gaweł*) in Poland.

In Scotland, where the Gaels settled from the 5th century onwards, particular names are sometimes associated with particular clans. So, for example, the name *Somerled* (*Somhairle* in Scottish Gaelic, Anglicized as *Sorley*) is traditionally associated with Clan Macdonald, the kindred of the Lords of the Isles. Mention of this name reminds us of the interplay between Gaelic names and Norse names. Gaelic *Amhlaoíbh*/*Amhlaidh*, *Somhairle*, *Tormod*, *Uisdean*, *Sgàire*, and even *Raghnall* (*Ronald*) are from Norse, while Norse names such as *Njall* and *Birgit* are from Gaelic.

In the 18th century, the rise of fashionable interest in the Celtic twilight led James Macpherson to compose a series of 'ancient epic poems' (1762–3) purporting to be by Ossian (*Oisín*, *Oisein*), son of Fingal. These poems were admired by Goethe and Schiller amongst others, and by Napoleon, with a curious sequel for the history of personal names. Some of Napoleon's godchildren were christened with 'Ossianic' names such as *Oscar*, *Selma*, *Morna*, and *Malvina*. When Napoleon's marshal Bernadotte accepted the invitation to take the throne of Sweden, the Ossianic name *Oscar* became established as a Scandinavian royal name.

Welsh names are of similar antiquity, though there are fewer traditional names surviving in Welsh than in Gaelic. Many of the old Welsh names that are now in use or being revived are found in the *Mabinogi*, a medieval collection of ancient legends. These names include *Branwen*, *Lleu*, *Geraint*, *Heilyn*, *Iorwerth*, *Rhiannon*, *Urien*, *Ynyr*, and *Pryderi*. Another group of traditional Welsh names commemorates heroes and princes who led resistance variously to the Romans (*Caradoc*), the Saxons (*Cadwaladr*), and the Normans (*Llewelyn*, *Glyndŵr*). Also found are Welsh forms of Norman and English names introduced in the Middle Ages and later (*Siôn*, *Siân*, *Siarl*).

By far the most important Welsh source of names, in many different European languages, is the cycle of Arthurian legends. The historical Arthur is a shadowy, legendary figure who led British resistance to the Saxon invasions of Britain in the 5th or 6th century AD. From the Middle Ages onwards a vast body of European literature grew up around the subject of King Arthur and his knights. Names derived from this tradition include *Elaine*, *Enid*, *Gavin* (*Gawain*), *Guinevere*, *Lancelot*, *Merlin* (*Myrddin*), *Percival*, and *Tristram* (*Tristan*) and *Isolde* (*Yseult*, Welsh *Esyllt*).

The present century is witnessing not only a revival of traditional Welsh names but also an influx of new coinages. These are mainly from vocabulary elements (e.g. *Eirwen* 'snow-pure', *Glenda* 'clean-good'), but also from place names such as *Arfon*, *Eifion*, *Dyfed*, and *Trefor*.

We are grateful to Professor Gwynedd Pierce for his advice on Welsh names.

The Influence of Literature, Film, and Popular Culture

Works of literature can have a profound influence on name choices. The widespread influence of Arthurian legend on European naming has already been mentioned. The names of some of Shakespeare's heroines have been used as given names, for example *Rosalind*, *Olivia*, *Portia*, *Perdita*, *Imogen*, *Juliet*, and *Cordelia*. However, on the whole, the names of Shakespeare's characters have been less influential than might have been expected. Many Shakespearean names are those of historical or supposedly historical characters (*Hal*, *Troilus*, *Macbeth*); others are Italianate (*Antonio*, *Claudio*, *Viola*); others, especially male names (*Florizel*, *Prospero*, *Hamlet*), seem to have been simply too outlandish to have achieved popular status.

Other writers have influenced particular names. Thus, *Pamela* and *Clarissa* probably owe much of their popularity to novels by Samuel Richardson; *Amelia* to Henry Fielding; *Nicol* to Sir Walter Scott; *Justine* to Lawrence Durrell; *Leila* to Byron and Lord Lytton; *Christabel* to Samuel Taylor Coleridge; *Maud* and *Vivien* to Alfred, Lord Tennyson; and *Pippa* to Browning. In the 19th century, the given name *Shirley* (which is derived via a surname from a place name) changed sex, becoming a conventional female name after publication of Charlotte Brontë's novel *Shirley* in 1849.

Literary influence is not, of course, confined to the English language. In Italy, for example, the same phenomenon may be observed in the name *Loredana*, which was coined by Luciano Zuccoli for a novel published in 1908, and *Ornella*, in Gabriele d'Annunzio's *Figlia de Ioro* (1904). The phenomenon is long established, as the influence of Dante and Petrarch on the names *Beatrice* and *Laura* bears witness.

The literary quality of a work is a less influential factor than its wide readership and ability to capture the popular imagination. All the writers mentioned above have enjoyed perennial popularity, but in addition some more ephemeral works have played a major part in establishing certain names. Paul Leicester Ford's novel *Janice Meredith*, published in 1899, is little read nowadays, but the name *Janice* owes its popularity to that work.

The most striking example of the influence of a work of literature on the choice of names is Margaret Mitchell's novel *Gone with the Wind* (1936), which was made into a popular film in 1939. The names of most of the characters were invented or revived by the author, and so their adoption as conventional given names can be pinpointed precisely and attributed to this work. It was largely or wholly responsible for the names *Bonnie*, *Rhett*, *Scarlett*, and *Careen* among others.

In the 20th century, films have had a considerable influence on the choice of names. *Tracy*, for example, underwent a great increase in popularity as a female name from the late 1950s onwards, after release of the 1956 film *High Society*, in which Grace Kelly played the character of Tracy Lord.

Not only fictional characters but also the actors who portray them can have an influence on the popularity of a name. *Greer*, *Cary*, and *Spencer*, for example, have been chosen as names in honour of the film stars Greer Garson, Cary Grant, and Spencer Tracy. *Claudette* increased in popularity in the English-speaking world because of the fame of the film actress Claudette Colbert. Where a film star, or a character in film or popular fiction, bears a name that is already well established the influence is more difficult to trace. However, the influence of glamour is undeniable: it seems very likely that the popular status of *Humphrey* was improved by Bogart, *Clark* by Gable, *Trevor* by Howard, *James* by Cagney and Dean, *Jean* by Harlow, *Jane* by Russell, and *Marilyn* by Monroe.

Another characteristically 20th-century influence is that of rock and pop music: the rise of *Elvis* is clearly traceable, but we can only guess how many present-day Johns and Pauls owe their name to Lennon and McCartney.

Soap operas, too, influence the choice of names, as witness the rise during the late 1980s of *Charlene*, in Britain as well as Australia. This is the name of a character played by Kylie Minogue in the Australian soap opera *Neighbours*. And of course the popularity of *Kylie* itself derives from the same source.

Surnames as Given Names

In the English-speaking world a large number of surnames are in use as given names: only those are recorded here that have acquired conventional status.

Surnames had been sporadically used as first names for several centuries, mainly among landed families: for example the Skeffingtons, among whom the surname *Clotworthy* was in regular use as a first name. In the 19th century, however, this phenomenon became more frequent. In most cases it originated because of a close relationship or connection between families—usually by marriage. A bride from a rich and powerful family would christen her first-born with her own maiden surname; the conjunction of the two names would be taken as symbolic of the union between the two families. Gradually, the practice became more and more widespread. Use of the mother's maiden name as a *second* given name has been an especially common practice among English speakers in the 20th century.

Some given names that were derived originally from surnames have become fully established as freely used first names in their own right (e.g. *Clifford, Dudley, Stanley*). Many more are fairly frequently used as such (e.g. *Kendal, Kingsley, Marshall*). In Britain such names are almost always borne by males, apart from a few conventionalized exceptions (e.g. *Shirley, Beverley, Kimberley*).

A number of Scottish surnames have become very common as conventional English given names, including *Keith, Douglas, Fraser, Graham*, and *Leslie*. The latter, in the *-ie* spelling, has become conventionalized as a male name. The spelling *Lesley* is used for both sexes.

Some Old English personal names have become modern first names by an indirect route, i.e. through the transferred use of surnames that were derived from them during the early Middle Ages. Examples are *Goddard, Goodwin*, and *Osborn*.

Other Sources of Given Names

We have now mentioned the main sources of traditional given names, but there are many other sources from which a personal name may be derived. Some of these can be rather ephemeral.

Since the 19th century, several different types of vocabulary word have been used as given names: in particular, words denoting precious stones (*Beryl, Ruby*) and flowers (*Daisy, Primrose*). Sometimes a vocabulary word denoting a desirable quality for the life ahead is bestowed on a baby, as in the case of the names *Joy, Happy; Fortunato, Bonifacio*, and *Felix*.

Occasionally, a place name will be found in use as a given name. Several of the Western Isles and other parts of Scotland have been used in this way, notably *Isla(y)* and *Iona*, less commonly *Lewis* and *Uist, Lorne* and *Athol*, and the river name *Clyde*. Otherwise, this source of given names is unusual except through the mediation of a surname.

Nicknames rarely become established as personal names, but pet forms such as *Peggy* and *Bill* can take on a life of their own. American examples include *Chuck* and *Bud*. Some short forms or pet forms are more commonly used than the more formal version, as in the case of *Reg/Reginald*. In other cases, a short name such as *Max* or *Kim* may be used in its own right, and strangers may wrongly identify it as a 'short form' of a longer name such as *Maxwell* or *Kimberley*.

The Slavonic languages are particularly rich in pet forms, and use of the official version of a person's name can sound cold and formal. However, there is very rarely any confusion in such languages as to what is an appropriate pet form and what is the full form to which each belongs. In English, by contrast, a name such as *Jack* can be taken variously as a pet form of *John* or *James* or as a name in its own right.

Masculine and Feminine

Many female names in Christian cultures are derived from male names—names such as *Joan, Jane, Janet*, and *Seònaid* (all members of the 'John' group), or *Petra, Paula, Georgina*, and *Simone*. One reason for this is that for the past two thousand years and more, European societies have been male-dominated and patrilineal. Another factor is that comparatively few women are mentioned by name in the gospels.

In languages such as Italian, where normally the inflection clearly indicates whether a name is male or female, there is no difficulty in creating a feminine equivalent of a male name, such as *Giovanna* from *Giovanni*, and vice versa in rarer cases such as *Carmela/Carmelo*.

In English and some other languages, certain diminutive suffixes have become conventional signs of feminine gender, for example *-et* as well as *-ette*, and *-een/-ene*, the latter being at least in part derived from Irish *-ín*. These endings are now commonly used as elements in the coining of new female names.

NAMING PRACTICES IN DIFFERENT CULTURES

English Coinages since the 17th Century

Some Old Testament names were in occasional use throughout the Middle Ages, but they became far more frequent during the 17th century, and more of them were brought into use under the influence of Puritan reformers. A few, such as *Jabez*, *Saul*, and *Solomon*, became for a while part of the common stock of usual first names. They subsequently declined in popularity, were modestly revived during the Victorian period, and are now once again uncommon, except as Jewish names. At the height of the vogue for Old Testament names in the 17th century, some very unlikely sounding names were taken from incidental mentions and genealogical lists, and even biblical place names were pressed into service, for example *Ebenezer*. Another innovation of the Puritans was the use of vocabulary words and phrases as first names: *Praisegod*, *Livewell*, *Truth*, *Increase*. These were for the most part nonce coinages, and the vogue quickly passed, but a few names denoting virtuous qualities (*Faith*, *Prudence*, *Patience*) have survived from that period as standard female names.

During the 18th century, the stock of first names was modestly increased by the adoption in real life of various consciously literary coinages or far-fetched borrowings, fanciful names bestowed on romantic heroines and then used in real life. Examples are *Clarinda*, *Pamela*, and *Vanessa*.

The Victorian era was a period of further expansion in the stock of first names, which occurred in two principal ways. On the one hand both Old English and Old Testament names were revived, while on the other hand new first names were created from surnames and from vocabulary words.

In the 20th century, the number of names used regularly has continued to grow apace. The use of vocabulary words as first names for women has increased, and the two categories mentioned earlier (gemstones and flowers) have been expanded to include other precious and desirable things (*Amber*, *Jade*, *Crystal*), plants (*Bryony*, *Fern*, *Poppy*), and birds (*Kestrel*, *Teale*). Names from other parts of the world have been enthusiastically adopted, beginning in the early years of the century with Russian names introduced via France (*Vera*, *Tanya*, *Natasha*). A couple of decades later, there was a vogue for names of Scandinavian origin (*Ingrid*, *Astrid*). Currently, certain fanciful inventions, combinations, and respellings are gaining ground, a process formerly more associated with America (see below).

Modern Given Names in America

The first European names to be established in America were those in use among Puritan settlers. Some of the more unusual Old Testament names (see above) remain in steady use, especially in rural areas: *Jed* (*Jedidiah*), *Zeke* (*Ezekiel*), *Hephzibah*, *Zillah*.

A later American naming practice, less common in Britain, is the adoption of surnames as first names, not because of any family connection, but out of admiration for some famous contemporary or historical figure so called (*Chauncey*, *Wesley*, *Sandford*). A number of American presidents have been so honoured, in particular *Washington* and *Lincoln*. From presidential forenames come the names *Franklin*, *Lyndon*, *Grover*, and *Woodrow*. The last two, incidentally, were surnames given as middle names and later preferred as forenames by their bearers. The full names of the presidents in question were *Stephen Grover Cleveland* and *Thomas Woodrow Wilson*.

Many first names derived from surnames are in America borne by women. A few are conventionalized in this use (*Brooke*, *Paige*) but many more are used equally for either sex, so that it is often not possible to determine the gender of a bearer from the name alone. Even conventional male first names, such as *Sean*, are coming increasingly to be bestowed on girls as well.

Another process of name creation long established in America is that of free invention. Formerly regarded as typical of the southern states, this has in the second half of the present century become more widespread. Most of the coined names are borne by women. Strategies include fanciful respelling (*Kathryn* (now the predominant form in America), *Madalynne*, *Ilayne*); minor alterations in currently popular names (*Jenna*, *Deloris*); the combining of syllables from existing names (*Jolene*, *Lolicia*); elaborations with productive feminine suffixes (such as *-elle*, *-ette*, *-ice*, *-inda*, *-ona*, *-yl*); and outright invention (*Luvenia*, *Tawana*).

Another feature more characteristic of America than Britain is the use of pet forms as fully fledged first names in their own right, so that a *Pam* is not necessarily to be addressed more formally as *Pamela*, nor *Bobby* as *Robert*. President Carter insisted that he be officially known as *Jimmy*, although he was in fact christened *James*. In the same way, some informal nicknames have come to be bestowed as official first names (*Bud*, *Ginger*, *Rusty*). Vocabulary words that denote titles such as *Duke*, *Earl*, and *Prince* are also regularly used as first names.

African-American, West Indian, and other Black Names

In both America and Britain, the names borne by African-Americans, West Indians, and other Black people differ to some extent from those of the White population. They contain a high proportion of freely invented names of the kind just mentioned. These are commonly borne by males as well as females.

Characteristic Black names also include adopted European forms (*Antonio*, *Antoine*, *Anton*, often in altered spellings such as *Antwan*) and some surname forms that are much less common among the population as a whole (*Curtis*, *Leroy*, *Winston*).

It is possible to detect certain fashionable processes at work in the forming of new Black names, for example the prefixing of *De-* to male names (*Dejuan*, *Deshawn*). This probably originated by extraction from Italian patronymic surnames such as *Deangelo* and *Demarco*. The practice is matched by the prefixing of *La-* and *Sha-* to female names (*Lashauna*, *Shafaye*).

Canada, Australia, and New Zealand

First names in Canada do not differ greatly from those of the United States. There are, however, a few names that are characteristically Canadian: for example *Lorne*, the recent feminine creation *Jaime*, and the hybrid respelling *Meaghan*.

Australia and New Zealand also share the same basic stock of English first names, with a rich admixture of names from other parts of Europe brought by a wide diversity of immigrants. Irish influence is strong in Australia, and the use of the surname *Kelly* as a girl's name seems to be of Australian origin. This in turn may have influenced the coinage of *Kylie*, which is usually said to be of Aboriginal origin.

Australia shares with some parts of America a convention of cheerful creativity in given names, especially female names. A characteristically Australian name is *Raelene*. *Charlene*, which is also sometimes regarded as characteristically Australian, is also found in the southern and western United States. It is not clear whether it was coined independently in the two places or whether it was borrowed by one from the other.

In New Zealand two names of Maori origin, *Ngaio* and *Nyree*, have achieved some currency.

French Names

In France the choice of first name is in theory legally restricted by a law of 1803 to names that have been borne by saints or by figures from ancient history. However, names occurring in the Bible (*Abel*, *Adam*) and in classical mythology (*Achille*, *Hercule*) have long been freely allowed. In the present century a much wider variety of names has become officially acceptable. In particular, words denoting flowers (*Garance*, *Guimauve*, *Pervenche*), largely drawn from the Revolutionary calendar, have passed into occasional use as girls' names. As in other Roman Catholic countries, the veneration of local and national patron saints is an important source of given names in France.

In the south of France a number of traditional Provençal names have long been in use. Some of these, such as *Mireille* and *Magali*, have become fashionable throughout France.

Breton first names are, not surprisingly, very much more restricted in geographical distribution. Although certain names such as *Guen(n)olé*, *Guenaèlle*, *Guyomard*, and *Judicael* have become well established in Brittany, there have been court battles over the more exotic names favoured by some Breton nationalists.

Italian Names

The common given names of Italy today are all derived from names borne by saints recognized by the Roman Catholic Church. In the Middle Ages there was a comparatively wide repertoire of names in Italian, including an extensive group of Germanic names of Lombard origin (*Galimberto*, *Garibaldo*). Some of these have given rise to surnames, but most of them are no longer in use as given names.

Vocabulary phrases intended to invoke a good omen (*Benvenuto* 'welcome', *Diotiguardi* 'God preserve you') were also formerly used as given names in Italy.

Many different dialects are spoken, and the sense of regional identity is strong. Regional influences, therefore, such as the veneration of local patron saints, are prominent. For example, *Romolo* is a typical name of the Rome area; *Brizio* is more or less limited to parts of Umbria.

Names in the Iberian Peninsula

In Spain the influence of the Roman Catholic Church is, if anything, more powerful than it is in Italy. Some of the well-established royal names, for example *Alfonso*, *Hernán* (*Fernando*), and *Rodrigo*, and a few other names, including *Elvira* and *Gonzalo*, are of Visigothic origin. Apart from the royal names, those that survived did so by virtue of having been borne by Christian saints. Veneration of the local patron saint is as strong in Spain as it is in Italy. St Ramiro of León, St Elodia of Huesca, and St Sandalio of Cordoba are examples of local patron saints who happened to bear Visigothic names. Of many of the other Germanic names introduced by the Visigoths (*Amalasunta*, *Sisebuto*) there is now little trace.

A striking feature of Spanish names is the large number of female names that refer to epithets or aspects of the cult of the Virgin Mary, mentioned earlier. Often these are affixed to the overwhelmingly common first name *María*, as, for example, *María de las Mercedes*, *María del Amor*. Some of these references (*Angosto*, *Aranzazu*) are to minor local cults, and many such names are confined to a particular region, within which they may be enormously popular.

A further, related group of names refers to festivals and symbolic objects associated with the Church and particularly with the adoration of the Virgin: *Concepción*, *Anunciación*, *Asunción*, *Resurección*, and *Rosario*. These names may in theory be borne by both men and women, but in practice they are nowadays largely confined to women, and are so marked in the dictionary. Similar names are to a lesser extent found in Italy (*Concetta*, *Assunta*) and Ireland (*Concepta*, *Assumpta*).

The Spanish language is also notable for its extensive use of affective forms of first names, readily employing a variety of diminutives (*Juanito*, *Teresita*), pet forms (*Charo*, *Chus*, *Manolo*, *Quique*), and contractions (*Maripi*, *Maica*).

In north-western Spain, speakers of Galician use forms such as *Xoán* and *Xosé*.

Catalan names are found in the north-east of Spain. Some of them are closely related to the Provençal names of southern France. The most typical of them is *Jordi*, the name of the patron saint of Catalonia.

In the Basque country are found saints' names (*Txomin*, *Gorka*) and vernacular religious names, some of which (*Jasone*, *Sorne*) have common Spanish equivalents. Others (*Arrene*, *Izaga*) are unique to Basque.

Portuguese names are very similar in character and often in form also to those of Spain. A peculiarly Portuguese feature is the adaptation of names from classical antiquity (*Péricles*, *Pompeu*, *Tucídides*, *Lucrécio*). These are, however, comparatively unusual.

German Names

In Germany and Austria some ancient Germanic names are still in use for which cognates are not found in other parts of Europe (e.g. *Helmut*, *Berthold*). Many of these have been in use continuously from the early Middle Ages to the present day, although they have from time to time faced strong competition from biblical names and the Greek and Latin names of early saints. Nowadays many of the less common Germanic names, especially women's names (*Waltraut*, *Gerlinde*), which were revived during the 19th century under the influence of Romantic enthusiasm for early Germanic mythology, are again out of fashion.

Names borne by members of the royal and imperial families in German-speaking countries were particularly well established, e.g. *Friedrich* and *Wilhelm* in Prussia, *Ernst* and *August* in Saxony, *Ludwig* in Bavaria, and *Franz*, *Josef*, and *Ferdinand* in Austria. However, the regional loyalties of German names were never as strong as those of Italy.

Another characteristic of German nomenclature is the group of pious names formed during the Reformation on the model of traditional dithematic names, but composed of elements of Christian significance, for example *Gottlob* and *Hilfgott*. These survived through the 19th century, but many of them are now felt to be rather old-fashioned.

Certain linguistic features may be regarded as characteristic of different regions of Germany. The Low German dialects in the north have many hypocoristic forms ending in -*ke*, and some names long common there have in the past couple of decades become more popular throughout northern Germany.

In southern Germany and Austria hypocoristic forms typically end in -*l* and -*i* (*Gretel*, *Poldi*). Certain names are characteristically Austrian, for example *Leopold*, the name of the country's patron saint. In Switzerland hypocoristic forms tend to end in -*i* and -*li* (*Mitzi*, *Resli*). Several names of local saints (*Regula*, *Reto*, *Pirmin*) are scarcely used outside Switzerland. The influence of the Roman Catholic Church, too, is strong in south Germany and in Austria, encouraging the use of names such as *Alois* and *Theresia*.

In the eastern regions of Germany, Slavonic influence can be observed on the choice of first names (*Wenzel*, *Stenzel*) and on hypocoristic forms (*Anja*, *Anke*, *Annuschke*).

Names in the Netherlands and Belgium

Some of the first names of the Netherlands are similar to the Low German names of north Germany. They are distinguished by a large number of pet forms, which are only with difficulty to be related to the base form (*Jaap*, *Joop*, *Mies*). Considering the small size of the country, Dutch has a particularly rich variety of different local forms of personal names.

Some Frisian names preserve what appear to be old Germanic monothematic bynames, often of uncertain derivation (*Boje*, *Ibbe*).

Among the Flemish speakers of Belgium, substantially the same names are used as in the Netherlands, often with slight differences in spelling, for example *Blaes* instead of the usual Dutch *Blaas*. Certain typically Belgian names of Germanic origin have been adopted by French-speaking Walloons in a French spelling, for example *Baudouin*.

Scandinavian Names

The most striking aspect of names in Scandinavia, outside Finland, is that a large number of Old Norse names have survived to the present day. Names of Christian origin are indeed found in Scandinavia, such as *Anders* (Andrew), *Johan* (John), and *Anna*, but they are rivalled by more ancient Norse names, which it has been fashionable to revive in all parts of Scandinavia since the 19th century. In some cases this revival has led to the coinage of new names not actually attested in Old Norse literature or inscriptions, but made up from combinations of elements found in the ancient names.

Many of these names go back to the characters of Norse legends and sagas (*Sigurd*, *Gunnar*, *Gudrun*). Generally they are dithematic—that is, they are composed of two parts etymologically, using such elements as *arn* 'eagle', *björn* 'bear', *úlfr* 'wolf', *sigr* 'victory', *gunr* 'strife', and *rún* 'secret lore'. Names of the old gods are found as elements too: in particular *Þórr*, the god of thunder.

In Scandinavia, as elsewhere, use of a name by a monarch has had a profound influence on its popularity: this is true not only of comparatively recent royal names such as *Gustav* and *Margrethe*, but also of more ancient ones such as *Knut*, *Olav*, and *Håkon*.

Some of the names derived from Old Norse forms are monothematic: these represent in part historic or modern shortenings of the more usual dithematic names (*Stein*, *Tor*), in part ancient or medieval bynames formed from vocabulary words (*Frode*, *Bror*).

Some Celtic influence on Scandinavian names is detectable, too. The patron saint of Sweden, *Birgit*, is one example, being of Irish origin. The influence of Ossianic names has already been mentioned in the section on the Celtic tradition.

There are few differences in most Scandinavian names between Danish, Swedish, and Norwegian forms, and those that exist are often no more than reflections of the different orthographic systems of the languages, e.g. Swedish *Björn* for Norwegian *Bjørn*. By the same token, we find Danish *Torbe(r)n* for Norwegian *Torbjørn*. However, not all Scandinavian names have cognate forms in all three languages. Examples of names that are characteristically Danish include *Abelone* and *Jytte*. Names found normally only in Norway include *Gro* and *Terje*, while typically Swedish names include *Birger* and *Göran*.

The given names of Finland differ greatly from those in use in the rest of Scandinavia, as a result of the distinct character of the Finnish language and culture. Finnish is not an Indo-European language. It is distantly related to Hungarian, and is quite unlike the Germanic and Slavic languages that are its neighbours. A few common first names in use in Finland have been borrowed from Swedish (*Pirjo*, *Pirkko*, *Oskari*). Others are derived from the names of saints, often in a heavily altered form (*Pentti*, *Ransu*). Others again are derived from vocabulary words of religious or ornamental significance (*Toivo*, *Usko*).

Our thanks are due to Professor Lena Peterson for her advice on Scandinavian names.

Russian Names

The overwhelming influence on Russian names has been the Orthodox Church. From an early date, the Church forbade the use of native Slavic names, and insisted on names that had been borne by saints of the Eastern Church. This had the curious effect of ensuring that the Russian naming tradition was derived mainly from Byzantine Greek, whence such names as *Arkadi*, *Gennadi*, and *Prokop*.

Names of the traditional Slavonic dithematic type became more common towards the end of the 19th century, for example *Vsevolod*, *Vyacheslav*, either from a reading of ancient literature or by borrowing from other Slavonic languages. However, they were never widespread. A few 20th-century names—e.g. *Ninel* (*Lenin* spelled backwards) and *Melor* (an acronym for *Marx*, *Engels*, *Lenin*, *October*, *Revolution*)—were created after the Revolution by enthusiasts for the new Socialist order, but these never achieved much currency either, and they are now no more than historical curiosities.

A noticeable feature of Russian naming practice is the very large number of pet forms of first names in familiar use, many of them differing greatly from the base form (e.g. *Dunya* from *Avdotya*, *Sasha* from *Aleksandr*). These in turn may have further hypocoristic suffixes added to them (*Dunyasha*, *Sashura*).

Our thanks are due to Mr Paul Falla for his advice on Russian and Eastern European names.

Polish Names

In Poland, by contrast, the majority of the population is staunchly Catholic. The names of the most popular saints are in some cases familiar in the West, albeit in an unfamiliar spelling. In addition, a number of traditional dithematic Slavic names are in common use (e.g. *Bogdan*, *Bronistaw*, *Faromierz*). Typical name-forming elements include *-slaw* glory, *-mierz* famous, *rad-* glad, and *jaro-* spring. As in other Slavic countries, short forms and pet forms (*Basia*, *Farek*, *Stanek*) are very widely used in Polish. In general, everyday conversation people normally use a pet form, while the full form of a name is usually reserved for formal and official situations.

Polish royal names include *Kazimierz*, *Mieczyslaw*, *Zygmunt* and *Wladyslaw*. All except *Zygmunt* are dithematic Slavic names. *Stanislaw* is famous both as a royal name and as the name of a martyred 11th-century bishop of Cracow.

Czech Names

The historic former kingdom of Bohemia (*Čechy*) forms what is now the Czech Republic. To the east of it is Slovakia, whose language is closely related to Czech. Some common Czech and Slovak given names are vernacular spellings of the saints' names that are the common heritage of the Western Church (e.g. *Ondřej* (Andrew), *Antonín* (Anthony), *Blažej* (Blaise), *Brož* (Ambrose), etc.). As in the case of Polish, there is also a substantial admixture of Slavic dithematic names (*Bohumíl*, *Břetislav*, *Dobroslav*, etc.).

Two names of special importance to Czechs are *Ludmila*, the name of a 10th-century Bohemian saint, and *Václav* (*Wenceslaus*), the name borne by five rulers of Bohemia, including the pious Duke of Bohemia known to English carol singers as 'Good King Wenceslas'.

Hungarian Names

Hungarian, like Finnish, to which it is distantly related, is a non-Indo-European language. Its form and structure are quite unlike those of the Indo-European languages by which it is surrounded (German, Czech, Slovak, Russian, Serbian, Croatian, Slovenian, and Romanian). However, its position as the language of a major central European power, which for many years was politically united to German-speaking Austria, among other factors, ensured that its names would be strongly influenced by the traditions of Western Christianity and of German speakers, as well as by those of the Slavic communities, many of which were at one time ruled from Budapest.

Even when they are of Latin, German, or Slavic origin, the given names of Hungary are often far removed from the forms they have in those languages. For example, among the most common male names are *István* (from Latin *Stephanus*), *Imre* (corresponding to German *Heinrich*), *László* (from Slavic *Vladislav*), and *Kálmán* (from Irish *Colman*, Latin *Columbānus*). Not one of these names is native to Hungary. In addition, a few given names based on Hungarian vocabulary elements have been formed as calques on names of Latin origin (e.g. *Virág* on *Flora*, *Vidor* on *Hilarius*). In Hungary, uniquely in Europe, the given name follows the surname.

Romanian Names

In spite of its location in eastern Europe, the language of Romania is of Romance origin, and the forms of the given names in use there are often quite similar to those of Italy and Spain (*Anghel*, *Ignatie*, *Rafail*, *Silvestru*). In addition, there are several names drawn from the neighbouring Slavic areas (*Cislau*, *Ladislau*, *Mirca*).

Modern Jewish Names

Traditional Jewish names, in every country of Europe where there were Jewish communities, were and are the names of the Bible. In many places these were altered in form to conform to the phonology of the local language, in particular Yiddish in northern and eastern Europe.

Many Jewish names are common to Gentiles and Jews alike (*Joseph*, *Deborah*). Others are traditional Hebrew names (*Asher*, *Baruch*, *Hyam*), Hebrew forms (*Moshe*, *Shelomo*), Yiddish forms (*Issur*, *Motke*), and Anglicized forms (*Morton*, *Milton*). The latter two examples are used for reasons of alliteration in place of *Mordecai* or *Moshe*. There are also modern revivals of biblical Hebrew names (*Ehud*, *Yael*) and modern Hebrew coinages (*Ilan*, *Semadar*).

Our thanks are due to Dr Joseph A. Reif for his contribution to the Jewish names in this dictionary.

P.W.H., F.M.H.
January 1990

Acknowledgements

A comparative work of this kind can only hope to succeed by drawing on the expertise of scholars from many different disciplines. Advisers for particular aspects have been mentioned in the course of the introduction; a summary list is given here of those scholars who kindly gave up a great deal of their time to read the first draft of this dictionary, giving detailed comments and suggestions for additions and improvements. We are profoundly grateful to them for their efforts, which have enabled us to improve the accuracy and usefulness of the book greatly. Any errors or shortcomings that remain are of course the responsibility of the authors.

Professor Tomás de Bhaldraithe, Royal Irish Academy
Ronald Black, Lecturer in Celtic, University of Edinburgh
P. S. Falla, Editor, *Oxford English–Russian Dictionary*
Professor Lena Peterson, University of Uppsala
Professor Emeritus Gwynedd Pierce, University of Wales College of Cardiff
Dr Joseph A. Reif, Bar-Ilan University

Aa

Aaron ♂ Biblical name, borne by the brother of Moses, who was appointed by God to be Moses' spokesman and became the first High Priest of the Israelites (Exodus 4:14–16, 7:1–2). It is of uncertain origin and meaning: most probably, like ▷Moses, of Egyptian rather than Hebrew origin. The traditional derivation from Hebrew *har-on* 'mountain of strength' is no more than a folk etymology. The name has been in regular use from time immemorial as a Jewish name and was taken up by the Nonconformists as a Christian name in the 16th century. Since the late 1990s it has been widely popular.

VARIANTS: **Aron, Arron, Arun** (modern respellings).

Abbie ♀ Pet form of ▷Abigail, frequently used as an independent given name.

VARIANTS: **Abby, Abbey, Ab(b)i**.

Abdul ♂ Arabic: short form of ▷Abdullah.

Abdullah ♂ Arabic name meaning 'servant of Allah'. See ʿAbd-Allāh in Arabic appendix.

Abe ♂ As a Jewish name it is either a short form of ▷Abraham or a Yiddish name of two syllables from Aramaic *abba* 'father', which was used as a personal name in Talmudic times instead of ▷Abraham. As an English name it is a short form of ▷Abraham.

Abel ♂ Biblical name, borne by the younger son of Adam and Eve, who was murdered for reasons of jealousy by his brother Cain (Genesis 4:1–8). The Hebrew form is *Hevel*, ostensibly representing the vocabulary word *hevel* 'breath, vapour', and so taken to imply vanity or worthlessness. Abel is considered by the Christian Church to have been a pre-Christian martyr (see Matthew 23:35), and is invoked as a saint in the litany for the dying. Nevertheless, his name has not been much used either before or after its brief vogue among the Puritans.

Abigail ♀ Biblical name, meaning 'father of exaltation' in Hebrew, borne by one of King David's wives, who had earlier been married to Nabal (1 Samuel 25:3), and by the mother of Absalom's captain Amasa (2 Samuel 1:25). The name first came into general use in Britain in the 16th century, under Puritan influence. It was a common name in literature for a lady's maid, for example in Beaumont and Fletcher's play *The Scornful Lady* (1616). The biblical Abigail refers to herself as 'thy servant' in addressing King David. In Ireland this name has traditionally been used as an Anglicized form of **Gobnat** (see Irish appendix), although the reasons for this are not clear. It was popular in the 17th century, especially among Puritans and Nonconformists, and has again enjoyed considerable favour since the 1990s.

VARIANTS: **Abigaile, Abbigail, Abbiegail, Ab(b)ygail, Abigayle**.

PET FORMS: **Abbie, Abbey, Abby, Abi**.

Abilene ♀ Mainly U.S.: a comparatively rare name. In the New Testament, Abilene is a region of the Holy Land (Luke 3:1); the name is of uncertain origin, but may be derived from a Hebrew word meaning 'grass'. Several places in America have been named from this reference, notably a city in Kansas, which was the boyhood home of President Dwight D. Eisenhower. Its adoption as a girl's given name was encouraged partly by its resemblance to ▷Abbie and partly by the fact that *-lene* is a productive suffix of girls' names (as in ▷Charlene).

Abishag ♀ Biblical name, possibly meaning 'wise, educated' in Hebrew. It was borne by a beautiful Shunammite virgin who was brought to the dying King David in a vain attempt to restore him to health and vigour. She was later used by David's son and successor Solomon as a reason for executing his half-brother and rival Adonijah (1 Kings 1–2): Adonijah had wanted to marry Abishag.
VARIANT: Jewish: **Avishag**.

Abital ♀ Biblical name meaning 'dewy', borne by a wife of King David (2 Samuel 3:4).
VARIANT: Jewish: **Avital**.

Abner ♂ Biblical name, meaning 'father of light' in Hebrew. It was borne by a relative of King Saul, who was in command of Saul's army (1 Samuel 14:50; 26:5). It is not common as a given name in England, but has enjoyed a steady, modest popularity in America, where it dates back to the time of the earliest Puritan settlements.
VARIANT: Jewish: **Avner**.

Abraham ♂ Biblical name, borne by the first of the Jewish patriarchs, with whom God made a covenant that his descendants should possess the land of Canaan. The Hebrew form is *Avraham*, and is of uncertain derivation. In Genesis 17:5 it is explained as 'father of a multitude (of nations)' (Hebrew *av hamon* (*goyim*)). It has always been a popular Jewish given name, and was also chosen by Christians, especially by Puritans and other fundamentalists from the 16th century onwards. Various early saints of the Eastern Roman Empire also bore this name. Its currency in the United States was greatly enhanced by the fame of President Abraham Lincoln (1809–65).
VARIANTS: Jewish: **Avraham**, **Avrom**.
SHORT FORM: **Abe**.

Abram ♂ Biblical name, a variant of ▷Abraham. It was probably originally a distinct name (meaning 'high father' in Hebrew). According to Genesis 17:5, the patriarch's name was changed by divine command from *Abram* to *Abraham*. From the Middle Ages, however, if not before, it was taken to be a contracted version.

Absalom ♂ Biblical name, probably meaning 'father of peace' in Hebrew. It was borne by the third son of King David, who to the great sorrow of his father rebelled against him and was eventually killed when he was caught by the hair in an oak tree as he fled (2 Samuel 15–18). The name has never been particularly common in the English-speaking world.
VARIANT: **Absolon**.

Acacia ♀ From the name of the flower, which is related to the mimosa. The plant was named by botanists in the 16th century with the Latin form, *acacia*, of Greek *akakia*, which had earlier been used in translations of the Bible to refer to the tree from whose wood the Arc of the Covenant was made. This word is of uncertain origin, probably a derivative of Greek *akē* 'point, thorn', but it has also been analysed as being from the Greek negative prefix *a-* + *kakos* 'bad', as if the flowers had the power to ward off evil influence. The given name is fairly frequent in Australia, where the acacia (usually known there as the *wattle*) is a common flower and popular national symbol. It is possible that in some cases ▷Keisha may be regarded as a shortened form of this name.

Ace ♂ Originally a nickname, now fairly commonly used as a given name, especially in the United States. It represents the colloquial term *ace*, referring to someone who is particularly good at something. This meaning derives, via the notion of being 'number one', from the word *ace* denoting a single item (as for example the lowest (and highest) value in a suit of playing cards). This probably derives from Latin *as*, the name of a coin of low value.

Achilles ♂ From Greek mythology. Achilles was the son of the sea nymph Thetis and the mortal Peleus. As a child he was immersed in the Styx by his mother, thereby making his body invulnerable except for the heel by which he was held. He was a leading warrior of the Greek army attacking Troy. In the *Iliad*, Homer relates how he withdrew from the siege as a result of a slight to his honour, until his lover Patroclus, wearing his armour, was killed by Hector. Thereupon Achilles rejoined the fray and killed Hector. Eventually, he was wounded by Paris in his unprotected heel and died. The Greek form of his name is *Akhilleus*, and is of unknown, possibly pre-Greek, origin; it may be connected with that of the River *Akheloös*. The name has been used only rarely in the English-speaking world, usually as a result of recent Continental influence. Although there were various minor early saints so named, it has normally been chosen by parents who wished to take advantage of the licence given by the Catholic Church to select names borne by classical heroes as well as those of saints.

Ada ♀ Of uncertain origin; it was not in general use before the late 18th century. It may be a Latinate variant of the biblical name ▷Adah. However, it has also been explained as a pet form of ▷Adele and ▷Adelaide, Germanic female names of which the first element is *adal* 'noble'. It was borne by a 7th-century abbess of Saint-Julien-des-Prés at Le Mans.

Adah ♀ Biblical name, meaning 'adornment' in Hebrew, borne by the wives of Lamech (Genesis 4:19) and of Esau (Genesis 36:2). See also ▷Ada.

Adam ♂ In the Bible, the name of the first man (Genesis 2–3). It probably derives from Hebrew *adama* 'earth'; it is a common feature of creation legends that God or a god fashioned the first human beings from earth or clay and breathed life into them. The name was subsequently borne by a 7th-century Irish abbot of Fermo in Italy. It has been very popular in the English-speaking world since the 1960s. In Hebrew it is a generic term for 'man' (Genesis 5:2) and has never been considered a personal name, although *Hava* 'Eve' has enjoyed popularity as a Jewish name.
COGNATES: Irish: Ádhamh. Scottish Gaelic: Àdhamh. German, Dutch: Adam. French: Adam. Spanish: Adán. Portuguese: Adão. Italian: Adamo. Polish: Adam. Finnish: Aatami. Hungarian: Ádám.

Adamina ♀ Rare feminine form of ▷Adam.

Addie ♀ Pet form of any of the female names beginning *Adel-*, e.g. ▷Adelaide, ▷Adela, ▷Adele, or ▷Adeline.
VARIANT: Addy.

Addison ♂ Transferred use of the surname, which originated as a patronymic derived from *Addie* or *Adie*, a medieval (and occasional modern) pet form of ▷Adam. This is now a moderately popular given name, especially in the United States.

Adela ♀ Latinate form of ▷Adele, especially popular in the late 19th century.
VARIANT: Adella.

Adelaide ♀ Of Germanic origin (via French Adélaïde), from *adal* 'noble' + *heid* 'kind, sort'. It was borne in the 10th century by the wife of the Holy Roman Emperor Otto the Great. She became regent after his death and was revered as a saint. The given name increased in popularity in England during the 19th century, when it was borne by the wife of King William IV; she was the daughter of the ruler of the German duchy of Saxe-Meiningen. The

Australian city of Adelaide was named in her honour.

PET FORM: English: Addi(e), Addy.

Adele ♀ From French Adèle, an ancient name popular in medieval Europe because of the fame of a 7th-century saint, a daughter of the Frankish king Dagobert II. It is of Germanic origin, from *adal* 'noble' (a short form of a two-element name such as *Adelheid*; see ▷Adelaide). It was the name of William the Conqueror's youngest daughter (*c.*1062–1137), who became the wife of Stephen of Blois. However, it died out in England in the later Middle Ages. It was revived in the 19th century, being the name of a character in Johann Strauss's opera *Die Fledermaus*. Its popularity was further reinforced in the 1930s as the name of a character in the novels of Dornford Yates.

VARIANTS: Adel, Adelle.

PET FORMS: Addi(e), Addy.

Adélie ♀ French elaboration of ▷Adele, now sometimes also used in the English-speaking world, with or without the accent. Adélie Land in Antarctica was named in 1840 by the French explorer Jules Dumont d'Urville in honour of his wife; the Adélie penguin (*Pygoscelis adeliae*) is so named because it breeds on that coastline.

Adelina ♀ Latinate form of ▷Adeline, which has enjoyed some favour in the English-speaking world. It was famously borne by the Spanish-born opera singer Adelina Pattie (1843–1919).

Adeline ♀ French diminutive of *Adèle* (see ▷Adele), used occasionally in England from the early 16th century onwards, and now also found in the wider English-speaking world.

Adil ♂ Arabic name meaning 'just, fair'.

Adina ♀, ♂ Mainly Jewish: in the Bible a male name, derived from Hebrew *adin* 'slender'. It is borne by a soldier in the army of King David, 'Adina the son of Shiza the Reubenite, a captain of the Reubenites' (1 Chronicles 11:42). In modern times it was revived as a male name among Zionists, but is now more commonly a female name, no doubt because of the characteristically feminine *-a* ending.

Adlai ♂ Biblical name, borne by a very minor character, the father of one of King David's herdsmen (1 Chronicles 27:29). It represents an Aramaic contracted form of the Hebrew name *Adaliah* 'God is just', and is one of a large number of minor biblical names taken up by the Puritans in the 17th century. Many of them, including *Adlai*, were taken to New England by the early settlers and have survived in North America. *Adlai* is particularly associated with the American statesman and Democratic presidential candidate Adlai Stevenson (1900–65), in whose family the name was traditional: it was also borne by his grandfather (1835–1914), who was vice-president in 1893–97.

Adolph ♂ Usual (hypercorrected) spelling of German Adolf (see German appendix), which was first introduced into Britain by the Normans, displacing the Old English equivalent *Æthelwulf* ('noble' + 'wolf'). It did not become at all common, however, until it was reintroduced by the Hanoverians in the 18th century. The association with Adolf Hitler (1889–1945) has meant that the name has been little used since the Second World War. The Latinized form Adolphus has been a recurring name in the Swedish royal family and has also been used occasionally in the English-speaking world.

VARIANT: Adolphus (Latinized form).

Adria ♀ Rare feminine form of ▷Adrian, recorded in the 17th century.

Adrian ♂ Usual English form of the Latin name *Hadrianus* 'man from Hadria'. Hadria was a town in northern Italy, which gave its name to the

Adriatic Sea; it is of unknown derivation. The initial *H-* has always been very volatile. The name was borne by the Roman emperor Publius Aelius Hadrianus, during whose reign (AD 117–138) Hadrian's Wall was built across northern England. The name was later taken by several early popes, including the only English pope, Nicholas Breakspeare (Adrian IV). It was in early use among immigrants from the Low Countries, and is found in some English regions from the mid-16th century. It has enjoyed considerable popularity in the English-speaking world since the late 20th century.

Adrianne ♀ Modern feminine form of ▷Adrian, less common than ▷Adrienne.
VARIANTS: **Adrian(n)a**.

Adrienne ♀ French feminine form of ▷Adrian, now also used in the English-speaking world.

Aegle ♀ From Latin, the name borne in classical mythology by various characters—a daughter of the Sun and sister of Phaeton; one of the Hesperides; and a nymph, daughter of Jupiter and Neaera. It derives from the Greek word *aiglē* 'brightness, splendour'.

Aeneas ♂ From Latin, the name of the hero of Virgil's *Aeneid*, a Trojan prince who sailed from Troy after its destruction by the Greeks and, after many adventures, settled in Latium (Italy), becoming the ancestor of the Roman people. The name is of unknown derivation; it appears in Homer as *Aineas*, and was associated by the Romans themselves with Greek *ainein* 'to praise'. In Scotland this name was sometimes used as a classicized form of ▷Angus.

Africa ♀ Name recorded in the U.S. since the 18th century and now favoured by African Americans conscious of their ancestral heritage.

Agatha ♀ Latinized version of the Greek name *Agathē*, from the feminine form of the adjective *agathos* 'good, honourable'. This was the name of a Christian saint popular in the Middle Ages; she was a Sicilian martyr of the 3rd century who suffered the fate of having her breasts cut off. According to the traditional iconography, she is depicted holding them on a platter. In some versions they look more like loaves, leading to the custom of blessing bread on her feast day (5 February). The name was revived in the 19th century, but has faded again since.
PET FORM: **Aggie**.

Aggie ♀ Pet form of ▷Agnes and ▷Agatha.

Agnes ♀ Latinized version of the Greek name *Hagnē*, from the feminine form of the adjective *hagnos* 'pure, holy'. This was the name of a young Roman virgin martyred in the persecutions instigated by the Roman emperor Diocletian in AD 303. She became a very popular saint in the Middle Ages. Her name was early associated with Latin *agnus* 'lamb', leading to the consistent dropping of the initial *H-* and to her representation in art accompanied by a lamb. The colloquial form *Annes* led to some confusion with *Ann(e)* in earlier centuries. Frequent in the medieval period, the name was revived in the 19th century, and has been especially popular in Scotland. See also ▷Annis.
PET FORM: **Aggie** (mainly Scottish).
COGNATES: Irish Gaelic: **Aignéis**. German, Dutch, Scandinavian: **Agnes**. French: **Agnès**. Spanish, Portuguese: **Inés**. Italian: **Agnese**. Russian: **Agnessa**. Polish: **Agnieszka**. Czech: **Anežka**. Finnish: **Aune**. Hungarian: **Ágnes**. Latvian: **Agnese**. Lithuanian: **Agné**.

Aharon ♂ Jewish: modern Hebrew form of ▷Aaron.

Ahmed ♂ Arabic name meaning 'highly commendable'. See Aḥmad in Arabic appendix.

Aidan ♂ Anglicized form of the ancient Gaelic name Áedán (see Irish appendix). The name was borne by various early Irish saints, notably an Irish disciple (d. 626) of St David of Wales, who later became bishop of Ferns and was noted for his kindness and generosity, and the one (d. 651) who brought Christianity to the English settlers of 7th-century Northumbria, founding the monastery on the island of Lindisfarne. The name was revived in the 20th century, in particular during the last couple of decades, by parents conscious of their Irish or Scottish ancestry and has also acquired considerable popularity among those without such connections.
VARIANTS: **Edan, Aedan, Aiden.**

Aileen ♀ Mainly Scottish variant spelling of ▷Eileen.

Ailie ♀ Pet form of ▷Aileen or an Anglicized form of Scottish Eilidh (see Scottish appendix).

Ailsa ♀ Modern Scottish name derived from *Ailsa Craig*, the name of a high rocky islet in the Clyde estuary off the Ayrshire coast, near the traditional estates of the Scottish Kennedys. Ailsa Craig (whose name is actually from Old Norse *Alfsigesey* 'Alfsigr's island') is known in Gaelic as *Allasa*, but popularly as *Creag Ealasaid* (see **Ealasaid** in Scottish appendix).

Aimée ♀ French: originally a vernacular nickname meaning 'beloved', from the past participle of French *aimer* 'to love' (Latin *amare*; compare ▷Amy). It has been in use in French since the Middle Ages, although it has never been very common. It is now also used, with or without the accent, as a given name in the English-speaking world.
VARIANT: **Aimi.**

Ainsley ♂, occasionally ♀ Transferred use of the Scottish surname, also spelled *Ainslie*, which is borne by a powerful family long established in the Scottish borders. It was originally a local name, taken north from either *Annesley* in Nottinghamshire or *Ansley* in Warwickshire. The former gets its name from the genitive case of the Old English name *Ān* (a short form of any of various compounds containing the word *ān* 'one, only') + Old English *lēah* 'wood, clearing'. The latter is from Old English *ānsetl* 'hermitage' + *lēah*. It is borne by the chef and television personality Ainsley Harriott.
VARIANTS: **Ainslee, Ainslie.**

Aisha ♀ Pronounced 'ayeesha'; of Arabic origin, now also in more general use in the English-speaking world. See Arabic appendix.
VARIANTS: **Aishah, Ayesha.**

Aizik ♂ Jewish: variant of Yiddish *Yitzhak* (see ▷Isaac).

Al ♂ Short form of any of the names beginning with this syllable.

Alaina ♀ Feminine form of Alain, the French equivalent of ▷Alan.
VARIANT: **Alayna.**

Alaine ♀ Variant of ▷Alaina or ▷Elaine.

Alan ♂ Of Celtic origin and uncertain derivation (possibly a diminutive of a word meaning 'rock'). It was introduced into England by Breton followers of William the Conqueror, most notably Alan, Earl of Brittany, who was rewarded for his services with vast estates in the newly conquered kingdom. In Britain the variants Allan and Allen are considerably less frequent, and generally represent transferred uses of surname forms, whereas in America all three forms of the name are approximately equally common. See also ▷Alun.
SHORT FORM: **Al.**

Alana ♀ Latinate feminine form of ▷Alan, a comparatively recent coinage.
VARIANTS: **Alanna, ▷Alannah, Alanah, Allana.**

Alanda ♀ Recent coinage, a feminine form of ▷Alan influenced by ▷Amanda.

Alanna ♀ Variant spelling of ▷Alana, possibly influenced by ▷Anna.

Alannah ♀ Variant spelling of ▷Alanna, possibly influenced by names of Hebrew origin such as ▷Hannah and ▷Susannah and by the Anglo-Irish term of endearment *alannah* (Gaelic *a leanbh* 'O child').

Alaric ♂ From a Germanic personal name composed of *ala* 'all' or *ali* 'stranger' + *rīc* 'power, ruler'. Now rare, it was introduced to Britain in this form by the Normans. The first element may also in part derive from a contracted form of *adal* 'noble'. The Blessed Alaricus or Adalricus (d. 975) was a Swabian prince who became a monk at the monastery of Einsiedeln in Switzerland.

Alba ♀ Italian, occasionally used in the English-speaking world. It appears to be from the feminine form of the Latin adjective *albus*, but may rather be a derivative of Germanic *alb* 'elf, supernatural being'.

Alban ♂ From the Latin name *Albanus*, which is of uncertain origin. It may be an ethnic name from one of the numerous places in the Roman Empire called *Alba* 'white', or it may represent a Latinized form of a British name derived from the Celtic word *alp* 'rock, crag'. Christian tradition has it that St Alban was the first martyr in Roman Britain, who was executed, probably in 209, at Verulamium (now known as St Albans). A Benedictine abbey was founded there and dedicated to the saint by King Offa. Derivation from *Albion*, a poetic name for Britain, is also a possibility.

PET FORMS: Albie, Alby.

Alberic ♂ Learned form of ▷Aubrey, derived from Latin *Albericus* in the 14th century. It enjoyed a slight and brief vogue in the 19th century, but is now rare.

Albert ♂ From an Old French name, *Albert*, of Germanic (Frankish) origin, derived from *adal* 'noble' + *berht* 'bright, famous'. This was adopted by the Normans and introduced by them to England, displacing the Old English form *Æþelbeorht*. The name is popular in a variety of forms in Western Europe, and has been traditional in a number of European princely families. It was out of favour in England for centuries, however, and the revival of its popularity in the 19th century was largely in honour of Queen Victoria's consort, Prince Albert of Saxe-Coburg-Gotha.

SHORT FORMS: Al, Bert.

PET FORMS: Albie, ▷Alby, Bertie.

Alberta ♀ Feminine form of ▷Albert, a name borne by one of Queen's Victoria's daughters (1848–1939), after whom the Canadian province was named.

Albertina ♀ Feminine pet form of ▷Albert.

Albie ♂ Variant spelling of ▷Alby.

Albina ♀ Latin feminine form of *Albinus*, a derivative of the Roman family name *Albius*, which is from *albus* 'white'. It is the name of a minor saint: St Albina, who was martyred in Caesarea in 250. She is particularly venerated in Campania, where her relics are preserved to this day.

SHORT FORM: ▷Bina.

Albion ♂ From the poetical name for Britain. This is often supposed to derive from Latin *albus* 'white' and to refer to the whiteness of cliffs spied from the sea, but in fact it more probably comes from the Celtic element *alp* 'rock, crag'. The given name has occasionally been chosen by parents in all parts of the English-speaking world who wish to commemorate their association with or affection for the British Isles.

Alby ♂ Pet form of ▷Albert, and sometimes of ▷Alban; also an Anglicized form of Irish Ailbhe (see Irish appendix).

VARIANT: **Albie.**

Aldous ♂ Pronounced 'awl-dus'; of uncertain origin, but probably a medieval short form of any of various Norman names, such as *Aldebrand*, *Aldemund*, and *Alderan*, containing the Germanic word *ald* 'old'. It was relatively common in East Anglia during the Middle Ages, but is now rare, known mainly as the given name of the novelist Aldous Huxley (1894–1963).

Alec ♂ English and Scottish short form of ▷Alexander, now less popular in England than ▷Alex.

Alesha ♀ Respelling of ▷Alicia.

Alethea ♀ A learned coinage, not found before the 16th century. It represents the Greek word *alētheia* 'truth', and seems to have arisen as a result of the Puritan enthusiasm for using terms for abstract virtues as girls' names. See also ▷Althea.

Alex ♂, ♀ Short form of ▷Alexander, ▷Alexandra, and ▷Alexis; also commonly used as a given name in its own right.

VARIANT: **Alix** (♀).

SHORT FORM: **Lex.**

Alexa ♀ Short form of ▷Alexandra or variant of ▷Alexis as a female name.

Alexander ♂ From the Latin form of the Greek name *Alexandros*, from *alexein* 'to defend' + *anēr* 'man, warrior' (genitive *andros*). The name became extremely popular in the post-classical period, and was borne by several individuals in the New Testament and some early Christian saints. Its use as a common given name throughout Europe, however, derives largely from the fame of Alexander the Great, King of Macedon (356–323 BC), around whom a large body of popular legend grew up in late antiquity, much of which came to be embodied in the medieval 'Alexander romances'.

SHORT FORMS (ALSO SCOTTISH): **Al, Alex, Alec, Alick.**

PET FORMS: ▷**Sandy** (chiefly Scottish; Gaelic **Sandaidh**); ▷**Lexy,** ▷**Lexie.**

COGNATES: Irish: **Alastar.** Scottish Gaelic: **Alasdair** (Anglicized as ▷**Alistair**). German, Dutch: **Alexander.** Scandinavian: **Alexander.** French: **Alexandre.** Spanish: **Alejandro.** Catalan: **Aleixandre.** Portuguese: **Alexandre.** Italian: **Alessandro.** Russian: **Aleksandr.** Polish: **Aleksander.** Czech: **Alexandr.** Croatian, Serbian, Bulgarian: **Aleksandar.** Slovenian: **Aleksander.** Finnish: **Aleksanteri.** Hungarian: **Sándor.**

Alexandra ♀ Latinate feminine form of ▷Alexander. It was very little used in the English-speaking world before the 20th century, when it was brought in from Scandinavia and Eastern Europe. It owes its sudden rise in popularity in Britain at the end of the 19th century to Queen Alexandra, Danish wife of Edward VII.

SHORT FORMS: **Alex, Alexa;** ▷**Sandra.**

PET FORMS: ▷**Sandy** (chiefly Scottish); **Lexy.**

Alexandria ♀ Variant of ▷Alexandra, influenced by the name of the city in Egypt, founded by Alexander the Great in 322 BC and named in his honour. This is now a relatively common given name in the United States, where it is also found as a place name, for example in Louisiana, Minnesota, and Virginia; the last was named in 1748 after a family of local landowners whose surname was *Alexander*.

Alexandrina ♀ Latinate derivative of ▷Alexandra. It was most common in the 19th century, and was in fact the first name of Queen Victoria.

Alexia ♀ Variant of ▷Alexis as a female name.

Alexis ♂, ♀ Variant (or female derivative) of *Alexius*, the Latin spelling of Greek *Alexios*, a short form of various compound personal names derived from *alexein* 'to defend'. St Alexius was a 5th-century saint of Edessa, venerated particularly in the Orthodox Church as a 'man of God'. *Alexis* was originally a boy's name, but is now more commonly given to girls.

Alf ♂ Short form of ▷Alfred.
PET FORM: Alfie.

Alfa ♂, ♀ Variant spelling of ▷Alpha.

Alfie ♂ Pet form of ▷Alfred, now popular as an independent given name.

Alfred ♂ From an Old English name derived from *ælf* 'elf, supernatural being' + *ræd* 'counsel'. It was a relatively common name before the Norman Conquest of Britain, being borne most notably by Alfred the Great (849–899), King of Wessex. After the Conquest it was adopted by the Normans in a variety of more or less radically altered forms (see ▷Avery). In some regions the forms *Alvery* and *Avery* never fell entirely out of favour and became locally popular in the 16th century. It provides a rare example (▷Edward is another) of a distinctively Old English name that has spread widely on the Continent. It was strongly revived in the 19th century, along with other names of pre-Conquest historical figures, faded in the mid-20th century, but has since recovered some popularity.

Alfreda ♀ Variant of ▷Elfreda, but now probably taken as a feminine equivalent of ▷Alfred.

Alger ♂ Transferred use of the surname, which is ultimately derived from an Old English name derived from *ælf* 'elf, supernatural being' + *gār* 'spear'. This form absorbed other names with different first elements: *æþel* 'noble', *eald* 'old', and *ealh* 'temple'.

The personal name was not common either before or after the Norman Conquest, although it was briefly revived in the 19th century, along with other Germanic names.

Algernon ♂ Of Norman French origin, originally a byname meaning 'with a moustache' (from Old French *grenon, gernon* 'moustache'). The Normans were as a rule clean-shaven, and this formed a suitable distinguishing nickname when it was applied to William de Percy, a companion of William the Conqueror. In the 15th century it was revived, with a sense of family tradition, as a byname or second given name for his descendant Henry Percy (1478–1527), and thereafter was regularly used in that family. It was subsequently adopted into other families connected by marriage with the Percys, and eventually became common property, although it is now used infrequently.
PET FORMS: Algy, Algie.

Ali ♂, ♀ As a girl's name it is a pet form of ▷Alison, ▷Alice (as in the case of American film actress Ali MacGraw, b. 1938), or any of the other female names formed with this first syllable. It is now also used as an independent given name. As a boy's name, it is used as a pet form of ▷Alistair and is also an independent given name from an Arabic word meaning 'sublime'; see ʿAli in Arabic appendix.

Alice ♀ Originally a variant of ▷Adelaide, representing an Old French spelling of a reduced form of Germanic *Adalheidis*. *Alice* and *Adelaide* were already regarded as distinct names in English during the medieval period. *Alice* enjoyed a surge of popularity in the 19th century and periods of favour ever since. It was the name of the central character of Lewis Carroll's *Alice's Adventures in Wonderland* (1865) and *Through the Looking Glass* (1872), who was based on his child friend Alice Liddell, daughter of the Dean of Christ Church, Oxford.

VARIANTS: Alys; Alis (Welsh).

Alicia ♀ Modern Latinate form of ▷Alice. It was borne by the British ballerina Alicia Markova (born Lilian Alicia Marks, 1910–2004).

VARIANTS: Alisia, Alisha; Alissa, Alyssa; Alesha.

Alick ♂ Variant of ▷Alec, which has gained some currency as a given name in its own right.

Alina ♀ Of uncertain origin. It is probably a variant of ▷Aline, but could also be of Arabic origin, from a word meaning 'noble' or 'illustrious'. It is also used in German-speaking countries, and in Scotland it has been used as a feminine form of ▷Alistair.

VARIANT: Allina.

Alinda ♀ In the English-speaking world this name is of recent origin, apparently a blend of ▷Alina and ▷Linda. It is, however, also used in German-speaking countries, where it is derived from the ancient Germanic personal name *Adelinde*, from *adal* 'noble' + *lind* 'soft, tender'.

Aline ♀ In the Middle Ages this represented a contracted form of ▷Adeline. In modern use it is either a revival of this or a respelling of ▷Aileen. In Scotland and Ireland it has sometimes been chosen as representing an Anglicized spelling of the Gaelic vocabulary word *àlainn* (Scottish), *álainn* (Irish), meaning 'lovely'.

Alisa ♀ Contracted form of ▷Alicia.

Alison ♀ From a very common medieval name, a Norman French diminutive of ▷Alice. Despite its early popularity, it became quite rare in England in the 16th century. However, it survived in Scotland, with the result that until its revival in England in the 20th century it had a strongly Scottish flavour.

VARIANTS: Allison (the usual North American spelling), Al(l)yson; Alysoun (a medieval English spelling, which was revived in the 20th century).

PET FORMS: Allie, Ally.

Alissa ♀ Contracted form of ▷Alicia.

Alistair ♂ Altered spelling of *Alasdair*, the Scottish Gaelic form of ▷Alexander. Alexander has long been a popular name in Scotland, having been borne by three medieval kings of the country. *Alistair* is now widely used in the English-speaking world, often by those without Scottish connections.

VARIANTS: Alisdair, Alastair, Alister, Al(l)aster, Alistar.

PET FORM: Aly.

Alix ♀ Variant of ▷Alex, used only as a feminine name. Its formation has probably been influenced by ▷Alice.

Aliyah ♀ Arabic: variant of Aliyya, feminine form of Ali (see Arabic appendix).

VARIANT: Aaliyah.

Aliza ♀ Jewish: modern Hebrew name meaning 'joyful'. Its popularity has been influenced by the English names ▷Gay and ▷Alice, and it has also been used as translation of the Yiddish name ▷Freyde.

Alizabeth ♀ Respelling of ▷Elizabeth.

Allan ♂ Variant spelling of ▷Alan, used mainly in Scotland and North America.

Allana ♀ Variant spelling of ▷Alana.

Allaster ♂ Scottish: variant spelling of ▷Alistair. It is borne, for example, by a minstrel in Sir Walter Scott's *Rob Roy* (1818), which ensured its 19th-century popularity.

Allegra ♀ From the feminine form of the Italian adjective *allegro* 'happy, jaunty' (familiar in English as a musical tempo). It seems to have been an original coinage when it was given to Byron's illegitimate daughter (1817–22), but since then it has been taken up by parents in many English-speaking countries. It is not normally used as a given name in Italy.

Allen ♂ Variant spelling of ▷Alan, in Britain generally found only as a surname, but in North America equally common as a given name.

Allie ♀ Pet form of ▷Alison, occasionally used as a given name in its own right.

VARIANTS: ▷Al(l)y.

Allina ♀ Variant spelling of ▷Alina.

Allison ♀ Respelling of ▷Alison. This is the more common form of the name in the United States.

Ally ♀ Pet form of ▷Alison, now increasingly used as a given name in its own right under the influence of the popular American television series *Ally McBeal*.

VARIANT: Aly.

Allyson ♀ Respelling of ▷Alison.

Alma ♀ Relatively modern creation, of uncertain origin. It had a temporary vogue following the Battle of Alma (1854), which is named from the river in the Crimea by which it took place; similarly, *Trafalgar* had occasionally been used as a girl's name earlier in the 19th century. Nevertheless, the historical event seems only to have increased the popularity of an existing, if rare, name. *Alma* is also the feminine form of the Latin adjective *almus* 'nourishing, kind' (compare the term *alma mater* 'fostering mother', denoting an educational establishment). The name was borne by Alma Bennett (1889–1958), American vamp of the silent screen. In Tennessee Williams's play *Summer and Smoke* (1948), a bearer of the name explains that it is 'Spanish for soul', but this seems to be no more than coincidental.

Aloha ♀ U.S.: modern name representing the Polynesian word meaning 'love' (familiar as a form of greeting and farewell in Hawaii and elsewhere in the South Pacific).

Aloisia ♀ Latinate feminine form of ▷Aloysius.

Aloysius ♂ Pronounced 'al-oo-**ish**-us'; of unknown origin, possibly a Latinized form of a Provençal version of ▷Louis. It was relatively common in Italy in the Middle Ages, and has subsequently enjoyed some popularity among Roman Catholics in honour of St Aloysius Gonzaga (1568–91), who was born in Lombardy.

Alpha ♂, ♀ Taken from the first letter of the Greek alphabet (ultimately of Semitic origin; compare Hebrew *āleph* 'ox'). It seems to have been chosen as a given name in the 19th and 20th centuries as a symbol of primacy and excellence, and is used for both boys and girls.

VARIANT: Alfa.

Alphonse ♂ French form of Spanish *Alfonso*, which is of Germanic (Visigothic) origin. It is probably a compound of *adal* 'noble' + *funs* 'ready, prompt'. Alternatively, the first element may be *ala* 'all', *hadu* 'struggle', or *hild* 'battle'; forms are found to support each derivation, so it is possible that several Visigothic names that were originally distinct have fallen together. The -*ph*- spelling is the result of classical influences (or classical pretensions). St Alphonsus was a 9th-century bishop of Astorga, who spent the last years of his life at the abbey of St Stephen de Ribas de Sil in Galicia. *Alphonse* has been occasionally used in the English-speaking world, especially among West Indians and African Americans. The Latinized form **Alphonsus** has been used in Ireland as an equivalent of the Gaelic name Anluan (see Irish appendix).

PET FORMS: Fonsie, Fonso.

Alphonsine ♀ French feminine diminutive of ▷Alphonse, now also used in the English-speaking world.

Alte ♀ Jewish: feminine form of *Alter* (see ▷Altman).

Althea ♀ From Greek mythology. Although sometimes considered to be a contracted form of ▷Alethea, it is actually a quite distinct name (Greek *Althaia*) of uncertain origin. It was borne in classical legend by the mother of Meleager, who was given a brand plucked from the fire at the instant of her son's birth, with the promise that his life would last as long as the brand did; some twenty years later she destroyed it in a fit of pique. The name was revived by the 17th-century poet Richard Lovelace as a poetic pseudonym for his beloved.

Althena ♀ Modern coinage, apparently a blend of ▷Althea and ▷Athene.

Altman ♂ Jewish: composed of Yiddish *alt* 'old' + *man* 'man'. Traditionally, it was a name given to children to protect them from the angel of death, who would be confused by the conflict between the name and its infant bearer, or else as an omen name intended to ensure that the bearer would live to a ripe old age. The nominal adjective *Alter* is also used as a given name.

Alton ♂ Mainly U.S.: transferred use of the English surname, which is from any of a number of places so called in England. These have various origins; the most common is from Old English *æwiell* 'source (of a river)' + *tūn* 'settlement, enclosure'. It was borne (but dropped) as a given name by the American bandleader and trombonist Alton Glenn Miller (1904–44).

Alun ♂ An ancient Welsh name, indirectly related to ▷Alan, of which it is now generally taken to be the Welsh equivalent. It is borne in the *Mabinogi* by Alun of Dyfed, a character mentioned in passing several times. It is also a river-name and a regional name in Wales, sometimes spelled *Alyn*. *Alun* was adopted as a bardic name by John

Blackwell (1797–1840) and became popular as a result of his fame. It is now used increasingly outside Wales as an alternative spelling of ▷Alan.

Alva ♀ Anglicized form of the traditional Irish name Ailbhe (see Irish appendix), which is derived from Old Irish *albho* 'white'. In medieval times this was also a boy's name, but it has been revived mainly as a girl's name. It is popularly taken as a feminine equivalent of ▷Alvin. In the 19th century it was occasionally conferred as a boy's name, a variant spelling of the biblical name *Alvah*, meaning 'height', which was borne by one of the leaders of Edom.

Alvar ♂ As a medieval name this was from the Old English personal name *Ælfhere*, composed of *ælf* 'elf, supernatural being' + *here* 'army, warrior'. In modern use it may be a revival of this, a transferred use of the surname derived from it, or an Anglicized form of Spanish *Álvaro*, a Visigothic personal name derived from Germanic *al* 'all' + *war* 'guard'.

Alvin ♂ From an Old English personal name derived from *ælf* 'elf, supernatural being' + *wine* 'friend'. This was not especially common in Britain either before or after the Norman Conquest, but it is popular in the United States. The reasons for this are not entirely clear; association with ▷Calvin may be a factor. A more plausible (though less elevated) explanation is that this was the name given to the naughty chipmunk in a popular television cartoon series of the 1960s.
VARIANTS: Alwyn, Aylwin.

Aly ♀ Variant spelling of ▷Ally.

Alys ♀ Variant spelling of ▷Alice.

Alyson ♀ Variant spelling of ▷Alison.

Alysoun ♀ Medieval spelling of ▷Alison, which has enjoyed some currency since the 20th century.

Alyssa ♀ Variant spelling of ▷Alissa.

Amabel ♀ From Latin *amabilis* 'lovable' via Old French. Although now very rare in the English-speaking world, this name lies behind the much commoner name ▷Annabel and also ▷Mabel. It gained some currency from being borne by the character Amabel Rose Adams in Angela Thirkell's *Barsetshire Chronicles* (1933 onwards).

Amadeus ♂ Medieval Latin name meaning 'love God', probably originally a deliberate calque of Greek *Theophilos* (see ▷Theophilus). The name was traditional in the royal house of Savoy; bearers include the Blessed Amadeus IX, Duke of Savoy (1435–72). In the English-speaking world it is famous chiefly as the second name of the composer Wolfgang Amadeus Mozart (1756–91), for whom it was a Latin version of German **Gottlieb** (see German appendix). It is occasionally bestowed by music-loving parents in his honour.

Amalia ♀ Latinized form of the Germanic name *Amal*, meaning 'work'. This was a first element in various names—now more or less obsolete—for which *Amal* was used as a short form. *Amalia* is chiefly German and Scandinavian, but is also found occasionally in the English-speaking world. Its popularity was enhanced in Germany in the 18th century by the fame of Anna Amalia, Duchess of Saxe-Weimar (1739–1807), a great patron of the arts, whose court attracted Goethe, Schiller, Herder, and many others.

Amanda ♀ A 17th-century literary coinage from the Latin gerundive (feminine) *amanda* 'lovable, fit to be loved', from *amare* 'to love'. This is evidently modelled on ▷Miranda; the masculine form *Amandus*, borne by various saints from the 4th to the 7th century, seems not to have been the direct source of the feminine form. The girl's name enjoyed considerable popularity in the mid-20th century.
SHORT FORM: **Manda**.

PET FORM: ▷**Mandy**.

Amaryllis ♀ Of Greek origin and uncertain derivation, possibly from *amaryssein* 'to sparkle'. It was borne in classical pastoral poetry, including Virgil's *Eclogues*, by a typical shepherdess or country girl. In modern times the name has probably sometimes been given because of association with the flower, named in the 19th century from the Arcadian heroine.

Amber ♀ From the word for the fossilized resin *amber*, a word derived via Old French and Latin from Arabic *ambar*. This was first used as a given name at the end of the 19th century. It enjoyed a surge in popularity following the publication of Kathleen Winsor's novel *Forever Amber* in 1944, and again in the 1990s.

Ambrose ♂ English form of the Late Latin name *Ambrosius*, from post-classical Greek *Ambrosios* 'immortal'. This was borne by various early saints, most notably a 4th-century bishop of Milan. The name has never been common in England, but has enjoyed considerably greater popularity in Roman Catholic Ireland, where the surname *Mac Ambrois* is Anglicized as *McCambridge*.
COGNATES: Irish: **Ambrós**. Welsh: **Emrys**. French: **Ambroise**. Spanish, Portuguese: **Ambrosio**. Catalan: **Ambròs**. Italian: **Ambrogio**. Polish: **Ambrozy**. Czech: **Ambrož**. Hungarian: **Ambróz**.

Amelia ♀ A blend of two medieval names: *Emilia* (which is of Latin origin: see ▷Emily) and the Latinized Germanic ▷Amalia. Henry Fielding is sometimes credited with having coined it for the heroine of his novel *Amelia* (1751), but forms such as *Meelia*, *Amaly* and *Aemelia* occur from the 17th century onwards.
VARIANTS: **Emelia, Emilia**.

Amélie ♀ French equivalent of ▷Amelia, now also used in the English-speaking world, with or without the accent; it received a boost in popularity with the release of the French film *Amélie* (2001), directed by Jean-Pierre Jennet.

Amias ♂ Rare, and of uncertain origin, possibly from the surname *Amias*, which is a local name for someone from Amiens in France. However, both surname and given name are rare. The ending *-ias* is found in biblical names (e.g. ▷Tobias), where it represents a Greek form of Hebrew *-iyah* 'God'; *Amias* may sometimes have been chosen in the belief that it was a biblical name, reinforced by the fact that *am-* is the Latin root meaning 'love'. See also ▷Amiaz and ▷Amyas.

Amiaz ♂ Jewish: modern Hebrew given name, meaning 'my people are strong'.

Amice ♀ From a medieval given name derived from Latin *ami(ci)tia* 'friendship'; see ▷Amity.

Amie ♀ Variant spelling of ▷Amy, corresponding in form to the French vocabulary word meaning '(female) friend'.

Amita ♀ Apparently a modern creation, an altered form of ▷Amity. In form it coincides with Latin *amita* 'maternal aunt'.

Amittai ♂ Jewish: biblical name, meaning 'true' or 'honest' in Hebrew, borne by the father of Jonah (2 Kings 14:25).

Amity ♀ Comparatively recent coinage from the learned, Latinate word meaning 'friendship'; compare ▷Amice.

Amnon ♂ Mainly Jewish: biblical name (meaning 'faithful' in Hebrew), borne by King David's eldest son, who raped and abandoned his half-sister Tamar and was killed by her brother Absolom.

Amos ♂ Biblical name, borne by a Hebrew prophet of the 8th century BC, whose sayings are collected in the book of the Bible that bears his name. This is of uncertain derivation, but may be connected with the Hebrew verb *amos* 'to carry'. In some traditions it is assigned the meaning 'borne by God'. The name is used among Christians as well as Jews, and was popular among the Puritans. In Britain it survived well into the 19th century, and has recently enjoyed a modest revival. Its popularity in the U.S. continues.

Amshel ♂ Jewish (Yiddish): variant of ▷Antshel.

Amy ♀ Anglicized form of Old French *Amee* 'beloved'. This originated in part as a vernacular nickname, in part as a form of Latin *Amata*. The latter is ostensibly the feminine form of the past participle of *amare* 'to love', but in fact it may have had a different, pre-Roman, origin; it was borne in classical mythology by the wife of King Latinus, whose daughter Lavinia married Aeneas and (according to the story in the *Aeneid*) became the mother of the Roman people.

VARIANT SPELLINGS: Ami(e), Aimie; Aimée (French form).

Amyas ♂ Of uncertain origin; possibly a variant of ▷Amias. It first occurs in Spenser's *Faerie Queene*, in which it is the name of a 'squire of low degree'.

Anaïs ♀ Catalan and Provençal derivative of *Ana* (see ▷Anne), now also used in the English-speaking world.

Anastasia ♀ Russian: feminine form of the Greek male name *Anastasios* (a derivative of *anastasis* 'resurrection'). It has always been popular in Eastern Europe, in honour of a 4th-century saint who was martyred at Sirmium in Dalmatia. It was also used occasionally in England in the Middle Ages and as late as the 17th century; more recently it has made a considerable comeback. One of the daughters of the last tsar of Russia bore this name. She was murdered by the Bolsheviks in 1918, along with the rest of her family, but in 1920 a woman claiming to be the

Romanov princess Anastasia came to public notice in Germany, and a film was later based on this story (1956).

Andra ♀ Modern feminine form of ▷Andrew. See also Scottish appendix.

André ♂ French form of ▷Andrew, now also used in the English-speaking world.

Andrea ♀ Of disputed origin. It has been in use since the 17th century. It is now generally taken as a feminine equivalent of ▷Andreas, and this probably represents its actual origin. However, it was not in use in the Middle Ages, and the suggestion has also been made that it represents a coinage in English from the Greek vocabulary word *andreia* 'manliness, virility'.

Andreas ♂ The original New Testament Greek form of ▷Andrew, used in the English-speaking world as a learned variant.

Andrew ♂ English form of the Greek name *Andreas*, a short form of any of various compound names derived from *andr-* 'man, warrior'. In the New Testament this is the name of the first disciple to be called by Jesus. After the Resurrection, St Andrew preached in Asia Minor and Greece. He is traditionally believed to have been crucified at Patras in Achaia. He was one of the most popular saints of the Middle Ages and was adopted as the patron of Scotland, Russia, and Greece. It has long been among the most popular boys' names in the English-speaking world, especially in Scotland. Its popularity in England was further enhanced by its use as a British royal name for Prince Andrew (b. 1960), the Duke of York.

SHORT FORM (MAINLY SCOTTISH): **Drew.**

PET FORM (ENGLISH AND SCOTTISH): **Andy.**

COGNATES: Irish: **Aindrias, Aindréas; Aindriú.** Scottish Gaelic: **Aindrea,**

Anndra. Welsh: Andras. German: Andreas. Dutch: Andries. Scandinavian: Anders. French: André. Spanish: Andrés. Catalan: Andreu. Portuguese: Andre. Italian: Andrea. Russian, Bulgarian: Andrei. Polish: Andrzej, Jędrzej. Czech: Andrej, Ondřej. Croatian, Serbian: Andrija. Slovenian: Andrej. Finnish: Antero. Hungarian: András, Endre. Lithuanian: Andrius. Latvian: Andrejs.

Andriana ♀ Modern coinage, apparently a blend of ▷Andrea and *Adriana* (see ▷Adrianne) or possibly ▷Arianna.

Andrine ♀ Comparatively rare feminine derivative of ▷Andrew with the characteristically feminine ending -*ine*.

Andy ♂ Pet form of ▷Andrew, now sometimes bestowed in its own right.

Aneurin ♂ Modern form of Welsh Aneirin (see Welsh appendix), occasionally bestowed outside the Welsh-speaking world in honour of the statesman Aneurin Bevan (1897–1960). This was the name of the first known Welsh poet, who lived AD *c.*600. The 'Book of Aneirin' is a 13th-century manuscript which purports to preserve his work, including the *Gododdin*, a long work about the defeat of the Welsh by the Saxons.

PET FORM: **Nye.**

Angel ♂, ♀ Very common Spanish boy's name (pronounced with a hard g and the stress on the second syllable), a vernacular derivative (via Latin) of Greek *angelos*, which meant 'messenger' in classical Greek, but in New Testament Greek acquired the specialized sense 'messenger of God', i.e. an angel. It is common in the U.S. In Britain it is now almost exclusively a girl's name, but it was used occasionally as a boy's name from the 1400s, if not earlier. As such it is familiar as the name of Angel Clare, the chief male character in Thomas Hardy's novel *Tess of the D'Urbervilles* (1891).

Angela ♀ From Church Latin, a feminine form of the boy's name *Angelus* (see ▷Angel). The older feminine form *Angelis* has been completely superseded by *Angela*, which increased greatly in popularity in Britain and America from the 18th century onwards.

PET FORM: Angie.

Angelica ♀ From Church Latin, from the feminine form of the Latin adjective *angelicus* 'angelic', or simply a Latinate elaboration of ▷Angela.

Angelina ♀ Latinate elaboration of ▷Angela.

VARIANT: Angeline (the French form, now also used in the English-speaking world).

Angie ♀ Pet form of ▷Angela.

Angus ♂ Anglicized form of the Scottish Gaelic name Aonghas (see Scottish appendix). Though still having a Scottish flavour, it has been used increasingly in modern times also by people without Scottish connections.

USUAL IRISH FORM: Aengus.

SHORT FORM: ▷Gus.

PET FORM: Angie (Scottish, pronounced 'an-ghee', representing Gaelic *Angaidh*).

Anise ♀ Modern coinage, apparently from the name of the aniseed plant (Old French *anis*, from Latin and Greek). For other modern first names derived from spices, see ▷Clove and ▷Juniper. It is possible that it was influenced by the medieval first name ▷Annis.

Anita ♀ Originally a Spanish pet form of *Ana*, the Spanish version of ▷Anne. It is now widely used in English-speaking countries with little awareness of its Spanish origin. In the 1950s it came to prominence as the name of the Swedish film actress Anita Ekberg

(b. 1931); more recently it has been associated with the British business woman and campaigner Anita Roddick (1943–2007).

Anitra ♀ Apparently a literary coinage by Henrik Ibsen, who used it as the name of an Eastern princess in *Peer Gynt* (1867). No Arabic original is known. It is now occasionally used as a given name, not only in Norway but also elsewhere in Scandinavia, Germany, and the English-speaking world.

Ann ♀ Variant spelling of ▷Anne. In the U.S. *Ann* is the more frequent spelling.

Anna ♀ Latinate variant of ▷Anne, in common use as a given name in most European languages. Among people with a classical education, it has from time to time been associated with Virgil's *Aeneid*, where it is borne by the sister of Dido, Queen of Carthage. This Phoenician name may ultimately be of Semitic origin, and thus related to the biblical *Anne*. However, the connection, if it exists, is indirect rather than direct.

Annabel ♀ Sometimes taken as an elaboration of ▷Anna, but more probably a dissimilated form of ▷Amabel. It has been common in Scotland since the 12th century and was still in use in England in the 1600s. Its recent revival in popularity in England and elsewhere dates from the 1940s.

VARIANTS: Annabell: Annabella (Latinized form); Annabelle (Gallicized form, under the influence of ▷Belle).

Annalisa ♀ Anglicized spelling of the German and Scandinavian compound name Anneliese (see German appendix), which has enjoyed increasing popularity in the English-speaking world in recent times.

VARIANTS: Annaliesa, Annalise, Annelise; Annelies.

Anne ♀ English form (via Old French, Latin, and Greek) of the Hebrew girl's name *Hanna* 'He (God) has favoured me (i.e. with a child)'. This is the name borne in the Bible by the mother of Samuel (see ▷Hannah), and according to non-biblical tradition also by the mother of the Virgin Mary. It is the widespread folk cult of the latter that has led to the great popularity of the name in various forms throughout Europe. The simplified form ▷Ann was much more common in the 19th century but the form with final -*e* grew in popularity during the 20th century, partly perhaps due to L. M. Montgomery's story *Anne of Green Gables* (1908), and partly due to Princess Anne (b. 1950). See also ▷Anna.

PET FORMS: Annie. Dutch: Anneke.

Anneka ♀ Latinate variant of the Dutch name Anneke, a pet form of ▷Anne, popularized in Britain in the 1980s by the television presenter Anneka Rice.

VARIANTS: An(n)ika.

Annelie ♀ Elaborated form of ▷Anne or an Anglicized spelling of Scandinavian *Anneli*, a shortened form of the originally German name Anneliese (see German appendix).

Annella ♀ Elaborated form of ▷Anne. It is favoured in the Highlands of Scotland.

Annemarie ♀ Compound name composed of ▷Anne and ▷Marie.

VARIANTS: Annmarie; Annamarie, Annamaria.

Annette ♀ French pet form of ▷Anne, now also widely used in the English-speaking world.

VARIANT: Annetta (Latinate form).

Annice ♀ Variant spelling of ▷Annis, based on the numerous women's names ending in -*ice*.

Annie ♀ Pet form of ▷Ann or ▷Anne.

VARIANT: Anni.

Annika ♀ Respelling of ▷Anneka.

Annis ♀ Scottish and English: a medieval vernacular form of ▷Agnes, which gave rise to a surname. Its modern use as a given name is probably at least in part a transferred use of the surname as well as a revival of the medieval given name.

VARIANTS: Annys, Annice.

Anona ♀ Of uncertain origin, apparently not recorded before the 1920s. It seems most likely that it arose as an artificial combination of elements from existing names, for example ▷Anne and ▷Fiona. In form it resembles Latin *annona* 'corn supply', but this is unlikely to have influenced the formation of the name. It is now rarely used.

Anouk ♀ French: said to be a pet form of ▷Anne. It is famous as the adopted name of the French film actress Anouk Aimée (b. 1952), and is now found also in the English-speaking world.

Anouska ♀ Anglicized spelling of Russian *Anuska*, a pet form of ▷Anna, now increasingly adopted in the English-speaking world.

VARIANT: Anoushka.

Anselm ♂ Of Germanic origin, a compound of *ans* 'divinity' + *helm* 'helmet'. It was brought from Italy to England by St Anselm, who was Archbishop of Canterbury in the late 11th and early 12th centuries, and is regarded as one of the Doctors of the Church. The name is now relatively infrequent and used mainly by Roman Catholics.

Anshel ♂ Jewish (Yiddish): variant of ▷Antshel.

Anthea ♀ Latinized spelling of Greek *Antheia*, a personal name derived from the feminine of the adjective *antheios* 'flowery'. This was used in the classical period as a byname of the goddess Hera at Argos, but as a modern given name it was reinvented in the 17th century by English pastoral poets such as Robert Herrick.

Anthonia ♀ Variant spelling of ▷Antonia, modelled on the spelling of ▷Anthony.

Anthony ♂ The usual English form of the old Roman family name *Antonius*, which is of uncertain (probably Etruscan) origin. The spelling with *-th-* (not normally reflected in the pronunciation) represents a learned but erroneous attempt to associate it with Greek *anthos* 'flower'. In the post-classical period it was a common name, borne by various early saints, most notably a 3rd-century Egyptian hermit monk, who is regarded as the founder of Christian monasticism.

VARIANT: **Antony.**

SHORT FORM: **Tony.**

COGNATES: Irish: **Antain(e).** German, Dutch, Scandinavian: **Anton.** French: **Antoine.** Spanish: **Antonio.** Catalan: **Antoni.** Portuguese: **António.** Italian: **Antonio.** Russian, Bulgarian: **Anton.** Polish: **Antoni.** Czech: **Antonín** (from Latin *Antoninus*). Croatian: **Ante, Antun.** Slovenian: **Anton.** Hungarian: **Antal.** Lithuanian: **Antanas** (from Latin *Antoninus*).

Antigone ♀ Classical name in occasional modern use, a compound of *anti* 'against, contrary' + *gen-*, *gon-* 'born'. In Greek mythology Antigone was a daughter of Oedipus by his accidental incestuous marriage to his own mother, Jocasta. After her brothers, Eteocles and Polynices, killed each other, she gave funeral rites to both of them, defying the order of her uncle Creon, King of Thebes, that the rebel Polynices should be left unburied. For this, Creon had her buried alive. Its choice as a modern given name is perhaps made with reference to her strength of character in doing what she perceived as right.

Antoine ♂ French equivalent of ▷Anthony, now also used in the English-speaking world.

VARIANT: **Antwan** (U.S. respelling).

Antoinette ♀ French feminine diminutive of ▷Antoine, which has become popular in the English-speaking world.

SHORT FORM: **Toinette.**

Anton ♂ Common European form of ▷Anthony (see cognates list), now also used in the English-speaking world.

Antonella ♀ Modern feminine form of ▷Anton, created by fusion with the productive feminine suffix *-ella*.

Antonia ♀ Latin feminine form of ▷Anthony, unaltered since classical times, when it was a common Roman feminine family name.

VARIANT: **Anthonia.**

PET FORM: **Toni.**

Antonietta ♀ Modern pet form of ▷Antonia.

Antonina ♀ Latin derivative of ▷Antonia, common in Poland and occasionally used in the English-speaking world.

Antonino ♂ Italian pet form of ▷Antonio, now also used in parts of the English-speaking world.

Antonio ♂ Italian and Spanish form of ▷Anthony, from Latin *Antonius*, also used in English-speaking countries.

Antony ♂ Variant spelling of ▷Anthony.

Antrim ♂ From the name of the region and county in Northern Ireland, in Gaelic *Aontraim*. This is probably derived from Gaelic *aon* 'one' + *treabh* 'house', and so referred originally to a single isolated dwelling that subsequently became the centre of a village and then of a town, which in turn gave its name to the county. The given name has occasionally been chosen by parents who have an association with this region.

Antshel ♂ Jewish (Yiddish): ultimately from Latin *angelus* 'angel'.

VARIANTS: **Anshel, Amshel.**

Anya ♀ Popular Anglicized form of Spanish Ana (see Spanish appendix).

Aphra ♀ Of uncertain origin. It could be an altered spelling of a Late Latin name, *Afra*. This was originally an ethnic name for a woman from Africa (in Roman times meaning the area around Carthage). It was used in the post-classical period as a nickname for a dark person, and eventually became a given name, being borne, for example, by saints martyred at Brescia under the Roman emperor Hadrian and at Augsburg under Diocletian. The respelling of the name may have been prompted by Micah 1:10 'in the house of Aphrah roll thyself in the dust', where *Aphrah* is often taken as a personal name, but is in fact a place name meaning 'dust'. As a given name it has never been frequent, and is known chiefly as the name of the writer Aphra Behn (1640–89).

Apollinaria ♀ Feminine form of Latin *Apollinaris* (itself from an adjectival form of the name of the god *Apollo*), influenced by ▷Apollonia. It has been used in Russian and occasionally in English.

Apollonia ♀ Latin feminine form of the Greek masculine name *Apollonios*, an adjectival derivative of the name of the sun god, *Apollo*. This is of uncertain origin, and may be pre-Greek. St Apollonia was an elderly deaconess martyred at Alexandria under the Emperor Decius in the mid 3rd century.

April ♀ From the month (Latin (*mensis*) *aprilis*, probably a derivative of *aperire* 'to open', as the month when buds open and flowers appear). It forms part of a series with ▷May and ▷June, all names taken from months associated with the spring, a time of new birth and growth, and may originally have been intended as an English version of the supposedly French name ▷Avril.

Arabella ♀ Of uncertain origin; probably an altered form of *An(n)abella* (see ▷Annabel). It occurs in Scotland and the North of England from the 1600s onwards.

VARIANT: Arabel (now rare, but commoner in earlier centuries, when it was also sometimes found as Orabel, apparently altered by folk etymology to conform with Latin *orabilis* 'invokable' (from *orare* 'to pray to'), i.e. a saint who could be invoked).

Aram ♂ Biblical name, meaning 'height' in Hebrew, borne by a son of Shem and grandson of Noah mentioned in a genealogy (Genesis 10: 22).

Archer ♂ Transferred use of the surname, in origin an occupational name for a bowman (Old French *arch(i)er*, from Latin *arc(u)arius*, a derivative of *arcus* 'bow'). In Australia it may sometimes have been chosen as a given name in tribute to the seven Archer brothers (Charles, John, David, William, Archibald, Thomas, and Colin) who were well-known pastoralists and explorers in 19th-century Queensland.

Archibald ♂ Of Norman French origin, from a Germanic (Frankish) personal name derived from *ercan* 'genuine' + *bald* 'bold, brave'. See also Scottish appendix.

VARIANT: Archibold.

PET FORMS: Archie, Archy; Scottish: Baldie.

Archie ♂ Pet form of ▷Archibald, adopted as an independent given name from the 19th century. Since the beginning of the 21st century it has enjoyed a burst of popularity.

Aretha ♀ Mainly U.S.: probably intended as a derivative of Greek *aretē* 'excellence'. It is principally associated with the singer Aretha Franklin (b. 1942), the 'goddess of soul'.

Ariadne ♀ From classical mythology: the name of a daughter of the Cretan king Minos. She gave the Athenian hero Theseus a ball of wool to enable him to find his way out of the Labyrinth after killing the Minotaur. He took her with him when he sailed from Crete, but abandoned her on the island of Naxos on the way back to Athens. Greek lexicographers of the Hellenistic period claimed that the name was composed of the Cretan dialect elements *ari-* (an intensive prefix) + *adnos* 'holy'. The name survived in the Christian era because of St Ariadne (d. *c.*130), an early Phrygian martyr.

VARIANTS: **Ariana** (simplified form); **Arianna** (Italian), **Arianne** (French).

Arianna ♀ Italian form of ▷Ariadne, now also used in English-speaking countries, especially the United States.

Ariel ♂, ♀ From the biblical place name *Ariel*, said to mean 'lion of God' in Hebrew. It is mentioned in the prophecies of Ezra (8:16) and Isaiah (29:1–2). This is relatively common as a boy's name in modern Israel, but in the United States it is more frequently used as a girl's name.

Arielle ♀ Recent coinage, a distinctively female form of ▷Ariel, now quite common in the United States.

VARIANT: **Ariella**.

Arjun ♂ Indian name meaning 'white' in Sanskrit; see Indian appendix.

Arke ♂ Jewish: Yiddish pet form of ▷Aaron.

Arlene ♀ Modern coinage, most common in North America. It is of unknown origin, probably a fanciful coinage based on ▷Marlene or ▷Charlene, or both. It became famous in the 1950s as the name of the American actress and beauty columnist Arlene Dahl (b. 1924).

VARIANTS: **Arleen, Arline**.

Arlette ♀ Of ancient but uncertain origin. It is apparently a Norman French double diminutive, from Germanic *arn* 'eagle'. It was the name of the mistress of Duke Robert of Normandy in the 11th century; their son was William the Conqueror.

Armani ♂, ♀ Modern coinage, inspired no doubt by the celebrated Italian fashion designer Giorgio Armani (b. 1935), whose surname is derived from the medieval personal name *Armanno*, a Lombardic name from Germanic *hariman* 'freeman'.

Armstrong ♂ Transferred use of the surname, which originated in the Scottish Borders, probably as a nickname for a man with strong arms.

Arn ♂ **1.** Jewish: Yiddish contracted form of ▷Aaron. **2.** English: short form of ▷Arnold.

PET FORM: **Arnie**.

Arnold ♂ From an Old French name, *Arnald, Arnaud*, which is of Germanic (Frankish) origin, from *arn* 'eagle' + *wald* 'ruler'. It was adopted by the Normans and introduced to Britain by them. An early saint of this name, whose cult contributed to its popularity, was a musician at the court of Charlemagne. He is said to have been a Greek by birth; it is not clear when and how he acquired his Germanic name. It never entirely went out of use in England, and came back into more general favour in the 19th century, along with several other medieval Germanic names.

SHORT FORM: **Arn**.

PET FORM: **Arnie**.

Aron ♂ Simplified form of ▷Aaron.

Arran ♂ Modern coinage, apparently taken from the name of the Isle of Arran off the west coast of Scotland. In part it may also be a respelling of ▷Aaron.

Arron ♂ Variant of either ▷Aaron or ▷Arran.

Art ♂ Short form of ▷Arthur. There is also a traditional Gaelic name of this form (from *art* 'bear'; see Irish appendix) which has generally been Anglicized as *Arthur*, although it in fact has no connection with that name. In the diminutive form *Artan* it has given rise to the Skye surname *Mac Artain*, Anglicized as *McCartan*.

Artemas ♂ Of New Testament Greek origin, from a name representing a short form of various compound names containing that of the goddess ▷Artemis (for example, *Artemidoros* 'gift of Artemis' and *Artemisthenes* 'strength of Artemis'). It is borne in the Bible by a character mentioned briefly in St Paul's letter to Titus (3:12). The name enjoyed some popularity among the Puritans in the 17th century, but fell out of use again.

VARIANT: **Artemus** (Latinized).

Artemis ♀ From the name of the Greek goddess of the moon and of hunting, equivalent to the Latin ▷Diana. It is of uncertain derivation, and may well be pre-Greek. As a given name it is rare, but is chosen occasionally by parents in search of something distinctive. It is borne by a granddaughter of Lady Diana Cooper, perhaps as an oblique tribute to the grandmother.

Artemus ♂ Variant of ▷Artemas.

Arthur ♂ Of Celtic origin. King Arthur was a British king of the 5th or 6th century, about whom virtually no historical facts are known. He ruled in Britain after the collapse of the Roman Empire and before the coming of the Germanic tribes, and a vast body of legends grew up around him in the literatures of medieval Western Europe. His name is first found in the Latinized form *Artorius*; it is of obscure etymology. The spelling with *-th-* was popular among the gentry families of West Yorkshire in the late 1400s, even before Henry VII, who may have hoped to capitalize on the legend, gave the name to his son. It remained in regular use in some areas and its popularity exploded in the early 19th century, largely as a result of the fame of Arthur Wellesley (1769–1852), Duke of Wellington, the victor at the Battle of Waterloo and subsequently prime minister. Further influences were Tennyson's *Idylls of the King* (1859–85), and the widespread Victorian interest, especially among the Pre-Raphaelites, in things medieval in general and in Arthurian legend in particular.

SHORT FORM: ▷Art.

Arye ♂ Jewish: meaning 'lion' in Hebrew. The lion is traditionally associated with the name ▷Judah (Hebrew *Yehuda*), because of Jacob's dying blessing, which included the words: 'Judah is a lion's whelp' (Genesis 49:9). The name became common during the Middle Ages when such animal names were popular in Europe (compare Yiddish ▷Leib).

Asa ♂ Biblical name, borne by one of the early kings of Judah, who reigned for forty years, as recorded in 1 Kings and 2 Chronicles. It was originally a byname meaning 'doctor, healer' in Hebrew, and is still a common Jewish name. It was first used among English-speaking Christians by the Puritans in the 17th century.

Asaph ♂ Biblical name, meaning 'collector' in Hebrew. It is found attached to some of the Psalms (50 and 73–83), and may have been the name of the writer or of a cantor. It is also mentioned at 1 Chronicles 6:39, 9:15, and 25:1; and other, apparently unrelated bearers of the name are mentioned at 2 Kings 18:37 and Isaiah 36:3 and 36:22. In more recent times the name was borne by Asaph Hall (1829–1907), the American astronomer who discovered the two satellites of Mars.

Asenath ♀ Biblical name, borne by Joseph's Egyptian wife (Genesis 41:45), who became the mother of Manasseh and Ephraim. The name is said to have meant 'she belongs to her father' in Ancient Egyptian.

Ashanti ♀ Modern coinage from the name of a people of south central

Ghana, used mainly by Blacks as a symbol of pride in their African roots.

Asher ♂ Jewish: meaning 'fortunate' or 'happy' in Hebrew. It was borne in the Bible by one of the sons of Jacob: 'and Leah said, Happy am I, for the daughters will call me blessed; and she called his name Asher' (Genesis 30:13). Outside the Jewish community, it is probably a transferred use of the surname, derived from a local name for someone who lived by an ash tree, Middle English *asche*.

VARIANT: **Osher**.

Ashley ♀, ♂ Originally male, but now an increasingly popular given name for girls, this is a transferred use of the surname, which comes from any of numerous places in England named with Old English *æsc* 'ash' + *lēah* 'wood'. It is recorded as a given name in the 16th century, but its wider use was probably inspired by Anthony Ashley Cooper (1801–85), 7th Earl of Shaftesbury, a noted humanitarian who inspired much of the legislation designed to improve conditions among the working classes. It became one of the three most popular girls' names in North America in the latter half of the 20th century, with a wide variety of spellings.

VARIANTS: **Ashlea, Ashleigh, Ashlee, Ashlie, Ashly** all ♀.

Ashling ♀ Anglicized form of the modern Irish name **Aisling** (pronounced 'ash-ling'; see Irish appendix).

Ashlyn ♀ Altered form of ▷Ashling, or else a combination of the first syllable of the popular girl's name ▷Ashley with the suffix -*lyn*.

VARIANTS: **Ashlynn, Ashlynne**.

Ashton ♀, ♂ Transferred use of the surname, a local name from any of the numerous places in England named with Old English *æsc* 'ash tree' + *tūn* 'enclosure, settlement'. This occurs occasionally as a boy's name in England

from the 1600s; it is now used also for girls, partly, perhaps, due to the vogue for ▷Ashley.

Asia ♀ Modern name, usually chosen with reference to the continent of Asia. The name of this is from Greek, of uncertain ultimate origin; it may derive from an Assyrian element *asu* 'east'. The given name may also sometimes be a shortened form of a name ending in these letters, such as Aspasia.

VARIANTS: **Ashia, Aysha**.

Aspen ♀ Mainly U.S.: from the name of the tree, a type of poplar with delicately quivering leaves. The word was originally an adjective, derived from the tree-name *asp* (Old English *æspe*), but came to be used as a noun in the 16th century. Development as a personal name may also have been influenced by the name of the fashionable ski resort, Aspen, Colorado.

Aston ♀, ♂ Generally a transferred use of the surname, a local name from any of the numerous places in England named with Old English *ēast* 'east' + *tūn* 'settlement', or occasionally *æsc* 'ash tree' + *tūn* 'settlement'. There is, however, a Middle English personal name, *Astan(us)* (probably a survival of Old English *Æðelstān*), which may have survived in some places in this form.

Astra ♀ Modern coinage meaning 'star', based on either Greek *aster* or Latin *astrum*.

Astrid ♀ Scandinavian name, derived from Old Norse *áss* 'god' + *fríðr* 'fair, beautiful'. It came into use in the English-speaking world during the 20th century, influenced to some extent by Queen Astrid of the Belgians (1905–35).

SHORT FORM: **Asta**.

Atalanta ♀ From classical mythology. Atalanta was a girl who was a swift runner and who took part in the hunt for the Calydonian boar. Meleager, leader of the hunt, gave her its pelt, for he had fallen in love with her. However, he died as a result of quarrels with his brothers. Atalanta undertook to marry only a man who could defeat her in a race; losers were condemned to death. Eventually, Hippomenes defeated her by dropping three golden apples which she stopped to pick up.

Atarah ♀ Biblical name from a Hebrew word meaning 'crown'. Atarah was one of the wives of Jerahmeel (1 Chronicles 2:26).

VARIANT: **Atara** (now a common modern Hebrew name, possibly as a translation of Yiddish ▷Kreine).

Athanasius ♂ Latin name of an early Christian saint (*c.*297–373), an Alexandrian theologian venerated particularly in the Eastern Church. His name is derived from the Greek vocabulary word *athanatos* 'immortal', and was popular among early Christians, since it expressed their confidence in eternal life.

Athene ♀ In classical mythology the name of the Greek goddess of wisdom and patron of Athens.

VARIANTS: **Athena, Athina.**

Atholl ♂, ♀ Transferred use of the Scottish place name, a district of Perthshire, seat of the dukes of Atholl. The place name is thought to derive from Gaelic *ath Fodla* 'new Ireland'.

VARIANTS: **Athol, Athole.**

Auberon ♂ From an Old French name of Germanic (Frankish) origin. There is some doubt about its origin; it may be connected with ▷Aubrey or be derived from *adal* 'noble' + *ber(n)* 'bear'. Its best-known bearer in recent times was the writer and journalist Auberon Waugh (1939–2001) and, as Oberon, it was borne by the king of the fairies in Shakespeare's *A Midsummer Night's Dream*.

VARIANT: **Oberon.**

SHORT FORM: **Bron.**

Aubrey ♂, ♀ From a Norman French form of the Germanic name *Alberic*,

from *alb* 'elf, supernatural being' + *ric* 'power'. This was the name, according to Germanic mythology, of the king of the elves. The native Old English form, *Ælfrīc*, borne by a 10th-century archbishop of Canterbury, did not long survive the Conquest. *Aubrey* was a relatively common given name during the Middle Ages, but later fell out of favour. Its occurrence since the 19th century may in part represent a transferred use of the surname derived from the Norman given name, as well as a revival of the latter. In the United States, this is mainly used as a girl's name, perhaps under the influence of ▷Audrey.

VARIANT: **Aubree** (feminine form).

Audley ♂ Transferred use of the surname derived from a place in Staffordshire named with the Old English female personal name *Aldgȳth* + *lēah* 'clearing'.

Audra ♀ Modern variant of ▷Audrey, used especially in the southern United States in forms such as **Audra Jo** and **Audra Rose**.

Audrey ♀ Much altered form of the Old English girl's name *Æðelþrȳð*, derived from *æðel* 'noble' + *þrȳð* 'strength'. This was the name of a 6th-century saint (normally known by the Latinized form of her name, *Etheldreda*), who was a particular favourite in the Middle Ages. According to tradition she died from a tumour of the neck, which she bore stoically as a divine punishment for her youthful delight in fine necklaces. The name went into a decline at the end of the Middle Ages, when it came to be considered vulgar, being associated with *tawdry*, that is, lace and other goods sold at fairs held in her name (the word deriving from a misdivision of *Saint Audrey*). Shakespeare bestowed it on Touchstone's comic sweetheart in *As You Like It*. In the 20th century, such associations largely forgotten, the name was revived, partly due in the

1950s and 60s to the popularity of the actress Audrey Hepburn (1929–93).

VARIANTS: Audrie, Audry.

Audrina ♀ Fanciful elaboration of ▷Audrey, of recent origin.

Augusta ♀ Latinate feminine form of ▷Augustus, which enjoyed a vogue in Britain towards the end of the 19th century but has since fallen out of favour.

Augustina ♀ Feminine form of ▷Augustus, a recent coinage.

Augustine ♂ English form of the Latin name *Augustinus* (a derivative of ▷Augustus). Its most famous bearer is St Augustine of Hippo (354–430), perhaps the greatest of the Fathers of the Christian Church. He formulated the principles followed by the numerous medieval communities named after him as Austin canons, friars, and nuns. Also important in England was St Augustine of Canterbury, who brought Christianity to Kent in the 6th century. See also ▷Austin.

COGNATES: Irish: Ághaistín, Aibhistín. German: Augustin. Dutch: Augustijn. French: Augustine. Spanish: Agustín. Catalan: Agustí. Portuguese: Agostinho. Italian: Agostino. Russian: Avgustin. Finnish: Tauno. Hungarian: Ágoston. Lithuanian: Augustinas.

Augustus ♂ Latin name, from the adjective *augustus* 'great, magnificent' (from *augere* 'to increase'). This word was adopted as a title by the Roman emperors, starting with Octavian (Gaius Julius Caesar Octavianus), the adopted son of Julius Caesar, who assumed it in 27 BC and is now generally known as the Emperor Augustus. This name, together with ▷Augusta, was revived in England in the 18th century, but it has now again declined in popularity.

SHORT FORM: Gus.

Aurelia ♀ Feminine form of Latin *Aurelius*, a family name derived from *aureus* 'golden'. The name was borne by several minor early saints, but its revival as a given name in the 17th century is probably due to its meaning rather than association with any of them.

Auriol ♀ From Latin *aureola*, feminine diminutive form of *aureus* 'golden'. It has been used selectively since the 19th century, making modest gains in popularity in recent decades.

VARIANTS: Auriel, Auriole.

Aurora ♀ From Latin *aurora* 'dawn', also used in the classical period as the name of the personified goddess of the dawn. It was not used as a given name in the post-classical or medieval periods, but is a reinvention of the Renaissance, and has generally been bestowed as a learned equivalent of ▷Dawn.

Austin ♂ Medieval vernacular form of the Latin name *Augustinus* (see ▷Augustine). Both forms were used selectively in various regions of England as late as the 17th century and they are found occasionally much later, but the present-day use of this form as a given name is normally a reintroduction from its survival as a surname. It is particularly popular in the United States.

VARIANTS: Austen, Austyn.

Autumn ♀ Mainly U.S.: from the name of the season (Latin *autumnus*). This is now more popular as a given name than ▷Summer, in spite of its less sunny connotations and the fact that in American English *autumn* is felt to be a rather formal word.

Ava ♀ Of uncertain origin, probably Germanic, from a short form of various female compound names containing the element *av* (of uncertain meaning). St Ava or Avia was a 9th-century abbess of Dinart in Hainault and a member of the Frankish royal family. However, evidence for the existence of the name between the early Middle Ages and the mid-20th century is lacking, and it may well be a modern invention. Its popularity since the 1950s is largely due to the film actress Ava Gardner (1922–90).

Avelina ♀ Latinate form of the Norman name ▷Evelyn.

Aveline ♀ Of Germanic origin, introduced to Britain by the Normans. It seems to represent an Old French pet form of the Germanic name ▷Avila (a derivative of ▷Avis), but it could also be an elaborated form of ▷Ava.

Averil ♀ Variant of ▷Avril.

Averill ♂ Mainly U.S.: transferred use of the surname, which originated in the Middle Ages from the Old English female personal name *Eoforhild* (see ▷Avril).

Avery ♀, ♂ Transferred use of the surname, which originated in the Middle Ages from a Norman French pronunciation of ▷Alfred. It is used mainly as a boy's name in Britain, while in North America it is more popular as a girl's name.

Avila ♀ Latinized form of a medieval Germanic name related to ▷Avis, in use in the Middle Ages. The modern name, however, is borne almost exclusively by Roman Catholics, among whom it is given in honour of St Theresa of Avila (1515–82).

Avis ♀ From a Norman French form of the ancient Germanic name *Aveza*, derived from a short form of one or more compound names containing the first element *av* (as in ▷Ava; the meaning is uncertain). The correspondence in form to the Latin word *avis* 'bird' is coincidental.

VARIANT: Avice.

Avishag ♀ Jewish: modern Hebrew form of ▷Abishag.

Avital ♀ Jewish: modern Hebrew form of ▷Abital.

Avner ♂ Jewish: modern Hebrew form of ▷Abner.

Avon ♂ From the name of any of several rivers in England (such as the one on which Stratford-on-Avon is situated or the one that runs through Bristol). All of these were originally named with a Celtic word meaning simply 'river' (Welsh *afon*, Gaelic *abhainn*). Use as a given name may in some cases have been influenced by the popularity of ▷Evan; a recent trend is to create new given names by varying the vowels or consonants of established ones.

Avraham ♀ Jewish: modern Hebrew form of ▷Abraham.

Avril ♀ Although generally taken as the French form of the name of the fourth month (see ▷April), this has also been influenced by an Old English female personal name derived from *eofor* 'boar' + *hild* 'battle'.

Avrom ♂ Jewish: Yiddish form of ▷Abraham.

Axel ♂ Scandinavian (Danish) form of ▷Absalom, also now used in parts of the English-speaking world.

PET FORM: Acke.

Ayesha ♀ Variant of ▷Aisha.

Aylwin ♂ Variant of ▷Alvin.

Aysha ♀ Apparently a fanciful respelling of ▷Asia.

Azalea ♀ Modern coinage from the name of the flowering shrub, one of the most recent of the names taken from terms denoting flora from the 19th century onwards. The shrub was named in the 18th century with the feminine form of Greek *azaleos* 'dry', because it flourishes in dry soil.

Azalia ♀ Modern coinage, an altered spelling of ▷Azalea, perhaps influenced by ▷Azania or ▷Azaria. *Azaliah* is also a male name (meaning 'reserved by God' in Hebrew) borne by a minor biblical character (2 Kings 22:3).

Azania ♀ *Azaniah* is a male name (meaning 'heard by God' in Hebrew) borne by a minor biblical character, which was occasionally used in England by Nonconformists, but this name is now bestowed chiefly with reference to the African nationalist name for South Africa, used as a symbol of resistance during the apartheid era.

Azaria ♀ From the male biblical name *Azariah* (meaning 'helped by God' in Hebrew). This was in occasional use in England from the 17th century onwards, probably in honour of the biblical prophet who recalled King Asa to a proper observance of religion (2 Chronicles 15:1–8). The name is borne by a number of other minor characters in the Bible, all of them male. However, the *-a* ending ensures that it is used as a girl's name in the modern English-speaking world.

VARIANT: **Azarias** (Greek form).

Azelia ♀ Modern coinage, apparently a variant of ▷Azalia, possibly influenced by Greek *azēlos* 'not jealous'.

Azriel ♂ Jewish: meaning 'God helps' in Hebrew. It is borne in the Bible by a character briefly mentioned as a leading member of the tribe of Manasseh (1 Chronicles 5:24).

Bb

Babette ♀ Pet form of ▷Barbara.

Babs ♀ Informal pet form of ▷Barbara.

Bailey ♂, ♀ Transferred use of the surname, which has various origins. Most commonly it was an occupational name for a bailiff or administrative official; in other cases it was a local name for someone who lived near a bailey, i.e. a city fortification; in others it may be a local name from *Bailey* in Lancashire, which gets its name from Old English *bēg* 'berry' + *lēah* 'wood, clearing'. In the United States this is now more popular as a girl's name than a boy's name, though the reverse is true in Britain.
VARIANTS: Bailie, Baily, Bailee, Baileigh; Baylie, Baylee, Bayley, Bayleigh.

Baldwin ♂ From an Old French name of Germanic (Frankish) origin, derived from *bald* 'bold, brave' + *wine* 'friend'. This was adopted by the Normans and introduced by them to Britain. In the Middle Ages it was a comparatively common name, which gave rise to a surname. It was borne by the Norman crusader Baldwin of Boulogne, who in 1100 was elected first king of Jerusalem, and by four further crusader kings of Jerusalem. It continued to be used by some families in England into the 17th century, but in modern times it normally represents a transferred use of the surname rather than a direct revival of the Norman given name.

Balthasar ♂ Name ascribed in medieval Christian tradition to one of the three wise men of the Orient who brought gifts to the infant Jesus. The name is a variant of that of the biblical king *Belshazzar* and means 'Baal protect the king'. It has never been a common given name in the English-speaking world.

VARIANT: Balthazar.

Baptist ♂ English form of Church Latin *baptista*, Greek *baptistēs* (a derivative of *baptein* 'to dip'), the epithet of the most popular of the numerous saints called ▷John. As an English given name it is used mainly in the United States by members of evangelical sects.

Barbara ♀ From Latin, meaning 'foreign woman' (a feminine form of *barbarus* 'foreign', from Greek, referring originally to the unintelligible chatter of foreigners, which sounded to the Greek ear like no more than *bar-bar*). St Barbara has always been one of the most popular saints in the calendar, although there is some doubt whether she ever actually existed. According to legend, she was imprisoned in a tower and later murdered by her father, who was then struck down by a bolt of lightning. Accordingly, she is the patron of architects, stonemasons, and fortifications, and of firework makers, artillerymen, and gunpowder magazines.
VARIANT: Barbra (a modern contracted spelling, as in the case of the singer, actress, and film director Barbra Streisand, b. 1942).
SHORT FORM: Barb (mainly North American, informal).
PET FORMS: Barbie, Babs, Babette.

Barclay ♂ Transferred use of the Scottish surname, which was from *Berkeley* in Gloucestershire, named with Old English *beorc* 'birch tree' + *lēah* 'wood, clearing'. It was taken to Scotland in the 12th century by Walter de *Berchelai*, who became chamberlain of Scotland in 1165. His descendants were one of the most powerful families in Scotland.

VARIANTS: **Berk(e)ley.**

Barnabas ♂ From the New Testament, where *Barnabas* represents a Greek form of an Aramaic name meaning 'son of consolation'. St Barnabas was a Jewish Cypriot, one of the earliest Christian missionaries, who sold his property and gave the proceeds to the Church. He worked with St Paul until about AD 48.

VARIANT: **Barnaby** (from a medieval vernacular form).

PET FORMS: **Barney, Barny.**

COGNATES: Dutch: **Barnabas.** French: **Barnabé.** Spanish: **Bernabé.** Polish: **Barnaba.** Czech: **Barnabáš.** Hungarian: **Barna.**

Barnaby ♂ Variant of ▷Barnabas, from a medieval vernacular form.

Barney ♂ Pet form of ▷Barnaby or its learned equivalent ▷Barnabas.

Baron ♂ From the title of nobility, along the lines of ▷Earl and ▷Duke. The title arose in the Norman feudal system and seems to be of Germanic origin, derived from Old English *beorn* 'young warrior' or a related continental Germanic form. In part the given name, and in particular the variant Barron, may represent the surname derived from the title.

Barrett ♂ Transferred use of the surname, which is of obscure origin. It is probably a nickname from Middle English *baret* 'dispute, argument'. The transferred use as a given name is recent.

Barrie ♂ Variant spelling of ▷Barry.

Barrington ♂ Transferred use of the surname, a local name from any of several places in England so named. The one in Gloucestershire is an Old English compound meaning 'settlement of Beorn's people'. In the Somerset place name the first element is an unattested Old English personal name *Bāra*, which also occurs, in the genitive form, as the first element of the Cambridgeshire place name. *Barrington* has also been used as an English form of Gaelic *Ó Bearáin*.

Barry ♂ Anglicized form of the Irish name Barra (see Irish appendix). Since the 20th century this name has become very popular in the English-speaking world, especially Australia.

VARIANT: **Barrie.**

PET FORMS: **Baz, Bazza** (Australian informal).

Barrymore ♂ Transferred use of the surname, apparently derived from any of numerous minor places in England and Scotland named Barmoor or Barmore. In some cases the name may have been chosen with reference to the famous theatrical dynasty, which includes most recently the actress Drew Barrymore (b. 1975).

Bart ♂ Short form of ▷Barton and ▷Bartholomew. It is borne by one of the principal characters in the popular TV cartoon series *The Simpsons*.

Bartholomew ♂ Of New Testament origin, the name of an apostle mentioned in all the synoptic gospels (Matthew, Mark, and Luke) and in the Acts of the Apostles. It is an Aramaic formation meaning 'son of Talmai', and has been assumed by many scholars to be a byname of the apostle ▷Nathaniel. *Talmai* is a Hebrew name, said to mean 'abounding in furrows' (Numbers 13:22).

SHORT FORM: **Bart.**

COGNATES: Irish: **Bairtliméad; Parthalán.** Scottish Gaelic: **Pàrlan.** German: **Bartholomäus.** Dutch: **Bartholomeus** (learned); **Bartel** (vernacular). French: **Barthélemy.** Spanish: **Bartolomé.** Portuguese: **Bartolomeu.** Italian: **Bartolo(m)meo.** Russian: **Varfolomei.** Polish: **Bartłomiej** (learned); **Bartosz** (vernacular). Czech: **Bartoloměj.** Finnish: **Perttu.** Hungarian: **Bartal, Bartos, Bartó.**

Barton ♂ Transferred use of the surname, originally a local name from any of the numerous places in England so called from Old English *bere* 'barley' + *tūn* 'enclosure, settlement'.

SHORT FORM: Bart.

Baruch ♂ Jewish: biblical name meaning 'blessed' in Hebrew. It is borne by a character who appears in the Book of Jeremiah.

Basil ♂ From the Greek name *Basíleios* 'royal' (a derivative of *basileus* 'king'). This name was borne by St Basil the Great (*c*.330–379), bishop of Caesarea, a theologian regarded as one of the Fathers of the Eastern Church. It was also the name of several early saints martyred in the East.

SHORT FORM: ▷Baz.

COGNATES: Dutch: Basiel. French: Basil. Spanish, Italian: Basilio. Portuguese: Basileu. Polish: Bazyli. Greek: Vasilios. Russian: Vasili. Finnish: Pasi.

Bathsheba ♀ Biblical name, meaning 'daughter of the oath' in Hebrew. It was the name of the woman who became the wife of King David, after he had disposed of her husband Uriah, and mother of King Solomon (2 Samuel 11–12). It was popular with the Puritans in England and is the name of the central character in Thomas Hardy's *Far from the Madding Crowd*, but it is found only occasionally today.

SHORT FORM: Sheba.

Baxter ♂ Transferred use of the surname, which originated in the Middle Ages as an occupational name for a baker, Old English *bæcestre*. The *-estre* suffix was originally feminine, but by the Middle English period the gender difference had been lost; *Baxter* was merely a regional variant of *Baker*.

Bay ♂, ♀ As a male name this is generally a short form of ▷Bailey, although it is sometimes used as an independent first name. As a female name it is likely to be, at least in part, a transferred use from the various plants

known as *bay* (Old French *baie*, Latin *baca*, earlier *bacca*, 'berry'). These are similar to the laurels (see ▷Laurel) and the leaves of several species are used as flavouring agents (compare ▷Juniper and ▷Cinnamon).

Baylie ♀ Variant spelling of ▷Bailey.

Baz ♂ **1.** Mainly Australian: informal pet form of ▷Barry. **2.** Short form of ▷Basil.

VARIANT: Bazza.

Bea ♀ Short form of ▷Beatrice or ▷Beatrix.

Beata ♀ Late Latin feminine form of *Beatus* 'blessed'. The name was borne by an early Christian saint martyred in North Africa. *Beata* is widely used among Roman Catholics in Germany, Poland, and elsewhere; it is less common in the English-speaking world.

Beatrice ♀ Italian and French form of ▷Beatrix, which was quite popular in England during the Middle Ages, and strongly revived in the 19th century. It is most famous as the name of Dante's beloved, and is borne by the elder (b. 1988) of the Duke of York's daughters.

SHORT FORMS: English: Bea, Bee.

PET FORMS: English: Beat(t)ie.

Beatrix ♀ From a Late Latin personal name, which was borne by a saint martyred in Rome, together with Saints Faustinus and Simplicius, in the early 4th century. The original form of the name was probably *Viatrix*, a feminine version of *Viator* 'voyager (through life)', which was a favourite name among early Christians. This was then altered by association with Latin *Beatus* 'blessed' (*Via-* and *Bea-* sometimes being pronounced the same in Late Latin). See also ▷Beatrice.

SHORT FORMS: Bea, Bee.

PET FORMS: Beat(t)ie.

Beatriz ♀ Spanish form of ▷Beatrix, now also used in the English-speaking world.

Beau ♂, ♀ Recent coinage as a given name, originally a nickname meaning 'handsome', as borne by the Regency dandy Beau Brummell (1778–1840), who was for a time a friend of the Prince Regent. The word was also used in the 19th century with the meaning 'admirer' or 'sweetheart'. Its adoption as a given name seems to have been due to the hero of P. C. Wren's novel *Beau Geste* (1924) or to the character of Beau Wilks in Margaret Mitchell's *Gone with the Wind* (1936), which was made into an exceptionally popular film in 1939. More recently, it has been associated with the American actor Beau Bridges (b. 1941) and has gained considerable currency. Its use as a girl's name is a recent development.

Becca ♀ Modern short form of ▷Rebecca.

Bechor ♂ Jewish: Hebrew name meaning 'firstborn'; it is borne particularly by Jews of Sephardic descent.

Beck ♀ Modern informal short form of ▷Rebecca.

Beckah ♀ Modern short form of ▷Rebecca.

Becky ♀ Pet form of ▷Rebecca. It was especially popular in the 18th and 19th centuries, and is now used independently.

Bee ♀ Variant spelling of ▷Bea.

Beige ♀ U.S.: modern coinage, apparently from the colour. This comes from French, and referred originally to undyed woollen cloth; its further derivation is unknown. Its use as a given name may have been influenced in part by the semantically similar ▷Fawn and the phonetically similar ▷Paige.

Beile ♀ Jewish: Yiddish name probably derived from the Slavic element *beli* 'white', although some believe it to be from the Romance adjective *bella* 'beautiful'.

VARIANT: **Beyle.**
PET FORM: **Beylke.**

Bekki ♀ Modern respelling of ▷Becky.

Belinda ♀ Of uncertain origin. It was used by Sir John Vanbrugh for a character in his comedy *The Provok'd Wife* (1697), was taken up by Alexander Pope in *The Rape of the Lock* (1712), and has enjoyed a steady popularity ever since. It is not certain where Vanbrugh got the name from. The notion that it is Germanic (with a second element *lind* 'soft, tender, weak') is not well founded. In Italian literature it is the name ascribed to the wife of Orlando, vassal of Charlemagne, but this use is not supported in Germanic sources. The name may be an Italian coinage from *bella* 'beautiful' (see ▷Bella) + the feminine name suffix *-inda* (compare, for example, ▷Lucinda).

Bella ♀ Shortened form of *Isabella*, the Italian version of ▷Isabel, but also associated with the Italian adjective *bella*, feminine of *bello* 'handsome, beautiful' (Late Latin *bellus*).

Bellarmino ♂ Catholic name used occasionally since the 20th century in honour of the Italian saint Roberto Bellarmino (1542–1621), a prominent Jesuit. He was canonized in 1930 and declared a Doctor of the Church in 1931.

Belle ♀ Variant of ▷Bella, reflecting the French feminine adjective *belle* 'beautiful'.

Ben ♂ Short form of ▷Benjamin, or less commonly of ▷Benedict or ▷Bennett. Since the mid-1980s it has also been very popular as an independent given name.
PET FORMS: **Benny, Bennie.**

Benedict ♂ From Church Latin *benedictus* 'blessed'. This was the name of the saint (*c*.480–*c*.550) who composed the Benedictine rule of Christian monastic life that is still followed in essence by all Western orders. He was born near Spoleto in Umbria, central Italy. After studying in Rome, he went to live as a hermit at Subiaco, and later organized groups of followers and imitators into monastic cells. In *c.*529 he moved to Monte Cassino, where he founded the great monastery that is still the centre of the Benedictine order. His rule is simple, restrained, and practical. See also ▷Bennett.

VARIANT: ▷Bennett.

COGNATES: Scottish Gaelic: Benneit. German, Dutch: Benedikt. Danish: Bendt, Bent. Norwegian: Bendik. Swedish: Bengt. French: Benoît. Spanish: Benito. Catalan: Benet. Portuguese: Bento. Italian: Benedetto. Russian: Venedikt. Polish: Benedykt. Czech: Benedikt. Finnish: Pentti. Hungarian: Benedek. Latvian: Bendikts.

Benedicta ♀ Feminine form of ▷Benedict, in occasional use in the English-speaking world.

VARIANT: Benedicte.

Benita ♀ Spanish feminine form of *Benito* (Spanish form of ▷Benedict), used since the early 20th century in various parts of the English-speaking world.

Benjamin ♂ Biblical name, borne by the youngest of the twelve sons of Jacob. His mother Rachel died in giving birth to him, and in her last moments she named him *Benoni*, meaning 'son of my sorrow'. His father, however, did not wish him to bear such an ill-omened name, and renamed him *Benyamin* (Genesis 35:16–18; 42:4). This means either 'son of the right hand' or more likely 'son of the south' (Hebrew *yamin* can also mean 'south'), since Benjamin was the only child of Jacob born in Canaan and not in Mesopotamia to the north. Another tradition is that the second element of the name is a variant of the Hebrew plural noun *yamim*, which means 'days' but is used idiomatically to mean 'year' or 'years'. The name would then mean 'son of (my) old age' and refer to the fact

that Benjamin was Jacob's youngest child. In the Middle Ages the name was often given to sons whose mothers had died in childbirth. Today it has no such unfortunate associations and it grew enormously in popularity following the release of the film *The Graduate* (1967), in which Dustin Hoffman played the role of Benjamin Braddock. It is used in Scotland as an Anglicized form of Gaelic Beathan (see Scottish appendix).

SHORT FORMS: Ben(n).

PET FORMS: Benny, Bennie, Benji(e), Benjy.

COGNATES: German, Dutch: Benjamin. French: Benjamin. Spanish: Benjamín. Portuguese: Benjamim. Italian: Beniamino. Russian: Venyamin. Hungarian: Benjámim.

Bennett ♂ The normal medieval vernacular form of ▷Benedict, borne by women as well as men in the past. Now sometimes used as an antiquarian revival, but more often a transferred use of the surname derived from the medieval given name.

VARIANTS: Benett, Bennet, Benet.

Benson ♂ Transferred use of the surname, which originated in part as a patronymic from *Ben(n)*, a short form of ▷Benedict, and in part as a local name from *Benson* (formerly *Bensington*) in Oxfordshire.

Bentley ♂ Transferred use of the surname, which originated as a local name from any of the dozen or so places in England so called from Old English *beonet* 'bent grass' + *lēah* 'wood, clearing'.

Benton ♂ Transferred use of the surname, a local name from either of two places in Northumberland named with Old English *bēan* 'beans' (a collective singular) or *beonet* 'bent grass' + *tūn* 'settlement, enclosure'.

Ber ♂ Jewish: from Yiddish *ber* 'bear', probably influenced by the early medieval European practice of giving animal names to people. It is often paired with ▷Dov in order to provide a Hebrew name in certain rituals.

Berenice ♀ From the Greek personal name *Berenikē*, which seems to have originated in the royal house of Macedon. It is almost certainly a Macedonian dialectal form of the Greek name *Pherenikē* 'victory bringer'. It was introduced to the Egyptian royal house by the widow of one of Alexander the Great's officers, who married Ptolemy I. It was also borne by an early Christian woman mentioned in Acts 25, for which reason it was felt to be acceptable by the Puritans in the 17th century. It has now fallen out of fashion again. See also ▷Bernice.

VARIANT: Bernice (the form used in the Authorized Version).

Beresford ♂ Transferred use of the surname, which originated as a local name from a place in Staffordshire named with Old English *beofor* 'beaver' (or possibly a byname from this word) + *ford* 'ford'.

Berkeley ♂ Variant of ▷Barclay. In the U.S. it may be chosen with reference to the place so named in California.

Berkley ♂ Variant of ▷Barclay.

Bernadette ♀ French feminine diminutive of ▷Bernard. Its use in Britain and Ireland is largely confined to Roman Catholics, who take it in honour of St Bernadette Soubirous (1844–79), a French peasant girl who had visions of the Virgin Mary and uncovered a spring near Lourdes where miraculous cures are still sought.

VARIANT: Bernardette.

Bernard ♂ From an Old French name of Germanic (Frankish) origin, derived from *ber(n)* 'bear' + *hard* 'hardy, brave, strong'. This was the name of three famous medieval churchmen: St Bernard of Menthon (923–1008), founder of a hospice on each of the Alpine passes named after him; the monastic reformer St Bernard of

Clairvaux (1090–1153); and the scholastic philosopher Bernard of Chartres. It was adopted by the Normans and introduced by them to England. A native Old English form, *Beornheard*, was superseded by the Norman form.

PET FORM: English: Bernie.

COGNATES: Irish: Bearnard. German: Bernhard(t), Bernd(t). Dutch: Bernhard. Scandinavian: Bernt. French: Bernard. Spanish, Portuguese, Italian: Bernardo. Catalan: Bernat. Hungarian: Bernát.

Bernardine ♀ Feminine form of ▷Bernard, formed by the addition of the feminine ending *-ine*. In the English-speaking world it is used mainly by Roman Catholics.

VARIANT: Bernadine.

Bernice ♀ Contracted form of ▷Berenice. This is the form that is used in the Authorized Version of the Bible, and it is now fairly popular in the English-speaking world.

PET FORM: Binnie.

Berry ♀ From the vocabulary word (Old English *berie*). This is one of the less common of the names referring to flowers, fruit, and vegetation that began to be used as given names in the 20th century.

Bert ♂ Short form of any of the various names containing this syllable as a first or second element, for example ▷Albert and ▷Bertram. See also ▷Burt.

PET FORM: Bertie.

Bertha ♀ Latinized version of a Continental Germanic name, a short form of various compound women's personal names derived from *berht* 'famous' (akin to Modern English *bright*). It probably existed in England before the Conquest, and was certainly reinforced by Norman use, but fell out of use in the 15th century. It was reintroduced into the English-speaking world from Germany in the 19th century, but has once again gone out of fashion.

Bertram ♂ From an Old French name of Germanic (Frankish) origin, from *berht* 'bright, famous' + *hramn* 'raven'. Ravens were traditional symbols of wisdom in Germanic mythology; Odin was regularly accompanied by ravens called Hugin and Munin. This name was adopted by the Normans and introduced by them to Britain. See also ▷Bertrand.

SHORT FORM: **Bert.**

PET FORM: **Bertie.**

Bertrand ♂ Medieval French variant of ▷Bertram, imported to Britain by the Normans. In modern times it has been made famous by the English philosopher Bertrand Russell (1872–1970), but is only in occasional use.

SHORT FORM: **Bert.**

Beryl ♀ One of several women's names that are taken from gemstones and that came into fashion at the end of the 19th century. Beryl is a pale green semiprecious stone (of which emerald is a variety). Other colours are also found. The word is from Greek, and is ultimately of Indian origin.

Bess ♀ Short form of ▷Elizabeth, in common use in the days of Queen Elizabeth I, who was known as 'Good Queen Bess'.

Bet ♀ Short form of ▷Elizabeth.

Beth ♀ Short form of ▷Elizabeth, not used before the 19th century, when it became popular in America and elsewhere after publication of Louisa M. Alcott's novel *Little Women* (1868), in which Beth March is one of the four sisters who are the central characters.

Bethan ♀ Originally a Welsh pet form of ▷Beth, now also popular elsewhere in the English-speaking world.

Bethany ♀ Of New Testament origin. In the New Testament it is a place name, that of the village just outside

Jerusalem where Jesus stayed during Holy Week, before going on to Jerusalem and crucifixion (Matthew 21:17; Mark 11:1; Luke 19:29; John 12:1). Its Hebrew name may mean 'house of figs' (*beth te'ena* or *beth te'enim*). Until recently the given name was favoured mainly by Roman Catholics, being bestowed in honour of Mary of Bethany, sister of Martha and Lazarus. She is sometimes identified with Mary Magdalene (see ▷Madeleine), although the grounds for this identification are very poor.

Betsy ♀ Pet form of ▷Elizabeth, a blend of *Betty* and *Bessie*, which is also used independently.

Bette ♀ Variant of ▷Bet, associated particularly with the film actress Bette Davis (1908–89), whose original name was Ruth Elizabeth Davis.

Bettina ♀ Latinate elaboration of ▷Betty.

VARIANT: **Bettine.**

Betty ♀ Pet form of ▷Elizabeth, dating from the 18th century. In the 17th century it is also found occasionally as a pet form of ▷Beatrice. It is now used as a name in its own right.

VARIANTS: **Bettie, Beti.**

Beulah ♀ Biblical name, pronounced '**byoo**-la': from the name (meaning 'married' in Hebrew) applied to the land of Israel by the prophet Isaiah (Isaiah 62:4). 'The land of Beulah' has sometimes been taken as a reference to heaven. It was taken up as a given name in England at the time of the Reformation and was used among the Puritans in the 17th century. It was borne by the American actress Beulah Bondi (1899–1981), and was immortalized by Mae West's instruction to her maidservant: 'Beulah, peel me a grape.'

Bevan ♂ Transferred use of the Welsh surname, a shortened form of the patronymic *ap Evan* 'son of Evan'.

b

Beverley ♀ Transferred use of the surname, which is from a place in East Yorkshire named with Old English *beofor* 'beaver' + *lēac* 'stream'. The spelling **Beverly** is the usual form of the name in America, where association with Beverly Hills in Los Angeles, the district where many film stars live, may have been a factor in its popularity.

VARIANT: **Beverly**.

Bevin ♀ Anglicized form of the Gaelic name Béibhinn (see Irish appendix).

Beynish ♂ Jewish (Yiddish): from the Czech given name *Beneš*, a form of ▷Benedict, adopted in part as a translation of ▷Baruch.

Bianca ♀ Italian: from *bianca* 'white' (i.e. 'pure', but see also ▷Blanche). The name was used by Shakespeare for characters in two of his plays set in an Italian context: the mild-mannered sister of Katharina, the 'shrew' in *The Taming of the Shrew*, and a courtesan in *Othello*. It came to prominence in the 1970s as the name of Bianca Jagger, the Nicaraguan fashion model, peace worker, and diplomat, who was for a time married to the rock singer Mick Jagger. Since then it has been used increasingly in the English-speaking world.

Biddy ♀ Of Anglo-Irish origin: pet form of **Bride** (see Irish appendix) or ▷Bridget. It was formerly quite common, but is now seldom used outside Ireland, partly perhaps because the informal expression 'an old biddy' in English has come to denote a tiresome old woman.

Bilal ♂ Arabic name meaning 'wetting'. Words denoting water, which is scarce in the desert, have positive associations in Arabic.

Bill ♂ Altered short form of ▷William, not used before the 19th century. The reason for the change in the initial consonant is not clear, but it conforms to the pattern regularly found when English words beginning with *w-* are borrowed into Gaelic. The nickname 'King Billy' for William of Orange is an early example from Ireland, which may have influenced English usage. It is bestowed occasionally as a name in its own right.

PET FORMS: **Billy**, ▷Billie.

Billie ♀, ♂ Variant of ▷Billy, now used mainly for girls, and sometimes bestowed at baptism as a female equivalent of ▷William.

Billy ♂, also ♀ Pet form of ▷William, now in favour as an independent name for boys, and also used occasionally for girls.

Bina ♀ **1.** Jewish (Yiddish): from Yiddish *bin(e)* 'bee'. This was used as a translation of the Hebrew name *Devorah* (see ▷Deborah), meaning 'bee'. However, it was often taken as being from Hebrew *bina* 'understanding'.**2.** Among Gentiles, it occasionally occurs as a short form of ▷Albina.

VARIANTS: **Binah**, **Bine**.

PET FORM: **Binke**.

Binnie ♀ Pet form of ▷Bernice, associated particularly with the actress and singer Binnie Hale (1899–1984).

Binyamin ♂ Jewish: modern Hebrew form of ▷Benjamin.

Blaine ♂ Anglicized form of the Gaelic personal name *Bláán*, originally a byname, a diminutive form of *blá* 'yellow'. This was the name of an early Celtic saint who lived in the 6th century.

VARIANTS: **Blain**, **Blane**.

Blair ♂, ♀ Transferred use of the Scottish surname, in origin a local name from any of various places named with Gaelic *blàr* 'plain', 'field'. Outside Scotland, where it is a male name, it is found chiefly in North America, where it is also popular for girls.

VARIANT: **Blaire**.

Blaise ♂, ♀ French, from the Latin name *Blasius*, probably from *blaesus* 'lisping'. It was the name of a saint who was popular throughout Europe in the Middle Ages but is almost forgotten today. He was a bishop of Sebaste in Armenia, and was martyred in the early years of the 4th century; these bare facts were elaborated in a great number of legends that reached Europe from the East at the time of the Crusades. As a boy's name it was in moderate use in England from the Middle Ages. It is now found only occasionally, but is also used for girls.

Blake ♂ Transferred use of the surname, which has two quite distinct etymologies. It is both from Old English *blæc* 'black' and from Old English *blāc* 'pale, white'; it was thus originally a nickname given to someone with hair or skin that was either remarkably dark or remarkably light. It is now quite popular as a boy's name.

Blanche ♀ Originally a nickname for a blonde, from *blanche*, feminine of Old French *blanc* 'white' (of Germanic origin). It came to be associated with the notion of whiteness as indicating purity, and was introduced into England as a given name by the Normans. A pale complexion combined with light hair was long an ideal of beauty in Europe (compare Modern English *fair*, which at first meant 'beautiful' and then, from the 16th century, 'light in colouring').

Blane ♂ Variant spelling of ▷Blaine.

Blossom ♀ 19th-century coinage, from the vocabulary word for flowers on a fruit tree or ornamental tree (Old English *blōstm*), used as an affectionate pet name for a young girl. A well-known bearer of the name is the jazz singer Blossom Dearie (b. 1926).

Blume ♂ Jewish: Yiddish name, originally an affectionate nickname meaning 'flower' (from Middle High German *bluome*).

PET FORM: **Blumke**.

Bly ♂ Transferred use of the surname, in origin an Anglicized form of Irish Gaelic *Ó Blighe* 'descendant of *Blighe*', a personal name probably derived from Old Norse *Blígr* (from *blígja* 'to gaze').

Blythe ♀ Modern coinage, apparently an altered spelling of the vocabulary word *blithe* 'carefree, cheerful' (Old English *blīðe* 'kind, pleasant, joyous'). In part it may represent a transferred use of the surname with this spelling, derived from the vocabulary word during the Middle Ages.

Boaz ♂ Biblical Hebrew name of uncertain origin, said by some to be from a word meaning 'swiftness'. In the Bible it is borne by a distant kinsman of Ruth, who treats her generously and eventually marries her. The given name was in infrequent use in England in the 17th and 18th centuries, but is now very rarely used except occasionally in Jewish families.

Bob ♂ Altered short form of ▷Robert, a later development than the common medieval forms *Hob*, *Dob*, and *Nob*, all of which, unlike *Bob*, have given rise to English surnames.

Bobbie ♀, ♂ Variant spelling of ▷Bobby, now used mainly for girls, as a pet form of ▷Roberta or ▷Robin or as an independent given name.
VARIANT: **Bobbi**♀.

Bobby ♂, ♀ Pet form of ▷Robert (for its development, see ▷Bob), now also used as an independent given name. It is also sometimes used as a girl's name, as a variant spelling of ▷Bobbie.

Bond ♂ Transferred use of the surname, originally denoting a medieval farmer who was a smallholder or peasant farmer. The word (Middle English *bonde*) is of Germanic origin and seems to have referred to a tenant farmer 'bound' to an overlord and owing him rent or service.

Boniface ♂ From the Late Latin name *Bonifatius*, derived from *bonum* 'good' + *fatum* 'fate'. In the early Middle Ages the name came to be alternatively written as *Bonifacius* (with the same pronunciation) and reanalysed as a compound of *bonum* + *facere* 'to do', i.e. 'doer of good deeds'. The name was borne by several early saints, including a 7th-century pope and an Anglo-Saxon missionary who evangelized extensively in Germany in the 8th century. The latter was originally named *Winfrid*, but took the name *Bonifacius* on entering holy orders.

Bonita ♀ Coined in the United States in the 1940s from the feminine form of Spanish *bonito* 'pretty'. This is not used as a given name in Spanish-speaking countries. *Bonita* looks like the feminine form of a medieval Latin male name, *Bonitus* (from *bonus* 'good'), which was borne by an Italian saint of the 6th century and a Provençal saint of the 7th. However, no medieval record of the feminine form in use as a given name is known.

PET FORM: ▷Bonnie.

Bonnie ♀ Originally an affectionate nickname from the Scottish word *bonnie* 'fine, attractive, pretty'. However, it was not until recently used as a given name in Scotland. Its popularity may be attributed to the character of Scarlett O'Hara's infant daughter Bonnie in the film *Gone with the Wind* (1939), based on Margaret Mitchell's novel of the same name. (Bonnie's name was really Eugenie Victoria, but she had 'eyes as blue as the bonnie blue flag'.) A famous American bearer was Bonnie Parker, accomplice of the bank robber Clyde Barrow; their life together was the subject of the film *Bonnie and Clyde* (1967). The name enjoyed a vogue in the second part of the 20th century, and has also been used as a pet form of ▷Bonita.

VARIANT: **Bonny.**

Booker ♂ Transferred use of the surname, in origin an occupational name for either a scribe or binder of books (a derivative of Middle English *boke* 'book', Old English *bōc*), or else a bleacher of cloth (a derivative of Middle English *bouken* 'to steep in lye', Middle Dutch *būken*).

Boone ♂ Transferred use of the surname, in origin a nickname from Old French *bon* 'good' (Latin *bonus*). Use as a given name may have been inspired by the legendary U.S. frontiersman Daniel Boone (1734–1820).

Booth ♂ Transferred use of the surname, which originally denoted someone who lived in a small hut or bothy, the typical dwelling of a cowherd or shepherd (Middle English *bōth(e)*, of Scandinavian origin). Use as a given name may have originated in honour of William Booth (1829–1912), founder of the Salvation Army.

Boris ♂ Russian: from the Tartar nickname *Bogoris* 'small'. Later, however, it was taken to be a shortened form of the Russian name *Borislav*, from *bor* 'battle' + *slav* 'glory'. The name was borne in the 9th century by a ruler of Bulgaria who converted his kingdom to Christianity and gave shelter to disciples of saints Cyril and Methodius when they were expelled from Moravia. The name was also borne by a 10th-century Russian saint, son of Prince Vladimir of Kiev and brother of St Gleb. It is as a result of his influence that *Boris* is one of the very few non-classical names that the Orthodox Church allows to be taken as a baptismal name (although the saint himself bore the baptismal name *Romanus*). It is borne by the British journalist and politician Boris Johnson (b. 1964).

PET FORMS: **Borya, Boba.**

Boyd ♂ Transferred use of the common Irish and Scottish surname, which is of uncertain derivation. It may originally have been a local name from the island of Bute in the Firth of Clyde, known in Gaelic as *Bod* (genitive case *Bóid*). The first known bearer of the surname is Robertus *de Boyd*, recorded in Scotland in the early 13th century.

Brad ♂ Mainly North American: short form of ▷Bradford and ▷Bradley. One of the best-known bearers of the name is U.S. film actor Brad Pitt (b. 1963).

Braden ♂ Transferred use of the Irish surname, Gaelic *Ó Bradáin* 'descendant of *Bradán*'. The latter is a personal name meaning 'salmon'.

VARIANTS: Braeden, Braiden, Brayden.

Bradford ♂ Mainly U.S.: transferred use of the surname, in origin a local name from any of the numerous places in England so called from Old English *brād* 'broad' + *ford* 'ford'. The surname was borne most famously by William Bradford (1590–1657), leader of the Pilgrim Fathers from 1621 and governor of Plymouth Colony for some 30 years. It was also the name of another William Bradford (1722–91), a printer who played an important part in the American Revolution.

Bradley ♂ Transferred use of the surname, in origin a local name from any of the numerous places in England so called from Old English *brād* 'broad' + *lēah* 'wood, clearing'. The most famous American bearer of this surname was General Omar N. Bradley (1893–1981). As a given name it used to be found mainly in North America but of late has come into fashion in Britain.

VARIANT: Bradleigh.

Brady ♂, ♀ Transferred use of the surname, which is of Irish origin, from Gaelic *Ó Brádaigh* 'descendant of *Brádach*'. *Brádach* is an old Irish byname of uncertain origin, possibly a contracted form of *brághadach* 'large-chested', from *brágha* 'chest'.

VARIANT: Braidy.

Bramwell ♂ Transferred use of the surname, apparently a local name in

origin, from a lost place so named, or perhaps a variant of *Bramhall*, from either of two places named with Old English *brōm* 'broom' + *halh* 'nook'.

Bran ♂ Welsh: traditional name from *brân* 'raven', now in wider use. In Welsh and Irish mythology, the name was borne by Bran the Blessed, a giant-sized god, the son of the sea god Mannannan Mac Lir. He had many heroic adventures before being mortally wounded in the foot with a poisoned spear while attempting to rescue his sister Branwen in Ireland. At his behest, his severed head was carried to the hill where the Tower of London now stands and buried there.

Brandon ♂ Transferred use of the surname, in origin a local name from any of various places so called, most of which get their name from Old English *brōm* 'broom, gorse' + *dūn* 'hill'. In some cases it may be an altered form of ▷Brendan. There has perhaps also been some influence from the surname of the Italian American actor Marlon Brando (1924–2004). In Britain the name has enjoyed a steady rise in popularity since the mid-1990s.

VARIANTS: Brandan, Branden, Brandyn.

Brandy ♀ Mainly U.S.: ostensibly from the vocabulary word for the type of liquor (earlier known as *brandy wine* or *brand(e)wine*, from Dutch *brandewijn* 'distilled wine'), but probably invented as a feminine form of ▷Brandon.

VARIANTS: Brandie, Brandi.

Brant ♂ Mainly U.S.: probably a variant of the rather more common ▷Brent. The English surname *Brant* is a relatively infrequent variant of *Brand*, derived from the Old Norse personal name *Brandr*, meaning 'sword' (compare ▷Brenda).

VARIANT: Brand.

Branton ♂ Mainly U.S.: variant of ▷Brandon or transferred use of the surname *Branton*. This is a local name from places in Northumberland and West Yorkshire so named from Old English *brōm* 'broom, gorse' + *tūn* 'enclosure, settlement'.

Brayden ♂ Respelling of ▷Braden.

Brayne ♀ Jewish (Yiddish): a back-formation from Brayndel, itself a pet form from Yiddish *broyn* 'brown'.

Braxton ♂ Transferred use of the surname, in origin a local name from an unidentified place. The place name seems to be composed of the genitive case of the Old English personal name *Bracc* + Old English *tūn* 'enclosure, settlement'. Use as a given name has been influenced by the popularity of names such as ▷Brant and ▷Branton, and the adoption as given names of similar-sounding surnames such as ▷Caxton and ▷Paxton.

Breanna ♀ Mainly U.S.: variant spelling of ▷Brianna.
VARIANT: Breanne.

Bree ♀ Anglicized form of Irish Brighe (see Irish appendix).
ALSO: Brie.

Brenda ♀ A very popular name, of uncertain derivation. Until the 20th century it was confined mainly to Scotland and Ireland. It is probably of Scandinavian rather than Celtic origin, however: a short form of any of the various compound names derived from Old Norse *brand* 'sword'. Its popularity in Gaelic-speaking countries has no doubt been influenced by its similarity to ▷Brendan.

Brendan ♂ Anglicized form of Irish Breandán (earlier *Bréanainn*); see Irish appendix. This was the name of two 6th-century Irish saints, Brendan the Voyager and Brendan of Birr. According to Irish legend, the former was the first European to set foot on North American soil.
VARIANT: Brendon.

Brenna ♀ Mainly U.S.: modern coinage, apparently created as a feminine form of ▷Brennan, but perhaps also influenced by ▷Brianna.

Brennan ♀ Mainly U.S.: transferred use of the Irish surname, Gaelic Ó *Braonáin* 'descendant of *Braonán*'. The latter is a personal name derived from a diminutive of *braon* 'moisture, drop'. It may also be taken as a contracted form of ▷Brendan.

Brent ♂ Mainly U.S.: transferred use of the surname, which is derived from any of several places in Devon and Somerset that are on or near prominent hills, and were named with a Celtic or Old English term for a hill.

Brenton ♂ Mainly U.S.: transferred use of the surname, in origin a local name from a place near Exminster in Devon, called in Old English *Brȳningtūn* 'settlement associated with *Brȳni*'. The latter is a personal name derived from *bryne* 'fire, flame'. The modern given name may also be a variant of ▷Branton.

Brett ♂ Transferred use of the surname, which originated in the Middle Ages as an ethnic name for one of the Bretons who arrived in England in the wake of the Norman Conquest. As a surname it is most common in East Anglia, where Breton settlement was particularly concentrated. As a given name, it enjoyed something of a vogue in the 1970s and has since remained modestly popular, especially in the United States.
VARIANT: Bret.

Brewster ♂ Mainly U.S.: transferred use of the surname, in origin an occupational name for a brewer, Middle English *brēowestre*. The *-estre* suffix was originally feminine, but by the Middle English period this grammatical distinction had been lost (compare ▷Baxter).

Brian ♂ Of Irish origin: perhaps from an Old Celtic word meaning 'high' or 'noble'. The name has been perennially popular in Ireland, in particular on account of the fame of Brian Boru (Gaelic *Brian Bóroimhe*) (*c.* 940–1014), a warrior who was credited with driving the Vikings from Ireland and who eventually became high king of Ireland. In the Middle Ages it was relatively common in East Anglia, where it was introduced by Breton settlers, and in northern England, where it was introduced by Scandinavians from Ireland. It was quite popular in Yorkshire in the early 16th century, largely because it had long been a family name among the Stapletons, who had Irish connections. They first used it after Sir Gilbert Stapleton married Agnes, the daughter of the great northern baron Sir Brian fitzAlan. In Gaelic Scotland it was at first borne exclusively by members of certain professional families of Irish origin.

VARIANT: **Bryan.**

Brianna ♀ A female equivalent of ▷Brian, found occasionally in England from the 16th century onwards. It has enjoyed a steady rise in popularity over recent years, especially in the United States.

VARIANTS: **Brianne, Brina; Breanna** (mainly U.S.).

Briar ♀ 20-century coinage from *briar* or *brier* (from Old English *brær*), denoting a thorny bush of wild roses (sweet briar) or brambles.

Brice ♂, occasionally ♀ Mainly U.S.: variant spelling of ▷Bryce.

Bridget ♀ Anglicized form of Gaelic Brighid (pronounced 'breed'); see Irish appendix. This was the name of an ancient Celtic goddess, which in Gaulish would have been *Brigindos*, meaning 'the exalted one'. St Brigid of Kildare (*c.*450–*c.*525) is one of the patron saints of Ireland. Very few facts are known about her life. She founded a religious house for women at Kildare, and is said to be have been buried at Downpatrick, where St Patrick and St Columba were also buried. Many of the stories of miracles told about St Brigid

seem to be Christianized versions of pagan legends concerning the goddess. The popularity of the name was further reinforced throughout Europe, especially in Scandinavia in the form Birgit, as the name of the patron saint of Sweden (1304–73). She was a noblewoman of Irish stock who, after the death of her husband, founded an order of nuns, the Bridgettines. Later she went to Rome and attempted to introduce religious reforms there.

VARIANTS: **Bri(d)gid, Bri(d)git.**

PET FORMS: ▷**Biddy, Bridie, Bridey.**

Brie ♀ Variant spelling of ▷Bree, altered in form to coincide with the name of a district in northern France (so called from Late Latin *bracia* 'marshland') famous for its production of a variety of soft cheese. This is now a relatively common first name in Australia.

Brigham ♂ Mainly U.S.: transferred use of the surname, originally a local name from places in Cumbria and North Yorkshire named with Old English *brycg* 'bridge' + *hām* 'homestead, settlement'. As a given name it has been adopted primarily in honour of the early Mormon leader, Brigham Young (1801–77). It is not known why he was given this name; he was the son of John and Abigail (née Howe) Young of Whitingham, Vermont.

Brighton ♂ Transferred use of the surname, in origin a local name from Breighton on the River Derwent, so called from Old English *brycg* 'bridge' + *tūn* 'enclosure, settlement'. The surname is unlikely to derive from Brighton in Sussex, as this was known as *Brighthelmestone* 'settlement of Brighthelm' until the end of the 18th century, but in some cases the first name may have been given with reference to it.

Brigitte ♀ French form of ▷Bridget. This spelling, associated with the French film star of the 1950s Brigitte

Bardot (b. 1934 as Camille Javal), has been adopted in the English-speaking world.

Brina ♀ **1.** Short form of names such as ▷Sabrina. **2.** Anglicized form of the Jewish name ▷Brayne. **3.** Variant of ▷Brianna.

Briony ♀ Variant spelling of ▷Bryony.

Brinley ♂ Transferred use of the surname, which is probably a variant of *Brindley*, a local name from a place in Cheshire, so named from Old English *berned* 'burnt' + *lēah* 'woodland clearing'.

VARIANT: **Brynley.**

Briony ♀ Variant spelling of ▷Bryony.

Britt ♀ Swedish: contracted form of *Birgit* (see ▷Bridget), made famous in the English-speaking world by the Swedish actress Britt Ekland (b. 1942; her surname was originally Eklund).

Brittany ♀ Mainly North American: modern coinage, taken from the traditionally Celtic-speaking region of north-west France, known in medieval Latin as *Britannia*, because it was settled by refugees from Cornwall and Devon following the establishment of the Anglo-Saxon kingdom of Wessex. Its adoption as a given name has also been influenced by ▷Britt, of which it is sometimes regarded as the full form. In recent years it has rapidly established itself as a popular name in the English-speaking world.

Britney ♀ Respelling of ▷Brittany, associated particularly with the American singer Britney Spears (b. 1981). This is the more frequent spelling in Britain.

Brock ♂ Transferred use of the surname, in origin a nickname for someone resembling a badger (Middle English *broc(k)*, Old English *brocc*, of Celtic origin).

Broderick ♂ Transferred use of the surname, which is a derivative

of the Welsh personal name Rhydderch (see Welsh appendix).

Brodie ♂, ♀ Transferred use of the Scottish surname, which is taken from Brodie Castle in Moray, probably so named from Gaelic *brothhach* 'muddy place'.

VARIANT: **Brody.**

Brogan ♂, ♀ Either an Anglicized form of the Irish male personal name *Brógán*, which is probably from a diminutive of Gaelic *bróg* 'shoe', or a transferred use of the surname derived from the personal name, used for both boys and girls.

Brontë ♀ Transferred use of the surname borne by the literary sisters Charlotte (1816–55), Emily (1818–48), and Anne (1820–49). The spelling Brontë was adopted by their father, Patrick, in place of the form *Prunty*. In 1799 King Ferdinand of the Two Sicilies conferred the title Duke of Bronte (the name of a place in Sicily) on the victorious British admiral Horatio Nelson, and this no doubt was what prompted Patrick Prunty to revise the spelling of his surname. The fact that the Greek word *bronte* means 'thunder' may have been an additional influence. *Prunty* is an Irish surname (Gaelic *Ó Proinntigh*) indicating descent from a bearer of the personal name *Proinnteach* 'bestower' (originally a byname for a generous person). Use as a given name seems to have been inspired by the character in the film *Green Card* (1990).

Brooke ♀, ♂ Transferred use of the surname, originally a local name for someone who lived near a brook or stream (Old English *bróc*). It is borne by the American actress Brooke Adams (b. 1949), but is probably more closely identified with her compatriot Brooke Shields (b. 1965).

VARIANT: **Brook.**

Brooklyn ♂, ♀ Modern coinage, apparently an adoption of the

American place name from a district of New York city, originally named by Dutch settlers as *Breukelen*. The choice of the name by David and Victoria Beckham for their eldest son (b. 1999) will no doubt have increased its popularity.

Bruce ♂ Transferred use of the Scottish surname, now used as a given name throughout the English-speaking world. In the 20th century it was particularly popular in Australia. The surname was originally a Norman baronial name, but a precise identification of the place from which it was derived has not been made (there are a large number of possible candidates). The Bruces were an influential Norman family in Scottish affairs in the early Middle Ages; its most famous member was Robert 'the Bruce' (1274–1329), who is said to have drawn inspiration after his defeat at Methven from the perseverance of a spider in repeatedly climbing up again after being knocked down. He ruled Scotland as King Robert I from 1306 to 1329.

Brunella ♀ Latinate feminine formation from ▷Bruno, its form possibly influenced by ▷Prunella.

Bruno ♂ From the Germanic word *brun* 'brown'. This was in use as a name in many of the ruling families of Germany during the Middle Ages. It was borne by a 10th-century saint, son of the Emperor Henry the Fowler, and by the Saxon duke who gave his name to Brunswick (German *Braunschweig*, i.e. 'Bruno's settlement'). Its use in the English-speaking world, which dates from the end of the 19th century, may have been partly influenced by Lewis Carroll's *Sylvie and Bruno* (1889), but more probably it was first used by settlers of German ancestry in the United States.

Brutus ♂ From an old Roman family name, borne most notably by the statesman Marcus Junius Brutus, who was one of the assassins of Julius

Caesar. It is therefore sometimes taken as symbolic of resistance to tyranny. It was originally a byname meaning 'dull' or 'stupid', and is still only occasionally used as a first name because of its association with the English vocabulary word 'brute'. Junius Brutus Booth (1796–1852), father of the actor Edwin Thomas Booth and Lincoln's assassin John Wilkes Booth, was explicitly named in admiration for the Roman who struck a blow for freedom in conspiring against an elected official who had become a tyrant.

Bryan ♂ Variant of ▷Brian, influenced by the usual spelling of the associated surname.

Bryant ♂ Transferred use of the surname, which is derived from the given name ▷Brian. The final -*t* arose as a result of a mishearing by English speakers of the devoicing of the -*n* in Gaelic, reinforced by association with names such as ▷Constant.

Bryce ♂ Transferred use of the Scottish surname derived from the medieval given name *Brice*, found in the Latinized forms *Bri(c)tius* and *Bricius*. It is probably of Gaulish origin, possibly derived from a word meaning 'speckled' (compare Welsh *brych*), and was the name of a saint who was a disciple and successor of St Martin of Tours.

VARIANT: **Brice**.

Brynley ♂ Respelling of ▷Brinley, possibly influenced by Welsh **Bryn** (see Welsh appendix).

Brynn ♂, ♀ Mainly U.S.: respelling of Welsh **Bryn** (see Welsh appendix). In the United States this is now used predominantly as a girl's name, perhaps by association with names such as ▷Lynn.

Bryon ♂ Mainly U.S.: respelling of ▷Brian.

Bryony ♀ From the name of the plant (Greek *bryonia*). This is one of the names

b

coined in the 20th century from
vocabulary words denoting flowers.
VARIANT: **Briony.**

Bryson ♂ Mainly U.S.: transferred use
of the surname, which has a double
origin. In part it represents a
patronymic derived from the given
name ▷Bryce, in part it is an Anglicized
form of the Irish Gaelic surname Ó
Briosáin, an altered form of Ó
Muirgheasáin 'descendant of
Muirgheasán'. The latter is a personal
name perhaps derived from muir 'sea'
+ gus 'vigour' + the diminutive suffix
-an. The Ó Muirgheasáins were
hereditary poets (and keepers of the
relics of St Columba) in Donegal and
Scotland.

Buck ♂ Mainly U.S.: from the
nickname Buck, denoting a robust and
spirited young man, from the
vocabulary word for a male deer (Old
English bucc) or a he-goat (Old English
bucca).

Bud ♂ Mainly U.S.: originally a short
form of the nickname or vocabulary
word buddy 'friend', which may be an
alteration, perhaps a nursery form, of
brother, or else derived from the
Scottish Gaelic vocative case a bhodaich
'old man'.
VARIANT: **Buddy.**

Buffy ♀ Informal pet form of
▷Elizabeth, based on a child's
unsuccessful attempts to pronounce
the name.

Bunem ♂ Jewish (Yiddish): from an
affectionate nickname derived from the
French phrase bon homme 'good man'.

Bunty ♀ Nickname and occasional
baptismal name, of uncertain
derivation. It seems most likely that it
derives from what was originally a
dialectal pet name for a lamb, from the
verb bunt 'to butt gently'.

Burgess ♂ Transferred use of the
surname, in origin a status name from
the Old French word burgeis 'freeman of

a borough' (a derivative of burg 'town',
of Germanic origin).

Burnett ♂, ♀ Transferred use of the
surname (from an Old French
diminutive of brun 'brown'), in origin
a nickname referring to brown
colouring of hair, complexion, or
clothing. As a female first name it may
have been chosen in some cases with
reference to the plant Sanguisorba minor,
known as burnet, whose leaves are used
for salad (compare ▷Sorrel and
▷Fennel).
VARIANT: **Burnet.**

Burt ♂ Mainly U.S.: of various origins.
In the case of the film actor Burt
Lancaster (1913–94) it is a short form of
▷Burton, but it has also been used as a
variant spelling of ▷Bert. The pianist
and composer Burt Bacharach (b. 1928)
was the son of a Bert Bacharach, and his
given name is presumably simply a
variation of his father's.

Burton ♂ Transferred use of the
surname, in origin a local name from
any of the numerous places in England
so called. In most cases the place name
is derived from Old English burh
'fortress, fortified place' + tūn
'enclosure, settlement'.

Buster ♂ Mainly U.S.: originally a
nickname from the slang term of
address buster 'smasher, breaker', a
derivative of the verb bust (altered
form of burst). It was the nickname of
the silent movie comedian Joseph
Francis 'Buster' Keaton (1895–1966).

Buxton ♂ Transferred use of the
surname, in origin a local name from a
place in Derbyshire noted for its
thermal springs. In the Middle Ages this
place was known as Buchestanes or
Bucstones, i.e. 'bowing stones', and was
probably named from logan stones
(boulders so poised that they rocked at
a touch) in the vicinity. Use as a given
name seems to have been influenced by
the popularity of names such as ▷Buck
and ▷Bud, and the adoption as given

names of similar-sounding surnames such as ▷Caxton and ▷Paxton.

Byron ♂ Transferred use of the surname, first bestowed as a given name in honour of the poet Lord Byron (George Gordon, 6th Baron Byron, 1784–1824). The surname derives from the Old English phrase *æt ðæm bȳrum* 'at the byres or cattlesheds', and denoted someone who lived there because it was his job to look after cattle.

b

Cc

Cade ♂ Transferred use of the surname, which originated as a nickname from a word denoting something round and lumpish. It is one of several given names that owe their origin to their use for a character in Margaret Mitchell's novel *Gone with the Wind* (1936).

VARIANT: **Kade**.

Caden ♂ Probably a transferred use of the surname, a reduced and altered form of Irish and Scottish *McCadden*, an Anglicized form of Gaelic *Mac Cadáin* 'son of Cadán'.

VARIANT: **Kaden**.

Caesar ♂ Mainly U.S.: Anglicized form of Italian *Cesare* or French *César*, or a direct adoption of the Roman imperial family name *Caesar*, of uncertain meaning. It has been connected with Latin *caesaries* 'head of hair', but this is no more than folk etymology; the name may be of Etruscan origin. Its most notable bearer was Gaius Julius Caesar (?102–44 BC) and it also formed part of the full name of his relative Augustus (Gaius Julius Caesar Octavianus Augustus). Subsequently it was used as an imperial title and eventually became a vocabulary word for an emperor (leading to German *Kaiser* and Russian *tsar*).

Cai ♂ Variant spelling of ▷Kai.

Caile ♂ Variant spelling of ▷Cale.

Caileigh ♀ Variant spelling of ▷Kayley.

Cain ♂ Biblical name, meaning 'acquired' in Hebrew, borne by the older son of Adam and Eve, who, out of jealousy, killed his brother, Abel (Genesis 4: 1–8). In spite of this unfortunate association, the name is now increasingly used.

Caitlín ♀ Irish equivalent of ▷Katherine, pronounced 'kat-leen'. It is being used increasingly in the English-speaking world, generally without the accent and with the pronunciation '**kate**-lin'.

VARIANTS: **Caitlyn, Kaitlyn**.

Caius ♂ Classical Latin personal name, also written *Gaius*, which is of extremely ancient origin and uncertain etymology. It was borne for example by the dictator Caius Julius Caesar, and in the early Christian period by numerous saints. Its use as a modern name is infrequent.

Cal ♂ Short form of ▷Calvin. Ulster variant of **Cathal** (see Irish appendix).

Cale ♂ Of uncertain origin; perhaps a variant of ▷Kale or a transferred use of a surname.

Caleb ♂ Biblical name, borne by an early Israelite, one of only two of those who set out with Moses from Egypt to live long enough to enter the promised land (Numbers 26:65). The name, which is apparently derived from the word for 'dog' in Hebrew, is said in some traditions to symbolize devotion to God. It was popular among the Puritans and was introduced by them to America. In recent years it has become quite popular both in the United States and Britain.

VARIANT: **Kaleb**.

Caleigh ♀ Variant spelling of ▷Kayley.

Calico ♀ Apparently from the name of the cotton fabric, originally so called because it was imported from the Indian port of Calicut (now Kozhikode) in Kerala. It may have come to be adopted as a first name by association with ▷Dimity.

Calista ♀ From the Late Latin name *Calixta*, feminine form of *Calixtus* (from Latin *calix* 'cup'), adopted by Christians with specific reference to the cup containing the wine of the Christian sacrament. The male name was borne by three popes, including a 3rd-century saint (d. 222); it never enjoyed great popularity in England, but it became common in Bohemia, especially among members of a Hussite sect calling themselves Calixtines, who believed that wine as well as bread should be given to the laity in the Eucharist. In modern times this name is borne by the actress Calista Flockhart, star of the TV show *Ally McBeal*. There is also an apparent association with Greek *kallista* (feminine form) 'fairest, most beautiful'.

Callie ♀ Of uncertain origin; probably a pet form of ▷Calista.
VARIANT: **Cally.**

Callum ♂ Variant spelling of **Calum**, the Scottish Gaelic form of the Late Latin personal name *Columba* 'dove'. This was popular among early Christians because the dove was a symbol of gentleness, purity, peace, and the Holy Spirit. St Columba was one of the most influential of all the early Celtic saints. He was born in Donegal in 521 into a noble family, and was trained for the priesthood from early in life. He founded monastery schools at Durrow, Derry, and Kells, and then, in 563, sailed with twelve companions to Scotland, to convert the people there to Christianity. He established a monastery on the island of Iona, and from there converted the Pictish and Irish inhabitants of Scotland. He died in 597 and was buried at Downpatrick. The name has recently enjoyed considerable popularity throughout the English-speaking world.
VARIANTS: **Calum** (the usual Scottish form); **Colm** (usual Irish form).

Calvin ♂ From the French surname, used as a given name among Nonconformists in honour of the French Protestant theologian Jean Calvin (1509–64). The surname meant originally 'little bald one', from a diminutive of *calve*, a Norman and Picard form of French *chauve* 'bald'. (The theologian was born in Noyon, Picardy.) Today the name possibly owes its popularity as much to the New York fashion designer Calvin Klein as to the theologian.
SHORT FORM: ▷**Cal.**

Cameo ♀ Apparently a transferred use of the vocabulary word (Italian *cammeo*, which is probably of Oriental origin) referring to the relief carving of a layered mineral carried out in such a way as to result in foreground and background of contrasting colours, and by extension to anything else—including a baby—that is small but perfectly formed.

Cameron ♂, ♀ Transferred use of the Scottish surname (see Scottish appendix). As a given name it has gained wide and popular currency in the English-speaking world, and is now also used as a girl's name.
VARIANT: **Camron; Kameron, Kamran** (modern respellings).

Camilla ♀ Feminine form of the old Roman family name *Camillus*, of obscure and presumably non-Roman origin. According to tradition, recorded by the Roman poet Virgil, Camilla was the name of a warrior maiden, Queen of the Volscians, who fought in the army of Aeneas (*Aeneid* 7:803–17).
SHORT FORM: **Milla.**
PET FORM: ▷**Millie, Milly.**

Camille ♀ French form of ▷Camilla, now also used in the English-speaking world.

Campbell ♂ Transferred use of the Scottish surname, borne by one of the great Highland clans, whose head is the Duke of Argyll. See Scottish appendix.

Candace ♀ The hereditary name of a long line of queens of Ethiopia. One of them is mentioned in the Bible, when the apostle Philip baptizes 'a man of Ethiopia, an eunuch of great authority under Candace queen of the Ethiopians, who had the charge of all her treasure' (Acts 8:27).

Candice ♀ Respelling of ▷Candace, perhaps influenced by ▷Clarice or by a folk etymology deriving the name from Late Latin *canditia* 'whiteness'. The name is best known as that of the American actress Candice Bergen (b. 1946).

Candida ♀ From Late Latin, meaning 'white'. The colour was associated in Christian imagery with purity and salvation (see Revelation 3:4 'thou hast a few names even in Sardis which have not defiled their garments; and they shall walk with me in white: for they are worthy'). This was the name of several early saints, including a woman supposedly cured by St Peter himself.

Candy ♀ Chiefly North American: short form of ▷Candace, ▷Candice, or ▷Candida. It is also an affectionate nickname derived from the vocabulary word *candy* 'confectionery'. The word *candy* is from French *sucre candi* 'candied sugar', i.e. sugar boiled to make a crystalline sweet. The French word is derived from Arabic *qandi*, which is in turn of Indian origin. The name was moderately popular in the United States in the 1960s, but has since fallen out of favour.

Canna ♀ Apparently from the name of a genus of plants that have attractive, brightly coloured flowers and are widely cultivated in parts of the world with a warm climate. This is now relatively well established as a first name in Australia. The botanical name represents Latin *canna* 'reed'.

Caprice ♀ From the vocabulary word referring to a whim or something whimsical. The word came into English via French from Italian *capriccio*, which originally referred to a sensation of horror making the hair stand on end (from Italian *capo* 'head' + *riccio* 'hedgehog'); its later meaning derives from association with the stubbornness of the goat (Italian *capra*).

Cara ♀ 20th-century coinage, from the Italian term of endearment *cara* 'beloved' or the Irish Gaelic vocabulary word *cara* 'friend'. This is not normally used as a given name in Italy, where such innovations are held in check by the hostility of the Roman Catholic Church to baptismal names that have not been borne by saints.

Careen ♀ Modern name of uncertain derivation. Its first appearance seems to have been in Margaret Mitchell's novel *Gone with the Wind* (1936), where it is borne by one of the sisters of Scarlett O'Hara. The name may represent a combination of ▷Cara with the diminutive suffix *-een* (of Irish origin, as in ▷Maureen), or it may be an altered form of ▷Corinne or ▷Carina.

Caren ♀ Variant spelling of ▷Karen.

Carenza ♀ Variant spelling of Cornish ▷Karenza.

Carey ♂, ♀ Variant spelling of ▷Cary, used mainly as a girl's name, under the influence of ▷Carrie. In Irish use, it is sometimes a transferred use of the surname, an Anglicized form of *Ó Ciardha* ('descendant of Ciardha') or *Mac Fhiachra* ('son of Fiachra').

Carin ♀ Variant spelling of ▷Karin or ▷Karen.

Carina ♀ Late 19th-century coinage, apparently representing a Latinate elaboration of the feminine adjective *cara* 'beloved'; in part it may also have been inspired by ▷Karin.

Caris ♀ Simplified spelling of ▷Charis.

Carissa ♀ Mainly U.S.: apparently a simplified spelling of ▷Charissa, or an elaborated form of ▷Carys.

Carl ♂ From an old-fashioned German spelling variant of Karl, the German version of ▷Charles. It is now increasingly used in the English-speaking world, and for some reason is particularly popular in Wales.

Carla ♀ Feminine form of ▷Carl.

Carlene ♀ Modern coinage, from ▷Carl + the feminine name suffix -ene (compare ▷Charlene).
VARIANT: **Carleen**.

Carlin ♀ Elaborated form of ▷Carla, apparently of German origin.
VARIANTS: **Carlyn, Carline**.

Carlo ♂ Italian form of ▷Charles, now also used in the English-speaking world.

Carlos ♂ Spanish and Portuguese form of ▷Charles, now also used in the English-speaking world, especially the United States.

Carlotta ♀ Italian equivalent of ▷Charlotte, occasionally used in the English-speaking world.

Carlton ♂ Transferred use of the surname, a local name from any of various places (in Beds., Cambs., Co. Durham, Leics., Lincs., Northants, Notts., Suffolk, and Yorks.) named with Old English carl '(free) peasant' + tūn 'settlement', i.e. 'settlement of the free peasants'. This is the same name as ▷Charlton, Ch- representing the southern (Anglo-Saxon) pronunciation, while C- represents the northern (Anglo-Scandinavian) version.

Carly ♀ Pet form of ▷Carla, ▷Carlin, etc. or an independent feminine form of ▷Carl.
VARIANT: **Carley, Carlie, Carli**.

Carlyle ♂ Transferred use of the surname, in origin a local name from Carlisle in Cumbria. The first syllable of the place name represents the British element ker 'fort'; the second derives from the Romano-British name of the settlement, Luguvalium. The surname is common in Northern Ireland as well as in northern England and Scotland. Use as a given name may also have originated as an elaborated form of ▷Carl.

Carmel ♀ Of early Christian origin, referring to 'Our Lady of Carmel', a title of the Virgin Mary. Carmel is the name (meaning 'garden' or 'orchard' in Hebrew) of a mountain in the Holy Land near modern Haifa, which was populated from very early Christian times by hermits. They were later organized into the Carmelite order of monks. The name is used mainly by Roman Catholics.
VARIANT: **Carmel(l)a**.
PET FORMS: **Carmelina, Carmelita**.

Carmen ♀ Spanish form of ▷Carmel, altered by folk etymology to the form of the Latin word carmen 'song'. It is now sometimes found as a given name in the English-speaking world, in spite of, or perhaps because of, its association with the tragic romantic heroine of Bizet's opera Carmen (1875), based on a short story by Prosper Mérimée.
VARIANT: **Carmine (English)**.

Carol ♀, originally ♂ Anglicized form of Carolus (see ▷Charles), or of its feminine derivative ▷Carola. It has never been common as a boy's name, and has become even less so since its growth in popularity as a girl's name. This seems to be of relatively recent origin (not being found much before the end of the 19th century). It probably originated as a short form of ▷Caroline.

Carola ♀ Feminine derivative of Carolus (see ▷Charles), which has been in infrequent use amongst English speakers since the 19th century at least.

Carole ♀ French form of ▷Carol, formerly quite commonly used in the

English-speaking world. In the 1930s it was associated particularly with the film star Carole Lombard (1908–42). Now that *Carol* is used almost exclusively for girls, the form *Carole* has become less frequent.

Caroline ♀ From the French form of Latin or Italian **Carolina**, a feminine derivative of *Carolus* (see ▷**Charles**). This name was used by certain gentry families from the 17th century onwards, no doubt in honour of the Stuart kings named *Charles*. It was famously borne by Lady Caroline Lamb (1785–1828), mistress of the poet Lord Byron.

VARIANT: **Carolyn.**

SHORT FORM: **Caro.**

PET FORM: ▷**Carrie.**

Carolina ♀ Variant of ▷**Caroline**, in some cases probably chosen with reference to the states of North and South Carolina in the U.S., which were named in honour of Charles II.

Carolyn ♀ Altered form of ▷**Caroline**.

VARIANTS: **Carolynn(e), Carolin.**

Caron ♀ Welsh: from *caru* 'love'. The name is also sometimes used outside Wales, possibly as a variant of ▷**Karen**.

Carrie ♀ Pet form of ▷**Caroline** or occasionally of other girls' names beginning with the syllable *Car-*, now often bestowed as a name in its own right.

Carson ♂, occasionally ♀ Mainly North American: transferred use of the mainly Scottish surname, which is of uncertain derivation. The first known bearer of the surname is a certain Robert *de Carsan* (or *de Acarson*), recorded in 1276; the 'de' suggests derivation from a place name, but no suitable place has been identified. Among Protestants in Northern Ireland, it is sometimes bestowed in honour of Edward Carson (1854–1935), the Dublin barrister and politician who was a violent opponent of Home Rule

for Ireland. In America the popularity of the name may have been affected by the legendary Missouri frontiersman Kit Carson (1809–68).

Carter ♂ Transferred use of the surname, which originated as an occupational name for someone who transported goods in a cart.

Cary ♂, sometimes ♀ Transferred use of the surname, which comes from one of the places in Devon or Somerset so called from an old Celtic river name. *Cary* became popular as a given name in the middle of the 20th century, due to the fame of the film actor Cary Grant (1904–89), who was born in Bristol and made his first theatrical appearances under his original name of Archie Leach.

VARIANT: ▷**Carey.**

Caryl ♀, occasionally ♂ Of uncertain origin, probably a variant of ▷**Carol**.

VARIANT: **Caryll.**

Carys ♀ Modern Welsh coinage, from *câr* 'love' + the ending *-ys*, derived by analogy with names such as ▷**Gladys**. It also enjoys considerable popularity outside Wales.

Casey ♂, ♀ Originally a North American name bestowed in honour of the American engine driver and folk hero 'Casey' Jones (1863–1900), who saved the lives of passengers on the 'Cannonball Express' at the expense of his own. He was baptized Johnathan Luther Jones in Cayce, Kentucky, and acquired his nickname from his birthplace. As a girl's name it is a variant of ▷**Cassie**. In recent decades it has become equally popular in Britain, particularly as a name for girls. In part, this may reflect a transferred use of the Irish surname, a reduced Anglicized form of *Ó Cahasaigh* 'descendant of Cathasach'.

VARIANTS: **Casy; Kacey, Kasey; Kaci(e)** ♀.

Caspar ♂ Dutch form of ▷**Jasper**, also found as a variant in English. According to legend, this was the name of one of the three Magi or 'wise men' who brought gifts to the infant Christ. The Magi are not named in the Bible, but early Christian tradition assigned them the names *Caspar*, *Balthasar*, and *Melchior*. Among the best known bearers in modern times is the U.S. statesman Caspar Weinberger (1917–2006).

VARIANT: **Casper**.

Cassandra ♀ From Greek legend. Cassandra was a Trojan princess blessed with the gift of prophecy but cursed with the fate that nobody would ever believe her. She was brought back to Greece as a captive concubine by Agamemnon, but met her death at the hands of his jealous wife Clytemnestra. Although it was never generally popular, this name was in occasional use from the Middle Ages until the 18th century, and has recently been revived by parents looking to the pages of classical mythology for distinctive names.

SHORT FORM: **Cass**.

PET FORMS: **Cassie**, **Cassy**.

Cassia ♀ Feminine form of ▷Cassius or ▷Cassian. It may also in part represent an adoption of the name of the spice (see ▷Kezia).

Cassian ♂ From Latin *Cassianus*, an elaboration of ▷Cassius. This name was borne by several early saints, most notably one martyred at Tangier in 298.

Cassidy ♀, ♂ Transferred use of the Anglicized form of the Irish surname *Ó Caiside*. Its use as a girl's name may be due to the *-y* ending, coupled with the fact that it could be taken as an expanded form of *Cass* (a medieval and modern short form of ▷Cassandra).

Cassie ♀ Pet form of ▷Cassandra, now also used as an independent given name.

Cassius ♂ From an old Roman family name, borne most notably by the senator Gaius Cassius Longinus, who led the conspiracy to assassinate Julius Caesar. The Latin name is of uncertain derivation, possibly connected with *cassus* 'empty, hollow'. Like other famous names from Roman history, such as ▷Caesar and *Pompey*, this name was commonly bestowed on slaves by their owners, and at one time it was fairly common among African Americans in the United States. Because of these associations it was repudiated by the boxer Cassius Clay (b. 1942), who changed his name to Muhammad Ali.

Cassy ♀ Pet form of ▷Cassandra.

Casy ♂, ♀ Variant spelling of ▷Casey.

Cath ♀ Short form of ▷Catherine.

Catherine ♀ Variant spelling of ▷Katherine. This form of the name is also used in France.

VARIANTS: **Catharin(e)**, **Cath(e)ryn**, **Cathrin(e)** (English only).

SHORT FORM: **Cath**.

PET FORMS: **Cathy**, **Cathie**.

Cathleen ♀ Variant spelling of ▷Kathleen.

Cathy ♀ Pet form of ▷Catherine.

Catrina ♀ Simplified spelling of ▷Catriona, now occasionally used in the English-speaking world.

Catriona ♀ Anglicized form of the Gaelic names **Ca(i)triona** (Scottish) and **Caitríona** (Irish), which are themselves forms of ▷Katherine. As the accents show, it is stressed on the second *i*. The name is now also used elsewhere in the English-speaking world, although it is still especially popular among people of Scottish ancestry. It attracted wider attention as the title of Robert Louis Stevenson's novel *Catriona* (1893), sequel to *Kidnapped*.

Caxton ♂ Transferred use of the surname, in origin a local name from a place in Cambridgeshire. The place name derives from the genitive case of the Old Norse byname *Kakkr* (apparently a derivative of *kokkr* 'lump') + Old English *tūn* 'enclosure, settlement'. The surname is well known, as it was borne by William Caxton (?1422–91), who established the first printing press in England, but the reason for its recent adoption as a given name is not clear.

Cayle ♂ Variant spelling of ▷Cale.

Cayleigh ♀ Variant spelling of ▷Kayley.

Cecil ♂ Transferred use of the surname of a great noble family, which rose to prominence in England during the 16th century. The Cecils were of Welsh origin, and their surname represents an Anglicized form of the Welsh given name Seissylt (see Welsh appendix). In the Middle Ages *Cecil* was occasionally used as an English form of Latin *Caecilius* (an old Roman family name derived from the byname *Caecus* 'blind'), borne by a minor saint of the 3rd century, a friend of St Cyprian.

Cécile ♀ French equivalent of ▷Cecily, now also quite common in the English-speaking world (usually without the accent). The form Cecile is found in 14th-century English records.

Cecilia ♀ From the Latin name *Caecilia*, feminine form of *Caecilius* (see ▷Cecil). This was a good deal more common than the masculine form, largely due to the fame of the 2nd- or 3rd-century virgin martyr whose name is still mentioned daily in the Roman Catholic Canon of the Mass. She is regarded as the patron saint of music and has inspired works such as Purcell's 'Ode on St Cecilia's Day', although the reasons for this association are not clear.

VARIANT: Cecelia.

PET FORMS: Cissie, Cissey; Sessy, Sissy.

Cecily ♀ Medieval vernacular English form of ▷Cecilia.

VARIANTS: Cecilie, Cicely.

Cedric ♂ Coined by Sir Walter Scott for the character Cedric of Rotherwood in *Ivanhoe* (1819). It seems to be an altered form of *Cerdic*, the name of the traditional founder of the kingdom of Wessex. Cerdic was a Saxon (Scott's novel also has a Saxon setting), and his name is presumably of Germanic origin, but the formation is not clear. The name has acquired something of a 'sissy' image, partly on account of Cedric Errol Fauntleroy, the long-haired, velvet-suited boy hero of Frances Hodgson Burnett's *Little Lord Fauntleroy* (1886). A well-known bearer was the film actor Sir Cedric Hardwicke (1893–1964).

Céleste ♀ French, now also in use in the English-speaking world (usually without the accent): from Latin *Caelestis* 'heavenly', a popular name among early Christians.

Célestine ♀ Pet form of ▷Céleste.

Celia ♀ From Latin *Caelia*, feminine form of the old Roman family name *Caelius* (of uncertain origin, probably a derivative of *caelum* 'heaven'). The name was not used in the Middle Ages, but was introduced to the English-speaking world as the name of a character in Shakespeare's *As You Like It*. It was popularized in the 1940s by the actress Celia Johnson (1908–82). This name is sometimes taken as a short form of ▷Cecilia.

Celina ♀ Variant spelling of ▷Selina.

Céline ♀ French, also found in the English-speaking world: apparently from Latin *Caelina*, a feminine form of *Caelinus*, which is a derivative of *Caelius* (see ▷Celia). It may alternatively be a short form of Marcelline (see French appendix).

Cerise ♀ Modern coinage, apparently from French *cerise* 'cherry' (see ▷Cherry) or the English word for the colour (which is borrowed from the French term). However, it may be simply a combination of elements, e.g. from **Ceri** (see Welsh appendix) and ▷**Louise**.

VARIANT: **Cherise**.

Cerys ♀ Variant of the modern Welsh name ▷**Carys**, now also in general use.

Chad ♂ Modern spelling of the Old English name *Ceadda*, the name of a 7th-century saint who was Archbishop of York. It is of uncertain derivation, but has enjoyed considerable popularity in recent years.

Chadwick ♂ Mainly U.S.: transferred use of the surname, in origin a local name from any of the various places in England named as the 'specialized farm or industrial centre (Old English *wīc*) of Ceadda (see ▷**Chad**) or Ceadel'. In modern use, this name is sometimes taken, wrongly, as a full form of *Chad*.

Chaim ♂ Jewish: variant of ▷**Hyam**.

Chalice ♀ Although coinciding in form with the term for the ecclesiastical vessel (via Old French from Latin *calix* 'cup') which features in many versions of the legend of the Holy Grail, this apparently originated as a first name from the combination of syllables found in other popular female names, such as ▷**Charlotte** and ▷**Alice**.

Chance ♂ Mainly U.S.: transferred use of the surname, in origin a nickname for an inveterate gambler or for someone who had survived an accident by a piece of luck, from Anglo-Norman *chea(u)nce* '(good) fortune'.

Chandler ♂, occasionally ♀ Transferred use of the surname, which originated as an occupational name for someone who made and sold candles (an agent noun from Old French *chandele* 'candle'). The extended sense 'retail dealer' arose in the 16th century. As a girl's name, it is used mainly in North America.

Chanel ♀ Transferred use of the French surname *Chanel*, bestowed no doubt with reference to Gabrielle

'Coco' Chanel (1883–1971), who founded a famous Parisian fashion house.

VARIANT: **Chanelle**.

Chantal ♀ French name also used in the English-speaking world. It was originally bestowed as a given name in honour of St Jeanne-Françoise Frémiot (1572–1641), a woman of great piety who in 1592 married the Baron de Chantal (whose title denoted a place in Saône-et-Loire). After her husband's death she adopted a strict religious life under the instruction of St Francis of Sales, and in 1610 founded an order of nuns, the Visitandines, devoted at first to charitable works, later (after official intervention by the clergy) to teaching and devotion to the Sacred Heart of Jesus.

Chantelle ♀ Altered spelling of ▷**Chantal**, influenced by the diminutive suffix *-elle*.

VARIANTS: **Chantel(l)**, **Shantell**.

Chapman ♂ Transferred use of the surname, which originated in the Middle Ages as an occupational name for a merchant or pedlar, from Old English *cēapmann* (a compound of *cēapan* 'to buy, sell, trade' + *mann* 'man').

Chardonnay ♀ Modern coinage, from the name of the wine (named from the variety of grape from which it is produced). It was borne by a character in the television serial *Footballers' Wives*.

Charis ♀ From Greek *kharis* 'grace'. This was a key word in early Christian thought, but was not used as a name in the early centuries after Christ or in the Middle Ages. As a given name it is a 17th-century innovation, probably chosen to express the Christian concept of charity. In later use it may sometimes have been selected as a classical reference to the three Graces (Greek *kharites*).

VARIANTS: **Karis**, **Caris**.

Charisma ♀ Modern name, from the vocabulary word denoting personal magnetism or charm (from Greek *kharisma* 'blessing', referring originally to the spiritual gifts conferred by the Holy Spirit on the Christian apostles). It may be chosen by parents in the hope that the child will have this quality, or it may simply represent an elaboration of ▷Charis.

Charissa ♀ Recent elaboration of ▷Charis, perhaps as a result of blending with ▷Clarissa.

VARIANT: Charisse.

Charity ♀ From the vocabulary word, denoting originally the Christian's love for his fellow man (Latin *caritas*, from *carus* 'dear'). This was taken up as a girl's name in the 16th century, but in spite of St Paul's words 'and now abideth faith, hope, charity, these three; but the greatest of these is charity' (1 Corinthians 13:13), *Charity* is less commonly used as a given name than the shorter ▷Faith and ▷Hope.

Charlene ♀ Chiefly Australian and North American: 20th-century coinage, from ▷Charles + the feminine name suffix *-ene*. It may have been influenced by the older but much rarer French name Charline, a feminine diminutive of ▷Charles.

VARIANT: Sharlene.

Charles ♂ From a Germanic word, *karl*, meaning 'free man', akin to Old English *ceorl* 'man'. The name, Latin form *Carolus*, owed its popularity in medieval Europe to the Frankish leader Charlemagne (?742–814), who in 800 established himself as Holy Roman Emperor. His name (Latin *Carolus Magnus*) means 'Charles the Great'. *Carolus*—or *Karl*, the German form— was a common name among Frankish leaders, including Charlemagne's grandfather Charles Martel (688–741). *Charles* is the French form. The name occurs occasionally in medieval Britain as *Karolus* or *Carolus*; it had a certain vogue in West Yorkshire from the

1400s, particularly among gentry families. The form *Charles* was chosen by Mary Queen of Scots (1542–87), who had been brought up in France, for her son, *Charles James* (1566–1625), who became King James VI of Scotland and, from 1603, James I of England. His son and grandson both reigned as King Charles, and the name thus became established in the 17th century both in the Stuart royal house and among English and Scottish supporters of the Stuart monarchy. In the 18th century it was to some extent favoured, along with ▷James, by Jacobites, supporters of the exiled Stuarts, opposed to the Hanoverian monarchy, especially in the Highlands of Scotland. In the 19th century the popularity of the name was further enhanced by romanticization of the story of 'Bonnie Prince Charlie', leader of the 1745 rebellion.

COGNATES: Irish: Séarlas. Scottish Gaelic: Teàrlach. Welsh: Siarl. German: Karl, ▷Carl. Dutch: Karel, C(h)arel. Scandinavian: Karl. French: Charles. Spanish: Carlos. Catalan: Carles. Portuguese: Carlos. Italian: Carlo. Polish: Karol. Czech: Karel. Finnish: Kaarle. Hungarian: Károly. Lithuanian: Karolis.

Charlie ♂, ♀ Pet form of ▷Charles and ▷Charlotte, now popular as an independent given name for both boys and girls.

VARIANT: Charley.

Charlotte ♀ French feminine diminutive of ▷Charles, used in England since the 17th century. It was particulary popular in the 18th and 19th centuries, in part due to the influence of firstly Queen Charlotte (1744–1818), wife of George III, and secondly the novelist Charlotte Brontë (1816–55); it has again come to prominence since the 1980s, especially in England and Australia.

PET FORMS: Charli(e), Lottie, Tottie.

Charlton ♂ Transferred use of the surname, originally a local name from any of numerous places, mainly in southern England, named in Old English as the 'settlement of the free peasants', Old English *ceorlatun* (compare ▷Carlton). Its use as a given name is largely as a result of the fame of the film actor Charlton Heston (1924–2008 as John Charles Carter; *Charlton* was his mother's maiden name).

Charmaine ♀ Possibly a variant of ▷Charmian, influenced by names such as ▷Germaine, but more probably an invented name based on the vocabulary word *charm* + *-aine* as in ▷Lorraine. It is not found before 1920, but has enjoyed some popularity since the 1960s, when it came to notice as the title of a hit song by The Bachelors.

Charmian ♀ From the Late Greek name *Kharmion* (a diminutive of *kharma* 'delight'). The name was used by Shakespeare in *Antony and Cleopatra* for one of the attendants of the Egyptian queen; he took it from Sir Thomas North's translation of Plutarch's *Parallel Lives*.

Charna ♀ Jewish (Yiddish): from a Slavic word meaning 'dark, black' (compare Polish *czarny*, Russian *cherny*).
VARIANT: **Cherna.**
PET FORMS: **Charnke, Charnele.**

Chas ♂ Short form of ▷Charles, originally from a written abbreviation.
VARIANT: **Chaz.**

Chase ♂ Especially North American: transferred use of the surname, which originated in the Middle Ages as a nickname for a huntsman, from Anglo-Norman *chase* 'chase, hunt'.

Chasity ♀ Mainly U.S.: a simplified form of ▷Chastity or a blend of that name with ▷Charity.

Chastity ♀ Mainly U.S.: from the vocabulary word, which is from Late Latin *castitas*, a derivative of *castus* 'pure, undefiled'. This was favoured by the Puritans in the 17th century, but is

now rarely used in the U.K. It came to notice in the late 60s when it was given by the singer and actress Cher Bono to her daughter.

Chauncey ♂ U.S. coinage from a well-known New England surname. It was first chosen as a given name in honour of the Harvard College president Charles Chauncy (1592–1672), the New England clergyman Charles Chauncy (1705–87), or the naval officer Isaac Chauncey (1772–1840). These three men were descended from a single family; the surname is found in England in the Middle Ages, and probably has a Norman baronial origin, but is now very rare in Britain.
VARIANT: **Chauncy.**

Chaya ♀ Jewish: from Hebrew *Hayya* 'alive' or 'animal'. In the first meaning it corresponds to ▷Chaim and names such as Vidal (see Spanish appendix), and in the second meaning it parallels animal names such as ▷Arye. See also ▷Eve.

Chaz ♂ Pet form of ▷Charles, derived in part from the use of ▷Chas as a written abbreviation for that name.

Chelle ♀ Informal short form of ▷Michelle or other names with this ending; see also ▷Shell.

Chelsea ♀ A 20th-century coinage enjoying a certain vogue. Ostensibly it is from the district of south-west London, which became known as the hub of the Swinging Sixties. (It was named in Old English as the 'chalk landing place', *cealc hȳð*.) It is also the name of several places in North America, the earliest of which, in Maryland, was named in 1739. It is the name of the daughter of former U.S. President Bill Clinton. Another influence on the coinage may have been the given name ▷Kelsey.
VARIANTS: **Chelsey, Chelsie.**

Cher ♀ Short form of ▷Cheryl or any of the other names formed with

Cher-, now sometimes used as an independent given name, influenced by French *cher* 'dear'. It is most famously borne by the U.S. singer and actress Cher (b. 1946 as Cherilyn Sarkisian).

Cherelle ♀ Apparently a respelling of ▷Cheryl, influenced by the popular feminine name ending *-elle* (originally a French feminine diminutive suffix).

Cherene ♀ Chiefly U.S.: modern coinage, a combination of *Cher-* (compare the many names following) with the feminine ending *-ene*.

Cherida ♀ Modern coinage, a blend of ▷Cheryl and ▷Phillida. It may also have been influenced by the Spanish feminine vocabulary word *querida* 'darling' (compare ▷Cherie).

Cherie ♀ Modern coinage from the French feminine vocabulary word *chérie* 'darling'.

VARIANTS: **Cheri, Chérie.**

Cherish ♀ Modern coinage, apparently an alteration of ▷Cheryth to match the vocabulary word *cherish* 'to treasure, care for' (brought into English in the Middle Ages from Old French *cherir*, a derivative of *cher* 'dear').

Cherith ♀ Variant spelling of ▷Cheryth.

Cherna ♀ Jewish (Yiddish): variant of ▷Charna.

PET FORMS: **Chernke, Chernele.**

Cherry ♀ 19th-century coinage, probably taken from the vocabulary word denoting the fruit (Middle English *cheri(e)*, from Old French *cherise*). However, in some cases it is derived from a transferred use of the surname *Cherry* (to which the naturalist and pioneer photographer Cherry Kearton owed his name). Dickens used *Cherry* as a pet form of ▷Charity: in *Martin Chuzzlewit* (1844) Mr Pecksniff's daughters Charity and Mercy are known as Cherry and Merry. In modern usage it is perhaps in some cases an Anglicization of French ▷Chérie.

VARIANT: **Cherrie.**

Cheryl ♀ Not found before the 1920s, and not common until the 1940s, but increasingly popular since, being borne, for example, by the American actress Cheryl Ladd (b. 1951). It appears to be a blend of ▷Cherry and ▷Beryl.

VARIANTS: **Cheryll, Cherryl, Cherril(l); Sheryl.**

Cheryth ♀ Evidently a blend of ▷Cherry with ▷Gwyneth, influenced by the biblical place name *Cherith*. The brook Cherith was a dry riverbed in which the prophet Elijah took refuge from the wrath of Ahab and Jezebel (1 Kings 17:3–5).

VARIANT: **Cherith.**

Chester ♂ Transferred use of the surname, in origin a local name from the city of *Chester*, so called from an Old English form of Latin *castra* 'legionary camp'. Use as a given name has become quite common since the 20th century.

Chevonne ♀ Anglicized spelling of Siobhán. See Irish appendix.

Cheyenne ♀ Modern coinage from the name of the American Indian people who once inhabited the land between the Missouri and Arkansas rivers. Their name is derived via Canadian French from Dakota *šahíyena*, from *šaia* 'speak incoherently', from *ša* 'red' + *ya* 'speak'.

Chiara ♀ Italian form of ▷Clara, pronounced 'kee-ah-ra', now also used in the English-speaking world. The name has always been particularly popular in Italy and has been borne by several Italian saints, notably Clare of Assisi (*c*.1193–1253), an associate of Francis of Assisi and founder of the order of nuns known as the Poor Clares. See also ▷Ciara.

Chloe ♀ Pronounced 'khloh-ee': from the Late Greek name *Khloë*, originally used in the classical period as an epithet of the fertility goddess Demeter. It may be indirectly connected with ▷Chloris. A person of this name receives a fleeting mention in the New Testament (1 Corinthians 1:11), and its use as a given name in the English-speaking world almost certainly derives from this reference, leading to its adoption in the 17th century among the Puritans. It has fared better since than many of the minor biblical names taken up at that time (see appendices 15–22), having in recent decades also appeared in combinations such as *Chloe-Anne*, *Chloe-Louise*, and *Chloe-Marie*.

Chloris ♀ From Greek mythology. *Khlōris* was a minor goddess of vegetation; her name derives from Greek *khlōros* 'green'. It was used by the Roman poet Horace for one of his loves (see also ▷**Lalage**) and was taken up by Augustan poets of the 17th and 18th centuries, but has since fallen from favour.

Chorine ♀ Apparently an altered form of ▷**Corinne**, coinciding with the vocabulary word formerly used to refer to a female dancer in music hall and variety shows (a French formation, from *chor-* 'dance' + the feminine diminutive suffix *-ine*).

Chris ♂, ♀ Short form of ▷**Christopher**, and of ▷**Christine** and the group of related girls' names. As a boy's name it is sometimes used independently.

Chriselda ♀ Elaboration of ▷**Chris**, apparently on the model of ▷**Griselda**.

Chrissie ♀ Pet form of ▷**Christine** and the group of related girls' names. An influence is the American singer-songwriter Chrissie Hynde (b. 1951).
VARIANT: **Chrissy**.

Christa ♀ Latinate short form of ▷**Christine** and ▷**Christina**. It seems to have originated in Germany, but is now also well established in the English-speaking world.

Christabel ♀ Medieval coinage from the name of *Christ* combined with the productive suffix *-bel* 'beauty' (see ▷**Belle**). This name is recorded in

Yorkshire from the mid 1400s onwards. Its popularity was enhanced by its use for the heroine of a poem (1816) by Samuel Taylor Coleridge (1772–1834). The name was borne by the pioneer suffragette Christabel Pankhurst (1880–1958), in whose honour it has sometimes been bestowed.
VARIANTS: **Christabelle**, **Christabella**; **Christobel**.

Christelle ♀ French altered form of ▷**Christine**, derived by replacement of the feminine diminutive suffix *-ine* with the equally feminine suffix *-elle*. The name is now also used in the English-speaking world, where its popularity has been enhanced by its resemblance to ▷**Crystal**, of which it may in some cases be a variant.
VARIANT: **Christel**.

Christene ♀ Variant spelling of ▷**Christine**, influenced by the productive feminine name suffix *-ene*.

Christian ♂, ♀ From Latin *Christianus* 'follower of Christ', in use as a given name from the Middle Ages onwards, especially as a girl's name. The name of *Christ* (Greek *Khristos*) is a translation of the Hebrew term *Messiah* 'anointed'.
VARIANT: **Christianne** ♀.
COGNATES (MASCULINE): Scottish Gaelic: ▷**Crisdean**. German: **Christian**, **Karsten**. Dutch: **Christiaan**, **Carsten**. Scandinavian: **Christer**. French: **Chrétien**. Spanish, Portuguese, Italian: **Cristiano**. Polish: **Krysztian**. Hungarian: **Krisztian**.

Christiana ♀ Medieval learned feminine form of ▷**Christian**. As a recent revival it represents an elaborated form of ▷**Christina**. It is also sometimes spelled **Christianna**, under the influence of the name ▷**Anna**.

Christie ♂, ♀ Pet form of ▷**Christine** or, particularly in Scotland and Ireland, of ▷**Christopher**, now also used independently.
VARIANTS: **Christy**, **Kristy**.

Christina ♀ Simplified form of Latin *Christiana*, feminine form of *Christianus* (see ▷Christian), or a Latinized form of Middle English *Christin* 'Christian' (Old English *christen*, from Latin).

SHORT FORMS: ▷Chris, Tina.

COGNATES: Irish: Crístíona. Scottish Gaelic: Cairistìona, Cairistìne. Welsh: Crystin. German: Christina, Kristin(a). Dutch: Christina, Kristina. Swedish: Kristina, Kerstin. French: ▷Christine. Spanish, Portuguese, Italian: Cristina. Russian: Kristina. Polish: Kr(z)ystyna. Czech: Kristina. Finnish: Kirs(t)i. Hungarian: Kriszti(á)na. Lithuanian: Kristina.

Christine ♀ French form of ▷Christina. It was popular in the medieval period, when it appears to have been used interchangeably with ▷Christian, and again in Britain at the end of the 19th century. In the United States it was particularly popular from the 1950s to the 1970s.

VARIANTS: ▷Christene, Christeen.

SHORT FORM: ▷Chris.

PET FORMS: Chrissie, Chrissy, ▷Christie, ▷Christy, ▷Kirstie.

Christmas ♂ From the festival celebrating the birth of Christ (so called from *Christ* (see ▷Christian) + *mass* 'festival'). It is sometimes given to a boy born on Christmas Day. See also ▷Noël and ▷Natalie.

Christopher ♂ From the Greek name *Khristophoros*, from *Khristos* 'Christ' + *pherein* 'to bear'. This was popular among early Christians, conscious of the fact that they were metaphorically bearing Christ in their hearts. A later, over-literal interpretation of the name gave rise to the legend of a saint who actually bore the Christ-child over a stream; he is regarded as the patron of travellers. In England the name was uncommon in the Middle Ages, but became very popular in the 16th century, especially in parts of the North.

VARIANT: Kristopher.

SHORT FORM: ▷Chris.

PET FORMS: Kit; Christie, ▷Christy (mainly Scottish and Irish).

COGNATES: Irish: Críostóir. German: Christoph. Dutch: Christofoor, Kristoffor. Scandinavian: Kristoffer. French: Christophe. Spanish: Cristóbal. Catalan: Cristòfol. Portuguese: Cristovão. Italian: Cristoforo. Polish: Krzysztof. Czech: Kryštof. Bulgarian: Hristo. Finnish: Risto. Hungarian: Kristóf. Latvian: Kristaps.

Christy ♂, ♀ Variant spelling of ▷Christie. In the British Isles this is a predominantly masculine form, but in the United States it is more frequent as a girl's name.

Chrystal ♀ Variant spelling of ▷Crystal, apparently influenced by Greek *khrysos* 'gold'.

VARIANT: Chrystalla (Latinate).

Chuck ♂ North American: now usually taken as a pet form of ▷Charles. It was originally a nickname, from an English term of endearment (as in Shakespeare's phrase 'dearest chuck'), probably from Middle English *chukken* 'to cluck'.

PET FORM: Chuckie.

Cian ♂ Traditional Irish name meaning 'ancient', now popular in the English-speaking world. It was borne by a son-in-law of Brian Boru, who played a leading role in the battle of Clontarf (1014).

Ciara ♀ Modern Irish coinage, created as a feminine form of ▷Ciarán, and now in vogue elsewhere in the English-speaking world.

ANGLICIZED FORMS: Kiara(h), Kiera.

Ciarán ♂ Traditional Irish name, now popular elsewhere in the English-speaking world (usually without the accent). It was originally a byname, a diminutive form of *ciar* 'black', which was borne by two Irish saints: a hermit of the 5th century and the founder of the monastery at Clonmacnoise (d. 547).

VARIANTS: **Cieran; Kieran, Kieron** (borne, for example, by the Irish actor Kieron Moore, 1925–2007), **Kieren, Keiran**. (Anglicized forms)

Cicely ♀ Variant of ▷Cecily. This was a common form of the name in the Middle Ages, and in the 20th century was well known as the name of the British actress and singer Cicely Courtneidge (1893–1980).

Cilla ♀ Pet form of ▷Priscilla, associated chiefly with the Liverpudlian singer and TV personality Cilla Black (b. 1943), whose real name is Priscilla White.

Cindy ♀ Pet form of ▷Cynthia or, less often, of ▷Lucinda, now very commonly used as a given name in its own right, especially in North America. It has sometimes been taken as a short form of the name of the fairytale heroine *Cinderella*, which is in fact unrelated (being from French *Cendrillon*, a derivative of *cendre* 'cinders').

VARIANT: **Sindy**.

Cinnamon ♀ Modern name, from the term for the spice (Greek *kinnamon*, of Semitic origin), in part perhaps referring to its warm brown colour. Use as a first name may have been influenced by other names which coincide in form with the names of spices, although they partly have other origins; see for example ▷Cassia and ▷Fennel.

Cissie ♀ Pet form of ▷Cecilia or ▷Cicely, which has sometimes been used as an independent given name in recent decades.

Claiborne ♂ U.S.: transferred use of the surname of a major American family. William Claiborne (*c.*1587–*c.*1677), the second son of Edmund Cliburne of Cliburn in Westmorland (now Cumbria), was a founding colonist in Virginia. His descendant William

Charles Claiborne (1775–1817) was the first governor of Louisiana.

Claire ♀ French form of ▷Clara. It was introduced to Britain by the Normans, but subsequently abandoned. This spelling was revived in the 19th century as a variant of ▷Clare.

VARIANT: **Clair**.

Clancy ♂ Mainly U.S.: transferred use of the Irish surname, an Anglicized form of Gaelic *Mac Fhlannchaidh* 'son of *Flannchadh*'. The latter is an ancient Irish personal name derived from *flann* 'red'.

VARIANT: **Clancey**.

Clara ♀ Post-classical Latin name, from the feminine form of the adjective *clarus* 'bright, famous'. In the modern English-speaking world it represents a re-Latinization of the regular English form ▷Clare. It was made famous in the early 20th century by the singer Dame Clara Butt (1873–1936) and the silent film actress Clara Bow (1905–65), known as 'the It girl' (because, whatever 'it' was, she had it).

Clare ♀ The normal English vernacular form of ▷Clara during the Middle Ages and since.

Clarence ♂ In use from the mid-19th century in honour of the popular elder son of Edward VII, who was created Duke of Clarence in 1890, but died in 1892. His title (*Dux Clarentiae* in Latin) originated with a son of Edward III, who in the 14th century was married to the heiress of Clare in Suffolk (which is so called from a Celtic river name and has no connection with the given name ▷Clare). The title has been held by various British royal princes at different periods in history. In the United States the name was borne most notably by the American defence lawyer Clarence Darrow (1857–1938), played in various films by Orson Welles, Spencer Tracy, and Henry Fonda.

Clarette ♀ Rare elaborated form of ▷Clare, with the French feminine diminutive suffix *-ette*. The formation may have been influenced by the wine *claret* (Medieval Latin (*vinum*) *claratum* 'clarified wine').

Clarice ♀ Medieval English and French form of the Latin name *Claritia*. This may have meant 'fame' (an abstract derivative of *clārus* 'famous'), but as a given name it may have been no more than an arbitrary elaboration of ▷Clara. It was borne by a character who features in some versions of the medieval romances of Roland and the other paladins of Charlemagne, and in recent times by the ceramic artist Clarice Cliff (1899–1972).

VARIANTS: **Clarisse**, **Claris** (modern).

Clarinda ♀ Rare elaboration of ▷Clara, formed with the suffix *-inda* (as in ▷Belinda and ▷Lucinda). *Clarinda* first appears in Spenser's *Faerie Queene* (1596). The formation was influenced by *Clorinda*, which occurs in Torquato Tasso's *Gerusalemme Liberata* (1580). This is itself an arbitrary elaboration of ▷Chloris. Robert Burns (1759–96) wrote four poems *To Clarinda*.

Clarissa ♀ Latinate form of ▷Clarice occasionally found in medieval documents. It was revived by Samuel Richardson as the name of the central character in his novel *Clarissa* (1748) and has since remained in moderate use.

Clark ♂ Transferred use of the surname, which originated as an occupational name denoting a clerk (Latin *clericus*), in the Middle Ages a man in minor holy orders who earned his living by his ability to read and write. It is recorded as a given name in Britain from the late 17th century onwards. Since the 1930s, when it was associated particularly with the film star Clark Gable (1901–60), it has been widely used as a given name, especially in North America.

VARIANT: **Clarke**.

Clarrie ♀, ♂ Pet form of ▷Clara and various similar women's names, and also of ▷Clarence. In popular culture it is borne by long-suffering Clarrie Grundy in the English radio soap *The Archers*.

Claude ♂ French: from the Latin name ▷Claudius. It was borne by various early saints, but its popularity in France is largely due to the fame of the 7th-century St Claude of Besançon. This form is widely used in the English-speaking world and has superseded Claud as the preferred spelling in Britain and the United States.

Claudette ♀ French: feminine diminutive form of ▷Claude, now also occasionally used in the English-speaking world. It gained considerable prominence in the 1930s as the name of the French film star Claudette Colbert (1903–96), a Hollywood favourite for many years. Her original name was Lily Claudette Chauchoin.

Claudia ♀ From the Latin female name, a feminine form of ▷Claudius. The name is mentioned in one of St Paul's letters to Timothy (2, 4:21 'Eubulus greeteth thee, and Pudens, and Linus, and Claudia, and all the brethren'), as a result of which it was taken up in the 16th century and has since maintained a steady popularity.

Claudine ♀ French: feminine diminutive form of ▷Claude. It was made popular at the beginning of the 20th century as the name of the heroine of a series of novels by the French writer Colette (1873–1954), and is now also occasionally used in the English-speaking world.

Claudius ♂ Old Roman family name derived from the Latin byname *Claudus* 'lame', used occasionally in the English-speaking world.

Claver ♂ Roman Catholic name given in honour of the Catalan saint Pere Claver (1581–1654), a Jesuit who worked among Negro slaves in Central

America. He was canonized in 1888. His surname is a Catalan occupational name for a locksmith.

Clay ♂ Either a shortened form of ▷Clayton or a transferred use of the surname *Clay*, a local name for someone who lived on a patch of land which had clay soil (Old English *clæg*).

Clayton ♂ Especially U.S.: transferred use of the surname, originally a local name from any of the several places in England (for example, in Lancs., Staffs., Sussex, and W. Yorks.) named with Old English *clæg* 'clay' + *tūn* 'enclosure, settlement'.

Clelia ♀ From Latin *Cloelia*, the name borne by a semi-mythological heroine of early Roman history. She was given as a hostage to the Etruscan invader Lars Porsenna, but made an escape back to Rome by swimming the Tiber.

Clem ♂, ♀ Short form of the boy's name ▷Clement and of girls' names such as ▷Clementine.
PET FORM: Clemmie ♀.

Clematis ♀ From the name of the plant (so named in the 16th century from Greek *klēmatis* 'climbing plant').

Clemence ♀ Medieval French and English form of Latin *Clementia*, a derivative of *Clemens* (see ▷Clement) or an abstract noun meaning 'mercy'. It was fairly popular in Britain from the late medieval period until the 17th century, but has since been used less often.
SHORT FORM: Clem.
PET FORM: Clemmie.

Clemency ♀ Rare variant of ▷Clemence or a direct use of the abstract noun, on the model of ▷Charity, ▷Faith, ▷Mercy, etc.

Clement ♂ From the Late Latin name *Clemens* (genitive *Clementis*) meaning 'merciful'. This was borne by several early saints, notably the fourth pope and the early Christian theologian Clement of Alexandria (Titus Flavius Clemens, AD ?150–?215).

SHORT FORM: Clem.
PET FORM: Clemmie.

Clementine ♀ Feminine form of ▷Clement, created with the French feminine diminutive suffix -*ine*. The name was first used in the 19th century, and for a time it was very popular. It is now largely associated with the popular song with this title. The Latinate form **Clementina** is also found.
SHORT FORM: Clem.
PET FORM: Clemmie.

Clemmie ♀, ♂ Pet form of ▷Clement and of girls' names such as ▷Clementine, borne more often by girls than by boys.

Cleo ♀ Short form of ▷Cleopatra, now used independently. It is famously borne by the jazz singer Cleo Laine (b. 1927). See also ▷Clio.

Cleopatra ♀ From the Greek name *Kleopatra*, derived from *kleos* 'glory' + *patēr* 'father'. This was borne by a large number of women in the Ptolemaic royal house of Egypt. The most famous (?69–30 BC) was the lover of Mark Antony, and has always figured largely in both literature and the popular imagination as a model of a passionate woman of unsurpassed beauty, who 'gave all for love' and in the process destroyed the man she loved. She had previously been the mistress of Julius Caesar.

Cleveland ♂ Transferred use of the surname derived from the regional name for the district around Middlesbrough, so named from Old English *clif* 'bank, slope' (genitive *clifa*) + *land* 'land'. Grover Cleveland (1837–1908) was the 22nd and 24th president of the U.S.; Cleveland is also the name of a city in Ohio: both of these may be factors influencing its use as a given name in the U.S.

Cliff ♂ Short form of ▷Clifford, now also sometimes of ▷Clifton. It has been used occasionally as a given name, especially since the advent in the 1950s of the pop singer Cliff Richard (real name Harry Webb). It has sometimes also been associated with ▷Clive.

Clifford ♂ Transferred use of the surname, recorded as a given name from the 17th century. There are several places (e.g. in Glos., Herefords., and Yorks.) so named, from Old English *clif* 'cliff, slope, riverbank' + *ford* 'ford'.

Clifton ♂ Transferred use of the surname, a local name from any of the numerous places named with Old English *clif* 'cliff, slope, riverbank' + *tūn* 'enclosure, settlement'. Use of this as a given name is more recent than that of ▷Clifford. It may in some cases have been adopted as an expanded form of ▷Cliff.

Clint ♂ Short form of ▷Clinton, now used as a given name in its own right, having been made famous by the actor Clint Eastwood (b. 1930).

Clinton ♂ Mainly North American: transferred use of the English surname, a local name from *Glympton* in Oxfordshire or *Glinton* in Northants. It was originally used as a given name in America in honour of the Clinton family, whose members included the statesman George Clinton (1739–1812), governor of New York, and his nephew De Witt Clinton (1769–1828), who was responsible for overseeing the construction of the Erie Canal. More recently it has no doubt been bestowed with reference to William Jefferson Clinton (b. 1946), 42nd president of the U.S., and it has enjoyed increasing popularity in the U.K.

Clio ♀ From Greek *Kleio*, the name borne in classical mythology both by one of the nymphs and by one of the Muses. It is probably ultimately connected with the word *kleos* 'glory'; compare ▷Cleopatra. The name is now sometimes used as a variant of ▷Cleo.

Clitus ♂ Mainly U.S.: Latinized form of Greek *Kleitos*, the name of one of

Alexander the Great's generals. This name is probably ultimately connected with *Kleio* (see ▷Clio).

Clive ♂ Transferred use of the surname, in origin a local name from any of the various places (e.g. in Cheshire, Shropshire) so called from Old English *clif* 'cliff, slope, bank'. As a given name it seems to have been originally chosen in honour of 'Clive of India' (Robert Clive, created Baron Clive of Plassey in 1760).

Clodagh ♀ Of recent Irish origin. It is the name of a river in Tipperary, and seems to have been arbitrarily transferred to use as a given name. There may be some association in the minds of givers with the Latin name *Clodia*, a variant of ▷Claudia borne by the mistress of the Roman poet Catullus. It is borne by the Northern Irish pop singer Clodagh Rogers (b. 1947) and is occasionally used in the wider English-speaking world.

Clove ♀ From the name of the spice (via Old French from Latin *clavus* 'nail', referring to the shape of the dried flower buds). In part it may also represent a short form of ▷Clover.

Clover ♀ Modern coinage taken from the word denoting the plant (Old English *clāfre*).

Clovis ♂ French derivative of the Germanic personal name *Hlodovic*, a compound of *hlōd* 'famous, clear' + *wīg* 'war'. The name, a doublet of ▷Louis, is also occasionally used in the English-speaking world.

Clyde ♂ Mainly North American: from the name of a river in south-west Scotland that runs through Glasgow, perhaps by way of a surname derived from the river name, although for many Scottish emigrants it was the point of departure from Scotland. The given name gained some currency, especially in the American South. The bank robber Clyde Barrow became something of a cult figure after the film

Bonnie and Clyde (1967), in which he was played by Warren Beatty.

Coby ♂ Transferred use of the surname, the origin of which is unexplained.

Cody ♂, ♀ Transferred use of the Irish surname, an Anglicized form of Gaelic *Ó Cuidighthigh* 'descendant of *Cuidightheach*' (originally a byname for a helpful person), or of *Mac Óda* 'son of *Óda*' (a personal name of uncertain origin). Use as a given name in the United States especially has been at least in part inspired by William Frederick Cody (1846–1917), better known as 'Buffalo Bill', the showman of the Wild West.

VARIANTS: **Codi, Codie, Codee** all ♀.

Colbert ♂ Transferred use of the surname, derived from an Old French given name of Germanic (Frankish) origin, from *kol* (akin to Old Norse *kollr* 'helmet') + *berht* 'bright, famous'. This given name was introduced to Britain by the Normans. It survived long enough to give rise to the surname, but its use as a given name died out soon after.

Colby ♂ Mainly U.S.: transferred use of the surname, in origin a local name from places in Norfolk and Cumbria, so called from the Old Norse personal name *Koli* (a byname for a swarthy person, from *kol* '(char)coal') + Old Norse *býr* 'settlement'. Use as a given name seems to have been influenced by the 1980s television serial *The Colbys*, a spinoff from *Dynasty*.

Cole ♂ Transferred use of the surname, itself derived from a medieval given name which may be a reduced form of ▷Nicholas or represent a survival into Middle English of the Old English byname *Cola* 'swarthy, coal-black', from *col* 'charcoal'. As a given name, it is associated with the songwriter Cole Porter (1893–1964) and has enjoyed a degree of popularity in recent times.

Coleen ♀ Variant spelling of ▷Colleen.

Coleman ♂ Variant of *Colman* (from Late Latin *Columbanus*, a derivative of *Columba* 'dove'; see ▷Callum). In part it also represents a transferred use of the surname, which derives in most cases from the Gaelic personal name *Colmán*, but in others may be an occupational term for a charcoal burner.

Colette ♀ French feminine diminutive form of the medieval name *Col(le)*, a short form of ▷Nicholas. It was given particular currency from the 1920s onwards by the fame of the French novelist Colette (1873–1954).

ENGLISH VARIANT: **Collette**.

Colin ♂ Diminutive form of the medieval name *Col(le)*, a short form of ▷Nicholas. The medieval name died out after the 14th century. In the 19th century *Colin* was reintroduced to England from Scotland, where it is an Anglicized form of the Gaelic name *Cailean*, particularly favoured among the Campbells and the MacKenzies, which relates to St Columba (see ▷Callum) as *Crisdean* does to Christ and *Moirean* to Mary.

VARIANT: **Collin**.

Coll ♂ From a medieval short form of ▷Nicholas. Its use as a modern given name in part represents a transferred use of the surname derived from the given name in the Middle Ages. In Scotland it has been used as an Anglicized form of the Gaelic name *Colla*, perhaps from an Old Celtic root meaning 'high'.

Colleen ♀ Mainly North American and Australian: from the Anglo-Irish vocabulary word *colleen* 'girl, wench' (Gaelic *cailín*). It became established as a name in the interwar years in North America, and was associated with the star of the silent screen Colleen Moore (1901–88), whose original name was Kathleen Morrison. It is not used as a given name in Ireland. It is sometimes taken as a feminine form of ▷Colin or a variant of ▷Colette.

VARIANTS: Coleen, Coline.

Collette ♀ Variant spelling of ▷Colette.

Collin ♂ Variant spelling of ▷Colin.

Colm ♂ Usual Irish form of ▷Callum, now also in use in the English-speaking world.

VARIANT: Colum.

Colton ♂ Mainly North American: transferred use of the surname, in origin a local name from any of various places in England so called. The place name is of varied origin: in most cases it derives from the Old English personal name *Cola*, a byname for a swarthy person (from *col* 'charcoal') + Old English *tūn* 'enclosure, settlement', and so is a doublet of ▷Colby.

Colum ♂ Variant of ▷Colm.

Columbine ♀ From Italian *Colombina*, a diminutive of *Colomba* 'dove'. In the tradition of the *commedia dell'arte* this is the name of Harlequin's sweetheart. The modern name, however, was coined independently as one of the many girls' names taken in the 19th century from vocabulary words denoting flowers. The columbine gets its name from the fact that its petals are supposed to resemble five doves clustered together.

Comfort ♀, ♂ From the abstract noun, on the model of ▷Charity, ▷Faith, ▷Mercy, etc. After a period of popularity following the Reformation, the name continued in infrequent use into the 19th century and recently enjoyed something of a revival, as a girl's name.

Conall ♂ Gaelic traditional name, now also used in the English-speaking world. It is composed of Old Celtic words meaning 'wolf' and 'strong', and was borne by many early chieftains and warriors of Ireland, including the Ulster hero Conall Cearnach, one of the two sons of Niall of the Nine Hostages. (The other was Eóghan.) Conall gave his name to *Tirconell*, otherwise known as Donegal.

VARIANT: Connell.

Conan ♂ Anglicized spelling of Conán (see Irish appendix). In historical times, the name was borne by a 7th-century saint, bishop of the Isle of Man. Sir Arthur Conan Doyle (1859–1930), creator of Sherlock Holmes, was born in Edinburgh, of Irish stock. The science-fiction creation Conan the Destroyer owes more to the villain of legend than to the bishop or the writer. For the most part this name is of Irish origin; however, it was in use in Yorkshire, especially among the Askes and the Bartons, from the 12th to the 16th centuries. In this case, the name was derived from Conan, Earl of Richmond, and is of Breton origin.

Conn ♂ Irish name meaning 'chief', also used as a short form of ▷Connor and of various non-Irish names beginning with the syllable *Con-*. See also Irish appendix.

Connie ♀ Pet form of ▷Constance, now also used independently.

Connor ♂ Anglicized form of the Gaelic name Conchobhar (see Irish appendix). In recent years the name has also become very popular outside Ireland.

VARIANT: Conor, Conner.

Conrad ♂ The usual English spelling of *Konrad*, a Germanic personal name derived from *kuon* 'bold' + *rad* 'counsel'. It was used occasionally in Britain in the Middle Ages in honour of a 10th-century bishop of Constance, but modern use in the English-speaking world is a reimportation from Germany dating mainly from the 19th century.

Constance ♀ Medieval form of the Late Latin name *Constantia*, which is either a feminine derivative of *Constans* (see ▷Constant) or an abstract noun meaning 'constancy'. This was a popular name among the Normans, and was borne by, amongst others, the formidable Constance of Sicily (1158–98), wife of the Emperor Henry VI.

PET FORM: Connie.

Constant ♂ Medieval form of the Late Latin name *Constans* 'steadfast' (genitive *Constantis*). This was not a common name in the Middle Ages, but was used particularly in the Maude family. The vernacular variant Costin is also found. The name was taken up more widely among Christians from the 17th century onwards, partly because of its transparent meaning and partly as expressing a determination to follow the exhortations of St Peter: 'Be sober, be vigilant; because your adversary the devil, as a roaring lion, walketh about, seeking whom he may devour; whom resist stedfast (*constant*) in the faith' (1 Peter 5:8–9).

Constantine ♂ From the Late Latin name *Constantinus*, a derivative of *Constans*; see ▷Constant. In early modern English the names *Constant* and *Constantine* were not always clearly distinguished. The Roman emperor Constantine the Great (?288–337) is specially honoured in the Christian Church as the first Christian emperor. The name was also borne by three kings of medieval Scotland, where it represents an Anglicized form of the Gaelic name ▷Conn, and is a traditional name in the Phipps (Marquesses of Normanby) family.

Conway ♂ Transferred use of the surname, which has multiple origins. It is a local name from places in Scotland, in the parish of Beauly, or (now Conwy) on the coast of North Wales. As an Irish name, it is an Anglicized form of various Gaelic names such as *Ó Connmhaigh* or *Mac Connmhaigh* 'descendant (or son) of *Connmhach*' (a personal name derived from *connmach* 'head smashing'), or *Ó Conbhuidhe* 'descendant of *Cú Bhuidhe*' (a personal name from *cú* 'hound' + *buidhe* 'yellow').

Cora ♀ Name apparently coined by James Fenimore Cooper for one of the characters in *The Last of the Mohicans* (1826). It could represent a Latinized form of Greek *Korē* 'maiden'. In classical mythology this was a euphemistic name of the goddess of the underworld, Persephone, and would not have been a well-omened name to take. Nevertheless, this has not proved an obstacle to its use in the English-speaking world.

Coral ♀ Late 19th-century coinage. This is one of the group of girls' names taken from the vocabulary of gemstones. Coral is a pink calcareous material found in warm seas; it actually consists of the skeletons of millions of tiny sea creatures. The word is from Late Latin *corallium* and is probably ultimately of Semitic origin.

Coralie ♀ Apparently an elaboration of ▷Cora or ▷Coral on the model of ▷Rosalie.

Corbin ♂ Mainly U.S.: of uncertain derivation, perhaps a short form of the rare given name ▷Corbinian, or a transferred use of the surname, in origin a nickname from a diminutive form of Anglo-Norman *corb* 'crow'.

Corbinian ♂ The name of a Frankish saint (?670–770) who evangelized Bavaria from a base at Freising, near Munich. His name was presumably originally Frankish, but in the form in which it has been handed down it appears to be an adjectival derivative of Latin *corvus* 'crow, raven', which had a Late Latin variant *corbus*. This may represent a translation of the Germanic personal name *Hraban*.

Cordelia ♀ Name used by Shakespeare for King Lear's one virtuous daughter. It is not clear where he got it from; it does not seem to have a genuine Celtic origin. It may be a fanciful elaboration of Latin *cor* 'heart' (genitive *cordis*). It has enjoyed modest favour in recent years.

Cordula ♀ Apparently a Late Latin diminutive form of *cor* 'heart' (genitive *cordis*). A saint of this name was, according to legend, one of Ursula's eleven thousand companions.

Coretta ♀ Elaborated form of ▷Cora, with the addition of the productive feminine suffix *-etta* (originally an Italian diminutive form). This is the name of the widow of the American civil rights campaigner Martin Luther King.

Corey ♂ Especially common as an African-American and Black-British name. The reasons for its popularity are not clear. It may well be a transferred use of the English surname *Corey*, which is derived from the Old Norse personal name *Kori*.
VARIANTS: **Cory, Corie**.

Corin ♂ French: from Latin *Quirinus*, the name of an ancient Roman divinity partly associated with the legendary figure of Romulus. It is of uncertain origin, possibly connected with the Sabine word *quiris* or *curis* 'spear'. In the early Christian period the name was borne by several saints martyred for the faith. The name is also used in the English-speaking world (where it is often regarded as a male equivalent of ▷Corinna), notably borne by the actor Corin Redgrave (b. 1939).

Corinna ♀ From the Greek name *Korinna* (probably a derivative of *Korē*; compare ▷Cora), borne by a Boeotian poetess of uncertain date, whose works survive in fragmentary form. The name was also used by the Roman poet Ovid for the woman addressed in his love poetry. This form has now been superseded in the English-speaking world by ▷Corinne.
VARIANTS: **Cor(r)ina**.

Corinne ♀ French form of ▷Corinna, now the more popular form in the English-speaking world.
ENGLISH VARIANTS: **Coreen, Corrin(n)e**.

Cormac ♂ Traditional Irish name, of uncertain origin. It has been a very

popular name in Ireland from the earliest times, and in modern times has been taken up in the wider English-speaking world. See Irish appendix.

Cornelia ♀ From the Latin feminine form of the old Roman family name ▷Cornelius. It was borne in the 2nd century BC by the mother of the revolutionary reformers Tiberius and Gaius Sempronius Gracchus. Its use in England dates from the 17th century, when it was probably brought in by Dutch immigrants.

Cornelius ♂ From an old Roman family name, *Cornēlius*, which is of uncertain origin, possibly a derivative of Latin *cornu* 'horn'. This was the name of a 3rd-century pope who is venerated as a saint. The name was particularly popular in the Low Countries, and immigrants contributed to its frequency in the north of England from the 1400s. However, it is now seldom used in Britain.

Cornell ♂ Medieval vernacular form of ▷Cornelius. In modern use it normally represents a transferred use of the surname, which has multiple origins.

Cory ♂ Variant spelling of ▷Corey.

Cosima ♀ Feminine form of ▷Cosmo, occasionally used in the English-speaking world. The name was borne by Cosima Wagner (1837–1930), daughter of Franz Liszt and devoted wife of Richard Wagner.

Cosmo ♂ Italian form of the Greek name *Kosmas* (see Italian appendix). This was borne by a Christian saint martyred, together with his brother Damian, at Aegea in Cilicia in the early 4th century. It was first brought to Britain in the 18th century by the Scottish dukes of Gordon, who had connections with the ducal house of Tuscany. The name was traditional among the Medicis, having been borne most famously by Cosimo de' Medici

(1389–1464), its founder and one of the chief patrons of the Italian Renaissance.

Costin ♂ Medieval pet form of ▷Constantine. See also ▷Constant.

Coty ♂ Mainly U.S.: transferred use of the surname, which is rare, apparently in origin a local name from a diminutive form of French *côte* 'riverbank'. Use as a given name has probably been influenced by its resemblance to ▷Cody.

Courtney ♀, ♂ Transferred use of the surname, originally a Norman baronial name from any of various places in northern France called *Courtenay*, the original meaning of which is 'domain of Curtius'. However, from an early period it was wrongly taken as a nickname derived from Old French *court nez* 'short nose'. In the U.K. it is found chiefly as a girl's name.

Coy ♂ U.S.: of uncertain origin. It is hardly likely to be from the modern English vocabulary word, which has both feminine and pejorative connotations. It probably represents a transferred use of the surname *Coy* or perhaps *McCoy*, a variant of *McKay*, meaning 'son of **Aodh**' (see Irish appendix).

Craig ♂ From a nickname from the Gaelic word *creag* 'rock', or in some cases a transferred use of the Scottish surname derived as a local name from this word. Though still particularly popular in Scotland, the given name is now used throughout the English-speaking world and is chosen by many people who have no connection with Scotland.

Crawford ♂ Transferred use of the surname, originally a local name from any of the various places so named from Old English with *crāwe* 'crow' + *ford* 'ford', for example in Dorset, Lanarkshire, and Lancashire.

Creighton ♂ Pronounced '**kry**-ton': transferred use of the Scottish surname, in origin a local name from *Crichton* in Midlothian, so called from Gaelic *crìoch* 'border, boundary' + Middle English *tune* 'settlement' (Old English *tūn*).

VARIANT: **Crichton**.

Cressa ♀ Modern name in occasional use, apparently originating as a contracted short form of ▷Cressida.

Cressida ♀ From a medieval legend, told by Chaucer and Shakespeare among others, set in ancient Troy. Cressida is a Trojan princess, daughter of Calchas, a priest who has defected to the Greeks. When she is restored to her father, she jilts her Trojan lover Troilus in favour of the Greek Diomedes. The story is not found in classical sources. Chaucer used the name in the form *Criseyde*, getting it from Boccaccio's *Criseida*. This in turn is ultimately based on Greek *Khryseis* (a derivative of *khrysos* 'gold'), the name of a Trojan girl who is mentioned briefly as a prisoner of the Greeks at the beginning of Homer's *Iliad*. Chaucer's version of the name was Latinized by Shakespeare as *Cressida*. In spite of the unhappy associations of the story, the name has enjoyed some popularity since the late 20th century.

Crichton ♂ Variant of ▷Creighton.

Crispian ♂ Medieval variant of ▷Crispin, now rarely used.

Crispin ♂ From Latin *Crispinus*, a derivative of the old Roman family name *Crispus* 'curly(-headed)'. St Crispin was martyred with his brother Crispinian in *c*.285, and the pair were popular saints in the Middle Ages.

Cristina ♀ Mainly U.S.: Italian, Spanish, and Portuguese form of ▷Christina, sometimes also used in the English-speaking world.

Crystal ♀ 19th-century coinage, which has recently enjoyed some popularity. This is one of the group of names taken from or suggestive of gemstones. The word *crystal*, denoting high-quality cut glass, is derived from

Greek *krystallos* 'ice'. As a boy's name, *Crystal* originated as a Scottish pet form of ▷Christopher, but it is rarely used today.

VARIANTS: **Krystal, Kristel, Krystle.**

Curt ♂ Originally an Anglicized spelling of the German name ▷Kurt, but now also used as a short form of ▷Curtis.

Curtis ♂ Transferred use of the surname, which originated in the Middle Ages as a nickname for someone who was 'courteous' (Old French *curteis*). At an early date, however, it came to be associated with Middle English *curt* 'short' + *hose* 'leggings'; compare ▷Courtney.

VARIANT: **Kurtis.**

Cushla ♀ From the Irish term of endearment *cushla macree*, Gaelic *cuisle mo croidhe* 'beat of my heart'. The word is not normally used as a given name in Ireland.

Cuthbert ♂ From an Old English personal name composed of *cūð* 'known' + *beorht* 'bright, famous'. This was borne by two pre-Conquest English saints: a 7th-century bishop of Lindisfarne and an 8th-century archbishop of Canterbury who corresponded with St Boniface. The name has been in more or less continuous use in the northern counties of England from the 13th century, though its use has declined over recent decades.

PET FORM: Lowland Scotland: **Cuddy.**

Cy ♂ Short form of ▷Cyrus, sometimes used in America as an independent given name.

Cynthia ♀ From Greek *Kynthia*, an epithet applied to the goddess Artemis, who was supposed to have been born on Mount *Kynthos* on the island of Delos. The mountain name is of pre-Greek origin. *Cynthia* was later used by the Roman poet Propertius as the name of the woman to whom he addressed his love poetry. The English given name

was not used in the Middle Ages, but dates from the classical revival of the 17th and 18th centuries.

PET FORM: **Cindy.**

Cyprian ♂ From the Late Latin family name *Cyprianus* 'native of Cyprus', borne by one of the leading figures in the history of the Western Church. A 3rd-century bishop of Carthage, he wrote widely on theological themes and did much to further the unity of the Church.

Cyril ♂ From the post-classical Greek name *Kyrillos*, a derivative of *kyrios* 'lord'. It was borne by several early saints, most notably the theologians Cyril of Alexandria and Cyril of Jerusalem. It was also the name of one of the Greek evangelists who brought Christianity to the Slavic-speaking regions of Eastern Europe, where, as a result, the name became very popular. In order to provide written translations of the gospels for their converts, they devised the alphabet still known as Cyrillic. In Yorkshire, England, this was a favourite name of the Arthington family, but in their case it started out as *Searle*, a personal name of Germanic origin introduced to Britain by the Normans. It is now out of fashion.

COGNATES: French: **Cyrille.** Russian, Bulgarian: **Kiril.**

Cyrille ♂, ♀ French form of ▷Cyril, now also occasionally used in the English-speaking world, sometimes as an elaborated spelling variant and sometimes as a feminine form.

Cyrus ♂ From the Greek form (*Kyros*) of the name of several kings of Persia, most notably Cyrus the Great (d. 529 BC). The origin of the name is not known, but in the early Christian period it was associated with Greek *kyrios* 'lord', and borne by various saints, including an Egyptian martyr and a bishop of Carthage. In recent times it has been borne most famously by Cyrus Vance, U.S. Secretary of State 1977–1980.

SHORT FORM: **Cy.**

Dd

Daffodil ♀ One of the rarer flower names, which perhaps originated as an expanded version of Daffy, a pet form of ▷Daphne. The flower got its name in the 14th century from a run-together form of Dutch *de affodil* 'the asphodel'.

Dahlia ♀ From the name of the flower, which was so called in the 19th century in honour of the pioneering Swedish botanist Anders Dahl (1751–89). His surname is from a Swedish word related to English ▷Dale.

Daisy ♀ From the word denoting the flower, Old English *dægesēage* 'day's eye', so called because it uncovers the yellow disc of its centre in the morning and closes its petals over it again at the end of the day. The name was used early on as a punning pet form of ▷Margaret, by association with French ▷Marguerite, which is both a version of that name and the word for the flower. It was taken up at the end of the 19th century as part of the general vogue for flower names, and has enjoyed a steady rise in popularity since the mid-1990s.

Dale ♂, ♀ Transferred use of the surname, originally a local name for someone who lived in a *dale* or valley. It is now fairly commonly used as a given name, along with other monosyllabic surnames of topographical origin (see for example ▷Dell and ▷Hale).

Daley ♂ From the Irish surname, the Gaelic form of which is *Ó Dálaigh* 'descendant of *Dálach*'. The latter is a personal name derived from *dál* 'assembly, gathering'.
VARIANT: Daly.

Dalia ♀ In part a simplified spelling of ▷Dahlia, in part a Jewish name derived from Modern Hebrew *dalia* 'flowering branch'.

VARIANT: Daliah (associated especially with the Israeli film actress Daliah Lavi, b. 1940), Dalya.

Dallas ♂, ♀ Mainly U.S.: transferred use of the surname, adopted in honour of George Mifflin Dallas, Vice-President 1845–49, after whom the city in Texas is named. The surname is of Scottish origin, derived from the village of Dallas in Morayshire, named in Gaelic as *Dalfhas* 'meadow stance', i.e. a meadow traditionally used as a night's resting place by cattle drovers.

Dalton ♂ Transferred use of the surname, in origin a local name from any of various places named in Old English as 'the settlement in the valley', from *dæl* 'valley' + *tūn* 'enclosure, settlement'. The name is borne by the celebrated pianist Dalton Baldwin (b. 1931).

Daly ♂ Variant spelling of ▷Daley.

Dalya ♀ Variant spelling of ▷Dalia, influenced by Russian names such as *Katya* and *Tanya*.

Damaris ♀ Mainly U.S.: name of a woman mentioned in the New Testament as being converted to Christianity by St Paul (Acts 17:34). Its origin is not clear, but it is probably Greek, perhaps a late form of *Damalis* 'calf'. It was taken up in the 16th century, along with the names of other characters fleetingly mentioned in the New Testament, and has been occasionally used ever since.

Damask ♀ Apparently from the name of the fabric, which is decorated with patterning of contrasting texture but the same colour. This is so called because it was originally imported from Damascus in Syria. Use as a first name may have been inspired by association

d

with names such as ▷Dimity and ▷Calico. It may also have been adopted with reference to the distinctive dusky pink colour of the damask rose (*Rosa damascena*).

Damian ♂ From Greek *Damianos*, the name of the brother of Kosmas (see ▷Cosmo). The two brothers were martyred together at Aegea in Cilicia in the early 4th century. The origin of the name is not certain, but it is probably akin to ▷Damon.

Damien ♂ French form of ▷Damian, now also used in the English-speaking world. In Britain it has become the more frequent form. It is borne by the controversial British artist Damien Hirst (b. 1965).

Damon ♂ From a classical Greek name, a derivative of *damān* 'to tame, subdue' (often a euphemism for 'kill'). This was made famous in antiquity by the story of Damon and Pythias. In the early 4th century BC Pythias was condemned to death by Dionysius, ruler of Syracuse. His friend Damon offered to stand surety for him, and took his place in the condemned cell while Pythias put his affairs in order. When Pythias duly returned to be executed rather than absconding and leaving his friend to his fate, Dionysius was so impressed by the trust and friendship of the two young men that he pardoned both of them. The name was not used in the early centuries of the Christian era or during the Middle Ages. Its modern use dates from the 1930s and is due at least in part to the fame of the American short-story writer Damon Runyon (1884–1946). It is sometimes taken as a variant of ▷Damian.

Dan ♂ In modern use this is taken as a short form of ▷Daniel, although increasingly used in its own right, but it is also an independent biblical name, meaning 'he judged' in Hebrew, borne by one of Jacob's twelve sons (Genesis 30:6).

PET FORM: **Danny**.

Dana ♀, ♂ Mainly North American: of unknown origin, perhaps a transferred use of a surname that is fairly common in the United States. This may be of Irish origin, although the surname is not known in Ireland. *Dana* or *Ana* was the name of an ancient Irish fertility goddess, and this was also used in medieval times as a girl's name. However, it is not clear whether there is any connection between this name and the modern given name, which is sometimes also used as a feminine form of ▷Dan or ▷Daniel. Modern use as a boy's given name began in honour of Richard Henry Dana (1815–82), author of *Two Years before the Mast*, who supported the rights of fugitive slaves before and during the Civil War. The popularity of the given name was increased by the fame of the film star Dana Andrews (1909–92).

Danaë ♀ Name borne in Greek mythology by the daughter of Acrisius, who was ravished by Zeus in the form of a shower of gold; as a result she gave birth to the hero Perseus. Her name is of uncertain derivation; she was a great-great-granddaughter of *Danaus*, the eponymous founder of the Greek tribe of the *Danai* or Argives.

Dane ♂ Transferred use of the surname, in origin a local name representing a dialect variant of ▷Dean that was common in south-east England, rather than an ethnic name for someone from Denmark. The latter sense may be behind the given name in some cases.

Daniel ♂ Biblical name (meaning 'God is my judge' in Hebrew), borne by the prophet whose story is told in the Book of Daniel. He was an Israelite slave of the Assyrian king Nebuchadnezzar, who obtained great favour through his skill in interpreting dreams and the 'writing on the wall' at the feast held by Nebuchadnezzar's son Belshazzar. His enemies managed to get him cast into a lions' den, but he was saved by God. This was a favourite tale in the Middle Ages, often represented in miracle plays. The name has been perennially popular among English speakers since the 16th century and has been particularly favoured since the 1980s.

VARIANT: Danyal.

SHORT FORM: ▷Dan.

PET FORM: Danny.

COGNATES: Scottish Gaelic: Dàniel. Welsh: Deiniol. German, Scandinavian: Daniel. Dutch: Daniël. French, Spanish, Portuguese: Daniel. Italian: Daniele. Russian: Daniil. Polish, Czech: Daniel. Finnish: Taneli. Hungarian: Dániel.

Daniella ♀ Feminine form of ▷Daniel.

VARIANT: Daniela.

Danielle ♀ French feminine form of ▷Daniel, now frequently used also in the English-speaking world.

Danika ♀ Eastern European name, now also used in the English-speaking world. It is derived from a Slavic word denoting the morning star.

VARIANT: Danica.

Danny ♂ Pet form of ▷Daniel, now also used as a given name in its own right.

VARIANT OR FEMININE FORM: Dannie.

Dante ♂ Italian name bestowed in honour of the medieval poet Dante Alighieri (1265–1321), also used in the English-speaking world. As a medieval given name *Dante* was a contracted form of *Durante* 'steadfast, enduring'. In an English context it was famously borne by the pre-Raphaelite poet and painter Dante Gabriel Rossetti (1828–1882), the son of an exiled Italian scholar and patriot.

Danya ♀ Modern coinage; apparently a feminine form of ▷Dan.

Danyal ♂ Fanciful respelling of ▷Daniel.

Daphne ♀ Name borne in Greek mythology by a nymph who was changed into a laurel by her father, a river god, to enable her to escape the attentions of Apollo. The name means 'laurel' in Greek. According to the myth the nymph gave her name to the shrub, but in fact of course it was the other way about: her name was taken from the vocabulary word (which is probably of pre-Greek origin). The name came into use in England at the end of the 19th century, when it was adopted as part of the vogue for plant names at that time.

Dara ♂ Irish: short form of Mac Dara 'son of oak' (see Irish appendix). This name, though still particularly associated with Connemara, is now found throughout Ireland and elsewhere in the English-speaking world. It was formerly often Anglicized as ▷Dudley.

Darby ♂ Transferred use of the surname, in origin a local name from the city of Derby or the district of West Derby near Liverpool. These are so called from Old Norse *diur* 'deer' + *býr* 'settlement'. In Ireland this name has been used as an Anglicized form of Gaelic Diarmaid (see also ▷Dermot).

Darcy ♀, ♂ Transferred use of the English and Irish surname, originally a Norman baronial name (*d'Arcy*) borne by a family who came from Arcy in northern France. The surname was well established in north central England from the Middle Ages onwards, and various gentry families used it as a male given name from the late 1500s. It has always had a somewhat aristocratic flavour, which has added to its popularity as a first name. It is the surname of the hero of Jane Austen's novel *Pride and Prejudice* (1813). Its use as a girl's name, often spelled Darcey—as in the case of the British ballerina Darcey Bussell (b. 1969)—is more recent and is now predominant.

Darell ♂ Mainly U.S.: variant spelling of ▷Darrell.

d

Daren ♂ Mainly U.S.: variant spelling of ▷Darren.

Daria ♀ Of classical Greek origin: feminine form of the male name ▷Darius. St Daria (d. 283) was a Greek woman married to an Egyptian Christian called Chrysanthus; they both lived at Rome and were martyred under the joint emperors Numerian and Carinus.

Darien ♂ Especially U.S.: of uncertain origin, perhaps a cross between ▷Darren and ▷Darius. Its identity in form with the name of a region of Panama and Colombia seems to be merely coincidental.

Darin ♂ Mainly U.S.: variant of ▷Darren, associated with the singer Bobby Darin (1936–73), who was originally called Walden Robert Cassotto. He chose the name that he made famous from the list of surnames in a telephone directory.

Darius ♂ From Greek *Dareios*, originally a transliterated version of the name of various ancient Persian kings. The original form of the name is said to have been *Darayavahush*, from *daraya(miy)* 'possess' or 'maintain' + *vahu* 'well, good'. An obscure saint of this name was martyred at Nicaea with three companions at an uncertain date.

Darlene ♀ Mainly Australian and North American: modern coinage, an alteration of the affectionate term of address *Darling*, by fusion with the suffix *-(l)ene*, found as an ending in other girls' names.

VARIANT: **Darleen**.

Darnell ♂ Of uncertain derivation. It may be a transferred use of the surname derived from *darnel*, a type of grass (from Old French), or it may be a variant of ▷Darrell, influenced by the plant name.

Darragh ♂ Irish and Scottish: popularly associated with the Scottish Gaelic vocabulary word *darach* 'oak' (Irish *dair*, genitive *darach*). As an Irish name it also functions as an Anglicized form of Dáire (see appendix). It is one of the Celtic names that is now spreading into more general use.

Darrell ♂ Mainly North American: transferred use of the surname, originally a Norman baronial name (*d'Airelle*) borne by a family who came from Airelle in Calvados. It was first used as a given name towards the end of the 19th century.

VARIANTS: **Darrel, Darell, Darryll**.

Darren ♂ 20th-century coinage, of uncertain derivation. It may be a transferred use of a surname (itself of obscure origin). It seems to have been first borne by the American actor Darren McGavin (1922–2006). It came to public notice as the name of a character in the popular American television comedy series *Bewitched*, made in the 1960s, and has remained steadily popular ever since.

VARIANTS: **Daren, Darran, Dar(r)in, Dar(r)on, Dar(r)yn**.

Darrene ♀ Feminine form of ▷Darren, formed by fusion with the productive feminine suffix *-ene*.

VARIANT: **Dareen**.

Darryl ♂, occasionally ♀ Variant of ▷Darrell. Like its variant Daryl, it is occasionally borne by women, no doubt by analogy with names such as ▷Cheryl. A recent influence on the girl's name is the actress Daryl Hannah (b. 1960).

VARIANTS: **Daryl(l)**.

Darwin ♂ Transferred use of the surname, which in turn probably derives from the Old English personal name *Dēorwine*, composed of the elements *dēor* 'dear, beloved' + *wine* 'friend'. Use as a given name seems to have originated in honour of Charles Darwin (1809–82), founder of the theory of evolution.

Dassah ♀ Jewish: shortened form of ▷Hadassah, as a result of erroneous association of the first syllable with the Hebrew definite article *ha*.

Dave ♂ Informal short form of ▷David, sometimes bestowed as an independent given name.

David ♂ Biblical name, borne by the greatest of all the kings of Israel, whose history is recounted with great vividness in the first and second books of Samuel and elsewhere. As a boy he killed the giant Philistine Goliath with his slingshot. As king of Judah, and later of all Israel, he expanded the power of the Israelites and established the security of their kingdom. He was also noted as a poet, many of the Psalms being attributed to him. The Hebrew derivation of the name is uncertain; it is said by some to represent a nursery word meaning 'darling'. It is a very popular Jewish name, but is almost equally common among Gentiles in the English-speaking world. It is particularly common in Wales and Scotland, having been borne by the patron saint of Wales (see Dewi in Welsh appendix) and by two medieval kings of Scotland.

SHORT FORM: Dave.

PET FORMS: Davy, Davey, Davie (mainly Scottish); ▷Dai (see Welsh appendix).

COGNATES: Irish: Dáibhídh. Scottish Gaelic: Dàibhidh. Welsh: ▷Dafydd, ▷Dewi. German, Dutch: David. French: David. Spanish: David. Italian: Davide. Russian: David. Polish: Dawid. Czech: David. Finnish: Taavi. Hungarian: Dávid.

Davina ♀ Latinate feminine form of ▷David. The name seems to have originated in Scotland, and is occasionally elaborated to Davinia, on the model of ▷Lavinia.

VARIANT: Davena.

Davis ♂ Mainly U.S.: transferred use of the surname, in origin a patronymic from the given name ▷Davy. Use as a given name is often in honour of Jefferson Davis (1808–89), President of the Confederate States during the Civil War.

VARIANT: Davies.

Davy ♂ Pet form of ▷David.

Dawn ♀ From the vocabulary word for daybreak, originally bestowed as a given name in the 1920s, no doubt because of the connotations of freshness and purity of this time of day. It may have originated as a translation of ▷Aurora. Twin girls are sometimes given the names *Dawn* and ▷Eve, although the latter name does not in fact have anything to do with the time of day. The name is also associated with the British actress Dawn Addams (1930–85), the British comedienne Dawn French (b. 1957), and the American singer Dawn Upshaw (b. 1960).

VARIANT: Dawne.

Dawson ♂ Transferred use of the surname, in origin a patronymic from *Daw*, a Middle English pet form of ▷David.

Dean ♂ Transferred use of the surname, which has a double origin. In part it is a local name for someone who lived in a valley (Middle English *dene*, Old English *denu*) and in part an occupational name for someone who served as a dean, i.e. ecclesiastical supervisor (Latin *decanus*). The given name also sometimes represents Italian *Dino* (a short form of names such as *Bernardino*), as in the case of the American actor and singer Dean Martin (1917–95).

VARIANTS: Deane, Dene.

Deanna ♀ Variant of ▷Diana, coined in 1936 by the Canadian film star and singer Deanna Durbin (b. 1921), whose original given names were Edna Mae. It is now sometimes used as a feminine form of ▷Dean.

VARIANT: Deana.

Deanne ♀ Variant of ▷Diane, also sometimes used as a feminine form of ▷Dean.

Deborah ♀ Biblical name (meaning 'bee' in Hebrew), borne by the nurse of Rebecca (Genesis 35:8) and by a woman judge and prophet (Judges 4–5) who led the Israelites to victory over the Canaanites. It has always been popular as a Jewish name. It was in use among Christians by the mid 16th century and was taken up by the Puritans in the 17th century, in part because the bee was a symbol of industriousness. Since then it has enjoyed enormous popularity, peaking in the 1960s. Among other famous bearers is the actress Deborah Kerr (1921–2007).
VARIANTS: Debora, Deb(b)ra, Debrah.
SHORT FORM: Deb.
PET FORMS: Debbie, Debbi, Debby, Debi, Debs.

Declan ♂ Anglicized form of Deaglán (see Irish appendix). The name has been strongly revived in Ireland and is one of the set of Celtic names which has become established in the wider English-speaking world since the mid-1990s.

Dee ♀, occasionally ♂ Pet form of any of the given names beginning with the letter D- (compare ▷Jay and ▷Kay), in particular ▷Dorothy. It is also used as an independent name, and may in some cases be associated with the River Dee (compare ▷Clyde).

Deforest ♂ U.S.: transferred use of the surname, apparently adopted in honour of John DeForest (1826–1906), the author of several novels, mostly set during the American Civil War, which enjoyed great popularity at the end of the 19th century.
VARIANT: Deforrest.

Deirdre ♀ Name borne in Celtic legend by a tragic heroine, sometimes referred to as 'Deirdre of the Sorrows'. The story goes that she was betrothed to Conchobhar, King of Ulster, but instead eloped with her beloved Naoise. Eventually, however, the jilted king murdered Naoise and his brothers, and Deirdre herself died of a broken heart. She is sometimes taken as symbolic of the fate of Ireland under English rule, but this has not stopped her name being used by English parents with no Celtic blood in them. It became popular in Ireland and elsewhere in the Edwardian era, following retellings of the legend by both the poet W. B. Yeats (1907) and the playwright J. M. Synge (1910). The name itself is of uncertain derivation; the earliest Celtic forms are very variable.
VARIANT: Deidre.

Del ♂ Colloquial pet form of ▷Derek, with alteration of the exposed -r of the short form to -l (compare ▷Hal and ▷Tel).

Delbert ♂ Apparently a modern coinage composed of the name elements Del (see ▷Delmar, ▷Delroy) + Bert. In the 1980s it was adopted by the comedian Lenny Henry as the name of one of his comic creations, Delbert Wilkins, and it is used chiefly by people with West Indian connections.

Delfina ♀ Italian and Spanish form of ▷Delphine, sometimes also used in the English-speaking world.

Delia ♀ From a classical Greek epithet of the goddess Artemis, referring to her birth on the island of Delos (compare ▷Cynthia). It was taken up by the pastoral poets of the 17th century, and has been moderately popular ever since. It is particularly associated with the cookery writer and broadcaster Delia Smith.

Delice ♀ Anglicized or Frenchified form of ▷Delicia.
VARIANT: Delyse.

Delicia ♀ Feminine form of the Late Latin name Delicius, a derivative of deliciae 'delight'. Use as a given name seems to be a modern phenomenon; it is not found in the Middle Ages.

VARIANT: **Delysia**.

Delilah ♀ Biblical name (of uncertain origin), borne by Samson's mistress, who wheedled him into revealing that the secret of his strength was in his hair, and then cut it off while he was asleep and betrayed him to the Philistines (Judges 16:4–20). Although the biblical Delilah was deceitful and treacherous, the name was in regular use in Britain and the U.S. from the mid 17th century to the late 18th century. Since then it has occasionally been revived as an exotic name.

VARIANT: **Delila**.

Delite ♀ Modern coinage, apparently based on the vocabulary word *delight* (from Old French *delit*, compare ▷Delicia; the *-gh-* of the modern spelling is not justified by the etymology).

Dell ♂ Transferred use of the surname, originally a local name for someone who lived in a *dell* or hollow.

Della ♀ Name which first appeared in the 1870s and has continued to grow steadily in popularity ever since. Its derivation is not clear; if it is not simply an arbitrary creation, it may be an altered form of ▷Delia or ▷Delilah, or a short form of ▷Adela. In modern use it is sometimes taken as a feminine form of ▷Dell.

Delmar ♀ Mainly U.S.: of uncertain derivation, possibly from Spanish *del mar* 'of the sea', which occurs in various place names as a distinguishing epithet and also in the Marian title *Reina del Mar* 'Queen of the Sea'. It may alternatively have originated as an alteration of ▷Elmer (compare ▷Delroy and ▷Elroy) or as a transferred use of the surname, a reduced form of *Delamar*, a local Norman name from any of the places in northern France called La Mare 'the pond'.

Delores ♀ Variant of ▷Dolores.

Delphine ♀ French, from Latin *Delphina* 'woman from Delphi'. The Blessed Delphina (1283–1358) was a Provençal nun, who was probably named in honour of the 4th-century St Delphinus of Bordeaux. In modern times the name may sometimes be chosen for its association with the *delphinium* flower.

Delroy ♂ Apparently an altered form of ▷Leroy, perhaps representing the Old French phrase *del roy* '(son/servant) of the king'. It is used chiefly among West Indians in Britain.

Demelza ♀ Modern Cornish name, which has no history as a Celtic personal name but is derived from a place name in the parish of St Columb Major. The given name began to be used in the 1950s and was given a boost by the serialization on British television of the 'Poldark' novels by Winston Graham, in which it is the name of the heroine.

Demetrius ♂ Latin form of Greek *Dēmētrios* 'follower of Demeter', classical goddess of fertility. This name was borne by several early Christian martyrs; its huge popularity in eastern Europe is due in particular to the fame of a 4th-century saint martyred under Diocletian. For some reason, it never achieved much popularity in western Europe.

COGNATES: Spanish, Portuguese, Italian: **Demetrio**. Greek: **Demétrios**. Russian: **Dmitri**. Bulgarian, Serbian: **Dimitar**.

Demi ♀ Modern coinage, popularized, if not first used, by the film actress Demi Moore (b. 1962 as Demetria Gene Guynes) as a pet form of Demetria, feminine form of ▷Demetrius.

Den ♂ Short form of ▷Dennis.

Dena ♀ Modern coinage, representing either a respelling of ▷Dina, or else a form created as a feminine version of ▷Dean.

Dene ♂ Variant spelling of ▷Dean.

Denese ♀ Altered spelling of ▷Denise.

Denice ♀ Altered spelling of ▷Denise.

Deneze ♀ Altered spelling of ▷Denise.

Denis ♂ Variant spelling of ▷Dennis. This is the usual French form of the name.

Denise ♀ French feminine form of ▷Denis, widely used in the English-speaking world since the 1920s. See also ▷Dionysia.
VARIANT: Denyse.

Dennis ♂ Vernacular English form, based on French *Denis*, of the Greek name *Dionysios*, Late Latin *Dionisius*, which was borne by several early Christian saints, including St Denis, a 3rd-century evangelist who converted the Gauls and became a patron saint of Paris. It was on his account that the name was popular in France and was adopted by the Normans. In classical times, the name was an adjective denoting a devotee of the god *Dionysos*, a relatively late introduction to the classical pantheon; his orgiastic cult seems to have originated in Persia or elsewhere in Asia.
VARIANT: Denis, Denys.
SHORT FORM: Den.
PET FORM: Denny.
COGNATES: French: Denis. Spanish, Portuguese: Dionisio. Russian: Denis. Polish: Dionizy. Hungarian: Dénes.

Denton ♂ Transferred use of the surname, originally a local name from any of the numerous places named in Old English as 'the settlement in the valley', from *denu* 'valley' + *tūn* 'enclosure, settlement'.

Denver ♂ Transferred use of the surname, which is from a place in Norfolk, named with Old English *Dene* 'Dane' (genitive *Dena*) + *fær* 'ford, crossing'.

Denzel ♂ From the Cornish surname *Denzell*, a local name from a place in Cornwall. It came to be used as a given name in the Hollis family in the 16th century, when the Hollis family and the Denzell family became connected by marriage, and spread from there into more general use. It is borne by the African American actor Denzel Washington (b. 1954).
VARIANT: Denzil.

Deon ♂ Variant spelling of ▷Dion.

Deonne ♀ Feminine form of ▷Deon.

Derek ♂ From a Low German or Dutch form of *Theodoric* (see ▷Terry), introduced into Britain during the Middle Ages by Flemish weavers, although it was not much used until a sudden explosion of popularity in the mid 20th century.
VARIANTS: Dereck, Der(r)ick, Dery(c)k.
PET FORM: Del.

Dermot ♂ Anglicized form of the Irish name Diarmaid (see Irish appendix), now also used elsewhere in the English-speaking world. In Irish legend, Diarmaid was the lover of Gráinne, who had been promised to the ageing hero Finn mac Cumhaill, leader of the Fianna. The lovers eloped, but were pursued for sixteen years by Finn; according to one version of the story, Diarmaid was eventually killed by a wild boar and Gráinne died of grief.

Derren ♂ Altered form of ▷Darren.

Derrick ♂ Variant spelling of ▷Derek.

Derrin ♂ Of uncertain origin, perhaps an elaboration of ▷Derry influenced by ▷Darren.

Derry ♂ Of uncertain origin, perhaps a blend of ▷Derek and ▷Terry.

Deryn ♀ Welsh: from (*a*)*deryn* 'blackbird'.

Des ♂ Informal short form of ▷Desmond.

Desdemona ♀ Name occasionally chosen by parents in search of an unusual name, who are no doubt attracted by the sweet nature and innocence of Shakespeare's character and not deterred by her tragic fate. She was murdered by her husband, Othello, in an ill-founded jealous rage, and her name is in fact particularly appropriate to her destiny, as it probably represents a Latinized form of Greek *dysdaimōn* 'ill-starred'.

Desirée ♀ French (now also used in the English-speaking world, usually without the accent), from Latin *Desiderata* 'desired'. This name was given by early Christians to a longed-for child or as a symbol of desire for eternal life, virtuous qualities, or other Christian attributes, but the French form is now often taken as suggesting that the bearer will grow up into a desirable woman.

Desmond ♂ Transferred use of an Irish surname derived from the Gaelic byname *Deasmhumhnach* '(man from) south Munster', an ancient Irish kingdom named after *Mumhu*, one of its early kings.

SHORT FORM: **Des.**

Destiny ♀ From the vocabulary word denoting the power of fate (Old French *destinee*, from Late Latin *destinata*). This has recently become established as a given name, with variant spellings such as **Destinie**, **Destiney**, and **Destinee**.

Devereux ♂ Transferred use of a surname, which was originally a Norman baronial name derived (with fused preposition *de*) from *Evreux* in Eure. It was the family name of the 16th-century earls of Essex: Robert Devereux, the 2nd earl, was a favourite of Queen Elizabeth I, later disgraced and executed for treason.

Devin ♂, ♀ Mainly U.S.: transferred use of the Irish surname, Gaelic *Ó Damháin* 'descendant of *Damhán*'. The latter is a byname meaning 'fawn'.

Devon ♂, ♀ Mainly North American: of uncertain origin. It is found among Jews as well as gentiles. Among the latter it is generally from the name of the English county, either directly or as a transferred use of the surname, which derives from a British tribal name said to mean 'worshippers of the god Dumnōnos'.

VARIANT: **Devonne** ♀.

Devorah ♀ Jewish: modern Hebrew form of ▷Deborah.

Dewey ♂ Mainly U.S.: of uncertain origin, perhaps a respelling of **Dewi** (see Welsh appendix) or transferred use of the surname.

VARIANT: **Dewy.**

Dexter ♂ Transferred use of the surname. Although this is now a male given name, the word that gave rise to the surname originally denoted a female dyer, from Old English *dēag* 'dye' + *-estre*, feminine ending of agent nouns. However, the distinction of gender was already lost in Middle English. The name coincides in form with Latin *dexter* 'right-handed, auspicious', and may sometimes have been chosen because of this.

SHORT FORM: **Dex.**

PET FORM: **Dexy.**

Dextra ♀ Modern name, apparently coined as a feminine equivalent of ▷Dexter. It represents the feminine form of Latin *dexter* 'right-handed, auspicious'.

Dharma ♀ From the Sanskrit word (meaning 'decree' or 'custom') used in Hinduism and Buddhism to refer to the body of central tenets of the belief system. It has achieved limited use as a first name in the English-speaking world as a result of increasing popular interest in Eastern spirituality; compare ▷Karma, ▷Nirvana, and ▷Samsara.

Di ♀ Short form of ▷Diana and ▷Diane.

Diahann ♀ Elaborated variant of ▷Diane, associated particularly with the American actress Diahann Carol (b. 1935).

Diamond ♀ Mainly U.S.: one of the most recent of the girls' names adopted from the vocabulary of gemstones.

Diana ♀ Name borne in Roman mythology by the goddess of the moon and of hunting, equivalent to the Greek Artemis. In mythology she is characterized as both beautiful and chaste. Her name is of ancient and uncertain derivation. It probably contains a first element that is also found in the name of the Greek god *Dionysos* (see ▷Dennis) and the Latin name of the supreme god *Jupiter*. It was adopted in Britain during the Tudor period as a learned name, a borrowing from Latin influenced by the French form ▷Diane. Although it was much used by Elizabethan poets celebrating the virgin goddess and alluding to the Virgin Queen, it was not particularly popular as a given name until the end of the 19th century. In earlier centuries some clergymen were reluctant to baptize girls with this pagan name, mindful of the riots against St Paul stirred up by worshippers of Diana of the Ephesians (Acts 19:24–41). In the late 20th century, its popularity received a boost because of its association with the late Diana, Princess of Wales (1961–97), who was renowned for her beauty, glamour, and compassion.

VARIANT: Dianna (by association with ▷Anna).

SHORT FORM: Di.

Diane ♀ French form of ▷Diana, now also widely used in the English-speaking world. It was especially popular among the Renaissance aristocracy, who loved hunting and were therefore proud to name their daughters after the classical goddess of the chase.

VARIANTS: Diann(e) (by association with ▷Ann(e)), Dian; Deanne; Dyan (U.S.).

SHORT FORM: Di.

Diandrea ♀ Modern coinage, apparently a blend of ▷Diana and ▷Andrea.

Dick ♂ Short form of ▷Richard. The alteration of the initial consonant is supposed to result from the difficulty that English speakers in the Middle Ages had in pronouncing the trilled Norman *r-*.

Dickie ♂ Pet form of ▷Dick, with the originally Scottish and northern English diminutive suffix *-ie*. This has more or less completely replaced the medieval diminutive ▷Dickon.

Dickon ♂ Medieval pet form of ▷Dick (with the Old French suffix *-on*), still in occasional use.

Digby ♂ Transferred use of the surname, in origin a local name from a place in Lincolnshire, so called from Old Norse *díki* 'ditch' + *býr* 'settlement'.

Diggory ♂ Rarely used name of uncertain derivation. It is associated by some with French *égaré* 'lost, gone astray' and may have owed its popularity in the medieval period to the 14th-century romance *Sir Degaré*. It is now associated chiefly with literary characters such as Diggory Venn in Thomas Hardy's *Return of the Native* and (in a variant spelling) Digory Kirke in C. S. Lewis's 'Narnia' books.

Dillon ♂ Variant spelling of ▷Dylan, based on an English surname of different origin. The surname *Dillon* or *Dyllon* derives in part from a now extinct Norman French personal name of Germanic origin; in part it is a local name from *Dilwyn* in Hereford.

Dilly ♀ Pet form of ▷Dilys and Dilwen (see Welsh appendix), now sometimes used as an independent given name.

Dilys ♀ Modern Welsh name, from the vocabulary word *dilys* 'genuine, steadfast, true', used occasionally by people without Welsh connections.

VARIANTS: Dylis, Dyllis.

Dimity ♀ Apparently from the name of the light cotton fabric, which came into English from Italian in the 15th century and is derived from the Greek prefix *di-* 'two, double' + Greek *mitos* 'warp thread'. However, since it is found primarily as an Irish name, it may have originated as a feminine equivalent of ▷Dermot (Gaelic *Diarmaid*, earlier *Diarm(u)it*).

Dina ♀ In part a variant spelling of ▷Dinah, with which it often shares the same pronunciation. In part, however, it derives from the Italian name *Dina*, a short form of diminutives such as *Bernardina*.

Dinah ♀ Biblical name (a feminine form derived from Hebrew *din* 'judgement'), borne by a daughter of Jacob. She was raped by Shechem but avenged by her brothers Simeon and Levi (Genesis 34). In modern times it is generally taken as a variant of the much more common ▷Diana.

Dion ♂ French, from Latin *Dio* (genitive *Dionis*), a short form of the various names of Greek origin containing as their first element *Dio-* Zeus. Examples include *Diodoros* 'gift of Zeus' and *Diogenes* 'born of Zeus'. It is also used in the English-speaking world, especially as a Black name.

Dionne ♀ Feminine form of ▷Dion, associated chiefly with the African American singer Dionne Warwick (b. 1940 as Marie Dionne Warrick).

Dionysia ♀ Latin form of ▷Denise; see ▷Dennis. This form was in use in northern England from the 14th to the 17th century; the short form Dye is the source of the surname *Dyson*.

Dionysius ♂ Latin form of ▷Dennis.

Dirk ♂ Flemish and Dutch form of ▷Derek. Its use in the English-speaking world since the 1960s is largely due to the fame of the actor Dirk Bogarde (1921–99, born Derek Niven van den Bogaerde). He was of Dutch descent, although he was actually born in Scotland. The manly image of the name

has been reinforced by its coincidence in form with Scottish *dirk* 'dagger' (from Gaelic *durc*).

Dittany ♀ From the name of a plant (Greek *diktamnon*, from Mount *Dikte* in Crete, where it grew in profusion) famed in classical times for its medicinal qualities.

Diva ♀ Apparently from the vocabulary word denoting a female opera singer or other highly admired woman. The word came into English from Italian in the 19th century and literally means 'goddess' (from the feminine form of Latin *divus* 'divine').

Dixie ♀ Mainly U.S.: name chosen as symbolic of the American South. The nickname is of uncertain origin. It is said to be from the ten-dollar bills printed in New Orleans, named in the Cajun dialect from French *dix* 'ten'.

Dobre ♀ Jewish (E. Yiddish): from the Slavic word *dobro* 'good, kind'.
VARIANT: **Dobe.**

Dodie ♀ Pet form of ▷Dorothy, derived from a child's unsuccessful attempts to pronounce the name.

Dolly ♀, in Scotland occasionally ♂ Originally (from the 16th century onwards) a pet form of ▷Dorothy; now also a pet form of ▷Dora and ▷Dolores. Since the 18th century, it has also been found as an independent given name (taken as being from the vocabulary word *doll*, which was in fact derived in the 17th century from the pet name for *Dorothy*). In Gaelic areas of Scotland it is found as a pet form of the boy's name ▷Donald.

Dolores ♀ Spanish: from *Maria de los Dolores* 'Mary of the Sorrows', a reference to the Seven Sorrows of the Virgin Mary. The feast of Our Lady's Dolours was established in 1423. The name is now also borne in the English-speaking world, mainly by

Roman Catholics. In part, it was popularized by the film star Dolores Del Rio (1905–83), born in Mexico as Dolores Asunsolo.

VARIANTS: Delores, Deloris.

PET FORMS: Lola, Lolita, Dolly.

Dominic ♂ From the Late Latin name *Dominicus*, a derivative of *dominus* 'lord'. It was used mainly by Roman Catholics, in honour of St Dominic (1170–1221), founder of the Dominican order of monks, but has enjoyed wider appeal since the 1970s.

VARIANT: Dominick (an old spelling, still in occasional use).

SHORT FORM: Dom.

Dominica ♀ Latinate feminine form of ▷Dominic. This name was borne by a saint martyred in Campania under the Emperor Diocletian and by a wealthy Roman widow who was an associate of St Laurence.

Dominique ♀ Feminine form of ▷Dominic, from a French form that is used as both a girl's and a boy's name.

Don ♂ Short form of ▷Donald. It is also a variant of the Irish name Donn (see Irish appendix).

PET FORMS: Donny, Donnie.

Donald ♂ Anglicized form of Gaelic Domhnall (see Scottish appendix). The final -d of the Anglicized form derives partly from misinterpretation by English speakers of the Gaelic pronunciation, and partly from association with Germanic-origin names such as ▷Ronald. This name is strongly associated with clan Macdonald, the clan of the medieval Lords of the Isles, but is now also widely used by families with no Scottish connections.

SHORT FORM: Don.

PET FORMS: Donny, Donnie; Dolly (in Gaelic Scotland).

Donella ♀ Scottish: coined as a feminine equivalent of ▷Donald.

Donna ♀ Of recent origin (not found as a name before the 1920s). It is derived from the Italian vocabulary word *donna* 'lady' (compare ▷Madonna), but it is now also used as a feminine form of ▷Donald.

Donnell ♂ Transferred use of the Scottish and Irish surname *Mac Dhomhnuill*, derived in the Middle Ages from the given name Domhnall (see Scottish appendix).

Donny ♂ Pet form of ▷Donald.

Donovan ♂ Transferred use of the Irish surname, Gaelic *Ó Donndubháin* 'descendant of *Donndubhán*'. The latter is a personal name from *donn* 'brown-haired man' or 'chieftain' + *dubh* 'black, dark' + the diminutive suffix *-án*. Its use as a given name dates from the early 1900s. The folk-rock singer Donovan had some influence on its increase in popularity in the 1960s.

Donya ♀ Recent coinage, perhaps an altered form of ▷Donna or ▷Danya.

Dora ♀ 19th-century coinage, representing a short form of ▷Isidora, ▷Theodora, ▷Dorothy, and any other name containing the Greek word *dōron* 'gift'. Wordsworth's daughter (1804–47), christened Dorothy, was always known in adult life as Dora. The name's popularity was enhanced by the character of Dora Spenlow in Dickens's novel *David Copperfield* (1850).

Doran ♂ Transferred use of the surname; see Irish appendix.

Dorcas ♀ From Greek *dorkas* 'doe, gazelle'. It was not used as a personal name by the ancient Greeks, but is offered in the Bible as an interpretation of the Aramaic name ▷Tabitha (Acts 9:36), and was taken up by the early Christians. It was much used among the Puritans in the 16th century, and has remained in occasional use ever since, having also been used as an Anglicized form of Gaelic Deòiridh (see Scottish appendix).

Doreen ♀ Anglicization of the Irish name **Dorean** (see Irish appendix). It may also be a derivative of ▷**Dora** with the addition of the productive suffix *-een*, representing an Irish pet form. It peaked in popularity in the first half of the 20th century but has since fallen from favour.

VARIANTS: **Dorene, Dorine.**

Doria ♀ Of uncertain origin, probably a back-formation from ▷**Dorian** or else an elaboration of ▷**Dora** on the model of the numerous women's given names ending in *-ia*.

Dorian ♂ Early 20th-century coinage, apparently invented by Oscar Wilde, as no evidence has been found of its existence before he used it for the central character in *The Portrait of Dorian Gray* (1891). Dorian Gray is a dissolute rake who retains unblemished youthful good looks; in the attic of his home is a portrait which does his ageing for him, gradually acquiring all the outward marks of his depravity. This macabre background has not deterred parents from occasionally bestowing the name on their children. Wilde probably took the name from Late Latin *Dorianus*, from Greek *Dōrieus*, denoting a member of the Greek-speaking people who settled in the Peloponnese in pre-classical times. *Dorian* would thus be a masculine version of ▷**Doris**. It may have been selected occasionally by admirers of ancient Sparta and its militaristic institutions, since the Spartans were of Dorian stock.

VARIANT: **Dorien.**

Dorinda ♀ Elaboration of ▷**Dora**, with the suffix *-inda* (as for example ▷**Clarinda**). The name was coined in the 18th century, and enjoyed a modest revival of interest in the 20th.

Doris ♀ From the classical Greek ethnic name meaning 'Dorian woman'. The Dorians were one of the tribes of Greece; their name was traditionally derived from an ancestor, *Dōros* (son of Hellen, who gave his name to the Hellenes, i.e. the Greek people as a whole), but it is more likely that *Dōros* (whose name could be from *dōron* 'gift') was invented to account for a tribal name of obscure origin. In Greek mythology, Doris was a minor goddess of the sea, the consort of Nereus and the mother of his daughters, the Nereids or sea-nymphs, who numbered fifty (in some versions, more). The name was especially popular from about 1880 to about 1930, and was borne by the American film star Doris Day (b. 1924 as Doris Kappelhoff), among others.

VARIANT: **Dorris.**

Doron ♂ Apparently a variant of ▷**Dorian** (perhaps influenced by the names ▷**Damian** and ▷**Damon**), although it corresponds in form with the Greek word *dōron* 'gift'. As a Jewish name, it is a modern coinage borrowed directly from the Greek.

Dorothea ♀ Latinate form of a post-classical Greek name, from *dōron* 'gift' + *theos* 'god' (the same elements as in ▷**Theodora**, but in reverse order). The masculine form *Dorotheus* was borne by several early Christian saints, the feminine by only two minor ones, but only the girl's name has survived. In modern use in the English-speaking world it represents either a 19th-century Latinization of ▷**Dorothy** or a learned reborrowing.

Dorothy ♀ Usual English form of ▷**Dorothea**. The name was not used in the Middle Ages, but was taken up in the 15th century and became common thereafter. It was borne by the American film star Dorothy Lamour (1914–1996, born Dorothy Kaumeyer).

VARIANTS: **Dorothee, Dorothie.**

SHORT FORM: **Dot.**

PET FORMS: **Dottie, Dotty, Dodie, Dolly.**

Dory ♀ Pet form of ▷**Dora**, now seldom used in that function and even less commonly bestowed as an independent given name.

Dot ♀ Short form of ▷Dorothy.

Dottie ♀ Pet form of ▷Dorothy, with the hypocoristic suffix *-ie*. The form Dotty is also used, and its popularity does not seem to have been adversely affected by the fact that it coincides in form with the slang word meaning 'crazy'.

Douglas ♂ Transferred use of the surname borne by one of the most powerful families in Scotland, the earls of Douglas and of Angus, also notorious in earlier times as Border reivers. In the 17th and 18th centuries it was used as a girl's name in northern England. It is now exclusively a boys' name, used throughout the English-speaking world.

SHORT FORM: Doug.

PET FORM: Duggie.

Dov ♂ Jewish: meaning 'bear' in Hebrew. It is a translation into Hebrew of an animal name that became popular in European languages in the early Middle Ages. The bear is often associated with the name ▷Issachar, although the reason for this is not clear. There was a famous rabbi named Issachar Dov, but this may have been simply a fortuitous pairing of the two names. Subsequently bearers may have been named after him.

Dove ♀ Modern name, from the vocabulary word denoting the bird (Middle English *douve*, from Old Norse *dōfa*), noted as a symbol of peace and gentleness.

Doyle ♂ Mainly U.S.: transferred use of the Irish surname, Anglicized form of *Ó Dubhghaill* 'descendant of *Dubhghall*', from *dubh* 'black', 'dark' + *gall* 'stranger' (compare Dougal in Scottish appendix). This was used as a byname for Scandinavians, in particular to distinguish the darker-haired Danes from fair-haired Norwegians.

Drake ♂ Mainly U.S.: transferred use of the surname, which is derived in part from the Old English byname *Draca* 'snake, dragon' (which survived into the Middle Ages as a given name), and in part from Middle English *drake* 'male duck' (imported from Middle Low German) used as a nickname. Use as a given name is likely to have originated in honour of the English explorer Sir Francis Drake (?1540–96).

Dreda ♀ Shortened form of ▷Etheldreda, quite commonly used as an independent given name in the 19th century, when the longer form was also in fashion. It has survived slightly better than the four-syllable original, but is nevertheless now rare.

Drew ♂, ♀ Scottish short form of ▷Andrew, often used as an independent given name in Scotland, and in recent years increasingly popular elsewhere in the English-speaking world, also as a girl's name, borne for example by the American actress Drew Barrymore (b. 1975).

Drogo ♂ Of Norman origin but uncertain meaning and derivation. Norman given names are most often of Continental Germanic derivation, and this one is possibly ultimately from Old Saxon *drog* 'ghost, phantom', or perhaps from Old High German *tragen* 'to carry'. However, most plausible is the suggestion that it was brought into Germanic from Slavic as a short form of a name formed with *dorogo* 'dear'.

Drusilla ♀ From a Late Latin name, a feminine diminutive of the old Roman family name *Dr(a)usus*, which was first taken by a certain Livius, who had killed in single combat a Gaul of this name and, according to a custom of the time, took his victim's name as a cognomen. Of the several women in the Roman imperial family who were called Livia Drusilla, the most notorious was Caligula's sister and mistress. The name is borne in the Bible by a Jewish woman, wife of the Roman citizen Felix, who was converted to

Christianity by St Paul (Acts 24:24). In England it was taken up as a given name in the 17th century as a result of the biblical mention and has remained in occasional use ever since.

Duane ♂ Anglicized form of the Irish name Dubhán (see Irish appendix) or of the surname (Ó Dubháin) derived from it. Its popularity in the English-speaking world in the mid-1950s was influenced by the U.S. guitarist Duane Eddy (b. 1938).

VARIANTS: **Dwane, Dwayne, Dwain.**

Dudley ♂ Transferred use of the surname of a noble family, who came originally from Dudley in the West Midlands, named in Old English as the 'wood or clearing of Dudda'. Their most famous member was Robert Dudley, Earl of Leicester (?1532–88), who came closer than any other man to marrying Queen Elizabeth I. This given name is much less common in North America than in England. One of its best-known recent bearers was the comedian and actor Dudley Moore (1935–2002).

SHORT FORM: **Dud.**

Duggie ♂ Pet form of ▷Douglas.

Duke ♂ In modern use this normally represents a coinage parallel to ▷Earl and ▷King, but it has been used as a short form of ▷Marmaduke from at least the early 1600s.

Dulcie ♀ Learned re-creation in the 19th century of the medieval name Dowse, Late Latin Dulcia, a derivative of dulcis 'sweet'. It is borne by the film and stage actress Dulcie Gray (b. 1919).

Duncan ♂ Anglicized form of the Gaelic name Donnchadh (see Scottish appendix), also used among people without Scottish connections. This was the name of a 7th-century Scottish saint (abbot of Iona) and two medieval kings of Scotland. The final -n in the Anglicized form seems to be the result of confusion with the Gaelic word ceann 'head' in the Latinized form Duncanus. Compare Irish **Donagh.**

Dunstan ♂ From an Old English personal name derived from dun 'dark' + stān 'stone', borne most notably by a 10th-century saint who was archbishop of Canterbury. The name is now used mainly by Roman Catholics.

Dustin ♂ Transferred use of the surname, which is of uncertain origin, probably a Norman form of the Old Norse personal name Þórsteinn, composed of elements meaning 'Thor's stone'. It is now used fairly regularly as a given name, largely as a result of the fame of the film actor Dustin Hoffman (b. 1937), who is said to have been named in honour of the less well-known silent film actor Dustin Farman (1870–1929).

Dusty ♂, ♀ Apparently a pet form, or in some cases a feminine form, of ▷Dustin. As a girl's name it was made familiar in the 1960s by the singer Dusty Springfield (1939–99, born Mary O'Brien).

Dvoire ♀ Jewish: Yiddish form of ▷Deborah (Hebrew ▷Devorah).

Dwayne ♂ Variant spelling of ▷Duane.

Dwight ♂ Transferred use of the surname, which probably comes from the medieval English female name Diot, a pet form of Dionysia (see ▷Dennis). It is found mainly in North America, where its increase in popularity after the Second World War was a result of the fame of the American general and president Dwight D. Eisenhower (1890–1969). He was named in honour of the New England philosopher Timothy Dwight (1752–1817) and his brother Theodore Dwight (1764–1846).

Dwyer ♂ Transferred use of the Irish surname, Anglicized form of Ó Duibhuidhir 'descendant of Duibhuidhir', a personal name composed of dubh 'dark, black' + odhar 'sallow, tawny' (or possibly eidhir 'sense, wisdom').

Dyan ♀ Mainly U.S.: modern variant spelling of ▷Diane.

Dylan ♂ Welsh: of uncertain origin, probably connected with a Celtic word meaning 'sea'. In the *Mabinogi* it is the name of the miraculously born son of Arianrhod, who became a minor divinity of the sea. Since the late 20th century the name has become popular outside Wales as a result of the fame of the Welsh poet Dylan Thomas (1914–53) and the American singer Bob Dylan (b. 1941), who changed his surname from Zimmerman as a tribute to the poet.

Dylanne ♀ Feminine form of ▷Dylan, a modern coinage based on the pattern of French names.

Dylis ♀ Modern respelling of ▷Dilys.

Dymphna ♀ This is the name of a medieval Flemish saint about whom little is known beyond the fact that she is regarded as the protector of lunatics and epileptics. According to legend, she was an Irish girl who had been abused by her father and killed by him when she opposed his wishes. Her relics are preserved at Gheel, near Antwerp in Belgium, where an important mental hospital of medieval foundation still bears her name. Her name has been identified, rightly or wrongly, with Irish Damhnait.

VARIANT: Dympna.

Ee

Eamon ♂ Pronounced 'ay-mon'; Anglicized spelling of Irish *Éamon(n)* or *Éaman(n)*, Irish forms of ▷Edmund. Although it still has an essentially Irish flavour, the name was popularized throughout Britain in the 1950s due to the fame of the broadcaster Eamon Andrews (1922–87).

VARIANT: **Eamonn.**

Earl ♂ North American: from the title originally adopted as a nickname parallel to ▷Duke, ▷King, etc. The title was used in England in Norman times as an equivalent of the French *comte* 'count'; it is from Old English *eorl* 'warrior, nobleman, prince'. In some cases the given name may have been taken from the surname *Earl*, which was originally either a nickname or a term denoting someone who worked in the household of an earl.

VARIANTS: **Earle, Erle.**

Earla ♀ Mainly U.S.: coined as a feminine form of ▷Earl.

VARIANT: **Erla.**

ELABORATED FORMS: **Earlina, E(a)rline, Earlene, Earleen.**

Earnest ♂ Mainly North American variant spelling of ▷Ernest.

Earnestine ♀ Mainly U.S.: variant spelling of ▷Ernestine.

Ebba ♀ 19th-century revival of an Old English female name, a contracted form of *Eadburga*, composed of *ēad* 'prosperity' + *burg* 'fortress'. St Ebba the Elder (d. 638) was the sister of Oswald, King of Northumbria, who founded a Benedictine abbey at Coldingham in Berwickshire; St Ebba the Younger (d. *c.*870) was abbess there and was murdered by marauding Danes.

Ebenezer ♂ Originally a biblical place name (meaning 'stone of help' in Hebrew). This was the site of the battle where the Israelites were defeated by the Philistines (1 Samuel 4:1). After they took their revenge, Samuel set up a memorial stone bearing this name (1 Samuel 7:12). It was taken up as a given name by the Puritans in the 17th century, possibly after being misread in the Bible as a personal name, or else because of its favourable etymological connotations. It now has unfavourable connotations because of the miserly character of Ebenezer Scrooge in Charles Dickens's *A Christmas Carol* (1843), but nevertheless is still occasionally used.

Ebony ♀ From the name of the deeply black wood (Late Latin *ebenius*, from Greek *ebenos*, ultimately of Egyptian origin). From the 1970s the name was adopted by African Americans as a symbol of pride in their colour and has enjoyed considerable popularity.

Echo ♀ In modern use, probably directly from the vocabulary word (Greek *ēkhō*, which reached English via Latin). In classical mythology, this was the name of a nymph who pined away with love for Narcissus until nothing remained except her disembodied voice. Although the Greek word purports to be derived from the name of the nymph, in fact the word is of Indo-European origin, and so the truth seems to be that the nymph was invented to explain the word.

Ed ♂ Short form of the various boys' names with the first syllable *Ed-*, especially ▷Edward.

Eddie ♂ Pet form of ▷Edward.

Eden ♀, ♂ This name is found as a variant or pet form of ▷Edith in Yorkshire from the 15th century onwards. It is recorded as a baptismal name in the 16th century. In present-day use it probably refers to the biblical 'Garden of Eden', so named from Hebrew *'eden* 'place of pleasure'. As a boy's name it may also represent a variant of ▷Aidan or a transferred use of a surname, itself derived in the Middle Ages from a given name *Edun* or *Edon*. This is of Old English origin, from *ēad* 'prosperity, riches' + *hūn* 'bear cub'.

Edgar ♂ From an Old English personal name derived from *ēad* 'prosperity, riches' + *gār* 'spear'. This was the name of an English king and saint, Edgar the Peaceful (d. 975), and of Edgar Atheling (?1060–?1125), the young prince who was chosen by the English to succeed Harold as king in 1066, but who was supplanted by the Normans. Although used only infrequently in Britain, it is still fairly popular in the United States.

Edie ♀ Pet form of ▷Edith.

Edith ♀ From an Old English female personal name derived from *ēad* 'prosperity, riches' + *gȳð* 'strife'. This was borne by a daughter (961–984) of Edgar the Peaceful. (She was named in accordance with the common Old English practice of repeating name elements within a family.) She spent her short life in a convent, and is regarded as a saint.

VARIANTS: **Edyth(e)**.

PET FORM: **Edie**.

Edmond ♂ French form of ▷Edmund, now in quite frequent use in the English-speaking world.

Edmund ♂ From an Old English personal name derived from *ēad* 'prosperity, riches' + *mund* 'protector'. It was borne by several early royal and saintly figures, including a 9th-century king of East Anglia killed by invading Danes, allegedly for his adherence to Christianity. In the 16th and 17th centuries, there was a good deal of interchange between *Edmund* and *Edward*.

Edna ♀ In Ireland this has been used as an Anglicized form of Eithne (see Irish appendix). The name occurs in the apocryphal Book of Tobit, where it is the name of the mother of Sarah and stepmother of Tobias. This is said to be from Hebrew *'ednah* 'pleasure, delight', and if so it is connected with the name of the Garden of ▷Eden. The earliest known uses of the given name in England are in the 16th century, when it was probably imported from Ireland, although the spelling *Ednah* supports the idea that it was taken from the Bible.

Edom ♂ Biblical name (meaning 'red' in Hebrew), which was the byname of Esau. It was given to him because he was born covered with red hair (Genesis 25:25) or because he sold his birthright for a bowl of red lentil soup. This was frequently used as a given name in medieval Scotland, where it was taken to represent a variant of ▷Adam. It is occasionally bestowed in modern times by parents with Scottish connections.

Edric ♂ From an Old English personal name composed of *ēad* 'prosperity, riches' + *rīc* 'power, rule'. It fell out of regular use after the Norman Conquest but has undergone a modest revival in recent years.

Edsel ♂ In Germanic mythology this name is a variant of *Etzel*, apparently derived from *adal* 'noble', or else from the nickname *Atta* 'father'. In modern times its best-known bearer was Edsel Ford, son of Henry Ford, founder of the Ford Motor Corporation. The family was partly of Dutch or Flemish descent, but the reason for the choice of given name is not known.

Edward ♂ From an Old English personal name derived from *ēad* 'prosperity, riches' + *weard* 'guard'. This has been one of the most successful of all Old English names, in frequent use from before the Conquest to the present day, and even being exported into other European languages. It was the name of three Anglo-Saxon kings and has been borne by eight kings of England since the Norman Conquest. It is also the name of the youngest son of Queen Elizabeth II. The most influential early bearer was King Edward the Confessor (?1002–66; ruled 1042–66). In a troubled period of English history, he contrived to rule fairly and (for a time at any rate) firmly. But in the latter part of his reign he paid more attention to his religion than to his kingdom. He died childless, and his death sparked off conflicting claims to his throne, which were resolved by the victory of William the Conqueror at the Battle of Hastings. His memory was honoured by Normans and English alike, for his fairness and his piety. Edward's mother was Norman; he had spent part of his youth in Normandy; and William claimed to have been nominated by Edward as his successor. Edward was canonized in the 12th century, and came to be venerated throughout Europe as a model of a Christian king.

DERIVATIVES: Scottish Gaelic: **Eideard**; **Eudard** (a dialectal variant). German, Dutch: **Eduard** (influenced by the French form). Scandinavian: **Edvard**. French: **Édouard**. Spanish: **Eduardo**. Portuguese: **Duarte**. Italian: **Edoardo**. Russian: **Edvard**. Czech: **Eduard**, **Edvard**. Finnish: **Eetu**.

SHORT FORMS: **Ed**, **Ned**, **Ted**.

PET FORMS: **Eddie**, **Neddy**, **Teddy**.

Edwin ♂ From an Old English personal name derived from *ēad* 'prosperity, riches' + *wine* 'friend'. It was borne by a 7th-century king of Northumbria, who was converted to Christianity by St Paulinus and was killed in battle against pagan forces, a combination of circumstances which led to his being venerated as a martyr. The name occurs occasionally from the mid 16th century, but in modern use it is largely the result of a 19th-century revival.

VARIANT: **Edwyn**.

Edwina ♀ 19th-century coinage, representing a Latinate feminine form of ▷Edwin or, in at least one case, of ▷Edward. Edwina Ashley (1901–60), a descendant of Lord Shaftesbury who became the wife of Earl Mountbatten, was so named in honour of Edward VII; the king had originally wished her to be called *Edwardina*.

Edwyn ♂ Variant spelling of ▷Edwin.

Edyth ♀ Variant spelling of ▷Edith.

Effemy ♀ Older vernacular form of ▷Euphemia.

Effie ♀, ♂ As a girl's name it is a pet form of ▷Euphemia or ▷Hephzibah (now rarely used in their full forms, but popular in the 19th century) and is occasionally bestowed independently or as an Anglicized form of Gaelic Oighrig (see Scottish appendix). As a boy's name it is a pet form of ▷Ephraim.

Egbert ♂ From an Old English personal name derived from *ecg* 'edge (of a sword)' + *beorht* 'bright, famous'. This was borne by two English saints of the 8th century and by a 9th-century king of Wessex. It survived for a while after the Conquest, but fell out of use by the 14th century. It was briefly revived in the 19th century, but is now seldom used.

Eglantine ♀ Flower name, used as a nickname by Chaucer, and occasionally as a given name in the 18th and 19th centuries, but not at present in use. The word is from an alternative name for the sweetbriar, derived in the 14th century from Old French *aiglent*, ultimately a derivative of Latin *acus* 'needle', referring to the prickly stem of the plant.

Ehud ♂ Jewish: probably meaning 'pleasant, sympathetic' in Hebrew; it is borne by a left-handed Benjaminite, who saved the Israelites by stabbing the Moabite king Eglon (Judges 3: 15–26).

Eileen ♀ Anglicized form of Eibhlín (see Irish appendix). This name became very popular in many parts of the English-speaking world in the early part of the 20th century.
VARIANT: Aileen (esp. Scottish).

Eireen ♀ Of recent origin, a respelling of ▷Irene under the influence of ▷Eileen.
VARIANT: Eirene.

Elaine ♀ Originally an Old French form of ▷Helen, but now generally regarded as an independent name. The Greek and Latin forms of the name had a long vowel in the second syllable, which produced this form (as opposed to ▷Ellen) in Old French. In Arthurian legend, Elaine is the name of one of the women who fell in love with Lancelot. The name occurs in this form in the 15th-century English *Morte d'Arthur* of Thomas Malory. In the 19th century it was popularized in one of Tennyson's *Idylls of the King* (1859). Most of the characters in Arthurian legend have names that are Celtic in origin, although subjected to heavy French influence, and it has therefore been suggested that *Elaine* may actually be derived from a Welsh word meaning 'hind' or 'fawn'.
VARIANTS: Elain, Elayne.

Eldon ♂ Transferred use of the surname, in origin a local name from a place in Co. Durham, so called from the Old English male personal name *Ella* + Old English *dūn* 'hill'.

Eleanor ♀ From an Old French respelling of the Old Provençal name *Alienor*. This has sometimes been taken as a derivative of ▷Helen, but it is more probably of Germanic derivation (the first element being *ali* 'other, foreign';

the second is obscure). The name was introduced to England by Eleanor of Aquitaine (1122–1204), who came from Aquitaine in south-west France to be the wife of King Henry II. It was also borne by Eleanor of Provence, the wife of Henry III, and Eleanor of Castile, wife of Edward I.
VARIANTS: Ellenor, Elinor. Elenor.
SHORT FORMS: ▷Nell, Ellen.
PET FORMS: ▷Nellie, Nelly.

Eleanora ♀ Latinate form of ▷Eleanor.

Eleazar ♂ Variant spelling of ▷Eliezer.

Elen ♀ Welsh form of ▷Helen, now also used outside Wales. It is identical with the Welsh vocabulary word *elen* 'nymph', but this is unlikely to be the origin. It is found in Welsh texts from an early period as an equivalent of *Helen*, for example as the name of the mother of Constantine, finder of the True Cross.
VARIANT: Elin.

Elena ♀ Italian and Spanish form of ▷Helen, now used quite frequently in the English-speaking world.

Eleonora ♀ Italian form of ▷Eleanor, now sometimes also used in the English-speaking world.

Elfleda ♀ Latinized form of the Old English female personal name Æðelflæd, composed of the elements *æðel* 'noble' + *flæd* 'beauty'. It was revived briefly in the 19th century.

Elfreda ♀ 19th-century revival of a Latinized form of the Old English female personal name Ælfþryð, from *ælf* 'elf, supernatural being' + *þryð* 'strength'. This form may also have absorbed the Old English name Æðelþryð, which was originally distinct (see ▷Audrey).
SHORT FORM: ▷Freda.

Eli ♂ Biblical name, from a Hebrew word meaning 'height'. This was borne by the priest and judge who brought up the future prophet Samuel (1 Samuel

4). It was especially popular among Puritans in the 17th century and has enjoyed a modest revival in recent years. As a Jewish name, it is also a short form of any of numerous names formed with *el* 'God', such as ▷Eliezer, ▷Elijah, and ▷Elisha.

Elias ♂ Biblical name, from the Greek form (used in the New Testament) of the name of the prophet ▷Elijah. It is one of a number of Old Testament names which have come back into favour since the latter part of the 20th century. See also ▷Ellis.

Eliezer ♂ Meaning 'God helps' in Hebrew; it is borne in the Bible by one of the sons of Aaron (Exodus 6:23). In the Authorized Version the name is rendered as Eleazar.

Elijah ♂ Biblical name (meaning 'Yahweh is God' in Hebrew), borne by an Israelite prophet whose exploits are recounted in the First and Second Book of Kings. Elijah's victory over the prophets of Baal on Mount Carmel played an important part in maintaining the Jewish religion, recognizing just one God. This story, and other stories in which he figures, including his conflicts with Ahab's queen, Jezebel, and his prophecies of doom, are among the most vivid in the Bible. For some reason it has not been much used as a given name by Christians, although it is found among the early Puritan settlers in New England and in the U.K. in the 18th century. In the 1960s and 70s it gained considerable popularity among Black Muslims.

Elin ♀ Variant spelling of ▷Elen.

Elinor ♀ Variant spelling of ▷Eleanor.

Eliot ♂ Variant spelling of ▷Elliot. VARIANT: Eliott.

Elisabeth ♀ The spelling of ▷Elizabeth used in the Authorized Version of the New Testament, and in most modern European languages. This was the name of the mother of John the Baptist (Luke 1:60). Etymologically, the name means 'God is my oath', and is therefore identical with *Elisheba*, the name of the wife of Aaron according to the genealogy at Exodus 6:23. The final element seems to have been altered by association with Hebrew *shabbāth* 'Sabbath'.

Élise ♀ French: short form of ▷Elisabeth. The name was introduced into the English-speaking world (where it is often written without the accent) in the late 19th century and has become fairly popularity in recent years.

Elisha ♀, ♂ Traditionally a male Biblical name derived from Hebrew *el* 'God' + *sha* 'to help or save'. It is borne in the Bible by a prophet, the disciple and successor of Elijah, whose story is told in the Second Book of Kings. It has long been popular among Christian fundamentalists as a boy's name, but is now increasingly frequent as a girl's name, perhaps influenced by ▷Alicia. VARIANT: Eleesha ♀.

Elita ♀ Modern coinage, apparently derived from the vocabulary word *elite*, denoting a select group of people, with the addition of the Latinate suffix -*a*. The word came into English from French in the 18th century; it derives from the past participle of *élire* 'to choose' (Latin *eligere*). Use as a given name seems to reflect a desire on the part of the parents that their daughter should achieve success in life or be a member of an élite.

Eliyahu ♂ Jewish: meaning 'Jehovah is God' in Hebrew. It is familiar in the English-speaking world in the form ▷Elijah.

Eliza ♀ Short form of ▷Elizabeth, first used in the 16th century, and popular in the 18th and 19th centuries as an independent given name. It was used by George Bernard Shaw for the main female character, Eliza Dolittle, in his play *Pygmalion* (1913), which was the basis for the musical and film *My Fair Lady*.

Elizabeth ♀ The usual spelling of ▷Elisabeth in English. It is recorded in the medieval period, but was made popular by being borne by Queen Elizabeth I of England (1533–1603). In the 20th century it again became extremely fashionable, partly because it was the name of Elizabeth Bowes-Lyon (1900–2002), who in 1936 became Queen Elizabeth as the wife of King George VI, and after his death in 1952 achieved great public affection as Queen Mother for nearly half a century. Even more influentially, it is the name of her daughter Queen Elizabeth II (b. 1926).

VARIANT: **Elisabeth**. See also ▷Elspeth and ▷Isabel.

SHORT FORMS: **Eliza, Elsa, Liza, Lisa, Liz; Beth, Bet, Bess; Lisbet(h), Lizbet(h), Lysbet(h)**.

PET FORMS: **Elsie, Bessie, Bessy, Betty, Betsy, Tetty, Libby, Lizzie, Lizzy, Buffy**.

COGNATES: Irish: **Eilís**. Scottish Gaelic: **Ealasaid**. German, Dutch: **Elisabeth**. Scandinavian: **Elisabet**. French: **Elisabeth**. Spanish: **Elisabet**. Portuguese: **Elisabete**. Italian: **Elisabetta**. Greek: **Elisavet**. Russian: **Yelizaveta**. Polish: **Elzbieta**. Czech: **Alžběta**. Slovenian: **Elizabeta**. Hungarian: **Erzsébet**.

Elkan ♂ Mainly Jewish: shortened form of the Hebrew name **Elkanah** 'possessed by God', borne in the Bible by several people, including the father of the prophet Samuel (1 Samuel 1:1).

Elke ♀ Jewish: Yiddish name, apparently adopted as a feminine form of ▷Elkan. The variant **Elkie** is well known as the name of the singer Elkie Brooks (b. 1946 as Elaine Bookbinder).

Ella ♀ Of Germanic origin, introduced to Britain by the Normans. It was originally a short form of any of various compound names containing *ali* 'other,

foreign' (compare ▷Eleanor). It is now often taken to be a variant or pet form of ▷Ellen. It was famously borne by the American jazz singer Ella Fitzgerald (1917–1996), and has become increasingly popular in Britain since the 1990s.

Elle ♀ Modern coinage of uncertain derivation. It may have arisen as an independent given name from a short form of a name beginning with the letter *L*- (compare ▷Dee, ▷Kay), coincidentally corresponding with French *elle* 'she'.

Ellen ♀ Originally a variant of ▷Helen, although now no longer associated with that name. Initial *H*- tended to be added and dropped rather capriciously, leading to many doublets (compare for example ▷Esther and ▷Hester). It is also sometimes used as a short form of ▷Eleanor, to which, however, it is unrelated.

SHORT FORM: ▷**Nell**.

PET FORMS: ▷**Nellie, Nelly**.

Ellena ♀ Either a variant of ▷Helena or possibly a fanciful spelling of ▷Eleanor, influenced by ▷Ellen.

Ellenor ♀ Variant spelling of ▷Eleanor, the result of blending with ▷Ellen.

Ellie ♀ Pet form of any of the numerous girls' names beginning with the syllable *El*-, in particular ▷Eleanor. At the beginning of the 21st century it enjoyed a surge in popularity as an independent given name, often also used in compounds such as *Ellie-Ann*, *Ellie-Mae*, and *Ellie-Louise*.

VARIANT: **Elly**.

Elliot ♂ Transferred use of the surname, itself derived from a medieval (Norman French) masculine given name. This was a diminutive of *Elie*, the Old French version of ▷Elias. It is borne by the American actor Elliott Gould (b. 1938 as Elliot Goldstein), and has been fairly popular since the latter half of the 20th century.

VARIANTS: **Elliott, Eliot(t)**.

Ellis ♂, ♀ From a medieval vernacular form of ▷Elias, in use as a given name in northern England from the 14th century onwards. In modern use it is often a transferred use of the surname derived from this name. In Wales it is now often taken as an Anglicized form of the Old Welsh name Elisud (see Welsh appendix). It has enjoyed considerable popularity in recent times, having also been taken up as a girl's name.

Elma ♀ U.S.: of uncertain derivation. It is thought in part to be a combination of elements from ▷Elizabeth and ▷Mary; in part a feminine equivalent of ▷Elmer.

Elmer ♂ Transferred use of the surname, itself derived from an Old English personal name derived from _æðel_ 'noble' + _mær_ 'famous'. This has been used as a given name in the United States since the 19th century, in honour of the brothers Ebenezer and Jonathan Elmer, leading activists in the American Revolution. It is also found in Canada.

Élodie ♀ French: derived from a Visigothic female personal name composed of _ali_ 'other, foreign' + _od_ 'riches, prosperity'. The name is now sometimes used in the English-speaking world (usually without the accent).

Éloise ♀ French name of uncertain but probably Germanic origin. Éloise or Héloïse was the name of the learned and beautiful wife (d. _c._1164) of the French philosopher and theologian Peter Abelard (1079–1142), whom she married secretly. A misunderstanding with her uncle and guardian, the powerful and violent Canon Fulbert of Notre Dame, led to Abelard being set upon, beaten up, and castrated. He became a monk and Héloïse spent the rest of her days as abbess of a nunnery, but they continued to write to each other. The name was brought to England by the Normans and remained in periodic use thereafter until it suddenly came into favour at the end of the 20th century; it is usually written without the accent.

VARIANTS: French: **Héloïse**. English: **Elouise**.

Elroy ♂ Variant of ▷Leroy. The initial syllable seems to be the result of simple transposition of the first two letters; it may also have been influenced by the Spanish definite article _el_ and taken as meaning 'the king'.

Elsa ♀ Shortened form of ▷Elisabeth or ▷Elizabeth. The name was borne by the English-born film actress Elsa Lanchester (1902–86). Elsa Belton was a character in Angela Thirkell's once widely read _Barsetshire Chronicles_. In the 1960s the name was also associated with the lioness named Elsa featured in the book _Born Free_, by Joy Adamson, which was made into a film.

Elsbeth ♀ Modern variant of ▷Elspeth.

Elsdon ♂ Mainly U.S.: transferred use of the surname, in origin a local name from a place in Northumberland. The place name is recorded in the 13th century in the forms _Eledene_, _Hellesden_, _Elisden_, and _Ellesden_; it is probably named as 'Elli's valley' (Old English _denu_).

Elsie ♀ Originally a Scottish simplified form of _Elspie_, a pet form of ▷Elspeth. This came to be used as an independent name in Scotland and beyond, and in the early 20th century proved more popular than _Elspeth_.

Elspeth ♀ Scottish contracted form of ▷Elizabeth, also found outside Scotland.

Elton ♂ Transferred use of the surname, in origin a local name from any of numerous places in England so called (mostly from the Old English masculine personal name _Ella_ + Old English _tūn_ 'enclosure, settlement'). In

England it is largely associated with the singer-songwriter Elton John; born Reginald Kenneth Dwight in 1947, he adopted the given name by which he is famous in honour of the saxophonist Elton Dean.

Elva ♀ Of uncertain origin and meaning; possibly a variant of ▷Alva.

Elvina ♀ Apparently a feminine form of ▷Alvin.

Elvira ♀ Spanish name of Germanic (Visigothic) origin (see Spanish appendix), very common in the Middle Ages. It was not used in the English-speaking world until the 19th century, when it was made familiar as the name of the long-suffering wife of Don Juan, both in Mozart's opera *Don Giovanni* (1789) and in Byron's satirical epic poem *Don Juan* (1819–24). In his comedy *Blithe Spirit* Noel Coward used it as the name of Charles Condomine's first wife, who returns to haunt him. It is also the name of the heroine of the Swedish film *Elvira Madigan* (1967), directed by Bo Widerberg, a romantic tragedy about a pair of lovers who would rather die than be separated.

Elvis ♂ Of obscure derivation, made famous by the American rock singer Elvis Presley (1935–77). It may be a transferred use of a surname, or it may have been made up, but it was certainly not chosen for the singer in anticipation of a career in show business, for his father's name was Vernon Elvis Presley. A shadowy Irish St Elvis, of the 6th century, is also known as *Elwyn*, *Elwin*, *Elian*, and *Allan*.

Elyse ♀ Altered spelling of ▷Élise.

Elysia ♀ Apparently a respelling of ▷Alicia, influenced by *Elysian* (meaning 'heavenly', from *Elysium*, in classical mythology the place to which dead heroes were conveyed by the gods).

Emanuel ♂ Variant spelling of ▷Emmanuel.

Emelia ♀ Variant of ▷Amelia.

Emeny ♀ Medieval name of uncertain origin. It appears in various forms such as *Emonie* and *Imanie* and seems to be of Germanic origin. It was Latinized as ▷Ismene.

Emerald ♀ Modern coinage from the name of the gemstone, representing a vernacular form of ▷Esmeralda.

Emerson ♂ Transferred use of the surname, derived in the Middle Ages from a patronymic meaning 'son of Emery'. It is sometimes bestowed in honour of the American poet Ralph Waldo Emerson (1858–1928), and is borne by various celebrities including Keith Emerson, keyboard player in the 1970s' pop group Emerson, Lake, and Palmer, and the Brazilian racing driver Emerson Fittipaldi (b. 1946).

Emery ♂ Transferred use of the surname, derived in the Middle Ages from a personal name introduced to England by the Normans. This was originally composed of the Germanic elements *amal* 'bravery, vigour' + *rīc* 'power', but soon assumed a variety of forms such as *Amauri* and *Emauri*.

Émile ♂ French: from the Latin name *Aemilius* (see ▷Emily). The name is now found in the English-speaking world, usually written without the accent.

Emilia ♀ Variant of ▷Amelia, first recorded in the medieval period.

Emily ♀ From a medieval form of the Latin name *Aemilia*, the feminine version of the old Roman family name *Aemilius* (probably from *aemulus* 'rival'). It was not common in the Middle Ages, but was revived in the 19th century and is extremely popular throughout the English-speaking world today. Its best-known 19th-century bearer was probably the novelist and poet Emily Brontë (1818–48).

VARIANT: **Emilie**.

Emma ♀ Old French name, of Germanic (Frankish) origin, originally a short form of compound names such as ▷Ermintrude containing the word *erm*(*en*), *irm*(*en*) 'entire'. It was adopted by the Normans and introduced by them to Britain, but its popularity in medieval England was greatly enhanced by the fact that it had been borne by the mother of Edward the Confessor, herself a Norman. In modern times, it was only in moderate use early in the 20th century but rose sharply in favour in the 1970s and has since remained perennially popular.

Emmaline ♀ Modern variant of ▷Emmeline, influenced by ▷Emma.

Emmanuel ♂ Biblical name (meaning 'God is with us' in Hebrew) used for the promised Messiah, as prophesied by Isaiah (7:14; referred to in Matthew 1:23). The Authorized Version of the Bible uses the Hebrew form *Immanuel* in the Old Testament, *Emmanuel* in the New.
VARIANT: **Emanuel**.

Emmarald ♀ Variant of ▷Emerald, influenced by the given name ▷Emma.

Emmeline ♀ Old French name of Germanic (Frankish) origin, introduced to Britain by the Normans. In origin it seems to have been a derivative of ▷Emma, but when it was revived in the 19th century there was some confusion with ▷Emily. It was born by the suffragette Emmeline Pankhurst (1858–1928), mother of Christabel and Sylvia.

Emmet ♂ Transferred use of the surname, itself derived from the medieval female given name *Emmet* or *Em*(*m*)*ot*, diminutive forms of ▷Emma. It may sometimes be used by parents with Irish connections, in honour of the rebel Robert Emmet (1778–1803), who led a disastrous attempt at rebellion against the English.
VARIANT: **Emmett**.

Emmie ♀ Pet form of ▷Emma, ▷Emily, and related names, now used increasingly as an independent given name.
VARIANT: **Emmy**.

Ena ♀ One of several Anglicized forms of the Gaelic name **Eithne** (see Irish appendix). In the case of Queen Victoria's granddaughter Princess Ena (Victoria Eugénie Julia Ena, 1887–1969) it had a different origin: it was a misreading by the minister who baptized her off a handwritten note of the originally intended name ▷Eva. In England, the name is remembered principally as that of the fearsome Ena Sharples in the television soap opera *Coronation Street*. See also ▷Ina.

Enid ♀ Celtic name of uncertain derivation, borne by a virtuous character in the Arthurian romances, the long-suffering wife of Geraint. The name was revived in the second half of the 19th century, following Tennyson's *Idylls of the King* (1859), which contains the story of Geraint and Enid, in which Enid recovers her husband's trust by patience and loyalty after he has suspected her, wrongly, of infidelity.

Ennis ♀, ♂ Probably a transferred use of the surname *Innis*, which is from some place named with Gaelic *inis* 'island'.
VARIANT: **Enis**.

Enoch ♂ Biblical name (possibly meaning 'experienced' in Hebrew), borne by the son of Cain (Genesis 4:16–22) and father of Methuselah (Genesis 5:18–24). The latter is said to have lived for 365 years. The apocryphal 'Books of Enoch' are attributed to him. In modern times the name was borne by the controversial Conservative politician Enoch Powell (1912–98).

Enos ♂ Biblical name (meaning 'mankind' in Hebrew), borne by a son of Seth and grandson of Adam (Genesis 4:26), who allegedly lived for 905 years.

Ephraim ♂ Biblical name, pronounced 'ee-frame'; borne by one of the sons of Joseph and hence one of the tribes of Israel. The name probably means 'fruitful' in Hebrew; it is so explained in the Bible (Genesis 41:52 'and the name of the second called he Ephraim: For God hath caused me to be fruitful in the land of my affliction'). This was used by the Puritans in the 16th century, but was used more widely in the 18th and 19th centuries. It is still a common Jewish given name.

Eppie ♀ Pet form of ▷Euphemia or ▷Hephzibah. It was fairly common in Victorian times but has since fallen out of favour. It is the name of the orphan child adopted by the eponymous hero of George Eliot's novel *Silas Marner*; in this case it represents a pet form of ▷Hephzibah.

Erasmus ♂ Latinized form of Greek *Erasmos*, a derivative of *erān* 'to love'. St Erasmus (d. 303) was a bishop of Formiae in Campania, martyred under Diocletian; he is numbered among the Fourteen Holy Helpers and is a patron of sailors. This is a rare given name in the English-speaking world. It is occasionally bestowed in honour of the great Dutch humanist scholar and teacher Erasmus Rotterodamus (c. 1469–1536).

Eric ♂ Of Old Norse origin, from *ei* 'ever, always' (or *einn* 'one, alone') + *ríkr* 'ruler' (see Eirik in Scandanavian appendix). It was introduced into Britain by Scandinavian settlers before the Norman Conquest. As a modern given name, it was revived in the mid 19th century and has remained in use since.
VARIANTS: Eri(c)k.
COGNATES: German: Erich. French: Éric.

Erica ♀ Latinate feminine form of ▷Eric, coined towards the end of the 18th century. It has also been reinforced by the fact that *erica* is the Latin word for 'heather'.
VARIANTS: Eri(c)ka.

Erin ♀, ♂ Anglicized form of Irish Éirinn (see Irish appendix). Erin has

been used as a poetic name for Ireland for centuries, and in recent years this has become a popular given name in the English-speaking world, even among people with no Irish connections.

Erla ♀ Variant spelling of ▷Earla.

Erle ♂ Variant spelling of ▷Earl.

Erline ♀ Apparently a feminine derivative of ▷Erle.

Ermine ♀ In origin perhaps a variant of German **Hermine** (see German appendix), but strongly influenced in popularity by association with the name of the fur (Old French *ermine*, Medieval Latin *armenius* (*mus*) 'Armenian mouse'), which in Britain is traditionally worn in ceremonies by members of the peerage.

Ermintrude ♀ Of Germanic origin, adopted from Old French by the Normans and introduced by them to Britain. It is derived from *erm(en)*, *irm(en)* 'entire' + *traut* 'beloved'. It did not survive long into the Middle Ages, but was occasionally revived in the 18th and 19th centuries. It is now completely out of fashion.

Ern ♂ Informal short form of ▷Ernest.

Erna ♀ Simplified version of *Ernesta*, created as a feminine form of ▷Ernest.

Ernest ♂ Of Germanic origin, derived from the Old High German vocabulary word *eornost* 'serious business, battle to the death'. The name was introduced into England in the 18th century by followers of the Elector of Hanover, who became George I of England. A variant spelling, **Earnest**, has arisen by association with the modern English adjective *earnest*.
SHORT FORM: Ern.
PET FORM: Ernie.

Ernestine ♀ Elaborated feminine form of ▷Ernest, created in the 19th century and now in only occasional use.
VARIANT: Ernestina.

Errol ♂ Transferred use of the Scottish surname, which derives from a place name. It was made famous by the film actor Errol Flynn (1909–59), noted for his 'swashbuckling' roles. He was born in Australia, but spent most of his career in Hollywood. *Errol* is now popular as an African-American and West Indian name, influenced by such figures as the jazz pianist Erroll Garner (1921–77).

VARIANTS: **Erol, Erroll; Eryl.**

Erskine ♂ Transferred use of the Scottish surname, which derives from the name of a place near Glasgow. The surname was also taken to Ireland by Scottish settlers, and was first brought to public attention as a given name by the half-Irish writer and political activist Erskine Childers (1870–1922).

Eryl ♂ Modern spelling of ▷Errol.

Esau ♂ Biblical name, borne by the elder twin brother of Jacob, to whom he sold his birthright for a bowl of soup ('a mess of potage' in the Authorized Version) when he came home tired and hungry from a hunt. The name seems to mean 'hairy' in Hebrew (Genesis 25:25 'and the first came out red, all over like an hairy garment; and they called his name Esau'). It is now rarely used as a given name in the English-speaking world.

Esdras ♂ Greek form of the Hebrew name ▷Ezra, used in the Douay Bible as the title of the Books of Ezra (1 Esdras) and Nehemiah (2 Esdras) and of two further books (3 and 4 Esdras) not included in the Protestant canon.

Esmé ♀, ♂ French male name, from Old French *esme* 'esteemed, loved' (from Latin *aestimare* 'to value, esteem'), which was introduced to Scotland in the 16th century. Since the 18th century it has also been in use in the English-speaking world as a female name and it is now much more popular as a name for girls than boys. It occurs in various forms, often written without the accent.

VARIANTS: **Esmée, Esmie** ♀.

Esmeralda ♀ From the Spanish vocabulary word *esmeralda* 'emerald'. Its occasional modern use as a given name dates from Victor Hugo's *Notre Dame de Paris* (1831), in which it is the nickname of the gypsy girl loved by the hunchback Quasimodo; she was given the name because she wore an amulet containing an artificial emerald.

VARIANT: **Esmerelda.**

Esmond ♂ From an Old English personal name derived from *ēast* 'grace, beauty' + *mund* 'protection'. A Norman French form is also found, reflecting a Continental Germanic original. However, it was not used in Britain as a given name between the 14th century and the late 19th century, when it was revived; it has since remained in very occasional use.

Esta ♀ Latinate respelling of ▷Esther.

Estelle ♀ Old French name meaning 'star' (Latin ▷Stella), comparatively rarely used during the Middle Ages. It was revived in the 19th century, together with the Latinate form **Estella**, which was used by Dickens for the cold but beautiful ward of Miss Havisham in *Great Expectations* (1861).

Esther ♀ Biblical name, borne by a Jewish captive who became the wife of the Persian king Ahasuerus. Her Hebrew name was *Hadassah* 'myrtle', and the form *Esther* is said to be a Persian translation of this, although others derive it from Persian *stara* 'star'. It may also be a Hebrew form of the name of the Persian goddess *Ishtar*. According to the book of the Bible that bears her name, Esther managed, by her perception and persuasion, to save large numbers of the Jews from the evil machinations of the royal counsellor Haman. See also ▷Hester.

Estrild ♀ From an Old English or Continental Germanic personal name composed of *Eastre* (the name of a goddess of spring, whose name lies behind modern English *Easter*) + *hild* 'battle'. According to legend, Estrildis was the name of a German princess who was captured and brought to Britain. She so enchanted King Locrine that he left his wife Gwendolen for her: in revenge, Gwendolen had both Estrildis and her daughter Sabrina thrown into the River Severn and drowned.

Ethan ♂ Biblical name (meaning 'firmness' or 'long-lived' in Hebrew) of an obscure figure, Ethan the Ezrahite, mentioned as a wise man whom Solomon surpassed in wisdom (1 Kings 4:31). The name was sparingly used even among the Puritans, but became famous in the United States since it was borne by Ethan Allen (1738–89), leader of the 'Green Mountain Boys', a group of Vermont patriots who fought in the American Revolution. Since the mid 1990s the name has enjoyed a great surge in popularity in Britain.

Ethel ♀ 19th-century revival of an Old English name, a short form of various female personal names containing *ethel* 'noble' as a first element, for example ▷Etheldreda. The name enjoyed great popularity for a period at the beginning of the 20th century but is at present out of fashion.

Etheldreda ♀ Latinized form of the Old English female personal name *Æðelþryð* (see ▷Audrey). It was taken up as a given name in the 19th-century, but is now very rare.

Etta ♀ Short form of the various names such as *Rosetta* and *Henrietta* ending in this element, originally an Italian feminine diminutive suffix.

Euan ♂ Anglicized form of Scottish Gaelic Eóghan, now also bestowed by parents without Scottish connections.

Eudocia ♀ Latinized form of the New Testament Greek names *Eudoxia* 'of good appearance' and *Eudokia* 'wellbeing, comfort'. The Byzantine

empress Eudocia (d. *c.*460) was the wife of the emperor Theodosius II. She was a devout Christian, of humble origin, and after the emperor's death in 450 she retired to Jerusalem and spent the last ten years of her life in quiet contemplation.

Eudora ♀ Ostensibly a Greek name, from *eu* 'well, good' + a derivative of *dōron* 'gift'. However, there is no saint of this name, and it is more probably a 19th-century learned coinage, made up of elements which are common in other given names.

Eugene ♂ From the Old French form of the Greek name *Eugenios* (from *eugenēs* 'well-born, noble'). This name was borne by various early saints, notably a 5th-century bishop of Carthage, a 7th-century bishop of Toledo, and four popes. It is sometimes used as an Anglicized form of Irish Eóghan and has also been used as an Anglicized form of the Irish name Aodh.
SHORT FORM: **Gene**.

Eugenia ♀ Feminine form of Greek *Eugenios* or Latin *Eugenius*; see ▷Eugene.

Eugénie ♀ French form of ▷Eugenia. The name was introduced to England as the name of the Empress Eugénie (Eugenia María de Montijo de Guzmán, 1826–1920), wife of the Emperor Napoleon III, and has since been occasionally used (sometimes without the accent) in the English-speaking world. In the British royal family it was borne by Princess Victoria Eugénie of Battenberg (1887–1969), a granddaughter of Queen Victoria, after whom Prince Andrew's younger daughter (b. 1990) was named.

Eulalia ♀ From a Late Greek personal name composed of *eu* 'well, good' + *lalein* 'to talk'. It was very common in the Middle Ages, when it was to a large extent confused with ▷Hilary, but is now rare.
MODERN VARIANT: **Eulalee**.
SHORT FORM: **Eula**.

Eunice ♀ From a Late Greek name, derived from *eu* 'well, good' + *nīkē* 'victory'. This is mentioned in the New Testament as the name of the mother of Timothy, who introduced him to Christianity (2 Timothy 1:5). This reference led to the name being taken up by the Puritans in the 16th century.

Euphemia ♀ Latin form of a Late Greek name derived from *eu* 'well, good' + *phēnai* 'to speak'. This was the name of various early saints, notably a virgin martyr said to have been burned at the stake at Chalcedon in 307. It had a limited popularity in some regions in the 16th and 17th centuries and returned to favour in the Victorian period, especially in the pet form ▷Effie. It is little used at present.

PET FORMS: ▷Effie, ▷Eppie.

Eustace ♂ From the Old French form of the Late Greek names *Eustakhios* and *Eustathios*. These were evidently of separate origin, the former derived from *eu* 'well, good' + *stakhys* 'grapes', the latter from *eu* + *stēnai* 'to stand'. However, the tradition is very confused. The name was introduced in this form to Britain by the Normans, among whom it was popular as a result of the fame of St Eustace, a Norman nobleman who was said to have been converted to Christianity by the vision of a crucifix between the antlers of the stag he was hunting.

Eva ♀ Popular Latinate form of ▷Eve, used also as an Anglicization of the Irish name Aoife (see Irish appendix).

Evadne ♀ From a Greek personal name derived from *eu* 'well, good' + another element of uncertain meaning. The name was borne by a minor figure in classical legend, who threw herself on to the funeral pyre of her husband, and was therefore regarded as an example of wifely piety. The modern spelling and pronunciation are the result of transmission through Latin sources. The name has never been common. It is associated with the character of Dr Evadne Hinge of the 1970s and 80s comedy duo Hinge and Bracket.

Evan ♂ As a Welsh name this represents an Anglicized form of Iefan, a later development of Ieuan (see Welsh appendix). As a Scottish name it is a variant of ▷Euan. It is now used throughout the English-speaking world.

Evander ♂ Latin form of Greek *Euandros*, composed of *eu* 'well, good' + *anēr* 'man' (genitive *andros*). In classical legend, *Evander* is the name of an Arcadian hero who founded a city in Italy where Rome was later built.

Evangeline ♀ Fanciful name derived from Latin *evangelium* 'gospel' (Greek *euangelion*, from *eu* 'good' + *angelma* 'tidings') + the suffix *-ine* (in origin a French feminine diminutive). *Evangeline* is the title of a narrative poem (1848) by the American poet Henry Wadsworth Longfellow, in which the central character is called Evangeline Bellefontaine.

Eve ♀ English vernacular form of the name borne in the Bible by the first woman, created from one of Adam's ribs (Genesis 2:22). It derives, via Latin *Eva*, from Hebrew *Havva*, which is considered to be a variant of the vocabulary word *hayya* 'living' or 'animal'. Adam gave names to all the animals (Genesis 2:19–20) and then to his wife, who was 'the mother of all living' (Genesis 3:20).

PET FORM: Evie.

Evelina ♀ Latinate form of the girl's name ▷Evelyn, or a combination of ▷Eve with the suffix *-lina*.

Evelyn ♀, ♂ Modern use of this as both a boy's and a girl's name derives from a transferred use of an English surname, from the Norman female name Aveline, an elaborated form of ▷Ava. At present it is used more frequently as a girl's name, and is also found as a variant Anglicization of Irish

Éibhleann or Aibhilín (see Irish appendix; see also Evlin).

VARIANTS: **Evelyne, Eveline, Eveleen,** all ♀.

Everard ♂ From an Old English personal name derived from *eofor* 'boar' + *hard* 'hardy, brave, strong'. This was reinforced at the time of the Norman Conquest by a Continental Germanic form introduced to Britain by the Normans. The modern given name may be a transferred use of the surname, but it was in regular use in the Digby family of Rutland from the 15th to the 17th centuries, probably as a survival of the Norman name. It alternated in this family with ▷Kenelm.

Everett ♂ Transferred use of the surname, a variant of ▷Everard.

Everton ♂ Transferred use of the surname, originally a local name from any of various places in Bedfordshire, Merseyside, and Nottinghamshire, so named from Old English *eorfor* 'wild boar' + *tūn* 'settlement'. Sometimes the name may be bestowed in honour of Everton Football Club.

Evette ♀ Respelling of ▷Yvette, influenced by ▷Eve.

Evie ♀ Pet form of ▷Eve or ▷Eva, occasionally also of ▷Evelyn as a girl's name. It is now also used independently.

Evonne ♀ Respelling of ▷Yvonne, influenced by ▷Eve.

Evron ♂ Jewish: Yiddish form of ▷Ephraim.

Ewan ♂ The usual Anglicized form in Scotland and Northern Ireland of Gaelic Eóghan (see Irish appendix). It is also found in northern England from the 14th century onwards, and since the late 1990s has been one of the Gaelic names that enjoy wider currency.

VARIANT: **Ewen.**

Ewart ♂ Transferred use of the Scottish surname, probably first used as a given name in honour of the Victorian statesman William Ewart Gladstone (1809–98). The surname has several possible origins: it may represent a Norman form of ▷Edward, an occupational name for a ewe-herd, or a local name from a place in Northumberland.

Eydl ♀ Jewish (Yiddish): originally an affectionate nickname meaning 'noble' (Yiddish *eydl*; compare modern German *edel*).

Ezekiel ♂ Biblical name, pronounced 'iz-**ee**-kee-el': meaning 'God strengthens' in Hebrew. This was borne by one of the major prophets. The book of the Bible that bears his name is known for its vision of a field of dry bones, which Ezekiel prophesies will live again (chapter 37). His prophecies were addressed to the Jews in Babylonian exile, after Nebuchadnezzar had seized Jerusalem in 597 BC.

SHORT FORM: **Zeke.**

Ezra ♂ Biblical name (meaning 'help' in Hebrew), borne by an Old Testament prophet, author of the book of the Bible that bears his name. This was one of the Old Testament names taken up by the Puritans in the 17th century.

Ff

Fabia ♀ Latin feminine form of the old Roman family name *Fabius* (see ▷Fabian).

Fabian ♂ From the Late Latin name *Fabianus*, a derivative of the old Roman family name *Fabius*, said to be a derivative of *faba* 'bean'. It was borne by an early pope (236–250), who was martyred under the Emperor Decius. The name was introduced into Britain by the Normans. It occurs occasionally in the 16th and 17th centuries, but was never much used in the English-speaking world until it achieved a modest currency in the last decade of the 20th century.

Fabienne ♀ French: feminine form of Fabien, French form of ▷Fabian, now used occasionally in the English-speaking world.

Fabiola ♀ Late Latin feminine diminutive form of the old Roman family name *Fabius* (see ▷Fabian). St Fabiola (d. *c.*400) was a Roman widow who founded the first Western hospital, originally a hostel to accommodate the flood of pilgrims who flocked to Rome, in which she tended the sick as well as accommodating the healthy.

Fae ♀ Variant spelling of ▷Fay.

Fairfax ♂ Transferred use of the surname, recorded from the early 17th century. It was originally a nickname for someone with beautiful long hair (Old English *fæger* 'lovely' + *feax* 'hair, tresses'). The surname is that of a prominent English family: the 3rd Baron Fairfax was the leader of the Roundhead army during the Civil War, and the 6th Baron Fairfax was a notable early colonist in Virginia.

Faith ♀ From the abstract noun denoting the quality of believing and trusting in God. The name began to be used in the 16th century, was very popular among the Puritans of the 17th, and is presently enjoying a modest comeback.

Faivish ♂ Jewish (Yiddish): probably from Greek *Phoîbos*, an epithet of the sun god Apollo. It is said to have been adopted as a learned equivalent of Hebrew *Shimshon* (see ▷Samson). However, it is more likely derived directly from the Greek, as the Greeks often named captured slaves after gods. It was often coupled with the Aramaic name ▷Shraga, since it was important for Jewish men to be called by a Hebrew or Aramaic name in certain religious rites.

Falk ♂ Jewish: from Yiddish *falk* 'falcon' (compare modern German *Falke*). It is sometimes taken as a translation of the Hebrew given name *Yehoshua* (see ▷Joshua). The association of various animals with the main Hebrew personal names is traditional in Jewish culture, and is usually to be explained on the basis of some biblical reference. The connection in this case, however, is unclear; it has been suggested that Joshua circled the Land of Canaan like a bird of prey before swooping down on it triumphantly.

Fancy ♀ From the vocabulary word referring to the quality of imagination (in origin it is a contracted form of *fantasy*) or to an unusual idea (compare ▷Caprice).

Fanny ♀ Pet form of ▷Frances, very popular in the 18th and 19th centuries, but now much rarer.

Fatima ♀ Usually a Muslim name, bestowed in honour of Muhammad's daughter. However, it is occasionally borne by Roman Catholics in honour of 'Our Lady of Fatima', who in 1917 appeared to three shepherd children from the village of Fatima, near Leiria in western Portugal.

Fay ♀ Late 19th-century coinage, from the archaic word *fay* 'fairy'. It was to some extent influenced by the revival of interest in Arthurian legend, in which Morgan le Fay is King Arthur's half-sister, a mysterious sorceress who both attempts to destroy Arthur and tends his wounds in Avalon after his last battle. She is sometimes identified with the 'Lady of the Lake'. Between the wars the name came to prominence as that of the British actress Fay Compton (1894–1979); more recently it has been associated with the writer Fay Weldon (b. 1931).
VARIANTS: Faye (now, the most frequent spelling, associated particularly with the American actress Faye Dunaway, b. 1941), Fae.

Fayge ♀ Jewish (Yiddish): variant of ▷Feige.

Fayvel ♂ Jewish (Yiddish): variant of ▷Feivel.

Feige ♀ Jewish: from Yiddish Feygl 'bird' (modern German *Vogel*; compare ▷Zipporah). The present form of the name was arrived at by back-formation, the final *-l* having been interpreted as a Yiddish diminutive suffix rather than an integral part of the word.
VARIANT: Fayge.

Feivel ♀ Jewish (Yiddish): pet form of ▷Faivish.

Felicia ♀ Latinate feminine form of ▷Felix. It was popular in Britain in the medieval period (with the vernacular forms Felice, Felis), but by the 16th century it had become confused with ▷Phyllis. In modern times it is in only occasional use.

Felicity ♀ From the abstract noun denoting luck or good fortune (via Old

French from Latin *felicitas*; compare ▷Felix), first used as a given name in the 17th century. It also represents the English form of the Late Latin personal name *Felicitas*, which was borne by several early saints, notably a slave who was martyred in 203 together with her mistress Perpetua and several other companions.
PET FORM: Flick.

Felix ♂ Latin name meaning 'happy, fortunate', which has from time to time been popular as a given name in Britain and elsewhere because of its auspicious omen. It was in use as a byname in Latin, applied for example to the dictator Sulla (138–178 BC). It was very popular among the early Christians, being borne by a large number of early saints.

Fenella ♀ Anglicized form of Scottish Gaelic Fionnuala (see Scottish appendix), bestowed occasionally by parents without Scottish connections.
VARIANT: Finella.

Fenicia ♀ Of uncertain origin, probably just an alteration of ▷Felicia. It could also be an Anglicized form of Latin *Phoenicia* 'Phoenician woman', although there does not seem to be a saint of that name, as is normally the case for names derived from Latin.

Fenn ♂ Transferred use of the surname, in origin a local name for someone who lived in a low-lying marshy area, from Old English *fenn* 'marsh, fen'. It is also found as a short form of ▷Fenton.

Fennel ♀ 19th-century coinage, from the name of the plant (Latin *faeniculum*, a diminutive of *faenum* 'hay'), whose seeds are used as a spice. This probably came to be used as a first name because of its resemblance to a short form of ▷Fenella.

Fenton ♂ Transferred use of the surname, in origin a local name from any of the various places (for example, in Cumbria, Lincolnshire, Northumberland, Nottinghamshire, Staffordshire, and Yorkshire) so called from Old English *fenn* 'marsh, fen' + *tūn* 'enclosure, settlement'.

SHORT FORM: **Fenn**.

Ferdinand ♂ From a Spanish name, originally *Ferdinando* (now *Hernán*), which is of Germanic (Visigothic) origin, derived from *farð* 'journey' (or possibly an altered form of *frið* 'peace') + *nand* 'ready, prepared'. This was a traditional name in the royal families of Spain from an early date. It appeared in Britain in the 16th century, having been introduced by Roman Catholic supporters of Queen Mary I, who married Philip II of Spain in 1554.

PET FORMS: **Ferdi(e)**.

Fergus ♂ Anglicized form of **Fearghas** (see Irish or Scottish appendix), one of the Gaelic names that has recently also been favoured by parents without Irish or Scottish connections.

Fern ♀ From the vocabulary word denoting the plant (Old English *fearn*). Modern use of this word as a given name dates from the 19th century, when it is also recorded occasionally as a boy's name in the United States. In some instances the given name may be a transferred use of the surname derived in the medieval period from the vocabulary word.

Ferrer ♂ Catholic name given in honour of the Valencian saint, Vicente Ferrer (*c.*1350–1418), who travelled throughout Europe seeking to heal the papal schism. His surname is a Catalan occupational name for a blacksmith.

Festus ♂ Latin name meaning 'firm, steadfast'. This was the name of the Roman procurator of Judea who refused to bow to pressure from the Jews and condemn St Paul to death for his preaching, although he was totally unconvinced by it (Acts 25; 26:30–32). It was also borne by some early minor saints, and has been used as a Latinized

form of the Irish names **Fachtna** and **Feichín** (see Irish appendix).

Fidelis ♂ Original Latin form of **Fidel** (see Spanish appendix), occasionally used as a given name in the English-speaking world.

Fiesta ♀ From the vocabulary word (borrowed from Spanish, from Latin (*dies*) *festa*) referring to a carnival or celebration. It seems to have been chosen as a first name because of its happy association, or perhaps to commemorate the rejoicing over the birth of a baby.

Fifi ♀ French nursery form of *Joséphine* (see ▷Josephine). It is used occasionally in the English-speaking world, even though it now has definite connotations of frivolity.

Filomena ♀ Respelling of ▷Philomena.

Fina ♀ Short form of ▷Seraphina. See also Irish appendix.

Finella ♀ Variant of ▷Fenella.

Finlay ♂, occasionally ♀ Anglicized form of the Scottish Gaelic name Fionnlagh (see Scottish appendix) or a transferred use of the surname derived from the given name. This is one of a set of Celtic names which in recent years has also been favoured increasingly among parents without Scottish connections. It is also used occasionally for girls.

VARIANTS: **Finley, Findlay**.

Finn ♂ Either a transferred use of the surname derived in the Middle Ages from the Old Norse personal name *Finnr* 'Finn', used both as a byname and as a short form of various compound names with this first element, or an adoption of the Irish name (see Irish appendix). The name has recently enjoyed considerable popularity.

Fiona ♀ Latinate derivative of the Gaelic word *fionn* 'white, fair'. It was first used by James Macpherson (1736–96), author of the Ossianic poems, which were supposedly translations from ancient Gaelic. It was subsequently used as a pen-name by William Sharp (1855–1905), who produced many romantic works under the name of Fiona Macleod, and has since become popular throughout the English-speaking world.

Fishl ♂ Jewish: from a diminutive of Yiddish *fish* 'fish' (modern German *Fisch*). It seems to have been adopted as a given name because of the biblical prophecy that the descendants of Ephraim and Manasseh would multiply as the fish in the sea (Genesis 48:16).

Fitz ♂ Either a short form of any of the numerous names representing a transferred use of a surname formed with the Anglo-Norman French prefix *fi(t)z* 'son of', as for example ▷Fitzgerald, ▷Fitzroy, or a transferred use of the surname *Fitz*, which may be of the same derivation, but applied originally to distinguish a son from a father bearing the same given name, or a local name from Fitz in Shropshire, named with the Old English personal name *Fitt* + *hōh* 'hill spur'.

Fitzgerald ♂ Transferred use of the surname, which is a patronymic from the personal name ▷Gerald formed by the addition of the Anglo-Norman French prefix *fi(t)z* 'son of'.

Fitzroy ♂ Transferred use of the Irish surname, in origin a patronymic formed from the Anglo-Norman French prefix *fi(t)z* 'son of' + ▷Roy in one or other of its senses, though it is usually taken to imply that the original bearer was a bastard son of the king.

Flair ♀ Modern name, apparently from the vocabulary word denoting a particular talent for something. The word came into English from French in the 19th century and is a derivative of *flairer* 'to smell out, discern'. Use as a given name seems to reflect a desire on the part of the parents that their

daughter should exhibit such talent in life; there may also be some influence from the similar sounding ▷Fleur.

Flavia ♀ Feminine form of the old Roman family name *Flavius* (from *flavus* 'yellow(-haired)'). This was the name of at least five minor early saints.

Fletcher ♂ Transferred use of the surname, in origin an occupational name for a maker of arrows, from Old French *flech(i)er*, an agent derivative of *fleche* (of Germanic origin). An early bearer of this as a given name was Fletcher Christian, leader of the mutiny on the *Bounty* in 1789.

Fleur ♀ From an Old French name meaning 'flower', occasionally used in the Middle Ages. Modern use, however, seems to derive mainly from the character of this name in John Galsworthy's *The Forsyte Saga* (1922).

Flick ♀ Informal pet form based on ▷Felicity.

Flinders ♂ Transferred use of the surname, an altered form of *Flanders*, which originally denoted someone who came to England from that region. Its occasional use as a given name is probably in honour of the explorer Matthew Flinders (1774–1814). Flinders Petrie (1853–1942) was a famous British archaeologist.

Flint ♂ For the most part from the vocabulary word denoting a type of particularly hard rock (Old English *flint*), chosen as representing qualities of strength, endurance, and determination. In some cases it may represent a transferred use of the surname, which was originally given to someone who lived by a significant outcrop of this rock.

Flo ♀ Short form of ▷Florence and ▷Flora, common in the early part of the 20th century, but now usually considered somewhat old-fashioned.

Floella ♀ Recent coinage, in Britain especially popular as a Black name. It is evidently a compound of ▷Flo and ▷Ella.

Flora ♀ Name borne in Roman mythology by the goddess of flowers and the spring (a derivative of Latin *flos* 'flower', genitive *floris*). It is also the feminine form of the old Roman family name *Florus*, likewise derived from *flos*. *Flora* was little used in England before the 18th century, when it was imported from Scotland. In 1746 Flora Macdonald (1722–90) of Milton in South Uist helped Bonnie Prince Charlie to escape from there to the Island of Skye, disguised as a woman, after his defeat at Culloden. In fact, *Flora* was merely an Anglicized form of her Gaelic name, *Fionnaghal*, a variant of *Fionnguala* (see Fionnuala in Scottish appendix). However, her fame made the name *Flora* popular in the Highlands and elsewhere.

SHORT FORM: Flo.

PET FORM: Scottish: Florrie (Gaelic *Flòraidh*).

Florence ♀, formerly also ♂ Medieval form of the Latin masculine name *Florentius* (a derivative of *florens* 'blossoming, flourishing') and its feminine form *Florentia*. In the Middle Ages the name was commonly borne by men (as, for example, the historian Florence of Worcester), but it is now exclusively a girl's name. This was revived in the second half of the 19th century, being given in honour of Florence Nightingale (1820–1910), the founder of modern nursing, who organized a group of nurses to serve in the Crimean War. She herself received the name because she was born in the Italian city of Florence (Latin *Florentia*, Italian *Firenze*).

VARIANT: Florance.

SHORT FORMS: Flo, Floss.

PET FORMS: Florrie, Flossie.

Florentina ♀ Feminine form of Latin *Florentinus*, an elaborated form of *Florens* (see ▷Florence). The name was borne by a 7th-century Spanish saint, the sister of the other saints Fulgentius, Isidore, and Leander.

Florida ♀ From the name of the U.S. state, originally so named in Spanish because of its lush vegetation (from Latin *floridus* 'flowery'). It may also in part have originated as an elaboration of ▷Flora or a more modern form of ▷Florence.

Florrie ♀ Scottish pet form of ▷Flora, now little used except in the Highlands. The name was also used elsewhere, especially in the 19th century, as a pet form of ▷Florence, and has occasionally been used as an independent name in recent times.

Flossie ♀ Pet form from a contraction of ▷Florence, common in the 19th century but no longer much used. The popularity of the name was perhaps enhanced by association with the soft downy material known as *floss*.

Flower ♀ From the vocabulary word (from Old French; compare ▷Fleur), which is also sometimes used as a term of endearment.

Floyd ♂ Transferred use of the Welsh surname, in origin a variant of ▷Lloyd. This form of the name results from an attempt to represent the sound of the Welsh initial *Ll-* using traditional English pronunciation and orthography. From the 1890s to the 1930s it was at its most popular in the United States.

Flynn ♂ Transferred use of the Irish surname, an Anglicized form of Gaelic *Ó Floinn* 'descendant of *Flann*' (a byname meaning 'red(dish), ruddy').

Forbes ♂ Transferred use of the Scottish surname, in origin a local name from the lands of Forbes in Aberdeenshire. These are named from the Gaelic word *forba* 'field, district' + the locative suffix *-ais*. In

Scotland this name was traditionally pronounced in two syllables, but a monosyllabic pronunciation is now the norm.

Ford ♂ Transferred use of the common surname, in origin a local name for someone who lived near a place where a river could be crossed by wading through it (Old English *ford*).

Forrest ♂ Mainly U.S.: transferred use of the surname, in origin a local name for someone who lived in or by an enclosed wood, Old French *forest*.
VARIANT: **Forest**. Compare ▷Deforest.

Foster ♂ Transferred use of the surname, an occupational name with at least four possible derivations: from Middle English *foster* 'foster parent', *for(e)ster* 'forester', *fors(e)ter* 'shearer', or *fu(y)ster* 'saddle-tree maker'.

Fox ♂ Generally a transferred use of the surname, which derives as a nickname from the animal (Old English *fox*). This may originally have been given to a cunning person, or to someone with red hair, or for some other anecdotal reason. Use as a given name may have originated in honour of George Fox (1624–91), founder of the Quaker movement. In Ireland it has also been used as an English translation of the Gaelic nickname *Sionnach* 'fox'. As a Jewish name it has been used as an Anglicized form of the Yiddish nickname *fiksl* 'fox'.

Fran ♀, ♂ Short form of ▷Frances, or less commonly of ▷Francis.

France ♂, ♀ Mainly U.S.: short form of ▷Francis or ▷Frances, or bestowed with reference to the country.

Francene ♀ Variant spelling of ▷Francine.

Frances ♀ Feminine form of ▷Francis. In the 16th century the two spellings were used indiscriminately for both sexes, the distinction in spelling not being established until the 17th century.

SHORT FORM: **Fran**.
PET FORM: **Fanny**.

Francesca ♀ Italian form of ▷Frances, now widely used in the English-speaking world. Originally a vocabulary word meaning 'French', it was bestowed from the 13th century onwards in honour of St Francis of Assisi. It has also been used independently as an English name. Its most famous bearer was Francesca di Rimini, daughter of Giovanni da Polenta, Count of Ravenna. A legendary beauty, she was betrothed by her father to the misshapen Giovanni Malatesta, Lord of Rimini, in return for military support. Malatesta's good-looking younger brother, Paolo, acted as his proxy in the betrothal, but Francesca and he fell in love. They were discovered, and put to death by Malatesta in 1289. Their tragedy is enshrined in the Fifth Canto of Dante's *Inferno*, as well as in several other works of literature and in a symphonic fantasy by Tchaikovsky.

Francine ♀ From a French diminutive pet form of *Françoise*, the French form of ▷Frances.
VARIANTS: **Francene, Franceen**.

Francis ♂ English equivalent of Italian **Francesco** (see Italian appendix), originally a vocabulary word meaning 'French' or 'Frenchman' (Late Latin *Franciscus*; compare ▷Frank). This was a nickname given to St Francis of Assisi (1181–1226) because of his wealthy father's business connections with France. His baptismal name was Giovanni. He had a pleasant, ordinary life as a child and young man, but after two serious illnesses, a period of military service, and a year as a prisoner of war in Perugia, he turned from the world and devoted himself to caring for the poor and sick. He was joined by groups of disciples, calling themselves 'minor friars' (*friari minores*). The main features of the Franciscan rule are humility, poverty, and love for all living creatures. The given name occurs occasionally in England as early as 1300, and more frequently from the early 16th century, when there was a surge of admiration for, and imitation of, Italian Renaissance culture.

SHORT FORMS: ▷Frank, Fran, France.

Francisco ♂ Spanish and Portuguese equivalent of ▷Francis, now used as a given name in the English-speaking world, perhaps on occasion with reference to the U.S. city of San Francisco (compare ▷Brooklyn, ▷Chelsea, ▷Rio).

Frank ♂ Of Germanic origin. The name referred originally to a member of the tribe of the Franks, who are said to have got the name from a characteristic type of spear that they used. When the Franks migrated into Gaul in the 4th century, the country received its modern name of France (Late Latin *Francia*) and the tribal term Frank came to mean 'Frenchman'. The name is now also used as a short form of ▷Francis or ▷Franklin.

Frankie ♂, ♀ Pet form of ▷Frank, also sometimes of ▷Frances, ▷Francesca, or ▷Francine. As a girl's name, it is perhaps most familiar as the name of the heroine of American folk song *The Ballad of Frankie and Johnny*.

Franklin ♂ Transferred use of the surname, derived from Middle English *frankeleyn* 'freeman', denoting a member of a class of men who were not of noble birth but who were nevertheless freeholders. The vocabulary word is derived from Old French *franc*, meaning both 'free' and 'Frankish'. The connection between freemen and Franks is reflected in the Late Latin term *francalia*, originally denoting lands held by Franks, which came to mean lands not subject to taxes. The given name is now quite common, especially in the United States, where it is often bestowed in honour of the statesman and scientist Benjamin Franklin (1706–90). A more

recent influence was President Franklin D. Roosevelt (1882–1945).

VARIANT: Franklyn.

Fraser ♂ Transferred use of the Scottish surname, which may be of Norman origin but uncertain derivation. See Scottish appendix.

VARIANTS: Frazer, Frazier.

Fred ♂ Short form of ▷Frederick or, occasionally, of ▷Alfred, now also used independently.

Freda ♀ Originally a short form of various names such as ▷Elfreda and ▷Winifred, also occasionally of ▷Frederica, but now used mainly (though infrequently) as an independent name. In some cases it may have been adopted as an English equivalent of the German name *Frieda*, a short form of such compound names as *Friedegund* and *Friedelind*, of which the common element is Germanic *frid-* 'peace'.

VARIANT: Frieda.

Freddie ♂, ♀ Pet form of ▷Frederick, also used independently. It is occasionally found as a pet form of ▷Frederica.

Freddy ♂ Pet form of ▷Frederick, also used independently.

Frederica ♀ Latinate feminine form of ▷Frederick.

SHORT FORM: Freda.

PET FORM: Freddie.

Frederick ♂ From an Old French name of Germanic origin, from *fred*, *frid* 'peace' + *rīc* 'power, ruler'. It was adopted by the Normans and introduced into Britain by them, but did not survive long. Modern use in Britain dates from the 17th century, and it became more frequent in the 18th among followers of the Elector of Hanover, who in 1714 became George I of England. It was reinforced by the vogue for Germanic names in Victorian times.

VARIANTS: Frederic, Fredrick, Fredric.

SHORT FORM: **Fred.**

PET FORMS: **Freddy, Freddie.**

COGNATES: German: **Friedrich.** Dutch: **Frerik, Freek.** Scandinavian: **Fredrik.** Danish, Norwegian: **Frederik.** French: **Frédéric.** Spanish: **Federico.** Portuguese: **Frederico.** Italian: **Federico.** Polish: **Fryderyk.** Czech: **Bedřich.** Finnish: **Rieti.** Hungarian: **Frigyes.**

Freya ♀ Of Old Norse origin. *Freya* or *Fröja* was the goddess of love in Scandinavian mythology. Her name is most probably derived from an ancient North Germanic word related to Old High German *frouwa* 'lady' (modern German *Frau*). The name has long been a traditional one in Shetland and is now in general use in England and Scotland. It came to prominence in the late 1990s. A notable modern bearer was the explorer and writer Freya Stark (1893–1993).

Freyde ♀ Jewish: meaning 'joy' in Yiddish (modern German *Freude*).

Frieda ♀ Variant spelling of ▷Freda, under the influence of German **Friede** (see German appendix).

Froim ♂ Jewish: Yiddish form of ▷Ephraim.

Frost ♂ Transferred use of the surname, in origin a nickname for someone of an icy or unbending disposition or who had white hair or a white beard. (Old English *frost* is a derivative of *frēosan* 'to freeze'.) As a first name it may sometimes be given to a child born during an exceptionally cold spell, or in honour of the American poet Robert Frost (1874–1963).

Frume ♀ Jewish: originally a nickname meaning 'pious, devout' in Yiddish (modern German *fromm*).

Fry ♂ Transferred use of the surname, in origin denoting either a free person rather than a serf (from Old English *frīg* 'free', a byform of *frēo*) or else a small person (from Old Norse *frió* 'seed'). Elizabeth Fry (1780–1845) was a celebrated Quaker prison reformer.

Fulk ♂ Of Germanic origin, introduced to Britain by the Normans. The name was originally a short form of various compound names containing the word *volk* 'people, tribe' (compare modern English *folk*). It has gradually died out of general use, but is still used in certain families, in particular the Grevilles. Fulke Greville, 1st Baron Brooke, was a leading figure at the court of Elizabeth I. See also ▷Greville.

VARIANT: **Fulke.**

Fulton ♂ Transferred use of the Scottish surname, which seems to have been originally a local name from a lost place in Ayrshire. Robert Fulton (1765–1815) was the American engineer who designed the first commercially successful steamboat. In Britain the name is associated with the Scottish actor Fulton McKay (1922–87).

Fulvia ♀ From the feminine form of the old Roman family name *Fulvius*, a derivative of Latin *fulvus* 'dusky, tawny' (ultimately akin to *flavus*; compare ▷Flavia). The name does not seem to have been much used among early Christians, and there are no saints Fulvia or Fulvius. In classical times its most famous bearer was the wife of Mark Antony, who opposed Octavian by force on her husband's behalf while he was in Egypt.

Gg

Gabriel ♂, ♀ Biblical name (meaning 'man of God' in Hebrew), borne by one of the archangels. Gabriel appeared to Daniel in the Old Testament (Daniel 8:16; 9:21), and in the New Testament to Zacharias (Luke 1:19; 26:27) and, most famously, to Mary to announce the impending birth of Christ (Luke 1:2). Used only infrequently in the 20th century, *Gabriel* has recently found favour as a given name in the English-speaking world, and is now sometimes bestowed on girls.
PET FORM: Gaby.

Gabriella ♀ Latinate feminine form of ▷Gabriel.
VARIANT: Gabriela.
PET FORMS: Gab(b)y.

Gabrielle ♀ French feminine form of ▷Gabriel, now well established in the English-speaking world.

Gaby ♀, ♂ Pet form of ▷Gabriella, ▷Gabrielle, or ▷Gabriel.

Gae ♀ From the English vocabulary word *gay* in its original meaning 'blithe' or 'cheerful'. This came to be used as a given name in the early 20th century because of its well-omened meaning, but fell out of favour again in the 1960s, when the vocabulary word acquired the meaning 'homosexual'; only the spelling *Gae* is still in use for the name.

Gael ♀ Fanciful spelling of ▷Gail, also occasionally written Gaelle.

Gaia ♀ From the name (a derivative of Greek *gē* 'earth') borne in classical mythology by the primeval goddess of the earth, who gave birth to Ouranos ('sky') and had children by him: Okeanos ('sea'), Kronos ('time'), and the Titans. It has been used as a modern first name since the popularization of

James Lovelock's conception of the whole earthly ecosystem as a living self-regulating entity under this name.

Gail ♀ Shortened form of ▷Abigail. It was not found as an independent given name before the middle of the 20th century; it became popular in the 1950s and 1960s, but has since fallen out of fashion.
VARIANTS: Gaile, Gale, Gayle, Gael(le).

Gala ♀ Of Russian origin, a contracted form of Galina, which is said to be from the Greek name *Galēnē* 'calm', although it may actually be a vernacular form of ▷Helen. The name is now adopted occasionally by English-speakers, perhaps influenced by the festive connotations of the vocabulary word.

Gale ♀ Variant spelling of ▷Gail.

Galen ♂ Mainly U.S.: from the name of the Graeco-Roman medical writer Claudius *Galenus* (AD 129–199). His name represents a Latinized form of a Greek name derived from *galēnē* 'calm'.

Galia ♀ Jewish: modern Hebrew name, meaning 'wave'.

Gallagher ♂ Transferred use of the Irish surname, an Anglicized form of *Ó Gallchobhair* 'descendant of Gallchobhar' (see Gallchobhar in Irish appendix).

Gamaliel ♂ Biblical name, apparently meaning 'benefit of God' in Hebrew, occurring in both the Old and the New Testaments. In the Old Testament it is the name of the prince of the tribe of Manasseh at the time of the Exodus (Numbers 1:10); in the New Testament it is borne by a wise Pharisee (Acts 5:34) and a teacher of St Paul (Acts 22:3), who may have been the same person. It was in limited use in England from the 15th century and was taken up by Puritans in the 17th century; in more recent times it has been associated with the U.S. president Warren Gamaliel Harding (1865–1923).

Gardner ♂ Transferred use of the surname, in origin an occupational name for someone responsible for the maintenance of the grounds of a manor house or abbey (a derivative of Middle English *gardin*, from Norman French, of Germanic origin).

Gareth ♂ Apparently of Celtic origin, but uncertain derivation. It first occurs in Malory's *Morte d'Arthur* as the name of the lover of Eluned, and seems to have been heavily altered from its original form, whatever that may have been (possibly the same as Geraint; see Welsh appendix). It is now very popular in Wales. ▷Gary, which is actually an independent name, is often taken to be a pet form of it.

Garfield ♂ Transferred use of the surname, in origin a local name for someone who lived near a triangular field, from Old English *gār* 'triangular piece of land' + *feld* 'open country'.

Garner ♂ Transferred use of the surname, in origin an occupational name for someone responsible for supervising the stores kept in a granary (Old French *gernier*, from Latin *granarium*, a derivative of *granum* 'grain, corn').

Garnet ♂, ♀ Transferred use of the surname, in origin probably an occupational name for a grower or seller of pomegranates (from a metathesized form of Old French (*pome*) *grenate*, Latin *pomum granatum* 'fruit full of seeds'). The name of the red-coloured precious stone derives from the same source, in reference to the fruit's bright red colour, and use as a modern first name may have been inspired by the adoption of other terms denoting gemstones as female names. It may also in part reflect the fame of the British field marshal Sir Garnet Wolseley (1833–1913).

VARIANT: **Garnett**.

Garret ♂ Transferred use of the surname, which is derived from the given names ▷Gerald and ▷Gerard. In Ireland it is often a direct Anglicization of *Gearóid*, the Gaelic form of ▷Gerald, and is the name of the former Taoiseach Garret Fitzgerald (b. 1926).

VARIANT: **Garrett**.

Garrick ♂ Mainly U.S.: transferred use of the surname, in some cases perhaps adopted in honour of the English actor-manager David Garrick (1717–79). He was of Huguenot descent, the grandson of a certain David *de la Garrique*. This is a Languedoc name, from *garrigue*, denoting a stretch of open limestone country.

Garrison ♂ Mainly U.S.: transferred use of the surname, originally a local name from Garriston in North Yorkshire or from a patronymic for the son of a man called ▷Garret. William Lloyd Garrison (1805–79) was a prominent American anti-slavery campaigner: the given name may originally have been bestowed in honour of him. It is now popularly associated with the American writer Garrison Keillor (b. 1942). Sometimes it is given to the sons of fathers who are called ▷Gary or ▷Garry.

Garry ♂ Variant spelling of ▷Gary, influenced by ▷Barry.

Garth ♂ Transferred use of a surname, but often taken to be a contracted form of ▷Gareth. As a surname it originated in the north of England, as a local name for someone who lived near an enclosure of some sort (Old Norse *garðr*). In modern times its popularity has been influenced by the virile superhero of this name, the main character in a long-running strip cartoon in the *Daily Mirror* newspaper.

Gary ♂ Transferred use of a surname, which is probably derived from a Norman personal name of Continental Germanic origin, a short form of any of the various compound names beginning with *gar* 'spear'. One bearer of this surname was the American industrialist Elbert Henry Gary (1846–1927), who gave his name to the steel town of Gary, Indiana (chartered in 1906). In this town was born the theatrical agent Nan Collins, who suggested *Gary* as a stage name for her client Frank J. Cooper, who thus became Gary Cooper (1901–61). His film career caused the name to become enormously popular from the 1930s to the present day. Its popularity has been maintained by the cricketer Gary Sobers (b. 1936; in his case it is in fact a pet form of ▷Garfield) and the footballer Gary Lineker (b. 1960). It is now often taken as a pet form of ▷Gareth.

VARIANT: **Garry.**

PET FORM: **Gaz** (informal).

Gavin ♂ Of Celtic origin, but uncertain ultimate derivation; it first appears in French sources as *Gauvain*. The name is borne in the Arthurian romances by one of the knights of the Round Table (more familiar in English versions as Sir *Gawain*). It was still in use in the north of England as late as the early 18th century and never died out in Scotland, whence it was reintroduced to England from the early 20th century. It is now very widely used in England, Wales, and elsewhere in the English-speaking world.

VARIANT: **Gawain.**

Gaye ♀ Variant of ▷Gae, used in preference to the now obsolete spelling Gay, which was generally a girl's name, but has also been borne by men, in Ireland, as a pet form of ▷Gabriel.

Gayle ♀ Variant spelling of ▷Gail. The popularity of this form was no doubt increased by the fame of the American film actress Gayle Hunnicutt (b. 1943).

Gaylord ♂ Transferred use of a surname, which is a form, altered by folk etymology, of the Old French nickname *Gaillard* 'dandy'. It was adopted as a first name from the 19th century, but it now seems to have

suffered the same fate as *Gay* (see ▷Gaye).

Gaynor ♀ Medieval form of the name of Arthur's queen, ▷Guinevere. It was popular in the 1960s but has since fallen out of fashion.

VARIANT: **Gayner, Gayna.**

Gaz ♂ Informal pet form of ▷Gary.

VARIANT: **Gazza.**

Ged ♂ Contracted form of ▷Gerald or ▷Gerard. See also ▷Jed.

Gemma ♀ From a medieval Italian nickname meaning 'gem, jewel'. It has been chosen in modern times mainly because of its transparent etymology. Among Roman Catholics it is sometimes chosen in honour of St Gemma Galgani (1878–1903), who was the subject of many extraordinary signs of grace, such as ecstasies and the appearance of the stigmata. It was extremely popular in the 1980s but has since faded slightly.

VARIANT: **Jemma.**

Gene ♂, ♀ Short form of ▷Eugene, now used as a boy's given name in its own right, especially in North America. It has been made familiar by film actors such as Gene Autry, Gene Hackman, Gene Kelly, and Gene Wilder. It is also occasionally used as a girl's name, in which case it represents a respelling of ▷Jean.

Genette ♀ Variant spelling of ▷Jeannette.

Geneva ♀ Of recent origin and uncertain derivation: possibly a variant of ▷Jennifer. In form it coincides with the name of the city in Switzerland (compare ▷Florence and ▷Venetia). It may alternatively have been intended as a short form of ▷Genevieve.

Genevieve ♀ The name of the patron saint of Paris, Geneviève in French. She was a 5th-century Gallo-Roman nun who encouraged the people of Paris in the face of the occupation of the city by the Franks and threatened attacks by the Huns. Her name is probably derived from Celtic words meaning 'people, tribe' and 'woman', but if so it has been heavily altered during its transmission through French sources. The name was introduced to Britain from France in the 19th century and is now in steady use.

Genine ♀ Altered spelling of ▷Jeannine.

Genista ♀ Modern coinage taken from the Latin name, *Genista*, of the genus of plants known as broom. It is from this word that the Plantagenet royal dynasty took its name: the founder, Geoffrey Plantagenet (1113–51), wore a sprig of broom (Latin *planta genesta*) to distinguish himself in battle.

Geoff ♂ Short form of ▷Geoffrey. See also ▷Jeff.

Geoffrey ♂ Of Germanic (Frankish and Lombard) origin, introduced to Britain by the Normans. It was in regular use among the counts of Anjou, ancestors of the English royal house of Plantagenet, who were descended from Geoffrey Plantagenet, Count of Anjou (1113–51). It was a particularly popular name in England and France in the later Middle Ages; notable bearers in England include the poet Geoffrey Chaucer (*c*.1340–1400) and in Wales the chronicler Geoffrey of Monmouth (d. 1155). The original form and meaning of the name is disputed. According to one theory, it is merely a variant of ▷Godfrey; others derive the first part from the Germanic word *gawia* 'territory', *walah* 'stranger', or *gisil* 'pledge'. Medieval forms can be found to support all these theories, and it is possible that several names have fallen together, or that the name was subjected to reanalysis by folk etymology at an early date.
VARIANT: ▷Jeffrey.

Geordie ♂ Pet form of ▷George, still used in Scotland and the north of England. It is from this name that the generic term *Geordie* for a Tynesider derives.

George ♂ Via Old French and Latin, from Greek *Georgios* (a derivative of *geōrgos* 'farmer', from *gē* 'earth' + *ergein* 'to work'). This was the name of several early saints, including the shadowy figure who is now the patron of England (as well as of Germany and Portugal). If the saint existed at all, he was perhaps martyred in Palestine in the persecutions of Christians instigated by the Emperor Diocletian at the beginning of the 4th century. The popular legend in which the hero slays a dragon is a medieval Italian invention. He was for a long time a more important saint in the Orthodox Church than in the West, and the name was not much used in England during the Middle Ages, even after St George came to be regarded as the patron of England in the 14th century. Its use increased from the 1400s, and by 1500 it was regularly among the most popular male names. This popularity was reinforced when George I came to the throne in 1714, bringing this name with him from Germany. It has been one of the most popular English boys' names ever since.
PET FORMS: Georgie, Geordie.
COGNATES: Irish: Seoirse. Scottish Gaelic: Seòras, Deòrsa. Welsh: Siôr, Sior(y)s. German: Georg; Jörg (dialectal); Jürgen (Low German in origin). Dutch: Joris, Joren, Jurg. Danish: Jørgen, Jørn. Swedish: Göran, Jöran, Jörgen, Örjan. French: Georges. Spanish: Jorge. Catalan: Jordi. Portuguese: Jorge. Italian: Giorgio. Russian: Georgi, Yuri, Yegor. Polish: Jerzy. Czech: Jiří. Croatian: Juraj, Jure. Slovenian: Jure. Finnish: Yrjö. Hungarian: György. Lithuanian: Jurgis. Latvian: Juris.

Georgena ♀ Altered spelling of ▷Georgina.

Georgene ♀ Altered form of ▷Georgine, by association with the productive suffix -*ene*.

Georgette ♀ French feminine diminutive of *Georges*, the French form of ▷George, now also used in the English-speaking world. The crêpe material so called derives its name from that of an early 20th-century French dressmaker, Georgette de la Plante.

Georgia ♀ Latinate feminine form of ▷George. It was borne by a 5th-century saint who became a recluse near Clermont in the Auvergne and, more recently, by the celebrated American artist Georgia O'Keeffe (1887–1986). It has been very popular since the mid-1990s.

VARIANT: **Jorja**.

Georgiana ♀ Elaborated Latinate form of ▷Georgia or ▷Georgina. It was famously borne by the 18th-century beauty Georgiana, Duchess of Devonshire (1757–1806).

Georgie ♀, ♂ Originally a pet form of ▷George, but now used more commonly as a girl's name, a pet form of ▷Georgia or ▷Georgina. It is also used independently for both boys and girls.

Georgina ♀ Latinate feminine derivative of ▷George. This feminine form originated in Scotland in the 18th century, when *George* itself became common among anti-Jacobites.

Georgine ♀ French form of ▷Georgina, now also used occasionally in the English-speaking world.

VARIANT: English: **Georgene**.

Gerald ♂ From an Old French name of Germanic (Frankish) origin, derived from *gār, gēr* 'spear' + *wald* 'rule'. It was adopted by the Normans and introduced by them to Britain. There has been some confusion with ▷Gerard. It died out in England at the end of the 13th century. However, it continued to be popular in Ireland, where it had been brought in the 12th century at the time of Strongbow's invasion. It was

used in England in the 17th century and revived in the 19th century, along with several other long-extinct names of Norman, Old English, and Celtic origin, and is now more common than *Gerard*, which survived all along as an English 'gentry' name.

VARIANT: **Jerrold**.

SHORT FORM: **Ged**.

PET FORMS: **Gerry, Jerry**.

Geraldine ♀ Feminine derivative of ▷Gerald, invented in the 16th century by the English poet the Earl of Surrey, in a poem praising Lady Fitzgerald. It remained very little used until the 18th century, when it suddenly increased in popularity.

PET FORM: **Gerry**.

Gerard ♂ Old French name of Germanic (Frankish) origin, introduced to Britain by the Normans. It is derived from *gār, gēr* 'spear' + *hard* 'brave, hardy, strong'. In the later Middle Ages this was a more common name than ▷Gerald, with which it was sometimes confused. Nowadays it is less common, surviving mainly among Roman Catholics, in honour of the many saints of this name.

VARIANTS: **Gerrard, Jerrard**.

SHORT FORM: **Ged**.

PET FORMS: **Gerry, Jerry**.

Gerardine ♀ Feminine form of ▷Gerard, created by the addition of the suffix -*ine* (in origin a French feminine diminutive).

Germaine ♀, ♂ Feminine form of the rarer French masculine name **Germain** (Late Latin *Germanus* 'brother'; the original reference may have been to the concept of Christian brotherhood). Germaine Cousin (*c.*1579–1601) was a Provençal saint, the daughter of a poor farmer. Her canonization in 1867 gave an additional impulse to the use of the name in France, from where it was imported into the English-speaking world. This form of the name is now also used occasionally as a boy's name. See also ▷Jermaine.

Gerrard ♂ Variant spelling of
▷Gerard, in part from the surname
derived from the given name in the
Middle Ages.

Gerry ♂, ♀ Pet form of ▷Gerald,
▷Gerard, or ▷Geraldine, occasionally
used independently. See also ▷Jerry.

Gershom ♂ Biblical name, borne by a
son of Moses (Exodus 2:22). It possibly
means 'exile' (i.e. a person in exile) in
Hebrew, but it is usually interpreted as
'sojourner', from Hebrew *ger sham* 'a
stranger there'.

Gershon ♂ Byform of ▷Gershom,
borne in the Bible by a son of ▷Levi
(Genesis 46:11).

Gertrude ♀ From a Germanic female
personal name, derived from *gār*, *gēr*
'spear' + *þrūþ* 'strength'. The name is
not found in England immediately after
the Conquest, but only in the later
Middle English period. It may have
been introduced by migrants from the
Low Countries who came to England in
connection with the cloth trade, and
was certainly in consistent use in some
areas throughout the 16th and 17th
centuries, although it was not generally
popular until the 19th century, when
many medieval names were revived. It
has now fallen from favour again.

SHORT FORM: **Gert.**
PET FORM: **Gertie.**

Gervaise ♂ Norman name of
unknown origin. It has been suggested
that it might be Germanic, formed from
gēr 'spear' and an unexplained second
element. The given name is bestowed
in honour of a certain St Gervasius,
whose remains, together with those of
Protasius, were discovered in Milan in
the year 386. Nothing is known about
their lives, but St Ambrose, who had
ordered the search for their remains,
declared that they were martyrs, and a
cult soon grew up. Given these
circumstances, we might expect their
names to be Greek or Latin, but if they
are, the origins are unknown. The

name is in use mainly among Roman
Catholics. *Protasius* has not survived as a
given name. See also ▷Jarvis.

VARIANT: **Gervase.**

Ghislain ♀ Of recent origin, or at any
rate a recent introduction to the
English-speaking world. It is evidently a
revival of the Old French oblique case
of ▷Giselle, in a spelling that suggests
Low German, Dutch, or Flemish
influence.

VARIANT: **Ghislaine.**

Gib ♂ Medieval and modern short
form of ▷Gilbert.

VARIANT: **Gibb.**

Gideon ♂ Biblical name meaning 'he
who cuts down' in Hebrew; it was
borne by an Israelite leader appointed
to deliver his people from the
Midianites (Judges 6:14). He did this by
getting his army to creep up on them
with their torches hidden in pitchers.
The name was popular among the 17th-
century Puritans, and has remained in
select use.

Gigi ♀ French pet form of ▷Giselle,
made famous in the English-speaking
world by Lerner and Loewe's
immensely popular musical *Gigi* (1958),
starring Leslie Caron in the title role.

Gilbert ♂ Old French name of
Germanic (Frankish) origin, derived
from *gisil* 'pledge' + *berht* 'bright,
famous'. It was adopted by the Normans
and introduced by them to Britain. This
was the name of the founder of the only
native British religious order (abolished
at the Dissolution of the Monasteries),
St Gilbert of Sempringham (?1083–
1189), in whose honour it is still
sometimes bestowed, especially among
Roman Catholics. It gained a wider
currency in the 19th century.

SHORT FORM: **Gib.**

Gilda ♀ Italian: apparently of
Germanic origin, representing a
feminine short form of names
containing the element *gild* 'sacrifice'

(compare e.g. **Hermengildo** in Spanish appendix). Its occasional use in the English-speaking world since the 19th century may have been prompted by the character in Verdi's *Rigoletto*, the innocent daughter of the hunchback jester Rigoletto, who becomes the object of the Duke of Mantua's affections and is murdered on her father's orders as the result of a series of misunderstandings.

Giles ♂ Much altered English vernacular form of the Late Latin name *Aegidius*, from Greek *Aigidios* (a derivative of *aigidion* 'kid, young goat'), via Old French *Gide*. It was the name of an 8th-century saint who, according to tradition, was an Athenian citizen who fled to Provence because he could not cope with the fame and adulation caused by his power to work miracles, in particular by healing the lame and crippled. This was not a particularly common name in the Middle Ages and its use seems to have been confined to certain families and localities.

VARIANT: **Gyles.**

Gill ♀ Short form of ▷Gillian, rather less frequent than ▷Jill.

Gillaine ♀ Modern name, representing an altered form of ▷Gillian inspired by the several women's names ending in *-aine*, such as ▷Lorraine. The name ▷Ghislain may also have been an influence.

Gillian ♀ Variant of ▷Julian, from which it was differentiated in spelling only in the 17th century.

VARIANT: **Jillian.**

SHORT FORMS: **Gill**, ▷**Jill.**

PET FORMS: **Gilly**, **Jilly.**

Gilroy ♂ Transferred use of the Irish and Scottish surname, perhaps influenced to some extent by ▷Elroy and ▷Leroy. The surname is of Gaelic origin, from *an giolla ruadh* 'the red-haired lad'.

Gina ♀ Short form of ▷Georgina, now also used as an independent given

name. As an Italian name it is a short form of *Giorgina* or *Luigina*, and was made famous by the actress Gina Lollobrigida (b. 1927).

Ginette ♀ Respelling of ▷Jeannette.

Ginevra ♀ Italian form of ▷Genevieve, now also occasionally used in the English-speaking world.

Ginger ♂, ♀ Originally a nickname for someone with red hair, occasionally used as a given name in the 20th century. As a girl's name it is sometimes a pet form of ▷Virginia, as in the case of the film star Ginger Rogers (1911–1995, born Virginia McMath).

Ginny ♀ Pet form of ▷Virginia or (occasionally) ▷Jane.

VARIANTS: **Ginnie**, **Jinny.**

Giselle ♀ French name of Frankish origin, from the Germanic word *gisil* 'pledge'. It was a common practice in medieval Europe to leave children as pledges for an alliance, to be brought up at a foreign court, and the name may be derived as a byname from this practice. This was the name by which the wife of Duke Rollo of Normandy (*c*.860–*c*.930) was known. On her account the name enjoyed considerable popularity in France from an early period. Use of the name in English-speaking countries is much more recent, and is due mainly to the ballet *Giselle* (first performed in 1841).

VARIANTS: **Gisel(l)a**, **Gisele.**

PET FORM: ▷**Gigi.**

Gitte ♀ Jewish: of Yiddish origin, originally a nickname meaning 'good' (modern German *gut*).

PET FORM: **Gittel.**

Gladstone ♂ Transferred use of the Scottish surname, in origin a local name from Gledstanes in Biggar, so called from Old English *glæd* 'kite' + *stān* 'rock' (the final *-s* is a later addition). As a given name it has sometimes been bestowed in honour of the Victorian Liberal statesman William Ewart

Gladstone (1809–98). It is now favoured by West Indians: the Warwickshire and England fast bowler Gladstone Small is of West Indian parentage.

Gladwin ♂ Transferred use of the surname, itself from a medieval given name derived from Old English *glæd* 'bright' + *wine* 'friend'.

Gladys ♀ From the Old Welsh name Gwladus, which is of uncertain derivation. It has been quite widely used outside Wales since the beginning of the 20th century, but is now out of fashion.

Glanville ♂ Transferred use of the surname, which can be either of Norman origin, from a place so named in Calvados, or from any of various places in England named with Old English *clǣne* 'clean' (i.e. free from undergrowth) + *feld* 'pasture, open country', such as Glanville in Somerset and Hampshire, or Clanfield in Hampshire.

Glen ♂ Modern coinage from the Scottish word *glen* 'valley' (Gaelic *gleann*), in some cases perhaps representing a transferred use of the surname derived from this word. In recent years it has been used far beyond Scotland as a given name. Among well-known bearers of the name is the U.S. country singer Glen Campbell (b. 1936). There has been some confusion with the Welsh name ▷Glyn, which has the same meaning.

VARIANT: ▷Glenn (as borne by the U.S. band leader Glenn Miller (1905–1944)).

Glenda ♀ Modern Welsh coinage, composed of the vocabulary words *glân* 'clean, pure, holy' + *da* 'good'. It is also used outside Wales, and is associated particularly with the actress and politician Glenda Jackson (b. 1937).

Glenn ♂, ♀ Variant spelling of ▷Glen, occasionally used as a girl's name, as in the case of the American actress Glenn Close (b. 1947).

Glenna ♀ Modern coinage, invented as a female form of ▷Glen.

Glenys ♀ Modern Welsh coinage; see Welsh appendix. In its various spellings it has also been used by English speakers.

VARIANTS: **Glen(n)is, Glenice, Glenice, Glenise, Glennys, Glyn(n)is.**

Gloria ♀ From the Latin word meaning 'glory', not used as a given name before the 20th century. It first occurs as the name of a character in George Bernard Shaw's play *You Never Can Tell* (1898), and was fairly popular in the 1940s and 1950s.

Glory ♀ Anglicized form of ▷Gloria, now occasionally used as a given name.

Glyn ♂ Welsh: from the Welsh place name element *glyn* 'valley'. This was adopted as a given name in the 20th century, as the result of a desire to bestow on Welsh children specifically Welsh names, and has since been taken up in the English-speaking world outside Wales.

VARIANT: **Glynn.**

Glynis ♀ Altered form of ▷Glenys.

Goddard ♂ From the Old English personal name *Godeheard*, composed of *god* 'god' + *heard* 'hardy, brave'. In modern use it is probably a transferred use of the surname derived from this in the Middle Ages, rather than a revival.

Godfrey ♂ From the Old French name *Godefroy*, which is of Germanic (Frankish) origin, from *god* 'god' (or *gōd* 'good') + *fred, frid* 'peace'. This was adopted by the Normans, and brought to England by immigrants from the Low Countries and France. It was borne by a Norman saint (*c.*1066–1115) who became bishop of Amiens. There has been considerable confusion with ▷Geoffrey.

Godiva ♀ Latinized form of an Old English female personal name composed of the elements *god* 'god' + *gyfu* 'gift'. The name was borne most notably by an 11th-century Mercian noblewoman who, according to a famous legend, rode naked on horseback through the streets of Coventry to dissuade her husband Earl Leofric from imposing a heavy tax on the townspeople. It is rarely, if ever, used as a modern given name.

Godwin ♂ From the Old English personal name *Godwine*, derived from *god* 'god' + *wine* 'friend'. This was borne in the 11th century by the Earl of Wessex, the most important man in England after the king. He was an influential adviser to successive kings of England, and father of the King Harold who was defeated at Hastings in 1066. The personal name continued in use after the Norman Conquest long enough to give rise to a surname. Modern use as a given name is probably a transferred use of the surname, rather than a revival of the Old English name.

Golda ♀ Jewish (Yiddish): originally a nickname meaning 'gold'. It was borne by the former Israeli prime minister Golda Meir (1898–1978), who Hebraicized her name from Golda Meyerson.

VARIANT: **Golde**.

Goldie ♀ From a nickname for a blonde, a girl with golden hair, as in the case of the actress Goldie Hawn (b. 1945).

Gomer ♂ Biblical name (meaning 'complete' in Hebrew), borne by a son of Japheth and grandson of Noah. It is in occasional use in the United States. *Gomer* is also an English surname, derived from an Old English personal name composed of *gōd* 'good' + *mǣr* 'famous', and the given name may also be a transferred use of this.

Goodwin ♂ Transferred use of the surname, which is derived from the Old English personal name *Gōdwine*, from *gōd* 'good' + *wine* 'friend'. There has

been considerable confusion with ▷Godwin.

Gordon ♂ Transferred use of the Scottish surname, which is derived from a place name. It is a matter of dispute whether it referred originally to the Gordon in Berwickshire or to a similarly named place in Normandy. As a given name it seems to have been taken up in honour of Charles George Gordon (1833–85), the British general who died at Khartoum.

Goretti ♀ Name bestowed by Roman Catholics in honour of the 20th-century Italian saint, Maria Goretti. In 1902, at the age of eleven, she was savagely assaulted by a neighbour in an attempted rape. She forgave her attacker before expiring in hospital, and was canonized in 1950 as an example to children of a saintly life at an early age.

Grace ♀ From the abstract noun (via Old French, from Latin *gratia*), this name occurs occasionally in the 15th century, and by the 1540s was among the most popular girls' names in some parishes. It has always been particularly popular in Scotland and northern England (borne, for example, by Grace Darling, the lighthouse keeper's daughter whose heroism in 1838, saving sailors in a storm, caught the popular imagination). In more recent times it was famous as the name of the actress Grace Kelly (1928–82), who became Princess Grace of Monaco. In Ireland it is used as an Anglicized form of Gráinne (see Irish appendix).

Gracie ♀ Pet form of ▷Grace, also used independently. It was made famous by the Lancashire singer and comedienne Gracie Fields (1898–1979), whose original name was Grace Stansfield.

Grafton ♂ Transferred use of the surname, in origin a local name from any of several places named with the Old English elements *grāf* 'grove' + *tūn* 'enclosure, settlement'. In the United

States it seems to have been adopted as a given name in honour of the third Duke of Grafton, Augustus Henry Fitzroy, who served as British Prime Minister 1767–70 and who favoured conciliation with the American colonies.

Graham ♂ Transferred use of a Scottish surname, in origin a local name from Grantham in Lincolnshire. This is recorded in Domesday Book not only in its current form but also as *Grandham*, *Granham*, and *Graham*; it was apparently named as the 'gravelly place', from Old English *grand* 'gravel' + *hām* 'homestead'. The surname was taken to Scotland in the 12th century by Sir William de Graham, founder of a famous clan. The earls of Montrose were among his descendants.

VARIANTS: **Grahame, Graeme.**

Grant ♂ Transferred use of the surname, common in Scotland, where it is the name of a famous clan. It is derived from a nickname meaning 'large' (Anglo-Norman *grand*). In the United States the name is sometimes bestowed in honour of the Civil War general and 18th president, Ulysses S. Grant (1822–85).

Granville ♂ From one of the Norman baronial names that subsequently became aristocratic English surnames and are now used intermittently as boys' given names. This one derives from any of several places in Normandy named with Old French *grand* 'large' + *ville* 'settlement'.

Gray ♂ See ▷Grey.

Grayson ♂ Transferred use of the surname, in origin a patronymic for someone who was the son of a steward (Middle English *greyve*, from Old Norse *greifi*).

Greer ♀ Transferred use of the Scottish surname, which originated in the Middle Ages from a contracted form of ▷Gregor. It has become known as a girl's name in the English-speaking

world through the fame of the actress Greer Garson (1908–96), whose mother's maiden name it was.

VARIANT: **Grier.**

Greg ♂ Short form of ▷Gregory and ▷Gregor.

VARIANT: **Gregg.**

Gregor ♂ Scottish form of ▷Gregory, now in wider use in the English-speaking world.

Gregory ♂ Via Latin *Gregorius* from the post-classical Greek name *Gregōrios* 'watchful' (a derivative of *gregōrein* 'to watch, be vigilant'). The name was a very popular one among the early Christians, who were mindful of the injunction 'be sober, be vigilant' (1 Peter 5:8). It was borne by a number of early saints. The most important, in honour of whom the name was often bestowed from medieval times onwards, were Gregory of Nazianzen (*c*.329–90), Gregory of Nyssa (d. *c*.395), Gregory of Tours (538–94), and Pope Gregory the Great (*c*.540–604). A famous bearer of the name in modern times is the film star Gregory Peck (1916–2003). The name has traditionally been popular in Scotland, where it is often found in the form **Gregor.**

SHORT FORMS: **Greg; Greg(g), Greig** (Scottish).

COGNATES: Irish: **Gréagóir.** Scottish Gaelic: **Griogair.** Welsh: **Grigor.** German: **Gregor.** Dutch: **Joris.** Scandinavian: **Greger.** Danish, Norwegian: **Gregers.** French: **Grégoire; Grégory** (Provençal in origin, now more fashionable than the traditional form). Spanish, Italian: **Gregorio.** Portuguese: **Grégorio.** Russian: **Grigori.** Polish: **Grzegorz.** Czech: **Řehoř.** Croatian: **Grgur.** Slovenian: **Gregor.** Finnish: **Reijo.** Hungarian: **Gergely.**

Grenville ♂ Transferred use of the surname, in origin a Norman name from Grainville-la-Teinturière in Seine-Inférieure. George Grenville (1712–70) and his son William (1759–1834) both achieved political prominence, the former serving as prime minister (1763–65), and his son, who was raised to the peerage in 1790, as home secretary and later as foreign secretary in William Pitt the Younger's administration, before himself serving briefly as prime minister (1806–7).

Greta ♀ Short form of *Margareta*, a Latinate form of ▷Margaret. As an independent given name it became fairly popular in the English-speaking world as a result of the fame of the Swedish-born film actress Greta Garbo (1905–92, born Greta Louisa Gustafsson).

VARIANT: **Gretta**.

Grete ♀ German and Danish: short form of *Margarete* (see ▷Margaret), now also occasionally used as an independent given name in the English-speaking world.

Greville ♂ Transferred use of the surname, which is a Norman baronial name from Gréville in La Manche. The Greville family were earls of Warwick, and held Warwick Castle from the time of Queen Elizabeth I, who granted it to her favourite Fulke Greville (1554–1628).

Grey ♂ Transferred use of the surname, in origin a nickname for someone with grey hair or a grey beard (from Old English *græg*). In Scotland and Ireland it has also been used as a translation of various Gaelic surnames derived from *riabhach* 'brindled, grey', such as *Mac Riabhaich*.

VARIANT: **Gray** (the usual U.S. form of the vocabulary word).

Grier ♀ Variant spelling of ▷Greer.

Griselda ♀ Of uncertain origin, possibly from a Germanic name derived from *gris* 'grey' + *hild* 'battle'. It became popular in the Middle Ages with reference to the tale of 'patient Griselda' (told by Boccaccio and Chaucer), who was taken as a model of the patient, long-suffering wife.

Grizel ♀ Medieval vernacular form of ▷Griselda, used particularly in Scotland, and in the north of England at least as late as the 18th century. The name has now died out, no doubt in part because of its similarity to the vocabulary word *grizzle* meaning 'to grumble or whine'.

Grover ♂ Transferred use of the surname, in origin a local name for someone who lived near a grove of trees (Old English *grāf*). Use as a given name is partly due to the U.S. president (Stephen) Grover Cleveland (1837–1908).

Gudrun ♀ Scandinavian: from an Old Norse female personal name composed of *guð* 'god' + *rūn* 'secret lore'. In Norse legend this was the name borne by the heroine of the *Volsungasaga*, sister of Gunnar and wife of Sigurd, whose destruction she brought about. The name was revived in the second part of the 19th century, and is now also used in Germany and occasionally in the English-speaking world, possibly under the influence of the character Gutrune in Wagner's *Götterdämmerung* or Gudrun Brangwen, one of the central characters in D.H. Lawrence's *Women in Love* (1920), which was made into a film in 1969.

Guinevere ♀ From the Old French form of the Welsh name **Gwenhwyfar**. It is famous as the name of King Arthur's wife, who in most versions of the Arthurian legends is unfaithful to him, having fallen in love with Sir Lancelot. See also ▷Gaynor and ▷Jennifer.

Guni ♂ Jewish: meaning 'painted, coloured' in Hebrew; it is borne in the Bible by a son of Naphtali and grandson of Jacob (Genesis 46:24).

Gus ♂ Short form of ▷Augustus, ▷Angus, or ▷Gustave. In the case of Gus the Theatre Cat, a character in T.S. Eliot's *Old Possum's Book of Practical Cats* (1939), it is a short form of *Asparagus*!

PET FORM: **Gussie**.

g

Gustave ♂ Anglicized form of the Scandinavian name **Gustav** (see Scandinavian appendix), used occasionally in the English-speaking world since the late 19th century.

Guy ♂ From an Old French name, of Germanic (Frankish) origin, originally a short form of a compound name starting with *witu* 'wood' or *wīt* 'wide'. This was adopted by the Normans and introduced by them to England. In Old French initial *w-* regularly became *gu-*. The usual Norman forms of the name were *Gy* or *Guido*. In medieval Latin the same name is found as *Wido*. It was a popular name among the Normans, enhanced no doubt by the romance of Guy of Warwick, recounting the exploits of a folk hero of the Crusades.

Gwen ♀ Short form of ▷Gwendolen or Gwenllian (see Welsh appendix), or an independent name from Welsh *gwen*, the feminine form of *gwyn* 'white, fair; blessed, holy'.

Gwendolen ♀ Welsh name (see Welsh appendix), borne, according to Geoffrey of Monmouth, by the wife of a mythical Welsh king Locrine, who abandoned her for a German princess called Estrildis. Gwendolen in revenge had Estrildis and her daughter Sabrina drowned in the River Severn. The name is borne by one of the principal characters in Oscar Wilde's play *The Importance of Being Earnest* (first performed in 1895). It became more widely used in the English-speaking world from the mid 19th century, though its popularity has waned since the 1930s.

VARIANTS: **Gwendolin(e)**, **Gwendolyn(e)**; **Gwendoline** (formed under the influence of ▷Caroline and other girls' names ending in *-ine*).

Gwyneth ♀ Welsh: altered form of Gwynedd (see Welsh appendix), used as a girl's name. Its popularity from the late 19th century, at first in Wales and then more widely in the English-speaking world, seems to have been due originally to the influence of the popular novelist Annie Harriet Hughes (1852–1910), who adopted the pen-name Gwyneth Vaughan.

VARIANT: **Gwynneth**.

Gyles ♂ Variant spelling of ▷Giles.

Gypsy ♀ From the vocabulary word for a Romany or traveller. The word derives from *Egyptian*, as in the Middle Ages the Romanies were believed to have come to Europe from Egypt; in fact they dispersed from an original home in north India. This name may sometimes be chosen by parents who hope that their daughter will exhibit a free spirit. The American dancer Gypsy Rose Lee may have been an influence, although in her case the name was a nickname.

Gytha ♀ From an Old English female personal name, a short form of various compound names formed with *gyð* 'strife'. This name was born in the 11th century by the wife of Godwin, Earl of Wessex. It was revived in Victorian times and has been used occasionally since then.

Hh

Habacuc ♂ Biblical name, meaning 'embrace' in Hebrew, borne by one of the twelve minor prophets, author of the book of the Bible that bears his name. The name is hardly, if ever, used in modern times, but was occasionally used by Puritans and Dissenters from the 17th century to the 19th.

VARIANT: Habakkuk (spelling used in the Authorized Version of the Bible).

Hadassah ♀ Hebrew form of ▷Esther, which is the Persian form of the name. (See Esther 2:7.) This form is now sometimes chosen as a modern Jewish given name.

SHORT FORM: Dassah.

Hadley ♂ Transferred use of the surname, which arose in the medieval period as a local name from various places named Hadley or Hadleigh; most were named with Old English *hǣd* 'heath, heather' + *lēah*.

VARIANT: Hadleigh.

Hagar ♀ Biblical name (meaning 'flight' in Hebrew, although the biblical character so called was Egyptian) borne by a handmaid of Abraham's wife Sarah. Sarah let Hagar conceive a child by Abraham since she herself was barren, but she later resented her and treated her so harshly that she fled. Hagar was sent back by an angel, and her son Ishmael became Abraham's first child.

Haidee ♀ As the name of a character in Byron's poem *Don Juan* (1819–24), this may have been intended to be connected with the classical Greek adjective *aidoios* 'modest'. In modern use it is taken as a variant of ▷Heidi.

Hailey ♀ Variant spelling of ▷Hayley.

Hal ♂ Short form of ▷Harry, of medieval origin; now used occasionally as a given name in its own right. It was used by Shakespeare in *King Henry IV* as the name of the king's son, the future Henry V. Similar substitution of -*l* for -*r* has occurred in derivatives of *Terry* (*Tel*), *Derek* (*Del*), and in girls' names such as *Sal(ly)* from *Sarah*.

Hale ♂ Transferred use of the surname, in origin a local name for someone living in a nook or recess (Old English *halh*).

Haley ♀ Mainly U.S.: variant spelling of ▷Hayley.

Hall ♂ Transferred use of the surname, which originated as a local name for someone, usually a servant or retainer, who lived at a manor house (Old English *heall*).

Hallie ♀ Variant spelling of ▷Hayley.

Hamilton ♂ Mainly North American: transferred use of the Scottish surname. This was brought to Scotland in or before the 13th century from a village (now deserted) called Hamilton or Hameldune, near Barkby in Leicestershire (named with Old English *hamel* 'blunt, flat-topped' + *dūn* 'hill'). It is the surname of an enormously widespread and influential family, who acquired many titles, including the dukedom of Hamilton. The town near Glasgow so called is named after the family, not vice versa. Use as a given name seems to have begun in the United States in honour of Alexander Hamilton (?1757–1804), who was Secretary of the Treasury under George Washington and did much to establish the political and financial system on which the industrial growth and prosperity of the United States came to

h

be founded. He was killed in a duel with the irascible Aaron Burr.

Hamish ♂ Anglicized spelling of the vocative case, *Sheumais*, of the Scottish Gaelic version of ▷James. Although still predominantly a Scottish name, it is now sometimes chosen by families with no Scottish connections.

Hamza ♂ Muslim name probably meaning 'steadfast'. See Ḥamza in Arab appendix.

VARIANT: **Hamzah**.

Handel ♂ From the surname of the composer, adopted as a given name particularly by the music-loving Welsh (cf. ▷Haydn). Georg Friedrich Handel (1685–1759), who came to England with George I when he succeeded to the English throne in 1714, is often regarded as the greatest exponent of the German baroque. His surname is derived from a diminutive form of the given name Hans (see German appendix).

Hank ♂ Originally a medieval back-formation from *Hankin*, which is composed of *Han* (a short form of *Jehan* ▷John) + the Middle English diminutive suffix -*kin*. However, the suffix was mistaken for the Anglo-Norman diminutive -*in*, hence the form *Hank*. *Hank* is now sometimes used as an independent given name in North America, where it is usually taken as a pet form of ▷Henry. It has more or less died out in Britain.

Hannah ♀ Biblical name, borne by the mother of the prophet Samuel (1 Samuel 1:2), Hebrew *Hanna*. It is derived from a Hebrew word meaning 'He (i.e. God) has favoured me (i.e. with a child)'. See also ▷Anne. This form of the name was taken up as a given name by the Puritans in the 16th and 17th centuries and remained popular until the late 19th century. Thereafter it fell somewhat from favour but has enjoyed a massive revival since the 1990s.

VARIANT: **Hanna, Hana**.

Hannibal ♂ Name of the Carthaginian general Hannibal Barca (247–182 BC), who led an army from Spain across the Alps and into Italy to attack the Romans. He was eventually defeated by Scipio at the battle of Zama, but not until he had shaken the Roman republic to its core. His name is composed of the Phoenician element *hann* 'grace, favour' + the name of the god *Baal* 'lord'. It has recently been made famous by the character of the cannibalistic maniac Hannibal Lecter, created by Thomas Harris in the novels *Red Dragon* (1981) and its sequels *Silence of the Lambs* (1988) and *Hannibal* (1999).

Happy ♀ Modern coinage from the vocabulary word (originally meaning 'prosperous', a derivative of *hap* 'chance, good luck', of Old Norse origin), occasionally used for the sake of the good omen of its meaning; compare ▷Merry.

Harding ♂ Mainly U.S.: transferred use of the surname, which is derived from a medieval English given name. The Old English form was *Hearding*, a derivative (originally patronymic in form) of *Heard* 'hardy, brave, strong', a byname or short form of the various compound personal names containing this element. Use as a given name may have been influenced by the U.S. president Warren Gamaliel Harding (1865–1923).

Hardy ♂ Mainly U.S.: transferred use of the surname, in origin a nickname for a brave or stout-hearted man (from Middle English, Old French *hardi*, of Germanic origin).

Harlan ♂ Mainly U.S.: transferred use of the surname, in origin a local name from any of various places in England called *Harland*, from Old English *hār* 'grey', *hær* 'rock, tumulus', or *hara* 'hare' + *land* 'tract of land'. Use as a given name honours the American judge John Marshall Harlan (1833–1911), a conservative Republican who was nevertheless a pioneering supporter of civil rights in the Supreme Court. He was a descendant of the Quaker George Harland from Durham, England, who emigrated to Delaware in 1687, and became governor there in 1695.

VARIANT: **Harland.**

Harley ♂, ♀ Transferred use of the surname, in origin a local name from places in Shropshire and West Yorkshire, so called from Old English *hær* 'rock, heap of stones' or *hara* 'hare' + *lēah* 'wood, clearing'. Among bikers it has been used with the Harley Davidson motorcycle in mind.

Harmony ♀ From the vocabulary word meaning 'concord, agreement'. The name has been in occasional use since the 19th century.

Harold ♂ From an Old English personal name derived from *here* 'army' + *weald* 'ruler'. In pre-Conquest England, this was reinforced by the related Old Norse name *Haraldr*, introduced by Scandinavian settlers. The name was not at all popular in England after the Conquest, probably because of its association with the unfortunate King Harold, killed at the Battle of Hastings in 1066. It was used in some parts of Nottinghamshire in the 16th and 17th centuries, and revived more generally, along with a number of other Old English names, in the 19th century, when it suddenly became extremely popular.

Harper ♂, ♀ Mainly U.S.: transferred use of the surname, in origin an occupational name for someone who played the harp. As a girl's name it is associated in particular with the southern American writer Harper Lee, author of *To Kill a Mockingbird* (1960).

Harriet ♀ Anglicized form of French *Henriette*, a feminine diminutive of ▷Henry (French *Henri*) coined in the 17th century. It was quite common in England in the 18th and early 19th centuries.

PET FORM: **Hattie.**

Harriette ♀ Variant of ▷Harriet, probably coined to look more feminine, but it could be a reconstructed form, blending ▷Harriet with its source ▷Henriette.

Harris ♂ Transferred use of the surname, in origin a patronymic from the medieval English personal name ▷Harry.

Harrison ♂ Transferred use of the surname, which originated as a patronymic meaning 'son of Harry'. Use as a given name may have been influenced by the U.S. presidents William Henry Harrison (1773–1841) and his grandson Benjamin Harrison (1833–1901). A more recent influence is the actor Harrison Ford (b. 1942).

Harry ♂ Pet form of ▷Henry. This was the usual English form of *Henry* in the Middle Ages and later. It was used by Shakespeare, for example, as the familiar name of the mature King Henry V (compare ▷Hal). Since the publication of the first of J. K. Rowling's Harry Potter titles (*Harry Potter and the Philosopher's Stone*) in 1997, *Harry* has become extremely popular as an independent given name.

Hartley ♂ Transferred use of the surname, in origin a local name from any of the numerous places so called. Most (for example, those in Berkshire, Dorset, Hampshire, and Kent) are so called from Old English *heorot* 'hart, male deer' + *lēah* 'wood, clearing'. One in Northumberland is from *heorot* + *hlāw* 'hill', and one in Cumbria is probably from *heard* 'hard' + *clā* 'claw', i.e. tongue of land in the fork of a river.

Harvard ♂ Mainly U.S.: transferred use of the surname, which is from the Old English personal name *Hereweard*, a compound of *here* 'army' + *weard* 'guard', which was borne by an 11th-century thane of Lincolnshire who led resistance against the advancing Normans. The Old Norse cognate *Hervarr* was also common in the north midlands of England. Use as a given name has no doubt been influenced by Harvard College in Cambridge, Massachusetts. This takes its name from John Harvard (1607–38), who emigrated from London in 1637 and left half his wealth and the whole of his library to support the newly founded college.

Harvey ♂ Transferred use of the surname, which is derived from a Breton personal name composed of *haer* 'battle' + *vy* 'worthy'. It was introduced to Britain by Bretons who settled in East Anglia and elsewhere in the wake of the Norman Conquest.

SHORT FORMS: **Harv(e)**.

Hassan ♂ Muslim name meaning 'good, beautiful'. See Hasan in Arabic appendix.

Hattie ♀ Pet form of ▷Harriet, now sometimes used independently.

Hawk ♂ From the term denoting the bird of prey (Middle English *hauk*, from Old English *hafoc*), or a transferred use of the surname derived from this word.

VARIANT: **Hawke**.

Hawkin ♂ Transferred use of the surname, in origin a medieval diminutive form of ▷Hal.

Haya ♀ Jewish: feminine form of ▷Hyam, meaning 'life' in Hebrew.

Haydn ♂ From the surname of the composer, adopted in his honour particularly by the music-loving Welsh (compare ▷Handel). Josef Haydn (1732–1809) was court composer and kapellmeister to the powerful Count Nicholas Esterhazy, and spent most of his working life at the Esterhazy palace near Vienna. His surname is a respelling of the nickname *Heiden* 'heathen' (Middle High German *heiden*, Old High German *heidano*).

VARIANTS: **Hayden, Haydon**.

Hayley ♀ Transferred use of the surname, which derives from a place name, probably Hailey in Oxfordshire, which was originally named from Old English *hēg* 'hay' + *lēah* 'clearing'. Use as a given name began in the 1960s, inspired perhaps by the actress Hayley Mills (b. 1946), daughter of Sir John Mills and Mary Hayley Bell, and enjoyed great popularity until the late 1990s.

VARIANTS: **Haylee, Hailey, Hailee, Haley, Haleigh, Hallie**.

Hazel ♀ From the vocabulary word denoting the tree (Old English *hæsel*), or its light reddish-brown nuts. This is one of the most successful of the names coined in the 19th century from words denoting plants.

Heath ♂ Transferred use of the surname, in origin a local name for someone who lived on a patch of heathland (Old English *hǣð*).

Heather ♀ From the vocabulary word denoting the hardy, brightly coloured plant (Middle English *hather*; the spelling was altered in the 18th century as a result of folk etymological association with *heath*). The name was first used in the late 19th century and became particularly popular from the mid-1940s.

Heaven ♀ Mainly U.S.: from the vocabulary word denoting the sky or the abode of God (Old English *heofon*), a place of eternal happiness.

Hebe ♀ Pronounced 'hee-bee': from a Greek name, a feminine form of the adjective *hēbos* 'young'. This was borne in Greek mythology by a minor goddess who was a personification of youth. She was a daughter of Zeus and the wife of Hephaistos; it was their duty to act as cup-bearer to the gods. The name was taken up in England in the late 19th century, but it has fallen out of fashion again.

Heber ♂ Anglicized form of Irish Éibhear (see Irish appendix). *Heber* is also a biblical name (meaning 'enclave' in Hebrew), borne by various minor characters in the Bible.

Hector ♂ Name borne in classical legend by the Trojan champion who was killed by the Greek Achilles. His name (Greek *Hektōr*) is probably an agent derivative of Greek *ekhein* 'to restrain'. It was never popular in England, but there are occasional examples from the Middle Ages. In Scotland it was used as a classicized form of the Gaelic personal name *Eachann*, which is composed of *each* 'horse' + *donn* 'brown'. It has been moderately popular in the United States since the 1940s.

Hedley ♂ Transferred use of the surname, in origin a local name from any of several places called Hedley or Headley, for example in Hampshire, Surrey, Durham, and Northumberland, all named from Old English *hǣ* 'heather' + *lēah* 'wood, clearing'.
VARIANT: **Headley**.

Heidi ♀ Swiss pet form of *Adelheid*, the German form of ▷Adelaide. The name is now also popular in the English-speaking world, largely due to Johanna Spyri's children's classic *Heidi* (1881).
VARIANT: **Heide**.

Helen ♀ English vernacular form of the name (Greek *Helēnē*) borne in classical legend by a famous beauty, wife of Menelaus, whose seizure by the Trojan prince Paris sparked off the Trojan War. Her name is of uncertain origin; it may be connected with a word meaning 'ray' or 'sunbeam'; compare Greek *hēlios* 'sun'. It has sometimes been taken as connected with the Greek word meaning 'Greek', *Hellēn*, but this is doubtful. In the early Christian period the name was borne by the mother of the Emperor Constantine, who is now usually known by the Latin version of her name, *Helena*. She is credited with having found the True Cross in Jerusalem. She was born in about 248, probably in Bithynia. However, in medieval England it was believed that she had been born in Britain, which greatly increased the popularity of the name there.

Helena ♀ Latinate form of ▷Helen, used also in Germany, the Netherlands, Scandinavia, and Eastern Europe.

Hélène ♀ French form of ▷Helen, now in fairly frequent use in the English-speaking world, usually without the accents.

Helga ♀ From an Old Norse female personal name, a derivative of the adjective *heilagr* 'prosperous, successful' (from *heill* 'hale, hearty, happy'). It was introduced to England before the Conquest, but did not survive long. It has been reintroduced to the English-speaking world in the 20th century from Scandinavia and Germany. See also ▷Olga.

Héloïse ♀ French variant of ▷Éloise, which enjoyed a revival of popularity in the 18th century after publication of Rousseau's philosophical novel *La Nouvelle Héloïse* (1761).

Henrietta ♀ Latinate form of French ▷Henriette. Henrietta Maria (1609–69), the wife of King Charles I, was the daughter of Henry IV of France, in whose honour the name was sometimes chosen by gentry families in the 17th century. It enjoyed a revival in the late 19th century. See also ▷Harriet.
PET FORMS: **Hennie, Hettie, Hattie**.

Henriette ♀ French: feminine diminutive of *Henri*, the French form of ▷Henry, now in occasional use in the English-speaking world.

Henry ♂ A perennially popular given name, of Continental Germanic origin, from *haim* 'home' + *rīc* 'power, ruler'. It was an Old French name, adopted by the Normans and introduced by them to Britain. It has been borne by eight kings of England. Not until the 17th century did the form *Henry* (as opposed to ▷Harry) become the standard vernacular form, mainly under the influence of the Latin form *Henricus* and French *Henri*.
PET FORMS: ▷**Hal**, ▷**Hank**, ▷**Harry**.
COGNATES: Irish: **Anraí, Éinrí**. Scottish Gaelic: **Eanraig**. German: **Heinrich; Henrik, Hinrich** (Low German). Dutch: **Hendrik**. Scandinavian: **Hen(d)rik**.

French: Henri. Spanish: Enrique. Catalan: Enric. Portuguese: Henrique. Italian: Enrico. Polish: Henryk. Czech: Jindřich. Slovenian: Henrik. Finnish: Heikki. Hungarian: Henrik. Lithuanian: Henrikas.

Hephzibah ♀ Biblical name (meaning 'my delight is in her' (i.e. a new-born daughter)), borne by the wife of Hezekiah, King of Judah; she was the mother of Manasseh (2 Kings 21). It is also used in the prophecies of Isaiah as an allusive name for the land of Israel (compare ▷Beulah).

VARIANT: Hepzibah.

PET FORMS: Hepsie, ▷Effie.

Herbert ♂ From an Old French name of Germanic (Frankish) origin, introduced to Britain by the Normans. It is derived from *heri*, *hari* 'army' + *berht* 'bright, famous'. An Old English form, *Herebeorht*, existed in England before the Conquest, but was superseded by the Norman form, which gave rise to an important surname. The family in question were earls of Pembroke in the 16th and 17th centuries; they included the poet George Herbert. By the end of the Middle Ages *Herbert* was little used, although it remained a favourite with some families, notably the Saint Quintins of East Yorkshire. Its greater frequency in Britain from the 19th century onwards is due partly to the trend for the revival of medieval names of Germanic origin and partly to the trend for the transferred use of surnames.

SHORT FORM: Herb.

PET FORM: Herbie.

Hercules ♂ Latin form of the name of the Greek mythological hero *Hēraklēs*, whose name means 'glory of Hera'. He was the son of Zeus, king of the gods, by Alcmene, a mortal woman. In many versions of the legend, despite the meaning of the name, Hera, chief goddess in the Greek pantheon and wife of Zeus, is portrayed as the implacable enemy of Hercules, the child of her unfaithful husband. Hercules was noted for his exceptional physical strength; according to the myth, he was set a daunting series of twelve labours, and after successfully completing them he was made a god. The name has occasionally been used in the English-speaking world, under European influence. In the Highlands of Scotland it has been used as an Anglicized form of the rare Gaelic name Athairne.

Herman ♂ English form of Hermann (see German appendix), from a Germanic personal name derived from *heri*, *hari* 'army' + *man* 'man'. The name was in use among the Normans and was borne by many immigrants from the Low Countries in the 15th century. Perhaps because of that it continued in occasional use well into the 1700s. It was revived more generally in Britain in the 19th century, when it also became common in America, most probably as a result of the influence of German immigrants.

Hermia ♀ Latinate derivative of the name of the Greek god *Hermes* (compare ▷Hermione). This was used by Shakespeare for the name of a character in *A Midsummer Night's Dream* (1595).

Hermione ♀ Name borne in classical mythology by a daughter of Helen and Menelaus, who grew up to marry her cousin Orestes. It is evidently a derivative of *Hermes*, name of the messenger god, but the formation is not clear. The name was used by Shakespeare for one of the main characters in *A Winter's Tale* (1610), and is still in occasional use.

Hershel ♂ Jewish (Yiddish): pet form of ▷Hirsh, derived from a dialect variant.

VARIANTS: Herschel, Heshel, Heshi.

Heskel ♂ Jewish: Yiddish form of ▷Ezekiel.

Hesketh ♂ Transferred use of the surname, in origin a local name from any of the various places in northern

England named with Old Norse *hestr* 'horse' + *skeiðr* 'racecourse'. Horse racing and horse fighting were favourite sports among the Scandinavian settlers in England.

Hester ♀ Variant of ▷Esther, of medieval origin. For a long while the two forms were interchangeable, the addition or dropping of *h-* being commonplace in a whole range of words, but now they are generally regarded as two distinct names.

Hettie ♀ Pet form of ▷Henrietta and occasionally also of ▷Hester.
VARIANT: **Hetty**.

Hewie ♂ Scottish and northern English: variant spelling of ▷Hughie.

Hilary ♀, ♂ From the medieval form of the (post-classical) Latin masculine name *Hilarius* (a derivative of *hilaris* 'cheerful') and its feminine form *Hilaria*. From the Middle Ages onwards, the name was borne principally by men (in honour of the 4th-century theologian St Hilarius of Poitiers). Now, however, it is given almost exclusively to girls.
VARIANTS: **Hillary** (the usual U.S. spelling), **Hilarie** ♀.

Hilda ♀ Of Germanic origin, a Latinized short form of any of several girls' names derived from *hild* 'battle'. Many of these are found in both Continental Germanic and Old English forms. St Hilda (614–80) was a Northumbrian princess who founded the abbey at Whitby and became its abbess. The name all but died out by the 14th century. It was strongly revived in the 19th century. Since the 1930s, however, it has again fallen from favour.
VARIANT: **Hylda**.

Hildegard ♀ From an old Germanic female personal name composed of *hild* 'battle' + *gard* 'enclosure'. It was borne by the second wife of Charlemagne and by the mystical writer Hildegard of

Bingen (1098–1179), in whose music and writings there has been great interest in recent decades.
VARIANT: **Hildegarde**.

Hill ♂ Transferred use of the surname, in origin a local name for someone who lived on or near a hill (Old English *hyll*). As a first name it may in part represent a short form of ▷Hilton.

Hillary ♀ Variant spelling of ▷Hilary, found mainly in North America.

Hillel ♂ Jewish: apparently derived from the Hebrew word meaning 'praise'. It was borne in the Bible by the father of one of the Judges of Israel (Judges 12:13). It was also the name of an outstanding 1st-century rabbi and has been a popular Jewish name as a result of his fame.

Hilly ♀ Pet form of ▷Hilary or ▷Hillary.

Hilton ♂ Transferred use of the surname, in origin a local name from any of the many places named with the Old English elements *hyll* 'hill' + *tūn* 'enclosure, settlement'. As a first name it is sometimes chosen because of its association with the chain of luxury hotels founded by Conrad Hilton (1887–1979).

Hinde ♀ Jewish: from Yiddish *hinde* 'hind, female deer' (modern German *Hinde*), originally an affectionate pet name or female equivalent of ▷Hirsh.

Hiram ♂ Biblical name, borne by a king of Tyre who is repeatedly mentioned in the Bible (2 Samuel 2:11; 1 Kings 5; 9:11; 10:11; 1 Chronicles 14:1; 2 Chronicles 2:11) as supplying wood, craftsmen, and money to enable David and Solomon to construct various buildings. It was also the name of a craftsman of Tyre who worked in brass for Solomon (1 Kings 7:13). The name is presumably of Semitic origin, but is probably a Phoenician name; if it is Hebrew, it may be a shortened form of *Ahiram* 'brother of the exalted'. In England, the name was taken up by the

h

Puritans in the 17th century, but soon dropped out of regular use. It is still used occasionally in the United States.

Hirsh ♂ Jewish: from a Yiddish vocabulary word meaning 'hart, deer' (modern German *Hirsch*).
VARIANT: Hirsch.

Hobart ♂ Transferred use of the surname, itself representing a variant of the given name ▷Hubert. In some cases the given name may derive from the city in Tasmania, named after Robert Hobart, 4th Earl of Buckingham, who was Secretary of State for War and the Colonies at the time (1804) when it was founded.

Holly ♀ From the vocabulary word denoting the evergreen shrub or tree (Middle English *holi(n)*, Old English *holegn*). The name was first used at the beginning of the 20th century, and has been particularly popular since the 1990s. It is bestowed especially on girls born around Christmas, when sprigs of holly are traditionally taken indoors to decorate rooms.
VARIANT: Hollie.

Homer ♂ English form of the name of the Greek epic poet *Homĕros*, now regularly used as a given name in the United States (compare ▷Virgil), where it has been immortalized by the cartoon character Homer Simpson in the television series *The Simpsons*. Many theories have been put forward to explain the origin of the name of the poet, but none is conclusive. It is identical in form with the Greek vocabulary word *homĕros* 'hostage'.

Honesty ♀ From the vocabulary word denoting the quality (via Old French, from Latin *honestas*, connected with *honor* 'honour'). It was rare as a name until the 20th century, but at least one exmple from the 17th century is recorded. Modern use may have also been influenced by the fact that there is a flowering plant named with this word.

Honey ♀ From the vocabulary word (Old English *huneg*). Honey was used throughout the Middle Ages in Europe as a sweetener; sugar was not introduced to Europe from the New World until the 16th century. The word has long been used as a term of endearment. Modern use as a given name was prompted by a character in Margaret Mitchell's novel *Gone with the Wind* (1936), made into a film in 1939.

Honor ♀ Variant spelling of ▷Honour; the dominant spelling of both the vocabulary word and the given name in the United States today. This is now the more frequent spelling of the name in Britain also, used, for example, for the actress Honor Blackman (b. 1926).

Honora ♀ Latinate elaboration of ▷Honor, used mainly in Ireland.
VARIANT: Honorah.

Honore ♀ French form of ▷Honoria, also used occasionally in the English-speaking world.

Honoria ♀ Feminine form of the Late Latin male name *Honorius* (a derivative of *honor* 'honour'), a name borne by various early saints, including a 7th-century archbishop of Canterbury. It is occasionally used in the English-speaking world as an elaborated form of ▷Honour.

Honour ♀ From the vocabulary word denoting the quality (via Old French, from Latin *honor*). The name was popular with the Puritans in the 17th century and has remained in modest use to the present day.
VARIANT: Honor.

Hope ♀ From the vocabulary word (Old English *hopa*) denoting the quality, in particular the Christian quality of expectation in the resurrection and in eternal life. The name was created by the Puritans and has been one of their most successful coinages.

Hopkin ♂ Transferred use of the surname, now found mainly in Wales. It is derived from a medieval given name, a pet form (with the diminutive suffix -*kin*) of *Hob*, a short form of ▷Robert that probably had its origin through English mishearing of the Norman pronunciation of *R-*.

Horace ♂ From the old Roman family name ▷Horatius. The name was once widely used among admirers of the Roman poet Horace (Quintus Horatius Flaccus), but it is at present out of fashion. See also ▷Horatio.

Horatia ♀ Feminine form of Latin ▷Horatius. It has never been common in the English-speaking world, but was borne, for example, by the daughter of Horatio Nelson.

Horatio ♂ Variant of ▷Horace, influenced by the Latin form ▷Horatius and the Italian form *Orazio*. It is chiefly known as having been borne by Admiral Horatio Nelson (1758–1805), victor of many sea battles with the French during the Napoleonic Wars, culminating in the Battle of Trafalgar, in which he was killed.

Horatius ♂ An old Roman family name, which is of obscure, possibly Etruscan, origin. Its most famous bearer was the Roman poet Quintus Horatius Flaccus (65–8 BC), generally known in English as ▷Horace. From the mid-19th century, the name has occasionally been used by English speakers in its original Latin form. This probably owes more to the *Lays of Ancient Rome* (1842) by Thomas Babbington Macaulay than to the poet Horace. Macaulay relates, in verse that was once enormously popular, the exploit of an early Roman hero, recounting 'How Horatius kept the bridge'.

Hortense ♀ French form of Latin *Hortensia*, the feminine version of the old Roman family name *Hortensius*. This is of uncertain origin, but may be

derived from Latin *hortus* 'garden'. The given name began to be used in the English-speaking world in the 19th century, but is not common today.

Howard ♂ Transferred use of the surname of an English noble family. The surname has a large number of possible origins, but in the case of the noble family early forms often have the spelling *Haward*, and so it is probably from a Scandinavian personal name derived from *hā* 'high' + *varðr* 'guardian'. (The traditional derivation from the Old English name *Hereweard* 'army guardian' is untenable.) It is now a widespread given name.

Howell ♂ Anglicized form of the Welsh name Hywel (see Welsh appendix), or a transferred use of the surname derived from that name.

Hrothgar ♂ Old English cognate form of ▷Roger. The name is borne in the Old English narrative poem *Beowulf* by the Danish king who suffered the depradations of the monster Grendel for twelve years. In modern times it has been borne by Hrothgar J. Habakkuk (1915–2002), a former vice-chancellor of Oxford University.

Hubert ♂ Old French name of Germanic (Frankish) origin, derived from *hug* 'heart, mind, spirit' + *berht* 'bright, famous'. It was popular among the Normans, who introduced it to Britain, where it was later reinforced by settlers from the Low Countries. An 8th-century St Hubert succeeded St Lambert as bishop of Maastricht and is regarded as the patron of hunters, since, like St Eustace, he is supposed to have seen a vision of Christ crucified between the antlers of a stag.

Hudson ♂ Transferred use of the surname, originally a patronymic from the medieval personal name *Hudde*, a name of complex origin. It is usually explained as a pet form of ▷Hugh, but there was a pre-existing Old English personal name, *Hūda*, which may well still have been in use at the time of the Norman Conquest and have subsequently been absorbed by Hugh and its many diminutives. It appears that Hudde was also regarded as a pet form of ▷Richard.

Hugh ♂ From an Old French name, *Hugues*, *Hugo*, of Germanic (Frankish) origin, derived from *hug* 'heart, mind, spirit'. It was originally a short form of various compound names containing this element. This was borne by the aristocracy of medieval France, adopted by the Normans, and introduced by them to Britain. It was consistently one of the most popular boys' names in the Middle Ages in England, but fell out of favour in the 16th century until it was revived in the 20th century. Little Hugh of Lincoln was a child supposed in the Middle Ages to have been murdered by Jews in about 1255, a legend responsible for several outbursts of anti-Semitism at various times. The story is referred to by Chaucer in *The Prioress's Tale*. He is not to be confused with St Hugh of Lincoln (1140–1200), bishop of Lincoln (1186–1200), who was noted for his charity and good works, his piety, and his defence of the Church against the State. Since the later Middle Ages *Hugh* has also been used as an Anglicized form of the Gaelic name Aodh (see Irish or Scottish appendix).

Hughie ♂ Pet form of ▷Hugh, also sometimes used independently.
VARIANTS: **Hewie, Huey.**

Hugo ♂ Latinized form of ▷Hugh, used throughout the Middle Ages in official documents, and now enjoying a revival as a given name.

Hulda ♀ Biblical name (meaning 'weasel' in Hebrew), borne by a prophetess who foretold to Josiah the destruction of Jerusalem (2 Kings 22).
VARIANT: **Huldah.**

Humbert ♂ From an Old French name of Germanic (Frankish) origin, derived from *hun* 'bear-cub, warrior' +

berht 'bright, famous'. It was adopted by the Normans and introduced by them to Britain. However, it was not common in Britain in the Middle Ages, and has always had a Continental flavour. It was used by Vladimir Nabokov for the name of the demented pederast, Humbert Humbert, who is the narrator in his novel *Lolita* (1955).

Humphrey ♂ From a Norman name, *Hunfrid*, of Germanic origin, derived from *hun* 'bear-cub, warrior' + *fred*, *frid* 'peace'. The Norman form absorbed the native Old English form, *Hunfrith*, which existed in England before the Conquest. The spelling with *-ph-* reflects classicizing influence. Since the 16th century it has enjoyed a modest popularity in England, having been borne most notably by the youngest son of King Henry IV, the Duke of Gloucester (1391–1447), known as 'Duke Humphrey'. He was noted as a patron of literature, and founded what became the Bodleian Library at Oxford. In modern times, probably the most famous bearer has been the film star Humphrey Bogart (1899–1957).
VARIANTS: **Humphry, Humfr(e)y.**

Hunter ♂ Especially North America: transferred use of the surname, in origin an occupational name. The term was used not only of hunters on horseback of game such as stags and wild boars, which was in the Middle Ages a pursuit restricted to the ranks of the nobility, but also of much humbler bird catchers and poachers seeking food.

Huw ♂ Welsh form of ▷Hugh, now sometimes also used in other parts of the English-speaking world.

Huxley ♂ Transferred use of the surname, in origin a local name from a place in Cheshire which is apparently so called from the genitive case of the Old English personal name *Hucc* + Old English *lēah* 'wood, clearing'. Use as a given name was in some cases in honour of the English biologist Thomas

Huxley (1825–95), a leading supporter of the evolutionary theories of Charles Darwin.

Hyacinth ♀ English form of the name (Greek *Hyakinthos*) borne in classical mythology by a beautiful youth who was accidentally killed by Apollo and from whose blood sprang a flower bearing his name (not the modern hyacinth, but a type of dark lily). The name was later borne by various early saints, principally one martyred in the 3rd century with his brother Protus. This encouraged its use as a male name in Christian Europe, including, occasionally, Britain. However, in Britain at the end of the 19th century there was a vogue for coining new girls' names from vocabulary words denoting plants and flowers (e.g. ▷Daisy, ▷Ivy). *Hyacinth* accordingly came to be regarded exclusively as a girl's name. It has never been common, and in the 1990s came to be associated with the character of the domineering snob Hyacinth Bucket in the British TV comedy series *Keeping Up Appearances*.

VARIANTS: **Jacinth, Jacintha.**

Hyam ♂ Jewish: from the Hebrew word *hayyim* 'life'. This is sometimes added to the existing given name of a seriously ill person during prayers for his recovery.

Hylda ♀ Variant spelling of ▷Hilda.

Hyman ♂ Jewish: altered form of ▷Hyam, influenced by *man* 'man', a common element of Yiddish names.

VARIANT: **Hymen** (altered form, perhaps under the influence of *Hymen* in Latin and Greek, which was the name of the god of marriage).

Hymie ♂ Jewish: pet form of ▷Hyman or ▷Hyam.

h

Ii

Ian ♂ Scottish form of ▷John, also much used in the wider English-speaking world.

Ianthe ♀ From Greek *ion* 'violet' + *anthos* 'flower'. This name was borne in Greek mythology by a daughter of the sea god Oceanus. In the 19th century it appeared in works by Byron and Shelley (who also bestowed it on his daughter), and it is now found in occasional use.

Ibrahim ♂ Arabic form of ▷Abraham; see also Ibrāhīm in Arabic appendix.

Ida ♀ Originally a Norman name, of Germanic origin, derived from *īd* 'work'. This died out during the later Middle Ages. It was revived in the 19th century, influenced by its use in Tennyson's *The Princess* (1847) for the central character, who devotes herself to the cause of women's rights and women's education in a thoroughly Victorian way. The name is also associated with Mount Ida in Crete, which was connected in classical times with the worship of Zeus, king of the gods, who was supposed to have been brought up in a cave on the mountainside. In the 1930s it became famous as the name of the film star Ida Lupino (1914–1995).

Idony ♀ Medieval name derived from the Old Norse female personal name *Iðunnr*, which is probably a derivative of *ið* 'again'. In Old Norse mythology *Iðunnr* was the goddess in charge of the gods' apples of eternal youth. The name has sometimes been Latinized as Idonea, as if from the feminine form of the Latin adjective *idoneus* 'suitable'.

Ignatius ♂ Late Latin name, derived from the old Roman family name *Egnatius* (of uncertain origin, possibly Etruscan). This was altered in the early Christian period by association with Latin *ignis* 'fire'. It was borne by various early saints, and more recently by St Ignatius Loyola (1491–1556), who founded the Society of Jesus (Jesuits). In the modern English-speaking world it is used mainly if not exclusively by Roman Catholics.

Igor ♂ Russian: variant form of ▷Ivor, one of the names taken to Russia at the time of the first Scandinavian settlement of Kiev in the 9th century. In the English-speaking world it is a 20th-century borrowing.

Ike ♂ English pet form of ▷Isaac. It was made famous in the 20th century as the nickname of the American general and president Dwight D. Eisenhower (1890–1969), although in this case, of course, it was based on his surname.

Ilayne ♀ Apparently a fanciful respelling of ▷Elaine.

Ilene ♀ Apparently a fanciful respelling of ▷Eileen.

Ilona ♀ Hungarian form of ▷Helen, now also sometimes used in the English-speaking world.

Immaculata ♀ Latin: from the Marian title *Maria Immaculata*, referring to the doctrine of the Immaculate Conception. It is used in Ireland by Roman Catholics.

Immanuel ♂ Variant spelling of ▷Emmanuel, a form generally used in the English-speaking world by Jews.

Imogen ♀ The name owes its existence to a character in Shakespeare's *Cymbeline* (1609), but in earlier accounts of the events on which the play is based this character is named as *Innogen*, a name of Celtic origin, from Gaelic *inghean* 'girl, maiden'. The modern form of the name is thus due to a misreading of these sources by Shakespeare, or of the play's text by his printer. It was in fairly select use until the 1990s, when it became quite popular.

Imogene ♀ Elaborated form of ▷Imogen.

Ina ♀ Short form of any of the numerous girls' names ending in these two syllables (representing a Latinate feminine suffix), for example *Christina* and *Georgina*. It is now occasionally used as an independent given name. See also ▷Ena.

Inanna ♀ From the name of a Sumerian goddess, queen of heaven and earth. Her name is of uncertain derivation, but it seems to lie behind the name *Anna* borne by the sister of Dido, Queen of Carthage, in Virgil's Aeneid; this a quite different name from the one of Hebrew origin that gave rise to the traditional European given name ▷Anna.

India ♀ From the name of the subcontinent, used as the name of a character in Margaret Mitchell's novel *Gone with the Wind* (1936). In the case of India Hicks, Lord Mountbatten's granddaughter, the name was chosen because of her family's association with the subcontinent.

Inés ♀ Spanish form of ▷Agnes, now also used, usually without the accent, in the English-speaking world.

Inga ♀ Respelling of the German and Scandinavian name *Inge*, a short form of ▷Ingrid or any of various other names (for example *Ingeborg*) based on the name of the old Germanic fertility god *Ing*.

Ingram ♂ Transferred use of the surname, which is derived from a medieval given name. This was originally a contracted form of the Norman name *Engelram*, composed of

the ethnic name *Engel* 'Angle' (or *Ing*, name of the Old Norse fertility god) + *hramn* 'raven'. As late as the 17th century *Engelram* and *Ingram* were still in occasional use as given names in the north of England.

Ingrid ♀ From an Old Norse female personal name composed of the name of the fertility god *Ing* + *fríðr* 'fair, beautiful'. It was introduced into the English-speaking world from Scandinavia in the 20th century and became very popular, largely because of the fame of the Swedish film actress Ingrid Bergman (1915–82).

Inigo ♂ From the medieval Spanish given name *Íñigo*, a vernacular derivative of ▷Ignatius, apparently the result of crossing with a name recorded in the Middle Ages as *Ennecus*. This is of uncertain, possibly Basque, origin. *Íñigo* is now rarely used as a given name in Spain. In the English-speaking world it is mainly associated with the architect and stage designer Inigo Jones (1573–1652). The name had previously been borne by his father, a London clothmaker, who may well have received it at around the time of Queen Mary's marriage to Philip of Spain, when Spanish ways and Spanish names were fashionable, especially among devout Roman Catholics. The architect passed it on to his son, but later examples are infrequent.

Innes ♂, occasionally ♀ Transferred use of the surname (see Scottish appendix). Use as a girl's name may have been influenced by the Spanish name ▷Inés.

Iolanda ♀ Respelling of ▷Yolanda.

Iolanthe ♀ Modern coinage based on Greek *iolē* 'violet' + *anthos* 'flower'. It is known chiefly as the name of the eponymous fairy heroine of a Gilbert and Sullivan opera, first performed in 1882.

Iola ♀ Variant of ▷Iole, now the more frequent spelling.

Iole ♀ Pronounced 'eye-**oh**-lee': name borne in classical mythology by a daughter of Eurytus of Oechalia. Herakles's infatuation with her led to his murder by his wife Deianeira. It represents the classical Greek vocabulary word meaning 'violet', and may in part have been chosen as a learned response to the 19th-century vogue for given names derived from words denoting flowers and plants.
VARIANT: Iola.

Iona ♀ From the name of the tiny sacred island in the Hebrides, off the west coast of Mull (see Scottish appendix). In 563 St Columba came from Ireland to found a monastery here. It became the most important centre of Christianity in northern Britain, from which missionaries went out all over Scotland and northern England, and from which the monastery at Lindisfarne was founded. The given name still has a distinctly Scottish flavour, although it is increasingly in general use.

Ione ♀ Pronounced 'eye-**oh**-nee': 19th-century coinage, apparently with reference to the glories of Ionian Greece in the 5th century BC. No such name exists in classical Greek.

Ira ♂ Biblical name (meaning 'watchful' in Hebrew), borne by a character mentioned very briefly in the Bible, one of the chief officers of King David (2 Samuel 20:26). It was taken up by the Puritans in the 17th century, and is still occasionally used, mainly in the United States. It was famously borne by the lyricist Ira Gershwin (1896–1983).

Irene ♀ From Greek *eirēnē* 'peace'; it was borne in Greek mythology by a minor goddess who personified peace, and by a Byzantine empress (752–803). The name was taken up in the English-speaking world at the end of the 19th century, and became popular in the 20th, partly as a result of being used as the name of a character in John Galsworthy's *The Forsyte Saga* (1922). It was formerly pronounced in three syllables, as in Greek, but is now thoroughly naturalized as an English name and usually pronounced as two syllables.

Iris ♀ From Greek *iris* 'rainbow'; it was borne in Greek mythology by a minor goddess, one of the messengers of the gods, who was so named because the rainbow was thought to be a sign from the gods to men. In English her name was used in the 16th century to denote both the flower and the coloured part of the eye, on account of their varied colours. In modern English use the name is often taken as being from the word for the flower, but it is also in use in Germany, where there is no such pattern of flower names.

Irma ♀ Pet form of various girls' names of Germanic origin beginning with the element *irm(en)*, *erm(en)* 'whole, entire', for example *Irmgard* and *Irmtraud*. It was introduced to the English-speaking world at the end of the 19th century and gained some currency following the release of the film *Irma la Douce* (1963), in which Shirley MacLaine plays the title role.

Irvin ♂ Mainly U.S.: variant of ▷Irvine or ▷Irving.

Irvine ♂ Mainly North American: Anglicized form of the German given name Erwin (see German appendix) or transferred use of the Scottish surname, in origin a local name from a place in the former county of Ayrshire. The place name is probably derived from a Celtic river name, akin to Welsh *ir*, *yr* 'green, fresh' + *afon* 'water'.

Irving ♂ Transferred use of the Scottish surname, in origin a local name from a place in the former county of Dumfriesshire, which has the same origin as ▷Irvine. In the case of the songwriter Irving Berlin (1888–1989), the name was adopted: he was of Jewish origin, and was originally called Israel Baline. *Irving* is now a fairly common given name in North America. Among Jewish bearers, it is generally taken as an English equivalent of ▷Israel.

Irwin ♂ Transferred use of the surname, which is derived from the medieval given name *Irwyn*, *Erwyn*, or *Everwyn*, from Old English *eofor* 'boar' + *wine* 'friend'. There has also been some confusion with ▷Irving.

Isa ♀ Originally a short form of ▷Isabel and related names (the mining centre of Mount Isa in Queensland, Australia, was named by the prospector John Campbell Miles after his sister Isabella), but now more commonly used as an independent first name, pronounced '**eye**-za'.

Isaac ♂ Biblical name, borne by the son of Abraham, who was nearly sacrificed by his father according to a command of God which was changed at the last moment. A ram, caught in a nearby thicket, was sacrificed instead (Genesis 22:1–13). Isaac lived on to marry Rebecca and become the father of Esau and Jacob. The derivation of the name is not certain; it has traditionally been connected with the Hebrew verb meaning 'to laugh'. It was borne by both Christians and Jews in the Middle Ages and was taken up by the Puritans in the 16th century.

SHORT FORMS: Zack, Zak, Zac.
PET FORM: Ike.

Isabel ♀ Originally a Spanish version of ▷Elizabeth, which was coined by deletion of the first syllable and alteration of the final consonant sound to one that can normally end a word in Spanish. The name was imported into France in the early Middle Ages, and thence into England. It was a royal name, and its enduring popularity may have been enhanced by the fact that it was borne by a queen of England— Isabella (1296–1358), daughter of Philip IV of France—even though she led a

turbulent life and eventually had her husband, Edward II, murdered.
VARIANTS: Isabell(e); Isobel(le), Isobella.
PET FORMS: ▷Izzy, Izzie.

Isabella ♀ Latinate form of ▷Isabel, which has been popular in England since the 18th century and has recently become the preferred form of the name.
VARIANT: Isobella.

Isabelle ♀ French form of ▷Isabel, now in frequent use in the English-speaking world.

Isadora ♀ Variant spelling of ▷Isidora, borne for example by the American dancer Isadora Duncan (1878–1927).

Isaiah ♂ Biblical name (meaning 'God is salvation' in Hebrew), borne by the most important of the major prophets. Rather surprisingly perhaps, until recently the name was not common in the English-speaking world, although it was occasionally used among the Puritans in the 17th century. Since the 1980s, it has steadily risen in general popularity, especially in the United States, as well as being well established as a Jewish name.

Iser ♂ Jewish: back-formation from Yiddish Iserl (a metathesized form of Israel), the final -l having been taken as a hypocoristic ending.
VARIANT: Issur.

Iseult ♀ French form of ▷Isolde, also occasionally used in the English-speaking world.

Ishmael ♂ Biblical name composed of Hebrew elements meaning 'to hearken' and 'God'. It is borne in the Bible by Abraham's first son, the offspring of his barren wife's Egyptian maidservant Hagar; an angel told Hagar, 'Behold, thou art with child, and shalt bear a son, and shalt call his name Ishmael' (Genesis 16:11). In Islamic tradition, Ishmael (or Ismail) is believed to have been the ancestor of the Arabs (see Ismā'īl in Arabic appendix).

Isidora ♀ Feminine form of ▷Isidore.
PET FORMS: **Izzy, Izzie.**

Isidore ♂ English form (via Old French and Latin) of the Greek name *Isidōros*, composed of the name of the goddess *Isis* (of Egyptian origin) + Greek *dōron* 'gift'. In spite of its pagan connotations the name was a common one among early Christians, and was borne for example by the great encyclopedist St Isidore of Seville (c.560–636). By the late Middle Ages, however, it had come to be considered a typically Jewish name (although originally adopted as a Christianized version of ▷Isaiah).
PET FORMS: ▷**Izzy, Izzie.**

Isla ♀ Pronounced 'eye-la', 20th-century Scottish coinage, now used more widely among English speakers. It is from Islay, the name of an island in the Hebrides.

Ismail ♂ Arabic form of ▷Ishmael. See also Ismā῾īl in Arabic appendix.

Ismene ♀ Borne in classical mythology by a daughter of Oedipus. After Oedipus has blinded himself on discovering that he has killed his father and that Jocasta is not only his wife but also his mother, Ismene deserts her father, while Antigone, her sister, stays with him and supports him. In spite of its grim associations, the name has been used occasionally in modern times.

Isobel ♀ Variant spelling of ▷Isabel.

Isolde ♀ The name of the tragic mistress of Tristan in the Arthurian romances. There are several versions of the story. The main features are that the beautiful Isolde, an Irish princess, is betrothed to the aged King Mark of Cornwall. However, through accidentally drinking a magic potion, she and the young Cornish knight Tristan fall in love, with tragic consequences. The story has exercised a powerful hold on the European imagination. The name was relatively common in Britain in the Middle Ages, but is much rarer today.
VARIANT: **Isolda.**

Israel ♂ Biblical name, originally the byname (meaning 'he who strives with God' in Hebrew) given to Jacob after he had wrestled with an angel: 'Thy name shall be called no more Jacob, but Israel: for as a prince hast thou power with God and with men, and hast prevailed' (Genesis 32:28). The name was later applied to his descendants, the Children of Israel, and was chosen as the name of the modern Jewish state. The given name was used by the Puritans in the 16th century, but is now once again almost exclusively a Jewish name.

Issachar ♂ Biblical name, probably meaning 'hireling' in Hebrew, borne by one of the sons of Jacob: 'And Leah said, God hath given me my hire, because I have given my maiden to my husband: and she called his name Issachar' (Genesis 30:18). The name is still borne by Jews, but is rare among Gentiles.

Issur ♂ Jewish: variant of ▷Iser.

Itamar ♂ Jewish: meaning 'palm island' in Hebrew; it is borne in the Bible by a son of Aaron and brother of Eleazar (Exodus 6:23; Leviticus 10:1–7).

Ivan ♂ Russian form of ▷John, also used quite frequently in the English-speaking world. In Northern Ireland it is sometimes found as a variant of ▷Ewan.

Ivo ♂ Form of ▷Yves used in Germany and occasionally in the English-speaking world. It represents the nominative case of the Latinized form of the name.

Ivon ♂ Variant of ▷Ivo, derived from the oblique case of the name.

Ivor ♂ Of Scandinavian origin, from an Old Norse personal name, *Yherr*, derived from *ýr* 'yew, bow' + *herr* 'army'. In the 1920s and 30s it came to prominence as the name of the songwriter and actor Ivor Novello (1893–1951).

Ivy ♀ From the vocabulary word denoting the plant (Old English *ifig*). This given name was adopted at the end of the 19th century together with a large number of other words denoting flowers and plants pressed into service as girls' names. It is currently somewhat out of fashion.

Izzy ♀, ♂ Pet form of ▷Isabel (and its variants), ▷Isidora, and, as a boy's name, ▷Isidore.

VARIANT: **Izzie** ♀.

Jj

Jabez ♂ Biblical name, meaning 'sorrowful' in Hebrew: 'and his mother called his name Jabez, saying, Because I bare him with sorrow' (1 Chronicles 4:9). The name is thus metathesized from Hebrew *ya'zeb*. The name is now out of fashion, but it was popular among the Puritans in the 17th century, as the mention of Jabez in the Bible lent support to the Protestant work ethic. Jabez was 'more honourable than his brethren'; he called on the Lord for protection and wealth: 'Oh that thou wouldest bless me indeed, and enlarge my coast, and that thine hand might be with me'; the Lord duly obliged.

Jacalyn ♀ Modern variant of ▷Jacqueline.

Jacinta ♀ Spanish form of ▷Hyacinth, now used occasionally in the English-speaking world.

Jack ♂ Originally a pet form of ▷John, but now a well-established given name in its own right. It is derived from Middle English *Jankin*, later altered to *Jackin*, from *Jan* (a contracted form of *Jehan* 'John') + the diminutive suffix *-kin*. This led to the back-formation *Jack*, as if the name had contained the Old French diminutive suffix *-in*. It is sometimes also used as an informal pet form of ▷James, perhaps influenced by the French form ▷Jacques. It has been the most popular boys' name in England and Wales since 1995. Well-known bearers include the actor Jack Nicholson (b. 1937) and the golfer Jack Nicklaus (b. 1940). See also Jock in Scottish appendix and ▷Jake.
VARIANT: Jak, Jac.

Jackalyn ♀ Modern variant of ▷Jacqueline.

Jackie ♀, ♂ As a girl's name this is a pet form of ▷Jacqueline, as in the case of Jackie Kennedy Onassis (1929–94). It was originally a boy's name, a pet form of ▷Jack. The racing driver Jackie Stewart (b. 1939) was originally named John Young Stewart.
VARIANTS: Jacki ♀, Jacky.

Jacklyn ♀ Modern variant of ▷Jacqueline, influenced by ▷Jack.

Jackson ♂ Transferred use of the surname, meaning originally 'son of Jack' and in modern times sometimes bestowed with precisely this meaning. In the United States it has also been used in honour of President Andrew Jackson (1767–1845), the Confederate general Thomas 'Stonewall' Jackson (1824–63), and more recently the painter Jackson Pollock (1912–56).
PET FORM: Jacky.

Jacky ♂, ♀ As a boy's name this is a pet form of both ▷Jack and ▷Jackson. As a girl's name it is a variant spelling of ▷Jackie.

Jaclyn ♀ Modern variant of ▷Jacqueline.

Jacob ♂ Biblical name, from Hebrew *Yaakov*. This was borne by perhaps the most important of all the patriarchs in the Book of Genesis. Jacob was the father of twelve sons, who gave their names to the twelve tribes of Israel. He was the son of Isaac and Rebecca and twin brother of Esau. According to the story in Genesis, he was the cunning younger twin, who persuaded his brother Esau to part with his right to his inheritance in exchange for a bowl of soup ('a mess of pottage'). Later, he tricked his blind and dying father into blessing him in place of Esau. The derivation of the name has been much discussed. It is traditionally explained as being derived from Hebrew *akev* 'heel' and to have meant 'heel grabber', because when Jacob was born 'his hand took hold of Esau's heel' (Genesis 25:26). This is interpreted later in the Bible as 'supplanter'; Esau himself remarks, 'Is he not rightly named Jacob? for he has supplanted me these two times' (Genesis 27:36). *Jacob* is especially common as a Jewish given name, although it also became very popular among the Puritans from the 16th century onwards, and has again been widely used since the 1990s. Compare ▷James.

COGNATES: Welsh: Iago. German: Jakob. Dutch: Jakob, Jaap. Scandinavian: Jakob. French: ▷Jacques. Spanish, Portuguese: Jacob, Jacobo. Italian: Giacobbe. Russian: Yakov. Polish: Jakub. Czech: Jakub. Croatian: Jakov. Finnish: Jaakko. Hungarian: Jákob.

Jacoba ♀ Feminine form of ▷Jacob.

Jacobus ♂ Latin form of the biblical name *Yaakov*; see ▷Jacob.

Jacqueline ♀ Originally a French feminine diminutive form of *Jacques*, the French version of ▷James. In the 1960s it became very popular in the United States and elsewhere, influenced in part by the fame and stylish image of Jacqueline Bouvier Kennedy Onassis (1929–94), whose family was of French extraction.

VARIANTS: Jackalyn, Jacalyn, Jacqualine, Jacquelene, Jacquelyn(e), Jacquelin(e), Jacquiline, Jacaline, Jacueline; Jacklyn, Jaclyn.

PET FORMS: Jacki, Jackie, Jacky, Jacqui, Jacquie; Jaqui; Jaki, Jakki.

Jacquelyn ♀ Respelling of ▷Jacqueline, influenced by the productive suffix *-lyn* (see ▷Lynn).

Jacques ♂ French form of ▷James and ▷Jacob. In French there is no distinction between a form corresponding to *Jacob* and a form corresponding to *James*. This is a perennially popular French given name, and *Jacques* or *Jacques Bonhomme* has been used (like *John Bull* in English) as a typification of the ordinary citizen. In Shakespeare's time it was also used as an English name, pronounced '**jay**-kwez', as in the case of the melancholy character Jacques in *As You Like It*. Though rarely, if ever, now used in Britain it is found in the United States.

Jacquetta ♀ Anglicized spelling (influenced by ▷Jacqueline) of the Italian name *Giachetta*, a feminine diminutive of *Giac(om)o*, the Italian form of ▷James.

Jacqui ♀ Pet form of ▷Jacqueline, occasionally used independently.

Jada ♀, ♂ Biblical name meaning 'he knows' in Hebrew, borne by a son of Onam. In modern usage, however, the name, being borne predominantly if not exclusively by girls, is more likely an altered and more obviously feminine form of ▷Jade rather than a revival of the biblical name.

Jade ♀ From the name of the precious stone, a word that reached English from Spanish (*piedra de*) *ijada*, which literally means '(stone of the) bowels'. It was so called because it was believed to have the magical power of providing protection against disorders of the intestines. The vogue for this word as a given name developed later than that for other gemstone names, possibly because it sounds the same as the vocabulary word denoting a broken-down old horse or a nagging woman. It came to notice in the early 1970s when the daughter of the English rock star Mick Jagger was so named, peaking in popularity through the 1990s. In 2002 the name became famous as that of Jade Goody, a remarkably cheerful but ill-informed contestant on Channel 4's reality TV show *Big Brother*.

Jael ♀ Jewish: variant of ▷Yael.

Jago ♂ Cornish form of ▷James, also found as a surname.

Jai ♂ Indian: variant of ▷Jay 2.

Jaime ♀, ♂ This is the Spanish form of ▷James, but in the United States and Canada, and subsequently elsewhere in the English-speaking world, it came to be used also as a girl's name, apparently a variant of the girl's name ▷Jamie. In Britain it is now more commonly used for girls than boys, while in North America it is still predominantly a boy's name.

VARIANT: **Jame.**

Jaimie ♀ Variant spelling of the girl's name ▷Jamie.

Jaine ♀ Variant spelling of ▷Jane.

Jake ♂ Variant of ▷Jack, of Middle English origin, which since the 1990s has come back into fashion as an independent given name. It is also sometimes used as a short form of ▷Jacob.

Jakob ♂ German and Scandinavian spelling of ▷Jacob, now also used in the English-speaking world.

Jamal ♂ Arabic name meaning 'good looks, beauty'. See also **Jamāl** in Arabic appendix.

James ♂ English form of the name borne in the New Testament by two of Christ's disciples, James son of Zebedee and James son of Alphaeus. This form comes from Late Latin *Iacomus*, a variant of *Iacobus*, Latin form of Greek *Iakobos*. This is the same name as Old Testament ▷Jacob (Hebrew *Yaakov*), but for many centuries now they have been thought of in the English-speaking world as two distinct names. In Britain, *James* is a royal name that from the beginning of the 15th century onwards was associated particularly with the Scottish house of Stewart: James I of Scotland (1394–1437; ruled 1424–37) was a patron of the arts and a noted poet, as well as an energetic ruler. King James VI of Scotland (1566–1625;

reigned 1567–1625) succeeded to the throne of England in 1603. His grandson, James II of England (1633–1701; reigned 1685–8) was a Roman Catholic, deposed in 1688 in favour of his Protestant daughter Mary and her husband William of Orange. From then on he, his son (also called James), and his grandson Charles ('Bonnie Prince Charlie') made various unsuccessful attempts to recover the English throne. Their supporters were known as Jacobites (from Latin *Iacobus*), and the name James became for a while particularly associated with Roman Catholicism on the one hand, and Highland opposition to the English government on the other. Nevertheless, it has since become one of the most perennially popular boys' names.

SHORT FORM: **Jim.**

PET FORMS: **Jamey, Jamie, Jimmy, Jimmie.**

COGNATES: Irish: **Séamas, Séamus, Seumas, Seumus.** Scottish Gaelic: **Seumas.** Scottish (Anglicized); ▷**Hamish.** Dutch: **Jaume.** French: ▷**Jacques.** Spanish: **Jaime.** Catalan: **Jaume.** Portuguese: **Jaime(s).** Italian: **Giacomo.**

Jamesina ♀ Feminine version of ▷James, formed with the Latinate suffix -*ina.*

Jameson ♂ Transferred use of the surname, in origin a patronymic meaning 'son of James'.

Jamie ♂, ♀ Originally a male pet form of ▷James and still so used, especially in Scotland and Northumberland. It is now also found as a girl's name, a feminine equivalent of *James*, especially in North America, where it is used more frequently for girls than boys. It is famously borne by the actress Jamie Lee Curtis (b. 1958), and is often used in combination with ▷Lee or its variants.

VARIANTS: **Jamey; Jamee, Jami; Jaimie, Jaimee** ♀.

Jamieson ♂ Transferred use of the northern English and Scottish surname, in origin a patronymic meaning 'son of Jamie'.

Jamila ♀ Arabic name meaning 'beautiful, graceful'.

Jan ♂, ♀ As a boy's name this represents a revival of Middle English *Jan*, a by-form of ▷John, or an adoption of the common European form with this spelling. As a girl's name it is a short form of names such as ▷Janet and ▷Janice.

Jana ♀ Distinctively feminine variant of ▷Jan; in the English-speaking world a 20th-century importation from Eastern Europe.

Jancis ♀ Modern blend of ▷Jan and ▷Frances, first used in the novel *Precious Bane* (1924) by Mary Webb, for the character of Jancis Beguildy, daughter of Felix and Hephzibah.

PET FORM: **Jancie**.

Jane ♀ Originally a feminine form of ▷John, from the Old French form *Je(h)anne*. Since the 17th century it has proved the most popular of the feminine forms of *John*, ahead of ▷Joan and ▷Jean. It now also commonly occurs as the second element in combinations such as *Sarah-Jane*. In Britain it is still one of the most frequent of all girls' names. It is not a royal name, but was borne by the tragic Lady Jane Grey (1537–54), who was unwillingly proclaimed queen in 1553, deposed nine days later, and executed the following year. Seventy years earlier, the name had come into prominence as that of Jane Shore, mistress of King Edward IV and subsequently of Thomas Grey, 1st Marquess of Dorset, Lady Jane's grandfather. Jane Shore's tribulations in 1483 at the hands of Richard III, Edward's brother and successor, became the subject of popular ballads and plays, which may well have increased the currency of the name in the 16th century. A 19th-century influence was its use as the name of the central character in Charlotte Brontë's novel *Jane Eyre* (1847). From 1932 to 1959 it was used as the name of a cheerful and scantily clad beauty whose adventures were chronicled in a strip cartoon in the *Daily Mirror*. It is also borne by the American film stars Jane Russell (b. 1921) and Jane Fonda (b. 1937).

VARIANT: **Jayne, Jaine, Jain**. See also ▷Jean, ▷Joan, and ▷Joanna.

PET FORMS: **Janey, Janie, Jaynie**.

COGNATES: Irish: **Síne**. Scottish Gaelic: **Sine**. Welsh: **Siân**. German: **Johanna, Hanne, Hansine**. Dutch: **Johanna, Jan(n)a**. Danish, Norwegian: **Johanna, Jensine; Jonna** (Danish). Swedish: **Johanna**. French: **Jeanne**. Spanish: **Juana**. Italian: **Giovanna, Gianna**. Polish: **Jana**. Czech: **Johana, Hana, Jana**. Slovenian: **Jana**.

Janeen ♀ Simplified spelling of ▷Jeannine.

Janelle ♀ Modern elaborated form of ▷Jane, with the feminine ending *-elle* abstracted from names such as ▷Danielle.

VARIANT: **Janella** (a Latinate form; for the ending, compare ▷Prunella).

Janene ♀ Simplified spelling of ▷Jeannine.

Janet ♀ Originally a diminutive of ▷Jane, already in common use in the Middle English period. It remained in use in Scotland and in some parts of England well into the 17th century and was revived at the end of the 19th century to much more widespread use, while still retaining its popularity in Scotland. Since the 1960s, however, it has rather gone out of fashion in Britain.

VARIANTS: **Jannet**, ▷Janette.

SHORT FORM: ▷Jan.

PET FORMS: ▷Janette, **Janetta** (Latinized form).

Janetta ♀ Latinized form of ▷Janette.

Janette ♀ Either an elaborated version of ▷Janet, with the distinctly feminine suffix -*ette*, or a simplified form of ▷Jeannette.

Janey ♀ Pet form of ▷Jane.

Janice ♀ Derivative of ▷Jane, with the addition of the suffix -*ice*, abstracted from girls' names such as ▷Candice and ▷Bernice. It seems to have been first used as the name of the heroine of the novel *Janice Meredith* by Paul Leicester Ford, published in 1899.
VARIANTS: Janis(e); Jannice.
SHORT FORM: ▷Jan.

Janie ♀ Pet form of ▷Jane, sometimes used as an independent given name.

Janine ♀ Simplified form of ▷Jeannine.

Janina ♀ Elaborated form of ▷Janine.

Janis ♀ Variant spelling of ▷Janice. It was quite popular in the United States in the 1960s and 70s by association with the rock singer Janis Joplin (1943–70).

Janita ♀ Apparently an English form of ▷Juanita, influenced perhaps by ▷Anita, which is also of Spanish origin.

Janna ♀ Latinate elaboration of the girl's name ▷Jan.

Jannette ♀ Variant spelling of ▷Janette.

Japheth ♂ Biblical name, from Hebrew *Yepheth* 'enlargement, expansion', borne by the eldest son of Noah (Genesis 9:27). The name enjoyed some popularity among the Puritans in the 17th century, but is now infrequent.

Jared ♂ Biblical name (probably meaning 'descent' in Hebrew), borne by a descendant of Adam (Genesis 5:15). According to the Book of Genesis, he became the father of Enoch at the age of 162, and lived for a further eight hundred years. This name was occasionally used by the Puritans. It

was briefly revived in the 1960s and again more recently.
VARIANTS: Jarred, Jarod, Jarrod.

Jarrett ♂ Transferred use of the surname, in origin a variant of ▷Garret.

Jarrod ♂ Transferred use of the surname, which was derived in the Middle Ages from the given name ▷Gerald.

Jarvis ♂ Transferred use of the surname, which is from a Middle English form of the Norman given name ▷Gervaise. Modern use may in part represent an antiquarian revival of the medieval given name.
VARIANT: Jervis.

Jaslyn ♀ Modern coinage, apparently a combination of the first syllable of ▷Jasmine with the productive suffix -*lyn*.

Jasmine ♀ From the vocabulary word denoting the climbing plant with its delicate, fragrant flowers (from Old French, ultimately from Persian *yasmin*). It has been much in favour since the 1990s.
VARIANTS: Jasmin, Jasmyn, Jazmin(e); ▷Yasmin, Yasmine; Jasmina, Yasmina (Latinized forms).

Jason ♂ English form of the Greek name *Iasōn*, borne in classical mythology by a hero, leader of the Argonauts, who sailed to Colchis in search of the Golden Fleece, enduring many hardships and adventures. The sorceress Medea fell in love with him and helped him to obtain the Fleece; they escaped together and should have lived happily ever after. However, Jason fell in love with another woman and deserted Medea. Medea took her revenge by killing her rival, but Jason himself survived to be killed in old age by one of the rotting timbers of his ship, the *Argo*, falling on his head. The classical Greek name *Iasōn* probably derives from Greek *iasthai* 'to heal'. In New Testament Greek, the name probably represents a classicized form of ▷Joshua. It was borne by an early Christian in Thessalonica, at whose house St Paul stayed (Acts 17:5–9; Romans 16:21). Probably for this reason, it enjoyed some use among the Puritans in the 16th and 17th centuries. The name has been used for various characters in films and television series, and in the mid-20th century it enjoyed a sudden burst of popularity, although it was also the subject of some rather surprising hostility. Among popular non-fictional bearers of the name are the film actor Jason Robards (1922–2000), his father (1893–1963), also a film actor, and, more recently, the Australian actor Jason Donovan (b. 1968).

VARIANT: **Jayson**.

Jasper ♂ The usual English form of the name assigned in Christian folklore to one of the three Magi or 'wise men', who brought gifts to the infant Christ at his birth (Matthew 2:1). The name does not appear in the Bible, and is first found in medieval tradition. It seems to be ultimately of Persian origin, from a word meaning 'treasurer'. There is probably no connection with the English vocabulary word *jasper* denoting a gemstone, which is of Semitic origin. The name was introduced into England from the Low Countries in the Middle Ages and, although it never became popular, continued to be widely used in parts of the north. Well-known bearers include British comedian Jasper Carrott (b. 1945 as Robert Davies) and the fashion designer Jasper Conran (b. 1959).

Javan ♂ Biblical name, borne by a son of Japheth (Genesis 10:2). It seems to be derived from a Hebrew word meaning 'wine'. Modern use as a given name has probably been influenced by names such as ▷Jevon.

Jay ♂, ♀ **1.** Short form of any of the given names beginning with the letter J- (compare ▷Dee and ▷Kay), now also used as an independent given name. **2.** Indian male name meaning 'victory' in Sanskrit.

VARIANTS: **Jaye** (of 1); **Jai** (of 2).

Jayden ♂ Modern coinage, apparently an elaboration of ▷Jay by way of a blend with *Hayden* (see ▷Haydn). It has become popular throughout the English-speaking world in recent years.

VARIANT: **Jaydon, Jaiden**.

Jaye ♀, ♂ Variant spelling of ▷Jay, used mainly for girls.

Jayne ♀ Elaborated spelling of ▷Jane, a form popularized no doubt by the American actress Jayne Mansfield (Vera Jayne Palmer, 1933–67) and British ice-dancer Jayne Torvill (b. 1957).

PET FORM: **Jaynie**.

Jaynia ♀ Modern coinage, an elaboration of ▷Jayne.

Jaynie ♀ Pet form of ▷Jayne.

Jayson ♂ Respelling of ▷Jason.

Jazz ♂ Mostly a nickname for the bearer of any given name beginning with J-, especially ▷James (in this case arising probably from the written abbreviation *Jas.*, which was formerly in common use), but sometimes used as an independent given name and in part associated with the vocabulary word referring to the style of music so called. This word came into English from African-American slang of the southern United States in the early 20th century, and is of unknown origin. (There have been innumerable speculations.)

Jean ♀, ♂ Like ▷Jane and ▷Joan, a medieval variant of Old French *Je(h)anne*. Towards the end of the Middle Ages this form became largely confined to Scotland. In the 20th century it became more widely used in the English-speaking world and enjoyed a period of great popularity, but it is now out of fashion. Among numerous well-known and influential bearers are the British novelists Jean Plaidy (Eleanor

Hibbert, 1910–93) and Jean Rhys (Ella Gwendolen Rees Williams, 1894–1979), British actress Jean Simmons (b. 1929), and American-born actress Jean Seberg (1938–79). It is also found as a variant spelling of the masculine name ▷Gene.

VARIANT: **Jeane** ♀.

PET FORMS: **Jean(n)ie** ♀.

Jeana ♀ Latinate elaboration of ▷Jean or a respelling of ▷Gina.

VARIANT: **Jeanna**.

Jeane ♀ Variant spelling of ▷Jean.

Jeanetta ♀ Latinate elaboration of ▷Jeanette.

Jeanette ♀ Variant spelling of ▷Jeannette, in the 1920s and 30s associated particularly with the Americam singer and film star Jeanette MacDonald (1902–65).

Jeanie ♀ Pet form of ▷Jean, occasionally used as an independent given name.

Jeanine ♀ Variant spelling of ▷Jeannine.

Jeanna ♀ Variant spelling of ▷Jeana.

Jeannette ♀ French diminutive form of *Jeanne*, feminine form of *Jean* 'John', now also used in the English-speaking world.

VARIANTS (ENGLISH): **Jeanette, Jeanett; Jenette, Jennet, Jenet, Gin(n)ette.**

Jeannie ♀ Pet form of ▷Jean.

Jeannine ♀ French diminutive form of *Jeanne*, feminine form of *Jean* 'John', now also used in the English-speaking world.

Jeavon ♂ Variant spelling of ▷Jevon.

Jed ♂ Originally a short form of the biblical name Jedidiah, now generally used as an independent given name. *Jedidiah* means 'beloved of God' in Hebrew, and was used as an alternative name of King Solomon (2 Samuel 12:25). It was a favourite with the Puritans, who considered themselves, too, to be loved by God, but the full

form fell out of favour along with other rare or unwieldy Old Testament names. See also ▷Ged.

Jeevan ♂ Variant spelling of ▷Jevon.

Jeff ♂ Short form of ▷Jeffrey, now also used as an independent given name, especially in North America.

Jefferson ♂ Transferred use of the surname, originally a patronymic meaning 'son of Jeffrey'. The given name is still sometimes so used. In the United States it has often been bestowed in honour of the statesman Thomas Jefferson (1743–1826), principal author of the Declaration of Independence, who became the third president of the Union. He is also remembered as a scientist, architect, and writer.

Jeffrey ♂ Variant spelling of ▷Geoffrey, common in the Middle Ages (as reflected in surnames such as *Jefferson*). This is now the usual spelling of the name both in North America and Britain. Well-known bearers include the novelist and former British politician Jeffrey Archer (b. 1940), the British conductor Jeffrey Tate (b. 1943), and the American soul singer Jeffrey Osborne (b. 1951).

VARIANTS: **Jeffery, Jeffry.**

SHORT FORM: **Jeff.**

Jem ♂ From a medieval vernacular form of ▷James. In modern use, however, it is often a short form of ▷Jeremy.

Jemima ♀ Biblical name (meaning 'dove' or 'bright as day' in Hebrew), borne by the eldest of the daughters of Job, born to him towards the end of his life when his prosperity had been restored (Job 42:14). The name is recorded from the early 1700s in England, and became common in the first part of the 19th century. It has continued in modest use since then.

Jemma ♀ Variant spelling of ▷Gemma.

Jen ♀ Short form of ▷Jennifer, occasionally used independently.

Jenefer ♀ Variant spelling of ▷Jennifer.

Jenessa ♀ Recent coinage, a blend of ▷Jennifer and ▷Vanessa.

Jenette ♀ Variant spelling of ▷Jeannette.

Jeni ♀ Variant spelling of ▷Jenny.

Jenifer ♀ Variant spelling of ▷Jennifer.

Jenine Either a simplified spelling of ▷Jeannine or an elaborated form of ▷Jen.

Jenkin ♂ Transferred use of the surname, which is derived from the medieval given name *Jankin*. This was a pet form of the boy's name ▷Jan, with the diminutive suffix *-kin*. The modern given name is popular in Wales, where the surnames *Jenkin* and *Jenkins* are common.

Jenna ♀ Fanciful alteration of ▷Jenny, with the Latinate feminine ending *-a*.
VARIANT: Jena.

Jennefer ♀ Variant spelling of ▷Jennifer.

Jennet ♀ Either a simplified spelling of ▷Jeannette or a revival of a medieval pet form of the female name ▷Jean.

Jenni ♀ Variant spelling of ▷Jenny, now sometimes used for the sake of variety or stylishness (*-i* as an ending of girls' names being in vogue; compare ▷Jacqui and ▷Toni).

Jennie ♀ Variant spelling of ▷Jenny.

Jennifer ♀ Of Celtic (Arthurian) origin, a Cornish form of the name of King Arthur's unfaithful ▷Guinevere. At the beginning of the 20th century, the name was merely a Cornish curiosity, but since then it has become enormously popular all over the English-speaking world, partly due to the influence of the film star Jennifer Jones (b. 1919 as Phyllis Isley). Another factor in its rise was probably Bernard Shaw's use of it for the character of Jennifer Dubedat in *The Doctor's Dilemma* (1905). See also ▷Gaynor. More recent well-known bearers include the American tennis player Jennifer Capriati (b. 1976) and the British comedienne Jennifer Saunders (b. 1958).
VARIANTS: Jenifer, Jenefer, Jennefer, Jannifer.
SHORT FORM: Jen.
PET FORM: ▷Jenny.

Jennine ♀ Simplified spelling of ▷Jeannine.

Jenny ♀ Now universally taken as a pet form of ▷Jennifer. In fact, this name existed during the Middle Ages as a pet form of ▷Jean. It is often used independently. Among many well-known bearers are the Swedish soprano Jenny Lind (originally Johanna Lind, 1820–87), the British racehorse trainer Jenny Pitman (b. 1946), and the British actress Jenny Agutter (b. 1952).
VARIANTS: Jennie, Jenni, Jeni, Jenna.
SHORT FORM: Jen.

Jenson ♂ Transferred use of the surname, which is probably a variant of *Janson* 'son of Jan', a medieval form of ▷John.

Jep ♂ Medieval pet form of ▷Geoffrey, used occasionally as an independent given name.

Jeremiah ♂ Meaning 'appointed by God' in Hebrew; it was borne in the Bible by a Hebrew prophet of the 7th–6th centuries BC, whose story, prophecies of judgement, and lamentations are recorded in the book of the Bible that bears his name. The Book of Lamentations is also attributed to him; it bewails the destruction of Jerusalem and the temple by the Babylonians in 587 BC. Despite (or because of) the gloomy subject matter of these texts, the name enjoyed some popularity among Puritans from the 16th century onwards and later

j

Christian fundamentalists, partly perhaps because Jeremiah also preached reconciliation with God after his wrath was assuaged. Since the 1970s it has found considerable favour in the United States.

Jeremy ♂ Anglicized form, used in the Authorized Version of the New Testament (Matthew 2:17; 27:9), of the biblical name ▷Jeremiah. Well-known British bearers include the politician Jeremy Thorpe (b. 1929), the actor Jeremy Irons (b. 1948), and the columnist and television presenter Jeremy Clarkson (b. 1960).

SHORT FORM: Jem.

PET FORM: Jerry.

Jermaine ♂ Variant spelling of ▷Germaine, now the more frequent form of the male name and popular in particular among African Americans.

Jerome ♂ Vernacular form of the Greek name *Hieronymos*, derived from *hieros* 'holy' + *onoma* 'name'. St Jerome (*c*.342–420) was a citizen of the Eastern Roman Empire, who bore the Greek names Eusebios Hieronymos Sophronios; he was chiefly responsible for the translation into Latin of the Bible, the Vulgate. He also wrote many works of commentary and exposition on the Bible, and is regarded as one of the Doctors of the Church. The Greek form of the name was used occasionally in England; it is recorded in Nottinghamshire, for example, in the late 16th century. Both *Jerome* and *Jeronimus* are found in Yorkshire and elsewhere from that date onwards. The name was borne by the British writer Jerome K. Jerome (1859–1927), the American songwriter Jerome Kern (1885–1945), and the American ballet dancer and choreographer Jerome Robbins (1918–98).

PET FORM: ▷Jerry.

Jerrard ♂ Rare variant spelling of ▷Gerard, probably influenced by the form of the modern surname, if not a transferred use.

Jerrie ♀ Variant spelling of ▷Jerry or ▷Gerry.

Jerrold ♂ Rare variant of ▷Gerald, probably a transferred use of the surname derived from the given name in the Middle Ages.

Jerry ♂, ♀ As a boy's name this is a pet form of ▷Jeremy or ▷Gerald, or occasionally of ▷Gerard and ▷Jerome. As a girl's name it is a variant spelling of ▷Gerry, and is sometimes bestowed as an independent given name, as in the case of the American model and actress Jerry Hall (b. 1956).

Jervaise ♂ Variant spelling of ▷Gervaise.

Jervis ♂ Infrequent variant of ▷Jarvis.

Jess ♀, ♂ Usually a girl's name, a short form of ▷Jessie or ▷Jessica. As a boy's name, it is a short form of ▷Jesse or ▷Jessie. It is also used independently, both for boys and girls.

Jessamine ♀ From an archaic variant of the flower name ▷Jasmine, possibly chosen as a first name because of association with ▷Jessica.

VARIANTS: Jessamyn; Jessamy.

Jesse ♂, ♀ Meaning 'gift' in Hebrew; it is borne by the father of King David (1 Samuel 16), from whose line (according to the New Testament) Jesus was ultimately descended. It was popular among the Puritans, and is still used frequently in the United States, less so in Britain. As a girl's name it is a respelling of ▷Jessie. Notable American bearers have included the outlaw Jesse James (1847–82), the athlete Jesse Owens (1913–80), and the politician Jesse Jackson (b. 1941).

VARIANT OR SHORT FORM: Jess.

Jessica ♀ Apparently of Shakespearean origin. This was the name of the daughter of Shylock in *The Merchant of Venice* (1596). Shakespeare's source has not been established, but he presumably intended it to pass as a typically Jewish name. It may be from a biblical name that appeared, in the translations available in Shakespeare's day, as *Jesca* (Genesis 11:29; *Iscah* in the Authorized Version). This occurs in a somewhat obscure genealogical passage; Iscah appears to have been Abraham's niece. Notable bearers of the name include the British actress Jessica Tandy (1909–94), the British writer Jessica Mitford (1917–96), and the American actress Jessica Lange (b. 1949). The name has been extremely popular since the 1990s.

VARIANT: Jessika.

SHORT FORM: Jess.

PET FORMS: Jessie, Jesse.

Jessie ♀, ♂ Usually a girl's name, a pet form of ▷Jessica, also recorded in Scotland from an early date as a pet form of ▷Jean, although the derivation is not clear. The Gaelic form is *Teasag*. It is now quite often used in Scotland and elsewhere as a given name in its own right. As a boy's name it is a respelling of ▷Jesse.

VARIANTS: Jessi, Jessye (as borne by US singer Jessye Norman, b. 1945), Jesse ♀.

SHORT FORM: Jess.

Jethro ♂ Biblical name, borne by the father of Moses's wife Zipporah (Exodus 3:1; 4:18). It seems to be a variant of the Hebrew name *Ithra*, said to mean 'excellence', which is found at 2 Samuel 17:25. It was popular among the Puritans, but then fell out of general use. It was borne by the agricultural reformer Jethro Tull (1674–1741). In 1968 a rock group in Britain adopted the name Jethro Tull, and shortly afterwards the given name *Jethro* enjoyed a revival of popularity.

Jetta ♀ Comparatively recent coinage, a Latinate derivative of the vocabulary word denoting the mineral *jet*. This word is derived from Old French *jaiet*, from Latin (*lapis*) *gagates* 'stone from Gagai'. The latter was a city in Lycia, Asia Minor.

Jevon ♂ Transferred use of the surname, originally a nickname from Anglo-Norman French *jovene* 'young' (Latin *iuvenis*). Use as a given name has probably been influenced by its similarity in sound to ▷Evan.

VARIANTS: Jeavon, Jeevan.

Jewel ♀ Recent adoption of the vocabulary word meaning 'gemstone' (from Old French *jouel*, diminutive of *jou* 'plaything, delight', Latin *iocus*). The given name may derive from its use as a term of affection, or may have been suggested by the vogue in the 19th century for creating given names from words denoting particular gemstones, e.g. ▷Beryl, ▷Ruby.

Jill ♀ Short form (respelled) of ▷Gillian, also used as a given name in its own right. It was already used as a prototypical girl's name in the phrase 'Jack and Jill' in the 15th century.

PET FORMS: Jillie, Jilly.

Jillian ♀ Variant spelling of ▷Gillian.

Jilly ♀ Pet form of ▷Jill or ▷Jillian, sometimes adopted independently. In Britain it is particularly associated with the popular writer Jilly Cooper (b. 1937).

VARIANT: Jillie.

Jim ♂ Short form of ▷James, already recorded as early as the Middle Ages and now also used independently. Well-known bearers of the name have included the Scottish racing driver Jim Clark (1936–68), the British comedian Jim Davidson (b. 1953), and the Canadian actor Jim Carrey (b. 1962).

Jimmy ♂ Pet form of ▷James or ▷Jim, also used as an independent given name.

VARIANTS: Jimmie, Jimi.

Jinny ♀ Variant spelling of ▷Ginny.

Jo ♀, ♂ Usually a girl's name, a short form of ▷Joanna, ▷Joanne, ▷Jody, or ▷Josephine, sometimes used independently or in combination with other names, for example *Nancy Jo* and *Jo Anne* (see ▷Joanne). Occasionally it is a boy's name, a variant spelling of ▷Joe. Famous female bearers include the American female pop singer Jo Stafford (1920–2008) and the British politician Jo Grimond (originally Joseph Grimond, 1913–93).

Joachim ♂ Biblical name, probably from the Hebrew name *Johoiachin*, meaning 'established by God'. This was borne by a king of Judah who was defeated by Nebuchadnezzar and carried off into Babylonian exile (2 Kings 24). His father's name was *Jehoiakim*, and there has clearly been some confusion between the two forms in the derivation of the modern name. The reason for its great popularity in Christian Europe is that in medieval tradition it was the name commonly ascribed to the father of the Virgin Mary. He is not named at all in the Bible, but with the growth of the cult of Mary many legends grew up about her early life, and her parents came to be venerated as saints under the names Joachim and Anne.

Joan ♀ Contracted form of Old French *Jo(h)anne*, from Latin *Io(h)anna* (see ▷Joanna). In England this was the usual feminine form of ▷John from the Middle English period onwards and was extremely popular, but in the 16th and 17th centuries it steadily lost ground to ▷Jane. It was strongly revived in the first part of the 20th century, partly under the influence of George Bernard Shaw's play *St Joan* (1923), based on the life of Joan of Arc (1412–31). Claiming to be guided by the voices of the saints, she persuaded the French dauphin to defy the occupying English forces and have himself crowned, and she led the French army that raised the siege of Orleans in 1429. The following year she was captured by the Burgundians and sold to the English, and a year later she was burned at the stake for witchcraft at the age of 18 or 19. Her story has captured the

imagination of many writers, and she is variously portrayed as a national and political hero, a model of apolitical straightforwardness and honesty, and a religious heroine. She was canonized in 1920. More recent influences have included the American film actress Joan Crawford (1908–77, born Lucille le Sueur), the British actress Joan Collins (b. 1933), the American comedienne Joan Rivers (b. 1933), and the West Indian pop singer Joan Armatrading (b. 1950).

PET FORMS: **Joanie, Joni.**

COGNATES: Irish: **Siobhán.** Scottish Gaelic: **Siubhan.** See also ▷Jane.

Joanna ♀ From the Latin form, *Io(h)anna*, of Greek *Iōanna*, the feminine equivalent of *Iōannēs* (see ▷John). In the New Testament, this name is borne by a woman who was one of Jesus's followers (Luke 8:3; 24:10). She was the wife of the steward of the household of King Herod Antipas. The name was regularly used throughout the Middle Ages in most parts of Europe as a feminine equivalent of ▷John, but in England it has only been in common use as a vernacular given name since the 19th century. Celebrated British bearers of the name include the novelist Joanna Trollope (b. 1943), the actress Joanna Lumley (b. 1946), and the concert pianist Joanna McGregor (b. 1959).

VARIANT: **Joana, Joannah.**

SHORT FORM: **Jo.**

Joanne ♀ From Old French *Jo(h)anne*, and so a doublet of ▷Joan. This too was revived as a given name in its own right in the first half of the 20th century. It has to some extent been influenced by the independently formed combination *Jo Anne*.

VARIANTS: **Johanne, Joann.**

SHORT FORM: **Jo.**

Job ♂ Biblical name, pronounced rhyming with 'robe'. It is borne in the Bible by the hero of the Book of Job, a man of exemplary patience, whose faith was severely tested by God's apparently motiveless maltreatment of him. His name, appropriately enough, means 'persecuted' in Hebrew. His story was a favourite one in the Middle Ages and frequently formed the subject of miracle plays. The name was used among Puritans and Christian fundamentalists, but is currently out of favour, although the form Jobe, presumably a respelling to fix the pronunciation, is occasionally found.

Joby ♂ Modern name of uncertain origin. It may represent a pet form of the name ▷Job.

VARIANT: Jobey.

Jocasta ♀ Name borne in classical legend by the mother of Oedipus, King of Thebes. As the result of a series of misunderstandings, she also became his wife and the mother of his children. The derivation of her name is not known. In spite of its tragic associations, the name has enjoyed a certain vogue in recent years.

Jocelyn ♀, ♂ Now normally a girl's name, but in earlier times more often given to boys. It is a transferred use of the English surname, which in turn is derived from an Old French masculine personal name introduced to Britain by the Normans in the form *Joscelin*. This was originally a derivative, *Gautzelin*, of the name of a Germanic tribe, the *Gauts*. The spelling of the first syllable was altered because the name was taken as a double diminutive (with the Old French suffixes *-el* and *-in*) of *Josce* (see ▷Joyce).

VARIANTS: Jocelyne, Joscelyn, Joselyn, Josceline, Joslyn ♀ .

SHORT FORM: Joss.

Jodene ♀ Recent fanciful coinage, formed from ▷Jody plus the productive suffix *-ene*.

Jody ♂, ♀ Of uncertain origin. It may have originated as a pet form of ▷Jude and/or ▷Judith.

VARIANTS: Jodie (associated particularly with the American actress Jodie Foster, b. 1962 as Alicia Christian Foster); Jodi.

Joe ♂ Short form of ▷Joseph. It has also been in favour as an independent given name since the 1990s.

VARIANT: ▷Jo.

PET FORM: Joey.

Joel ♂ Biblical name, composed of two different Hebrew elements, *Yah(weh)* and *El*, both of which mean 'God'; the implication of the name is that the Hebrew God, *Yahweh*, is the only true god. This is a common name in the Bible, being borne by, among others, one of King David's 'mighty men' (1 Chronicles 11:38), and a minor prophet who lived in the 8th century BC. The name has been perennially popular as a Jewish name; it was also taken up by the Puritans and other Christian fundamentalists. The name has long been in regular use in North America but was uncommon in Britain until the 1990s. Well-known bearers of the name include the American singer and entertainer Joel Grey (b. 1932), the West Indian cricketer Joel Garner (b. 1952), and the American film director Joel Coen (b. 1954). The French form Joël is also used in the English-speaking world.

Joelle ♀ Borrowing of the fashionable French name *Joëlle*, a feminine form of ▷Joel. Its selection as a given name may also have been influenced by the fact that it can be taken as a combination of ▷Jo and the productive suffix *-elle* (originally a French feminine diminutive ending).

Joely ♀ Modern name, apparently a pet form of ▷Jolene, influenced in spelling by the boy's name ▷Joel. It may also represent an Anglicized pronunciation of ▷Jolie.

Joey ♂ Pet form of ▷Joseph or ▷Joe, also used as an independent given name.

Johanna ♀ Latinate feminine form of *Johannes* (see ▷John).

VARIANT: Johannah.

Johanne ♀ Variant of ▷Joanne.

John ♂ English form of Latin *Io(h)annes*, New Testament Greek *Iōannēs*, a contracted form of the Hebrew name *Johanan* 'God is gracious' (the name of several different characters in the Old Testament, including one of King David's 'mighty men'). *John* is the spelling used in the Authorized Version of the New Testament. The name is of great importance in early Christianity: it was borne by John the Baptist (the precursor of Christ himself, who baptized sinners in the River Jordan), by one of Christ's disciples (John the Apostle, a fisherman, brother of James), and by the author of the fourth gospel (John the Evangelist, identified in Christian tradition with the apostle, but more probably a Greek-speaking Jewish Christian living over half a century later). The name was also borne by many saints and by twenty-three popes, including John XXIII (Giuseppe Roncalli, 1881–1963), whose popularity was yet another factor influencing people to choose this given name. It was also a royal name, being borne by eight Byzantine emperors and by kings of Hungary, Poland, Portugal, France, and elsewhere. Among numerous bearers of note in recent times have been American president John F. Kennedy (1917–63) and British pop singer John Lennon (1940–80). In its various forms in different languages, it has been the most perennially popular of all Christian names.

COGNATES: Irish: **Eoin, Seán**. Scottish: **Ian, Iain, Eòin, Seathan**. Welsh: **Ieuan, Siôn**. German: **Johann, Johannes**. Dutch: **Jan**. Danish, Norwegian: **Jens, Johan, Jan**. Swedish: **Johan, Jöns, Jon, Jan**. French: **Jean**. Spanish: **Juan**. Catalan: **Joan**. Portuguese: **João**. Italian: **Giovanni, Gianni**. Greek: **Ioannis, Iannis**. Russian: **Ivan**. Polish: **Jan**. Czech: **Jan**. Finnish: **Juhani, Jussi, Hannu**. Hungarian: **János**. Latvian: **Janis, Jānis**.

PET FORMS: **Johnny, Johnnie, ▷Jack, ▷Hank**.

Johnathan ♂ Respelling of ▷Jonathan, as if a combination of ▷John and ▷Nathan.

Johnathon ♂ Mainly U.S.: respelled form of ▷Jonathan, influenced by ▷John.

Johnny ♂, occasionally ♀ Pet form of ▷John, also used as an independent given name from the 16th century onwards. In the United States it is occasionally also used as a girl's name. Famous bearers include the American country singer Johnny Cash (1932–2003) and the film actor Johnny Depp (b. 1963).
VARIANT: **Johnnie, Jonny**.

Johnson ♂ Transferred use of the surname, meaning originally 'son of John' and in modern times sometimes bestowed with precisely this meaning.

Johnston ♂ Transferred use of the surname, derived originally from a place in Scotland (notably the one in Annandale) named in Old English as 'John's settlement', or a variant of ▷Johnson.
VARIANT: **Johnstone**.

Jolene ♀ Mainly U.S.: recent coinage, combining the short form ▷Jo with the productive suffix *-lene*, extracted from names such as ▷Marlene. It seems to have originated in the United States in the 1940s. It was made famous by a hit song with this title, recorded by Dolly Parton in 1979.
VARIANT: **Joleen**.

Jolie ♀ From the French nickname or term of endearment *jolie* 'pretty one'. This is the feminine form of the adjective *joli*, which originally meant 'gay' or 'festive' and may derive from Old Norse *jōl* 'Yule'.

Jolyon ♂ Medieval variant spelling of ▷Julian. Its occasional use in modern Britain derives from the name of a character in John Galsworthy's sequence of novels *The Forsyte Saga* (1922), which was serialized on television in the late 1960s.

Jon ♂ Simplified spelling of ▷John or a short form of ▷Jonathan. The name is

borne by the Canadian singer Jon
Vickers (b. 1926) and the American
actor Jon Voight (b. 1938).

VARIANT: **Jonn.**

PET FORM: ▷**Jonny.**

Jonah ♂ Biblical name meaning
'dove' in Hebrew; it is borne by a
prophet whose adventures are the
subject of one of the shorter books of
the Bible. God appeared to Jonah and
ordered him to go and preach in
Nineveh. When Jonah disobeyed, God
caused a storm to threaten the ship in
which Jonah was travelling. His
shipmates, realizing that Jonah was the
cause of their peril, threw him
overboard, whereupon the storm
subsided. A 'great fish' swallowed Jonah
and delivered him, willy-nilly, to the
coasts of Nineveh. This story was
immensely popular in the Middle Ages,
and a favourite subject of miracle plays.
There has been a recent modest revival
in the name's popularity.

Jonas ♂ Variant of ▷Jonah, from the
New Testament Greek form of the
name. Both *Jonah* and *Jonas* were used
by the Puritans, the latter from the
1560s at least.

Jonathan ♂ Biblical name, meaning
'God has given', composed of the same
elements as those of ▷Matthew, but in
reverse order. This is the name of
several characters in the Bible, most
notably a son of King Saul, who was a
devoted friend and supporter of the
young David, even when David and
Saul were themselves at loggerheads
(1 Samuel 31; 2 Samuel 1:19–26). The
name is often taken as symbolic of
steadfast friendship and loyalty. Well-
known bearers of the name include the
Irish clergyman and writer Jonathan
Swift (1667–1745), British theatre
director Jonathan Miller (b. 1934),
British actor Jonathan Pryce (b. 1947),
and British television presenter
Jonathan Ross (b. 1960).

VARIANTS: **Jonathen, Jonathon;
Johnathan, Johnathon.**

SHORT FORM: **Jon.**

PET FORM: ▷**Jonny.**

Jones ♂ Transferred use of the
English and Welsh surname, meaning
originally 'son of Jon(e)' (see ▷John).

Joni ♀ Modern respelling of *Joanie*, pet
form of ▷Joan. It is particularly
associated with the Canadian folk
singer Joni Mitchell (b. 1943 as Roberta
Joan Anderson).

Jonina ♀ Name coined recently as a
feminine form of ▷John, preserving the
connection more clearly than ▷Jane,
▷Jean, and ▷Joan, each of which has
acquired a distinctive status of its own.

Jonn ♂ Variant spelling of ▷Jon or
John.

Jonny ♂ Simplified spelling of
▷Johnny or a pet form of ▷Jon, also
used independently.

VARIANT: **Jonnie.**

Jonquil ♀ From the name of the
flower, which was taken into English
from French *jonquille* (a diminutive of
Spanish *junco*, Latin *juncus* 'reed'). This is
one of the latest and rarest of the flower
names, which enjoyed a brief vogue
during the 1940s and 50s.

Jools ♂, ♀ Respelling of the English
pet name ▷Jules, clearly indicating the
difference in pronunciation from the
French name of the same form. It is
associated with the British jazz
musician and television presenter Jools
Holland (b. 1958 as Julian Holland).

Jordan ♂, ♀ Originally a name given
to a child of either sex baptized in holy
water that was, purportedly at least,
brought from the River Jordan, whose
Hebrew name, *ha-yarden*, means
'flowing down'. It was in this river that
Christ was baptized by John the Baptist,
and medieval pilgrims to the Holy Land
usually tried to bring back a flask of its
water with them. The modern given
name is either a revival of this, or else a
transferred use of the surname that was
derived from the medieval given name.

j

It is more popular as a boy's name in Britain and as a girl's name in the United States.

VARIANTS: Jorden, Jordin, Jordon; Jordyn ♀.

SHORT FORM: Judd ♂ (rare).

Jordana ♀ Feminine form of ▷Jordan.

Jorja ♀ Respelling of ▷Georgia, which is popular in New Zealand.

Jory ♀ Pet form of ▷Marjorie.

Jos ♂, ♀ Short form of ▷Joseph, ▷Josiah, or ▷Jocelyn.

Josceline ♀ Variant of ▷Jocelyn as a girl's name.

Joscelyn ♀ Respelling of ▷Jocelyn.

José ♂ Spanish equivalent of ▷Joseph, now also used in the English-speaking world, usually without the accent.

Josef ♂ German, Dutch, Scandinavian, and Czech spelling of ▷Joseph, now also in use in the English-speaking world.

Josefina ♀ Latinate variant of ▷Josephine.

Joselyn ♀ Respelling of ▷Jocelyn as a girl's name.

Joseph ♂ English form of the biblical Hebrew name *Yosef*, meaning '(God) shall add (another son)'. This was borne by the favourite son of Jacob, whose brothers became jealous of him and sold him into slavery (Genesis 37). He was taken to Egypt, where he rose to become chief steward to Pharaoh, and was eventually reconciled to his brothers when they came to buy corn during a seven-year famine (Genesis 43–7). In the New Testament *Joseph* is the name of the husband of the Virgin Mary. It is also borne by a rich Jew, Joseph of Arimathea (Matthew 27:57; Mark 15:43; Luke 23:50; John 19:38), who took Jesus down from the Cross, wrapped him in a shroud, and buried him in a rock tomb. According to medieval legend, Joseph of Arimathea brought the Holy Grail to Britain. The name was uncommon in Britain in the Middle Ages but was revived in the mid 16th century and had become popular by the 1630s, remaining so ever since.

VARIANT: Josef.

SHORT FORMS: Joe, Jo.

COGNATES: Irish: Seosamh. Scottish Gaelic: Ìoseph. German: Josef. Dutch: Jozef. Scandinavian: Josef. French: Joseph. Spanish: José. Catalan: Josep. Portuguese: José. Italian: Giuseppe. Russian, Bulgarian: Iosif. Polish: Józef. Czech: Josef. Croatian, Slovenian: Josip. Finnish: Jooseppi. Hungarian: József, Osip. Latvian: Jāzeps. Lithuanian: Juozapas.

Josephina ♀ Variant of ▷Josephine with the Latinate ending *-a*.

Josephine ♀ From French *Joséphine*, a feminine equivalent of ▷Joseph formed with the diminutive suffix *-ine*. It is now widely used in the English-speaking world. Notable bearers have included the British social reformer Josephine Butler (1828–1906) and the American-born French dancer and singer Josephine Baker (1906–75).

SHORT FORM: Jo.

PET FORMS: Josie, Josette, ▷Fifi, ▷Posy.

Josette ♀ Modern French pet form of *Joséphine*, which has sometimes also been used in the English-speaking world since the 20th century.

Josh ♂ Short form of ▷Joshua, now quite frequent in Britain as an independent given name.

Joshua ♂ Meaning 'God is salvation' in Hebrew; it is borne in the Bible by the Israelite leader who took command of the Children of Israel after the death of Moses and led them, after many battles, to take possession of the Promised Land. The name, long favoured by Jews and Nonconformist Christians, enjoyed a great surge in popularity in the 1990s. Well-known bearers of the name include the

American pianist and conductor Joshua Rifkin (b. 1944) and the American-born violinist Joshua Bell (b. 1967).

Josiah ♂ Meaning 'God heals' in Hebrew; it is borne by a king of Judah, whose story is recounted in 2 Kings 22–23. This was fairly frequently used as a given name in the English-speaking world, especially among Dissenters, from the 18th to the late 19th century. Following several decades of disuse, this name has become increasingly fashionable since the 1970s, especially in the U.S. The spelling Josias was also in use among Puritans from the 16th century. The most famous English bearer is the potter Josiah Wedgwood (1730–95). In North America this was a recurrent name in the Quincy family of Massachusetts; the best-known Josiah Quincy (1744–75) was a pre-Revolutionary patriot, who died while returning from arguing the cause of the American colonists in London.

Josiane ♀ French: elaborated form of *Josée* (French feminine form of ▷Joseph), now occasionally also used in the English-speaking world.

Josie ♀ Pet form of ▷Josephine, now widely used as an independent given name.

Joslyn ♀ Respelling of ▷Jocelyn, as a girl's name.

Joss ♂, ♀ Short form of ▷Jocelyn, also occasionally used as an independent given name. In part it may also be a revival of a medieval boy's name (see ▷Joyce). The name is borne by the British actor Joss Ackland (b. 1928) and the female pop singer Joss Stone (b. 1987 as Jocelyn Eve Stoker).

Joy ♀ From the vocabulary word (Old French *joie*, Late Latin *gaudia*). Being 'joyful in the Lord' was a duty that the Puritans took seriously, so the name became popular in the 17th century under their influence. In modern times, it is generally bestowed with reference to the parents' joy in their new-born child, or with the intention of wishing her a happy life.

Joyce ♀, formerly ♂ Apparently from the Norman male name *Josce* (Middle English *Josse*), which in turn is from *Jodocus*, a Latinized form of a Breton name, *Iodoc*, meaning 'lord', borne by a 7th-century Breton saint. The name was in use in England among Breton followers of William the Conqueror. However, although this was fairly common as a male given name in the Middle Ages, it had virtually died out by the 14th century. There is evidence of its use as a girl's name from the 16th century onwards in parishes with strong Puritan links, which suggests that it may have been associated with the vocabulary word *joy*; see ▷Joy. It was strongly revived in the 19th century under the influence of popular fiction. It is borne by characters in Mrs Henry Wood's *East Lynne* (1861) and Edna Lyall's *In the Golden Days* (1885). Modern use may well have been influenced also by the common Irish surname derived from the medieval Norman male name. See also ▷Joss.

Jozefa ♀ Anglicized spelling of *Josefa*, a feminine form of ▷Joseph, found in Spanish, Portuguese, the Scandinavian languages, and Czech.

Juan ♂ Spanish form of ▷John, now also used as a given name in English-speaking countries, in spite of the unfavourable associations with Don Juan, the heartless seducer of Mozart's opera *Don Giovanni* (1788) and libertine hero of Byron's satirical epic (1819–24).

Juana ♀ Spanish feminine form of ▷Juan. It is now also occasionally used in the English-speaking world, to which it was introduced mainly by Hispanic settlers in the United States.

Juanita ♀ Spanish feminine pet form of ▷Juan. It is now also occasionally used in the English-speaking world, to which it was introduced mainly by Hispanic settlers in the United States.

j

Judah ♂ Biblical name, said to mean 'praised' in Hebrew, borne by the fourth son of Jacob (Genesis 29:35), who gave his name to one of the twelve tribes of Israel and to one of its two kingdoms.

Judas ♂ Greek form of ▷Judah, borne in the New Testament by several characters, but most notably by Judas Iscariot, the apostle who betrayed Christ in the Garden of Gethsemane. There was another apostle called *Judas* (see ▷Jude), and the name was also borne by Judas Maccabbaeus, who liberated Judea briefly from the Syrians in 165 BC, but was killed in battle (161). His story was very popular in the Middle Ages. However, the association with Iscariot has ensured that this name has hardly ever been used as a Christian name, and that *Jude* has always been much rarer than other apostles' names.

Judd ♂ Medieval short form of ▷Jordan, now restored to use as a given name from the derived surname.

Jude ♂, occasionally ♀ Short form of ▷Judas, occasionally used in the New Testament and elsewhere to distinguish the apostle Jude (Judas Thaddaeus), to whom one of the Epistles in the New Testament is attributed, from the traitor Judas Iscariot. It is also borne by the central character in Thomas Hardy's gloomy novel *Jude the Obscure* (1895), a film adaptation of which was released in 1996. The Lennon and McCartney song 'Hey Jude' (1968) and the British actor Jude Law (b. 1972) may have contributed to the popularity of the name in recent times. As a girl's name it is a short form of ▷Judith or ▷Judy, and is sometimes used independently.

Judge ♂ Generally, no doubt, a transferred use of the surname, rather than a coinage with direct reference to the legal officer (Old French *juge*, from Latin *iudex*). As a

Jewish name it represents a translation of the Hebrew name *Dayan*, which denotes a rabbinic judge.

Judi ♀ Variant spelling of ▷Judy, as borne by the British actress Judi Dench (b. 1934 as Judith Olivia Dench).

Judith ♀ Biblical name, meaning 'Jewess' or 'woman from Judea', borne by a Jewish heroine whose story is recorded in the Book of Judith in the Apocrypha. Judith is portrayed as a beautiful widow who delivers her people from the invading Assyrians by gaining the confidence of their commander, Holofernes, and cutting off his head while he is asleep; without their commander, the Assyrians are duly routed. This has been a perennially popular Jewish name. In the English-speaking world it was taken up in the 16th century, having been in occasional use among Gentiles before this: for example, it was borne by a niece of William the Conqueror. It enjoyed great popularity between the 1940s and the 1960s. Today's notable bearers include the American novelist Judith Krantz (b. 1928) and the Scottish composer Judith Weir (b. 1954).
PET FORMS: Judy, Judi, Judie.

Judy ♀ Pet form of ▷Judith, recorded from the 17th century. It was the name adopted by the singer and film star Judy Garland (1922–69), original name Frances Gumm), and has since increasingly been used as an independent name.
VARIANTS: Judi, Judie.

Jules ♂, sometimes ♀ French form of ▷Julius. It is a very common given name in France and is used in the English-speaking world, where it is also fairly common as an informal pet form of ▷Julian, ▷Julie, and ▷Juliet.

Juli Variant spelling of ▷Julie.

Julia ♀ Feminine form of the old Roman family name ▷Julius. A woman called Julia is mentioned in Paul's Epistle to the Romans (Romans 16:15), and the name was borne by numerous early saints. Its frequency increased with the vogue for classical names in the 18th century, and it continues to enjoy considerable popularity, although the recent introduction of ▷Julie to the English-speaking world has reduced this somewhat. Well-known bearers include the British actress Julia Foster (b. 1941) and American actress Julia Roberts (b. 1967 as Julie Fiona Roberts).

COGNATES: Italian: **Giulia**. French: ▷**Julie**. Czech: **Julie**.

Julian ♂, occasionally ♀ From the common Late Latin name *Julianus*, a derivative of ▷Julius. In classical times *Julianus* was a name borne not only by various minor early saints, but also by the Roman emperor Julian 'the Apostate', who attempted to return the Roman Empire from institutionalized Christianity to paganism. For many centuries the English name *Julian* was borne by women as well as men, for example by the Blessed Julian of Norwich (*c.*1342– after 1413). The differentiation in form between *Julian* and ▷Gillian did not develop until the 16th century. *Julian* is still occasionally used as a girl's name. Notable bearers include the British classical guitarist Julian Bream (b. 1933) and the British jazz pianist and bandleader Julian Joseph (b. 1966).

VARIANTS: **Julyan**; ▷**Jolyon** ♂.

Juliana ♀ Latin feminine form of *Julianus* (see ▷Julian), which was revived in England in the 18th century and has been used occasionally ever since.

Julianna ♀ Modern combination of the given names ▷Julie and ▷Anna, perhaps sometimes intended as a form of ▷Juliana.

Julianne ♀ Modern combination of the given names ▷Julie and ▷Anne, perhaps sometimes regarded as a feminine form of ▷Julian.

VARIANT: **Juliane, Julieann, Julieanne**.

Julie ♀ French form of ▷Julia. This was imported to the English-speaking world in the 1920s, and soon became a great favourite. Its popularity was increased in the 1960s by the fame of the British actresses Julie Harris (b. 1925), Julie Andrews (b. 1935 as Julia Wells), Julie Christie (b. 1940), and, more recently, of Julie Waters (b. 1950).

Julien ♂ French form of ▷Julian, now also found in the English-speaking world.

Juliet ♀ Anglicized form of French ▷Juliette or Italian *Giulietta*, diminutive forms of ▷Julia. The name is most famous as that of the 'star-crossed' heroine of Shakespeare's tragedy *Romeo and Juliet*. Well-known bearers include the British actresses Juliet Mills (b. 1941) and Juliet Stevenson (b. 1956).

Juliette ♀ French diminutive of ▷Julie, used also in the English-speaking world. It is borne by the French actress Juliette Binoche (b. 1964).

Julio ♂ Spanish form of ▷Julius. It is now also used in the English-speaking world, to which it was introduced mainly by Hispanic settlers in the United States.

Julitta ♀ Of uncertain origin, probably a Late Latin form of ▷Judith, influenced by ▷Julia. This was the name borne by the mother of the infant saint Quiricus; she was martyred with him at Tarsus in 304.

Julius ♂ Roman family name, of obscure derivation, borne most notably by Gaius Julius Caesar (?102–44 BC). It was in use among the early Christians, and was the name of an early and influential pope (337–52), as well as of a later pope (1443–1513) who attempted to combat the corruption of the Renaissance papacy. The name is used occasionally in the English-speaking world, one of its best-known bearers being the writer John Julius Norwich (b. 1929).

Julyan ♂ Modern respelling of ▷Julian.

Junaid ♂ Muslim (Sufi) name bestowed in honour of the 10th-century mystic Abū'l-Qāsim al-Junayd.

June ♀ One of the names coined in the early 20th century from the names of months of the year. It was very popular in the 1930s but has since fallen from favour (compare ▷April and ▷May).

Junior ♂ From the common nickname used to distinguish a son from his father or for any young male, used occasionally since the early 20th century as an independent given name, mainly in the United States.

Juniper ♀ From the name of the plant (derived in the Middle Ages from Late Latin *iuniperus*, of uncertain origin). The term is also used in the Authorized Version of the Old Testament as a translation of Hebrew *rothem*, a substantial desert shrub whose wood was used in the building of the temple of Solomon. This is not a particularly common given name; there may have been some influence from ▷Jennifer, and in some cases it may represent a transferred use of the surname (which is in part derived from *Jennifer*).

Junita ♀ English variant of ▷Juanita, perhaps influenced by the name of the Roman goddess *Juno* or by the given name ▷June, or by both.

Juno ♀ Anglicized form of the Irish name Úna (see Irish appendix), assimilated to the name of the Roman goddess *Juno*, consort of Jupiter.

Justin ♂ English form of the Latin name *Justinus*, a derivative of ▷Justus. The name was borne by various early saints, notably a 2nd-century Christian apologist and a (possibly spurious) boy martyr of the 3rd century. *Justin* has enjoyed considerable popularity since the second half of the 20th century, reinforced latterly perhaps by the popularity of American singer Justin Timberlake (b. 1981).
VARIANT: **Justyn**.

Justina ♀ Feminine form of ▷Justin, from Latin *Justina*. This was the name of an early virgin martyr executed at Padua under Diocletian.

Justine ♀ Feminine form of ▷Justin. It is recorded in England in the 14th century, but the modern name is probably a borrowing from French. Its use in Britain since the 1960s was partly due to the influence of Lawrence Durrell's novel of this name.

Justus ♂ Mainly U.S.: Latin name meaning 'just' or 'fair'.

Kk

Kacey ♂, ♀ Variant spelling of ▷Casey.
VARIANT: **Kaci.**

Kade ♂ Respelling of ▷Cade.

Kaden ♂ Respelling of ▷Caden.

Kai ♂, occasionally ♀ German and Scandinavian: pet form of any of various Germanic names beginning with *K-* or *G -*. It has been connected with **Gerhard** and **Klaus** (see German appendix). It also may alternatively be from Latin *Gaius*, an ancient Roman personal name (see ▷Caius) or even from *Caietanus* (see **Kajetan** in German appendix), although the latter is primarily a Roman Catholic (South German) name, while *Kai* is predominantly North German. The reasons for its adoption and recent meteoric rise in popularity in the English-speaking world are unclear. In the United States, it may also in part represent a Hawaiian word meaning 'the sea'.

Kailey ♀ Variant spelling of ▷Kayley.

Kaitlyn ♀ Mainly North American: fanciful respelling of ▷Caitlín.

Kale ♂ Of uncertain origin, perhaps an Anglicized form of the Irish name **Cathal**. It may have been invented as a masculine equivalent of ▷Kayley and its variants.
VARIANTS: **Caile, Cayle, Cale, Kail(e), Kayle.**

Kaleb ♂ Respelling of ▷Caleb.

Kaley ♀ Variant spelling of ▷Kayley.

Kallum ♂ Apparently a respelling of ▷Callum.

Kamran ♂ Fanciful respelling of ▷Cameron.

Kane ♂ Anglicized form of the Irish Gaelic name **Cathán**, now also used elsewhere in the English-speaking world.

Kara ♀ Respelling of ▷Cara.

Karen ♀ Danish equivalent of ▷Katherine. It was first introduced to the English-speaking world by Scandinavian settlers in America; it has been used in Britain only since the 1940s, but had become very popular by the 1960s.

Karenza ♀ Cornish: meaning 'loving', a derivative of *car* 'love'.

Karin ♀ Swedish and Norwegian equivalent of ▷Katherine, found as a less common variant of ▷Karen in North America and Britain.

Karis ♀ Variant spelling of ▷Charis.

Karl ♂ German and Scandinavian equivalent of ▷Charles, also used in the English-speaking world. See also ▷Carl.

Karla ♀ German and Scandinavian feminine form of ▷Karl, now also used in the English-speaking world.

Karlene ♀ Modern coinage, a feminine form of ▷Karl, created by the addition of the female productive name suffix *-ene*.
VARIANT: **Karleen.**

Karma ♀ From the Sanskrit word (meaning 'action' or 'effect') used in Hinduism and Buddhism to refer to the principle by which a person's actions in this world determine the fate that awaits him or her after death. In English the word is sometimes used more loosely to refer to the processes of destiny, and it has sometimes been chosen as a given name with reference to this idea.

k

Karolyn ♀ Respelling of ▷Carolyn.

Kasey ♀ Variant spelling of ▷Casey.

Katarina ♀ Swedish equivalent of ▷Katherine, also occasionally used in the English-speaking world.

Kate ♀ Short form of ▷Katherine (or any of its variant spellings), reflecting the French pronunciation with -*t*- for -*th*-, which was also usual in medieval England. This short form has been continuously popular since the Middle Ages, and is now frequently used as an independent given name. It was used by Shakespeare for two important characters: the daughter of the King of France who is wooed and won by King Henry V, and the 'shrew' in *The Taming of the Shrew*.

Katelyn ♀ Elaboration of ▷Kate with the suffix -*lyn* (see ▷Lynn), or a respelling of ▷Caitlín.

Katerina ♀ Russian equivalent of ▷Katherine. This is a popular form in Russia, which is also occasionally used in the English-speaking world.

Kath ♀ Short form of ▷Katherine and its variants and of ▷Kathleen.

Katha ♀ Altered form of ▷Kathy or elaborated form of ▷Kath, with the Latinate feminine suffix -*a*.

Katharine ♀ Variant of ▷Katherine, associated by folk etymology with Greek *katharos* 'pure'. This is the preferred spelling in Germany. It is also the one used in the name of the American film star Katharine Hepburn (1907–2003).

Katherine ♀ English form of the name of a saint martyred at Alexandria in 307. The story has it that she was condemned to be broken on the wheel for her Christian belief. However, the wheel miraculously fell apart, and so she was beheaded instead. There were many elaborations on this story, which was one of the most popular in early Christian mythology, and she has been the object of a vast popular cult. The earliest sources that mention her are in Greek and give the name in the form *Aikaterinē*. The name is of unknown etymology; the suggestion that it may be derived from *Hēcatē*, the pagan goddess of magic and enchantment, is not convincing. From an early date, it was associated with the Greek adjective *katharos* 'pure'. This led to spellings with -*th*- and to a change in the middle vowel (see ▷Katharine). Several later saints also bore the name, including the mystic St Katherine of Siena (1347–80) who both led a contemplative life and played a role in the affairs of state of her day. *Katherine* is also a royal name: in England it was borne by the formidable and popular Katherine of Aragon (1485–1536), the first wife of Henry VIII, as well as by the wives of Henry V and Charles II.

VARIANTS: **Katharine, Kath(e)ryn, Katharyn, Kath(e)rin, Catherine, Catharine, Cathryn.**

SHORT FORMS: ▷**Kate, Kath, Cath, Cate.**

PET FORMS: **Kathy, Kathie, Kat(e)y, Kati(e), Kit(ty), Cathy.**

COGNATES: Irish: **Caitríona, Caitrín, Catraoine, Caitlín.** Scottish Gaelic: ▷**Catriona, Ca(i)triona.** Welsh: **Catrin.** German: **Kat(h)arine, Katrine.** Dutch: **Katrien, Katrijn.** Danish, Norwegian, Swedish: **Katarina.** French: **Catherine.** Spanish: **Catalina.** Catalan: **Caterina.** Portuguese: **Catarina.** Italian: **Caterina.** Greek: **Ekateríni.** Russian: **Yekaterina; Katerina** (popular form). Polish: **Katarzyna.** Czech: **Kateřina.** Croatian, Serbian, Slovenian: **Katarina.** Bulgarian: **Ekatarina.** Finnish: **Kaarina.** Hungarian: **Katalin.**

Katheryn ♀ Altered spelling of ▷Katherine, influenced by the productive name suffix -*yn*.

Kathleen ♀ Of Irish origin: traditional Anglicized form of ▷Caitlín.

VARIANTS: **Kathlene, Cathleen.**

SHORT FORM: **Kath.**

PET FORM: **Kathy.**

Kathlyn ♀ Respelling of ▷Kathleen, influenced by the productive suffix -*lyn*; see ▷Lynn.

Kathryn ♀ Variant of ▷Katherine.

Kathy ♀ Pet form of ▷Katherine and of ▷Kathleen, occasionally used as an independent given name.

Katia ♀ Variant spelling of ▷Katya.

Katie ♀ Pet form of ▷Katherine, also frequently used as an independent given name, which has been extremely popular since the 1980s. It is often found in combination with other names such as *Ann*, *Jane*, *Leigh*, *Louise*, and *Mae*.
VARIANT: **Katy.**

Katlyn ♀ Variant of ▷Katelyn.

Katrina ♀ Variant spelling of ▷Catrina.

Katrine ♀ German and Danish contracted form of **Katharine**, now also occasionally used in the English-speaking world.

Katriona ♀ Variant spelling of ▷Catriona.

Katy ♀ Variant spelling of ▷Katie, recorded as an independent given name since the 18th century.

Katya ♀ Russian pet form of *Yekaterina* (see ▷Katherine), now sometimes used as a given name in the English-speaking world.
VARIANT: **Katia.**

Kay ♀, ♂ Pet form of any of the various names beginning with the letter *K*- (compare ▷Dee and ▷Jay), most notably ▷Katherine and its many variants. It is also used independently. As a boy's name it may in part make reference to the name of the Arthurian knight Sir Kay, although he is not a particularly attractive character. His name is probably a Celticized form of Latin *Gaius*, an ancient Roman personal name of uncertain derivation. As a girl's name it was famous as that of the actress Kay Kendall (1926–59, original name Justine McCarthy).

Kaye ♀ Variant spelling of ▷Kay as a girl's name.

Kayla ♀ Altered form of ▷Kayley, a recent coinage now enjoying a considerable vogue in North America.
VARIANT: **Kaylah.**

Kayley ♀ Of recent origin and uncertain derivation, occurring in a remarkably large number of different spellings. It is probably a transferred use of the Irish surname *Kayley*, an Anglicized form of Gaelic *Ó Caollaidhe* 'descendant of *Caollaidhe*'. The latter is an ancient (male) personal name derived from *caol* 'slender'. Its adoption as a modern given name has probably also been influenced by the popularity of ▷Keeley, ▷Kelly, ▷Kylie, and ▷Callie.
VARIANTS: **Kayly, Kayli(e), Kaylee, Kayleigh, Kail(e)y, Kailee, Kaileigh, Kaley, Kalie, Kalee, Kaleigh; Cayleigh, Caileigh, Caleigh.**

Kaz ♀ Mainly Australian: informal pet form of ▷Karen.

Keane ♂ Anglicized form of the Irish name ▷Cian, also used elsewhere by English speakers.
VARIANT: **Kean.**

Keanu ♂ Hawaiian name meaning 'cool breeze blowing down from the mountains', made popular by the film actor Keanu Reeves (b. 1965).

Keaton ♂ Transferred use of the surname, in origin a local name from Keaton in Ermington, Devon, Ketton in Durham, or Ketton in Rutland.

Keegan ♂ Transferred use of the Irish surname, an Anglicized form of Gaelic *Mac Aodhagáin*, a patronymic from the personal name *Aodhagán* (see **Aogán** in Irish appendix).

Keelan ♂ Transferred use of the surname, which has two possible sources: either it is a reduced form of the Irish surname *Keelahan*, an

Anglicized form of Gaelic *Ó Céileacháin*, from a diminutive of *céile* 'companion', or alternatively it is Welsh in origin, a local name from any of various townships called *Cilan*.

Keeley ♀ Of recent origin and uncertain etymology, possibly an alteration of **Keelin** (see Irish appendix) to fit in with the pattern of girls' names ending in -(*e*)*y* or -*ie*. The Irish surname *Keeley* is a variant of ▷**Kayley**.

VARIANTS: Keely, Keelie, Keeleigh, ▷Keighley.

Keenan ♂ Transferred used of the Irish surname, Gaelic *Ó Cianáin* 'descendant of *Cianán*'. The latter is a personal name, a diminutive of ▷**Cian**.

Keeva ♀ Anglicized form of the Gaelic name Caoimhe (see Irish appendix).

Keighley ♀ Fanciful respelling of ▷**Keeley**, inspired by the Yorkshire town of *Keighley*, which is, however, pronounced 'keeth-lee'.

Keiller ♂ Chiefly Canadian: transferred use of the Scottish surname *Keiller*, from a village of this name in Perthshire. It is bestowed chiefly in honour of the Hon. Keiller Mackay (1888–1970), chief justice and later lieutenant governor of Ontario.

Keir ♂ Transferred use of the Scottish surname, pronounced 'keer', in origin a variant of ▷**Kerr**. The name has sometimes been chosen in honour of the trade unionist and first Labour MP, James Keir Hardie (1856–1915), whose mother's maiden name was Keir.

Keira ♀ Modern coinage: apparently a feminine form of ▷**Keir** or a respelling of ▷**Kiera**.

Keiran ♂ Anglicized form of ▷**Ciarán**, influenced by ▷**Keir**.

Keisha ♀ Pronounced 'kay-sha': modern coinage of uncertain origin. It is mainly used by Blacks and may derive from a West African language.

One suggested meaning is 'favourite daughter', from *nkisa*.

Keith ♂ Transferred use of the Scottish surname (see Scottish appendix). The principal family bearing this surname were hereditary Earls Marischal of Scotland from 1455 to 1715. This is one of a number of Scottish aristocratic surnames that have become well established since the 19th century as boys' names throughout the English-speaking world, not just in Scotland. Others include ▷Bruce, ▷Douglas, and ▷Graham.

Kellen ♂ Of uncertain derivation, perhaps an altered form of Irish **Kelan**, or a shortened form of the Scottish surname *McKellen* (Gaelic *Mac Ailein* 'son of Alan' or *Mac Cailein* 'son of Colin').

Kelly ♀, ♂ Originally an Anglicized form of the ancient Irish male name Ceallach (see Irish appendix). It is now very widely used in the English-speaking world, mainly as a girl's name. This is a transferred use of the surname *Ó Ceallaigh* 'descendant of Ceallach'.

VARIANTS: Kelley, Kellie ♀.

Kelsey ♀, ♂ Transferred use of the surname, which is from an Old English masculine personal name *Cēolsige*, derived from *cēol* 'ship' + *sige* 'victory'. Its use as a girl's name may have been influenced by names such as ▷**Elsie**. In the United States the spelling *Kelsey* is reserved chiefly for boys.

VARIANTS: Kelsi(e) ♀.

Kelvin ♂ Modern given name, first used in the 1920s and increasing in popularity from the 1950s onwards. It is taken from the name of the Scottish river which runs through Glasgow into the Clyde (compare ▷Clyde). Its choice as a given name may also have been influenced by names such as ▷Kevin and ▷Melvin and the fame of the scientist Lord Kelvin (1824–1907).

VARIANT: Kelvyn.

Kemp ♂ Transferred use of the surname, which originated in the Middle Ages as an occupational name or nickname from Middle English *kempe* 'athlete, wrestler' (from Old English *kempa* 'warrior, champion').

Ken ♂ Short form of ▷Kenneth, or occasionally of various other boys' names with this first syllable. It is occasionally used independently.

Kenda ♀ Modern name, apparently a shortened form of ▷Kendall. It has perhaps been created by analogy with the pair of names ▷Linda and ▷Lindall.

Kendall ♀, ♂ Transferred use of the surname, which is at least in part a local name, either from *Kendal* in Cumbria (formerly the county town of Westmorland), so named because it stands in the valley of the river Kent, or from *Kendale* in Driffield, Humberside, where the first element is Old Norse *keld* 'spring'. The surname may in some cases be derived from the Welsh personal name *Cynddelw*, which is of uncertain origin, perhaps from an Old Celtic word meaning 'high, exalted' + *delw* 'image, effigy').

VARIANTS: **Kendal, Kendel(l), Kendle.**

Kendra ♀ Mainly U.S.: recently coined name, probably as a feminine form of ▷Kendrick.

Kendrick ♂ In modern use a transferred use of the surname, the origins of which are complex. The source in many cases is the Old Welsh personal name *Cynwrig*. This is of uncertain derivation: it may be composed of elements meaning 'high, exalted' + 'hill' or 'summit'. The Scottish surname *Ken(d)rick* is a shortened form of *MacKen(d)rick* (Gaelic *Mac Eanraig* 'son of Henry'); Scottish bearers are descended from a certain Henry MacNaughton, and the (Mac)Ken(d)ricks are a sept of Clan MacNaughton. As an English surname, *Ken(d)rick* is derived, at least in part, from the Middle English given name

Cenric, in which two Old English personal names have fallen together: *Cēnerīc* (from *cēne* 'keen' + *rīc* 'power') and *Cynerīc* (from *cyne* 'royal' + *rīc* 'power'). *Cenric* survived as a given name into the 17th century.

VARIANT: **Kenrick.**

Kenelm ♂ From an Old English personal name derived from *cēne* 'keen, bold' + *helm* 'helmet, protection'. The name was popular in England during the Middle Ages, when a shadowy 9th-century Mercian prince of this name was widely revered as a saint and martyr, although his death seems to have been rather the result of personal and political motives. It has remained in occasional use ever since, especially in the Digby family, where it tended to alternate with ▷Everard. The most famous Sir Kenelm Digby (1603–65) was noted as a writer, scientist, adventurer, diplomat, and lover.

Kennard ♂ Transferred use of a surname, derived from a Middle English personal name in which several earlier names have fallen together. The first element is either *cēne* 'keen' or *cyne* 'royal'; the second is either *weard* 'guardian' or *heard* 'hardy, brave, strong'.

Kennedy ♀, ♂ Anglicized form of Irish Gaelic **Cinnéidigh** (see Irish appendix). In recent years it has sometimes been used as a given name in the English-speaking world in honour of the assassinated American president John F. Kennedy (1917–63) and his brother Robert (1925–68).

Kenneth ♂ Of Scottish origin: Anglicized form of two different Gaelic names, *Cinaed* and *Cainnech*. The former was the Gaelic name of Kenneth mac Alpin (d. 858), first king of the united Picts and Scots. The latter survives today in Scotland as the common Gaelic name **Coinneach** (see Scottish appendix). Since early in the 20th century *Kenneth* has been in regular use and enjoyed great popularity as a given

k

name well beyond the borders of Scotland.

VARIANT: **Kennith**.

SHORT FORM: **Ken**.

PET FORM: ▷**Kenny**.

Kenny ♂ Either a pet form of ▷Kenneth, also used as an independent given name, or an Anglicized form of Irish **Cainneach** (see Irish appendix).

Kenrick ♂ Contracted form of ▷Kendrick.

Kent ♂ Transferred use of the surname, in origin a local name from the English county. This is probably named with a Celtic word meaning 'border'. Use as a given name is of recent origin, but it is now quite popular. It may in part be seen as a short form of ▷Kenton.

Kenton ♂ Transferred use of the surname, in origin a local name from any of various places so called. The one in Devon gets its name from the British river name *Kenn* + Old English *tūn* 'enclosure, settlement'; the one in north-west London is from the Old English personal name *Cēna* + *tūn*; the one in Northumberland is from Old English *cyne-* 'royal' + *tūn*.

Kenzie ♂, occasionally ♀ Modern name, a short form of ▷Mackenzie. As a girl's name it may in part have been influenced by ▷Keziah.

Keren ♀ Shortened form of the biblical name *Keren-happuch*, borne by the third of Job's daughters (Job 42:14). The name meant 'horn of eye-paint' in Hebrew.

VARIANTS: **Keran**, **Ker(r)in**, **Keron**.

Kerena ♀ Latinate elaboration of ▷Keren.

VARIANT: **Kerina**.

Keri ♀ Respelling of either ▷Kerry or Ceri (see Welsh appendix).

Kermit ♂ Mainly U.S.: of Irish and Manx origin, from the Gaelic surname form *Mac Dhiarmaid* 'son of Diarmaid'

(see ▷Dermot). The name was borne by a son of the American president Theodore Roosevelt, and by a frog puppet, created in the 1970s for Jim Henson's *Muppet Show*.

Kerr ♂ Transferred use of the surname, which is a northern English local name for someone who lived by a patch of wet ground overgrown with brushwood (Old Norse *kjarr*).

Kerry ♀, ♂ Of Australian origin, a modern coinage, probably from the name of the Irish county. It is also quite common in Britain and elsewhere in the English-speaking world, especially as a girl's name.

VARIANTS: **Kerrie**, **Kerri**, ▷**Keri**, all ♀.

Kester ♂ Medieval Scottish form of ▷Christopher, occasionally revived as a modern given name.

Kestrel ♀ One of the rarer girls' names derived from vocabulary words denoting birds that came into use in the 20th century. The word itself derives from Old French *cresserelle*, apparently a derivative of *cressele* 'rattle'.

Keturah ♀ Biblical name, meaning 'incense' in Hebrew, borne by the woman Abraham married after Sarah's death (Genesis 25:1). The name is occasionally chosen in the English-speaking world by parents in search of an unusual name.

Kevin ♂ Anglicized form of the Gaelic name **Caoimhín** (see Irish appendix). Since the early 20th century it has been widely adopted throughout the English-speaking world.

VARIANTS: **Keven**, **Kevan** (from Gaelic *Caoimheán*, with a different diminutive suffix), **Kevyn**.

Kezia ♀ From the Hebrew word for the cassia tree (the English name of which is derived, via Latin and Greek, from Hebrew or a related Semitic source). It is borne in the Bible by one of Job's daughters, born to him towards the end of his life, after his prosperity had been restored (Job 42:14).

VARIANT: Keziah.

PET FORMS: Kizzie, Kizzy.

Kia ♀ Modern name of uncertain origin, possibly an arbitrary coinage. In New Zealand and Australia it may have been inspired by the Maori phrase *kia ora* 'be well', which is used as a greeting or to wish someone good luck.

Kian ♂ Anglicized spelling of Irish ▷Cian, now in general use.

Kiara ♀ Respelling of ▷Ciara.

VARIANT: Kiarah.

Kiera ♀ Recently coined feminine form of ▷Kieran; see also ▷Ciara.

Kieran ♂ Anglicized form of Irish ▷Ciarán, one of several names of Celtic origin that suddenly became popular throughout the English-speaking world during the 1990s.

Kilroy ♂ Transferred use of the surname, which is in origin a variant of ▷Gilroy.

Kim ♀, ♂ Originally a short form of ▷Kimberley, now established as an independent given name. The hero of Rudyard Kipling's novel *Kim* (1901) bore the name as a short form of *Kimball* (a surname used as a given name). In recent years, as a girl's name it has been borne by a number of well-known people, including the film stars Kim Novak (b. 1933) and Kim Basinger (b. 1953).

VARIANT: Kym.

Kimberley ♀, ♂ The immediate source of the given name is the town in South Africa, the scene of fighting during the Boer War, which brought it to public notice at the end of the 19th century. The town was named after a certain Lord Kimberley, whose ancestors derived their surname from one of the places in England called Kimberley. The first part of the place

name derives from various Old English personal names; the second (from Old English *lēah*) means 'wood' or 'clearing'.

VARIANTS: Kimberly (the more common North American spelling), Kimberli(e), Kimberlee, Kimberleigh, all ♀.

King ♂ From the vocabulary word for a male monarch, bestowed, especially in America, with a hint of the notion that the bearer would have kingly qualities; compare ▷Duke and ▷Earl. In some cases it may be a transferred use of the surname (originally a nickname or an occupational name given to someone who was employed in a royal household). Its frequency among African Americans is no doubt partly attributable to the civil rights leader Martin Luther King (1929–68). It is also used as a short form of ▷Kingsley.

Kingsley ♂, occasionally ♀ Transferred use of the surname, originally a local name derived from various places (in Cheshire, Hampshire, Staffordshire) named in Old English as *Cyningeslēah* 'king's wood'.

VARIANTS: Kingsly, Kingslie.

SHORT FORM: King.

Kira ♀ Variant spelling of ▷Kyra.

Kirk ♂ Transferred use of the surname, originally a northern English and Scottish local name for someone who lived near a church (from Old Norse *kirkja*). Recent use has probably been influenced to some extent by the film actor Kirk Douglas (b. 1916 as Issur Danielovich Demsky).

Kirsten ♀ Danish and Norwegian form of ▷Christine, now also well established in the English-speaking world. A well-known bearer of the name was the Norwegian opera singer Kirsten Flagstad (1895–1962).

Kirstie ♀ Scottish pet form of ▷Kirstin, now used as an independent given name throughout the English-speaking world.

k

VARIANTS: **Kirsty, Kirsti; Chirsty** (the usual spelling in the Scottish Highlands).

Kirstin ♀ Scottish vernacular form of ▷Christine, now also used outside Scotland.

Kirsty ♀ Variant spelling of ▷Kirstie.

Kit ♂, ♀ Pet form of ▷Christopher; also of ▷Katherine and its variants. In the medieval period it was a pet form of ▷Christian and ▷Christiana.

Kitty ♀ Pet form of ▷Katherine, derived from the pet form ▷Kit + the hypocoristic suffix -y. It is also used as an independent given name.

Kizzy ♀ Pet form of ▷Kezia; like the variant form Kizzie, it is also occasionally used as a given name in its own right.

Koppel ♂ Jewish: Yiddish pet form of *Jakob* (see ▷Jacob).

Kreine ♀ Jewish: from a dialect form of Yiddish *kroine* 'crown' (equivalent to modern German *Krone*, from Latin *corōna*). See also ▷Atarah.

Kris ♂, ♀ Short form of ▷Christopher, ▷Kristina, ▷Kristine, ▷Kristen, or any other name beginning with this syllable. It is occasionally used as an independent given name for boys.

Krista ♀ Mainly U.S.: variant spelling of ▷Christa.

Kristel ♀ Fanciful spelling of ▷Crystal.

Kristen ♀, ♂ As a girl's name this is a variant of ▷Kirsten or ▷Christine; it is quite popular in the United States. As a boy's name, it appears to be a recent borrowing of the Danish equivalent of ▷Christian.

Kristian ♂, ♀ Respelling of ▷Christian, also used as a girl's name in the United States.

Kristie ♀ Mainly U.S.: variant of the girl's name ▷Christie, under the influence of the Scottish name ▷Kirstie.

Kristina ♀ Respelling of ▷Christina. This coincides with the Swedish and Czech form of the name.

Kristine ♀ Mainly U.S.: fanciful respelling of ▷Christine, under the influence of ▷Kristina.
VARIANTS: **Kristeen, Kristene.**

Kristopher ♂ Mainly U.S.: respelling of ▷Christopher.

Kristy ♀ Variant spelling of ▷Kristie.

Krystal ♀ Respelling of ▷Crystal.

Kurt ♂ German: contracted form of *Konrad* (see ▷Conrad), now also used in the English-speaking world.

Kurtis ♂ Respelling of ▷Curtis, influenced by ▷Kurt, to which, however, it is not related.

Kyla ♀ Recently coined name, created as a feminine form of ▷Kyle or else a variant of ▷Kylie.

Kyle ♂, occasionally ♀ Of Scottish origin but now widely used in the English-speaking world. It is derived from a topographic term denoting a narrow strait or channel and in part is a transferred use of the surname, a local name from the region in Ayrshire so called. As a girl's name it appears to have been largely superseded by ▷Kyla.

Kylie ♀ Of Australian origin, said to represent an Aboriginal term for the boomerang. However, it seems more likely that the name is an invention, influenced by ▷Kyle and ▷Kelly. It has been very popular in Australia and, in part due to the Australian singer Kylie Minogue (b. 1968), has also acquired currency in Britain and elsewhere in the English-speaking world.
VARIANTS: **Kyley, Kylee, Kyleigh.**

Kylin ♀ Apparently an elaboration of ▷Kyla or ▷Kylie, perhaps by association with the Irish name **Keelin** (see Irish appendix). The fact that it is pronounced much the same as a

Chinese word denoting a mythological creature resembling the unicorn is presumably no more than coincidence.

Kym ♀, ♂ Respelling of ▷Kim.

Kynaston ♂ Transferred use of the surname, which originated in the Middle Ages as a local name from places in Hereford and Shropshire so called from Old English *Cyneþrípestūn* 'settlement of *Cyneþríp*', a male personal name composed of *cyne* 'royal' + *þríp* 'peace'.

Kyra ♀ Either from medieval Greek *kyra* 'lady' (classical Greek *kyria*) or a variant spelling of *Cyra*, a feminine form of ▷Cyrus. In other cases it is a name formed as a feminine equivalent of ▷Kyran.

VARIANT: **Kira**.

Kyran ♂ Variant spelling of ▷Kieran.

Ll

Lacey ♀, occasionally ♂ Transferred use of the surname, originally a Norman baronial name from *Lassy*, Calvados. The Lacey family was powerful in Ireland during the early Middle Ages.

VARIANT: **Lacy.**

Lachlan ♂ From Scottish Gaelic *Lachlann* (earlier *Lochlann*), said to refer originally to a migrant from Norway, the 'land of the lochs'. The name was traditionally used only in families with some Highlands connection and still retains a very Scottish flavour. However, it has now acquired wide popular appeal, especially in Australia and New Zealand.

PET FORMS: Scottish: **Lachie.** Canadian: **Lockie.**

FEMININE FORM: Scottish Highlands: **Lachina.**

Ladislas ♂ Latinate form of Polish *Wadisław*, Czech *Vladislav*, or Hungarian *László* (an old Slavic name composed of *volod* 'rule' + *slav* 'glory'), occasionally used in Britain and elsewhere, but mainly as a translation name.

VARIANT: **Ladislaus.**

Laetitia ♀ Pronounced 'le-**tish**-a': Latin form of ▷Lettice. This form has now been largely superseded by the various modern simplified spellings, which are particularly popular among Blacks in the English-speaking world.

VARIANTS: **Latisha, Leticia.**

Laila ♀ Variant spelling of ▷Leila.

Lalage ♀ Classical name, pronounced '**lal**-a-jee' or '**lal**-a-ghee'. It was used by Horace in his *Odes* as the name of his beloved of the moment. This was a literary pseudonym derived from Greek *lalagein* 'to chatter, babble'. It has

enjoyed a modest popularity among classically educated parents since the 19th century. It is the name of the narrator in E. Arnot Robertson's *Ordinary Families* (1933) and it also occurs in John Fowles's *The French Lieutenant's Woman* (1969).

PET FORMS: **Lally, Lallie; Lal(l)a.**

Lambert ♂ Transferred use of the surname, which is from an Old French given name of Germanic origin, from *land* 'land, territory' + *beorht* 'famous'. This was introduced to Britain by the Normans, but its frequency in Britain in later centuries owed something to immigrants from the Low Countries, and it continued in occasional use into the 18th century at least. St Lambert of Maastricht was a 7th-century saint who aided St Willibrord in his evangelical work.

Lamont ♂ Mainly U.S.: transferred use of the Irish and Scottish surname, derived from the medieval given name *Lagman*, from Old Norse *Logmaðr*, from *log* 'law' + *maðr* 'man'. The final *t* of the surname is not etymological, but in the medieval period *d* and *t* were added or dropped capriciously at the ends of words after *n* (for the reverse process, compare ▷Rosalyn).

Lana ♀ Of uncertain origin. If not simply an invention, it may have been devised as a feminine equivalent of ▷Alan (of which it is an anagram), or a shortened form of ▷Alana. It seems to have been first used by the American film actress Lana Turner (1920–1995), whose original name was Julia.

Lance ♂ Old French form of the Germanic personal name *Lanzo*, a short form of various compound names beginning with *land* 'land, territory' (compare ▷Lambert), but associated from an early date with Old French *lance* 'lance' (the weapon, from Latin *lancea*). The modern use as a given name most probably arose as a transferred use of the surname derived from the medieval given name, although it is also commonly taken as a short form of ▷Lancelot.

Lancelot ♂ The name borne by one of King Arthur's best and most valued knights, who eventually betrayed his trust by becoming the lover of Queen Guinevere. The name is of uncertain origin. It is probably, like other Arthurian names, of Celtic derivation, but has been heavily distorted by mediation through French sources.

Landon ♂ Mainly U.S.: transferred use of the surname, in origin a local name from any of various places in England called *Langdon*, from Old English *lang* 'long' + *dūn* 'hill'.

Lane ♂, occasionally ♀ Mainly U.S.: apparently a transferred use of the surname, in origin a local name for someone who lived in or by a lane (Old English *lane*, originally denoting a narrow pathway between hedges or banks).

Lani ♀ Pronounced 'lah-nee': modern coinage from the Polynesian word meaning 'sky, heaven', which is commonly used in Hawaii in compound names such as Leilani 'flower of heaven'.

Lanie ♀ Recent coinage, apparently originally a pet form of ▷Elaine, pronounced 'lay-nee', this is now found in the United States as an independent first name.
VARIANT: Laney.

Lanna ♀ Shortened form of ▷Alanna.

Lara ♀ Russian short form of ▷Larissa, introduced in the early 20th century to the English-speaking world. It enjoyed some popularity as

the name of one of the principal characters in Boris Pasternak's novel *Dr Zhivago* (1957), which was made into a film in 1965, but it was not until almost forty years later that the name acquired widespread currency in Britain.

Laraine ♀ Mainly U.S., especially African-American: of uncertain origin; in part it seems to be a variant spelling of ▷Lorraine and in part it may be derived from French *la reine* 'the queen' (compare ▷Raine).
VARIANTS: Larraine, Lareine, Lareina.

Larch ♀ Mainly U.S.: from the name of the tree (adopted in the 16th century from German *larche*, ultimately from Latin *larix*).

Larissa ♀ Russian name of uncertain origin, now also used in the English-speaking world (see Russian appendix).
PET FORM: ▷Larry.

Lark ♂, ♀ Mainly North American and Australian: from the name of the bird (Old English *lāwerce*). The given name is recorded from the 1830s in the United States. The lark is traditionally associated with early rising and cheerfulness, and is noted for its sweet song.

Larry ♂, ♀ Pet form of ▷Laurence or ▷Lawrence, sometimes used as an independent given name, as in the case of the American actor Larry Hagman (b. 1931). As a girl's name it is a pet form of ▷Larissa.

Latasha ♀ Mainly U.S., especially African-American: a recent coinage, blending ▷Latisha and ▷Natasha.

Latisha ♀ Recent coinage, a simplified spelling of ▷Laetitia.
SHORT FORM: Tisha.

Laura ♀ Feminine form of the Late Latin male name *Laurus* 'laurel'. St Laura was a 9th-century Spanish nun who met her death in a cauldron of molten lead. Laura is also the name of the woman addressed in the love poetry of the Italian poet Petrarch (Francesco Petrarca, 1304–74), and it owes much of its subsequent popularity to this. There have been various speculations about her identity, but it has not been established with any certainty. He first met her in 1327 while living in Avignon, and she died of the plague in 1348. The popularity of the given name in the English-speaking world has endured since the 19th century, when it was probably imported from Italy.

Lauraine ♀ Respelling of ▷Lorraine, influenced by ▷Laura.

Laureen ♀ Modern coinage, formed from ▷Laura with the addition of the productive suffix -een.
VARIANT: Laurene, Laurine.

Laurel ♀ 19th-century coinage from the vocabulary word for the tree (Middle English lorel, a dissimilated form of Old French lorer). However, Laurel is also recorded in the 16th and 17th centuries, when it was probably a pet form of ▷Laura.

Laurelle ♀ Elaborated form of ▷Laurel.

Lauren ♀ Apparently modelled on ▷Laurence, this was first used, or at any rate first brought to public attention, by the film actress Lauren Bacall (b. 1924 as Betty Jean Perske), famous for her partnership with Humphrey Bogart. They appeared together in several films, notably To Have and Have Not (1943) and The Big Sleep (1946). The name was extremely popular throughout the 1990s. See also ▷Loren.
VARIANT: Lauryn.

Laurence ♂ From a French form of Latin Laurentius 'man from Laurentum'. Laurentum was a town in Latium, which may have got its name from Latin laurus 'laurel', although it is more probably of pre-Roman origin. The given name was moderately popular in the Middle Ages (when it was used for girls as well as boys), under the influence of a

3rd-century saint who was one of the seven deacons of Rome. He was martyred in 258. The legend is that, having been required to hand over the Church's treasures to the civil authorities, he assembled the poor and sick and presented them. For this act of Christian defiance, he was roasted to death on a gridiron. In England the name is also associated with St Laurence of Canterbury (d. 619). A more recent influence has been the actor Sir Laurence Olivier (1907–89). See also ▷Lawrence.
PET FORMS: Larry, Laurie.
COGNATES: Irish: Labhrás. Scottish Gaelic: Labhrainn. German: Lorenz. Dutch: Laurens. Scandinavian: Lars. French: Laurent. Spanish: Lorencio. Catalan: Llorenç. Portuguese: Lourenço. Italian: Lorenzo. Greek: Lavrentios. Russian: Lavrenti. Polish: Laurencjusz (vernacular spelling of Latin Laurentius); Lawrenty; Wawrzyniec (vernacular form). Czech: Vavřinec. Slovenian: Lovrenc. Finnish: Lauri, Lasse, Lassi. Hungarian: Lőrinc.

Lauretta ♀ Italian diminutive form of ▷Laura, also sometimes used in the English-speaking world.
VARIANTS: Lor(r)etta, Lorette.

Laurie ♀, ♂ Pet form of ▷Laura, ▷Laurel, and ▷Laurence, also used as an independent given name.

Lauryn ♀ Respelling of ▷Lauren.

Lavender ♀ From the vocabulary word denoting the herb with sweet-smelling flowers (Old French lavendre, from Late Latin lavendula). It is recorded as a given name for both men and women in the 18th and 19th centuries, but has since become an exclusively female name.

Laverne ♀ Mainly U.S.: modern coinage of uncertain derivation. It has been suggested that it is from Vern (a short form of ▷Vernon), feminized by the addition of the French feminine definite article, la, and a final -e.

VARIANT: **Lavern.**

Lavinia ♀ Name, according to Roman mythology, of the wife of Aeneas, and thus the mother of the Roman people. Legend had it that she gave her name to the Latin town of *Lavinium*, but in fact she was almost certainly invented to explain the place name, which is of pre-Roman origin. She was said to be the daughter of King Latinus, who was similarly invented to account for the name of *Latium*. The name *Lavinia* is recorded in England from the 17th century onwards.

Lawrence ♂ Anglicized spelling of ▷Laurence. This is the usual spelling of the surname, and is now becoming increasingly common as a given name, especially in North America.

PET FORMS: ▷**Larry, Lawrie.**

Lawson ♂ Transferred use of the surname, in origin a patronymic from *Law*, a Middle English short form of ▷Laurence. In Australia it has been fairly regularly used as a given name in honour of the explorer William Lawson (1774–1850) and the writer Henry Lawson (1867–1922).

Layla ♀ Variant of ▷Leila, now the more commonly used spelling.

Layton ♂ Variant of ▷Leighton, from a variant spelling of the surname reflecting the pronunciation.

Laz ♂ Modern informal pet form of ▷Larry (compare *Baz* from *Barry* and *Gaz* from *Gary*).

Lazarus ♂ Name borne in the New Testament by two different characters: the brother of Martha and Mary, who was raised from the dead by Jesus (John 11:1–44), and the beggar who appears in the parable of Dives and Lazarus narrated by Jesus (Luke 16:19–31). The form *Lazarus*, used in the Authorized Version, is a Latinate version of Greek *Lazaros*, itself a transliteration of Aramaic *Lazar*, an aphetic short form of Hebrew *Eleazar*

'God is my help'. Because the beggar Lazarus was 'full of sores' the name was often used in the Middle Ages as a generic term for a leper, and so has never been common as a given name.

Lea ♀ Variant spelling of ▷Leah or ▷Lia, or occasionally possibly a shortened form of ▷Azalea. It is sometimes a variant of the girl's name ▷Lee, from an alternative form of the surname, pronounced as a single syllable.

Leaf ♂ From the vocabulary word for the part of a plant (Old English *lēaf*). This was one of the names taken from the world of nature in the 1960s under 'hippy' influence, and it has not been enduringly popular. Choice as a given name may have been influenced by the Scandinavian name *Leif*, from Old Norse *Leifr*, meaning 'heir'.

Leah ♀ Biblical name (meaning 'languid' in Hebrew), borne by the elder sister of Rachel (Genesis 29:23). Jacob served her father Laban for seven years in return for the hand of Rachel, but was deceived into marrying Leah first. He was then given Rachel as well, but had to labour seven more years afterwards. For a long time the name was mainly Jewish, although it also enjoyed some favour among the Puritans in the 16th century. It was taken up again in the 1980s and has been widely popular since the 1990s.

VARIANT: ▷**Lea, Leia.**

Leander ♂ Latin form of the Greek name *Leandros*, derived from *leōn* 'lion' + *anēr* 'man' (genitive *andros*). In Greek legend, Leander swam across the Hellespont every night to visit his beloved Hero and back again every morning; he was eventually drowned during a storm. In Christian times, the name was borne by a 6th-century saint, the brother of Sts Fulgentius, Isidore, and Florentina. He was a leading ecclesiastical figure of his day, a friend of Gregory the Great, and became archbishop of Seville. In modern times, the name has occasionally been used as an elaboration of the boy's name ▷Lee.

Leanne ♀ Modern combination of ▷Lee and ▷Anne, or else a respelling of ▷Liane.

VARIANTS: **Leann, Leanna.**

Leda ♀ Name borne in classical mythology by a queen of Sparta, who was ravished by Zeus in the shape of a swan. She gave birth to two eggs which, when hatched, revealed the two sets of twins: Castor and Pollux, and Helen and Hermione.

Lee ♂, occasionally ♀ Transferred use of the surname, in origin a local name from any of numerous places so called from Old English *lēah* 'wood, clearing'. In the United States, it is sometimes chosen in honour of the great Confederate general Robert E. Lee (1807–70). As a girl's name it is commonly used in compounds such as *Casey-Lee* and *Jamie-Lee*.

Leena ♀ Variant spelling of ▷Lena.

Leesa ♀ Respelling of ▷Lisa, influenced by ▷Lee.

Leia ♀ Variant spelling of ▷Leah.

Leib ♂ Jewish: Yiddish name, meaning 'lion' (compare modern German *Löwe*). See also ▷Arye.

Leigh ♀, ♂ Variant of ▷Lee, from an alternative spelling of the surname. As a girl's name it is frequently an element of compound names such as *Abbie-Leigh*, *Jodie-Leigh,* and *Katie-Leigh*.

Leighton ♂ Transferred use of the surname, in origin a local name from any of several places named with Old English *lēac* 'leek' + *tūn* 'enclosure, settlement', for example Leighton Buzzard in Bedfordshire.

VARIANT: ▷**Layton.**

Leila ♀ Of Arabic origin, now fairly common in the English-speaking world, having been used as a name for an oriental beauty both by Byron, in *The*

Giaour (1813) and *Don Juan* (1819–24), and by Lord Lytton for the heroine of his novel *Leila* (1838). In Arabic it means 'night', apparently alluding to a dark complexion.

VARIANTS: **Laila, Layla, Leyla, Lela, Lila.**

Leland ♂ Mainly U.S.: transferred use of the surname, in origin a local name for someone who lived by a patch of fallow land, from Middle English *lay, ley* 'fallow' + *land* 'land'. The surname is well established in the United States. It was borne by the humorous writer Charles Leland (1824–1903), author of *The Breitmann Ballads*, and it is also the name of a city in Mississippi.

Lemuel ♂ Possibly meaning 'devoted to God' in Hebrew; it was borne in the Bible by an obscure king who was lectured by his mother on the perils of strong drink and the virtues of a dutiful wife (Proverbs 31). He is mentioned by Chaucer in *The Canterbury Tales*, where his name is carefully distinguished from the more familiar ▷Samuel. Lemuel Gulliver was the unusual name of the hero of Jonathan Swift's *Gulliver's Travels* (1726).

Len ♂ Short form of ▷Leonard, also occasionally of ▷Lionel and ▷Lennox.

Lena ♀ Abstracted from various names ending in these syllables, such as *Helena* and *Magdalena*. In the United States it was particularly associated with the singer Lena Horne (1917–91).

VARIANT: **Leena.**

Lenda ♀ 20th-century coinage, an arbitrary alteration of ▷Linda.

Lennard ♂ Variant spelling of ▷Leonard, in part a transferred use of the surname, which was derived from the given name in the Middle Ages.

Lennie ♂ Pet form of ▷Leonard, sometimes used as an independent given name.

Lennon ♂ Transferred used of the Irish surname, Anglicized form of Gaelic *Ó Leannáin* 'descendant of

Leannán' (see Irish appendix) or
Ó Lonáin 'descendant of **Lonán**' (see Irish
appendix). Its use as a given name is no
doubt in honour of John Lennon of the
Beatles (1940–80).

Lennora ♀ Variant spelling of
▷Lenora.

Lennorah ♀ Variant spelling of
▷Lenora.

Lennox ♂ Transferred use of the
Scottish surname, which is also the
name of an earldom. It originated as a
local name from a district north of
Glasgow formerly known as *The
Levenach*. As a given name it was borne
by the British composer Sir Lennox
Berkeley (1903–89).

Lenny ♂ Pet form of ▷Leonard, also
used as an independent given name.

Lenora ♀ Originally a contracted
form of ▷Leonora, although sometimes
chosen as an expanded version
of ▷Lena.
VARIANTS: **Lennora, Len(n)orah.**

Leo ♂ From a Late Latin personal
name, meaning 'lion', which was borne
by a large number of early Christian
saints, most notably Pope Leo the Great
(?390–461).

Leon ♂ Derivative of ▷Leo, from the
oblique case. This form is common as a
Jewish name, but recently has also
acquired wider currency. The lion is an
important symbol among Jews because
of Jacob's dying pronouncement that
'Judah is a lion's whelp' (Genesis 49:9).

Leona ♀ Latinate feminine form of
▷Leo.

Leonard ♂ From an Old French
personal name of Germanic origin,
derived from *leon* 'lion' + *hard* 'hardy,
brave, strong'. This was the name of a
5th-century Frankish saint, the patron
of peasants and horses. Although it was
introduced into Britain by the
Normans, *Leonard* was an uncommon
name during the Middle Ages. It was

revived in some areas towards the end
of the 1400s, and in the 19th-century
became very popular. It is now also
common as a Jewish name (compare
▷Leon).
VARIANT: **Lennard.**
SHORT FORM: **Len.**
PET FORMS: **Lenny, Lennie.**

Leonardo ♂ Italian, Spanish, and
Portuguese equivalent of ▷Leonard,
now also used in the English-speaking
world, quite possibly with reference to
its most famous bearer, the
Renaissance genius Leonardo da Vinci
(1452–1519). He is remembered
principally as a painter and sculptor,
but also as an architect, engineer, and
scientist.

Léonie ♀ French: from Latin *Leonia*
(see French appendix). It is now also
widely used (frequently without the
accent) in the English-speaking world.
VARIANT: **Leoni.**

Léonne ♀ French: feminine form of
Léon (see ▷Leon), occasionally also used
(normally without the accent) in the
English-speaking world.

Leonora ♀ Shortened form of
▷Eleonora.

Léontine ♀ French form of Leontina
(see Italian appendix), occasionally also
used (normally without the accent) in
the English-speaking world.

Leopold ♂ From an Old French name
of Germanic (Frankish) origin, from *liut*
'people' + *bold* 'bold, brave'. The first
element was altered by association
with Latin *leo* 'lion'. A name of this
origin may have been introduced into
Britain by the Normans, but if so it did
not survive long. It was reintroduced to
Britain from the Continent towards the
end of the 19th-century in honour of
Leopold, King of the Belgians (1790–
1865) and uncle of Queen Victoria, to
whom he was an influential adviser in
her youth: she named one of her sons
after him.

Leroy ♂ Now considered a typically African-American given name, but formerly also extensively borne by White Americans. It is from a French nickname meaning 'the king', but it is not entirely clear why this particular form should have become such a popular given name in English.

VARIANT: ▷Elroy.

Les ♂ Short form of ▷Leslie.

Lesley ♀, ♂ Variant of ▷Leslie, now the usual form of the girls' name. Its first recorded use as such is in a poem by Robert Burns.

Leslie ♂, ♀ Transferred use of the Scottish surname derived from the lands of *Lesslyn* in Aberdeenshire (a place name perhaps named in Gaelic as *leas cuilinn* 'garden of hollies'). Surnames and clan names have been used as given names more readily and from an earlier date in Scotland than elsewhere, and this is the name of an ancient family, who in the 14th and 15th centuries were close associates of the Scottish royal house of Stewart and who have held the earldom of Rothes since 1457. The British film actor Leslie Howard (1890–1943), who was of Hungarian origin, had a considerable influence on the popularity of the name, especially in the United States, where he appeared in *Gone with the Wind* (1939). A famous female bearer is the French film actress Leslie Caron (b. 1931).

SHORT FORM: **Les** (♂).

Lester ♂ Transferred use of the surname, in origin a local name from the city of *Leicester*. The place name is recorded in the 10th century as *Ligora cæster*, representing a British name of obscure origin + Old English *cæster* 'Roman fort'.

Leticia ♀ Simplified spelling of ▷Laetitia.

Letitia ♀ Simplified spelling of ▷Laetitia, which has recently enjoyed a rise in popularity in Britain, notably among West Indians.

Lettice ♀ From the medieval vernacular form of the Latin name ▷Laetitia. It was in use in Britain in the Middle Ages, but then fell out of use until revived by the Victorians. It is now once again out of fashion.

PET FORMS: **Letty**, **Lettie**.

Levi ♂ Meaning 'associated' in Hebrew; in the Bible it was given by Jacob's wife Leah to her third son as an expression of her hope, 'Now this time will my husband be joined unto me, because I have born him three sons: therefore was his name called Levi' (Genesis 29:34). The Levites (a Jewish priestly caste) are descended from Levi. In the New Testament, *Levi* is a byname of the apostle and evangelist Matthew. In modern times the name has been mainly Jewish, although its appeal is now widening. Probably its most famous bearer was Levi Strauss (1829–1902), designer of the tough canvas jeans which still bear his name.

Levon ♂ This is the Armenian form of ▷Leon, but it is used independently as a given name in the U.S., perhaps influenced by the fame of the rock musician, Levon Helm (b. 1942 in Arkansas as Mark Lavon Helm), drummer with The Band.

Lew ♂ Short form of ▷Lewis or respelling of ▷Lou, as borne by the impresario Lew Grade (1906–98, originally Louis Winogradsky).

Lewie ♂ Anglicized spelling of ▷Louis, or a pet form of ▷Lewis.

Lewin ♂ Transferred use of the surname derived in the Middle Ages from the given name *Lewyn*, from the Old English personal name *Lēofwine*, a compound of *lēof* 'dear, beloved' + *wine* 'friend'.

Lewis ♂ English form, since the Middle Ages, of the French name ▷Louis. In modern use it is also in part a transferred use of the surname derived from this given name, or from

Anglicized forms of Gaelic *Mac Lughaidh* 'son of Lughaidh' (see Irish appendix) or Welsh Llewelyn (see Welsh appendix).
VARIANT: **Lewys** (modern spelling).
PET FORMS: **Lewi(e)**.

Lex ♂ Shortened form of ▷Alex, also occasionally used as a given name in its own right.

Lexie ♀, ♂ Pet form of ▷Alexandra, also used as an independent given name, and of ▷Alexis and ▷Alex.
VARIANT: **Lexy**.

Lexine ♀ Apparently an elaboration of ▷Lexie with the addition of the originally French feminine diminutive suffix *-(i)ne*, which has long been productive in forming English female names.

Lexis ♀, ♂ Short form of ▷Alexis.

Lexy ♀, ♂ Variant spelling of ▷Lexie.

Lia ♀ Italian name of uncertain derivation, probably a short form of *Rosalia* (see ▷Rosalie). It is also found in the English-speaking world, where it may also be a respelling of ▷Leah.

Liam ♂ Short form of Irish Uilliam (Irish equivalent of ▷William). It is now generally used as an independent given name and since the 1990s has been in vogue throughout the English-speaking world, in common with a number of other names of Celtic origin.

Liane ♀ Probably a short form of French *Éliane* (see French appendix), from Latin *Aeliana*, the name of an early martyr at Amasea in Pontus. *Aelianus* was an old Roman family name, perhaps a hypercorrected form of *Elianus* or *Helianus*, from Greek *hēlios* 'sun'.
VARIANTS: **Lian, Liana; Liann, Lianne, Lianna** (influenced by ▷Ann(e) and ▷Anna).

Libby ♀ Pet form of ▷Elizabeth, based originally on a child's

mispronunciation. It is now popularly used as a given name in its own right.

Libe ♀ Jewish: Yiddish name, meaning 'love' (compare modern German *Liebe*).

Liberty ♀ From the vocabulary word meaning 'freedom', chosen as a given name by parents for whom this is an important value. The word came into English via Old French from Latin *lībertās*, a derivative of *līber* 'free'.

Lila ♀ Simplified spelling of ▷Leila.

Lilac ♀ From the vocabulary word denoting the shrub with large sprays of heavily scented purple, pink, or white flowers. The word is from French, which derived it via Spanish from Arabic *līlak*, from Persian *nīlak* 'bluish', a derivative of *nīl* 'blue'.

Lili ♀ Either an adoption of the German name, a pet form, originally a reduplicated nursery form, of ▷Elisabeth (associated in particular with the Second World War popular song *Lili Marlene*) or a modern respelling of ▷Lily.

Lilian ♀ Of uncertain origin, first recorded in the late 16th century, and probably derived from a nursery form of ▷Elizabeth. It is now sometimes regarded as a derivative of the flower name ▷Lily, but this was not used as a given name in England until the 19th century.
VARIANT: **Lillian**.

Lilith ♀ The name borne, according to medieval tradition, by a wife of Adam prior to Eve. She is said to have been turned into an ugly demon for refusing to obey him. *Lilith* occurs in the Bible as a vocabulary word meaning 'night monster' or 'screech owl' (Isaiah 34:14), and in Jewish folklore is the name of an ugly demon. In spite of its unpleasant connotations, it has occasionally been used in modern times, perhaps in part being taken as an elaborated form of ▷Lily.

Lillian ♀ Variant spelling of ▷Lilian, now the more frequent form.

Lily ♀ From the vocabulary word for the flower (via Old French, from Latin *lilium*), regarded in Christian imagery as a symbol of purity. In recent times, it has become a popular component of compound names such as *Lily-Anne*, *Lily-May*, *Lily-Rose*, and *Tigerlily*.

VARIANTS: Lillie (borne, for example, by the actress Lillie Langtry, 1853–1929), Lilly, ▷Lili, Lilli.

Lin ♀ Short form of ▷Linda, ▷Lindsay, ▷Linnet, or any other female given name beginning with this syllable.

Lincoln ♂ Transferred use of the surname, in origin a local name from the name of the city of Lincoln. This is found in the 7th century as *Lindum colonia*, probably from an Old Welsh word meaning 'lake' (compare modern Welsh *llyn*) + the Latin defining term *colonia* 'colony, settlement'. As a given name it was in use in the United States in the 18th century. Rising in popularity in the 19th century, it has no doubt sometimes been bestowed in honour of Abraham Lincoln (1809–65), 16th president of the United States, who led the Union to victory in the Civil War and enforced the emancipation of slaves.

Linda ♀ Of relatively recent origin and uncertain etymology. It is first recorded in the 19th century. It may be a shortened form of ▷Belinda, an adoption of Spanish *linda* 'pretty', or a Latinate derivative of any of various other Germanic female names ending in -*lind* meaning 'weak, tender, soft'. It was popular in the 20th century, especially in the 1950s.

VARIANT: Lynda.

PET FORMS: Lindie, Lindy.

Lindall ♀ Transferred use of the surname, in origin a local name from *Lindal* in Lancashire. The place name is derived from Old English *līn* 'flax' + *dæl* 'valley'. Use as a given name seems to have originated as an elaborated form of ▷Linda.

VARIANTS: Lindal, Lindell.

Linden ♀ Ostensibly from the vocabulary word denoting the lime tree (originally the adjectival form, derived from Old English *linde*). The given name is recorded in the United States in the late 19th century as a boy's name. Use as a girl's name is of more recent, probably 20th-century, origin and it is more likely that this is simply an elaboration of ▷Linda.

Lindie ♀ Pet form of ▷Linda.

Lindon ♂ Variant spelling of ▷Lyndon.

Lindsay ♀, occasionally ♂ Transferred use of the Scottish surname, originally borne by Sir Walter de Lindesay, one of the retainers of King David I of Scotland (1084–1153), who took the name to Scotland from Lindsey in Lincolnshire. The place name is first recorded in the form *Lindissi*, apparently a derivative of the British name of Lincoln. To this was later added Old English *eg* 'island', since the place was virtually cut off by the surrounding fenland. As a given name Lindsay was at first used for boys, and in Scotland and Australia it remains in occasional use as a male name, but elsewhere it is now used for girls.

VARIANTS: ▷Lindsey, Linsay, Linsy, Linzi(e), Lynsey, all ♀.

Lindsey ♀ Either a variant spelling of ▷Lindsay, or a transferred use of the English surname derived in the Middle Ages from Lindsey in Suffolk, which is named with the Old English personal name *Lelli* + Old English *eg* 'island'.

VARIANTS: Lins(e)y, Linzi(e), Lyndsey, Lynsey.

Lindy ♀ Pet form of ▷Linda.

Linette ♀ Variant spelling of ▷Lynette.

Linford ♂ Transferred use of the surname, a local name from any of various places, most of which are named with Old English *līn* 'flax' or *lind* 'lime tree' + *ford* 'ford'. In the case of Great and Little Linford in Berkshire, the first element is Old English *hlyn* 'maple'. As a given name it is associated in particular with the British former athlete Linford Christie (b. 1960).

VARIANT: Lynford.

Linnet ♀ Variant spelling of ▷Lynette, strongly influenced in popularity by the vocabulary word for the small songbird (Old French *linotte*, a derivative of *lin* 'flax', on the seeds of which it feeds).

Linnette ♀ Variant spelling of ▷Lynette.

Linsay ♀ Simplified spelling of ▷Lindsay.

Linsey ♀ Simplified spelling of ▷Lindsey.

Linton ♂ Transferred use of the surname, originally a local name from any of numerous places in England so called. Most get the name from Old English *līn* 'flax, cotton' or *lind* 'lime tree' + *tūn* 'enclosure, settlement'.

VARIANT: Lynton.

Linus ♂ Latin form of the Greek name *Linos*, which is of uncertain origin. In Greek mythology, Linus was a famous musician who taught music to Hercules; it is also the name of an infant son of Apollo who was exposed to die on a mountainside in Argos. The name may have been invented to explain the obscure refrain, '*ailinon*', of the so-called 'Linus song', traditionally sung at harvest time in Argos. In the Christian era, *Linus* was the name of the second pope, St Peter's successor, who was martyred in *c*.76. He has been tentatively identified with the Linus to whom Paul sends greetings in 2 Timothy 4:21. Nowadays, the given name is associated with a character in the popular *Peanuts* strip cartoon series, a little boy inseparable from his security blanket.

Linzi ♀ Fanciful respelling of ▷Lindsay or ▷Lindsey.

Liona ♀ Altered form of ▷Leona, influenced by ▷Lionel.

Lionel ♂ From a medieval diminutive of the Old French name *Léon* (see ▷Leo) or the Middle English nickname *Lion*.

Lis ♀ Variant spelling of ▷Liz. See also ▷Lys.

Lisa ♀ Variant of ▷Liza, influenced by French *Lise* and German *Liese*.

Lisbet ♀ Shortened form of ▷Elizabeth.

Lisette ♀ French diminutive form of *Lise* (itself a reduced form of ▷Elisabeth), now also used in the English-speaking world.

VARIANT: Lysette.

Lisha ♀ Modern coinage, a shortened and respelled form of names such as ▷Delicia and ▷Felicia, on the model of ▷Trisha from ▷Patricia.

Lissa ♀ Short form of ▷Melissa. See also ▷Lyssa.

Lita ♀ Apparently a short form of Melita (see ▷Melitta), used occasionally as an independent given name.

Livia ♀ In modern use often taken as a short form of ▷Olivia, but originally a distinct name, a feminine form of the Roman family name *Livius*. This is of uncertain derivation, perhaps connected with *lividus* 'bluish'.

Liz ♀ Short form of ▷Elizabeth.

Liza ♀ Short form of ▷Eliza, also used independently.

VARIANT: Lisa.

Lizzie ♀ Pet form of ▷Elizabeth.

VARIANT: Lizzy.

Lloyd ♂ Transferred use of the Welsh surname, originally a nickname meaning 'grey(-haired)', now also

widely used outside Wales. See also
▷Floyd.

Lockie ♂ Canadian pet form of
▷Lachlan.

Logan ♂, ♀ Transferred use of the
Scottish surname, in origin a local
name from a place so called in
Ayrshire. Although it retains a
distinctly Scottish flavour, the
name is also used elsewhere in the
English-speaking world, being
particularly popular in Canada and
New Zealand.

Lois ♀ New Testament name of
unknown origin, borne by the
grandmother of the Timothy to whom
St Paul wrote two epistles (see 2
Timothy 1:5). Both Timothy and his
mother Eunice bore common Greek
names, but *Lois* remains unexplained.
In popular fiction the name is borne by
Lois Lane, the reporter girlfriend of
Superman.

Lola ♀ Spanish pet form (originally a
nursery form) of ▷Dolores, now
established as an independent given
name in the English-speaking world. It
owes some of its popularity to the fame
of Lola Montez (1818–1861), the stage
name adopted by Marie Gilbert, an Irish
dancer and courtesan who had affairs
with Liszt, Dumas, and others. From
1846–8 she so captivated the elderly
Ludwig I of Bavaria that she became the
virtual ruler of the country,
precipitating riots, a constitutional
crisis, and the abdication of the king.
She arrived in New York in 1851, and
spent the last years of her life working
to help prostitutes.

Lolicia ♀ Mainly U.S.: modern
coinage, an elaborated form of ▷Lola,
with the addition of a suffix derived
from names such as ▷Delicia.

Lolita ♀ Spanish diminutive form of
▷Lola. This was once quite common as a
given name in its own right in America,
with its large Hispanic population, but
has since been overshadowed by its

association with Vladimir Nabokov's
novel *Lolita* (1955). The Lolita of the title
is the pubescent object of the narrator's
desires, and the name is now used as a
generic term for any sexually
precocious girl.

Lonnie ♂ Of uncertain origin,
possibly an Anglicized or pet form of
the Spanish name *Alonso* or a variant of
▷Lenny. It is associated in Britain with
the skiffle singer Lonnie Donegan
(1931–2002, born Anthony Donegan),
famous in the 1950s and 60s.

Lora ♀ Probably a respelling of
▷Laura, that coincides in form with the
German spelling of the same name and
also with the medieval English given
name.

Lorcan ♂ Anglicized form of the
Gaelic name Lorcán (see Irish
appendix). In recent times, the name
has also been taken up by English
speakers having no Irish connections.

Loreen ♀ Elaboration of ▷Lora, with
the addition of the suffix *-een* (originally
an Irish diminutive, Gaelic *-ín*).
VARIANT: **Lorene**.

Lorelle ♀ Elaboration of ▷Lora, with
the addition of the suffix *-elle* (originally
a French feminine diminutive).

Loren ♀, occasionally ♂ Variant
spelling of ▷Lauren. In the United
States, this is used rather more
frequently for boys than girls, although
this is not the case in Britain.

Lorena ♀ Latinate elaboration of the
girl's name ▷Loren.

Lorene ♀ Variant spelling of ▷Loreen.

Loreto ♀ Religious name borne by
Roman Catholics, referring to the
town in central Italy to which in the
13th century the Holy House of the
Virgin is supposed to have been
miraculously transported from
Nazareth by angels.

Loretta ♀ Variant of ▷Lauretta,
normally borne by Roman Catholics,

among whom it is associated with
▷Loreto.

Lori ♀ Pet form of ▷Lorraine or variant
spelling of ▷Laurie.

Lorin ♂ Mainly U.S.: variant spelling
of the boy's name ▷Loren.
VARIANT: **Lorrin.**

Lorinda ♀ Elaboration of ▷Lora,
with the addition of the productive
feminine suffix -*inda* (compare
▷Belinda, ▷Clarinda, and
▷Lucinda).

Lorna ♀ Invented by R. D. Blackmore
for the heroine of his novel *Lorna Doone*
(1869), child captive of the outlawed
Doones on Exmoor, who is eventually
discovered to be in reality Lady Lorna
Dugal, daughter of the Earl of Dugal.
Blackmore seems to have derived the
name from the Scottish place name
Lorn(*e*) (Gaelic *Latharna*), a territory in
Argyll.

Lorne ♂ Mainly Canadian: of
uncertain derivation, but most
probably taken from the name of the
territory of *Lorn*(*e*) in Argyll (and thus a
masculine form of ▷Lorna). One of the
earliest bearers was the Canadian actor
Lorne Greene (1915–1987), and the
given name is now also found in
Scotland.

Lorraine ♀ Transferred use of the
surname, in origin denoting a migrant
from the province of *Lorraine* in eastern
France. This derives its name from
Latin *Lotharingia* 'territory of the people
of *Lothar*'. The latter is a Germanic
personal name derived from *hlud* 'fame'
+ *heri*, *hari* 'army'. *Lorraine* began to be
used as a girl's name in Scotland in the
19th century, and for a time in the
second half of the 20th century enjoyed
great popularity, which has since
waned.
VARIANTS: **Lorrain, Lorrayne.**
PET FORMS: **Lor(r)i.**

Lorrin ♂ Mainly U.S.: variant spelling
of the boy's name ▷Loren.

Lottie ♀ Pet form of ▷Charlotte. It was
a common girl's name in the 19th
century, and is currently enjoying a
modest revival as an independent given
name.
VARIANT: **Lotty.**

Lou ♂, ♀ Short form of ▷Louis or, less
commonly, ▷Louise.

Louella ♀ Modern coinage from the
first syllable of ▷Louise + the productive
suffix -*ella* (an Italian or Latinate
feminine diminutive). It is
particularly associated with the
Hollywood gossip columnist Louella
Parsons (1880–1972).
VARIANT: **Luella.**

Loughlin ♂ Irish: Anglicized form of
Lochlainn (see Irish appendix).

Louie ♂ Variant spelling of ▷Lewie or
▷Louis, currently in fashion.

Louis ♂ French name, of Germanic
(Frankish) origin, from *hlōd* 'fame' + *wīg*
'war'. It was very common in French
royal and noble families. Louis I (778–
840) was the son of Charlemagne, who
ruled as both King of France and Holy
Roman Emperor. Altogether, the name
was borne by sixteen kings of France up
to the French Revolution, in which
Louis XVI perished. Louis XIV, 'the Sun
King' (1638–1715), reigned for seventy-
two years (1643–1715), presiding in the
middle part of his reign over a period of
unparalleled French power and
prosperity. In modern times Louis is
also found in the English-speaking
world (usually pronounced '**loo**-ee'). In
Britain the Anglicized form ▷Lewis is
rather more common, whereas in
America the reverse is true.
VARIANTS: **Lewie, Lewi, Louie** (Anglicized
spellings).
SHORT FORM: **Lou.**
COGNATES: Scottish Gaelic: **Luthais.**
German: **Ludwig.** Dutch: **Lodewijk.**
Scandinavian: **Ludvig, Lovis.** Spanish:
Luis. Catalan: **Lluis.** Portuguese: **Luis.**
Italian: **Luigi, Lodovico.** Polish: **Ludwik.**

Czech, Slovenian: Ludvik. Hungarian: Lajos. Lithuanian: Liudvikas.

Louisa ♀ Latinate feminine form of ▷Louis, commonly used as an English given name since the 18th century.

SHORT FORM: **Lou.**

PET FORM: **Lulu.**

Louise ♀ French feminine form of ▷Louis, introduced to England in the 17th century. Like ▷Louisa, it has remained perennially popular and is currently frequently used as a component of compound names such as *Ella-Louise*, *Sophie-Louise*, and *Tia-Louise*.

SHORT FORM: **Lou.**

PET FORM: **Lulu.**

Lourdes ♀ Religious name borne by Roman Catholics, referring to the place in southern France where a shrine was established after a young peasant girl, Bernadette Soubirous, had visions of the Virgin Mary and uncovered a healing spring in 1858. Lourdes has since become a major centre for pilgrimage, especially by people suffering from various illnesses or physical handicaps.

Lovell ♂ Transferred use of the surname, which originated in the Middle Ages from the Old (Norman) French nickname *Louvel* 'wolf-cub', a diminutive of *lou* 'wolf'.

Lowell ♂ Mainly U.S.: transferred use of the surname of a well-known New England family, whose members included the poet Robert Lowell (1917–77). The surname is a variant of ▷Lovell.

Lowri ♀ Welsh form of ▷Laura, brought to wider notice in Britain by the broadcaster Lowri Turner (b. 1964).

Loyal ♂ Mainly U.S.: name derived from the modern English adjective (from Old French *leial*, from Latin *legalis* 'legal').

Luana ♀ It appears in records of the late 18th century and was the name of a Polynesian maiden in King Vidor's 1932 film *The Bird of Paradise*. It is apparently an arbitrary combination of the syllables *Lu-* and *-ana*.

VARIANTS: **Luanna, Luanne, Luan.**

Luca ♂ Italian equivalent of ▷Luke, now also used in the English-speaking world.

VARIANT: **Luka** (Anglicized spelling).

Lucas ♂ In part a learned form of ▷Luke, in part a transferred use of the surname derived from it in the Middle Ages. The Latin form *Lucas* was often used in the Middle Ages in written documents in place of the spoken vernacular form *Luke*, hence the common surname. It is also the spelling preferred in the Authorized Version of the New Testament, which has had some influence on its selection as a given name. There has been a sharp rise in its popularity since the turn of the century. *Lucas* is now also used as an Anglicized form of various Eastern European equivalents (see the cognates listed at ▷Luke).

Lucetta ♀ Fanciful elaboration of ▷Lucia or ▷Lucy, formed with the productive suffix *-etta*, originally an Italian feminine diminutive suffix. The name is found in Shakespeare, where it is borne by Julia's waiting woman in *Two Gentlemen of Verona*, but it is not much used in Italy and has generally been infrequent in England.

Luci ♀ Modern respelling of ▷Lucy.

Lucia ♀ Feminine form of the old Roman given name *Lucius*, which is probably a derivative of Latin *lux* 'light'. The girl's name is common in Italy and elsewhere, and is found as a learned, Latinate doublet of ▷Lucy in England. St Lucia of Syracuse, who was martyred in 304, was a very popular saint in the Middle Ages; she is often represented in medieval art as blinded and with her eyes on a platter, but the tradition that she had her eyes put out is probably based on nothing more than the association between light and eyes.

PET FORM: Lucilla.

Lucian ♂ From Latin *Lucianus*, a derivative of ▷Lucius. Saints Lucian, Maximian, and Julian were three missionaries to Gaul matryred at Beauvais at the end of the 3rd century. The British painter Lucian Freud was born in Berlin in 1922, the grandson of Sigmund Freud.

VARIANT: Lucien (French form).

Luciana ♀ Feminine form of ▷Lucian. It is the name of one of the principal characters in Shakespeare's *Comedy of Errors*.

Lucie ♀ French spelling of ▷Lucy, now also used in the English-speaking world.

Lucien ♀ French equivalent of ▷Lucian, also used in the English-speaking world.

Lucienne ♀ Feminine form of ▷Lucien, also used occasionally in the English-speaking world.

Lucilla ♀ Latin derivative of ▷Lucia, with the diminutive feminine suffix *-illa*. This name was borne by various minor early saints, including one martyred at Rome in *c.*258.

Lucille ♀ French form of ▷Lucilla, used also in the English-speaking world. A well-known bearer of the name was the American comedy actress Lucille Ball (1910–89).

Lucinda ♀ Derivative of ▷Lucia, with the addition of the productive suffix *-inda*. The formation is first found in Cervantes's *Don Quixote* (1605), but was not much in use in the 17th century except as a literary name. *Lucinde* was used by both Molière (in *Le Médecin malgré lui*, 1665) and Friedrich von Schlegel (in his novel *Lucinde*, 1799). It enjoyed considerable popularity in England in the 18th century, and has been in use ever since.

PET FORMS: Sinda, Sindy, Cindy; ▷Lucy.

Lucius ♂ Old Roman given name, probably ultimately a derivative of Latin *lux* 'light'. This is occasionally used as a given name in the English-speaking world, especially in America, but it is not as common as its feminine counterpart, ▷Lucia. Lucius was the name of two early Christians mentioned in the New Testament (Acts 13:1; Romans 16:21), and it was also borne by three popes.

Lucrece ♀ Vernacular form of ▷Lucretia, used, for example, in Shakespeare's narrative poem *The Rape of Lucrece*.

Lucretia ♀ Feminine form of the Roman family name *Lucretius*, which is of unknown derivation. In Roman legend, this is the name of a Roman maiden of the 5th century BC who killed herself after being raped by the King of Rome; the resulting scandal led to the end of the monarchy. It was also borne by a Spanish martyr who perished under Diocletian, but it is now chiefly remembered as the name of Lucrezia Borgia (1480–1519), regarded in legend as a demon poisoner who had incestuous relations with her father, Pope Alexander VI, and her brother Cesare. Although these allegations cannot now be disproved, history records her, after her marriage in 1501 to Alfonso d'Este, Duke of Ferrara, as being in reality a beautiful, intelligent, and fair-minded woman, and a generous patron of the arts.

Lucy ♀ From Old French *Lucie*, the vernacular form of ▷Lucia. It is sometimes assumed that *Lucy* is a pet form of ▷Lucinda, but there is no etymological justification for this assumption. It was in fairly widespread use in the Middle Ages, and increased greatly in popularity in the 18th century and again in the 1990s. In Ireland it serves as an Anglicized form of Irish Luíseach (see appendix).

Ludovic ♂ From Latin *Ludovicus*, the form used in medieval documents to represent the Germanic name *Hludwig* (see ▷Louis). In the west of Scotland it came to be used as an Anglicized form of the Gaelic name *Maol Dòmhnaich*, pronounced 'meel **dauv**-nach' and meaning 'devotee of the Lord', probably because both contain the same succession of consonants: l-d-v-c(h). It is borne by the writer and broadcaster Ludovic Kennedy (b. 1919).
SHORT FORM: **Ludo**.

Ludovica ♀ Latinate feminine form of ▷Ludovic, used occasionally in the English-speaking world.

Luella ♀ Variant spelling of ▷Louella.

Luis ♂ Spanish form of ▷Louis, also used in the English-speaking world.

Luisa ♀ Spanish form of ▷Louisa, now also used in the English-speaking world.

Luka ♂ Anglicized respelling of ▷Luca.

Luke ♂ Middle English vernacular form of ▷Lucas, Latin form of the post-classical Greek name *Loukas* 'man from Lucania'. This owes its perennial popularity throughout Christian Europe to the fact that, from the 2nd century onwards, the third gospel in the New Testament has been ascribed to the Lucas or Luke mentioned at various places in Acts and in the Epistles. Little is known about him beyond the facts that he was a doctor, a Gentile, and a friend and convert of St Paul. The name was borne by the character Luke Skywalker in the film *Star Wars* (1977), and rose sharply in popularity in the 1990s.
COGNATES: Irish: Lúcás. Scottish Gaelic: Lùcas. German: Lukas. Dutch: Lucas. French: Luc. Spanish, Portuguese: Lucas. Catalan: Lluc(h). Italian: Luca. Russian: Luka. Polish: Łukasz. Czech: Lukáš. Croatian, Serbian, Slovenian: Luka. Finnish: Luukas. Hungarian: Lukács.

Lulu ♀ Pet form, originally a reduplicated nursery form, of *Luise*, the German form of ▷Louise. It is now also used in the English-speaking world, both as a pet form of *Louise* and as an independent given name. It is particularly associated with the Scottish pop singer Lulu (b. 1948 as Marie McDonald McLaughlin Lawrie).

Luther ♂ From the German surname, which is from a Germanic personal name derived from *liut* 'people' + *heri*, *hari* 'army'. It is commonly bestowed among evangelical Protestants, in honour of the ecclesiastical reformer and theologian Martin Luther (1483–1546). In recent times it has also been bestowed in honour of the assassinated civil rights leader Martin Luther King (1929–68). It was at its most popular in the United States from the 1880s up to 1910 but has since steadily declined.

Luvenia ♀ English: apparently an arbitrary coinage, perhaps influenced by ▷Lavinia, originating in the southern United States.

Lyall ♂ Transferred use of the Scottish surname, which is probably derived from the Old Norse personal name *Liulfr*, composed of an unexplained first element + Old Norse *úlfr* 'wolf'. See also ▷Lyle.

Lydia ♀ Of Greek origin, meaning 'woman from Lydia', an area of Asia Minor. The name is borne in the Bible by a woman of Thyatira who was converted by St Paul and who entertained him in her house (Acts 16:14–15, 40). It has enjoyed steady popularity in the English-speaking world since the 17th century.

Lyle ♂ Transferred use of the mainly Scottish surname, in origin a local name for someone who came 'from the island' (Anglo-Norman *de l'isle*). (The island in question would in many cases have been an area of higher, dry ground in a marsh or fen, rather than in a sea or river.)

There may have been some confusion with ▷Lyall.

Lyn ♀ Variant spelling of ▷Lynn.

Lynda ♀ Variant spelling of ▷Linda.

Lynden ♂, ♀ Respelling of ▷Lyndon or ▷Linden.

Lyndon ♂ English: transferred use of the surname, derived from Lyndon, a place in the former county of Rutland (now part of Leicestershire), so called from Old English *lind* 'linden, lime tree' + *dūn* 'hill'. Its modern use as a male given name owes something to the American president Lyndon Baines Johnson (1908–73).
VARIANT: Lynden, Lindon.

Lyndsay ♀ Occasional variant spelling of ▷Lindsay.

Lyndsey ♀ Mainly U.S.: variant spelling of ▷Lindsey, possibly also of ▷Lindsay.

Lynette ♀ In modern use a derivative of ▷Lynn, formed with the French feminine diminutive suffix *-ette*. However, this is not the origin for the name as used in Tennyson's *Idylls of the King* (1859–85), through which it first came to public attention. There, it represents an altered form of some Celtic original; compare Welsh ▷Eluned.

VARIANTS: Lynnette, Lin(n)ette, Linnet.

Lynn ♀ Of uncertain origin: possibly an altered short form of ▷Linda, or a derivative of the French name *Line*, which originated as a short form of various girls' names ending in this syllable, for example *Caroline*. The element *-lyn(n)* has been a productive suffix of English girls' names since at least the middle of the 20th century, *Lynn* itself having enjoyed considerable popularity in the 1950s and 60s, especially.
VARIANT: Lynne.

Lynsay ♀ Respelling of ▷Lindsay.

Lynsey ♀ Respelling of ▷Lindsey.

Lynton ♂ Respelling of ▷Linton.

Lyra ♀ Modern coinage, apparently from Latin *lyra* 'lyre'; choice as a given name evokes images of gentle music and harmony.

Lys ♀ Variant spelling of ▷Lis, apparently inspired by medieval French (*fleur de*) *lys* 'lily'.

Lysette ♀ Variant spelling of ▷Lisette.

Lyssa ♀ Short form of ▷Alyssa. In form it coincides with the name, in Greek mythology, of the personification of madness or frenzy. See also ▷Lissa.

Mm

Mab ♀ Short form of ▷Mabel. See also ▷Maeve.

Mabel ♀ Originally a nickname from the Old French vocabulary word *amabel*, *amable* 'lovely' (akin to modern English *amiable* 'friendly, good-humoured'). The initial vowel began to be lost as early as the 12th century (the same woman is referred to as both *Mabilia* and *Amabilia* in a document of 1185), but a short vowel in the resulting first syllable was standard, giving a rhyme with *babble*, until the 19th century, when people began to pronounce the name to rhyme with *table*.

Mabelle ♀ Elaborated form of ▷Mabel, under the influence of the French phrase *ma belle* 'my beautiful one'.

Macey ♀, ♂ Transferred use of the surname, in origin a Norman baronial name from any of the places in northern France called *Massey* (Latin *Macciacum*, a derivative of the Gallo-Roman personal name *Maccius*). Use as a first name has been influenced by the rhyming *Stacey*, *Tracy*, *Lacey*, and *Pacey*.

VARIANTS : (all ♀) Macie; Macy as borne by the female pop singer Macy Gray (b. 1970 as Natalie McIntyre).

Mack ♂ Originally a common nickname for bearers of any of the Scottish and Irish patronymic surnames beginning with *Mac* or *Mc*, this is now sometimes used as an independent first name, especially in the U.S.

Mackenzie ♂, ♀ Transferred use of the Scottish surname, which is from Gaelic *Mac Coinnich*, a patronymic from *Coinneach* 'comely'. The *z* of the surname represents the medieval letter yogh, which was pronounced as a 'y' glide. In North America this is more commonly used for girls than boys.

VARIANTS: Makenzie, Makensie, Mckenzie.

Maddie ♀ Pet form of ▷Madeleine, also used as an independent given name.

Maddison ♀, occasionally ♂ Variant spelling of ▷Madison.

Maddy ♀ Pet form of ▷Madeleine and its variants, also used as an independent given name. In the United States it is sometimes found as a pet form of the modern girl's name ▷Madison.

VARIANT: Maddie

Madelaine ♀ Variant spelling of ▷Madeleine.

Madeleine ♀ The French form of the byname of a character in the New Testament, Mary *Magdalene* 'Mary of Magdala'. Magdala was a village on Lake Galilee, a few miles north of Tiberias. The woman 'which had been healed of evil spirits and infirmities' (Luke 8:2) was given this name in the Bible to distinguish her from other bearers of the very common name ▷Mary. It was widely accepted in Christian folk belief that she was the same person as the repentant sinner who washed Christ's feet with her tears in the previous chapter (Luke 7), but there is no support in the text for this identification.

VARIANTS: Madelaine, Madelene, Madeline, Mad(e)lyn, Madalene, Madaline, Madoline; ▷Magdalen.
PET FORMS: Maddie, Maddy.

Madge ♀ Pet form of ▷Margaret, a palatalized version of *Mag(g)* (see ▷Maggie).

Madison ♀, ♂ Transferred use of the surname, in origin a metronymic from the medieval woman's given name

Madde, a short form of ▷Madeleine or ▷Maud. It was taken up in the United States, its use as a given name apparently influenced by the statesman James Madison (1751–1836), who was president during the War of 1812 and took part in drafting the U.S. constitution and Bill of Rights. It is currently enjoying something of a vogue as a girl's name, perhaps in Britain more closely associated with the streets of New York than the politician.

VARIANT: **Maddison.**

PET FORMS: **Maddy, Maddie** ♀.

Madlyn ♀ Modern variant of ▷Madeleine, influenced by the productive suffix *-lyn*; see ▷Lynn.

Madoline ♀ Modern respelling of ▷Madeleine.

Madonna ♀ From an Italian title of the Virgin Mary (literally 'my lady'), applied to countless Renaissance paintings of a beautiful young woman (with and without an infant), representing the mother of Christ. Its use as a given name is a fairly recent phenomenon, arising among Americans of Italian descent. Since the 1980s, the name has been particularly associated with the American pop star Madonna Ciccone (b. 1958).

Madrona ♀ Jewish: from the Romance name *Matrona*. The name was apparently chosen in the hope that the baby would live to become a mother herself.

Mae ♀ Variant spelling of ▷May, possibly influenced by ▷Maeve. It was borne by the American film actress Mae West (1892–1980), whose prominent bust led to her name being given, by members of the RAF, to a type of inflatable life jacket used in the Second World War. This spelling is not much used, except in compounds such as *Ellie-Mae*, *Lily-Mae*, and *Daisy-Mae*.

Maeve ♀ Anglicized form of Meadhbh (see Irish appendix).

VARIANTS: **Mave, Meave.**

Magdalen ♀ Older English form of ▷Madeleine, usually pronounced 'maud-lin'. This was the usual form of the given name in the Middle Ages.

VARIANT: **Magdalene.**

Magdalena ♀ Latinate form of ▷Madeleine.

Maggie ♀ Pet form of ▷Margaret, now also used as an independent given name. In the Middle Ages the short form *Mag(g)* was common, as a result of the early loss in pronunciation of the English preconsonantal r; it is no longer used as a given name, but it did give rise to the surname *Maggs*.

Magnus ♂ Originally a Latin byname meaning 'great', this was first extracted from the name of *Charlemagne* (recorded in Latin chronicles as *Carolus Magnus* 'Charles the Great') and used as a given name by the Scandinavians. It was borne by seven medieval kings of Norway, including Magnus I (1024–47), known as Magnus the Good, and Magnus VI (1238–80), known as Magnus the Law Mender. There are several early Scandinavian saints called Magnus, including an earl of Orkney (d. 1116), to whom Kirkwall cathedral is dedicated. The name was imported to Scotland and Ireland during the Middle Ages.

Mahalia ♀ Apparently a cross between the two biblical masculine personal names *Mahali* (Exodus 6:19) and *Mahalah* (1 Chronicles 7:18), both fleetingly mentioned in genealogies.

Maia ♀ See ▷Maya.

Maisie ♀ Scottish pet form derived from *Mairead*, the Gaelic form of ▷Margaret, with the Scottish and northern English diminutive suffix *-ie*. The name is now widely used both in Scotland and beyond as an independent given name.

VARIANT: **Maisy.**

Maitland ♂, ♀ Transferred use of the surname, which is of uncertain origin. It may have arisen from a nickname for

m

an ungracious individual, from Anglo-Norman French *maltalent, mautalent* 'bad temper'; or possibly it denoted someone from Mautalant, a place in Pontorson, France, which was named for its unproductive soil.

Majella ♀ Name given by Roman Catholics in honour of St Gerard Majella (1725–55), an Italian Redemptorist monk who was the focus of a number of miraculous phenomena and who was canonized in 1904.

Makenzie ♀ Simplified spelling of the girl's name ▷Mackenzie.

VARIANT: **Makensie.**

Malachi ♂ Biblical name, borne by the last of the twelve minor prophets of the Old Testament; he foretold the coming of Christ and his name means, appropriately, 'my messenger' in Hebrew. The name was adopted by the Puritans in the 17th century, but until a recent modest revival was rarely used among English speakers outside Ireland. In Ireland, written **Malachy**, it is a traditional name, representing an adaptation of more than one medieval Gaelic name to the biblical name. It was used to refer to an Irish king who defeated the Norse invaders in an important battle. His baptismal name was *Maoíleachlainn* 'devotee of St Seachnall or Secundinus', but in medieval sources telling of his life this has already been altered to coincide with that of the biblical prophet.

Malcolm ♂ Anglicized form of the medieval Gaelic name *Mael Coluim* 'devotee of St Columba'. Columba was a 6th-century monk of Irish origin who played a leading part in the conversion to Christianity of Scotland and northern England; see also ▷Callum and ▷Colm. He has always been one of the most popular saints in Scotland, but in the Middle Ages it was felt to be presumptuous to give the names of saints directly to children; instead their blessing was invoked by prefixing the name with *mael* 'devotee of' or *gille*

'servant of'. Since the 1930s the given name has been used widely in the English-speaking world, not just by those with Scottish connections.

Malerie ♀ Modern coinage, apparently a respelling of ▷Mallory influenced by ▷Valerie.

Malkah ♀ Jewish: from Hebrew *malkah* 'queen'. This name does not appear in the Hebrew scriptures, but represents an affectionate nickname used from the Midde Ages onwards.

VARIANT: **Malka.**

Mallory ♀, occasionally ♂ Especially North American: transferred use of the surname, which originated as a Norman French nickname for an unfortunate person, from Old French *malheure* 'unhappy' or 'unlucky'. Use as a boy's name dates from the 17th century and has always been infrequent, but as a girl's name it is well established in North America and is also occasionally found in Britain.

VARIANTS: **Mallery, Malerie.**

Malvina ♀ Semi-fictional name, based on Gaelic *mala mhín* 'smooth brow', invented by James Macpherson (1736–96), the Scottish antiquarian poet who published works allegedly translated from the ancient Gaelic bard Ossian. The name became popular in Scandinavia because of the admiration of the Emperor Napoleon for the Ossianic poems: he was godfather to several of the children of his marshal Jean Baptiste Bernadotte (who ruled Norway and Sweden (1818–44) as Karl XIV Johan) and imposed his own taste in naming practices on them, hence the frequency of Ossianic given names in Scandinavia. *Las Malvinas* is the Argentinian name for the Falkland Islands, but it has no connection with the Ossianic name, being derived from the name of the French seaport St Malo.

Mamie ♀ Short form of ▷Margaret or ▷Mary, originating as a nursery form. It is occasionally used as an independent given name. It was the name by which the wife of President Eisenhower was usually known.

Manda ♀ Shortened form of ▷Amanda.

Mandel ♂ Jewish: variant of ▷Mendel, but assumed by folk etymology to be from German *Männl*, a diminutive of *Mann* 'man'. It probably has no connection with the Yiddish vocabulary word *mandel* 'almond'.

Mandy ♀, ♂ Pet form of ▷Amanda, now sometimes used as an independent given name. As a male name it is an Anglicized form of the Jewish name ▷Mandel.

VARIANTS: **Mandi(e)**.

Manfred ♂ From an old Germanic personal name, usually said to be from *man* 'man' + *fred*, *frid* 'peace'. However, it is more likely that the first element was *magin* 'strength' (the usual Norman form being *Mainfred*) or *manag* 'much'. This name was in use among the Normans, who introduced it to Britain. However, it did not become part of the common stock of English given names, and was reintroduced from Germany in the 19th century. It was a traditional name among the Hohenstaufens, and was borne by the last Hohenstaufen king of Sicily (1258–66), who died in battle against papal forces at Benevento. The name was also used by Byron for the central character in his poetic drama *Manfred* (1817), a brooding outcast, tormented by incestuous love for his half-sister.

Manley ♂ Transferred use of the surname, which in most cases originated as a local name from places in Devon and Cheshire, named in Old English as 'the common wood or clearing', from *(ge)mǣn* 'common, shared' + *lēah* 'wood, clearing'. Its choice as a first name may have been influenced by association with the vocabulary word *manly* and the hope that the qualities denoted by the

adjective would be attributes of the bearer. This word may also lie behind some cases of the surname, as a nickname for a 'manly' person.

Manny ♂ Pet form of ▷Emmanuel, found mainly as a Jewish name.

Manon ♀ French pet form of ▷Marie, common in the 18th and 19th centuries, and now also used in the English-speaking world. The name is familiar in the English-speaking world through the Abbé Prévost's story *Manon Lescaut* (1731), which was given operatic treatment by both Puccini and Massenet. In it the young Chevalier des Grieux elopes with the heroine, who supports them by becoming a courtesan and is eventually deported to Louisiana, where she dies.

Mara ♀ Of biblical origin, from Hebrew *Mara* 'bitter', a name referred to by Naomi when she went back to Bethlehem because of the famine in the land of Moab and the deaths of her husband and two sons: 'Call me not Naomi, call me Mara: for the Almighty hath dealt very bitterly with me' (Ruth 1:20).

Maralyn ♀ Respelling of ▷Marilyn.

Marc ♂ French form of ▷Mark, now also quite popular in the English-speaking world. It was given some currency in England in the 1960s by the pop singer Marc Bolan (1947–77).

Marcel ♂ French: from the Latin name *Marcellus*, originally a diminutive of ▷Marcus. The name has always been popular in France as it was borne by a 3rd-century missionary to Gaul, martyred at Bourges with his companion Anastasius. It is also used in the English-speaking world.

Marcella ♀ Feminine form of *Marcellus*; see ▷Marcel. St Marcella was a Roman noblewoman of the late 4th century who lodged St Jerome for three years.

m

March ♂ Transferred use of the surname. This has two origins: as a local name for someone who lived on the border between two territories, especially in the Marches between England and Wales or England and Scotland (from Norman French *march* 'boundary', of Germanic origin); and as a nickname for someone with some association with the month of March (Old French *march(e)*, Latin (*mensis*) *Martius*, a derivative of *Mars*; compare ▷Martin). In part this name may also have been adopted as a first name by association with the female names ▷April, ▷May, and ▷June, bearing in mind that Mars, the roman god of war, after whom the month is named, is male.

Marcia ♀ Often used as a feminine equivalent of ▷Mark, but in fact a feminine form of *Marcius*, itself a derivative of ▷Marcus. One St Marcia is commemorated in a group with Felix, Luciolus, Fortunatus, and others; another with Zenais, Cyria, and Valeria; and a third with Ariston, Crescentian, Eutychian, Urban, Vitalis, Justus, Felicissimus, Felix, and Symphorosa. None is individually very famous.

VARIANT: **Marsha.**

PET FORMS: **Marcie, Marcy, Marci.**

Marcus ♂ The original Latin form of ▷Mark, of unknown derivation; it may possibly be connected with *Mars*, the name of the Roman god of war, or the adjective *mas* 'male, virile' (genitive *maris*). This was one of the very small number of Roman given names of the classical period. There were only about a dozen of these in general use, with perhaps another dozen confined to particular families. *Marcus* has been in use in the English-speaking world since the 16th century if not earlier; in the 20th century it enjoyed a considerable increase in popularity. As an African-American name it is sometimes bestowed in honour of the Black Consciousness leader Marcus Garvey (1887–1940).

Marea ♀ Altered spelling of ▷Maria.

Marga ♀ Short form of ▷Margaret or any of the large number of related names beginning with these two syllables. It is sometimes used as an independent given name.

Margaret ♀ An extremely common given name from the Middle Ages onwards, derived via Old French *Marguerite* and Latin *Margarita* from Greek *Margarītēs*, from *margaron* 'pearl', a word ultimately of Hebrew origin. The name was always understood to mean 'pearl' throughout the Middle Ages. The first St Margaret was martyred at Antioch in Pisidia during the persecution instigated by the Emperor Diocletian in the early 4th century. However, there is some doubt about her name, as the same saint is venerated in the Orthodox Church as ▷Marina. There were several other saintly bearers of the name, including St Margaret of Scotland (d. 1093), wife of King Malcolm Canmore and daughter of Edmund Ironside of England. It was also the name of the wife of Henry VI of England, Margaret of Anjou (1430–82), and of Margaret Tudor (1489–1541), sister of Henry VIII, who married James IV of Scotland and ruled as regent there after his death. See also ▷Margery, ▷Marjorie.

VARIANTS: **Margaret(t)a** (Latinate forms).

SHORT FORMS: ▷**Meg,** ▷**Peg, Madge, Marge.**

PET FORMS: ▷**Maggie, Meggie, Peggy, Peggie, Peggi, Margie,** ▷**May.** See also ▷Daisy.

COGNATES: Irish: **Mairéad.** Scottish Gaelic: **Mair(gh)ead.** Welsh: **Mar(g)ed, Mererid.** German: **Margaret(h)a, Margaret(h)e, Margrethe;** vernacular: **Margrit, Margret, Meta.** Dutch: **Margriet.** Danish, Norwegian: **Margaret(h)a, Margrethe.** Swedish: **Margaret(h)a.** Scandinavian (vernacular): **Margit; Marit** (Norwegian, Swedish); **Merete, Mereta, Mette** (Danish). French: ▷**Marguerite.** Spanish: **Margarita.** Portuguese: **Margarida.** Italian: **Margherita.**

Russian: Margarita. Polish: Małgorzata. Czech: **Markéta**. Croatian, Serbian, Slovenian: **Margareta**. Finnish: **Marketta**. Hungarian: **Margit**. Latvian: Margrieta. Lithuanian: **Margarita**.

Margarita ♀ Spanish equivalent of ▷Margaret, now widely adopted in the English-speaking world.

Margaux ♀ Fanciful respelling of ▷Margot, inspired by a village near Bordeaux noted for its red wine.

Margery ♀ The usual medieval vernacular form of ▷Margaret (now also commonly spelled ▷Marjorie). This form of the name is preserved in the nursery rhyme 'See-saw, Margery Daw'.

Margie ♀ Pet form of ▷Margaret or ▷Margery, from the informal short form *Marge*.

Margot ♀ French pet form of ▷Marguerite, now used as an independent given name. In England it is still usually pronounced in the French way, but in Eastern Europe the final consonant is sounded, and this has had some influence in America.

VARIANTS: **Margo, Margaux**.

Marguerita ♀ Latinate form of ▷Marguerite.

Marguerite ♀ French form of ▷Margaret, also used in the English-speaking world, where its use has been reinforced by the fact that the name was adopted in the 19th century for a garden flower, a large cultivated variety of daisy. *Margaret* was earlier used in English as a dialect word denoting the ox-eye daisy, and the French equivalent was borrowed into English just in time to catch the vogue for deriving girls' names from vocabulary words denoting flowers. See also ▷Daisy.

Maria ♀ Latin form of ▷Mary. It arose as a back-formation from the early Christian female name ▷Mariam, which was taken as a Latin accusative case. In fact, however, it is an indeclinable Aramaic alternative form of the Hebrew name ▷Miriam. In the English-speaking world *Maria* is a learned revival dating from the 18th century, pronounced both 'ma-**ree**-a' and, more traditionally, 'ma-**rye**-a'. This form of the name is also in common use in most European languages, either as the main local form of the name, as in Italian, Spanish, Portuguese, German, Dutch, Scandinavian, Polish, and Czech, or as a learned doublet of a vernacular form. In Spain not only is the name *María* itself enormously common, but a large number of Marian epithets and words associated with the cult of the Virgin are also used as female given names. *Maria* is also used as a male name in combinations such as *Gianmaria* (Italian) and *José María* (Spanish).

SHORT FORM: **Ria**.

Mariah ♀ Elaborated spelling of ▷Maria, influenced by the many girls' names of Hebrew origin ending in -*a* plus an optional final *h*.

Mariam ♀ Aramaic alternative form of the Hebrew name ▷Miriam, which now has currency in the English-speaking world.

Mariamne ♀ The form of ▷Miriam used by the Jewish historian Flavius Josephus, writing in Latin in the 1st century BC, as the name of the wife of King Herod. On the basis of this evidence, it has been thought by some to be closer to the original form of the name actually borne by the Virgin Mary, and has therefore been bestowed in her honour.

Marian ♀ Originally a medieval variant spelling of ▷Marion. However, in the 18th century, when combined names began to come into fashion, it was sometimes understood as a combination of ▷Mary and ▷Ann.

Marianne ♀ Extended spelling of ▷Marian, reinforcing the association of the second element with ▷Ann(e). It also represents a French assimilated form of ▷Mariamne. *Marianne* is the name used for the symbolic figure of the French Republic.

m

VARIANTS: **Mariann, Marieanne, Marian(n)a** (Latinate form).

Maribella ♀ Latinate combination of ▷Maria with the name ▷Bella or the productive suffix -*bella* (cf. ▷Annabel and ▷Christabel).

Marice ♀ Respelling of ▷Maris, or else a combination of the first syllable of ▷Mary or ▷Margaret with the name suffix -*ice* (compare for example ▷Janice).

Marie ♀ French form of ▷Maria. When first introduced to England in the Middle Ages, it was Anglicized in pronunciation and respelled ▷Mary. This French form was reintroduced into the English-speaking world as a separate name in the 19th century, and is still pronounced more or less in the French manner, although sometimes with the stress on the first syllable. It is now often used in combination with other names such as *Ellie*, *Chloe*, and *Lisa*.

Mariel ♀ Either a shortened form of ▷Mariella or an altered form of ▷Muriel or ▷Meriel.

Mariella ♀ Italian diminutive form of ▷Maria, now sometimes used as an independent given name in the English-speaking world.

Marielle ♀ French pet form of ▷Marie, now also used as an independent given name in the English-speaking world.

Marietta ♀ Italian pet form of ▷Maria, now occasionally used as a given name in the English-speaking world. In Gaelic Scotland *Mar(i)etta* is sometimes found as an Anglicized form of *Mairead*, the Gaelic equivalent of ▷Margaret.

Marigold ♀ One of the older of the group of names that were adopted from words for flowers in the late 19th and early 20th centuries. The Old English name of the flower was *golde*, presumably from *gold* (the precious metal) in reference to its colour. At some time before the 14th century the flower became associated with the Virgin Mary, and its name was extended accordingly to *marigold*. The name is rarely used at present.

Marika ♀ Slavic pet form of ▷Maria, sometimes used as an independent given name in the English-speaking world.

Marilee ♀ Modern coinage, a combination of ▷Mary and ▷Lee.

Marilene ♀ Modern coinage, a combination of the name ▷Mary with the productive suffix -*lene*, or else a variant of ▷Marilyn.

Marilla ♀ Apparently an arbitrary elaboration of ▷Maria, with the syllable -*illa* derived from names such as ▷Priscilla.

Marilyn ♀ Elaboration of ▷Mary, with the addition of the productive suffix -*lyn* (see ▷Lynn). It is recorded in the 18th century, possibly as a blend of ▷Mary and ▷Ellen, but first came into regular use in the 20th century, peaking in the 1940s and 50s. Since then its use has been surprisingly moderate, considering the enduring popularity of the film star Marilyn Monroe (1926–62), baptized Norma Jeane Baker.

VARIANTS: **Marilynn(e), Marylyn(n), ▷Marilene.**

Marina ♀ From a Late Latin name, a feminine form of the family name *Marinus*. This was in fact a derivative of ▷Marius, a traditional name of uncertain derivation, but even during the early centuries AD it was widely assumed to be identical with the Latin adjective *marinus* 'of the sea'. The early saints of this name are all of very doubtful historical authenticity.

Marion ♀, ♂ Originally a medieval French diminutive form of ▷Marie, introduced to Britain in the Middle Ages. In some places it was taken as a pet form of ▷Margaret or ▷Margery. As a male name, it is an altered form of the Continental male name *Marian*, a derivative of Latin *Marianus* (from ▷Marius), but is now rarely, if ever, used. It was the birth name of the American film star John Wayne (1907–79).

Maris ♀ Modern name of uncertain origin. It may derive from the second word of the Marian epithet *stella maris* 'star of the sea'.

Marisa ♀ 20th-century elaboration of ▷Maria, with the suffix *-isa* abstracted from such names as *Lisa* and *Louisa*.

Marissa ♀ Variant of ▷Marisa, with the suffix *-issa*, abstracted from names such as *Clarissa*.

Marius ♂ Latin name occasionally used in English and other languages. It is of uncertain origin: it may be connected with *Mars*, the name of the god of war, or perhaps *mas, maris* 'virile'. The Italian, Spanish, and Portuguese equivalent, Mario, is extremely popular, being taken as the masculine form of ▷Maria and therefore associated with the cult of the Virgin Mary.

Marjie ♀ Pet form of ▷Margaret or ▷Margery, a variant spelling of ▷Margie, also found as Marjy and Marji.

Marjorie ♀ The usual modern spelling of ▷Margery. It seems to have arisen as the result of folk etymological association with that of the herb *marjoram* (compare ▷Rosemary). This word is of uncertain origin; its Middle English and Old French form was *majorane*, without the first *-r-*.

VARIANT: **Marjory.**

Mark ♂ From the Latin name ▷Marcus, borne by the Evangelist, author of the second gospel in the New Testament, and by several other early and medieval saints. In Arthurian legend, King Mark is the aged ruler of Cornwall to whom Isolde is brought as a bride by Tristan; his name was presumably of Celtic origin, perhaps derived from the element *march* 'horse'. This was not a particularly common name in the Middle Ages but was in more frequent use by the end of the 16th century.

COGNATES: Irish and Scottish Gaelic: Marcas. German, Dutch: Markus. French: Marc. Spanish: Marco, Marcos. Portuguese: Marcos. Italian: Marco. Russian: Mark. Polish, Czech: Marek. Croatian, Serbian, Slovenian: Marko. Finnish: Markku. Hungarian: Márk.

Marla ♀ English: modern creation, representing an altered form of ▷Marlene, or else a name invented as a feminine equivalent of ▷Marlon.

Marlene ♀ Contracted form of Latin *Maria Magdalene* (see ▷Madeleine). The name is of German origin, but is now also widely used in the English-speaking world, normally in a pronunciation with two syllables (compare ▷Arlene and ▷Charlene). Probably the first, and certainly the most famous, bearer of the name was the film star Marlene Dietrich (1901–92), who was born Marie Magdalene. The name was further popularized in the 1940s by the wartime German song 'Lili Marlene', which was immensely popular among both German and British troops in North Africa.

Marley ♂ Transferred use of the surname, a local name from any of various places so called, for example in Devon, Kent, and West Yokshire. The first element of these names is respectively Old English (*ge*)*mǣre* 'boundary', *myrig* 'pleasant', and *mearð* '(pine) marten'. The second element in each case is *lēah* '(woodland) clearing'. Use of the surname as a given name has probably been influenced to some extent by the popularity of the Jamaican singer Bob Marley (1945–81).

Marlon ♂ Name apparently first brought to public attention by the American actor Marlon Brando (1924–2004). The name was borne also by his father. It is of uncertain origin, possibly derived from ▷Marc with the addition of the French diminutive suffix *-lon* (originally a combination of two separate suffixes, *-el* and *-on*). The actor's family was partly of French extraction.

Marmaduke ♂ Of uncertain derivation. It is generally held to be an Anglicized form of the Old Irish name *Mael-Maedóc* 'devotee of Maedóc'. The name *Maedóc* was borne by various early Irish saints, most notably a 6th-century abbot of Clonmore and a 7th-century bishop of Ferns. Mael-Maedóc Ó Morgair (1095–1148) was a reformer of the Church in Ireland and a friend of Bernard of Clairvaux. However, the modern Gaelic form (from *c*.1200) is *Maol-Maodhóg* (pronounced 'mul-**may**-og'), so that the name would have had to have been borrowed into English before this loss of the *d*. *Marmaduke* has never been common except in Yorkshire. Its most notable bearer in recent times has been Marmaduke Hussey (1923–2006), a former chairman of the governors of the BBC.

SHORT FORM: ▷Duke.

Marnie ♀ Pet form of the Swedish name *Marna* (see Scandinavian appendix), now also used as an independent given name in the English-speaking world.

Marquis ♂ Mainly U.S.: taken from the vocabulary word denoting the rank of nobility (compare ▷Earl, ▷Prince, ▷King). This derives from Old French *marchis*, i.e. 'lord of the marches (border districts)'. The spelling was later influenced by the Provençal and Spanish equivalents. Use as a given name may also have been influenced by the Scottish surname *McMarquis*, Gaelic *Mac Marcuis*, a patronymic from ▷Marcus.

Marsh ♂ Transferred use of the surname, in origin a local name for someone who lived on a patch of marshy ground, from Middle English *mersche* (Old English *mersc*). It is also used as an informal short form of ▷Marshall, and possibly also as a masculine equivalent of ▷Marsha, by back-formation.

Marsha ♀ Phonetic spelling of ▷Marcia, associated particularly with the American film star Marsha Hunt (b. 1917).

Marshall ♂ Transferred use of the surname, derived from a Norman French occupational term that originally denoted someone who looked after horses, ultimately from Germanic *marah* 'horse' + *scalc* 'servant'. By the time it became fixed as a surname it had the meaning 'shoeing smith'; later it came to denote an official whose duties were to a large extent ceremonial. The surname is pronounced the same as the Latin name *Martial* (from Latin *Mars*, genitive *Martis*; compare ▷Martin). This may have contributed something to its use as a given name.

VARIANT: **Marshal**.

Martha ♀ New Testament name, of Aramaic rather than Hebrew origin, meaning 'lady'. It was borne by the sister of Lazarus and Mary of Bethany (John 11:1). According to Luke 10:38, when Jesus visited the house of Mary and Martha, Mary sat at his feet, listening to him, while Martha 'was cumbered about much serving', so that she complained to Jesus, 'Lord, dost thou not care that my sister hath left me to serve alone?' For this reason, the name *Martha* has always been associated with hard domestic work, as opposed to the contemplative life.

COGNATES: German: **Marthe**. Scandinavian: **Mart(h)a, Mart(h)e**. French: **Marthe**. Spanish, Italian: **Marta**. Polish, Czech, Slovenian: **Marta**. Finnish: **Martta**. Hungarian: **Márta**.

Marti ♀ Short form of ▷Martina or ▷Martine.

VARIANTS: **Martie, Marty**.

Martin ♂ English form of the Latin name *Martinus*. This was probably originally derived from *Mars* (genitive *Martis*), the name of the Roman god of war (and earlier of fertility). *Martin* became very popular in the Middle Ages, especially on the Continent, as a result of the fame of St Martin of Tours. He was born the son of a Roman officer in Upper Pannonia (an outpost of the Roman Empire, now part of Hungary), and, although he became a leading figure in the 4th-century Church, he is chiefly remembered now for having divided his cloak in two and given half to a beggar. The name was also borne by five popes, including one who defended Roman Catholic dogma against Eastern Orthodox theology. He died after suffering imprisonment and privations in Naxos and public humiliation in Constantinople, and was promptly acclaimed a martyr by supporters of the Roman Church. Among Protestants, the name is sometimes bestowed in honour of the German theologian Martin Luther (1483–1546); *Martin* was used as a symbolic name for the Protestant Church in satires by both Dryden and Swift. A further influence may be its use as the given name of the civil-rights leader Martin Luther King (1929–68).

VARIANT: **Martyn.**

PET FORM: **Marty.**

COGNATES: Irish: **Máirtín, Mártan.** Scottish Gaelic: **Màrtainn.** German: **Martin, Merten.** Dutch: **Martin Maarten, Martijn.** Danish, Norwegian: **Morten.** Swedish: **Mårten.** French: **Martin.** Spanish: **Martín.** Catalan: **Martí.** Portuguese: **Martinho.** Italian: **Martino.** Polish: **Marcin.** Czech: **Martin.** Croatian, Serbian, Slovenian: **Martin.** Finnish: **Martti.** Hungarian: **Márton.**

Martina ♀ Feminine form of the Latin name *Martinus* (see ▷Martin). It was in use from an early period, being borne by a notorious poisoner mentioned by the historian Tacitus. The 3rd-century saint of the same name is of doubtful authenticity. Modern use of the name in the English-speaking world seems to be the result

of German or Eastern European influence, as in the case of the American tennis player Martina Navratilova (b. 1956), who was born in the Czech Republic.

Martine ♀ French form of ▷Martina, also used in the English-speaking world.

Marty ♂, ♀ Short form of ▷Martin or of ▷Martina and ▷Martine. It has sometimes been used as an independent boy's name since the latter part of the 20th century, being associated particularly with the comedian Marty Feldman (1933–83), the pop singer Marty Wilde (b. 1939 as Reginald Smith), and the country-and-western singer Marty Robbins (1925–82).

Martyn ♂ Variant spelling of ▷Martin.

Marva ♀ Modern creation, apparently invented as a feminine form of ▷Marvin. The fanciful name **Marvalee** represents an elaboration of this.

Marvin ♂ Medieval variant of ▷Mervyn, resulting from the regular Middle English change of *-er-* to *-ar-*. Modern use may represent a transferred use of the surname derived from this in the Middle Ages. It is popular in the United States, where it is associated in particular with the American singer Marvin Gaye (1939–84) and the boxer Marvin Hagler (b. 1954).

Mary ♀ Originally a Middle English Anglicized form of French ▷Marie, from Latin ▷Maria. This is a New Testament form of ▷Miriam, which St Jerome derives from elements meaning 'drop of the sea' (Latin *stilla maris*, later altered by folk etymology to *stella maris* 'star of the sea'). *Mary* was the name of the Virgin Mary, mother of Jesus Christ, who has been the subject of a cult from earliest times. Consequently, the name was extremely common among early Christians, several saints among them, and by the Middle Ages was well established in every country in Europe

m

at every level of society. It has been in use ever since, its popularity in England having been relatively undisturbed by vagaries of fashion until the 1960s, when it began to decline sharply. In the New Testament, *Mary* is also the name of several other women: Mary Magdalene (see ▷Madeleine); Mary the sister of Martha, who sat at Jesus's feet while Martha served (Luke 10:38–42; John 11:1–46; 12:1–9) and who came to be taken in Christian tradition as symbolizing the value of a contemplative life; the mother of St Mark (Colossians 4:10); and a Roman matron mentioned by St Paul (Romans 16:6).

PET FORMS: ▷May, ▷Molly.

COGNATES: In most European languages, including English: ▷Maria. Irish: Máire (see also ▷Moira, ▷Maura); Máiria (a learned form). Scottish Gaelic: Màiri, Màili. Welsh: Mair, Mari. Dutch: Marja. French: ▷Marie. Spanish: María. Russian: Mar(i)ya. Czech, Croatian, Serbian, Slovenian: Marija. Finnish: Marja. Hungarian: Marica. Lithuanian: Marija.

Maryam ♀ Variant spelling of ▷Mariam.

Marylyn ♀ Variant spelling of ▷Marilyn.

VARIANT: ▷Marylynn.

Mason ♂ Transferred use of the surname, which originated in the early Middle Ages as an occupational name for a worker in stone, Old French *maçon* (of Germanic origin, connected with Old English *macian* 'to make').

Masterman ♂ Transferred use of the surname, which originated in Scotland as a term denoting a retainer or servant: the 'man' of the 'master'. This was used in particular for the eldest sons of barons and the uncles of lords. As a given name it is principally known from the central character of Captain Frederick Marryat's novel *Masterman Ready* (1841).

Mathew ♂ Variant spelling of ▷Matthew.

Mathias ♂ Variant spelling of ▷Matthias.

Matilda ♀ Latinized form of a Germanic personal name derived from *maht, meht* 'might' + *hild* 'battle'. This was the name of an early German queen (895–968), wife of Henry the Fowler, who was noted for her piety and generosity. It was also the name of the wife of William the Conqueror and of the daughter of Henry I of England (see ▷Maud). The name was introduced into England by the Normans, and this Latinized form is the one that normally occurs in medieval records, while the vernacular form *Maud* was the one in everyday use. *Matilda* was revived in England as a learned form in the 18th century.

VARIANT: Mathilda.

SHORT FORM: Tilda.

PET FORMS: Mattie, Matty; Tilly, Tillie.

COGNATES: German: Mecht(h)ilde. Dutch: Machteld. Danish, Norwegian: Mat(h)ilde. Swedish: Mat(h)ilda. French: Mathilde. Spanish, Portuguese, Italian: Matilde. Polish, Czech: Matylda. Finnish: Martta. Hungarian: Matild.

Matt ♂ Short form of ▷Matthew, also sometimes used as a given name in its own right.

Matthew ♂ English form of the name of the Christian evangelist, author of the first gospel in the New Testament. His name is a form of the Hebrew name *Mattathia*, meaning 'gift of God', which is fairly common in the Old Testament, being rendered in the Authorized Version in a number of different forms: *Mattan(i)ah, Mattatha(h), Mattithiah, Mattathias*, and so on. In the Authorized Version, the evangelist is regularly referred to as *Matthew*, while the apostle chosen to replace Judas Iscariot is distinguished as ▷Matthias. A related name from the same Hebrew roots, but reversed, is ▷Jonathan. Throughout the English-speaking world *Matthew* has been particularly popular since the 1970s.

VARIANT: **Mathew.**

SHORT FORM: **Matt.**

COGNATES: (also of ▷**Matthias**): Irish: Maitiú, Maitias. Scottish Gaelic: Mata; Matha (a dialectal variant). German: Matthäus. Dutch: Matthijs. Danish: Mads, Mathies. Norwegian, Swedish: Mats. French: Mathieu. Spanish: Mateo. Catalan: Mateu. Portuguese: Mateus. Italian: Matteo, Mattia. Russian: Matvei. Polish: Mateusz, Maciej. Czech: Matěj, Matyáš. Croatian, Serbian, Slovenian: Matija. Finnish: Matti. Hungarian: Mátyás, Máté.

Matthias ♂ New Testament Greek form of the Hebrew name *Mattathia* (see ▷**Matthew**), or rather of an Aramaic derivative. The Latin form of the name is *Matthaeus*. In English the form *Matthias* is used in the Authorized Version of the New Testament to distinguish the disciple who was chosen after the treachery of Judas to make up the twelve (Acts 1:23–26) from the evangelist *Matthew*. However, this distinction is not observed in other languages, where *Matthias* (or a version of it) is often a learned doublet existing alongside a vernacular derivative.

VARIANT: **Mathias.**

Maud ♀ Medieval vernacular form of ▷**Matilda**. This form was characteristically Low German (i.e. including medieval Dutch and Flemish). The wife of William the Conqueror, who bore this name, was the daughter of Baldwin, Count of Flanders. In Flemish and Dutch the letter -*t*- was generally lost when it occurred between vowels, giving forms such as *Ma(h)auld*. *Maud* or *Matilda* was also the name of the daughter (1102–67) of Henry I of England; she was married early in life to the Holy Roman Emperor Henry V, and later disputed the throne of England with her cousin Stephen. In 1128 she married Geoffrey, Count of Anjou. A medieval chronicler commented, 'she was a good woman, but she had little bliss with him'. The name *Maud* became quite common in England in the 19th century, when its popularity was influenced in part by Tennyson's poem *Maud*, published in 1855, but has not been much used since the early decades of the 20th century.

Maude ♀ Variant of ▷**Maud**, the usual spelling of the name in North America.

Maura ♀ Of Celtic origin. St Maura was a 5th-century martyr, of whom very little is known; her companion is variously named as *Britta* (of Celtic origin) and *Baya* (of Latin origin). In Ireland *Maura* is now commonly regarded as a form of ▷**Mary**.

Maureen ♀ Anglicized form of Máirín (see Irish appendix). Among other influences, the name was popularized by the film actress Maureen O'Hara (b. 1920). See also ▷**Moreen**.

VARIANTS: **Maurene, Maurine.**

SHORT FORM: ▷**Mo.**

Maurice ♂ From the Late Latin name *Mauricius*, a derivative of *Maurus* (a byname meaning 'Moor', i.e. 'dark, swarthy'), borne by, among others, an early Byzantine emperor (*c*.539–602). It was introduced to Britain by the Normans and was popular in the Middle English period, but was not widely adopted by the nobility and became rare in the 17th century. Between the mid-19th century and the 1940s, it was moderately popular but has since faded again. See also ▷**Morris**.

SHORT FORM: ▷**Mo.**

Mave ♀ Variant spelling of ▷**Maeve**, also sometimes used as an informal short form of ▷**Mavis**.

Mavis ♀ One of the small class of girls' names taken from vocabulary words denoting birds. *Mavis* is another word for the song thrush, first attested in Chaucer. It is from Old French, and probably ultimately of Breton origin.

The given name is not found before the last decade of the 19th century; it was popular in the 1930s and 40s but has since gone out of fashion.

Max ♂ Short form of ▷Maximilian, now also of ▷Maxwell and various other names with this first syllable. It is often used as an independent given name.

Maxie ♂, ♀ Pet form of any of the male or female names with *Max-* as the first syllable, such as ▷Maxwell, ▷Maxine. It is also occasionally used as a girl's name in its own right.
VARIANT: **Maxi** ♀.

Maxim ♂ Russian: from the Latin cognomen ▷Maximus 'greatest', later used as a given name. This was the name of a very large number of early saints, including a Byzantine theologian and mystic (*c*.580–662) who was persecuted under the Emperor Constans. *Maxim* Gorki was the pseudonym adopted by the Russian writer Alexei Maximovich Peshkov (1868–1936). The name is now also used in the English-speaking world.

Maximilian ♂ From the Latin name *Maximilianus* (a diminutive of ▷Maximus). This was borne by a 3rd-century saint numbered among the 'Fourteen Holy Helpers'. Although already existing, the name was reanalysed in the 15th century by the Emperor Friedrich III, who bestowed it on his first-born son (1459–1519), as a blend of the names *Maximus* and *Aemilianus*, intending thereby to pay homage to the two classical Roman generals Q. Fabius Maximus 'Cunctator' and P. Cornelius Scipio Aemilianus. The name became traditional in the Habsburg family in Austria-Hungary and also in the royal house of Bavaria. It was borne by an ill-fated Austrian archduke (1832–67) who was set up as emperor of Mexico but later overthrown and shot.
VARIANTS: **Maximillian, Maximilien.**

Maximus ♂ Latin cognomen meaning 'greatest'. Its use as a given name in the English-speaking world is recent.

Maxine ♀ Modern coinage, first recorded around 1930. It is a derivative of ▷Max by addition of the feminine ending *-ine*.

Maxwell ♂ Transferred use of the Scottish surname, in origin a local name from a minor place on the River Tweed, named as 'the stream (Old English *well*(*a*)) of *Mack*'. The latter is a form of ▷Magnus. Maxwell was the middle name of the newspaper tycoon William Maxwell Aitken, Lord Beaverbrook (1879–1964), who was born in Canada, and it has been used as a given name among his descendants. It is now also frequently taken as an expansion of ▷Max.

May ♀ Pet form of both ▷Margaret and ▷Mary. The popularity of this name, which was at its height in the early 20th century, has been reinforced by the fact that it fits into the series of month names with ▷April and ▷June, and also belongs to the group of flower names, being another word for the hawthorn, whose white flowers blossom in May. It is now not much used independently but is a common component of compounds such as *Ella-May*, *Lily-May*, and *Daisy-May*.

Maya ♀ Latinate version of ▷May or a respelled form of the name of the Roman goddess *Maia*, influenced by the common English name *May*. The goddess Maia was one of the Pleiades, the daughters of Atlas and Pleione; she was the mother by Jupiter of Mercury. Her name seems to be derived from the root *mai-* 'great', seen also in Latin *maior* 'larger'. In the case of the American writer Maya Angelou (b. 1928 as Marguerite Johnson), *Maya* is a nickname which she acquired in early childhood as a result of her younger brother's referring to her as 'mya sista'.
VARIANT: **Maia.**

Maybelle ♀ Altered form of ▷Mabel, influenced by the independent names ▷May and ▷Belle.

Maynard ♂ Transferred use of the surname, which is derived from a Norman French given name of Germanic origin, from *magin* 'strength' + *hard* 'hardy, brave, strong'.

Meagan ♀ Recent, pseudo-Irish spelling of ▷Megan.
VARIANT: **Meaghan**.

Medea ♀ Name borne in classical mythology by a Colchian princess who helped Jason to steal the Golden Fleece from her father. Later, however, she was abandoned by Jason in favour of Creusa (or, in some versions, Glauce). She took her revenge by killing the two children previously born to Jason and herself. The name may derive from the Greek verb *mēdesthai* 'to reflect, meditate, or ponder'.

Meg ♀ Short form of ▷Margaret, also used as an independent given name. It is an alteration of the obsolete short form *Mag(g)* (as in ▷Maggie). Until recently *Meg* was a characteristically Scottish form, but it is now used more widely. Its popularity may owe something to Meg March, one of the four sisters who are the main characters in Louisa M. Alcott's novel *Little Women* (1855).

Megan ♀ In origin a Welsh pet form of ▷Meg; nowadays it is much used as an independent first name throughout Britain and in America and elsewhere in the English-speaking world.
VARIANTS: **Meghan**, **Meag(h)an** (pseudo-Irish spellings).

Meggie ♀ Pet form of ▷Margaret, ▷Meg, or ▷Megan, as in the case of the central character of Colleen McCullough's novel *The Thorn Birds* (1977).

Meghan ♀ Recent, pseudo-Irish spelling of ▷Megan.

Mehalia ♀ Apparently an altered form of ▷Mahalia.

Mehetabel ♀ Biblical name (meaning 'God makes happy' in Hebrew), borne by a character, 'the daughter of Matred, the daughter of Mezahab', who is mentioned in passing in a genealogy (Genesis 36:39). The name achieved some currency among the Puritans in the 17th century but had gone out of regular use by the 19th century. Nowadays, it is chiefly associated with the companion (a cat) of Archy, the cockroach in the poems of Don Marquis (1927).
VARIANT: **Mehitabel**.

Meir ♂ Jewish: traditional name, meaning 'giving light' in Hebrew.
VARIANTS: **Meier, Meyer, Myer, Maier, Mayr** (generally assimilations to German surname forms).

Mel ♂, ♀ Short form of ▷Melvin or ▷Melville or, in the case of the girl's name, of ▷Melanie or the several other girls' names beginning with this syllable. It is also found independently as an Irish boy's name (see Irish appendix).

Melanie ♀ From an Old French form of Latin *Melania*, a derivative of the feminine form, *melaina*, of the Greek adjective *melas* 'black, dark'. This was the name of two Roman saints of the 5th century, a grandmother and granddaughter. St Melania the Younger was a member of a rich patrician family. She led an austere and devout Christian life and, on inheriting her father's wealth, she emancipated her slaves, sold her property, and gave the proceeds to the poor. She also established several contemplative houses, including one on the Mount of Olives, to which she eventually retired. The name *Melanie* was introduced to England from France in the Middle Ages, but died out again. It was reintroduced and became popular in the late 20th century.
VARIANTS: **Melany**, ▷**Melony, Mellony, Mel(l)oney**.

Melchior ♂ From the name assigned by medieval tradition to one of the three Magi. It is said to be of Persian origin, composed of the elements *melk* 'king' + *quart* 'city'.

Melek ♂ Jewish: from a vocabulary element meaning 'king' in Hebrew. It originated in part as a nickname, in part as a short form of various compound names containing this element, for example *Elimelek* 'God is king'.

Melinda ♀ Modern coinage, derived from the first syllable of names such as ▷Melanie and ▷Melissa, with the addition of the productive suffix *-inda* (as in ▷Lucinda).

Melissa ♀ From the Greek word *melissa* 'honey bee'. It is the name of the good witch who releases Rogero from the power of the bad witch Alcina in Ariosto's narrative poem *Orlando Furioso* (1532). The name was fairly popular in the 1990s, along with other girls' names sharing the same first syllable.
VARIANTS: **Melit(t)a**.

Melitta ♀ Variant of ▷Melissa, from an ancient Greek dialectal variant of *melissa* 'honey bee'.

Melody ♀ Modern transferred use of the vocabulary word (Greek *melōdía* 'singing of songs', from *melos* 'song' + *aeidein* 'to sing'), chosen partly because of its pleasant associations and partly under the influence of other girls' names with the same first syllable.

Melony ♀ Variant of ▷Melanie, perhaps influenced by ▷Melody.
VARIANTS: **Mellony, Mel(l)oney**.

Melville ♂ Mainly North American: transferred use of the Scottish surname, which originated as a Norman baronial name borne by the lords of a place in northern France called *Malleville* 'bad settlement', i.e. settlement on infertile land. The name was taken to Scotland as early as the 12th century and became an important

surname there; use as a given name seems also to have originated in Scotland.

Melvin ♂ Modern name of uncertain origin, probably a variant of the less common ▷Melville. The variant Melvyn is associated particularly with the film star Melvyn Douglas (1901–81).

Menahem ♂ Jewish: name meaning 'comforter' in Hebrew. It was borne in the Scriptures by an evil king of Israel who massacred pregnant women (2 Kings 15:14–18), but the name has nevertheless always been a popular one among Jews; in earlier times it was given particularly to a child born after the death of a sibling and seen as a comfort to his parents. See also ▷Mendel.
VARIANT: **Menachem**.

Mendel ♂ Jewish: Yiddish form of Hebrew ▷Menahem. It seems to have originated as a result of substitution of the Yiddish diminutive suffix *-l* (plus an intrusive *-d-*) for *-hem*, which was taken erroneously as the German diminutive suffix *-chen*.

Mercedes ♀ Spanish name associated with the cult of the Virgin Mary, from the liturgical title *Maria de las Mercedes* (literally, 'Mary of Mercies'; in English, 'Our Lady of Ransom'). Latin *mercedes* (plural) originally meant 'wages' or 'ransom'. In Christian theology, Christ's sacrifice is regarded as a 'ransom for the sins of mankind', hence an 'act of ransom' was seen as identical with an 'act of mercy'. There are feasts in the Roman Catholic calendar on 10 August and 24 September to commemorate the Virgin under this name. As a given name, this is now occasionally used in England, and more commonly in the United States, but normally only by Roman Catholics. It is associated with the American film actress Mercedes McCambridge (1916–2004). A more materialistic association with the high-class German brand of car so named may also be having an influence on the continued use of the name in this increasingly secular age.

PET FORM: **Merche**.

Mercer ♂ Transferred use of the surname, in origin an occupational name for a trader (Old French *mercier*, from Late Latin *mercarius*, a derivative of *merx* 'merchandise'). Use as a given name in the United States may have originated in honour of General Hugh Mercer, killed at the battle of Princeton in 1777. It may sometimes also have been chosen as a kind of male equivalent of ▷Mercy.

Mercia ♀ Latinate elaboration of ▷Mercy, coinciding in form with the name of the Anglo-Saxon kingdom of Mercia, which dominated England during the 8th century under its king, Offa.

Mercy ♀ From the vocabulary word denoting the quality of magnanimity, and in particular God's forgiveness of sinners, a quality much prized in Christian tradition. The word is derived from Latin *merces*, which originally meant 'wage' or 'reward' (see ▷Mercedes). The name was in regular use from the mid 15th century onwards and was favoured by the Puritans; Mercy is the companion of Christiana in the second part of John Bunyan's *Pilgrim's Progress* (1684). Subsequently, it fell out of use as a given name. In modern use, this is often an Anglicized form of *Mercedes*.

Meredith ♀, ♂ From an Old Welsh male personal name (see Welsh appendix). In recent years the name has been given to girls, especially in the United States, a choice possibly influenced by the female character so named in Enid Bagnold's novel *National Velvet* (1935), which was made into a film (1944).

Meriel ♀ Variant of ▷Muriel, in origin a Breton form of the underlying Celtic name. It is recorded in England from the 15th century onwards.

Merle ♀, ♂ Probably a contracted form of ▷Meriel, but also associated with the small class of girls' names derived from birds, since it is identical in form with Old French *merle* 'blackbird' (Latin *merula*). The name came to public notice in the 1930s with the actress Merle Oberon (1911–79, born Estelle Merle O'Brien Thompson).

Merlin ♂ Usual English form of the Welsh name Myrddin (see Welsh appendix). The name is most famous as that of the legendary magician who guides the destiny of King Arthur. The English form has been distorted by mediation through Old French sources, which associated the second element with the diminutive suffix -*lin*.

VARIANT: **Merlyn** (occasionally given to girls, as if containing the productive suffix of girls' names -*lyn*).

Merrill ♂ Transferred use of the surname, which was derived in the Middle Ages from the female name ▷Meriel or ▷Muriel.

Merrily ♀ Mainly U.S.: apparently a respelling of ▷Marilee, reshaped to coincide with the adverb derived from the adjective *merry*.

Merrilyn ♀ Recent coinage, a blend of ▷Marilyn and ▷Merry.

Merry ♀ Apparently an assimilated form of ▷Mercy. In Dickens's novel *Martin Chuzzlewit* (1844), Mr Pecksniff's daughters Charity and Mercy are known as Cherry and Merry. Nowadays the name is usually bestowed because of its association with the adjective denoting a cheerful and jolly temperament (compare ▷Happy). In the accent of Canada and the central and northern United States there is no difference in pronunciation between *Merry* and *Mary*.

Mertice ♀ Recent coinage, found in the southern United States. It seems to be an entirely arbitrary invention.

Merton ♂ Transferred use of the surname, in origin a local name from any of several places named in Old English as *mere tūn* 'settlement by the lake'. Use as a given name may have been influenced by its similarity in sound to the traditional given name ▷Martin.

Mervyn ♂ Anglicized form of Welsh Merfyn (see Welsh appendix), now also widely used outside Wales.

VARIANT: **Mervin**.

SHORT FORM: **Merv**.

Meryl ♀ Recent coinage, associated chiefly with the American actress Meryl Streep (b. 1949 as Mary Louise Streep).

Meshulam ♂ Jewish: Hebrew name, apparently meaning either 'paid for' or 'friend'. It is borne by a minor character in the Old Testament (2 Kings 22:3); the spelling *Meshullam* is used in the Authorized Version.

Mia ♀ Danish and Swedish pet form of ▷Maria. It came to be used in the English-speaking world largely as a result of the fame of the actress Mia Farrow (b. 1945) and has enjoyed a sharp rise in popularity since the late 1990s.

Micah ♂ Biblical name (meaning 'who is like Yahweh?' in Hebrew, and thus a doublet of ▷Michael). This was the name of a prophet, author of the book of the Bible that bears his name and that dates from the late 8th century BC.

Michael ♂ English form of a common biblical name (meaning 'who is like God?' in Hebrew) borne by one of the archangels, the protector of the ancient Hebrews, who is also regarded as a saint of the Catholic Church. In the Middle Ages, Michael was regarded as captain of the heavenly host (see Revelation 12:7–9), symbol of the Church Militant, and patron of soldiers. He was often depicted bearing a flaming sword. The name is also borne by a Persian prince and ally of Belshazzar mentioned in the Book of Daniel. Since the early 1900s it has been one of the most enduringly

popular boys' names in the English-speaking world. See also ▷Michal.

COGNATES: Irish: Mícheál. Scottish Gaelic: Mìcheal. Welsh: Meical, Mihangel. German: Michael. Dutch: Michaël, Machiel. Scandinavian: Mikael. Danish, Norwegian: Mikkel. French: Michel. Spanish, Portuguese: Miguel. Catalan: Miquel. Italian: Michele. Russian: Mikhail. Polish: Michał. Czech: Michal. Croatian: Mihovil. Serbian: Mihajlo. Slovenian: Mihael. Finnish: Mikko. Hungarian: Mihály.

SHORT FORMS: **Mike**, **Mick**.

PET FORMS: **Mick(e)y**, **Mikey**.

Michaela ♀ Latinate feminine form of ▷Michael.

VARIANT: **Mikayla** (modern respelling).

Michal ♀ Biblical name (meaning 'brook' in Hebrew) borne by a daughter of Saul who married King David. It is probably through confusion with this name that ▷Michael has occasionally been used as a girl's name in the English-speaking world.

Michèle ♀ French feminine form of *Michel* (see ▷Michael), also used in the English-speaking world (with or without the accent).

Michelle ♀ French feminine form of *Michel*, the French form of ▷Michael. This name is now also used extensively in the English-speaking world. It was popular in the 1970s and 80s, possibly influenced in part by a Beatles song with this name as its title (1966).

SHORT FORMS: **Chelle**, ▷**Shell**.

Mick ♂ Short form of ▷Michael; now common as a generic, and often derogatory, term for a Catholic or an Irishman.

Mickey ♂ Pet form of ▷Michael, now occasionally used independently.

VARIANT: **Micky**.

Mickenzie ♀ Altered form of ▷Mackenzie, influenced by the name ▷Mick.

Mignonette ♀ Pronounced 'mee-nyon-**et**': probably a direct use of the French nickname *mignonette* 'little darling', a feminine diminutive of *mignon* 'sweet, cute, dainty'. Alternatively, it may belong to the class of names derived from vocabulary words denoting flowers (the word in English is used for various species of *Reseda*).

Mikayla ♀ Modern respelling of ▷Michaela.

Mike ♂ Usual short form of ▷Michael. It is also used as an independent given name, particularly in the United States.

Mikey ♂ Pet form of ▷Michael, also used as an independent given name.

Milan ♂ Czech: from a short form of various compound names formed with *mil* 'grace, favour', now also used in the English-speaking world. Sometimes, however, it may be chosen with reference to the northern Italian city (Italian *Milano*), the capital of Lombardy.

Mildred ♀ From an Old English female personal name *Mildþrȳð*, derived from *mild* 'gentle' + *þrȳð* 'strength'. This was the name of a 7th-century abbess, who had a less famous but equally saintly elder sister called *Mildburh* and a younger sister called *Mildgȳð*; all were daughters of a certain Queen Ermenburh. Their names illustrate clearly the Old English pattern of combining and recombining the same small group of name elements within a single family. This name was in fairly regular localized use until the early 18th century and it enjoyed a strong revival throughout England in the 19th century. Its use declined from the 1930s onwards.

Miles ♂ Of Norman origin but uncertain derivation. Unlike most Norman names it is, as far as can be ascertained, not derived from any known Old French or Germanic name element. It may be a greatly altered pet form of ▷Michael, which came to be associated with the Latin word *miles* 'soldier' because of the military attributes of the archangel Michael. However, the usual Latin form of the name in the Middle Ages was *Milo*. There is a common Slavic name element *mil* 'grace, favour', with which it may possibly have some connection. The name has been in regular use in England since the 16th century. See also ▷Milo and ▷Myles.

Milla ♀ Shortened form of ▷Camilla, also sometimes used as an independent given name.

Millenna ♀ Name chosen for some of the babies born at the turn of the millennium (from Latin *mille* 'thousand' + *annus* 'year'), in 2000. It may also have been influenced by the Czech name *Milena*, a short form of various compound Slavic names containing the element *mil* 'grace, favour' (compare ▷Miles).

Miller ♂ Transferred use of the surname, in origin an occupational name for someone who ran a mill, grinding grain into flour. This is from Middle English *mille*, *milne*, from Old English *mylen*.

Millicent ♀ From an Old French name, *Melisende*, of Germanic (Frankish) origin, from *amal* 'labour' + *swinth* 'strength'. This was the name of a daughter of Charlemagne. It was adopted by the Normans and introduced by them to Britain.
PET FORMS: ▷Millie, Milly, Mills.

Millie ♀ Pet form of ▷Millicent, and also, less commonly, of names such as ▷Mildred, ▷Camilla, and ▷Emily. It is now also a popular given name in its own right.
VARIANT: **Milly.**

Milo ♂ Latinized form of ▷Miles, regularly used in documents of the Middle Ages, and revived as a given name in the 19th century.

Milton ♂ Transferred use of the surname, in origin a local name from the numerous places so called, a large number of which get their name from Old English *mylentūn* 'settlement with a mill'. Others were originally named as 'the middle settlement (of three)', from Old English *middel* 'middle' + *tūn* 'settlement'. The surname is most famous as that of the poet John Milton (1608–74), and the given name is sometimes bestowed in his honour. Its most illustrious bearer in recent times has been the economist Milton Friedman (1912–2006).

SHORT FORM: Milt.

Mimi ♀ Italian pet form of ▷Maria, originally a nursery name. The heroine of Puccini's opera *La Bohème* (1896) announces 'They call me Mimi', and since that time the name has occasionally been used in the English-speaking world.

Mimosa ♀ Modern coinage, from the word denoting the yellow flowering plant, which was named in the 17th century, probably as a derivative of Latin *mīmus* 'mime, mimic'; the idea is that it mimics an animal in its sensitivity to touch.

Mina ♀ Short form of various names with this ending (for example ▷Wilhelmina), also used as an independent given name since the 19th century. See also Scottish appendix.

Minette ♀ Of uncertain origin. Although ostensibly a French name, it is not in fact used in France. It is possibly a contracted form of ▷Mignonette.

Minnie ♀ Pet form of ▷Wilhelmina, at its peak of popularity in the latter half of the 19th century, when several names were introduced into Britain from Germany in the wake of Queen Victoria's consort, Prince Albert of Saxe-Coburg-Gotha, whom she married in 1840. It lost favour in the 20th century, partly because German names in general became unacceptable in Britain during the First World War, and later perhaps also because of association with cartoon characters such as Minnie Mouse (in Walt Disney's animations) and Minnie the Minx (in the *Beano* children's comic). More recently, however, it has made a modest recovery, influenced perhaps by the British actress Minnie Driver (b. 1970 as Amelia Driver).

Mirabelle ♀ French, from Latin *mirabĭlis* 'wondrous, lovely' (a derivative of *mirari* 'to wonder at, admire'; compare ▷Miranda). This name is found in Italian in the form Mirabella. Both the French and Italian forms were quite common in the later Middle Ages. The form Mirabel is found occasionally in France and England as a boy's name. By the 16th century, both forms were rare.

VARIANT: Mirabella (Latinate form).

Miranda ♀ Invented by Shakespeare for the heroine of *The Tempest* (1611). It represents the feminine form of the Latin gerundive *mirandus* 'admirable, lovely', from *mirari* 'to wonder at, admire'; compare ▷Amanda for a similar formation.

SHORT FORM: Randa.

PET FORMS: ▷Randy, Randie.

Mireille ♀ French: apparently first used, in the Provençal form *Mireio*, as the title of a verse romance by the poet Frédéric Mistral (1830–1914). The name is probably a derivative of Provençal *mirar* 'to admire' (compare ▷Miranda). The poet himself declared it to be a form of ▷Miriam, but this was apparently in order to overcome the objections of a priest to baptizing his god-daughter with a non-liturgical name. The name is also used occasionally in the English-speaking world.

Miriam ♀ Biblical name: the Old Testament form of the Hebrew name ▷Maryam. Of uncertain ultimate origin, this is first recorded as being borne by the elder sister of Moses (Exodus 15:20).

Since the names of both Moses and his brother Aaron are probably of Egyptian origin, it is possible that this female name is too. It was enthusiastically taken up as a given name by the Israelites, and is still found mainly, but by no means exclusively, as a Jewish name.

VARIANT: ▷Mariamne.

Missy ♀ Modern coinage from a pet form of the vocabulary word *miss*, applied to a young girl (compare Maidie in Irish appendix). It is common as a pet name and form of address in the southern United States. The vocabulary word *miss* originated in Middle English as a short form of *mistress*.

Misty ♀ Modern coinage, apparently from the vocabulary word, a derivative of *mist* 'thin fog' (Old English *mist*).

Mitchell ♂ Transferred use of the surname, itself derived from a common medieval form of ▷Michael, representing an Anglicized pronunciation of the French name *Michel*, introduced to Britain by the Normans.

SHORT FORM: Mitch.

Mo ♀, ♂ Short form of ▷Maureen and, less commonly, of ▷Maurice.

Mohammed ♂ Muslim name meaning 'praiseworthy, possessing fine qualities'. See Muḥammad in Arabic appendix.

VARIANTS: Mohammad, Mohamed, Muhammad, Muhammed.

Moira ♀ Anglicized form of Irish Máire (see Irish appendix), now used throughout the English-speaking world.

VARIANT: Moyra.

Molly ♀ Pet form of ▷Mary, which, like the now obsolete variant Mally, seems to have been coined in the 18th century. Since the 1990s it has been increasingly popular in many parts of the English-speaking world.

VARIANT: Mollie.

Mona ♀ Anglicized form of the Gaelic name Muadhnait (see Irish appendix). It is no longer restricted to people with Irish connections, and has sometimes been taken as connected with Greek *monos* 'single, only' or chosen with reference to Leonardo da Vinci's painting *Mona Lisa*.

Monica ♀ Of uncertain ultimate origin. This was the name of the mother of St Augustine, as transmitted to us by her famous son. She was a citizen of Carthage, so her name may well be of Phoenician origin, but in the early Middle Ages it was taken to be a derivative of Latin *monere* 'to warn, counsel', since it was as a result of her guidance that her son was converted to Christianity.

Monique ♀ French form of ▷Monica, now sometimes used in the English-speaking world.

Monroe ♂ Transferred use of the Scottish surname, usually spelled *Munro*. The ancestors of the Scottish Munros are said to have originally come from Ireland, apparently from a settlement by the River Roe in County Derry; their name is therefore supposed to be derived from Gaelic *bun Rotha* 'mouth of the Roe'. In the United States the popularity of the given name may have been influenced by the fame of James Monroe (1758–1831), fifth president of the United States and propounder (in 1823) of the Monroe Doctrine, asserting that European powers should not seek to colonize in North or South America and that the United States would not intervene in European affairs.

VARIANTS: Monro, Munro(e).

Montague ♂ Transferred use of the surname, originally a Norman baronial name borne by the lords of *Montaigu* in La Manche. The place name is from Old French *mont* 'hill' (Latin *mons*, genitive *montis*) + *aigu* 'pointed' (Latin *acutus*). A certain Drogo of Montaigu is known to have accompanied William the

m

Conqueror in his invasion of England in 1066, and *Montague* thus became established as an aristocratic British family name.

Montgomery ♂ Transferred use of the surname, originally a Norman baronial name from various places in Calvados. The place name is derived from Old French *mont* 'hill' + the Germanic personal name *Gomeric* 'power of man'. It has never been common as a given name, although it was given additional currency by the American actor Montgomery Clift (1920–66), and during and after the Second World War by the British field marshal, Bernard Montgomery (1887–1976).

Montmorency ♂ Transferred use of the surname, originally a Norman baronial name from a place in Seine-et-Oise. The place name is derived from Old French *mont* 'hill' + the Gallo-Roman personal name *Maurentius*. The given name enjoyed a brief vogue in the 19th century, but is now regarded as affected and so hardly ever used.

Monty ♂ Short form of ▷Montgomery or of the much rarer ▷Montague and ▷Montmorency. It is now also found as an independent given name. As a Jewish name, it was originally used as an approximate English equivalent of ▷Moses.

Moray ♂ Variant ▷Murray.

Mordecai ♂ Biblical name, borne by Esther's cousin and foster-father, who secured her introduction to King Ahasuerus (Esther 2–9). The name is of Persian origin and seems to have meant 'devotee of the god Marduk'. It had some currency among English Puritans in the 17th century and Nonconformists in the 18th and 19th centuries, but has always been, and still is, mainly Jewish.

PET FORMS: Yiddish: Motke, Motl.

Moreen ♀ Anglicized form of Gaelic Móirín (see Irish appendix). It has now

been to a large extent confused with ▷Maureen.

Morgan ♂, ♀ Anglicized form of Welsh Morcant (see Welsh appendix), traditionally a boy's name. In Britain since the late 1990s the name has become equally popular as a girl's name, perhaps adopted with conscious reference to King Arthur's jealous stepsister Morgan le Fay. Elsewhere in the English-speaking world, especially in North America, where it also enjoys considerable popularity, it is used predominantly for girls.

Morgana ♀ Modern feminine variant of ▷Morgan.

Morley ♂ Transferred use of the surname, in origin a local name from any of the numerous places named with Old English *mōr* 'moor, marsh' + *lēah* 'wood, clearing'.

Morris ♂ Variant of ▷Maurice. The spelling *Morris* was quite common as a given name in the Middle Ages, but it fell out of use and was readopted in modern times, in part from the surname earlier derived from the given name. Among Jews it has been adopted as an Anglicized form of ▷Moses.

Mortimer ♂ Transferred use of the surname, in origin a Norman baronial name borne by the lords of *Mortemer* in Normandy. The place name meant 'dead sea' in Old French, and probably referred to a stagnant marsh. It was not used as a given name until the 19th century. Among Jews it has been adopted as an Anglicized form of ▷Moses and in Ireland as an Anglicized form of Muiriartach (see Irish appendix).

Morton ♂ Transferred use of the surname, in origin a local name from any of the numerous places so called from Old English *mōrtūn* 'settlement by or on a moor'. It is also widely used as a Jewish name, having been adopted as

an approximate English equivalent of
▷Moses.

SHORT FORM: Mort.

Morwenna ♀ Cornish and Welsh:
from an Old Celtic personal name
derived from an element akin to Welsh
morwyn 'maiden'. The name was borne
by a somewhat obscure Cornish saint of
the 5th century; churches in her
honour have named several places in
Cornwall.

VARIANT: Morwen.

Moses ♂ Biblical name, the English
form of the name of the patriarch
(*Moshe* in Hebrew) who led the Israelites
out of Egypt (Exodus 4). His name is
thought to be of Egyptian origin, most
probably from the same root as that
found in the second element of names
such as *Tutmosis* and *Rameses*, where it
means 'born of (a certain god)'. Various
Hebrew etymologies have been
proposed, beginning with the biblical
'saved (from the water)' (Exodus 2:10),
but none is convincing. It is now mainly
a Jewish name, although until the mid-
20th century it also enjoyed
considerable popularity among
Christians in England, especially
among Puritans and Nonconformists.

Moss ♂ Transferred use of the
surname derived from the usual
medieval vernacular form of ▷Moses,
or a revival of this form. In Wales it
has in recent years also been used as a
short form of Mostyn (see Welsh
appendix).

Motke ♂ Jewish: Yiddish pet form of
▷Mordecai.

VARIANT: Motl.

Moya ♀ Modern name of uncertain
origin; it may be derived from ▷Moyra.

Moyra ♀ Variant spelling of ▷Moira.

Muhammad ♂ Variant spelling of
▷Mohammed. See Muḥammad in
Arabic appendix.

Munroe ♂ Variant spelling of
▷Monroe.

Murgatroyd ♂ Transferred use of
the Yorkshire surname, in origin a local
name from an unidentified place
named as 'the clearing (Yorkshire
dialect *royd*) belonging to (a certain)
Margaret'.

Muriel ♀ Of Celtic origin (see Muireall
in Scottish appendix). Forms of the
name are found in Breton as well as in
Irish and Scottish Gaelic, and in the
form ▷Meriel it was in use in the heart
of England in the Middle Ages. The
surname *Merrill* is derived from it. As
Muriel it was at first used mainly in
Scotland, but became more widely
popular during the first half of the 20th
century. Since then it has fallen from
favour again.

Murray ♂ Transferred use of the
Scottish surname, in origin a local
name from the region now called
Moray. It is well known as the name of
the motor-racing commentator Murray
Walker (b. 1923).

VARIANT: Moray.

Mustafa ♂ Muslim name meaning
'pure' or 'chosen'. See Muṣṭafa in
Arabic appendix.

Mya ♀ Modern coinage of uncertain
derivation; possibly a respelling of
▷Maya or ▷Mia, influenced by ▷Myra.

Myles ♂ **1.** Variant spelling of ▷Miles;
2. Anglicized form of Maolra (see Irish
appendix).

Myra ♀ Invented in the 17th century
by the poet Fulke Greville (1554–1628).
It is impossible to guess what models he
had consciously or unconsciously in
mind, but it has been variously
conjectured that the name is an
anagram of ▷Mary; that it is a simplified
spelling of Latin *myrrha* 'myrrh,
unguent'; and that it is connected with
Latin *mirari* 'to wonder at, admire' (see
▷Miranda).

Myriam ♀ Variant spelling of
▷Miriam. This is the usual spelling of
the name in France.

m

Myrna ♀ Anglicized form of Gaelic Muirne (see Irish appendix), now also used elsewhere in the English-speaking world. It is associated with the American film star Myrna Loy (1905–93).

VARIANT: **Morna**.

Myron ♂ From a classical Greek name, derived from Greek *myron* 'myrrh'. The name was borne by a famous sculptor of the 5th century BC. It was taken up with particular enthusiasm by the early Christians because they associated it with the gift of myrrh made by the three kings to the infant Christ, and because of the association of myrrh (as an embalming spice) with death and eternal life. The name was borne by various early saints, notably a 3rd-century martyr of Cyzicus and a 4th-century bishop of Crete. Their cult is greater in the Eastern Church than the Western.

Myrtle ♀ From the vocabulary word denoting the plant (Old French *myrtille*, Late Latin *myrtilla*, a diminutive of classical Latin *myrta*). This is one of the group of plant names that became popular as girls' names in the late 19th century. It has since gone out of fashion.

m

Nn

Nadia ♀ French and English spelling of Russian *Nadya* (a pet form of *Nadezhda* 'hope'). This name has been moderately popular in the English-speaking world since the 20th century.

Nadine ♀ French elaboration of ▷Nadia, also used in the English-speaking world. Many names of Russian origin became established in France and elsewhere in the early 20th century as a result of the popularity of the Ballet Russe, established in Paris by Diaghilev in 1909.

Nahman ♂ Jewish: an Aramaic-influenced form of ▷Nahum 'comforter', from the same root as ▷Menaham. This name has been in use from the Middle Ages to the present day.

Nahum ♂ Biblical name (meaning 'comforter' in Hebrew), borne by a prophet of the 7th century BC. He was the author of the book of the Bible that bears his name, in which he prophesies the downfall of Nineveh, which fell in 612 BC. This is a well-established Jewish name, which was also used by 17th-century Puritans. It was borne by the minor Restoration dramatist Nahum Tate (1652–1715), who rewrote Shakespeare's *King Lear* with a happy ending.

Nan ♀ Originally a pet form of ▷Ann (for the initial *N-*, compare ▷Ned). It is now also widely used as a short form of ▷Nancy.

Nancy ♀ Of uncertain origin. From the 18th century it is clearly used as a pet form of ▷Ann (see ▷Nan), but it may originally have been a similar formation deriving from the common medieval given name ▷Annis, a vernacular form of ▷Agnes. Nowadays it is an independent name, and was especially popular in America in the 1930s, 40s, and 50s.

VARIANTS: **Nancie, Nanci**.

SHORT FORMS: **Nan, Nance**.

Nanda ♀ In origin a short form of Italian *Ferdinanda* or Spanish *Hernanda*, which are the vernacular feminine equivalents of ▷Ferdinand. It is now in occasional use in the English-speaking world as an independent first name, perhaps in part as an elaboration of ▷Nan by association with names such as ▷Glenda and ▷Linda.

Nanette ♀ Elaboration of ▷Nan, with the addition of the French feminine diminutive suffix *-ette*.

Naomi ♀ Biblical name (meaning 'pleasantness' in Hebrew), borne by the wise mother-in-law of Ruth. The name has long been regarded as typically Jewish, but it occurs occasionally from the 17th century and came into wide general use around the 1980s.

Naphtali ♂ Biblical name, probably meaning 'wrestling' in Hebrew, borne by one of the sons of Jacob. The traditional explanation is given in the following quotation: 'and Rachel said, with great wrestlings have I wrestled with my sister, and I have prevailed: and she called his name Naphtali' (Genesis 30:8).

Napoleon ♂ Occasionally bestowed in modern times in honour of the French emperor Napoleon Bonaparte (1769–1821), who was born in Corsica into a family that was ultimately of Italian origin. *Napoleone* is a rare Italian given name, used in Abruzzo, Latium, Umbria, and Tuscany. It is probably of Germanic origin, perhaps connected with the name of the elvish *Nibelungen* 'sons of the mist' (compare modern German *Nebel*). It was later altered by association with Italian *Napoli* 'Naples' (Greek *nea polis* 'new city') and *leone* 'lion'.

Narcissus ♂ Latin form of the Greek name *Narkissos*. In classical mythology, Narcissus was a beautiful youth who fell in love with his own reflection in a pool of water and remained there transfixed until he faded away and turned into a flower. The legend purports to account for the name of the flower, a kind of lily, known in Greek as *narkissos*. The name is almost certainly of pre-Greek origin, but attempts have been made to link it with Greek *narkē* 'numbness'. The vocabulary word in English and horticultural Latin denotes the genus of flowers that includes the daffodil. The name was common among slaves and freedmen in the early Christian era, and a Roman citizen bearing this name is mentioned in St Paul's Epistle to the Romans (16:11). One St Narcissus was bishop of Jerusalem in 195; another was a Spanish bishop put to death at Gerona under Diocletian in *c.*307.

Narelle ♀ Australian: of uncertain origin. It has been in use since the 19th century and seems to represent an elaboration of an unidentified word or name from an Aboriginal language. *Narellan* is a town in eastern New South Wales, south-west of Sydney; the names may be connected, but if so the details may be unclear. As a given name this became widely popular in the 1940s; it is still in fairly frequent use.

Nat ♂ Short form of ▷Nathan and ▷Nathaniel.

Natalia ♀ Russian name, now also used in the English-speaking world. It is from the Late Latin name *Natalia*, a derivative of Latin *natalis* (*dies*) 'birthday', especially Christ's birthday, i.e. Christmas (compare ▷Noël). St Natalia was a Christian inhabitant of Nicomedia who is said to have given succour to the martyrs, including her husband Adrian, who suffered there in persecutions under Diocletian in 303. She is regarded as a Christian saint, although she was not herself martyred.
VARIANT: **Natalya**.

Natalie ♀ French form of ▷Natalia, adopted from Russian in the early 20th century, probably, like ▷Nadine, under the influence of Diaghilev's Ballet Russe, which was established in Paris in 1909. The name is now very common in France and in the English-speaking world, where it was borne by the actress Natalie Wood (1938–81). She was born Natasha Gurdin, in San Francisco. Her father was of Russian descent, her mother of French extraction.
VARIANT: **Nathalie**.

Natasha ♀ Russian pet form of ▷Natalia, now widely adopted as an independent name in the English-speaking world and elsewhere. Like ▷Noël, it is sometimes given to girls born on or about Christmas Day.

Nathalie ♀ Variant spelling of ▷Natalie. The *th* is a mere elaboration in the French spelling and has not yet had any effect on the pronunciation.

Nathan ♂ Biblical name, meaning 'he (God) has given' in Hebrew (compare ▷Nathaniel). This was the name of a prophet who had the courage to reproach King David for arranging the death in battle of Uriah the Hittite in order to get possession of the latter's wife Bathsheba (2 Samuel 12:1–15). It was also the name of one of David's own sons. In modern times this name has often been taken as a short form of ▷Nathaniel or of ▷Jonathan. Since the 1990s it has been much favoured throughout the English-speaking world.
VARIANT: **Nathen**.

Nathaniel ♂ English form of a New Testament name, which is derived from the Greek form of a Hebrew name meaning 'God has given' (compare

▷Nathan, which is sometimes taken as a short form of this name). It was borne by one of the less prominent of Christ's apostles (John 1:45; 21:2), who in fact is probably identical with ▷Bartholomew. The spelling used in the Authorized Version of the New Testament is Nathanael, but this is in much less frequent use as a given name in the English-speaking world.

Neal ♂ Variant spelling of ▷Neil.

Ned ♂ Short form of ▷Edward, originating in the misdivision of phrases such as *mine Ed* (compare ▷Nan). It was common in the Middle Ages and up to the 18th century, but in the 19th was almost entirely superseded in the role of short form by ▷Ted. It is now, however, enjoying a modest revival, also as an independent given name.

Neil ♂ Anglicized form of the enduringly popular Gaelic name ▷Niall. From the Middle Ages onwards, this name was found mainly in Ireland, the Highlands of Scotland, and the English-Scottish Border region. However, since the 20th century it has spread to enjoy considerable popularity in all parts of the English-speaking world, although in England it has recently been overtaken by the Gaelic form.
VARIANTS: Neal(e). See also ▷Nigel.

Nell ♀ Medieval short form of ▷Eleanor, ▷Ellen, and ▷Helen. For the initial *N-*, compare ▷Nan and ▷Ned. It was the name by which Charles II's mistress Eleanor Gwyn (1650–87) was universally known to her contemporaries, and at about that time it also became established as an independent name.
PET FORMS: Nellie, Nelly.

Nelson ♂ Transferred use of the surname, which originated in the Middle Ages as either a patronymic from ▷Neil or a metronymic from ▷Nell. Use as a given name probably began as a tribute to the British admiral

Lord Nelson (1758–1805), the victor of the Battle of Trafalgar; see also ▷Horatio. It is, however, now much more common in the United States than in Britain, its popularity there in the 1930s and 40s no doubt having been influenced by the American film actor and singer Nelson Eddy (1901–67). Nowadays the name is universally associated with the South African statesman Nelson Mandela (b. 1918).

Nena ♀ Variant spelling of ▷Nina.

Neo ♂ Modern coinage, apparently from the prefix derived from Greek *neos* 'new'. In some instances, however, the name may be African in origin, from a Tswana word meaning 'gift'.

Nerida ♀ Apparently an elaborated form of Nerys (see Welsh appendix), probably influenced by ▷Phillida, a variant of ▷Phyllis. Alternatively it may derive from Greek *nērēis* 'sea sprite' (see ▷Nerissa).

Nerissa ♀ Of Shakespearean origin. It is the name of a minor character in *The Merchant of Venice*, Portia's waiting woman, who marries Gratiano. The name seems to be a Latinate elaboration of Greek *nērēis* 'sea sprite'.

Neroli ♀ From the name of the fragrant oil, which was named after the Italian princess Anne Marie de la Tremoïlle of Neroli, who is said to have discovered it.

Nessa ♀ Originally a short form of *Agnessa*, a Latinate form of ▷Agnes, but in modern use usually a short form of ▷Vanessa. See also Irish appendix.

Nestor ♂ Mainly U.S.: name borne in classical legend by one of the leaders of the Greeks at Troy, the aged but still vigorous king of Pylos. It may represent a derivative of Greek *nostos* 'homecoming'.

Netta ♀ Apparently a Latinate variant of ▷Nettie.

n

Nettie ♀ Pet form derived from various girls' names ending in the syllable *-nette*, for example ▷Annette and ▷Jeannette, with the diminutive suffix *-ie*. It had a brief vogue in the late 19th and early 20th centuries.

Neve ♀ Anglicized spelling of the Gaelic name Niamh (see Irish appendix), now quite frequently chosen by parents without Irish connections.

Neville ♂ Transferred use of the surname, in origin a Norman baronial name from any of several places in Normandy called *Néville* or *Neuville* 'new settlement'. It was used as a given name first in the 16th century, and with increasing regularity from the second half of the 19th to the 1930s; since then it has steadily declined in popularity.

Newton ♂ Transferred use of the surname, in origin a local name from any of the very numerous places so called, from Old English *nēowe* 'new' + *tūn* 'enclosure, settlement'. This is said to be the commonest of all English place names. The most famous bearer of the surname is probably Sir Isaac Newton (1642–1727), the English scientist. As a given name it was modestly popular in the United States in the early part of the 20th century but has since fallen from favour.

SHORT FORM: **Newt.**

Ngaio ♀ New Zealand name, pronounced '**nye**-oh': apparently from the Maori word *ngaio* which means, among other things, 'clever'. *Ngai* is also a prefix meaning 'tribe, clan'; the given name may have originated as a tribal name. It was borne by New Zealander Ngaio Marsh (1895–1982), the author of more than 30 crime novels.

Ngaire ♀ New Zealand (Maori) name, pronounced '**nye**-ree': of unknown origin. It is usually Anglicized as ▷Nyree.

Nia ♀ When not of Welsh origin (see Welsh appendix), this is an African name, possibly derived from a Swahili vocabulary word meaning 'purpose'.

VARIANT: **Nyah** (of the African name).

Niall ♂ Of disputed derivation; it may mean 'cloud', 'passionate', or perhaps 'champion'. It was adopted by the Scandinavians in the form *Njal* and soon became very popular among them. From the Middle Ages onwards, this name was found mainly in Ireland, the Highlands of Scotland, and the English-Scottish Border region. However, it has been strongly revived among non-Gaelic speakers since the latter part of the 20th century.

ANGLICIZED FORMS: **Neal(e).**

Niamh ♀ Meaning 'brightness' or 'beauty' in Gaelic; this is one of a number of Celtic names which has been in vogue in the English-speaking world since the 1990s. It was borne in Irish mythology by the daughter of the sea god, who fell in love with the youthful Oisín, son of Finn mac Cumhaill (Finn MacCool), and carried him off over the sea to the land of perpetual youth, *Tír na nÓg*, where there is no sadness, no ageing, and no death.

VARIANT: **Neve** (Anglicized form).

Nichelle ♀ Modern coinage, an altered form of ▷Michelle influenced by ▷Nicole.

Nichola ♂ Variant spelling of ▷Nicola.

Nicholas ♂ English form of the post-classical Greek personal name *Nikolaos*, derived from *nikē* 'victory' + *laos* 'people'. The spelling with *-ch-* first occurred as early as the 12th century, and became firmly established at the time of the Reformation, although Nicolas is still occasionally found. St Nicholas was a 4th-century bishop of Myra in Lycia, about whom virtually nothing factual is known, although a vast body of legend grew up around him, and he became the patron saint of Greece and of Russia, as well as of children, sailors, merchants, and pawnbrokers. His feast day is 6 December, and among the many roles which legend has assigned to him is that of bringer of Christmas presents, in the guise of 'Santa Claus' (an alteration of the Dutch form of his name, *Sinterklaas*).

VARIANTS: Nicolas, Nickolas.

SHORT FORMS: Nick, Nik, Nico.

PET FORM: Nicky.

COGNATES: Irish: Nioclás. Scottish Gaelic: Neacal. German: Nikolaus, Niklaus. Dutch: Nicolaas, Nik(o)laas. Danish: Niels. Norwegian: Niklas; Nils. Swedish: Niklas; Nils. French: Nicolas. Spanish: Nicolás, Nicolao. Catalan: Nicolau. Portuguese: Nicolau. Italian: Nicola, Nic(c)olò. Greek: Nikolaos. Russian: Nikolai. Bulgarian: Nikolai. Polish: Mikołaj. Czech: Mikoláš, Mikuláš. Croatian, Serbian: Nikola. Slovenian: Nikolaj. Finnish: Niilo. Hungarian: Miklós. Lithuanian: Mykolas.

Nichole ♀ Variant spelling of ▷Nicole.

Nicholl ♂ Variant spelling of ▷Nicol.

Nick ♂ Short form of ▷Nicholas, occasionally used as an independent given name.

Nicki ♀ Pet form of ▷Nicola.

Nickie ♀ Pet form of ▷Nicola.

Nickolas ♂ Mainly U.S.: variant spelling of ▷Nicholas, influenced by the short form ▷Nick.

Nicky ♂, ♀ Pet form of ▷Nicholas and of ▷Nicola, occasionally used as a given name in its own right.

Nico ♂, occasionally ♀ Modern short form of both ▷Nicholas and ▷Nicola. As a boy's name it is also used independently.

Nicodemus ♂ Latinized form of the Greek name *Nikodēmos*, composed of *nikē* 'victory' + *dēmos* 'people,

population'. This is the name borne in the New Testament by one of the leading Greek Jews who spoke up for Jesus at his trial (John 7:50) and was present at his burial (John 19:39).

Nicol, ♀ ♂ Originally a common medieval vernacular form of ▷Nicholas. In modern use, except in Scotland where it is still bestowed mainly on boys, it is found more frequently as a girl's name, possibly being taken as a variant of ▷Nicole.

VARIANTS: Nicoll, Nichol(l) ♂.

Nicola ♀ Latinate feminine form of ▷Nicholas.

PET FORMS: Nicky, Nickie, Nicki, Nikki.

Nicolas ♀ Variant spelling of ▷Nicholas.

Nicole ♀ French feminine form of ▷Nicholas, now also in frequent use throughout the English-speaking world.

Nicolette ♀ French pet form of ▷Nicole, also used as an independent given name in the English-speaking world.

Nicoll ♂ Variant spelling of ▷Nicol.

Nigel ♂ Anglicized form of the medieval name *Nigellus*, a Latinized version (ostensibly representing a diminutive of Latin *niger* 'black') of the vernacular *Ni(h)el*, i.e. ▷Neil. Although it is frequently found in medieval records, this form was probably not used in everyday life before its revival by antiquarians such as Sir Walter Scott in the 19th century.

Nigella ♀ Latinate feminine form of ▷Nigel. Adoption as a given name may also have been encouraged by the fact that this is an alternative name (from its black seed) for the flower known as 'love-in-a-mist'.

Nik ♂ Modern variant spelling of ▷Nick.

Nikita ♂, ♀ Originally a Russian boy's name, from Greek *Anikētos* 'unconquered, unconquerable'. In recent years, however, the name has begun to be used in the English-speaking world, mainly as a girl's name, perhaps being taken as an elaboration of ▷Nikki with the feminine diminutive suffix -ita.

Nikki ♀ Pet form of ▷Nicola, now sometimes used as an independent given name.

Nile ♂ Apparently from the name of the river in Africa. This seems, like many of the major rivers of the world, to have been originally named with a word meaning simply 'river'. However, it may be a variant of ▷Niall, respelled to coincide with the river name.
VARIANT: **Niles**.

Nina ♀ Russian name (originally a short form of names such as *Antonina*). It is now also quite common in the English-speaking world, influenced perhaps by the American singer Nina Simone (1933–2003).
VARIANT: **Nena**.

Ninette ♀ French diminutive form of ▷Nina. Like ▷Nadine, this was one of the names brought to the English-speaking world from Russian via French in the early 20th century, and was famously borne by the ballerina, choreographer, and founder of the Royal Ballet, Ninette de Valois (1898–2001, born Edris Stannus).

Ninian ♂ Of uncertain origin. This was the name of a 5th-century British saint who was responsible for evangelizing the northern Britons and the Picts. His name first appears in the Latinized form *Ninianus* in the 8th century; this appears to be identical to the *Nynnyaw* recorded in the *Mabinogi*. The given name was used in his honour until at least the 16th century in Scotland and is also recorded in Yorkshire during the 16th–18th centuries.

Nirvana ♀ From the Sanskrit word (meaning 'extinction') used in

Buddhism and Hinduism to refer to the desirable ultimate state of absorption into the ground of all being. For its use as a modern first name, compare ▷Dharma, ▷Karma, and ▷Samsara.

Nita ♀ Short form of various names that end in these syllables, as for example ▷Anita and ▷Juanita.

Noah ♂ English form of the name of the biblical character whose family was the only one saved from the great Flood ordained by God to destroy mankind because of its wickedness. The origin of the name is far from certain; in the Bible it is implied that it means 'rest' (Genesis 5:29, 'and he called his name Noah, saying, This same shall comfort us concerning our work and toil of our hands, because of the ground which the Lord hath cursed'). One tradition indeed explains it as derived from the Hebrew root meaning 'to comfort' (see ▷Nahum) with the final consonant dropped. It was taken up by the Puritans in the 17th century, and is presently enjoying a revival throughout the English-speaking world.

Noam ♂ Modern Jewish name, from a Hebrew vocabulary word meaning 'delight, joy, pleasantness' (compare ▷Naomi, which is from the same Hebrew root). Its most famous bearer is the American linguist Noam Chomsky (b. 1928).

Noble ♂ Mainly U.S.: name derived from the modern English adjective (via Old French from Latin *nobilis*). The idea behind it may have been to imply aristocratic origin or to suggest qualities of character. In part there may be some influence from the surname, which arose in the Middle Ages from a descriptive nickname in the first sense.

Noël ♂, ♀ From Old French *noel, nael* 'Christmas', from Latin *natalis dies* (*Domini*) 'birthday (of the Lord)'. The meaning is still relatively transparent, partly because the term occurs as a synonym for 'Christmas' in the refrain of well-known carols. The name is often given to children born at Christmas time, though it is now little used as a girl's name in Britain.

VARIANTS: Noel; Noëlle, Noelle (feminine forms).

Nola ♀ Anglicized short form of the Gaelic name Fionnuala (see Irish appendix). It is now also used as a feminine form of ▷Nolan.

Nolan ♂ Transferred use of the Irish surname, Gaelic Ó Nualláin 'descendant of Nuallán'. The latter is an ancient Gaelic personal name, originally a byname representing a diminutive of *nuall* 'chariot-fighter, champion'.

Nolene ♀ Mainly Australian: name created as a feminine form of ▷Nolan.

VARIANT: Noleen.

Noll ♂ Pet form of ▷Oliver, frequent in the Middle Ages and occasionally revived in modern times. The initial consonant seems to derive from the misdivision of a vocative phrase; compare ▷Ned and ▷Nan.

Nona ♀ From the feminine form of the Latin ordinal *nonus* 'ninth', sometimes used as a given name in Victorian times for the ninth-born child in a family if it was a girl, or even for the ninth-born girl (compare ▷Quintus, ▷Sextus, ▷Septimus, and ▷Octavius). At the present day, when few people have nine children, let alone nine daughters, it has passed into more general, if only occasional, use.

Nonie ♀ Pet form of ▷Ione or of ▷Nora, also used to a limited extent as an independent given name.

Nora ♀ Short form of names such as ▷Leonora and ▷Honora, also used as an independent given name. At one time it was regarded as a peculiarly Irish name (see Nóra in Irish appendix).

VARIANT: Norah.

Norbert ♂ From an Old French name of Germanic (Frankish) origin, from *nord* 'north' + *berht* 'bright, famous'. The best-known bearer of this name was an 11th-century saint who founded an order of monks known as Norbertians (also called Premonstratensians from their first home at Premontré near Laon). *Norbert* was one of several names of Germanic origin that were revived in Britain in the late 19th century, but it is now rather more common in North America than in Britain.

Noreen ♀ Originally an Anglicized form of the Gaelic name Nóirín (see Irish appendix). It is now used as an independent given name in the English-speaking world.

VARIANTS: Norene, Norine.

Norma ♀ Apparently invented by Felice Romani in his libretto for Bellini's opera of this name (first performed in 1832). It is identical in form with Latin *norma* 'rule, standard', but there is no evidence that this word was the source of the name. In recent times, it has come to be taken in England and the Scottish Highlands as a feminine equivalent of ▷Norman.

Norman ♂ Of Germanic origin, from *nord* 'north' + *man* 'man', i.e. 'Norseman'. This name was in use in England before the Conquest, and was reinforced by its use among the Norman invaders themselves. The Normans were the inhabitants of Normandy in northern France, whose name is a reference to the Vikings who took control of the region in the 9th century. In the 11th and 12th centuries they achieved remarkable conquests, including not only Britain but also Sicily, southern Italy, and Antioch. In the Scottish Highlands it is used as the Anglicized equivalent of Tormod (see Scottish appendix).

n

Norris ♂ Transferred use of the surname, which is derived from Norman French *norreis* (in which the stem is the Germanic element *nord* 'north'), originally a local designation for someone who had migrated from the north.

Norton ♂ Transferred use of the surname, in origin a local name from any of the numerous places so called from Old English *norð* 'north' + *tūn* 'enclosure, settlement'.

Nuala ♀ Short form of **Fionnuala** (see Irish appendix), now in general use as an independent given name.

Nyree ♀ New Zealand: Anglicized spelling of a Maori name usually transcribed as ▷**Ngaire**. It is relatively common in New Zealand and was taken up to some extent in Britain due to the fame of the New Zealand-born actress Nyree Dawn Porter (1940–2001), who played Irene in the 1967 television serialization of Galsworthy's *Forsyte Saga*.

n

Oo

Oakley ♂ Transferred use of the surname, in origin a local name from any of the numerous places named with Old English *ā* 'oak' + *lēah* 'wood, clearing'.

Obadiah ♂ From a biblical name meaning 'servant of God' in Hebrew (compare Arabic ▷Abdullah, which has the same meaning). This was the name of a prophet who gave his name to one of the shorter books of the Bible, and of two other minor biblical characters: a porter in the temple (Nehemiah 12:25), and the man who introduced King Ahab to the prophet Elijah (1 Kings 18).

Oberon ♂ Variant spelling of ▷Auberon.

Ocean ♀, ♂ Modern coinage; one of a set of names taken from the world of nature in the second half of the 20th century.

Octavia ♀ Of Latin origin, representing a feminine form of ▷Octavius. It was borne by various female members of the Roman imperial family.

Octavian ♂ Usual English form of the Latin name *Octavianus*, a derivative of ▷Octavius. The first Roman emperor, now generally known by the imperial title *Augustus*, was born Gaius Octavius; when he was adopted by Julius Caesar he became Gaius Julius Caesar Octavianus. Another Octavianus was a 5th-century Carthaginian saint who was put to death with several thousand companions by the Asiatic Vandal king Hunneric.

Octavius ♂ From the Roman family name, derived from Latin *octavus* 'eighth'. The name is recorded from the 16th century and was fairly frequently given to a male eighth child (or the eighth son), particularly in large Victorian families (compare ▷Quintus, ▷Sextus, ▷Septimus, and ▷Nona). It is much less common these days, when families rarely extend to eight children, but is occasionally selected for reasons of family tradition or for some other reason without regard to its original meaning.

Oded ♂ Jewish: Hebrew name, meaning 'upholder, encourager', borne in the Bible by a prophet who persuaded the Israelites to release the captives that they had taken from the kingdom of Judah (2 Chronicles 28:9–15). It is a popular modern Hebrew name.

Odette ♀ French feminine diminutive form of the Old French male name *Oda*, which is of Germanic origin (see French appendix). Although the original boy's name has dropped out of use, this feminine derivative has survived and has been in occasional use in the English-speaking world since the 20th century.

Odile ♀ French: from the medieval Germanic name *Odíla* (see French appendix). The name is in occasional use in the English-speaking world.

Ofra ♀ Variant spelling of ▷Ophrah.

Olaf ♂ Scandinavian: from an Old Norse personal name composed of the elements *anu* 'ancestor' + *leifr* 'heir, descendant'. St Olaf, King of Norway (995–1030), aided the spread of Christianity in his kingdom. The name was introduced to Britain before the Norman Conquest, but modern use as a given name in the English-speaking world originated in America, where it was taken by recent Scandinavian immigrants.

Olga ♀ Russian name of Scandinavian origin, originally derived from the Old Norse adjective *heilagr* 'prosperous, successful'. It was imported by the Scandinavian settlers who founded the first Russian state in the 9th century. St Olga of Kiev (d. 969) was a Varangian noblewoman who was baptized at Byzantium in about 957 and set about converting her people. The name was introduced to the English-speaking world in the late 19th century, but retains a distinctively Russian flavour.

Olive ♀ Originally a medieval given name, *Oliff(e)*, derived via French from the Late Latin name *Oliva*, which was borne by two obscure early saints. It in turn is derived from the Latin name for the olive tree, and was no doubt adopted at first because of the associations of the olive tree with peaceful productivity and fruitfulness; the olive branch has been a symbol of peace since biblical times. Like many names denoting plants and flowers, it was particularly popular in the early decades of the 20th century. See also ▷Olivia.

Oliver ♂ From a French name, *Olivier*, recorded as the name of one of Charlemagne's paladins (retainers), the close companion in arms of Roland in the *Chanson de Roland*. Whereas Roland is headstrong and rash, Oliver is thoughtful and cautious. Ostensibly this name derives from Late Latin *olivarius* 'olive tree' (compare ▷Olive), but Charlemagne's other paladins all bear solidly Germanic names, so it is more probably an altered form of a Germanic name, perhaps distantly connected with Old Norse *Óleifr* 'ancestral relic'. It has remained in more or less continuous use since the medieval period, becoming ever more popular since the 1980s.

PET FORMS: **Ollie**, ▷**Noll**.

Olivia ♀ Latinate name, first used by Shakespeare for the rich heiress wooed by the duke in *Twelfth Night* (1599). Shakespeare may have taken it as a feminine form of ▷Oliver or he may have derived it from Latin *oliva* 'olive'. In the 1970s it was particularly associated with the Australian pop singer and actress Olivia Newton-John (b. 1948). Since the 1990s it has been very popular throughout the English-speaking world.

Ollie ♂ Pet form of ▷Oliver, associated particularly with the comic film actor Oliver Hardy (1892–1957), the rotund partner of Stan Laurel. It now has some currency as an independent given name.

Omar ♂ Biblical name (apparently meaning 'talkative' in Hebrew) borne by a character mentioned in a genealogy (Genesis 36:11). It has been occasionally used from Puritan times down to the present day, especially in America. More often, however, it is of Arabic origin, as in the case of the film actor and international bridge player Omar Sharif (b. 1932 in Egypt).

VARIANT: **Umar**.

Omri ♂ Jewish: Hebrew name, possibly derived from an element meaning 'sheaf of grain'. It is borne in the Bible by a king of Israel who built the city of Samaria, but who also 'wrought evil in the eyes of the Lord' (1 Kings 16:23–28). This has not prevented *Omri* from being used as a modern given name.

Ona ♀ Apparently a short form of any of the given names ending in these letters, for example, ▷Fiona and ▷Anona, now well established as an independent given name.

Opal ♀ One of the rarer girls' names created in the late 19th century from vocabulary words for gemstones. This English word is ultimately derived (via Latin and Greek) from an Indian language (compare Sanskrit *upala* 'precious stone').

Opaline ♀ Comparatively recent coinage: an elaboration of ▷Opal with the addition of *-ine*, a productive suffix of girls' names (originally a French diminutive suffix).

Ophelia ♀ The name of a character in Shakespeare's *Hamlet*, the beautiful daughter of Polonius; she loves Hamlet, and eventually goes mad and drowns herself. In spite of the ill omen of this literary association, the name has enjoyed moderate popularity since the 19th century. It was first used by the Italian pastoral poet Jacopo Sannazzaro (1458–1530), who presumably intended it as a feminine form of the Greek name *Ōphelos* 'help'. Shakespeare seems to have borrowed the name from Sannazzaro, without considering whether it was an appropriate name for a play set in medieval Denmark.

Ophrah ♀, ♂ Hebrew name meaning 'fawn'. In the Old Testament it is borne by a man (1 Chronicles 4:14), but it is now more commonly used as a girl's name.

VARIANTS: **Ophra, Ofra.**

Oprah ♀ Of uncertain origin: presumably a variant of either ▷Ophrah or ▷Orpah. It is particularly associated with the American television personality Oprah Winfrey (b. 1954).

Orpah ♀ Biblical name, borne by the sister-in-law of Ruth, who unlike Ruth did not accompany their mother-in-law Naomi on her return from Moab to Bethlehem. It seems to be derived from a Hebrew word meaning 'hind, female deer'.

Oralie ♀ Of uncertain origin, possibly an altered form of French *Aurélie* (see ▷Aurelia).

VARIANT: **Oralee.**

Oren ♂ Biblical name, apparently meaning 'pine tree' in Hebrew,

mentioned in a genealogy (1 Chronicles 2:25). This name is in use in a number of different spellings. There may have been some confusion with the Irish name **Oran** (see Irish appendix), of which this is sometimes a variant spelling.

VARIANTS: **Orin, Orren, Orrin.**

Oriana ♀ Latinate name first found in the medieval tale of *Amadis of Gaul* as the name of the daughter of Lisuarte, King of England, courted and eventually won by the model knight Amadis. It may be a derivative of Old French *or*, Spanish *oro* 'gold' (Latin *aurum*).

Orla ♀ Anglicized spelling of Órla (see Irish appendix). Although it retains a distinctly Irish flavour, it is now sometimes chosen by parents without Irish connections.

Orlando ♂ Italian form of ▷Roland, also used as a given name in the English-speaking world. It is the name of the hero in Shakespeare's comedy *As You Like It*.

Orson ♂ From a Norman French nickname meaning 'bear-cub' (a diminutive of *ors* 'bear', Latin *ursus*). This was occasionally used as a given name in the Middle Ages, but in modern times it probably represents a transferred use of the surname derived from the medieval nickname. Its most famous bearer of the 20th century was the American actor and director Orson Welles (1915–85), who dropped his more prosaic first name, George, in favour of his middle name before embarking on a career in films.

Orville ♂ Though in appearance a surname of Norman baronial origin, this name was in fact invented (with the intention of evoking such associations) by the novelist Fanny Burney for the hero, Lord Orville, of her novel *Evelina* (1778).

Osbert ♂ From an Old English personal name derived from *ōs* 'god' +

beorht 'bright, famous'. It is not now common, but in the earlier 20th century it enjoyed a modest vogue in Britain, being borne for example by the cartoonist Osbert Lancaster (1908–86) and the writer Osbert Sitwell (1892–1969).

Osborn ♂ From a Late Old English personal name composed of *ōs* 'god' + *beorn* 'bear, warrior' (both of Scandinavian origin). As a modern given name it generally represents a transferred use of the surname that was derived from this name during the Middle Ages.
VARIANTS: **Osborne, Osbourne.**

Oscar ♂ Old Irish name (see Irish appendix), which is borne in the Fenian sagas by a grandson of Finn mac Cumhaill (Finn MacCool). It was resuscitated by the antiquarian poet James Macpherson (1736–96), author of the Ossian poems. It is now also a characteristically Scandinavian name; it was introduced to Sweden because Napoleon, an admirer of the works of Macpherson, imposed the name on his godson Oscar Bernadotte, who became King Oscar I of Sweden in 1844 (see also ▷Malvina). In more recent times it has been associated particularly with the Irish writer and wit Oscar Wilde (1854–1900), and with the annual awards for achievement in the film industry made by the American Academy of Motion Picture Arts and Sciences. Oscar is one of a number of Celtic names that have recently come into general use and have become increasingly popular since the 1990s.

Osian ♂ Anglicized form of Oisín (see Irish appendix), a name found in Irish mythology and resuscitated in 1760 by James Macpherson (1736–96) as the name of the supposed author of some ancient Gaelic poetry which Macpherson claimed to have translated, though in all probability he wrote it himself. In recent times the name has become very popular in the English-speaking world, both in its Anglicized and Irish forms.
VARIANT: **Ossian.**

Osmond ♂ 19th-century revival of an Old English personal name composed of *ōs* 'god' + *mund* 'protector'. The name was also in use among the Normans and was borne by an 11th-century saint who was appointed to the see of Salisbury by William the Conqueror. As a modern given name it may be in part a transferred use of the surname derived from this name.
VARIANT: **Osmund.**

Oswald ♂ From an Old English personal name, derived from *ōs* 'god' + *weald* 'rule'. This was the name of two English saints. The first was a 7th-century king of Northumbria, who was killed in battle in 641. He was a Christian, a convert of St Aidan's, and his opponent, Penda, was a heathen, so his death was counted as a martyrdom by the Christian Church. The second St Oswald was a 10th-century bishop of Worcester and archbishop of York, of Danish parentage, who effected reforms in the English Church. The name was well established in northern England from the late 15th century, particularly in parishes where the church was dedicated to St Oswald. It enjoyed a modest revival in the 19th century as part of the vogue for pre-Conquest English names.

Oswin ♂ 19th-century revival of an Old English personal name composed of *ōs* 'god' + *wine* 'friend'. St Oswin was a 7th-century king of Northumbria, a cousin of King Oswald, who is likewise venerated as a martyr. However, the reasons for his death at the hand of his brother Oswy seem to have been political and personal rather than religious.

Otis ♂ Transferred use of the surname, in origin a patronymic derived from the genitive case of the medieval given name *Ote* or *Ode* (of Norman, and ultimately Germanic, origin; compare ▷Odette). In northern England the medieval given name survived into the 19th century. It came to be used as a given name in America in honour of the Revolutionary hero James Otis (1725–83); in modern times it has been bestowed in honour of the American soul singer Otis Redding (1941–67).

Ottilie ♀ French and German: from the medieval female given name *Odila* (see ▷Odile), now also used occasionally in the English-speaking world.

Otto ♂ Originally a short form of any of the various Germanic compound personal names containing the element *od*, *ot* 'prosperity, wealth' (compare Old English *ēad* in names such as ▷Edward and ▷Edwin). St Otto of Bamberg (d. 1139) was a missionary to the Pomeranians. Otto the Great (912–73) is generally regarded as the founder of the Holy Roman Empire, and the name has been borne by several members of German and Austrian royal houses. It was recorded occasionally among immigrants to England from the Low Countries in the 14th century, but failed to establish itself. Since the 19th century it has again been used occasionally in the English-speaking world, mostly among immigrants from Germanic countries.

Ottoline ♀ French diminutive of ▷Ottilie. The name acquired some currency in the English-speaking world in the early 20th century, partly due to the influence of the literary hostess Lady Ottoline Morrell (1873–1938).

Owain ♂ Welsh: of uncertain origin (see Welsh appendix), now also in general use.

Owen ♂ Modern form of the Welsh name Owain (see appendix) or a transferred use of the surname derived from the personal name. It is also used as an Anglicized form of Gaelic Eóghan (see Scottish and Irish appendices), which is probably ultimately a cognate of the Welsh name. Although retaining its Welsh flavour, this is one of a number of Celtic names which have recently come into general use and have become increasingly popular since the 1990s.

Oz ♂ Short form of ▷Oswald or any of the various other names beginning with *Os-*.

Ozzy ♂ Pet form of ▷Oswald or any of the various other names beginning with *Os-*, now also used occasionally as an independent given name.
VARIANT: **Ozzie**.

O

Pp

Pacey ♂ Transferred use of the surname, in origin a Norman baronial name from any of the places in northern France called *Passy* (Latin *Pacciacum*, a derivative of the Gallo-Roman personal name *Paccius*). Use as a first name may have been influenced by the rhyming ▷Stacey, ▷Tracy, ▷Lacey, and ▷Macey.

Paddy ♂ Pet form of ▷Patrick, now also used as an independent given name. The formation in *-y* is in origin characteristic of Lowland Scots, and this pet form seems to have arisen in Ulster in the 17th century. Since the 19th century it has come to function in English as a generic nickname for an Irishman.

Paige ♀ Transferred use of the surname, a less common variant of *Page*, originally an occupational name given to someone who served as a page to a great lord. It was taken up as a girl's name in the 20th century in the United States and is now popular throughout the English-speaking world.

VARIANT: **Page**.

Palmer ♂ Transferred use of the surname, which originally denoted someone who had made a pilgrimage to the Holy Land. Such pilgrims generally brought back a palm branch as proof that they had actually made the journey.

Pamela ♀ Invented by the Elizabethan pastoral poet Sir Philip Sidney (1554–86), in whose verse it is stressed on the second syllable. There is no clue to the sources that influenced Sidney in this coinage. It was later taken up by Samuel Richardson for the name of the heroine of his novel *Pamela* (1740). In Henry Fielding's *Joseph Andrews* (1742), which started out as a parody of *Pamela*, Fielding comments that the name is 'very strange'.

VARIANT: **Pamella** (a modern spelling).

Pancras ♂ Middle English form of Greek *Pankratios*, from the Greek epithet *pankratios* 'all-powerful' (from *pan* 'all, every' + *kratein* 'to rule'. This was a major title of Christ in Byzantine Greek, and was used as a personal name among early Christians. It was borne by a saint of the 1st century, who was stoned to death at Tauromenium (now Taormina) in Sicily. In England the name was popular during the early Middle Ages because in the 7th century the pope had sent to an Anglo-Saxon king relics of a saint so called (an obscure 3rd-century martyr, not the more famous Sicilian saint). It is now very rare, and modern instances are probably adaptations of the Italian name *Pancrazio*.

Pandora ♀ Name borne in classical mythology by the first woman on earth, created by the fire god Hephaistos as a scourge for men in general, in revenge for Prometheus's act of stealing fire on behalf of mankind. Pandora was given as a wife to Prometheus's foolish brother Epimetheus, along with a box which she was forbidden to open. Being endowed with great curiosity, she nevertheless did open it, and unleashed every type of hardship and suffering on the world, Hope alone being left inside the box. The name itself is ironically derived from the Greek words *pan* 'all, every' + *dōron* 'gift'.

Pansy ♀ 19th-century coinage, from the word for the garden flower, which is named from Old French *pensee* 'thought'. This was never particularly popular, and is seldom chosen at all now that the word *pansy* has acquired a derogatory slang sense denoting an effeminate man.

Paris ♀, ♂ As a male name in occasional use from the Middle Ages on, this was taken from Greek legend. Paris was the son of Priam who carried off Helen from Sparta to Troy and so caused the Trojan War; his name is of uncertain, probably non-Greek, derivation. Its more frequent use as a modern first name for boys and more especially girls seems to represent an adoption of the name of the French capital (derived from the name of a Gaulish tribe, known in Latinized form as the *Parisii*, who once lived on the site where the city came to be built).

Parker ♂ Mainly U.S.: transferred use of the common surname, in origin an occupational name for a gamekeeper employed in a medieval game park.

Parry ♂ Transferred use of the surname, originally a Welsh patronymic meaning 'son (Welsh *ap*) of Harry'. Use as a first name may have been influenced by the recent popularity of ▷Perry, and the rhyming ▷Barry and ▷Larry.

Parthenope ♀ Name borne in classical mythology by one of the Sirens, who drowned herself in frustration when Odysseus managed to avoid her lures by having himself tied to the mast and ordering his companions to block their ears with wax. Her name seems to be a derivative of Greek *parthenos* 'maiden' (an epithet of Athena) + *ōps* 'face, form'. This name was borne by a sister of Florence Nightingale who was born at Naples, where the body of the Siren is said to have been washed ashore. It is rarely, if ever, used today.

Pascal ♂ French name from Late Latin *Paschalis* 'relating to Easter' (Latin *Pascha*, from Hebrew *pesach* 'Passover'). This was taken up by the early Christians as a personal name, partly in honour of the great Christian festival, but mainly as a name for sons born at this time of the year. It was borne by two medieval popes, neither of whom achieved anything particularly notable. Its popularity may have been influenced by the fame of the French philosopher Blaise Pascal (1623–62), whose *Pensées* ('Thoughts') were published posthumously in 1670. The name is now occasionally used in the English-speaking world, mainly by Roman Catholics.

Pascale ♀ Feminine form of ▷Pascal.

Pat ♂, ♀ Short form of both ▷Patrick and ▷Patricia.

Patience ♀ From the vocabulary word denoting one of the Seven Christian Virtues. The vocabulary word is derived from Latin *pati* 'to suffer', and was associated by the early Christians with those who endured persecution and misfortune without complaint or loss of faith. It was a favourite with the Puritans, but fell out of regular use in the 20th century.

Patrice ♀, ♂ Medieval French form of both the male and female Latin names *Patricius* (see ▷Patrick) and ▷Patricia. In modern French it is used only as a boy's name, but in the English-speaking world it is used mainly for girls, apparently under the influence of names such as ▷Bernice.

Patricia ♀ From Latin *Patricia*, feminine form of *Patricius*; see ▷Patrick. SHORT FORMS: Pat, Tricia, Trish(a). PET FORMS: Patty, Pattie, Patti, ▷Patsy.

Patrick ♂ Name of the apostle and patron saint of Ireland (*c*.389–461), Gaelic *Pádraig*. He was a Christian Briton and a Roman citizen, who as a young man was captured and enslaved by raiders from Ireland. He escaped and went to Gaul before returning home to Britain. In about 419 he felt a call to do missionary work in Ireland. He studied for twelve years at Auxerre, and in 432 returned to Ireland. For the rest of his

p

life it is difficult to distinguish fact from fiction. He apparently went to the court of the high kings at Tara and made some converts there; then he travelled around Ireland making further converts until about 445, when he established his archiepiscopal see at Armagh. By the time of his death almost the whole of Ireland is said to have been converted to Christianity. He is also credited with codifying the laws of Ireland. In his Latin autobiography, as well as in later tradition, his name appears as *Patricius* 'patrician' (i.e. belonging to the Roman senatorial or noble class), but this may actually represent a Latinized form of some lost Celtic (British) name. In Ireland in particular, it has been one of the most enduringly popular boys' names.

SHORT FORM: **Pat**.

PET FORMS: ▷**Paddy**, ▷**Patsy**.

COGNATES: Irish: **Pádraig, Páraic**. French: **Patrick, Patrice**. Spanish, Portuguese: **Patricio**. Italian: **Patrizio**.

Patsy ♀, ♂ Pet form of ▷**Patricia** or ▷**Patrick**. It is generally a girl's name; as a boy's name it is almost completely restricted to Irish communities. Its popularity does not seem to have been seriously affected by its use in derogatory senses in the general vocabulary, in America meaning 'a dupe' and in Australia 'a homosexual'. It is sometimes used as an independent girl's name.

Patty ♀ Pet form of ▷**Patricia**. However, it is recorded as an independent given name as early as the 1700s—long before the coinage of ▷**Patricia**. It is said to have been a pet form of ▷**Martha**

VARIANTS: **Pattie, Patti**.

Paul ♂ From Latin *Paulus*, a Roman family name, originally a nickname meaning 'small', used in the post-classical period as a given name. Pre-eminently this is the name of the saint who is generally regarded, with St Peter, as co-founder of the Christian Church.

Born in Tarsus, and originally named *Saul*, he was both a Roman citizen and a Jew, and at first found employment as a minor official persecuting Christians. He was converted to Christianity by a vision of Christ while on the road to Damascus, and thereafter undertook extensive missionary journeys, converting people, especially Gentiles, to Christianity all over the eastern Mediterranean. His preaching aroused considerable official hostility, and eventually he was beheaded at Rome in about AD 65. He is the author of the fourteen epistles to churches and individuals which form part of the New Testament. It has been in continuous use in the British Isles since the 16th century.

COGNATES: Irish: **Pól**. Scottish Gaelic: **Pàl** (in secular use, the form *Pòl* being reserved for the name of the saint). German: **Paul**. Dutch: **Paul, Pauwel**. Danish: **Poul**. Swedish: **Pål, Påvel**. French: **Paul**. Spanish: **Pablo**. Catalan: **Pau**. Portuguese: **Paulo**. Italian: **Paolo**. Greek: **Pavlos**. Russian, Bulgarian: **Pavel**. Polish: **Paweł**. Czech: **Pavel**. Croatian: **Pavao**. Serbian: **Pavle**. Slovenian: **Pavel**. Finnish: **Paavo**. Hungarian: **Pál**. Lithuanian: **Paulius**.

Paula ♀ Latin feminine form of ▷**Paul**, borne by various minor early saints and martyrs.

Paulette ♀ French diminutive feminine form of ▷**Paul**. It is widely used in the English-speaking world, where it is a more recent and less popular importation than ▷**Pauline**.

Paulina ♀ Latin feminine form of the Late Latin name *Paulinus*, a derivative of *Paulus* (see ▷**Paul**). It was borne by several minor early martyrs.

Pauline ♀ French form of the Latin name *Paulina* (feminine of *Paulinus*, a derivative of the family name *Paulus* 'small') that has long been in use also in the English-speaking world.

Payton ♀, ♂ Mainly U.S.: transferred use of the surname, in origin a local name from *Peyton* in Sussex, probably named in Old English as 'Pǣga's settlement'. *Peyton Place* was the name of a novel by Grace Metalious, which was the basis for an American television soap opera in the 1950s.

VARIANT: **Peyton.**

Pearce ♂ Variant of ▷Pierce, normally a transferred use of the English surname derived from the given name in the Middle Ages.

Pearl ♀ One of the group of names coined in the 19th century from words for precious and semi-precious stones. It has a longer history as a Jewish name, representing an Anglicized form of Yiddish *Perle* (see also ▷Peninnah).

Peg ♀ Pet form of ▷Margaret. Variant of ▷Meg, The reason for the alternation of *M*- and *P*-, which occurs also in *Molly/Polly*, is not known; it has been ascribed to Celtic influence, but this particular alternation does not correspond to any of the usual mutational patterns in Celtic languages.

Peggy ♀ Pet form of ▷Margaret, frequently used as an independent given name in the 1920s and 30s; see ▷Peg.

Peleg ♂ Biblical name, meaning 'division' in Hebrew, borne by a minor figure mentioned in a genealogy (Genesis 10:25). The name was in use among the Puritans, but has become very rare in the modern English-speaking world. In Israel, however, it has been taken up, and is now both a given name and a surname.

Pelham ♂ Transferred use of the surname, in origin a local name from a place in Hertfordshire, so called from the Old English personal name *Pēo(t)la* + *hām* 'homestead'. From 1715 a family bearing this surname held the dukedom of Newcastle.

Pen ♀ Short form of ▷Penelope, and sometimes also of ▷Peninnah.

Penelope ♀ Name borne in Greek mythology by the wife of Odysseus who sat patiently awaiting his return for twenty years, meanwhile, as a supposed widow, fending off by persuasion and guile a pressing horde of suitors for her hand in marriage. Her name would seem to derive from Greek *pēnelops* 'duck', and play is made with this word in the *Odyssey*. However, this may obscure a more complex origin, now no longer recoverable. The name is recorded in England from the 16th century onwards.

SHORT FORM: **Pen.**

PET FORM: **Penny.**

Peninnah ♀ Jewish traditional name, meaning 'coral' in Hebrew. It was borne in the Bible by the co-wife (with Hannah) of Elkanah, the father of Samuel. In modern Hebrew it means 'pearl' and has become a popular name, often being substituted for Yiddish *Perle* and English ▷Pearl.

VARIANTS: **Peninna, Penina.**

Penn ♂ Mainly U.S.: transferred use of the surname, for the most part originally a local name from any of various places named with the British element *pen* 'hill', which was adopted into Old English. In other cases it may have referred to someone who lived near a sheep pen (Old English *penn*). The given name is sometimes chosen in honour of the founder of Pennsylvania, the Quaker William Penn (1644–1718), who was born in London into a family of Gloucestershire origin.

Penny ♀ Pet form of ▷Penelope, now sometimes also used as an independent given name.

Perce ♂ Variant of ▷Pierce or informal short form of ▷Percy or ▷Percival.

Percival ♂ From Old French versions of the Arthurian legend, where the name is spelled *Perceval*. According to Chrétien de Troyes (12th century) and

p

Wolfram von Eschenbach (c.1170–1220), Perceval (German *Parzifal*) was the perfectly pure and innocent knight who alone could succeed in the quest for the Holy Grail (a cup or bowl with supernatural powers, which in medieval legend was identified with the chalice that had received Christ's blood at the Crucifixion). Later versions of the Grail legend assign this role to Sir Galahad. The name *Perceval* probably represents a drastic remodelling of the Celtic name *Peredur*, as if from Old French *perce(r)* 'pierce' + *val* 'valley'. This may well have been influenced by ▷Percy, which was similarly analysed as a compound of *perce(r)* 'pierce' + *haie* 'hedge'.

Percy ♂ Originally a transferred use of a famous surname, but long established as a given name. From medieval times it was often used as a pet form of ▷Piers, and now often as a pet form of ▷Percival. The surname originated as a Norman baronial name, borne by a family who had held a fief in Normandy called *Perci* (from Late Latin *Persiacum*, composed of the Gallo-Roman personal name *Persius* and the local suffix *-acum*). As a given name it was taken up in the early 18th century in the Seymour family, which had intermarried with the Percy family. The poet Percy Bysshe Shelley (1792–1822) was also distantly connected with this family, and it was partly due to his influence that the given name became more widespread. It is out of fashion at present.

Perdita ♀ A Shakespearean coinage, borne by a character in *The Winter's Tale* (1610). The feminine form of Latin *perditus* 'lost', it has a clear reference to the events of the play, and this is explicitly commented on in the text. The name is now more closely associated in some people's minds with a (canine) character in Dodie Smith's *One Hundred and One Dalmatians* (1956), made into a film by Walt Disney.

PET FORM: **Perdie**.

Peregrine ♂ From Latin *Peregrinus* 'foreigner, stranger', a name borne by various early Christian saints, perhaps referring to the belief that men and women are merely sojourners upon the earth, their true home being in heaven. In modern times the name is rare, borne mostly by Roman Catholics, who choose it in honour of those saints.

Peronel ♀ Common medieval simplified form of ▷Petronel, occasionally revived in modern times as a given name.

Perry ♂ Pet form of ▷Peregrine, or transferred use of the surname *Perry*, in origin a local name for someone who lived by a pear tree (Old English *pirige*). In modern times, it has been borne by the American singer Perry Como (1912–2001), whose name was originally Nick Perido.

Perse ♂ Variant of ▷Pierce.

Persis ♀ Of New Testament origin, from Greek *Persis*, originally an ethnic name meaning 'Persian woman'. This name is borne by a woman mentioned fleetingly by St Paul—'the beloved Persis, which laboured much in the Lord' (Romans 16:12)—and was taken up from there at the time of the Reformation.

Pesah ♂ Jewish: Hebrew name meaning 'Passover' (compare ▷Pascal). It has traditionally been given to boys born during this period.

VARIANT: **Pesach**.

Pet ♀ Short form of ▷Petula, in part influenced by the common affectionate term of address 'pet', derived from the vocabulary word for a tame animal kept for companionship.

Peta ♀ Modern feminine form of ▷Peter, not used before the 1930s.

Petal ♀ From the vocabulary word for the part of a flower, also used as a term of endearment.

Pete ♂ Short form of ▷Peter.

Peter ♂ English form of the name of the best-known of all Christ's apostles, traditionally regarded as the founder of the Christian Church. The name derives, via Latin, from Greek *petros* 'stone, rock'. This is used as a translation of the Aramaic byname *Cephas*, given to the apostle Simon son of Jona, to distinguish him from another of the same name (Simon Zelotes). 'When Jesus beheld him, he said, Thou art Simon the son of Jona: thou shalt be called Cephas, which is by interpretation, A stone' (John 1:42). According to Matthew 16:17–18, Christ says more explicitly, 'Blessed art thou, Simon Bar-jona ... thou art Peter, and upon this rock I will build my church'. The name has been in continuous use since the Middle Ages.

SHORT FORM: **Pete.**

COGNATES: Gaelic: **Peadar.** Welsh: **Pedr.** German: **Peter.** Dutch: **Piet, Pieter.** Scandinavian: **Peter** (learned form); **Per** (vernacular form). Swedish: **Petter; Pär** (vernacular forms). French: **Pierre.** Spanish, Portuguese: **Pedro.** Catalan: **Pere.** Italian: **Pietro, Piero.** Russian: **Pyotr.** Polish: **Piotr.** Czech: **Petr.** Croatian, Serbian, Bulgarian: **Petar.** Slovenian: **Peter.** Finnish: **Pekka; Pietari** (learned form). Hungarian: **Péter.** Latvian: **Pēteris.** Lithuanian: **Petras.**

Petra ♀ Feminine form of ▷Peter, representing a hypothetical Latin name *Petra*; *petra* is in fact the regular Late Latin word for 'stone' (Greek *petra*), of which *petrus* is a by-form.

Petronel ♀ From Latin *Petronilla*, originally a feminine diminutive of the Roman family name *Petronius* (of uncertain derivation). The name *Petronilla* was borne by a 1st-century martyr, and early in the Christian era came to be connected with ▷Peter, so that in many legends surrounding her she is described as a companion or even the daughter of St Peter.

Petula ♀ Of uncertain origin, not used before the 20th century. It is possibly a Christian coinage intended to mean 'supplicant, postulant', from Late Latin *petulare* 'to ask', or there may be some connection with the flower name *petunia*. Alternatively, it may be an elaboration of the vocabulary word *pet* used as a term of endearment, with the suffix *-ula* abstracted from names such as ▷Ursula.

SHORT FORM: **Pet.**

Peyton ♀, ♂ Mainly U.S.: transferred use of the surname, a variant of ▷Payton.

Phil ♂, ♀ Short form of ▷Philip, ▷Phyllis, or of any of the various other names (male and female) beginning with the syllable *Phil-*.

Philbert ♂ From a Germanic personal name composed of the elements *fila* 'much' + *berht* 'bright, famous'. The first element has later been associated with the Greek name element *phil-* 'love'. St Philibert (*c*.608–84) was a Frankish monk who founded several abbeys.

Philip ♂ From the Greek name *Philippos*, meaning 'lover of horses', from *philein* 'to love' + *hippos* 'horse'. This was popular in the classical period and since. It was the name of the father of Alexander the Great. It was also the name of one of Christ's apostles, of a deacon ordained by the apostles after the death of Christ, and of several other early saints. See also ▷Philippa.

SHORT FORMS: **Phil, Pip.**

COGNATES: Irish: **Pilib.** Scottish Gaelic: **Filib.** German: **Philipp.** Dutch: **Filip.** Scandinavian: **Filip.** French: **Philippe.** Spanish: **Felipe.** Catalan: **Felip.** Portuguese: **Filipe.** Italian: **Filippo.** Polish, Czech: **Filip.** Finnish: **Vilppu.** Hungarian: **Fülöp.** Latvian: **Filips.**

Philippa ♀ Latin feminine form of ▷Philip. In England during the Middle Ages the vernacular name *Philip* was borne by women as well as men, but female bearers were distinguished in Latin records by this form. It was not,

p

however, used as a regular given name until the 19th century.

Philippina ♀ Latinate elaboration of ▷Philippa. In the Middle Ages it was sometimes interpreted as a compound of Greek *philein* 'to love' + *poinē* 'pain, punishment', since Christians were supposed to rejoice in purging themselves of their sins by pain and punishment, such as flagellation and the wearing of hair shirts.

VARIANTS: Philipina, Phillip(p)ina.

Phillida ♀ Variant of ▷Phyllis, derived from the genitive case (Greek *Phyllidos*, Latin *Phyllidis*) with the addition of the Latin feminine ending *-a*.

VARIANT: Phyllida.

Phillip ♂ Variant spelling of ▷Philip, in part a reflection of the surname, which is usually spelled *Phillips*.

Philo ♂ From the Late Greek personal name *Philōn*, a derivative of the element *phil-* 'love', in part as a short form of the various compound names containing this element. The name was borne by a 2nd-century saint, a deacon of St Ignatius.

Philomena ♀ From the name of an obscure saint (probably of the 3rd century) with a local cult in Italy. In 1527 the bones of a young woman were discovered under the church altar at San Severino near Ancona, together with a Latin inscription declaring them to be the body of St Filomena. Her name seems to be a feminine form of Latin *Philomenus*, Greek *Philomenēs*, from *philein* 'to love' + *menos* 'strength'. The name became popular in the 19th century, as a result of the supposed discovery in 1802 of the relics of another St Philomena in the catacombs at Rome. All the excitement, however, resulted from the misinterpretation of the Latin inscription *Filumena pax tecum* 'Peace be with you, beloved' (from Greek *philoumena* 'beloved').

VARIANT: Filomena.

Phineas ♂ Biblical name, borne by two minor characters. One was a grandson of Aaron, who preserved the purity of the race of Israel and deflected God's wrath by killing an Israelite who had taken a Midianite woman to wife (Numbers 25:6–15); the other, a son of the priest Eli, was killed in combat with the Philistines over the Ark of the Covenant (1 Samuel 1:3; 4:6–11). The name is spelled *Phinehas* in the Authorized Version, and has been taken to mean 'serpent's mouth' (i.e. 'oracle') in Hebrew, but this is an incorrect popular etymology. It is in fact derived from the Egyptian name *Panhsj*, originally a byname meaning 'the Nubian' and used as a personal name in Ancient Egypt. *Phineas* was popular among the Puritans in the 17th century, and has been occasionally used since, especially in America.

Phoebe ♀ Pronounced 'fee-bee': Latin form of the name of a Greek deity, *Phoibē* (from *phoibos* 'bright'), partly identified with Artemis, goddess of the moon and of hunting, sister of the sun god Apollo, who was also known as *Phoibos* (Latin *Phoebus*). The name was very popular in the late 17th century and has again enjoyed considerable popularity since the 1990s.

Phoenix ♂, ♀ Recent coinage as a given name, from the name of the mythological bird (Latin *phoenix*, Greek *phoinix*), which is said to live for an immensely long period and then, after being dead and consumed by fire, to rise again from the ashes of its corpse. The town that became the state capital of Arizona was so named because traces of ancient indigenous dwellings were seen in the area, and the new settlement was thus taken to represent a fresh cycle of habitation on the site.

Phyllicia ♀ Elaborated form of ▷Phyllis, influenced by ▷Felicia.

VARIANT: Phylicia.

Phyllida ♀ Variant spelling of ▷Phillida.

Phyllis ♀ Name of a minor character in Greek mythology who killed herself for love and was transformed into an almond tree; the Greek word *phyllis* means 'foliage', so clearly her name doomed her from the start.

Pia ♀ From the feminine form of Latin *pius* 'pious'. The name is common in Italy, and is also regularly used in Eastern Europe and Scandinavia. It has recently been reintroduced to the English-speaking world.

Pierce ♀ Variant of ▷Piers, borne for example by the Irish-born film actor Pierce Brosnan (b. 1953). In many cases it may represent a transferred use of the surname derived from the given name in the Middle Ages.

VARIANTS: **Pearce, Perse.**

Piers ♂ Regular medieval vernacular form of ▷Peter (from the Old French nominative case, as against the oblique *Pier*, modern *Pierre*). In the form *Pierce* it survived into the 18th century, although in part this may be a transferred use of the surname derived from the medieval given name. *Piers* was revived in the mid-20th century, perhaps partly under the influence of William Langland's great rambling medieval poem *Piers Plowman* (1367–86), in which the character of Piers symbolizes the virtues of hard work, honesty, and fairness.

Pinchas ♂ Yiddish form of ▷Phineas, still in regular use as a Jewish name. It is borne by the virtuoso violinist Pinchas Zuckerman (b. 1948).

Pip ♂, ♀ Contracted short form of ▷Philip or ▷Philippa. It is best known as the name of the main character in Charles Dickens's *Great Expectations* (1861), whose full name was Philip Pirrip.

Piper ♀ Transferred use of the surname derived from Middle English *pipere*, an occupational name for someone who played the pipes.

Pippa ♀ Contracted pet form of ▷Philippa, now also used as an independent given name. It was popularized in the 19th century by Browning's narrative poem *Pippa Passes* (1841), in which the heroine is a child worker in an Italian silk mill, whose innocent admiration of 'great' people is ironically juxtaposed with their sordid lives. The name is presumably supposed to be Italian, but is not in fact used in Italy.

Pitt ♂ Transferred use of the surname, which was originally given to someone who lived near to a hollow in the ground or a claypit. Use as a given name probably originated in honour of the British statesman William Pitt the Younger (1759–1806), who did much to undermine French power in Europe.

Polly ♀ Variant of ▷Molly, established as an independent given name since the 18th century. The reason for the interchange of *M*- and *P*- is not clear; compare ▷Peg.

SHORT FORM: **Poll.**

Poppy ♀ From the word denoting the flower, Old English *popæg* (from Latin *papaver*). It has been used as a given name since the latter years of the 19th century. It reached a peak of popularity in the 1920s and since the late 1990s has again been back in fashion.

Porter ♂ Transferred use of the surname, in origin an occupational name, either for someone who worked as a carrier of goods (Old French *porteour*, from a derivative of Latin *portāre* 'to carry') or else for a gatekeeper (Old French *portier*, from a derivative of Latin *porta* 'door, gate').

Portia ♀ This is the name of two characters in the works of Shakespeare. The most celebrated of them is an heiress in *The Merchant of Venice* who, disguised as a man, shows herself to be a brilliant advocate and delivers a stirring speech on the quality of mercy. It is also the name of the wife of Brutus

p

in *Julius Caesar*. The historical Brutus's wife was called *Porcia*, feminine form of the Roman family name *Porcius*, which is apparently a derivative of Latin *porcus* 'pig'.

VARIANT: **Porsha** (modern respelling).

Posy ♀ Pet form (originally a nursery version) of ▷Josephine. It has also been associated with the vocabulary word *posy* 'bunch of flowers' (originally a collection of verses, from *poesy* 'poetry'). It is occasionally used as an independent given name, fitting into the series of names associated with flowers that arose in the 19th century.

Potter ♂ Transferred use of the surname, in origin an occupational name for someone who made and sold pots (an agent derivative of *pot*, Old English *pott*). In the Middle Ages the term denoted workers in metal (who made pots and pans) as well as those using clay.

Precious ♀, ♂ From the vocabulary word meaning 'valuable, treasured', in use in the United States as a given name for both boys and girls at least since the 18th century, and now used elsewhere in the English-speaking world, mainly for girls.

Preston ♂ Transferred use of the surname, in origin a local name from any of the numerous places in England named with Old English *prēost* 'priest' + *tūn* 'enclosure, settlement'.

Price ♂ Transferred use of the Welsh surname derived from the patronymic *ap Rhys* 'son of Rhys' (see Welsh appendix).

VARIANT: **Pryce**.

Primrose ♀ One of the several girls' names taken from words for flowers in the late 19th century. The word is from Latin *prima rosa* 'first rose', although it does not in fact have any connection with the rose family.

Prince ♂ Originally a nickname from the royal title, Old French *prince* (Latin *princeps*). The name is popular among Blacks in Britain and the United States, influenced perhaps by the fame of the American singer Prince (b. 1958 as Prince Rogers Nelson).

Prisca ♀ Of New Testament origin: feminine form of the Roman family name *Priscus* (originally a nickname meaning 'ancient'). Prisca (2 Timothy 4:19) and Priscilla (Acts 18:3) are apparently the same person, but it is the diminutive form which became established as a common given name.

Priscilla ♀ Of New Testament origin: from a post-classical Latin personal name, a feminine diminutive of the Roman family name *Priscus* 'ancient'. *Priscilla* was the name of a woman with whom St Paul stayed at Corinth (Acts 18:3), referred to elsewhere as *Prisca*. The name was in regular use in the late 16th century and enjoyed a modest vogue in the 19th century.

PET FORM: **Prissy**.

Prosper ♂ From the Latin name *Prosperus*, derived from the adjective *prosper* 'fortunate, prosperous' (originally 'according to one's wishes', Latin *pro spe*). This was the name of various early saints, including a 5th-century theologian and contemporaneous bishops of Orleans and Reggio. It was a favourite among the English Puritans, partly because of its association with the English vocabulary word *prosper*, but is now rare. In France it is best known as the given name of the writer Prosper Mérimée (1803–70).

Pru ♀ Short form of ▷Prudence and ▷Prunella.

VARIANT: **Prue**.

Prudence ♀ Originally a medieval form of the Latin name *Prudentia*, a feminine form of *Prudentius*, from *prudens* 'provident'. The Blessed Prudentia was a 15th-century abbess who founded a new convent at Como in Italy. Later, among the Puritans in

17th-century England, *Prudence* was associated with the vocabulary word for the quality.

SHORT FORMS: Prue, ▷Pru.

Prunella ♀ Latinate name, probably one of the names coined in the 19th century from vocabulary words for plants and flowers, in this case from a diminutive derived from Late Latin *pruna* 'plum'.

SHORT FORMS: Prue, ▷Pru.

Psyche ♀ Pronounced '**sigh**-kee'; from the Greek word *psykhē*, meaning both 'butterfly' and 'soul' or 'spirit'. Use as a given name may derive in part from the nymph in classical mythology beloved by Cupid; in other cases it has been chosen by parents interested in exploring the potential of the human spirit.

p

Qq

Queenie ♀ Pet form from the affectionate nickname *Queen*, with the addition of the diminutive suffix *-ie*. In the Victorian era it was sometimes used as an allusive pet form for ▷Victoria. The vocabulary word *queen* goes back to Old English *cwēn*, akin to *cwene* 'woman', with a fanciful respelling.

Quentin ♂ From the Old French form of the Latin name *Quintinus*, a derivative of the given name ▷Quintus. The name was borne by a 3rd-century saint who worked as a missionary in Gaul.

VARIANTS: Quintin, ▷Quinton.

Quincy ♂ Mainly U.S.: transferred use of the English surname, in origin a Norman baronial name borne by a family that held lands at *Cuinchy* in Pas-de-Calais, Normandy. The place name is derived from the Gallo-Roman personal name ▷Quintus. This was the surname of a prominent New England family in the colonial era. Josiah Quincy (1744–75) was a lawyer and Revolutionary patriot, a close friend of John Adams (1735–1826) who became second president of the United States (1797–1801). The latter's son, John Quincy Adams (1767–1848), also served as president (1825–9). His middle name may have been chosen in honour of Josiah Quincy, or it may have been taken from the township of Quincy, Massachusetts, where he was born and where the Adams family had their seat.

VARIANT: Quincey.

Quinn ♂ Transferred use of the Irish surname, Anglicized form of *Ó Cuinn* 'descendant of Conn' (see Irish appendix). In some instances it may be a short form of ▷Quincy or ▷Quintin.

Quintin ♂ Variant of ▷Quentin.

Quinton ♂ Mainly U.S.: variant of ▷Quentin, influenced by the surname so spelled. The surname is a local name from any of several places named with Old English *cwēn* 'queen' + *tūn* 'enclosure, settlement'.

Quintus ♂ An old Roman given name meaning 'fifth'. It has been used in the English-speaking world, mainly in the 19th century, for the fifth-born son or a male fifth child in a family (compare ▷Sextus, ▷Septimus, ▷Octavius, and ▷Nona).

q

Rr

Rachael ♀ Variant spelling of ▷Rachel, influenced by ▷Michael.

Rachel ♀ Biblical name (meaning 'ewe' in Hebrew), borne by the beloved wife of Jacob and mother (after long barrenness) of Joseph (Genesis 28–35) and of Benjamin, at whose birth she died. In the Middle Ages and subsequently this was regarded as a characteristically Jewish name, but it is now also popular among Gentiles.

Rachelle ♀ Elaborated form of ▷Rachel, as if from French, but actually a recent coinage in English.

Rae ♀ Mainly Australian: probably originally a short form of ▷Rachel, but now generally taken as a feminine form of ▷Ray or ▷Raymond, or simply a derivative of *ray* meaning 'sunbeam'. In some cases it may be a transferred use of the Scottish surname *Rae*, originally either a short form of *MacRae* (from a Gaelic personal name meaning 'son of grace') or a nickname from the roebuck. It is often used in combinations such as *Rae Ellen* and *Mary Rae*.

Raelene ♀ Australian: fanciful coinage of recent origin, from ▷Rae + the productive feminine suffix -*lene*.

Rafe ♂ Spelling representation of the traditional pronunciation of the name ▷Ralph, a pronunciation now largely restricted to the upper classes in England.

Rafferty ♂, ♀ Transferred use of the Irish surname. The Gaelic form of this is *Ó Rabhartaigh* or *Ó Robhartaigh*, meaning 'descendant of **Robhartach**' (see Irish appendix). It has come into fairly regular use in Britain and the United States, usually as a boy's name.

Rainbow ♀ From the vocabulary word (from Old English *regn* 'rain' + *boga* 'bow, arch'). This is one of the names taken from the world of nature in the 1960s under the influence of the 'flower power' movement. It has not proved enduringly popular.

Raine ♀ Of modern origin and uncertain derivation. It is possibly a respelling of the French vocabulary word *reine* 'queen' (compare ▷Regina), or a transferred use of the surname *Raine* or *Rayne*. The surname is derived from a medieval given name, a short form of various Germanic compound names derived from *ra(g)in* 'advice, decision'. In modern times, this given name is borne by the Countess Spencer (b. 1929) daughter of the romantic novelist Barbara Cartland and stepmother of the Princess of Wales.

Ralph ♂ From a Norman French name, *Raulf*, a contracted form of the Germanic personal name *Radulf*, derived from *rād* 'counsel' + *wulf* 'wolf'. The spelling with -*ph* is due to classical influence in the 18th century.
VARIANTS: Ralf, ▷Rafe.

Ramona ♀ Spanish: feminine form of Ramón (see Spanish appendix). This has achieved some popularity in recent decades among non-Hispanic people in America and, to a lesser extent, in Britain, partly due to the influence of a popular song (1959) about a girl called Ramona.

Ramsay ♂ Transferred use of the Scottish surname, in origin a local name imported to Scotland from *Ramsey* in Huntingdonshire (so called from Old English *hramsa* 'wild garlic' + *ēg* 'island'). In the 12th century David, brother of King Alexander I of Scotland, was brought up at the English court, and acquired the earldoms of Huntingdon and Northampton. When he succeeded his brother as king, he took many of his retainers and associates with him to Scotland, and some of them took their surnames with them from places in eastern England. This explains why some famous Scottish surnames, such as *Ramsay*, *Lindsay*, *Graham*, etc., are derived from place names in that part of England. Some of these surnames have in turn gone on to be used as given names.

VARIANT: **Ramsey.**

Ran ♂ Short form of the various names beginning with this syllable, as, for example, ▷Randolf.

Randa ♀ Modern coinage, probably a shortened form of ▷Miranda. See also ▷Randy.

Randall ♂ Mainly U.S.: medieval vernacular form of ▷Randolf. This was in common use as a given name into the 17th century and gave rise to a surname. In modern use the given name is often a transferred use of this surname.

VARIANTS: **Randal, Randel(l), Randle.**

Randolf ♂ From a Norman given name, Old Norse *Rannulfr*, derived from *rand* 'rim, shield' (or *hrafn* 'raven') + *úlfr* 'wolf'.

VARIANT: **Randolph.**

Randy ♂, occasionally ♀ Mainly North American and Australian: as a boy's name this originated as a pet form of ▷Randall, ▷Randolf, or ▷Andrew. As a girl's name it may have originated either as a transferred use of the boy's name or else as a pet form of ▷Miranda (compare ▷Randa). It is now fairly commonly used as an independent name, mainly by men, in spite of the unfortunate connotations of the colloquial adjective meaning 'lustful'.

VARIANTS: **Randie, Randi** ♀.

Ranulf ♂ From an Old Norse personal name, *Reginulfr*, derived from *regin* 'advice, decision' + *úlfr* 'wolf'. This was introduced into Scotland and northern England by Scandinavian settlers in the early Middle Ages and modern use is largely confined to these areas.

Raphael ♂ From early Christian tradition, in which it is the name of one of the archangels (see also ▷Gabriel and ▷Michael). It is composed of Hebrew vocabulary elements meaning 'to heal' and 'God'. Raphael is not named in the canonical text of the Bible, but plays a part in the apocryphal tale of Tobias. The shorter form *Rapha* 'he (God) heals' (compare ▷Nathaniel and ▷Nathan) is borne by several characters in the Old Testament. The name has always been much more common in southern Europe than in Britain, and use in the English-speaking world today generally reflects southern European influence. It has also become a popular modern Hebrew name.

Raquel ♀ Spanish form of ▷Rachel, now in regular use in the English-speaking world. It was brought to public attention by the celebrity of the film actress Raquel Welch (b. 1940 as Raquel Tejada, in Chicago). Her father was Bolivian, her mother of English stock.

VARIANT: **Raquelle.**

Rastus ♂ Of New Testament origin, where it is a shortened form of the Latin name *Erastus* (Greek *Erastos*, from *erān* 'to love'). This was the name of the treasurer of Corinth converted to Christianity by St Paul (Romans 16:23).

Raven ♂, ♀ From the word denoting the bird (Old English *hræfn*), which has strikingly black plumage. It is in occasional use as a given name for both boys (incidentally paralleling the Old Norse byname *Hrafn*) and girls (falling into a set with other given names derived from birds, such as ▷Dove and ▷Teal).

Ravenna ♀ Apparently from the name of the city in north-east Italy (compare ▷Siena and ▷Venetia for other names derived from the names of Italian cities). The place name is probably of Etruscan origin. Use as a given name may in part also represent an elaborated or more clearly feminine form of ▷Raven.

Ray ♂ Short form of ▷Raymond, now also used as an independent given name, especially in North America. In some instances it may represent a transferred use of the surname *Ray*, which for the most part originated as a nickname, from Old French *rei*, *roi* 'king' (compare ▷Roy and ▷Leroy).

Raymond ♂ From an Old French name, *Raimund*, of Germanic origin, from *ragin* 'advice, decision' + *mund* 'protector'. This was adopted by the Normans and introduced by them to Britain. Subsequently it dropped out of use, but was revived in the middle of the 19th century, together with several other given names of Old English and Norman origin.

SHORT FORM: ▷Ray.

Rayner ♂ From a Norman personal name of Old French origin (*Rainer*), derived from a Germanic name composed of the elements *ragin* 'advice, decision' + *heri*, *hari* 'army'. This survived in use as an English given name at least until the end of the 15th century. In modern use it may also be a transferred use of the surname.

Read ♂ Transferred use of the English surname, which for the most part originated as a nickname for someone with red hair or a ruddy complexion (from Old English *rēad* 'red'; compare ▷Reid). In other cases, it may have arisen as a local name, from Old English *hrēod* 'reeds' or *rēod* 'cleared land'.

Reagan ♂, ♀ Transferred use of the Irish surname *Re(a)gan* (Gaelic *Ó Riagáin* 'descendant of Riagán'), no doubt chosen in the United States in honour of American president Ronald Reagan (1911–2004). As a girl's name it may

also be a respelling of the Shakespearean name ▷Regan, influenced by the surname.

Reanna ♀ Modern coinage, a variant of ▷Rhianna influenced by the spelling of ▷Deanna.

VARIANT: **Reanne**.

Rearden ♂ Anglicized form of Ríordán (see Irish appendix).

Reba ♀ Modern coinage, apparently derived from the first and last syllables of ▷Rebecca.

Rebecca ♀ Biblical name, from the Latin form of the Hebrew name *Rebekah*, borne by the wife of Isaac, who was the mother of Esau and Jacob (Genesis 24–27). The Hebrew root occurs in the Bible only in the vocabulary word *marbek* 'cattle stall', and its connection with the name is doubtful. In any case, Rebecca was Aramean, and the name probably has a source in Aramaic. It has always been common as a Jewish name; in England and elsewhere it began to be used also by Christians from the 14th century onwards and especially at the time of the Reformation, when Old Testament names became popular. It was very common among the Puritans in the 17th century, and has enjoyed a tremendous vogue in England since the latter part of the 20th century, among people of many different creeds. In Scotland this is found as an Anglicized form of **Beathag** (see Scottish appendix).

SHORT FORMS: **Becca, Beck**.

PET FORM: **Becky**.

Reece ♂ Anglicized spelling of Rhys (see Welsh appendix). The name is now in widespread and frequent use outside Wales, in many cases representing a transferred use of the surname so spelled, which is derived from the given name.

Reenie ♀ Respelling of ▷Renée, representing an Anglicized pronunciation of the name. Sometimes

r

it is a pet form of various names ending in the syllable -reen, such as ▷Doreen and ▷Maureen.

Rees ♂ Anglicized spelling of Welsh Rhys, in some cases representing a transferred use of the surname so spelled, which is derived from the Welsh given name.

VARIANT: Reese.

Reg ♂ Short form of ▷Reginald, often preferred by bearers of that name for use in almost all situations, but rarely actually bestowed as a baptismal name.

Regan ♂, ♀ As a boy's name, this is a transferred use of the Irish surname Re(a)gan (Gaelic Ó Riagáin; see ▷Reagan). The girl's name, however, may at least in part be from the name of one of the three daughters in Shakespeare's King Lear (1605), a most unattractive character, who flatters her father into giving her half his kingdom and then turns him out into a raging storm at night. It is not known where Shakespeare got the name; he presumably believed it to be of Celtic origin. It can be identified with the Irish Gaelic word ríogan 'queen' (pronounced 'ree-gan').

Reggie ♂ Pet form of ▷Reg, common in the 19th and early 20th centuries, but now less so.

Regina ♀ From the Latin vocabulary word meaning 'queen'. It was occasionally used as a given name among the early Christians; a St Regina, probably of the 3rd century, was venerated as a virgin martyr at Autun from an early date. In modern use it is normally borne by Roman Catholics in allusion to the epithet Regina Coeli 'Queen of Heaven', a cult title of the Virgin Mary since the 8th century.

Reginald ♂ Of Norman origin, derived from Reginaldus, a Latinized form of ▷Reynold influenced by Latin regina 'queen'. The full form is now regarded as very formal, and bearers

generally shorten it to ▷Reg in ordinary usage.

Reid ♂ Transferred use of the Scottish and northern English surname, in origin a nickname for someone with red hair or a ruddy complexion (from Old English rēad 'red'; compare ▷Read).

Reisel ♀ Jewish: Yiddish pet form of Reise, itself a Yiddish form of ▷Rose.

VARIANT: Reisl.

Rella ♀ Jewish: from Yiddish Rele, originally a pet form of ▷Rachel, ▷Rebecca, or ▷Reisel, but now used as an independent given name.

Remus ♂ According to ancient Roman tradition, the name of the brother of Romulus, co-founder with him of the city of Rome. In America this rare given name is associated particularly with the 'Uncle Remus' stories of Joel Chandler Harris (1848–1908), Uncle Remus being a Black who is the narrator of the stories.

Rena ♀ Of recent origin: an altered form of ▷Renée, from its Anglicized pronunciation (see ▷Reenie), a short form of ▷Serena, or else a variant spelling of ▷Rina.

Renata ♀ The original Latin form of ▷Renée. It is common in Italy (although it was seldom used there until the mid-19th century), and is also used occasionally in the English-speaking world.

René ♂, ♀ French: from the Late Latin name Renatus 'reborn', used by early Christians as a baptismal name celebrating spiritual rebirth in Christ. It is found in the English-speaking world, especially North America, where it is usually written without the accent. It occurs occasionally as a girl's name, presumably a modified spelling of ▷Renée or a short form of ▷Irene and similar names.

Renée ♀ French: from the Late Latin name Renata, feminine of Renatus 'reborn', used by early Christians as a baptismal name celebrating spiritual rebirth in Christ. The name is also used in the English-speaking world, often without the accent and in a highly Anglicized pronunciation (compare ▷Reenie).

Reuben ♂ Biblical name (said to mean 'behold, a son' in Hebrew), borne by one of the twelve sons of Jacob, and so the name of one of the twelve tribes of Israel. Genesis 29:32 explains it as follows: 'and Leah conceived, and bare a son, and she called his name Reuben: for she said, Surely the Lord hath looked upon my affliction; now therefore my husband will love me'. In Genesis 30:14–15, Reuben is depicted as a devoted son to his mother, but he incurred his father's wrath for seducing his concubine Bilhah and on his deathbed Jacob, rather than blessing him, cursed Reuben because of this incident (Genesis 49:4). Despite this, the name has enjoyed steady popularity as a Jewish name. Among Christians (chiefly Nonconformists) it came into use after the Reformation, survived into the 20th century, and is currently enjoying a modest revival.

VARIANT (ESP. JEWISH): **Reuven.**

Reuel ♂ Biblical name (meaning 'friend of God' in Hebrew) borne by a character mentioned in a genealogy (2 Chronicles 9:8).

Rex ♂ From the Latin vocabulary word meaning 'king'. This was not used as a personal name in Latin of the classical or Christian periods, and its adoption as a given name seems to have been a 19th-century innovation. Its popularity was increased by the fame of the British actor Rex Harrison (1908–90), who was christened Reginald Carey.

Rexanne ♀ Altered form of ▷Roxane or feminine equivalent of ▷Rex.

Reynard ♂ From an Old French name of Germanic (Frankish) origin, derived

from *ragin* 'advice, decision' + *hard* 'hardy, brave, strong'. In French, *renard* has become the generic term for a fox, as a result of the popularity of medieval beast tales featuring *Re(y)nard le goupil* 'Reynard the Fox'. The name was adopted by the Normans and introduced by them to Britain.

Reynold ♂ From an Old French name, *Reinald*, *Reynaud*, of Germanic (Frankish) origin, derived from *ragin* 'advice, decision' + *wald* 'ruler'. This was adopted by the Normans and introduced by them into England. In modern use, the given name sometimes represents a transferred use of the surname derived from the Norman personal name.

VARIANT: ▷Reginald. See also ▷Ronald.

Rhea ♀ The name borne, according to Roman tradition, by the mother (Rhea Silvia) of Romulus and Remus, who grew up to be the founders of the city of Rome. It was also a title of the goddess Cybele, introduced to Rome from Phrygia. Its meaning is unknown. Its use in the modern world, though not frequent, has recently increased.

Rhett ♂ Transferred use of a surname well established in South Carolina, an Anglicization of the Dutch surname *de Raedt* (from Middle Dutch *raet* 'advice'). This was brought to North America in 1694 by William Rhett (1666–1723). Robert Barnwell Rhett (1800–76) was a South Carolina congressman and senator, a noted secessionist. The name was used by Margaret Mitchell in *Gone with the Wind* (1936) for the character of the black sheep and charmer Rhett Butler. Like some of the other unusual names in that novel, it has attained a modest currency.

Rhetta ♀ Name coined as a feminine form of ▷Rhett.

Rhianna ♀ Modern name, an altered and more clearly feminine form of Welsh Rhiannon.

VARIANTS: Reanna, ▷Rianna.

Rhoda ♀ From the post-classical Greek name *Rhoda*, derived either from *rhodon* 'rose', or as an ethnic name meaning 'woman from Rhodes' (Greek *Rhodos*). In the New Testament Rhoda was a servant in the house of Mary the mother of John, where Peter went after his release from prison by an angel (Acts 12:13). In the Scottish Highlands *Rhoda* is used as a feminine form of ▷Roderick.

Rhona ♀ Of uncertain derivation, apparently originating in Scotland sometime around 1870. The spelling *Rona* is also found, and it is probable that the name was devised as a feminine form of ▷Ronald. It has also been suggested that it may be associated with the Hebridean island name *Rona* (cf. ▷Ailsa, ▷Iona, ▷Isla). In either case the spelling would then have been altered by association with ▷Rhoda.

Rhonda ♀ Modern coinage, a blend of ▷Rhoda and ▷Rhona. It is now often taken to be a Welsh name derived from *rhon* 'pike, lance' (as in Rhonwen; see Welsh appendix) + *-da* 'good', as in ▷Glenda. The name is associated particularly with the American film actress Rhonda Fleming (b. 1923 as Marilyn Louis).

Ria ♀ Short form of ▷Maria, of German origin but now also moderately popular in the English-speaking world.

Rianna ♀ Modern name, a variant of ▷Rhianna or a feminine equivalent of Irish ▷Ryan.

Ricarda ♀ Latinate feminine form of ▷Richard.

Rich ♂ Short form of ▷Richard. There was a medieval given name *Rich(e)*, but it is connected only indirectly with the modern form. It is a short form of several medieval names, including not only *Richard* but also other, rarer names of Old French (Germanic) origin with the same first element, as, for example, *Rich(i)er* 'power army' and *Richaud* 'power rule'.

Richard ♂ One of the most enduringly successful of the Old French personal names introduced into Britain by the Normans. It is of Germanic (Frankish) origin, derived from *rīc* 'power' + *hard* 'strong, hardy'. It has enjoyed continuous popularity in England from the Conquest to the present day, influenced by the fact that it was borne by three kings of England, in particular Richard I (1157–99). He was king for only ten years (1189–99), most of which he spent in warfare abroad, taking part in the Third Crusade and costing the people of England considerable sums in taxes. Nevertheless, he achieved the status of a folk hero, and was never in England long enough to disappoint popular faith in his goodness and justice. He was also Duke of Aquitaine and Normandy and Count of Anjou, fiefs which he held at a time of maximum English expansion in France. His exploits as a leader of the Third Crusade earned him the nickname 'Coeur de Lion' or 'Lionheart' and a permanent place in popular imagination, in which he was even more firmly enshrined by Sir Walter Scott's novel *Ivanhoe* (1820).

SHORT FORMS: Rick, ▷Dick, ▷Rich.

PET FORMS: Ricky, Rickie; Dicky, Dickie; ▷Richie.

COGNATES: Irish: Ristéard. Scottish Gaelic: Ruiseart. Welsh: Rhisiart. German: Richard. Dutch: Richard, Rikhart. Scandinavian: Rik(h)ard. French: Richard. Spanish, Portuguese: Ricardo. Italian: Riccardo. Polish: Ryszard. Czech: Richard. Slovenian: Rihard. Finnish: Rik(h)ard. Hungarian: Rikárd. Latvian: Rihards.

Richelle ♀ Modern feminine form of ▷Richard, derived from the first syllable of that name + *-elle*, feminine diminutive suffix of French origin. It may also have been influenced by ▷Rachelle and ▷Rochelle.

Richie ♂ Pet form of ▷Richard. The suffix *-ie* was originally characteristic of

Scotland and northern England, but the name is now found elsewhere. It is also used as a given name in its own right, in some cases representing a transferred use of the surname derived from the pet name.

VARIANT: Ritchie (probably also a transferred use of the surname spelled thus).

Rick ♂ Short form of ▷Richard, or, less frequently, of ▷Frederick or other names ending in -ric(k). It is also used as an independent given name, especially in North America.

Ricky ♂, ♀ Pet form of ▷Richard or, less frequently, of ▷Frederick or other names ending in -ric(k). It is also used as an independent given name both for boys and (occasionally) girls.

VARIANTS: Rickie; Ricki, Rikki ♀.

Ridley ♂ Transferred use of the surname, in origin a local name from any of various places so named. Those in Essex and Kent are from Old English *hrēod* 'reeds' + *lēah* 'wood, clearing'. The two in Cheshire and Northumberland are from *rydde* 'cleared land' + *lēah*. The given name may have been chosen in some cases by ardent Protestants in honour of Bishop Nicholas Ridley (?1500–55), burned at the stake for his Protestantism under Mary Tudor. More recently it has been associated with the film director Ridley Scott (b. 1973).

Rikki ♀ Variant spelling of the girl's name ▷Ricky.

Riley ♂, ♀ In some cases a transferred use of the English surname, a local name from a place named with Old English *ryge* 'rye' + *lēah* 'wood, clearing'. There is one such place in Devon and another in Lancashire. In other cases it probably represents a respelling of the Irish surname *Reilly*, which is from an old Irish personal name, *Raghallach*, of unknown origin. While it is presently more popular for boys than girls in

Britain, the converse is true in the United States.

VARIANT: Ryley ♂.

Rina ♀ Short form of any of the girls' names with this ending, such as ▷Katerina, ▷Carina, and ▷Sabrina, or an Anglicized form of Ríonach (see Irish appendix).

Rio ♂, ♀ Modern coinage, apparently from Spanish *rio* 'river'. It may have been adopted with reference to Rio de Janeiro (literally 'River of January') in Brazil, noted for its beach life, night life, and carnival.

Rita ♀ Originally a short form of *Margarita*, the Spanish form of ▷Margaret, but now commonly used as an independent given name. Its popularity in the 1940s and 50s was influenced no doubt by the fame of the American film star Rita Hayworth (1918–87).

Ritchie ♂ Variant spelling of ▷Richie.

Ritzy ♀ Modern coinage, apparently from the colloquial term meaning 'luxurious, elegant'. This word derives from the chain of luxury hotels founded in the 19th century by the Swiss entrepreneur César Ritz.

River ♂ From the vocabulary word (Anglo-Norman *river(e)*). This is one of the names taken from the world of nature in the 1960s under 'hippy' influence, and, unlike some, it has survived to the present day. Use as a given name may have been influenced by the surname *Rivers*, in origin a Norman baronial name from various places in northern France called *Rivières*.

Rob ♂ Short form of ▷Robert or other names with this first syllable.

Robbie ♂, ♀ Pet form of ▷Robert, also of ▷Robin and ▷Roberta. It is also used as an independent given name.

Robert ♂ One of the many French names of Germanic origin that were

r

introduced into Britain by the Normans; it has since remained in continuous use. It is derived from the nearly synonymous elements *hrōd* 'fame' + *berht* 'bright, famous', and had a native Old English predecessor of similar form (*Hreodbeorht*), which was supplanted by the Norman name. Two dukes of Normandy in the 11th century bore the name: the father of William the Conqueror (sometimes identified with the legendary Robert the Devil), and his eldest son. It was borne also by three kings of Scotland, notably Robert the Bruce (1274–1329), who freed Scotland from English domination. The altered short form *Bob* is very common, but *Hob* and *Dob*, which were common in the Middle Ages and gave rise to surnames, are extinct. See also ▷Rupert.

SHORT FORMS: Bob, Rob.

PET FORMS: Bobby, Robbie, ▷Robin.

COGNATES: Irish: Roibéard. Scottish Gaelic: Raibeart. German: Robert, Rupprecht. Dutch: Robrecht, Rob(b)ert. Scandinavian: Robert. French: Robert. Spanish, Portuguese, Italian: Roberto. Czech: Robert. Finnish: Roopertti. Hungarian: Róbert. Latvian: Roberts.

Roberta ♀ Latinate feminine form of ▷Robert.

Robin ♂, ♀ Originally a pet form of ▷Robert, from the short form ▷Rob + the diminutive suffix -*in* (of Old French origin), but now nearly always used as an independent name. In recent years it has been increasingly used as a girl's name, partly under the influence of the vocabulary word denoting the bird.

VARIANT: Robyn ♀.

Rocco ♂ Italian name of Germanic origin, derived from the element *hrok* 'rest', and now also used in the English-speaking world.

Rochelle ♀ Of uncertain origin, probably a feminine diminutive form of the French boy's name *Roch* (from Germanic *hrok* 'rest'),

borne by a 14th-century saint, patron of the sick. This girl's name is little used in France, though widely used in the English-speaking world. It may in part represent a respelling of ▷Rachelle.

Rocky ♂ Mainly U.S.: of recent origin, originally a nickname for a tough individual. The name came to public notice through the American heavyweight boxing champion Rocky Marciano (1923–69). He was of Italian extraction, and Anglicized his original name, ▷Rocco, into a form that seems particularly appropriate for a fighter. It was later taken up in a series of films as the name of a boxer played by the muscular actor Sylvester Stallone, and it has also been adopted as a nickname among devotees of body building.

Rod ♂ Short form of ▷Roderick and ▷Rodney.

Roda ♀ Variant spelling of ▷Rhoda.

Roddy ♂ Pet form of ▷Roderick and ▷Rodney, also occasionally used as an independent given name.

Roderick ♂ Of Germanic origin, from *hrōd* 'fame' + *rīc* 'power'. This name was introduced into England, in slightly different forms, first by Scandinavian settlers in the Danelaw and later by the Normans. However, it did not survive beyond the Middle English period. It owes its modern use to a poem by Sir Walter Scott, *The Vision of Don Roderick* (1811), where it is an Anglicized form of the related Spanish name *Rodrigo*, borne by the last Visigothic king of Spain, whose vision is the subject of the poem. It is now also very commonly used as an Anglicized form of two unrelated Celtic names: Scottish Gaelic Ruairidh and Welsh Rhydderch (see respective appendices).

SHORT FORM: Rod.

PET FORM: Roddy.

Rodge ♂ Informal short form of ▷Roger.

Rodger ♂ Variant spelling of ▷Roger, in part from the surname derived from the given name in the Middle Ages.

Rodney ♂ Originally a transferred use of the surname, but in independent use as a given name since the 18th century, when it was bestowed in honour of Admiral Lord Rodney (1719–92), who defeated the French navy in 1759–60. The surname probably derives ultimately from a place name, but the location and etymology of this are uncertain. Stoke Rodney in Somerset is named for the family: the manor was held by Richard de *Rodene* in the early 14th century. Rodden in Somerset was Reddene in Domesday Book; this may be the source of the surname.

SHORT FORM: **Rod**.

PET FORM: **Roddy**.

Roger ♂ From an Old French personal name, *Rog(i)er*, of Germanic (Frankish) origin, from *hrōd* 'fame' + *gār*, *gēr* 'spear'. This was adopted by the Normans and introduced by them to Britain, replacing the native Old English form *Hrōðgār*. *Roger* was one of the most popular boys' names throughout the medieval period, but less so after the Reformation, though it has continued in regular use to the present day. Roger, Count of Sicily (*c*.1031–1101), son of Tancred, recovered Sicily from the Arabs. His son, also called Roger, ruled Sicily as king, presiding over a court noted for its splendour and patronage of the arts.

VARIANT: **Rodger**.

Rohan ♂ Indian name from Sanskrit; see Indian appendix.

Roland ♂ From an Old French personal name of Germanic (Frankish) origin, from *hrōd* 'fame' + *land* 'land, territory'. This was adopted by the Normans and introduced by them to Britain. In Old French literature it is borne by a legendary Frankish hero, a vassal of Charlemagne, whose exploits are told in the *Chanson de Roland*. The subject of the poem is Roland's death at the Battle of Roncesvalles in the Pyrenees in 778, while protecting the rearguard of the Frankish army on its retreat from Spain. Roland is depicted in literature and legend as headstrong and impulsive. His devoted friendship with the prudent Oliver is also legendary.

VARIANT: **Rowland**.

PET FORMS: **Roly, Rowley**.

Rolf ♂ Contracted version of an old Germanic personal name derived from *hrōd* 'fame' + *wulf* 'wolf'. This is found in Old Norse as *Hrólfr*. As an English given name, it represents in part the survival of a form imported by the Normans, in part a much more recent (19th-century) importation of the modern German name. See also ▷Rudolf.

Rollo ♂ Latinized form of *Roul*, the Old French version of ▷Rolf. This form appears regularly in Latin documents of the Middle Ages, but does not seem to have been used in everyday vernacular contexts. It is the form by which the first Duke of Normandy (*c*.860–932) is generally known. He was a Viking who, with his followers, settled at the mouth of the Seine and raided Paris, Chartres, and elsewhere. By the treaty of St Clair he received the duchy of Normandy from Charles III, on condition that he should receive Christian baptism. Use of this name in English families in modern times seems to be a consciously archaistic revival.

Roly ♂ Pet form of ▷Roland. See also ▷Rowley.

Roman ♂ Russian, Polish, and Czech: from the Late Latin personal name *Romanus*, originally an ethnic name meaning 'Roman' (a derivative of *Roma*; compare **Romolo** in Italian appendix). This name was borne by a large number of early saints, and in the 10th century was given as a baptismal name to Boris, son of Vladimir, the ruler who Christianized Kievan Russia. Boris and his brother Gleb were murdered by

r

their brother Svyatopolk and canonized as martyrs. Use of the name in the English-speaking world is recent, influenced perhaps by the film director Roman Polanski (b. 1933 as Raimund Liebling).

Romeo ♂ Italian: from the medieval religious name *Romeo* 'pilgrim to Rome' (Late Latin *Romaeus*, a derivative of *Roma*; compare **Romolo** in Italian appendix). For his romantic tragedy, Shakespeare derived the name of the hero, the lover of Juliet, from a poem by Arthur Brooke, *The Tragicall Historye of Romeus and Juliet*. This is ultimately derived from a story by the Italian writer Matteo Bandello (1485–1561), whose works are the source of the plots of several Elizabethan and Jacobean plays. The sudden rise in frequency of the name in Britain may have been influenced at least in part by David and Victoria Beckham, who bestowed it on their second son (b. 2002). The reasons for their choice are not known.

Romy ♀ Pet form of *Rosemarie* (see ▷Rosemary), made famous by the Austrian film actress Romy Schneider (1938–82).
VARIANT: **Romey**.

Ron ♂ Short form of ▷Ronald. It is sometimes used as a given name in its own right.

Rona ♀ Variant spelling of ▷Rhona.

Ronald ♂ From the Old Norse personal name *Rögnvaldr* (composed of *regin* 'advice, decision' (also, 'the gods') + *valdr* 'ruler'). This name was regularly used in the Middle Ages in northern England and Scotland, where Scandinavian influence was strong. It is now widespread throughout the English-speaking world.
SHORT FORM: **Ron**.
PET FORMS: ▷Ronnie, ▷Roni.

Ronan ♂ Anglicized spelling of Rónán (see Irish appendix), now moderately popular outside Ireland.

Roni ♂, ♀ Pet form of ▷Ronald, or of ▷Veronica, occasionally used as an independent name.

Ronnie ♂, ♀ Pet form of ▷Ronald, or of ▷Veronica, also used as an independent given name for boys and (occasionally) girls.

Roo ♂, ♀ Modern informal short form of names such as ▷Rupert and ▷Ruth. In A. A. Milne's *Winnie the Pooh*, Roo is the name of the irrepressible child of Kanga, whose name therefore represents the second element of the word *kangaroo*.

Rory ♂ Anglicized form of the Gaelic name found in Ireland as **Ruaidhrí** and in Scotland as **Ruairidh** (see respective appendices). In Scotland this is further Anglicized to ▷Roderick. In recent times, *Rory* has come into popular general use.

Ros ♀ Short form of ▷Rosalind and ▷Rosamund.

Rosa ♀ Latinate form of ▷Rose.

Rosaleen ♀ Variant of ▷Rosalyn, influenced by the suffix *-een* (in origin the Irish Gaelic diminutive *-ín*). 'Dark Rosaleen' was the title of a poem by James Clarence Mangan (1803–49), based on the Gaelic poem *Róisín Dubh*; in it the name is used as a figurative allusion to the Irish nation.

Rosalie ♀ French form of the Latin name *Rosalia* (a derivative of *rosa* 'rose'), introduced to the English-speaking world in the latter part of the 19th century. St Rosalia was a 12th-century Sicilian virgin, and is the patron of Palermo.

Rosalind ♀ From an Old French personal name of Germanic (Frankish) origin, from *hros* 'horse' + *lind* 'weak, tender, soft'. It was adopted by the Normans and introduced by them to Britain. In the Middle Ages it was reanalysed by folk etymology as if from Latin *rosa linda* 'lovely rose'. Its popularity as a given name owes much to its use by Edmund Spenser for the character of a shepherdess in his pastoral poetry, and by Shakespeare as the name of the heroine in *As You Like It* (1599).

Rosaline ♀ Originally a variant of ▷Rosalind; compare ▷Rosalyn and ▷Rosaleen. It is the name of a minor character in Shakespeare's *Love's Labour's Lost* and is used for another, who does not appear but is merely mentioned, in *Romeo and Juliet*.

Rosalyn ♀ Altered form of ▷Rosalind. *Rosalin* was a common medieval form, since the letters *d* and *t* were often added or dropped capriciously at the end of words after *n*. The name has been further influenced by the productive suffix *-lyn* (see ▷Lynn).

VARIANTS: Rosalynn(e), Rosaleen.

Rosamund ♀ From an Old French personal name of Germanic (Frankish) origin, from *hros* 'horse' + *mund* 'protection'. This was adopted by the Normans and introduced by them to Britain. In the later Middle Ages it was reanalysed by folk etymology as if from Latin *rosa munda* 'pure rose' or *rosa mundi* 'rose of the world', titles given to the Virgin Mary. The spelling Rosamond has been common since the Middle Ages, when scribes used *o* for *u*, to distinguish it from *n* and *m*, all of which consisted of very similar downstrokes of the pen. 'Fair Rosamond' (Rosamond Clifford) was a legendary beauty who lived at Woodstock in Oxfordshire in the 12th century. She is said to have been the mistress of King Henry II, and to have been murdered by the queen, Eleanor of Aquitaine, in 1176.

Rosanne ♀ Modern coinage, a combination of the names ▷Rose and ▷Anne, possibly influenced by ▷Roxane. The form Rosanna is recorded in Yorkshire in the 18th century.

VARIANTS: Roseanne, Rosanna; Rosannagh (a fanciful respelling).

Roscoe ♂ Transferred use of the surname, in origin a local name from a place in northern England named with Old Norse *rá* 'roe deer' + *skógr* 'wood, copse'.

Rose ♀ Ostensibly from the vocabulary word denoting the flower (Latin *rosa*). However, the name was in use throughout the Middle Ages, long before any of the other girls' names derived from flowers, which are generally of 19th-century origin. In part it may refer to the flower as a symbol of the Virgin Mary, but it seems more likely that it also has a Germanic origin, probably as a short form of various girls' names based on *hros* 'horse' or *hrōd* 'fame'. The Latinate form *Rohesia* is commonly found in documents of the Middle Ages. As well as being a name in its own right, it is currently used as a short form of ▷Rosemary and, less often (because of their different pronunciation), of other names beginning *Ros-*, such as ▷Rosalind and ▷Rosamund.

PET FORM: Rosie.

Roselle ♀ Modern coinage, a combination of the given name ▷Rose with the productive suffix *-elle* (originally a French feminine diminutive suffix).

Rosemary ♀ 19th-century coinage, from the name of the herb (which is from Latin *ros marinus* 'sea dew'). It is often also assumed to be a combination of the names ▷Rose and ▷Mary.

VARIANT: Rosemarie.

PET FORM: Rosie.

Rosetta ♀ Italian pet form of ▷Rosa, occasionally also used in the English-speaking world.

Rosie ♀ Pet form of ▷Rose and ▷Rosemary. It was first used as an independent baptismal name in the 19th century.

Rosita ♀ Spanish pet form of ▷Rosa, sometimes used by English speakers.

r

Ross ♂ Either an adoption of the Gaelic topographic term *ros* 'headland' (compare ▷Glen, ▷Kyle) or a transferred use of the Scottish surname, which is borne by a large and ancient family whose members have played a major role in Scottish history. Although still very popular in Scotland, the name is now in widespread general use.

Rowan ♂, ♀ As a boy's name this is a transferred use of the surname, which is of Irish origin, being an Anglicized form of the Gaelic byname *Ruadhán* 'little red one'. It was borne by a 6th-century saint who founded the monastery of Lothra, and is the name of the present Archbishop of Canterbury, Dr Rowan Williams (b. 1950). As a girl's name it seems to be from the vocabulary word (of Scandinavian origin) denoting the tree, an attractive sight with its clusters of bright red berries.

Rowena ♀ Latinized form of a Saxon name of uncertain form and derivation. It is perhaps from Germanic *hrōd* 'fame' + *wynn* 'joy'. It first occurs in the Latin chronicles of Geoffrey of Monmouth (12th century) as the name of a daughter of the Saxon invader Hengist, and was taken up by Sir Walter Scott as the name of a Saxon woman, Lady Rowena of Hargottstanstede, who marries the eponymous hero of his novel *Ivanhoe* (1819).

Rowland ♂ Variant spelling of ▷Roland, or a transferred use of the surname derived from that given name in the Middle Ages.

Rowley ♂ Variant of ▷Roly, or a transferred use of the surname, a local name from any of the various places in England named with Old English *rūh* 'rough, overgrown' + *lēah* 'wood, clearing'.

Roxane ♀ From Latin *Roxana*, Greek *Roxanē*, recorded as the name of the wife of Alexander the Great. She was the daughter of Oxyartes the Bactrian,

and her name is presumably of Persian origin; it is said to mean 'dawn'. In English literature it is the name of the heroine of a novel by Defoe (1724), a beautiful adventuress who, deserted by her husband, enjoys a glittering career as a courtesan but eventually dies in a state of penitence, having been thrown into prison for debt. In modern use, the variant forms are more frequent.

VARIANTS: **Roxanne, Roxanna**.

Roxy ♀ Pet form of ▷Roxane, influenced also by the British colloquial term meaning 'flashy, glamorous'. This word derives from the chain of cinemas founded by the U.S. entrepreneur Samuel L. Rothafel ('red apple'), who was known by the nickname *Roxy*.

Roy ♂ Originally a Scottish name, representing an Anglicized spelling of the Gaelic nickname *Ruadh* 'red'. It has since spread to other parts of the English-speaking world, where it is often reanalysed as Old French *roy* 'king' (compare ▷Leroy).

Royce ♂ Mainly U.S.: transferred use of the surname, in origin a derivative of the vernacular form of the medieval female name *Rohesia* (see ▷Rose). As a modern first name it may in part be taken as a short form of ▷Royston.

Royle ♂ Transferred use of the surname, in origin a local name from a place in Lancashire, so called from Old English *ryge* 'rye' + *hyll* 'hill'. In part it may have been adopted as a given name because of association with the vocabulary word *royal* (compare ▷Noble and ▷King).

Royston ♂ Transferred use of the surname, in origin a local name from a place in Hertfordshire, named as the 'settlement of *Royce*'. The latter is an obsolete variant of *Rohesia* (see ▷Rose). *Royston* is now widely used as a given name, especially among West Indians, although the reasons for its popularity in that community are not known.

Roz ♀ Variant spelling of ▷Ros, with the final consonant altered to represent the voiced sound of the names from which it derives.

Rozanne ♀ Variant of ▷Rosanne or *Roxanne* (see ▷Roxane).

Rube ♂, ♀ Informal short form of ▷Reuben and ▷Ruby.

Ruben ♂ Variant spelling of ▷Reuben; this is the more frequent form in use in the United States.

Ruby ♀ From the vocabulary word for the gemstone (Latin *rubinus*, from *rubeus* 'red'). The name was chiefly common in the late 19th century and up to the middle of the 20th, and is presently enjoying a revival in parts of the English-speaking world.

Rudolf ♂ From a Latinized version, *Rudolphus*, of the Germanic name *Hrōdwulf* (see ▷Rolf). It was introduced to the English-speaking world from Germany in the 19th century. *Rudolf* was a hereditary name among the Habsburgs, the Holy Roman Emperors and rulers of Austria, from the Emperor Rudolf I (1218–91) to the Archduke Rudolf, Crown Prince of Austria-Hungary, who died in mysterious circumstances at his country house at Meyerling in 1889. Rudolf Rassendyll was the central character of Anthony Hope's adventure stories *The Prisoner of Zenda* (1894) and *Rupert of Hentzau* (1898), in which he is an English gentleman who bears a great physical resemblance to the King of Ruritania, to whom he is distantly related. He successfully impersonates the king for reasons of state. In the early 20th century the popularity of this name was further enhanced by the American silent-film actor Rudolph Valentino (1895–1926), born in Italy as Rodolfo di Valentina d'Antonguolla. It has not been used much in recent times, perhaps being inextricably associated

with 'the red-nosed reindeer' of the Christmas song.
VARIANT: **Rudolph**.

Rudy ♂ Pet form of ▷Rudolf, now established as an independent given name.
VARIANT: **Rudi** (German form).

Rufus ♂ From a Latin nickname meaning 'red(-haired)'. It is mentioned in the Bible (Mark 15:21) as the name of a son of Simon the Cyrenian, the man who was forced by the Romans to carry Jesus's cross to Golgotha. It was the nickname of William II (William Rufus, son of William the Conqueror, who was noted for his ruddy complexion), and was sometimes used in medieval documents as a translation of various surnames with the same sense. It began to be used as a given name in the 17th century.

Rupert ♂ Low German form of ▷Robert, first brought to England by Prince Rupert of the Rhine (1618–92), a dashing military leader who came to help his uncle, Charles I, in the Civil War. In Britain the name is inextricably linked with the children's comic strip character Rupert Bear, which first appeared in the *Daily Express* in 1920.

Russ ♂ Short form of ▷Russell, now also used occasionally as an independent given name. In some cases it may represent a transferred use of the surname *Russ*, from Old French *rous* 'red'.

Russell ♂ Transferred use of the common surname, originally from the Old French nickname *Rousel* 'little red one' (a diminutive of *rous* 'red', from Latin *russus*). Use as a given name may have been inspired by the philosopher Bertrand Russell (1872–1970), who was noted for his liberal agnostic views and his passionate championship of causes such as pacifism (in the First World War), free love, and nuclear disarmament. He was the grandson of the Victorian statesman Lord John Russell (1792–1878).

Rusty ♂, ♀ Nickname for someone with reddish-brown hair, a derivative of modern English *rust* (Old English *rūst*), also used in the United States as an independent given name.

Ruth ♀ Biblical name (of uncertain derivation) of a Moabite woman who left her own people to remain with her mother-in-law Naomi, and afterwards became the wife of Boaz and an ancestress of David. Her story is told in the book of the Bible that bears her name. It was used among the Puritans in England in the 16th century, partly because of its association with the English vocabulary word *ruth* meaning 'compassion'. It has always been popular as a Jewish name, but is now also widespread among people of many different cultures and creeds.

PET FORMS: **Ruthi, Ruthie.**

Ryan ♂, ♀ From the Irish surname, Gaelic *Ó Riain* 'descendant of Rian' (see Irish appendix). *Ryan* is associated with the film actor Ryan O'Neal (b. 1941) and is one of several names of Celtic origin that have become very popular throughout the English-speaking world since the 1990s. It is also now well established in North America as a girl's name.

Ryanne ♀ Modern name, coined as a feminine equivalent or more obviously feminine form of ▷Ryan.

Ryley ♂ Respelling of ▷Riley.

r

Ss

Sabella ♀ Modern name, apparently derived from ▷Isabella by the dropping of the initial vowel.

Sabina ♀ Latin name meaning 'Sabine woman', used occasionally in England since the 14th century. The Sabines were an ancient Italic race whose territory was early taken over by the Romans. According to tradition, the Romans made a raid on the Sabines and carried off a number of their women, but when the Sabines came for revenge the women succeeded in making peace between the two groups. The name *Sabina* was borne by three minor early Christian saints, in particular a Roman maiden martyred in about 127.

Sabrina ♀ From the name of a character in Celtic legend, who supposedly gave her name to the River Severn. In fact this is one of the most ancient of all British river names, and its true origins are obscure. Legend, as preserved by Geoffrey of Monmouth, had it that Sabrina was the illegitimate daughter of a Welsh king called Locrine, and was drowned in the river on the orders of the king's wife, Gwendolen. The river name is found in the form *Sabrina* in the Latin writings of Tacitus, Gildas, and Bede. Geoffrey of Monmouth comments that in Welsh the name is *Habren* (modern Welsh *Hafren*). The name of the legendary character is almost certainly derived from that of the river, rather than vice versa.

Sacha ♂ French version of ▷Sasha. This is one of the many names of Russian origin that were introduced to the English-speaking world, via French, at the time when Diaghilev's Ballet Russe made its great impact in Paris (1909–20).

Sacheverell ♂ Pronounced 'sash-ev-er-ell': transferred use of the surname, apparently originally a baronial name of Norman origin (from an unidentified place in Normandy believed to have been called *Saute-Chevreuil*, meaning 'roebuck leap'). It was made familiar as a given name by the writer Sacheverell Sitwell (1897–1985), who was named in honour of his ancestor William Sacheverell (1638–91), a minor Whig statesman.
PET FORM: **Sachie**.

Sadie ♀ Originally a pet form of ▷Sarah, but now generally considered to be an independent name. The exact formation is not clear: probably a nursery form.

Saffron ♀ From the name of the yellow food colouring and flavouring, derived from the stamens of a species of crocus. The word is from Old French *safran*, ultimately of Arabic origin: the bulb was introduced to Europe from the East in the early Middle Ages. As a given name it is most often given to babies born with strikingly golden hair.

Sage ♀, ♂ Mainly U.S.: apparently from the name of the herb (Middle English *sauge*, via Old French from Latin *salvia*); compare ▷Sorrel and ▷Bay. In part it may also have been taken from the vocabulary word meaning 'wise' (from Latin *sapius*).

Sal ♀, ♂ Short form of ▷Sally. In the U.S. it is used also as a short form of the Spanish male name **Salvador** or its Italian cognate, **Salvatore** (see respective appendices).

Sally ♀ In origin a pet form of ▷Sarah, but from the 20th century normally considered an independent name. It is frequently used as the first element in combinations such as *Sally-Anne* and *Sally-Jane*.

SHORT FORM: Sal.

Salome ♀ Greek form of an unrecorded Aramaic name, akin to the Hebrew word *shalom* 'peace'. It was common at the time of Christ, and was borne by one of the women who were at his tomb and witnessed the Resurrection (Mark 16:1–8). This would normally have led to its common use as a Christian name, and it is indeed found as such in medieval times. However, according to the Jewish historian Josephus, it was also the name of King Herod's stepdaughter, the daughter of Queen Herodias. In the Bible, a daughter of Herodias, generally identified as this Salome, danced for Herod and so pleased him that he offered to give her anything she wanted. Prompted by her mother, she asked for (and got) the head of John the Baptist, who was in one of Herod's prisons (Mark 6:17–28). This story so gripped medieval imagination that the name Salome became more or less taboo until the end of the 19th century, when Oscar Wilde wrote a play about her and some unconventional souls began to choose the name for their daughters.

Sam ♂, ♀ Short form of ▷Samuel (or, less frequently, of ▷Samson), and of ▷Samantha, now also used as an independent given name, especially for boys. It is also found as a short form of the Arabic names Samīr and Samīra (see appendix).

Samantha ♀ Of problematic and much debated origin. It arose in the United States at the end of the 18th century, possibly as a combination of *Sam* (from ▷Samuel) + a newly coined feminine suffix *-antha* (perhaps suggested by ▷Anthea).

Sami ♂ See Sāmi in Arabic appendix.

Sameer ♂ Respelling of Samīr (see Arabic appendix).

Sammy ♂, ♀ Pet form of ▷Samuel or ▷Samson or much less frequently of ▷Samantha. It is used as an independent given name, mainly for boys, and as a pet form of Samīr and Samīra (see Arabic appendix).

VARIANTS: Sammie, Sammi ♀.

Samsara ♀ From the Sanskrit word (meaning 'passing through') used in Hinduism and Buddhism to refer to the cycle of birth, death, and rebirth. It has sometimes been chosen as a given name by parents with an interest in Oriental spirituality.

Samson ♂ Biblical name (Hebrew *Shimshon*, probably derived from *shemesh* 'sun'), borne by a Jewish champion and judge famous for his prodigious strength. He was betrayed by his mistress, Delilah, and enslaved and blinded by the Philistines; nevertheless, he was able to bring the pillars of the temple of the Philistines crashing down in a final suicidal act of strength (Judges 13–16). This famous story provided the theme for Milton's poetic drama *Samson Agonistes* (1671), which is modelled on ancient Greek tragedy. In the Middle Ages the popularity of the given name was increased in Celtic areas by the fame of a 6th-century Celtic saint who bore it, probably as a classicized form of some ancient Celtic name. He was a Welsh monk who did missionary work in Cornwall and afterwards established a monastery at Dol in Brittany.

VARIANT: Sampson (usually a transferred use of the surname, derived from the given name in the Middle Ages).

Samuel ♂ Biblical name (Hebrew *Shemuel*), possibly meaning 'He (God) has hearkened' (presumably to the prayers of a mother for a son). It may also be understood as a contracted form of Hebrew *sha'ulme'el* meaning 'asked of God'. In the case of Samuel the son of Hannah, this would be more in keeping with his mother's statement 'Because I have asked him of the Lord' (1 Samuel

1:20). Living in the 11th century BC, Samuel was a Hebrew judge and prophet of the greatest historical importance, who established the Hebrew monarchy, anointing as king both Saul and, later, David. In the Authorized Version two books of the Old Testament are named after him, although in Roman Catholic and Orthodox versions of the Bible they are known as the first and second Book of Kings. The story of Samuel being called by God while still a child serving in the house of Eli the priest (1 Samuel 3) is of great vividness and has moved countless generations. In England and America the name was particularly popular among the 16th-century Puritans and among Nonconformists from the 17th to the 19th century. It became fashionable again in the 1990s.

SHORT FORM: **Sam.**

PET FORM: **Sammy.**

Sandford ♂ Mainly U.S.: transferred use of the surname (see ▷Sanford).

Sandra ♀ Short form of *Alessandra*, the Italian form of ▷Alexandra. A major influence in establishing this as a common given name in the English-speaking world was George Meredith's novel *Sandra Belloni* (1886), originally published as *Emilia in England* (1864); the heroine, Emilia Sandra Belloni, is a beautiful, passionate young singer.

Sandy ♀, ♂ Pet form, originally Scottish, of ▷Alexander and ▷Alexandra. As a girl's name, particularly, it is sometimes used independently, especially in the United States. It is also used as a nickname for someone with a crop of 'sandy' (light reddish-brown) hair.

VARIANT: **Sandie** ♀.

Sanford ♂ Mainly U.S.: transferred use of the surname, in origin a local name from any of numerous places in England called *Sandford*, from Old English *sand* 'sand' + *ford* 'ford'. Use as a given name honours Peleg Sanford, an early governor (1680–3) of Rhode Island.

VARIANT: **Sandford.**

Sapphire ♀ From the word for the gemstone (via Old French and Latin from Greek *sappheiros*, probably ultimately of Semitic origin). The Greek term seems to have originally denoted lapis lazuli, but was later transferred to the translucent blue stone. As a given name this is typically bestowed on a girl with deep blue eyes.

Sappho ♀ Name occasionally given in honour of the Greek lyric poet Sappho, who lived in the 6th century BC. Nothing is known about her life beyond what can be deduced from her poetry, which is fragmentary and may or may not be autobiographical, and the origin of her name is quite obscure. Her verse is noted for its lesbian passion; the name is now sometimes chosen by feminists in token of their liberation.

Sara ♀ Variant of ▷Sarah. This is the form used in the Greek of the New Testament (Hebrews 11:11).

Sarabeth ♀ Recent American coinage, a blend of ▷Sara and ▷Beth.

Sarah ♀ Biblical name, borne by the wife of Abraham and mother of Isaac. According to the Book of Genesis, she was originally called *Sarai* (possibly meaning 'contentious' in Hebrew), but had her name changed by God to the more auspicious *Sarah* 'princess' in token of a greater blessing (Genesis 17:15, 'And God said unto Abraham, As for Sarai thy wife, thou shalt not call her name Sarai, but Sarah shall her name be'). This has been one of the most enduringly popular girls' names.

VARIANTS: **Sara**, ▷**Zara.**

PET FORMS: ▷**Sally**, ▷**Sadie.**

Sarita ♀ Spanish diminutive form of ▷Sara, now also sometimes used as an independent first name in the English-speaking world.

S

Sasha ♀, ♂ English spelling of a Russian pet form of ▷Alexander and ▷Alexandra. It has been used in the English-speaking world as an independent name, introduced in the 20th century via France. Use as a girl's name in the English-speaking world is encouraged by the characteristically feminine *-a* ending.

Saskia ♀ Dutch name of uncertain derivation, now also used in the English-speaking world. It has been in use since the Middle Ages, and was borne, for example, by the wife of the artist Rembrandt. It may be derived from Germanic *sachs* 'Saxon'.

Satin ♀ From the vocabulary word denoting the sleek and luxurious fabric. The term reached English from French in the 14th century, and comes from Arabic *zaitūni*, a derivative of the place name *Tsingtung*, in southern China, from which the fabric was at first exported to the West.

Saul ♂ Biblical name (from a Hebrew word meaning 'asked for' or 'prayed for'), borne by one of the first kings of Israel. It was also the name of St Paul before his conversion to Christianity (Acts 9:4). It enjoyed some popularity among the Puritans, and has recently been revived somewhat, while remaining a mainly Jewish name.

Saundra ♀ Scottish variant of ▷Sandra, reflecting the same development in pronunciation as is shown by surnames such as *Saunders* and *Saunderson*, originally from a short form of ▷Alexander.

Savannah ♀ Mainly U.S.: apparently from the name of cities in Georgia and South Carolina. Both are on the Savannah River, ostensibly named with the word for a treeless plain (derived via Spanish from a native South American word). However, the river name may be an adaptation of some other name existing prior to European settlement. The given name may be taken directly from the vocabulary word, more under the influence of its sound than its meaning. In this case, it could be regarded as no more than a fanciful elaboration of ▷Anna or ▷Hannah.
VARIANT: **Savanna**.

Scarlett ♀ Name popularized by the central character in the novel *Gone With the Wind* (1936) by Margaret Mitchell, later made into a famous film. The characters in the novel bear a variety of unusual given names, which had a remarkable influence on naming practices throughout the English-speaking world in the 20th century. According to the novel, the name of the central character was Katie Scarlett O'Hara (the middle name representing her grandmother's maiden surname), but she was always known as Scarlett. The surname *Scarlett* is in origin an occupational name for a dyer or for a seller of rich, bright fabrics, from Old French *escarlate* 'scarlet cloth' (Late Latin *scarlata*, of uncertain, probably Semitic, derivation).
VARIANT: **Scarlet**.

Scott ♂ Although this was in use as a personal name both before and after the Norman Conquest, modern use in most cases almost certainly represents a transferred use of the surname. This originated as a byname for someone from Scotland or, within Scotland itself, for a member of the Gaelic-speaking people who originally came from Ireland. The given name is now often chosen by parents conscious of their Scottish ancestry and heritage, but it is also used more widely.

Seamus ♂ Anglicized spelling of *Séamas* or *Séamus*, Irish equivalents of ▷James. This is now sometimes used also by parents with no Irish connections.
VARIANT: **Shamus** (Anglicization).

Sean ♂ Anglicized spelling of Seán (pronounced 'shawn'), Irish equivalent of ▷John. The name has always been common in Ireland, but since the 1960s has frequently been chosen (usually without the accent) by parents who

S

have no Irish connections. One influence on its popularity has been the actor Sean Connery (b. 1930), of James Bond fame. See also Irish appendix.

VARIANTS: **Shaun, Shawn** (Anglicizations).

Sebastian ♂ From Latin *Sebastianus*, the name of a 3rd-century saint, a Roman soldier martyred by the arrows of his fellow officers. His sufferings were a favourite subject for medieval artists. The name means 'man from *Sebastē*', a city in Asia Minor so called from Greek *sebastos* 'august, venerable', used as a translation of the Latin imperial title *Augustus*.

SHORT FORM: **Seb.**

Selena ♀ Variant (the usual American form) of ▷Selina.

Selig ♂ Jewish: from the Yiddish vocabulary word *selig* 'happy, fortunate' (modern German *selig*), used as a vernacular translation of the Hebrew name ▷Asher.

VARIANT: **Zelig.**

Selima ♀ Of uncertain origin. Its first known occurrence is in a poem by Thomas Gray (1716–71), recording the death of Horace Walpole's cat Selima, 'drowned in a tub of gold fishes'. The metre shows that the name was stressed on the first syllable, but there is no clue as to its derivation. Gray (or Walpole) was possibly influenced by the Arabic name *Selim* 'peace'.

Selina ♀ Of uncertain origin. It is first found in the 17th century, and it may be an altered form of *Selena* (Greek *Selēnē*), the name of a goddess of the moon, or of *Celina* (Latin *Caelina*), a derivative of ▷Celia.

VARIANTS: **Selena, Celina.**

Selma ♀ Of uncertain origin, probably a contracted form of ▷Selima. It has also been occasionally used in Germany and Scandinavia, probably because it occurs as the name of Ossian's castle in Macpherson's ballads.

Selwyn ♂ Transferred use of the surname, which is of disputed origin.

There was a given name *Selewyn* in use in the Middle Ages, which probably represents a survival of an unrecorded Old English name derived from *sēle* 'prosperity' or *sele* 'hall' + *wine* 'friend'. Alternatively, the surname may be Norman, derived from *Seluein*, an Old French form of the Latin name *Silvanus* (from *silva* 'wood'; compare ▷Silas).

VARIANT: **Selwin.**

Sender ♂ Jewish: Yiddish form of ▷Alexander.

Septimus ♂ From a Late Latin name derived from Latin *septimus* 'seventh'. It was fairly commonly used in large Victorian families for the seventh son or a male seventh child, but is now rare (compare ▷Quintus, ▷Sextus, ▷Octavius, and ▷Nona).

Seraphina ♀ Latinate derivative of Hebrew *seraphim* 'burning ones', the name of an order of angels (Isaiah 6:2). It was borne by a rather shadowy saint who was martyred at the beginning of the 5th century in Italy, Spain, or Armenia.

VARIANT: **Serafina.**

SHORT FORM: **Fina.**

Serena ♀ From a Latin name, representing the feminine form of the adjective *serenus* 'calm, serene'. It was borne by an early Christian saint, about whom little is known. In her biography she is described as wife of the Emperor Domitian (AD 51–96), but there is no mention of her in any of the historical sources that deal with this period. In recent years the name has been associated with the American tennis player Serena Williams (b. 1981).

Sessy ♀ Pet form of ▷Cecilia.

Seth ♂ Biblical name (from a Hebrew word meaning 'appointed, placed'), borne by the third son of Adam, who was born after the murder of Abel (Genesis 4:25, 'And Adam knew his wife again; and she bare a son, and called his name Seth: For God, said she, hath appointed me another seed instead of Abel, whom

S

Cain slew'). It is recorded in England from the 1400s and was popular among the Puritans (particularly for children born after the death of an elder sibling). By the 20th century it had become rare. It was used for the darkly passionate rural character Seth Starkadder in Stella Gibbons's satirical novel *Cold Comfort Farm* (1932), and has recently enjoyed a revival. See also Indian appendix.

Sextus ♂ Traditional Latin given name, meaning 'sixth'. It was taken up in England during the Victorian period, often for a sixth son or a male sixth child, but it is now little used (compare ▷Quintus, ▷Septimus, ▷Octavius, and ▷Nona).

Seymour ♂ Transferred use of the surname, originally a Norman baronial name from *Saint-Maur* in Normandy. This place was so called from the dedication of its church to St *Maurus* (compare ▷Maurice).

Shabbetai ♂ Jewish: Hebrew name derived from *shabbāth* 'Sabbath' (itself a derivative of *shābath* 'rested'). It has been given to boys born on this day of the week.

VARIANT (CONTRACTED FORM): **Shabtai.**

Shae ♂, ♀ Modern variant of ▷Shea.

Shalene ♀ Modern variant of ▷Charlene.

Shalom ♂ Jewish: from the Hebrew vocabulary word meaning 'peace'.

Shamus ♂ See ▷Seamus.

Shan ♀ Informal short form of ▷Shantelle, ▷Shannon, or other names with this first syllable.

Shana ♀ Modern coinage, apparently an altered and more obviously feminine form of ▷Siân.

Shanae ♀ Modern name which seems to represent an elaboration of ▷Shana by association with names such as ▷Fae and ▷Gae.

Shandy ♀ Modern coinage, apparently from the term for the drink (earlier *shandigaff*, of uncertain origin); compare ▷Brandy and ▷Sherry. It may also have arisen as a combination of names such as ▷Shanelle and ▷Shantelle with ▷Mandy.

Shane ♂, occasionally ♀ Anglicized form of Irish Gaelic Seán (see ▷Sean), representing a Northern Irish pronunciation of the name. It has sometimes also been used as a girl's name.

Shanee ♀ Anglicized form of Welsh *Siani* (see ▷Siân).

Shanelle ♀ Recent coinage, apparently an elaborated form of ▷Chanel.

Shania ♀ Recent coinage, an elaborated form of ▷Shana, popularized by the singer Shania Twain. It is pronounced with the stress on the *i*, as in the traditional pronunciation of ▷Maria.

Shanice ♀ Modern coinage, a combination of the first syllable of ▷Shantelle, ▷Shannon or some other name with this first syllable with the name suffix *-ice* (compare for example ▷Janice).

Shanna ♀ Recent coinage, apparently an altered, more obviously feminine form of ▷Shannon.

Shannagh ♀ Variant of ▷Shannah or a transferred use of the Irish surname *Shannagh*, Gaelic Ó *Seanaigh* 'descendant of *Seanach*'. The latter is a Gaelic personal name derived from *sean* 'old, wise'.

Shannah ♀ Variant of ▷Shanna or a short form of *Shoshana*, the Hebrew form of ▷Susanna.

Shannon ♀, ♂ From the name of a river in Ireland. It is not clear why it has become so popular as a given name; compare ▷Clodagh. In part it may also be a transferred use of the Irish surname, Gaelic Ó *Seanáin* 'descendant of *Seanán*' (a diminutive of *Seán*). *Shannon* is not found as a traditional given name in Ireland itself.

Shantelle ♀ Recent coinage, apparently a respelled elaboration of ▷Chantal.

Shari ♀ Mainly U.S.: Anglicized spelling of *Sári*, the Hungarian form of ▷Sarah.

Sharissa ♀ Modern name, most often borne by African Americans. It is probably an elaborated form of ▷Sharon influenced by names such as ▷Clarissa and ▷Nerissa.

Sharlene ♀ Variant spelling of ▷Charlene.

Sharman ♂, ♀ As a boy's name this represents a transferred use of the surname, a variant of ▷Sherman. As a girl's name it is an altered form of ▷Charmaine.

Sharon ♀ From a biblical place name. The derivation is from the phrase 'I am the rose of Sharon, and the lily of the valleys' (Song of Solomon 2:1). The plant name 'rose of Sharon' is used for a shrub of the genus *Hypericum*, with yellow flowers, and for a species of hibiscus, with purple flowers. *Sharon* is recorded in the United States from the 18th century, as a name of both boys and girls. Since the 20th century, however, it has been used predominantly if not exclusively for girls.
VARIANT: **Sharron**.

Sharona ♀ Latinate elaborated form of ▷Sharon, now used in the English-speaking world.

Sharonda ♀ Elaboration of ▷Sharon, with the suffix *-da* abstracted from names such as ▷Glenda and ▷Linda.

Sharron ♀ Variant spelling of ▷Sharon.

Shaughan ♂ Variant spelling of ▷Shaun, probably influenced by ▷Vaughan.
VARIANT: **Shaughn**.

Shaun ♂, ♀ Anglicized spelling of Irish *Seán*; see ▷Sean. In Canada it is also found as a girl's name.

Shauna ♀ Name invented as a feminine form of ▷Shaun.

Shaw ♂ Transferred use of the surname, in origin a local name meaning 'wood, copse' (Old English *sceaga*, Old Norse *skógr*).

Shawn ♂, ♀ Anglicized spelling of Irish *Seán* (see ▷Sean), used mainly in North America. In Canada it is also found as a girl's name.

Shawna ♀ Recently coined feminine form of ▷Shawn.

Shay ♂, ♀ Variant spelling of ▷Shea.

Shayla ♀ Recent coinage, apparently a variant of ▷Sheila.

Shayna ♀ Modern name, either taken from a Yiddish name derived from German *Schön(e)* 'beautiful', or else a variant of ▷Sheena.

Shea ♂, ♀ Transferred use of the Irish surname, Gaelic *Ó Séaghdha* 'descendant of Séaghdha' (see Irish appendix).
VARIANTS: Shay, Shaye, Shae.

Sheba ♀ Short form of ▷Bathsheba.

Sheela ♀ Modern respelling of ▷Sheila.

Sheena ♀ Anglicized spelling of Sìne (Scottish) or Síne (Irish), Gaelic equivalents of ▷Jane (see respective appendices).

Sheila ♀ Anglicized spelling of *Síle*, the Irish Gaelic form of ▷Cecily. This name has become so common and widespread that it is hardly felt to be Irish any longer. In Australia since the 19th century it has been a slang generic term for any woman.
VARIANTS: Sheela, Sheelah, She(e)lagh.

Sheine ♀ Jewish (Yiddish): variant of ▷Shayna.

Shelagh ♀ Variant of ▷Sheila. The final consonants in the written form seem to have been added to give a Gaelic feel to the name. There is no etymological justification for them.

Shelby ♀, ♂ Mainly U.S.: transferred use of the surname (now more common in America than Britain). This has the form of a northern English local name, but no place bearing it has been identified. The chief inspiration for its use as a given name seems to be Isaac Shelby (1750–1826), Revolutionary commander and first governor of Kentucky.

Sheldon ♂ Transferred use of the surname, which originated as a local name from any of the various places so called. Examples occur in Derbyshire, Devon, and the West Midlands. The place name has a variety of different origins.

Shell ♀ Generally, this is a shortened form of ▷Michelle, respelled by association with the vocabulary word. In some cases it may be a shortened form of ▷Shelley.

Shelley ♀, occasionally ♂ Transferred use of the surname, the most famous bearer of which was the English Romantic poet Percy Bysshe Shelley (1792–1822). The surname is in origin a local name from one of the various places (in Essex, Suffolk, and Yorkshire) named in Old English as the 'wood (or clearing) on (or near) a slope (or ledge)'. The name is now used almost exclusively for girls, in part perhaps as a result of association with ▷Shirley (the actress Shelley Winters, 1922–2005, was born Shirley Schrift), and in part due to the characteristically feminine ending -(e)y.

Sheree ♀ Respelling of ▷Cherie.

Sheridan ♂, ♀ Transferred use of the surname made famous by the Irish playwright Richard Brinsley Sheridan (1751–1816). The surname is from Gaelic Ó Sirideáin (see Sirideán in Irish appendix). This is now occasionally also used as a girl's name. In the United States the inspiration is probably the Unionist commander General Philip Henry Sheridan (1831–88).

Sherman ♂ Transferred use of the surname, which is an occupational name for someone who trimmed the nap of woollen cloth after it had been woven, from Old English scēara 'shears' + mann 'man'. In the United States it is sometimes bestowed in honour of the Civil War general William Tecumseh Sherman (1820–71).

Sherry ♀ Probably in origin a respelled form of ▷Cherie, but now associated with the fortified wine, earlier sherry wine, so named from the port of Jérez in southern Spain.
VARIANTS: Sherrie, Sherri.

Shevaun ♀ Anglicized form of Irish ▷Siobhán.

Sheryl ♀ Variant spelling of ▷Cheryl.

Shifra ♀ Jewish: from Hebrew shifra 'beauty, grace'. Spelled Shiphrah in the Authorized Version, it was the name of one of the midwives who defied Pharaoh's order to drown all newborn Hebrew boys (Exodus 1:15–19).
VARIANT: Shiphrah.

Shilla ♀ Modern coinage, apparently an altered form of ▷Sheila.

Shiphrah ♀ Jewish: variant of ▷Shifra.

Shireen ♀ Variant of ▷Shirin, by association with the productive suffix -een, abstracted from names such as ▷Maureen and ▷Doreen.

Shirin ♀ Muslim name of Persian or Arabic origin, now beginning to be used quite widely in the English-speaking world.
VARIANTS: Shirrin, Shireen.

Shirley ♀, formerly ♂ Transferred use of the surname, in origin a local name from any of the various places (in the West Midlands, Derbyshire, Hampshire, and Surrey) named in Old English from scīr 'county, shire' or scīr 'bright' + lēah 'wood, clearing'. It was given by Charlotte Brontë to the heroine of her novel Shirley (1849). According to the novel, her parents had selected the name in prospect of a male child and used it regardless. *Shirley* had earlier been used as a boy's name (Charlotte Brontë refers to it as a 'masculine cognomen'), but this literary influence fixed it firmly as a girl's name. It was strongly reinforced during the 1930s and 40s by the popularity of the child film star Shirley Temple (b. 1928).

Shneur ♂ Jewish: Yiddish name, apparently derived from Latin *senior* 'elder'. Alternatively, it may have a Hebrew origin meaning 'two lights', a reference to illustrious ancestors on both sides of the child's family.

Shona ♀ Anglicized form of **Seonag** or **Seònaid** (see Scottish appendix). In America the name is pronounced identically with ▷Shauna, and may be used as a variant spelling of that name. It has also become popular as a Black name, probably in part because it is spelled the same as the name of a central African people. Compare ▷Zula for a similar formation.

Shraga ♂ Jewish: Aramaic name meaning 'fire, lantern'. It is usually paired with ▷Faivish as its Aramaic equivalent.

Shula ♀ As a Jewish name this is a short form of ▷Shulamit. It has been adopted by non-Jews in the English-speaking world as an independent given name. Its popularity has been influenced by its use as the name of a character in *The Archers*, the long-running radio soap opera.

Shulamit ♀ Hebrew name meaning 'peacefulness', a derivative of *shalom* 'peace'. The name occurs as a personification in the Song of Solomon (6:13): 'Return, return, O Shulamite; return, return, that we may look upon thee'. It is a popular modern Hebrew name.

VARIANTS: Shulamith, Shulamite.

Shaz ♀ Modern informal pet form of ▷Sharon.

VARIANT: Shazza.

Siân ♀ Welsh form of ▷Jane, derived from Anglo-Norman form *Jeanne*. It is now quite widely used in the English-speaking world, often without the accent.

PET FORMS: Siana, Siani.

Sibb ♀ Short form of ▷Sibyl, popular in the Middle Ages, but now rare.

Sibyl ♀ Variant spelling of ▷Sybil. Even in classical times there was confusion between the two vowels in this word.

Sidney ♂, ♀ Transferred use of the surname, which is usually said to be a Norman baronial name from *Saint-Denis* in France. However, at least in the case of the family of the poet and soldier Sir Philip Sidney (1554–86), it appears to have a more humble origin, being derived from lands in Surrey named as the 'wide meadow' (Old English *sīdan* 'wide' (dative case) + *ēg* 'island in a river, riverside meadow'). Evidence of use as a given name dates back to the 18th century, and the popularity of the boy's name increased considerably in the 19th century, probably due in part to Sydney Carton, hero of Dickens's novel *A Tale of Two Cities* (1859). As a girl's name it arose in part as a contracted form of ▷Sidony; coincidentally it represents an altered form of ▷Sindy. In recent years, the girls' name, usually written Sydney, has become popular throughout the English-speaking world, especially in North America.

VARIANT: Sydney.

SHORT FORM: Sid.

Sidony ♀ From Latin *Sidonia*, feminine of *Sidonius*, in origin an ethnic name meaning 'man from Sidon' (the city in Phoenicia). This came to be associated with the Greek word *sindon* 'winding sheet'. Two saints called Sidonius are venerated in the Catholic Church: Sidonius Apollinaris, a 4th-century bishop of Clermont, and a 7th-century Irish monk who was the first abbot of the monastery of Saint-Saëns

S

(which is named with a much altered form of his name).

VARIANT: **Sidonie**.

Siena ♀ Apparently from the name of the city in central Italy (compare ▷Ravenna and ▷Venetia). The place name is derived from that of a Gaulish tribe who once occupied the area, recorded in Latin sources as the *Senones*. Use as a given name may in part also have been inspired by the name ▷Sierra.

VARIANT: **Sienna**.

Sierra ♀ Mainly North American: apparently from the Spanish vocabulary word denoting a mountain range (from Latin *serra* 'saw', referring to the saw-toothed appearance). The reasons for its adoption and popularity are not clear, but it has remained among the most frequent girls' names in the United States since the late 1980s. Compare ▷Savannah.

Sigmund ♂ From an old Germanic personal name composed of the elements *sige* 'victory' + *mund* 'protector'. It was introduced to Britain both before and after the Norman Conquest, from Scandinavia and Normandy respectively, but it eventually fell out of use. As a modern given name in the English-speaking world it is a recent reintroduction from Scandinavia and Germany.

Sigrid ♀ From an Old Norse female personal name derived from *sigr* 'victory' + *fríðr* 'fair, beautiful'. The name is now also occasionally used in the English-speaking world.

Silas ♂ Of New Testament origin: Greek name, a contracted form of *Silouanus* (Latin *Silvanus*, a derivative of *silva* 'wood'). This name was borne by a companion of St Paul, who is also mentioned in the Bible in the full form of his name. The Eastern Church recognizes two separate saints, Silas and Silvanus, but honours both on the same day (20 July).

Silver ♀, ♂ From the name of the precious metal (Old English *siolfor*). It is sometimes given to babies born with very fair hair. It is also occasionally used as a pet form of the names ▷Silvestra and ▷Silvester.

Silvester ♂ From a Latin name, meaning 'of the woods'. It was borne by various early saints, most notably by the first pope to govern a Church free from persecution (314–35). His feast is on 31 December, and in various parts of Europe the New Year is celebrated under his name. The name has been continuously, if modestly, used from the Middle Ages to the present day.

VARIANT: **Sylvester**.

Silvestra ♀ Latin feminine form of ▷Silvester.

Silvia ♀ From Roman legend. Rhea *Silvia* was, according to Roman tradition, the mother of the twins Romulus and Remus, who founded Rome. Her name probably represents a reworking, by association with Latin *silva* 'wood', of some pre-Roman form. It was borne by a 6th-century saint, mother of Gregory the Great, and has always been relatively popular in Italy. Shakespeare used it as a typically Italian name in *Two Gentlemen of Verona*. It is also well established as an independent name in English-speaking countries.

VARIANT: **Sylvia**.

Sim ♂ Short form of ▷Simon, now rare, but more common in the Middle Ages, when it gave rise to the surnames *Simms* and *Simpson*.

Simcha ♂, ♀ Jewish: Hebrew name, meaning 'joy'. It was originally a female name, but is now more commonly given to males among Ashkenazic Jews.

Simeon ♂ Biblical name, from a Hebrew word meaning 'hearkening'. It is borne by several Old and New

Testament characters, rendered in the Authorized Version variously as *Shimeon*, *Simeon*, and *Simon*. In the New Testament, it is the spelling used for the man who blessed the infant Christ (Luke 2:25).

Simmie ♂ Pet form of ▷Simon, used mainly in Scotland.

Simon ♂ Usual English form of ▷Simeon, borne in the New Testament by various characters: two apostles, a brother of Jesus, a Pharisee, a leper, a tanner, a sorcerer (who offered money for the gifts of the Holy Ghost, giving rise to the term *simony*), and the man who carried Jesus's cross to the Crucifixion.

COGNATES: Irish: Síomón. Scottish Gaelic: Sim, Simidh. Dutch: Siemen. Scandinavian: Simon. French: Simon. Portuguese: Simão. Italian: Simone. Russian: Semyon. Polish: Szymon. Czech: Šimon. Slovenian: Simon. Finnish: Simo. Hungarian: Simon.

Simone ♀ French feminine form of ▷Simon, now also quite frequently used in the English-speaking world.

Simran ♀, ♂ Recent coinage, unexplained.

Sinclair ♂ Transferred use of the Scottish surname, in origin a Norman baronial name borne by a family that held a manor in northern France called *Saint-Clair*, probably Saint-Clair-sur-Elle in La Manche. It is an extremely common Scottish surname: the Norman family received the earldoms of Caithness and Orkney. They merged with the Norse- and Gaelic-speaking inhabitants of their domains to form one of the most powerful of the Scottish Highland families. The name of the novelist Sinclair Lewis (1885–1951) may have had some influence on recent use of this as a given name.

Sinda ♀ Variant of ▷Sindy.

Sindy ♀ Variant spelling of ▷Cindy that came into use in about 1950 and is most frequent in America.

Sinéad ♀ Irish Gaelic form of ▷Janet, pronounced 'shin-**aid**', derived from the French form *Jeanette*. It is now quite popular outside Ireland, usually written without the accent, as in the case of the Irish actress Sinead Cusack (b. 1948).

Siobhán ♀ Irish Gaelic form of ▷Joan, pronounced 'shiv-**awn**' or '**shoo**-an', derived from the Anglo-Norman form *Jehanne*. It became widely known and adopted in the English-speaking world, written without the accent, through the actress Siobhan McKenna (1923–86).

VARIANTS: Shevaun, Chevonne (Anglicized).

Sissy ♀ Pet form of ▷Cecilia.

VARIANTS: Sissey, Sissie.

Skipper ♂ Originally a nickname from the vocabulary word *skipper* 'boss' (originally denoting a ship's captain, from Middle Dutch *schipper*), or else representing an agent derivative of *skip* 'to leap or bound' (probably of Scandinavian origin). It is now sometimes used as an independent given name in the United States.

SHORT FORMS: Skip, Skipp.

Sky ♀, occasionally ♂ From the vocabulary word (from Old Norse *ský* 'cloud'). This was one of the names taken from the world of nature (compare ▷Rainbow, ▷Leaf, ▷River) during the 1960s under the influence of the hippy and flower-power movements. It continues to enjoy a modest popularity.

Skylar ♀, ♂ Mainly U.S.: modern coinage, apparently derived from the Dutch surname *Schuyler* (meaning 'scholar, school teacher') and possibly adopted in honour of Philip Schuyler (1733–1804), a member of Congress and a leading figure in the American Revolution. As a given name it was earlier borne mainly by boys but is now more popular for girls.

Skye ♀ Elaborated spelling of ▷Sky, influenced by the name of the island of *Skye* in the Hebrides, which is of Gaelic origin. Compare ▷Ailsa, ▷Iona, and ▷Isla for similar derivations.

Slaney ♂, ♀ Transferred use of the surname, which has recently come to be used fairly regularly in the United States as a given name for boys and less frequently also for girls.

Slater ♂ Transferred use of the surname, in origin an occupational name for a builder who specialized in fixing slates on roofs.

Sloan ♂ Transferred use of the Irish surname, Gaelic form *Ó Sluaghhadáin* ('descendant of *Sluaghadhán*'). The latter is a diminutive of the personal name *Sluaghadh*, meaning 'expedition, raid'. Recently the surname has occasionally been used as a given name, mainly in the United States.

Sloane ♀ In origin a variant of ▷Sloan. In the latter half of the 20th century it was associated with Sloane Square in west London, where a particular kind of fashionable young, upper-class women (known colloquially as 'Sloane Rangers') tended to live.

Sly ♂, ♀ Mainly U.S.: recent coinage. The reasons for its adoption as a given name are not clear. In the case of the American actor Sylvester Stallone, it is used as a contracted pet form of his given name. As a girl's name it may have originated as a pet form of ▷Selina. The fact that it coincides in form with the vocabulary word *sly*, meaning 'cunning' or 'devious', does not seem to have inhibited its current use as a given name.

Sofia ♀ Variant spelling of ▷Sophia.

Sofie ♀ Variant spelling of ▷Sophie.

Solomon ♂ Biblical name (Hebrew *Shlomo*, derived from *shalom* 'peace'), borne by one of the great kings of Israel, son of David and Bathsheba, who was legendary for his wisdom (2 Samuel 12–24; 1 Kings 1–11; 2 Chronicles 1–9). The books of Proverbs and Ecclesiastes were ascribed to him, and the Song of Solomon, otherwise known as the Song of Songs, bears his name. It has been sporadically used among Gentiles since the Middle Ages, but is still mainly a Jewish name.
SHORT FORM: **Sol.**
PET FORM: **Solly.**

Sondra ♀ Of recent origin, apparently an altered form of ▷Sandra.

Sonia ♀ Russian pet form of *Sofya* (see ▷Sophia), used as a given name in its own right in Britain and elsewhere since the 1920s.
VARIANT: **Sonya.**

Sonny ♂ Originally a nickname, from a pet form of the word *son* used as an affectionate term of address, but now used quite frequently as a first name in its own right. In communities of Italian origin, it is sometimes used as an English equivalent of **Sandro** (see Italian appendix).

Sonya ♀ Variant spelling of ▷Sonia.

Soo ♀ Recent coinage, a fanciful respelling of ▷Sue.

Sophia ♀ From the Greek word meaning 'wisdom'. The Eastern cult of St Sophia arose as a result of misinterpretation of the phrase *Hagia Sophia* 'holy wisdom' as if it meant 'St Sophia'. The name became popular in England in the 17th and 18th centuries—the heroine of Fielding's novel *Tom Jones* (1749) is called Sophia Weston—and has been increasing in popularity since the 1990s. In Scotland it has been used as an Anglicized form of the Gaelic name **Beathag** (see Scottish appendix).
VARIANT: **Sofia.**

Sophie ♀ French form of ▷Sophia. In the English-speaking world, where it is often taken as a pet form of that name, it has been popular since the 18th century, and has become particularly fashionable since the 1990s.

VARIANTS: **Sofie, Sophy.**

Sorrel ♀ From the vocabulary word for the plant (Old French *surele*, apparently a derivative of *sur* 'sour' (of Germanic origin), alluding to the acid taste of its leaves).

VARIANTS: **Sorrell, Sorell, Sorel.**

Spencer ♂ Transferred use of the surname, in origin an occupational name for a 'dispenser' of supplies in a manor house. This is the name of a great English noble family, traditionally supposed to be descended from someone who performed this function in the royal household. Its popularity as a given name was influenced in the mid-20th century by the American film actor Spencer Tracy (1900–67).

Spike ♂ Normally a nickname, but sometimes used as a given name in recent years, owing to the influence of the bandleader Spike Jones (1911–65) and the comedian Spike Milligan (1918–2002, born Terence Alan Milligan). As a nickname it usually refers to an unruly tuft or 'spike' of hair.

Sprite ♀ Modern coinage, from the vocabulary word denoting a small supernatural creature, mischievous yet benevolent (from Old French *esprit*, Latin *spiritus* 'spirit, incorporeal being').

Sroel ♂ Jewish: Yiddish form of ▷Israel.

Stacey ♀, occasionally ♂ Of uncertain derivation. *Stacey* and *Stace* are recorded as given names in the Middle Ages, probably pet forms of ▷Eustace. The medieval name seems to have fallen out of use by the 16th century, and the modern given name is probably a transferred use of the surname, which is likewise derived from ▷Eustace. It is not clear why this name should have become so common in the 1970s and

80s as a girl's name (less commonly as a boy's name).

VARIANTS: **Stacy, Stacie, Staci.**

Stafford ♂ Transferred use of the surname, in origin a local name from any of various places so called from Old English *stæð* 'landing place' + *ford* 'ford', most notably the county town of Staffordshire. This was the surname of the family that held the dukedom of Buckingham in the 15th and 16th centuries.

Stamford ♂ Transferred use of the surname, in origin a variant of ▷Stanford. Use as a given name may in part have been influenced by the city of Stamford in Connecticut (established in 1642) and by Sir Thomas Stamford Raffles (1781–1826), British founder of Singapore.

Stan ♂ Short form of ▷Stanley, also used as an independent given name.

Standish ♂ Transferred use of the English surname, in origin a local name from a place in Lancashire named with the Old English elements *stān* 'stone' + *edisc* 'pasture'. This was borne most famously by Miles Standish (?1584–1656), soldier, military leader, and law-enforcement officer of the Pilgrim Fathers, the subject of a historically inaccurate poem by Longfellow.

Stanford ♂ Transferred use of the surname, in origin a local name from the very numerous places named with the Old English elements *stān* 'stone' + *ford* 'ford'. Use as a given name may have been influenced by the prestigious Californian university named after Senator Leland Stanford, on whose land it was built. It may also in some cases have been adopted as an alternative elaboration of ▷Stan.

Stanislas ♂ Latinized form of an old Slavonic personal name composed of *stan* 'government' + *slav* 'glory'. St Stanislas Szczepanowski (1030–79) was a bishop of Cracow who was killed by King Bolesaw the Cruel of Poland. The

S

name recurs in a Sussex family named Browne from the 16th to the 18th century. It is still found occasionally in the English-speaking world, used sometimes as an Anglicized form of Irish Anéislis (see Irish appendix).

VARIANT: **Stanislaus.**

Stanley ♂ Transferred use of the surname, in origin a local name from any of numerous places (in Derbys., Durham, Gloucs., Staffs., Wilts., and Yorks.) so called from Old English *stān* 'stone' + *lēah* 'wood, clearing'. This is well established as a given name, and has been widely used as such since the 1880s. It had been in occasional use over a century earlier. Its popularity seems to have stemmed at least in part from the fame of the explorer Sir Henry Morton Stanley (1841–1904), who was born in Wales as John Rowlands but later took the name of his adoptive father, a New Orleans cotton dealer.

SHORT FORM: **Stan.**

Star ♀ Modern name, a vernacular equivalent of ▷Stella.

VARIANT: **Starr.**

Steel ♂ From the name of the hard and durable metal (Middle English *steel*, from Old English *stȳle*), in part a transferred use of the surname derived from this word as a nickname or occupational name.

VARIANT: **Steele.**

Stefan ♂ Scandinavian, German, Dutch, Polish, and South Slavic form of ▷Stephen, now also quite commonly used in the English-speaking world.

Steff ♀ Short form of ▷Stephanie.

Steffany ♀ Variant spelling of ▷Stephanie.

Stella ♀ From Latin *stella* 'star'. This was not used as a given name before the 16th century, when Sir Philip Sidney seems to have been the first to use it (as a name deliberately far removed from the prosaic range of everyday names) in the sonnets

addressed by Astrophel to his lady, Stella. *Stella Maris* 'star of the sea' was, however, established long before that as a byname of the Virgin Mary, and may have had some influence on the choice of the word as a name.

Steph ♀ Short form of ▷Stephanie.

Stephan ♂ Variant of ▷Stephen, preserving the vowels of the Greek name.

Stephanie ♀ From French *Stéphanie*, vernacular form of Latin *Stephania*, a variant of *Stephana*, which was in use among early Christians as a feminine form of *Stephanus* (see ▷Stephen). It is very popular in the United States.

VARIANTS: **Steffany, Stefanie** (as borne by the American film actress Stefanie Powers, b. 1942).

SHORT FORMS: **Steff, Steph.**

PET FORMS: **Steffie, Steffy, Stevie.**

Stephen ♂ Usual English spelling of the name of the first Christian martyr (Acts 6–7), whose feast is accordingly celebrated next after Christ's own (26 December). His name is derived from the Greek word *stephanos* 'garland, crown'.

VARIANTS: **Steven, Stephan.**

SHORT FORM: **Steve.**

PET FORM: **Stevie.**

COGNATES: Irish: **Stiofán, Stiana.** Scottish Gaelic: **Steaphan.** Welsh: **Steffan.** German: **Stefan, Stephan.** Dutch: **Steffen.** Scandinavian: **Stefan.** Swedish: **Staffan.** French: **Étienne, Stéphane.** Spanish: **Estéban.** Catalan: **Esteve.** Portuguese: **Estévão.** Italian: **Stefano.** Russian: **Stepan, Stefan.** Polish: **Szczepan, Stefan.** Czech: **Štěpán.** Croatian: **Stjepan.** Serbian: **Stevan.** Slovenian: **Štefan.** Hungarian: **István.** Lithuanian: **Steponas.**

Sterling ♂ Mainly U.S.: transferred use of the surname, a variant of ▷Stirling. As a given name, however, it is likely to have been chosen because of its association with the vocabulary word occurring in such phrases as 'sterling qualities' and 'sterling worth'. This is derived from the Middle English word *sterrling* 'little star': some Norman coins had a little star on them. A 20th-century influence on the name was the American film actor Sterling Hayden (1916–86).

Steve ♂ Short form of ▷Stephen and ▷Steven, also used as an independent given name. It is associated with the American film stars Steve McQueen (1930–80), noted for his 'tough guy' roles, and Steve Martin (b. 1945).

Steven ♂ Variant of ▷Stephen, reflecting the normal pronunciation of the name in the English-speaking world.

Stevie ♂, ♀ Pet form of ▷Stephen and of ▷Stephanie. Well-known bearers have included the poetess Stevie Smith (1902–71), whose baptismal name was Florence Margaret Smith, and the American singer Stevie Wonder (b. 1950 as Steveland Judkins).

Stewart ♂ Variant of ▷Stuart, less common as a given name, although more common as a surname.

Stirling ♂ Transferred use of the surname, in origin a local name from the town in Scotland. The place name is of uncertain derivation, perhaps from Old Welsh *ystre Velyn* 'dwelling of Melyn'.

St John ♂ Name expressing devotion to St John, generally pronounced 'sin-jen'; it has been in use in the English-speaking world, mainly among Roman Catholics, from the last two decades of the 19th century up to the present day.

Stone ♂ Probably for the most part a transferred use of the surname, which originally denoted someone who lived near a large boulder or outcrop. In other cases it may derive directly from the vocabulary word (Old English *stān*), and be chosen as representing qualities of strength and endurance.

Storm ♀, ♂ Apparently a 20th-century coinage, although it may have been in use slightly earlier. The name is presumably derived from the vocabulary word, adopted by admirers of *Sturm und Drang*. It is used mainly for girls in Britain, but as a boy's name in the United States.

Stuart ♂ From the French version of the surname *Stewart*. This form was introduced to Scotland in the 16th century by Mary Stuart, Queen of Scots, who was brought up in France. The surname originated as an occupational or status name for someone who served as a *steward* in a manor or royal household. The Scottish royal family of this name are traditionally supposed to be descended from a family who were hereditary stewards in Brittany before the Conquest. Use as a given name originated in Scotland, but is now widespread throughout the English-speaking world.
VARIANT: **Stewart.**
SHORT FORMS: **Stu, Stew.**

Sue ♀ Short form of ▷Susan and, less commonly, of ▷Susanna and ▷Suzanne.
VARIANTS: **Su, Soo.**

Sukie ♀ Pet form of ▷Susan, very common in the 18th century, but now rare.
VARIANT: **Sukey.**

Summer ♀ From the vocabulary word for the season (Old English *sumor*), used in modern times as a given name because of its pleasant associations and currently in vogue.

Sunny ♀ From the vocabulary word used to describe someone with a bright and cheerful personality (a derivative of *sun*, referring to the light and warmth provided by that heavenly body). Compare ▷Sonny.

Susan ♀ English vernacular form of ▷Susanna. Among well-known bearers are the American film stars Susan

S

Hayward (1918–75) and Susan Sarandon (b. 1946 as Susan Tomalin).

VARIANT: **Suzan.**

SHORT FORMS: **Sue, Su, Soo.**

PET FORMS: **Susie, Suzie, Susy, Suzy, Sukie, Sukey.**

Susanna ♀ New Testament form (Luke 8:3) of the Hebrew name *Shoshana* (from *shoshan* 'lily', which in modern Hebrew also means 'rose').

VARIANTS: **Susana, Suzanna(h), ▷Susannah.**

COGNATES: English: **Susan.** Scottish Gaelic: **Siùsan, Siùsaidh.** German: **Susanne, Susanna.** Dutch: **Susanna.** Scandinavian: **Susanne.** French: **Suzanne.** Spanish, Portuguese: **Susana.** Italian: **Susanna.** Polish: **Zuzanna.** Czech: **Zuzana.** Croatian, Serbian: **Suzana.** Finnish: **Susanna.** Hungarian: **Zsuzsanna.**

Susannah ♀ Variant of ▷Susanna, in 2003 the most common in this group of names. It is the form of the name used in the Old Testament. The tale of Susannah, wife of Joachim, and the elders who falsely accused her of adultery, is to be found in the apocryphal book that bears her name, and was popular in the Middle Ages and later.

Susie ♀ Pet form of ▷Susan and, less commonly, of ▷Susanna(h) and ▷Suzanne. It is occasionally used as an independent given name.

Suzanne ♀ French form of ▷Susanna, now also used in the English-speaking world.

Suzette ♀ French pet form of ▷Suzanne, now also used in the English-speaking world as an independent given name.

Suzie ♀ Pet form of ▷Susan and, less commonly, of ▷Susanna(h) and ▷Suzanne. It is occasionally used as an independent given name.

Sven ♂ Swedish: from the Old Norse byname *Sveinn* 'boy, lad'. It is now also used occasionally in England, perhaps with reference to the England (football team) coach, Sven Göran Eriksson (b. 1948), and in the United States.

Swift ♂ Probably from the name of the bird, so called because of its rapid, darting flight (Old English *swift*, referring to a sweeping motion). In part it may represent a transferred use of the surname, in origin usually a nickname for a fast runner. As an Irish surname it represents an Anglicized form of Gaelic *Ó Fuada* 'descendant of *Fuada*', a personal name derived from *fuad* 'haste'.

Sybil ♀ From the name (Greek *Sibylla* or *Sybilla*, with confusion over the vowels from an early period) of a class of ancient prophetesses inspired by Apollo. According to medieval theology, they were pagans denied the knowledge of Christ but blessed by God with some insight into things to come and accordingly admitted to heaven. It was thus regarded as a respectable name to be borne by Christians. This name was introduced to England by the Normans and enjoyed considerable popularity in the Middle Ages.

VARIANTS: **Sybilla (Latinate), Sybille (from French); Sibyl, Sibilla, Sibella.**

Sydney ♀, ♂ Variant spelling of ▷Sidney. (It was a medieval practice to write *y* for *i*, for greater clarity since *i* was easily confused with other letters.) Although traditionally a boy's name, it suddenly came into fashion as a girl's name at the beginning of the 21st century and, in this form, is now used more frequently for girls than boys in England and North America.

Sylphide ♀ From the vocabulary word referring to one of the invisible spirits supposed to populate the air (from French, a derivative of *sylpha*, a Latinate term apparently coined by Paracelsus).

Sylvester ♂ Variant spelling of
▷Silvester.

Sylvestra ♀ Variant spelling of
▷Silvestra.

Sylvia ♀ Variant spelling of ▷Silvia,
now rather more common than the
plain form.

Sylvie ♀ French form of ▷Silvia, now
also used in the English-speaking world.

Tt

Tabitha ♀ Aramaic name, meaning 'doe' or 'roe', borne in the New Testament by a woman who was restored to life by St Peter (Acts 9:36–41). In the biblical account this form of the name is given together with its Greek equivalent, ▷Dorcas. It was one of the names much favoured by Puritans and Dissenters from the 16th to the 19th centuries.

PET FORM: **Tabby** (obsolete).

Tacey ♀ As a medieval given name this is derived from the Latin imperative *tace* 'be silent', regarded as a suitable admonition to women. As a modern name, it is a pet form of ▷Tacita or perhaps derived from ▷Tracy.

Tacita ♀ From Latin *Tacita*, feminine form of the Roman family name *Tacitus*, originally a byname meaning 'silent'.

Tad ♂ Normally an Anglicized form of Gaelic **Tadhg** (see Irish appendix), but sometimes a short form of ▷Thaddeus. It is also used as an independent given name, especially in America.

Talbot ♂ Transferred use of the surname. This is of much debated origin, but seems most likely to be from a Norman French personal name of Germanic origin, composed of the elements *tal* 'to destroy' + *bod* 'message, tidings'. This is the surname of an ancient Irish family of Norman origin, who have held the earldoms of Shrewsbury and Waterford since the 15th century. The old word *talbot*, denoting a kind of hunting dog, is from the surname.

Talia ♀ Variant spelling of ▷Thalia or a short form of ▷Natalia.

VARIANT: **Talya**.

Talitha ♀ Of New Testament origin: from an Aramaic word meaning 'little girl'. Jesus raised a child from the dead with the words 'Talitha cumi; which is, being interpreted, Damsel, I say unto thee, arise' (Mark 5:41).

Tallulah ♀ Either a variant of **Talulla** (see Irish appendix); or it may be taken from the place name Tallulah Falls, Georgia, which is of American Indian origin. It is best known as the name of the American actress Tallulah Bankhead (1903–68). In spite of its exotic appearance, her given name was not adopted for the sake of her career but inherited from her grandmother. It has recently become modestly fashionable.

Tamara ♀ Russian: probably derived from the Hebrew name *Tamar*, from a vocabulary word meaning 'date palm', with the addition of the feminine suffix *-a*. The name Tamar is borne in the Bible by two female characters: the daughter-in-law of Judah, who is involved in a somewhat seamy story of sexual intrigue (Genesis 38), and a daughter of King David (2 Samuel 13), the full sister of Absalom, who is raped by her half-brother Amnon, for which Absalom kills him. It is rather surprising, therefore, that it should have given rise to such a popular given name. However, Absalom himself later has a daughter named Tamar, who is referred to as 'a woman of a fair countenance' (2 Samuel 14:27), and the name may derive its popularity from this reference. The name is now also used in the English-speaking world.

Tammy ♀ Pet form of ▷Tamara and ▷Tamsin, also used as an independent given name.

Tamsin ♀ Contracted form of Latinate *Thomasina*, a feminine form of ▷Thomas. This was relatively common throughout Britain in the Middle Ages, but confined to Cornwall immediately before its recent revival.

VARIANT: **Tamzin** (modern respelling).

Tania ♀ Variant spelling of ▷Tanya.

Tanner ♂ Mainly U.S.: transferred use of the common surname, in origin an occupational name for someone who treated animal skins to form leather (via Old English and Old French from a Late Latin word apparently derived from a Celtic name for the oak, whose bark was used in the process).

Tansy ♀ From the vocabulary word for the flower (Old French *tanesie*, derived from Greek *athanasia* 'immortal').

Tanya ♀ Russian pet form of ▷Tatiana, now quite commonly used as an independent given name in the English-speaking world.

VARIANT: **Tania**.

Tara ♀ From the name of a place in Meath, seat of the high kings of Ireland, named with Gaelic *teamhair* 'hill'. It has been used as a girl's name in America since the 1940s, probably as a result of the success of the film *Gone with the Wind* (1939), in which the estate of this name has great emotional significance. In Britain it was not much used before the late 1960s. Its popularity then was influenced by the character Tara King in the television series *The Avengers*.

VARIANT: **Tarra**.

Taree ♀ Occasionally used as a given name in Australia. It appears to represent an elaboration of ▷Tara, influenced by the name of a place in New South Wales. The place name probably derives from an Aboriginal word for a type of fig tree found in the area.

Tarquin ♂ The name borne by two early kings of Rome, Tarquinius Priscus 'the Old' (616–578 BC) and Tarquinius Superbus 'the Proud' (534–510 BC). It is of uncertain, probably Etruscan, origin; many of the most ancient Roman institutions and the vocabulary associated with them, as well as many Roman family names, were borrowed from the Etruscans. The name is now occasionally used in the English-speaking world.

Tarra ♀ Variant of ▷Tara.

Tasha ♀ Short form of ▷Natasha, now also used as an independent given name.

Tate ♂, ♀ Transferred use of the surname, which was derived in the medieval period from the Old English personal name *Tāta*.

Tatiana ♀ Russian: of early Christian origin. This was the name of various early saints honoured particularly in the Eastern Church. In origin it is a feminine form of Latin *Tatianus*, a derivative of *Tatius*, a Roman family name of obscure origin. Titus Tatius was, according to tradition, a king of the Sabines who later shared with Romulus the rule over a united population of Sabines and Latins. The name is now also used in the English-speaking world, though not so commonly as the pet form ▷Tanya. See Tatyana in Russian appendix.

Tawny ♀ From the vocabulary word denoting a light brown hair colour (Anglo-Norman *tauné*, Old French *tané* 'tanned'). This is probably a modern name created on the lines of examples such as ▷Ginger and ▷Sandy. However, it may also be a transferred use of the surname *Tawney*, which is a Norman baronial name from one of two places in Normandy: *Saint-Aubin-du-Thenney* or *Saint-Jean-du-Thenney*.

VARIANT: **Tawney**.

Taylor ♂, ♀ Transferred use of the surname, in origin an occupational name for a tailor (Anglo-Norman *taillour*, a derivative of *taillier* 'to cut', Late Latin *taleare*). Use as a given name was influenced by the U.S. president Zachary Taylor (1784–1850), hero of the Mexican War. As a girl's name it became well established in North America in the 1980s and has since also taken root in Britain.

VARÍANT: **Tayler**, **Tayla**.

Teal ♀ One of the girls' names taken from birds in the latter part of the 20th century. The teal is a kind of small duck; its name is attested in English since the 14th century and is probably connected with Middle Low German *tēlink*, Middle Dutch *tēling*.

VARIANT: **Teale**.

Ted ♂ Short form of ▷Edward, now also used as an independent given name.

Teddy ♂, occasionally ♀ Originally a pet form of ▷Theodore, but now generally used for ▷Edward, and also as an independent given name. Teddy bears were so named after the American president Theodore Roosevelt (1858–1919). Occasionally it is also used as a girl's name, in part as a pet form of ▷Edwina.

Tegan ♀ Welsh: modern coinage based on *teg* 'lovely', now also in general use outside Wales.

VARIANTS: **Teagan** (♀, ♂); **Teigan**, **Tiegan**.

Tel ♂ Altered short form of ▷Terry or ▷Terence, of recent origin. For the substitution of -*l* for -*r*, compare ▷Hal.

Tempe ♀ Pronounced 'tem-pee': from the name of a valley in eastern Greece, situated between Mount Olympus and Mount Ossa. In classical times it was regarded as the home of the Muses. The place name may be derived from Greek *temnein* 'to cut', referring to a valley carved between mountains.

Tempest ♂, ♀ Transferred use of the surname, which most probably originated as a nickname for someone with a stormy temperament, from the Middle English and Old French vocabulary word *tempeste*, from Latin *tempestas*. This was used in Yorkshire as a given name from the 1570s onwards, almost always in families with some connection with the Tempest family of Broughton Hall. In the 20th century the name has sometimes been adopted independently from the vocabulary word, especially as a female name.

Terence ♂ From the Latin name *Terentius*, which is of uncertain origin. It was borne by the Roman playwright Marcus Terentius Afer (who was a former slave, and took his name from his master, Publius Terentius Lucanus), and later by various minor early Christian saints. As a modern given name it is a 'learned' back-formation from the supposed pet form ▷Terry. It has become common in Ireland through being used as an Anglicized form of **Toirdhealbhach** (see Irish appendix).

VARIANTS: **Terrance**, **Terrence**.

SHORT FORM: **Tel**. See also ▷Terry.

Teresa ♀ Italian and Spanish form of ▷Theresa. In the English-speaking world the name is often chosen in this spelling by Roman Catholics, with particular reference to the Spanish saint, Teresa of Ávila (Teresa Cepeda de Ahumada, 1515–82).

Terrance ♂ The most common American spelling of ▷Terence.

Terrell ♂ Transferred use of the surname, a variant of ▷Tyrell.

Terrence ♂ Variant spelling of ▷Terence.

Terri ♀ Mid 20th-century coinage, originating either as a pet form of ▷Theresa or as a feminine spelling of ▷Terry. It is now well established as an independent given name.

Terry ♂ As a medieval given name this is a Norman form of the French name *Thierry*, from Germanic *Theodoric*, from *þeud* 'people, race' + *rīc* 'power, ruler'. This was adopted by the Normans and introduced by them to Britain. In modern English use it seems at first to have been a transferred use of the surname derived from the medieval given name, and later to have been taken as a pet form of ▷Terence.

SHORT FORM: **Tel**.

Terryl ♀ Modern coinage, apparently an elaboration of ▷Terri with the suffix -*yl* seen in names such as ▷Cheryl.

Tess ♀ Short form of ▷Tessa, also used as an independent given name.

Tessa ♀ Now generally considered to be a pet form of ▷Theresa, although often used independently. However, the formation is not clear, and it may be of distinct origin. Literary contexts of the late 19th century show that the name was thought of as Italian, although it is in fact unknown in Italy.

SHORT FORM: **Tess**.

PET FORMS: **Tessie, Tessy**.

Tetty ♀ Pet form of ▷Elizabeth, common in the 18th century (when it was used, for example, by Samuel Johnson's wife) but now rare or obsolete.

VARIANT: **Tettie**.

Tex ♂ Mainly U.S.: in origin a nickname for someone from Texas. The name of the state derives from an Indian tribal name, meaning 'friends', recorded as early as 1541 in the form *Teyas* and subsequently transmitted through Spanish sources.

Thaddeus ♂ Latin form of a New Testament name, the byname used to refer to one of Christ's lesser-known apostles, whose given name was *Lebbaeus* (Matthew 10:3). It is of uncertain origin, possibly derived via Aramaic from the Greek name *Theodōros* 'gift of God' or *Theodotos* 'given by God'.

SHORT FORMS: **Thad**, ▷**Tad**.

Thalia ♀ Name borne in classical mythology by the Muse of comedy; it is derived from Greek *thallein* 'to flourish', and in recent years has been in select use in the English-speaking world.

VARIANT: **Talia**.

Thea ♀ Short form of ▷Dorothea, also used independently.

Thecla ♀ Contracted form of the Greek name *Theokleia*, derived from *theos* 'God' + *kleia* 'glory'. The name was borne by a 1st-century saint (the first female martyr), who was particularly popular in the Middle Ages because of the lurid details of her suffering recorded in the apocryphal 'Acts of Paul and Thecla'.

Theda ♀ Latinate short form of the various ancient Germanic female personal names derived from *þeud* 'people, race'. It enjoyed a brief popularity in the United States from about 1915 to 1925, due to the popularity of the silent-film actress Theda Bara (1890–1955), the original 'vamp'. Her original name was Theodosia Goodman.

Thelma ♀ First used by the novelist Marie Corelli for the heroine of her novel *Thelma* (1887). She was supposed to be Norwegian, but it is not a traditional Scandinavian name. Greek *thelēma* (neuter) means 'wish' or '(act of) will', and the name could perhaps be interpreted as a contracted form of this.

Thelonius ♂ Latinized form of the name of St Tillo (see **Till** in German appendix). The variant spelling Thelonious is particularly associated with the American jazz pianist Thelonious Monk (1920–82).

Theo ♂ Short form of ▷Theodore and, less commonly, of ▷Theobald, now quite popular as an independent given name.

Theobald ♂ From an Old French name of Germanic (Frankish) origin,

t

derived from *peud* 'people, race' + *bald* 'bold, brave'. The first element was altered under the influence of Greek *theos* 'god'. This name was adopted by the Normans and introduced by them to Britain.

SHORT FORM: **Theo.**

Theodora ♀ Feminine form of ▷Theodore, borne most notably by a 9th-century empress of Byzantium, the wife of Theophilus the Iconoclast. It means 'gift of God'; the elements are the same as those of ▷Dorothea, but in reverse order.

Theodore ♂ From the French form of the Greek name *Theodōros*, derived from *theos* 'god' + *dōron* 'gift'. The name was popular among early Christians and was borne by several saints.

SHORT FORMS: **Theo, Ted.**

PET FORM: **Teddy.**

COGNATES: German, Danish: **Theodor.** Dutch: **Theodoor.** Norwegian, Swedish: **Teodor.** French: **Théodore.** Spanish, Portuguese, Italian: **Teodoro.** Russian: **Feodor, Fyodr.** Polish: **Teodor.** Bulgarian: **Todor.** Finnish: **Teuvo.** Hungarian: **Tivadar, Tódor.** Latvian: **Teodors.**

Theodosia ♀ Greek name derived from *theos* 'god' + *dōsis* 'giving'. It was borne by several early saints venerated in the Eastern Church, and is only very occasionally used in the English-speaking world today.

Theophilus ♂ New Testament name: the Latin form of the name of the addressee of St Luke's gospel and the Acts of the Apostles; also borne by various early saints. It is composed of the Greek words *theos* 'god' + *philos* 'friend', and was popular among early Christians because of its well-omened meaning 'lover of God' or 'beloved by God'.

Thera ♀ Of uncertain derivation: it could represent a shortened form of ▷Theresa, or be derived from the name of the Greek island of *Thēra*.

Theresa ♀ Of problematic origin. The name seems to have been first used in Spain and Portugal, and, according to tradition, was the name of the wife of St Paulinus of Nola, who spent most of his life in Spain; she was said to have originated (and to have derived her name) from the Greek island of *Thēra*. However, this story is neither factually nor etymologically confirmed.

VARIANTS: **Teresa, Treeza.**

PET FORMS: ▷**Terri,** ▷**Tessa.**

Thessaly ♀ From the name of the region in eastern central Greece. The place name is of ancient Illyrian origin and uncertain meaning.

Thirzah ♀ Variant of ▷Tirzah.

Thos ♂ Written abbreviated form of ▷Thomas.

Thomas ♂ New Testament name, borne by one of Christ's twelve apostles, referred to as 'Thomas, called Didymus' (John 11:16; 20:24). *Didymos* is the Greek word for 'twin', and the name is the Greek form of an Aramaic byname meaning 'twin'. The given name has always been popular throughout Christendom, in part because St Thomas's doubts have made him seem a very human character.

SHORT FORM: **Tom.**

PET FORM: **Tommy.**

COGNATES: Irish: **Tomás.** Scottish Gaelic: **Tòmas; Tàmhas.** Welsh: **Tomos.** German, Dutch, Scandinavian: **Thomas.** French: **Thomas.** Spanish: **Tomás.** Portuguese: **Tomás.** Italian: **Tommaso.** Russian: **Foma.** Polish: **Tomasz.** Czech: **Tomáš.** Croatian: **Toma.** Slovenian: **Tomaz.** Finnish: **Tuomo.** Latvian: **Toms.** Lithuanian: **Tomas.**

Thorn ♂ Short form of ▷Thornton or transferred use of the surname (originally denoting someone who lived near a large thorn bush), or a direct adoption of the vocabulary word because of its association with natural hardiness. As a given name, this is recorded in England as early as the 16th century, but the modern name appears to have arisen in 19th-century America.

Thornton ♂ Transferred use of the surname, in origin a local name from the very numerous places named with Old English *þorn* 'thorn bush' + *tūn* 'enclosure, settlement'. The given name is associated with the American writer Thornton Wilder (1897–1975).

Tia ♀ Recent coinage, of uncertain derivation. It coincides in form and pronunciation with the Spanish and Portuguese word meaning 'aunt', but this is an unlikely source. It may be a short form of names like ▷Laetitia and ▷Lucretia.

Tiana ♀ Recent coinage, apparently an elaborated form of ▷Tia or a shortened form of ▷Christiana.
VARIANT: **Tianna**.

Tiara ♀ Recent coinage, apparently from the vocabulary word for a woman's jewelled headdress (via Latin, from Greek *tiara(s)*, originally denoting a kind of conical cap worn by the ancient Persians). Compare ▷Tierra.

Tiernan ♂ Transferred use of the Irish surname, Gaelic *Ó Tighearnáin* 'descendant of Tighearnán' (see Tighearnán in Irish appendix).

Tierney ♂, ♀ Transferred use of the Irish surname, Gaelic *Ó Tighearnaigh* 'descendant of Tighearnach' (see Tighearnach in Irish appendix). This is now also well established as a girl's name. Its use in North America is due in part at least to the influence of the film actress Gene Tierney (1920–91).

Tierra ♀ Mainly U.S.: recent coinage, of uncertain derivation, ostensibly from Spanish *tierra* 'land, earth' (Latin *terra*), but compare ▷Tiara.

Tiffany ♀ Usual medieval English form of the Greek name *Theophania* 'Epiphany', from *theos* 'god' + *phainein* 'to appear'. This was once a relatively common name, given particularly to girls born on the feast of the Epiphany (6 January), and it gave rise to an English surname. As a given name, it fell into disuse until revived in the 20th century under the influence of the famous New York jewellers, Tiffany's, and the film, starring Audrey Hepburn, *Breakfast at Tiffany's* (1961). This is a very popular African-American name.

Tikvah ♀ Jewish: Hebrew name meaning 'hope'. The name is borne in the Bible by a male character mentioned in passing (2 Kings 22:14), but is now a female name chosen for the sake of its good omen.
VARIANT: **Tikva**.

Tilda ♀ Short form of ▷Matilda, also occasionally used independently.

Tilly ♀ Pet form of ▷Matilda, much used from the Middle Ages to the late 19th century, when it also came to be used as an independent given name. In recent times it has begun to make a comeback.
VARIANT: **Tillie**.

Tim ♂ Short form of ▷Timothy, also used occasionally as an independent given name, and in Ireland as an Anglicized form of Tadhg (see Irish appendix).
PET FORM: **Timmy** (normally used only for young boys).

Timothy ♂ English form, used in the Authorized Version of the Bible (alongside the Latin form *Timotheus*), of the Greek name *Timotheos*, from *timē* 'honour' + *theos* 'god'. This was the name of a companion of St Paul; according to tradition, he was stoned to death for denouncing the worship of Diana. It was not used in England before the Reformation but has been in steady use since the 18th century.
SHORT FORM: **Tim**.
PET FORM: **Timmy** (normally used only for young boys).

Tina ♀ Short form of ▷Christina and other girls' names ending in -*tina*; now often used as an independent given name.

Tirzah ♀ Biblical name, meaning 'pleasantness' or 'delight' in Hebrew, borne by a minor character mentioned in a genealogy (Numbers 26:33). It is also a biblical place name.

VARIANTS: **Tirza, Thirzah, Thirza.**

Tisha ♀ In origin a respelling of a reduced form of ▷Laetitia or ▷Patricia. It is now fairly commonly used as an independent given name.

Tita ♀ Either a short form of names ending in these two syllables, as for example *Martita*, or a feminine form of ▷Titus.

Titus ♂ From an old Roman given name, of unknown ultimate origin. It was borne by a companion of St Paul who became the first bishop of Crete, and also by the Roman emperor who destroyed Jerusalem in AD 70. It is remembered in England as the name of the clergyman and anti-Catholic conspirator Titus Oates (1649–1705), who fabricated the so-called Popish Plot (1678) to kill Charles II and his Protestant supporters. The name has never been very common in the English-speaking world, but is recorded regularly in some families from the 17th century onwards.

Tobias ♂ Greek form of Hebrew *Tobiah* 'God is good', borne by several characters in the Bible (appearing in the Authorized Version also as *Tobijah*). In the Middle Ages, however, it was principally associated with the tale of 'Tobias and the Angel'. According to the Book of Tobit in the Apocrypha, Tobias, the son of Tobit, a rich and righteous Jew of Nineveh, was lucky enough to acquire the services of the archangel Raphael as a travelling companion on a journey to Ecbatana. He returned wealthy, married, and with a cure for

his father's blindness. A historical St Tobias was martyred (*c*.315) at Sebaste in Armenia, together with Carterius, Styriacus, Eudoxius, Agapius, and five others.

Toby ♂, occasionally ♀ English vernacular form of ▷Tobias, now in frequent use as an independent given name. Its occasional use as a girl's name is recent.

Todd ♂ Transferred use of the surname, which was originally a nickname from an English dialect word meaning 'fox'.

Todos ♂ Jewish: Aramaic form of Greek *Theodōros* (see ▷Theodore). The name has been in use among Jews since the Hellenistic period.

Toinette ♀ Short form of ▷Antoinette.

Toltse ♀ Jewish: Yiddish name, probably from the Italian affectionate nickname *Dolce* 'sweet, lovely' (compare ▷Dulcie).

Tom ♂ Short form of ▷Thomas, in use since the Middle Ages. It is recorded as an independent name since the 18th century, and as such was very popular in the late 1990s.

Tomas ♂ Respelling of ▷Thomas, possibly in some cases representing Irish **Tomás**, Scottish Gaelic **Tòmas**, or (in the United States particularly) Spanish **Tomás**.

Tommy ♂ Pet form of ▷Thomas, also used as an independent given name.

Tone ♂ Transferred use of the English surname, which originated as a local name for someone who lived in the main settlement of a village (Middle English *tone*, from Old English *tūn*) rather than an outlying dwelling. This name is also used as an informal pet form of ▷Anthony; compare ▷Tony.

Toni ♀ Feminine form of ▷Tony, in part used as a pet form of ▷Antonia but more commonly as an independent given name, as for example by the American novelist Toni Morrison (b. 1931 as Chloe Ardelia Wofford).

Tonia ♀ Short form of ▷Antonia, now also used occasionally as an independent given name.

Tony ♂, occasionally ♀ Short form of ▷Anthony, sometimes used as an independent given name. As a girl's name it is a pet form of ▷Antonia.

Tonya ♀ Variant of ▷Tonia.

Topaz ♀ One of the rarer examples of the class of modern girls' names taken from vocabulary words denoting gemstones. The topaz gets its name via French and Latin from Greek; it is probably ultimately of Oriental origin. In the Middle Ages this was sometimes used as a boy's name, being taken as a form of ▷Tobias.

Torquil ♂ Anglicized form of Scandinavian Torkel (see Scandinavian appendix).

Tory ♀, ♂ Pet form of ▷Victoria. In the United States this is also a boy's name, no doubt representing a transferred use of the surname derived from a Scandinavian personal name: Old Norse Þórir or Old Danish Thori(r).
VARIANT: Tori ♀.

Tottie ♀ Pet form of ▷Charlotte, a rhyming variant of ▷Lottie. The name was most common in the 18th and 19th centuries, like ▷Tetty.
VARIANT: Totty.

Tracy ♂, ♀ Transferred use of the surname, in origin a Norman baronial name from places in France called *Tracy*, from the Gallo-Roman personal name *Thracius* + the local suffix *-acum*. In former times, *Tracy* was occasionally used as a boy's name, as were the surnames of other English noble families. Later, it was also used as a girl's name, generally being taken

as a pet form of ▷Theresa. It became a very popular girl's name in the 1960s and 70s, but has gradually declined since. It continues to be used as a boy's name in the United States but is rarely, if ever, so used in Britain.
VARIANTS: Tracey, Tracie ♀.

Travis ♂ Transferred use of the surname, in origin a Norman French occupational name (from *traverser* 'to cross') for someone who collected a toll from users of a bridge or a particular stretch of road. It is now widely used as a given name, especially in the United States.

Traynor ♂ Transferred use of the Irish surname, Gaelic *Mac Thréinfhir* 'son of *Thréinfear*', a byname meaning 'champion' (from *tréan* 'strong' + *fear* 'man').

Treena ♀ Variant spelling of ▷Trina.

Treeza ♀ Modern contracted spelling of ▷Theresa or Anglicization of Irish Treasa (see appendix).

Tremaine ♂ Transferred use of the Cornish surname, in origin a local name from any of several places named with Cornish *tre* 'homestead, settlement' + *men* 'stone'.

Trent ♂ Especially U.S.: from the name of the river that flows through the British Midlands (compare ▷Clyde), or a transferred use of the surname derived from it. The river name is of British origin: it may be composed of elements meaning 'through, across' and 'travel, journey', or it may mean 'traveller' or 'trespasser', a reference to frequent flooding. The given name may also in some cases be used as a short form of ▷Trenton.

Trenton ♂ Mainly U.S.: from the name of the city in New Jersey, the site of a decisive defeat of the British (1776) by Washington during the American Revolution. The city was founded in the late 17th century by a group of English Quakers under

t

the leadership of a certain William Trent. It was originally *Trent's Town*, reduced within half a century to *Trenton*.

Trevelyan ♂ Transferred use of the Cornish surname, in origin a local name from a place mentioned in Domesday Book as *Trevelien*, i.e. 'homestead or settlement (Cornish *tref*) of *Elian*'. The latter is an ancient Celtic personal name of obscure origin (compare ▷Elvis).

Trevor ♂ Transferred use of the Welsh surname, in origin a local name from any of the many places in Wales called *Trefor*, from *tref* 'settlement' + *for*, mutated form of *mawr* 'large'. In the mid-20th century it came to enjoy considerable popularity in the English-speaking world among people with no connection with Wales; for example the actor Trevor Howard (1916–88) was born in Kent.

SHORT FORM: **Trev.**

Trey ♂ Mainly U.S.: apparently from the vocabulary word, denoting the three in a suit of playing cards (from Old French *treis*, Latin *tres*). It may sometimes be given to a third son, but often it is regarded as no more than a variant of ▷Troy.

Tricia ♀ Short form of ▷Patricia. In North America, especially, it is sometimes used independently.

VARIANT: **Trisha.**

Trina ♀ Short form of ▷Catrina.

VARIANT: **Treena.**

Trinette ♀ English: modern elaboration of ▷Trina, using the originally French feminine diminutive suffix *-ette*.

Trinity ♀ From the vocabulary word denoting the three persons of the Christian Godhead: Father, Son, and Holy Ghost. It appears to have been adopted as a given name at the time of the Reformation, its use until recently, however, having been very select.

Trisha ♀ Respelling of ▷Tricia, also used as an independent given name.

Trista ♀ Mainly U.S.: name invented as a feminine form of ▷Tristan.

Tristan ♂ From Celtic legend, the name borne by a hero of medieval romance. There are many different versions of the immensely popular tragic story of Tristan and his love for Isolde. Generally, they agree that Tristan was an envoy sent by King Mark of Cornwall to bring back his bride, the Irish princess Isolde. Unfortunately, Tristan and Isolde fall in love with each other, having accidentally drunk the love potion intended for King Mark's wedding night. Tristan eventually leaves Cornwall to fight for King Howel of Brittany. Wounded in battle, he sends for Isolde. She arrives too late, and dies of grief beside his bier. The name *Tristan* is of unknown derivation, though it may be connected with Pictish *Drostan*; it has been altered from an irrecoverable original as a result of transmission through Old French sources that insisted on associating it with Latin *tristis* 'sad', a reference to the young knight's tragic fate.

VARIANT: **Trystan** (mainly Welsh).

Tristram ♂ Variant of ▷Tristan. Both forms of the name occur in medieval and later versions of the legend. In Laurence Sterne's comic novel *Tristram Shandy* (1759–67), the name is bestowed on the narrator through a misunderstanding and is regarded by his father as a great misfortune. Since the name originally intended for him was *Trismegistus*, the degree of misfortune may be taken as somewhat exaggerated.

VARIANTS: **Tristam, Trystram.**

Trixie ♀ Pet name derived from ▷Beatrix.

VARIANT: **Trixi.**

Troy ♂, occasionally ♀ Probably originally a transferred use of the surname, which is derived from *Troyes* in France. Nowadays, however, the given name is principally associated with the ancient city of Troy in Asia Minor, whose fate has been a central topic in epic poetry from Homer onwards. The story tells how Troy was sacked by the Greeks after a siege of ten years; according to classical legend, a few Trojan survivors got away to found Rome (and, according to medieval legend, another group founded Britain).

Trudy ♀ Pet form of ▷Gertrude or ▷Ermintrude, now used mainly as an independent given name.
VARIANT: **Trudie, Trudi.**

Truman ♂ Mainly U.S.: transferred use of the surname, in origin a nickname from Old English *trēowe* 'true, trusty' + *mann* 'man'. Use as a given name was boosted by the fame of Harry S. Truman (1884–1972), president of the United States (1945–52), although it was in occasional use before he became president.
VARIANT: **Trueman.**

Trystan ♂ Mainly Welsh variant of ▷Tristan.

Tucker ♂ Mainly U.S.: transferred use of the surname, in origin an occupational name for a fuller (from Old English *tūcian* 'to torment').

Turner ♂ Transferred use of the surname, in origin an occupational name for someone who made articles of wood, bone, or metal by turning them on a lathe. Among Blacks in the United States it is sometimes used as a given name in honour of Nat Turner, a slave who in 1831 led an insurrection against local landowners before being captured and executed.

Ty ♂ Short form of ▷Tyler and ▷Tyrone, often used as an independent given name.

Tybalt ♂ The usual medieval form of ▷Theobald, rarely used nowadays. It occurs in Shakespeare's *Romeo and Juliet*

as the name of a brash young man who is killed in a brawl.

Tycho ♂ Latinized form of the name of St Tychon (d. *c.*450), bishop of Amathus in Cyprus, who worked to suppress the last remnants of the cult of Aphrodite on the island. The Greek name *Tychōn* means 'hitting the mark', and was chosen for the sake of its good omen. The most famous modern bearer of the given name was the Danish astronomer Tycho Brahe (1546–1601).

Tye ♂ Either a variant spelling of ▷Ty or a transferred use of the surname, a local name for someone who lived by a common pasture, Middle English *tye*.

Tyler ♂, ♀ Transferred use of the surname, in origin an occupational name for a tiler (an agent derivative of Old English *tigele* 'tile', from Latin *tegula* 'covering'). John Tyler (1790–1862) was the tenth president of the United States. As a girl's name, it was in regular use in North America by the 1980s and soon after spread to other parts of the English-speaking world.

Tyrese ♂ Recent coinage, apparently an elaborated form of ▷Ty.
VARIANT: **Tyreece.**

Tyrone ♂ From the name of a county in Northern Ireland and a city in Pennsylvania. Its use as a given name seems to be due to the influence of the two film actors (father and son) called Tyrone Power, especially the younger one (1913–58).

Tyrell ♂ Transferred use of the surname, which is common in Ireland, but of uncertain derivation. It may have originated as a nickname for a stubborn person, from Old French *tirel*, used of an animal which pulls on the reins, a derivative of *tirer* 'to pull'.
VARIANT: **Tyrrell.**

Tyson ♂ Mainly U.S.: transferred use of the surname, which is of dual origin. In part it is a metronymic

t

from the medieval woman's given name *Dye*, a pet form of ▷Dionysia, and in part it is a nickname for a hot-tempered person, from Old French *tison* 'firebrand'. As a given name it is often taken as an expanded form of or patronymic from ▷Ty.

Uu

Ughtred ♂ From the rare Old English personal name *Uhtrǣd*, composed of the elements *uht* 'dawn' + *rǣd* 'counsel, advice'. This is a very uncommon given name in the English-speaking world, but remains in use in the Shuttleworth family.

Ulric ♂ In the Middle Ages, this represented an Old English name composed of the elements *wulf* 'wolf' + *rīc* 'power'. In its occasional modern use, it is probably an Anglicized spelling of German Ulrich (see appendix).

VARIANT: Ulrick.

Ulysses ♂ Latin form of the Greek name *Odysseus*, borne by the famous wanderer of Homer's *Odyssey*. The name is of uncertain derivation (it was associated by the Greeks themselves with the verb *odyssesthai* 'to hate'). Moreover, it is not clear why the Latin form should be so altered; mediation through Etruscan has been one suggestion. As an English given name it has occasionally been used in England from the 16th century and more commonly in America in the 19th and 20th centuries (like other names of classical origin such as ▷Homer and ▷Virgil). It was the name of the 18th president of the United States, Ulysses S. Grant (1822–85). It has also been used in Ireland as a classicizing form of Ulick (see Irish appendix).

Una ♀ Anglicized form of Irish Úna (see appendix). In Irish legend Úna is the mother of the hero Conn Cétchathach (Conn of the Hundred Battles). It was also the name of the beloved of the 17th-century poet Tomás Láidir Costello: banned by her parents from seeing him, Úna fell into a decline and died, leaving him to mourn her in

his verse. The Anglicized form of the name is sometimes taken to be from the feminine of Latin *unus* 'one'. It is the name used by Spenser for the lady of the Red Cross Knight in *The Faerie Queene*: he probably had Latin rather than Irish in mind, even though he worked in Ireland for a while. The Irish name has also been Anglicized as ▷Unity, ▷Juno, ▷Winifred, and ▷Agnes.

Unity ♀ From the vocabulary word for the quality (Latin *unitas*, a derivative of *unus* 'one'). It achieved some currency among the Puritans, but has been mainly used in Ireland as a kind of Anglicized extended form of ▷Una.

Urban ♂ From the Latin name *Urbanus* 'city dweller'. This was borne by numerous early saints, and was adopted by several popes.

Uri ♂ Jewish: from a Hebrew word meaning 'light' (compare ▷Uriah and ▷Uriel). There is no connection with the Russian name ▷Yuri.

Uriah ♂ Biblical name (from Hebrew, meaning 'God is light'), borne by a Hittite warrior treacherously disposed of by King David after he had made Uriah's wife Bathsheba pregnant (2 Samuel 11). The Greek form *Urias* occurs in the New Testament (Matthew 1:6). The name was used occasionally from the 16th century onwards, but is now most closely associated with the character of the obsequious Uriah Heep in Dickens's *David Copperfield* (1850) and has consequently undergone a sharp decline in popularity.

Uriel ♂ Biblical name derived from Hebrew *uri* 'light' + *el* 'God', and so a doublet of ▷Uriah. It is borne by two minor characters mentioned in genealogies (1 Chronicles 6:24; 2 Chronicles 13:2).

Ursula ♀ From the Latin name *Ursula*, a diminutive of *ursa* '(she-)bear'. This was the name of a 4th-century saint martyred at Cologne with a number of companions, traditionally said to have been eleven thousand, but more probably just eleven, the exaggeration being due to a misreading of a diacritic mark in an early manuscript. This name was moderately popular in the 16th century, but its use in the English-speaking world today is selective. A more recent influence has been the film actress Ursula Andress (b. 1936 in Switzerland).

Uzi ♂ Mainly Jewish: name, meaning 'power' or 'might' in Hebrew, borne in the Bible by six minor characters mentioned in genealogies. In the Authorized Version the spelling Uzzi is used. The name seems to represent a short form of the theophoric names ▷Uzziah and ▷Uzziel.

Uzziah ♂ Biblical name meaning 'power of Yahweh (God)' in Hebrew. It is borne by several characters in the Old Testament, including one of the kings of Judea.

VARIANT: Uziah.

Uzziel ♂ Biblical name, meaning 'power of God' in Hebrew. It is borne by several minor characters mentioned in Old Testament genealogies and has enjoyed some popularity as a given name among Jews.

VARIANT: Uziel.

u

V v

Val ♂, occasionally ♀ Short form of ▷Valerie, and sometimes also of ▷Valentine.

Valda ♀ 20th-century coinage, an elaboration of the girl's name ▷Val with the suffix *-da*, extracted from names such as ▷Glenda and ▷Linda.

Valene ♀ 20th-century coinage, an elaboration of the girl's name ▷Val with the productive feminine suffix *-ene*.

Valentina ♀ Latinate feminine form of ▷Valentine.

Valentine ♂, occasionally ♀ English form of the Latin name *Valentinus*, a derivative of *valens* 'healthy, strong'. This was the name of a Roman martyr of the 3rd century, whose feast is celebrated on 14 February. This was the date of a pagan fertility festival marking the first stirrings of spring, which has survived in an attenuated form under the patronage of the saint.
SHORT FORM: **Val.**

Valerie ♀ From the French form of the Latin name *Valeria*, feminine of *Valerius*, an old Roman family name apparently derived from *valere* 'to be healthy, strong'. The name owes its popularity as a male name in France to the cult of a 3rd-century saint who was converted to Christianity by Martial of Limoges. The masculine form **Valery** is found occasionally in England in the 16th century, but by the 17th century had fallen into disuse.
SHORT FORM: **Val.**

Valetta ♀ 20th-century coinage, an elaboration of the girl's name ▷Val with the ending *-etta*, originally an Italian feminine diminutive suffix. *Valetta* or *Valletta* is (apparently coincidentally) the name of the capital of Malta.

Valmai ♀ Name used fairly regularly in Australia since the 1920s, with some currency to the present day. It is said to be of Welsh origin, meaning 'mayflower'. However, no Welsh word of appropriate meaning equating to the first element can be identified, and the letter *v* is not used in Welsh. It may have been inspired by the ancient Welsh boys' name *Gwalchmai* (from *gwalch* 'falcon' + *May* 'May'), but it seems more likely to be an elaboration of ▷Val.

Van ♂ Short form of ▷Ivan or ▷Evan, as in the case of the American film actor Van Heflin (1910–71, born Emmett Evan Heflin) and the Northern Irish singer Van Morrison (b. 1945 as George Ivan Morrison).

Vanessa ♀ Name invented by Jonathan Swift (1667–1745) for his friend Esther Vanhomrigh. It seems to have been derived from the first syllable of her (Dutch) surname, with the addition of the suffix *-essa* (perhaps influenced by the first syllable of her given name). The name became fairly popular in the 20th century, being borne for example by the actress Vanessa Redgrave (b. 1937).
SHORT FORM: **Nessa.**

Vaughan ♂ Transferred use of the Welsh surname, in origin a nickname from the mutated form (*fychan* in Welsh orthography) of the Welsh adjective *bychan* 'small'.
VARIANT: **Vaughn.**

Velma ♀ Of modern origin and uncertain derivation, possibly based on ▷Selma or ▷Thelma.

Venessa ♀ Modern altered form of ▷Vanessa.

V

Venetia ♀ Of uncertain origin, used occasionally since the late Middle Ages. In form the name coincides with that of the region of northern Italy.

Venus ♀ From the name borne in classical mythology by the goddess of love and feminine beauty (the Latin equivalent of Greek Aphrodite; her name is related to *venustas* 'beauty, delight'). In recent years the name has been made famous by the American tennis player Venus Williams (b. 1980).

Vera ♀ Russian name, meaning 'faith'. It coincides in form with the feminine form of the Latin adjective *verus* 'true'. It was introduced to Britain at the beginning of the 20th century and was popular in the early decades, notably borne by the singer Vera Lynn, 'The Forces Sweetheart' (b. 1917 as Vera Welch), but has since gone out of fashion.

Vere ♂ Transferred use of the surname, in origin a Norman baronial name, from any of the numerous places in northern France so called from Gaulish *ver(n)* 'alder'.

Verena ♀ Characteristically Swiss name, first borne by a 3rd-century saint who lived as a hermit near Zurich. She is said to have come originally from Thebes in Egypt, and the origin of her name is obscure. This name is now occasionally used in the English-speaking world, where it is taken as an elaboration of ▷Vera.

VARIANT: **Verina**.

Vergil ♂ Variant spelling of ▷Virgil.

Verina ♀ Variant spelling of ▷Verena.

Verity ♀ From the archaic abstract noun meaning 'truth' (via Old French from Latin *veritas*, a derivative of *verus* 'true'; compare ▷Vera). It was a popular Puritan name, and is still occasionally used in the English-speaking world.

Verna ♀ Mainly U.S.: name coined in the latter part of the 19th century,

perhaps as a contracted form of ▷Verena or ▷Verona, or as a feminine form of ▷Vernon.

Vernon ♂ Transferred use of the surname, in origin a Norman baronial name from any of various places so called from Gaulish elements meaning 'place of alders' (compare ▷Vere).

SHORT FORM: **Vern**.

Verona ♀ Of uncertain origin. It seems to have come into use towards the end of the 19th century, and may either represent a shortened form of ▷Veronica or be taken from the name of the Italian city. It became more widely known from Sinclair Lewis's novel *Babbitt* (1923), in which it is borne by the daughter of the eponymous hero.

Veronica ♀ Latin form of ▷Berenice, influenced from an early date by association with the Church Latin phrase *vera icon* 'true image', of which this form is an anagram. The legend of the saint who wiped Christ's face on the way to Calvary and found an image of his face imprinted on the towel seems to have been invented to account for this derivation. Use of the name in modern times may to some extent be influenced by the flowering plant so called from the personal name.

PET FORMS: **Ronnie, Roni**.

Vessa ♀ Modern creation, a contracted form of ▷Vanessa or an assimilated form of ▷Vesta.

Vesta ♀ From the Latin name of the Roman goddess of the hearth, akin to the name of a Greek goddess with similar functions, *Hestia*, but of uncertain derivation. It is only rarely used as a given name in the English-speaking world, but was borne as a stage name by the Victorian music-hall artiste Vesta Tilley (1864–1952). In some cases it may represent a simplified form of ▷Silvestra.

Vi ♀ Short form of ▷Violet, ▷Vivien, or ▷Vivian.

V

Vic ♂ Short form of ▷Victor.

Vicky ♀ Pet form of ▷Victoria, now also used as an independent given name. VARIANTS: Vickie, Vicki, Vikki.

Victor ♂ From a Late Latin personal name meaning 'conqueror'. This was popular among early Christians as a reference to Christ's victory over death and sin, and was borne by several saints. An influence on the choice of the name in more recent times was the American actor Victor Mature (1915–99).
SHORT FORM: Vic.

Victoria ♀ Feminine form of the Latin name *Victorius* (a derivative of ▷Victor), also perhaps a direct use of Latin *victoria* 'victory'. It was little known in England until the accession in 1837 of Queen Victoria (1819–1901), who got it from her German mother, Mary Louise Victoria of Saxe-Coburg. It did not begin to be a popular name among commoners in Britain until the 1940s, reaching a peak in the 1990s.
PET FORMS: Vicky, Vickie, Vicki, Vikki; ▷Tory.

Vienna ♀ From the name of the capital of Austria (so called from the river on which it stands, thought to have derived its name from the Celtic element *vindo* 'white'). Modern adoption as a female first name follows the pattern of other female-sounding city names such as ▷Verona, ▷Siena, ▷Ravenna, and ▷Paris.

Vikki ♀ Respelling of ▷Vicky.

Vince ♂ Short form of ▷Vincent, in use at least from the 17th century, and probably earlier, since it has given rise to a surname. It is occasionally used as an independent given name.

Vincent ♂ From the Old French form of the Latin name *Vincens* 'conquering' (genitive *Vincentis*). This name was borne by various early saints particularly associated with France,

most notably the 5th-century St Vincent of Lérins.
SHORT FORM: Vince.
PET FORM: Vinnie.
COGNATES: Irish: Uinseann. German: Vinzenz (from Latin *Vincentius*). Dutch, Danish, Swedish: Vincent. French: Vincent. Spanish, Portuguese: Vicente. Catalan: Vicenç. Italian: Vincente; Vincenzo (from *Vincentius*). Polish: Wincenty (from *Vincentius*). Czech: Vincenc (from *Vincentius*). Croatian: Vinko. Hungarian: Vince. Lithuanian: Vincentas.

Viola ♀ From Latin *viola* 'violet'. The name is relatively common in Italy and was used by Shakespeare in *Twelfth Night*, where most of the characters have Italianate names. Its modern use in English has been influenced by the vocabulary word denoting the flower.

Violet ♀ From the name of the flower (Old French *violette*, Late Latin *violetta*, a diminutive of *viola*). This was one of the earliest flower names to become popular in Britain, being used as early as 1700 and becoming well established in the 19th century, although it is now somewhat out of favour.
SHORT FORM: Vi.

Viona ♀ Apparently an altered form of ▷Fiona, resulting from a blend with ▷Viola or ▷Violet.

Virgil ♂ Mainly U.S.: usual English form of the name of the most celebrated of Roman poets, Publius Vergilius Maro (70–19 BC). The correct Latin spelling is *Vergilius*, but it was early altered to *Virgilius* by association with *virgo* 'maiden' or *virga* 'stick'. Today the name is almost always given with direct reference to the poet, but medieval instances may have been intended to honour instead a 6th-century bishop of Arles or an 8th-century Irish monk who evangelized Carinthia and became archbishop of Salzburg, both of whom also bore the name. In the case of the later saint, it was a classicized form of the Gaelic name **Fearghal** (see Irish appendix).

VARIANT: **Vergil**.

Virginia ♀ From the feminine form of Latin *Virginius* (more correctly *Verginius*; compare ▷Virgil), a Roman family name. It was borne by a Roman maiden killed, according to legend, by her own father to spare her the attentions of an importunate suitor. It was not used as a given name in the Middle Ages. It was bestowed on the first American child of English parentage, born at Roanoke, Virginia, in 1587 and has since remained in constant, if modest, use. Both child and province were named in honour of Elizabeth I, the 'Virgin Queen'. Among modern influences on the choice of the name has been the actress Virginia McKenna (b. 1931).

PET FORM: **Ginny**. See also ▷Ginger.

Vita ♀ 19th-century coinage, either directly from Latin *vita* 'life', or else as a feminine form of the male name *Vitus*. It has been borne most notably by the English writer Vita Sackville-West (1892–1962), in whose case it was a pet form of the given name *Victoria*.

Viv ♂, ♀ Short form of ▷Vivian and ▷Vivien.

Vivi ♀ Feminine pet form of ▷Vivien and ▷Vivian.

Vivian ♀, occasionally ♂ Originally a boy's name, from an Old French form of the Latin name *Vivianus* (probably a derivative of *vivus* 'alive'), but now more frequent as a girl's name. The name was borne by a 5th-century bishop of Saintes in western France, remembered for protecting his people during the invasion of the Visigoths.

VARIANTS: **Vivien, Vyvyan**.

SHORT FORMS: **Viv; Vi; Vivi** ♀.

Vivien ♀, formerly ♂ Earlier generally taken as a variant of the boy's name ▷Vivian, but now also rarely used for boys. This spelling was quite common in Old French. Its use as a girl's name in the English-speaking world was influenced by Tennyson's *Merlin and Vivien* (1859). This name, from Arthurian legend, may represent an altered form of a Celtic name (perhaps akin to the Irish Gaelic name *Béibhinn* 'white lady', pronounced 'bee-**veen**'). The actress Vivien Leigh (1913–67) was christened *Vivian*.

SHORT FORMS: **Viv; Vi; Vivi** ♀.

Vivienne ♀ French feminine form of ▷Vivien, used in the English-speaking world as an unambiguously female form of the name.

Volf ♂ Jewish: Yiddish form of ▷Wolf.

Vyvyan ♂ Fanciful respelling of ▷Vivian.

Ww

Wade ♂ Transferred use of the surname, in origin either a local name from the medieval vocabulary word *wade* 'ford' (old English *(ge)wæd*), or else from a medieval given name representing a survival of Old English *Wada*, a derivative of *wadan* 'to go', borne, according to legend, by a great sea-giant.

Waldo ♂ From a Latinate short form of various old Germanic personal names derived from *wald* 'rule'. This gave rise in the Middle Ages to a surname, borne notably by Peter Waldo, a 12th-century merchant of Lyons, who founded a reformist sect known as the Waldensians, which in the 16th century took part in the Reformation movement. In America the name is particularly associated with the poet and essayist Ralph Waldo Emerson (1803–82), whose father was a Lutheran clergyman.

Walker ♂ Mainly U.S.: transferred use of the surname, in origin an occupational name for a fuller, Old English *wealcere*, a derivative of *wealcan* 'to walk, tread'; the fulling process involved treading cloth in vats of lye.

Wallace ♂ Transferred use of the surname, in origin an ethnic byname from Old French *waleis* 'foreign', used by the Normans to denote members of various Celtic races in areas where they were in the minority: Welshmen in the Welsh marches, Bretons in East Anglia, and surviving Britons in the Strathclyde region. The given name seems to have been first used in Scotland, being bestowed in honour of the Scottish patriot William Wallace (*c.*1270–1305).

Wally ♂ Pet form of ▷Walter or, less commonly, of ▷Wallace. It has dropped almost completely out of fashion, especially since the advent in the 20th century of the slang term, denoting a stupid or incompetent person.

Walter ♂ From an Old French personal name of Germanic (Frankish) origin, derived from *wald* 'rule' + *heri*, *hari* 'army'. This was adopted by the Normans and introduced by them to England, superseding the native Old English form, *Wealdhere*. It was a very popular name in medieval England, normally pronounced 'Water'.

SHORT FORMS: **Wat, Walt.**

Wanda ♀ Of uncertain origin. Attempts have been made to derive it from various Germanic and Slavic roots. It was certainly in use in Poland in the 19th century, and is found in Polish folk tales as the name of a princess. The derivation may well be from the ethnic term *Wend* (see ▷Wendell). The name was introduced to the English-speaking world by Ouida (Marie Louise de la Ramée), who used it for the heroine of her novel *Wanda* (1883).

Ward ♂ Transferred use of the surname, originally an occupational name from Old English *weard* 'guardian, watchman'.

Warner ♂ Transferred use of the surname, which is from a medieval personal name introduced to Britain by the Normans. It is of Germanic origin, from *war(in)* 'guard' + *heri*, *hari* 'army'.

Warren ♂ Transferred use of the surname, which is of Norman origin, a coalescence of two different surnames, one derived from a Germanic personal name based on the element *war(in)* 'guard' and the other from a place in Normandy called *La Varenne* 'the game

W

park'. The Norman personal name survived at least into the 17th century in Yorkshire, where it was particularly associated with the Scargill family. In America this name has sometimes been chosen in honour of General Joseph Warren, the first hero of the American Revolution, who was killed at Bunker Hill (1775). Among modern influences on the choice of the name has been the film actor Warren Beatty (b. 1937).

Warwick ♂ Transferred use of the surname, in origin a local name from the city in the West Midlands. The place name is probably from Old English *wær, wer* 'weir, dam' + *wīc* 'industrial or processing site'.

Washington ♂ Especially U.S.: transferred use of the surname of the first president of the United States, George Washington (1732–99), whose family came originally from Northamptonshire in England. They had been established in Virginia since 1656. The surname in this case is derived from the village of Washington in Co. Durham (now Tyne and Wear), so called from Old English *Wassingtūn* 'settlement associated with Wassa'.

Wat ♂ The usual medieval short form of ▷Walter, now occasionally revived.

Watkin ♂ Either a revival of the medieval given name, a pet form of ▷Walter (from ▷Wat + the diminutive suffix *-kin*), or a transferred use of the surname derived from it.

Wayne ♂ Transferred use of the surname, in origin an occupational name for a carter or cartwright, from Old English *wægen* 'cart, waggon'. It was adopted as a given name in the second half of the 20th century, mainly as a result of the popularity of the American film actor John Wayne (1907–79), who was born Marion Michael Morrison; his screen name was chosen in honour of the American Revolutionary general Anthony Wayne (1745–96).

Webster ♂ Transferred use of the surname, in origin an occupational name for a weaver, Old English *webbestre* (a derivative of *webb* 'web'). The *-estre* suffix was originally feminine, but by the Middle English period the gender distinction had been lost. Use as a given name in America no doubt owes something to the politician and orator Daniel Webster (1782–1852) and the lexicographer Noah Webster (1758–1843).

Wenceslas ♂ Latinized form of an East European Slavic name, composed of the elements *ventie* 'more, greater' + *slav* 'glory'. St Wenceslas was a 10th-century duke of Bohemia noted for his piety, the grandson of St Ludmilla. He is regarded as the patron of Bohemia. This was also the name of four kings of Bohemia in the period covering the 13th to the 15th century.

Wenda ♀ Recent coinage, an altered form of ▷Wendy (compare ▷Jenna from ▷Jenny), probably also influenced by ▷Wanda. In the early Middle Ages a female name of this form was in occasional use on the Continent as a short form of various female compound names (such as *Wendelburg* and *Wendelgard*) formed with the ethnic name of the Wends (compare ▷Wendell) as their first element.

Wendell ♂ Mainly U.S.: from the surname derived in the Middle Ages from the Continental Germanic personal name *Wendel*, in origin an ethnic name for a Wend, a member of the Slavic people living in the area between the Elbe and the Oder, who were overrun by Germanic migrants in the 12th century. It has been adopted as a given name as a result of the fame of the American writer Oliver Wendell Holmes (1809–94) and his jurist son, also Oliver Wendell Holmes (1841–1935), members of a leading New England family.

Wendy ♀ This name was apparently coined by the playwright J. M. Barrie, who used it for the 'little mother' in his play *Peter Pan* (1904). He took it from the nickname *Fwendy-Wendy* (i.e. 'friend') used for him by a child acquaintance, Margaret Henley. It has also been suggested that this name may have originated as a pet form of ▷Gwendolen. After peaking in the 1960s, use of the name declined quite rapidly.

VARIANT: **Wendi.**

Wentworth ♂ Transferred use of the surname, in origin a local name from places in Cambridgeshire and South Yorkshire. These were named with Old English *winter* 'winter' and *worð* 'enclosure'; the reference was to settlements that were inhabited only in winter, the inhabitants taking their flocks to other pastures in summer. In Australia it probably came into use as a given name in honour of D'Arcy Wentworth (?1762–1827), who was born in Ireland and played an important role in the early days of the Botany Bay settlement, and his son William Wentworth (1790–1872), an explorer and politician known as 'the Australian patriot' because of his advocacy of self-government.

Wesley ♂ From the surname of the founder of the Methodist Church, John Wesley (1703–91), and his brother Charles (1707–88), who was also influential in the movement. Their family must have come originally from one or other of the various places in England called *Westley*, the 'western wood, clearing, or meadow'. The given name was at first confined to members of the Methodist Church, but is now widely used without reference to its religious connotations.

SHORT FORM: **Wes.**

Weston ♂ Mainly U.S.: transferred use of the surname, in origin a local name from any of the very many places in England named in Old English as 'the western enclosure', from *west* 'west' + *tūn* 'enclosure, settlement'.

Whitley ♀ Mainly North American: transferred use of the surname, a local name from any of various places in England named with Old English *hwīt* 'white' + *lēah* 'wood, clearing'. Use as a girl's name may have been influenced by the adoption of ▷Whitney for the same purpose.

Whitney ♂, occasionally ♀ Mainly North American: transferred use of the surname, in origin a local name from any of various places in England named with the Middle English phrase *atten whiten ey* 'by the white island'. In the 1980s its popularity as a girl's name was enhanced by the fame of the American singer Whitney Houston (b. 1963).

Wilberforce ♂ Transferred use of the surname, in origin a local name from *Wilberfoss* in North Yorkshire, so called from the Old English female personal name *Wilburg* (see ▷Wilbur) + Old English *foss* 'ditch' (Latin *fossa*). It was taken up as a given name in honour of the anti-slavery campaigner William Wilberforce (1759–1833). It is now sometimes taken as an extended form of *Wilbur*.

Wilbur ♂ Mainly North American: transferred use of a comparatively rare surname, which is probably derived from a medieval female given name composed of Old English *will* 'will, desire' + *burh* 'fortress'. Its popularity in the United States peaked in the second decade of the 20th century but has since steadily declined.

Wilfrid ♂ From an Old English personal name, derived from *wil* 'will, desire' + *frið* 'peace'. This was borne by two Anglo-Saxon saints: there is some doubt about the exact form of the name of the more famous, who played a leading role at the Council of Whitby (664); it may have been *Walfrið* 'stranger peace'. Wilfrid the Younger was an 8th-century bishop of York. The name enjoyed some favour in Yorkshire (often in the form **Wilfrey**) in the 16th and 17th centuries. Influenced

w

by a character of this name in Sir Walter Scott's novel *Ivanhoe*, it was revived more widely in the 19th century, becoming quite popular then and in the early part of the 20th century.

VARIANT: Wilfred.

SHORT FORM: Wilf.

Wilhelmina ♀ Feminine version of *Wilhelm*, the German form of ▷William, formed with the Latinate suffix *-ina*. This name was introduced to the English-speaking world from Germany in the 19th century. It is now very rarely used.

SHORT FORM: ▷Mina.

PET FORM: ▷Minnie.

Will ♂ Short form of ▷William, in use since the early Middle Ages, when it was occasionally used also for various other given names of Germanic origin containing the first element *wil* 'will, desire' (e.g. *Wilbert* and ▷Wilmer). It is now also used as an independent given name.

Willa ♀ Name coined as a feminine form of ▷William, by appending the characteristically feminine ending *-a* to the short form ▷Will.

Willard ♂ Especially U.S.: transferred use of the surname, which is probably derived from the Old English personal name *Wilheard*, from *wil* 'will, desire' + *heard* 'hardy, brave, strong'. It is associated with the Jamaican opera singer Willard White (b. 1946).

William ♂ Probably the most successful of all the Old French names of Germanic origin that were introduced to England by the Normans. It is derived from Germanic *wil* 'will, desire' + *helm* 'helmet, protection'. The fact that it was borne by the Conqueror himself does not seem to have inhibited its favour with the 'conquered' population: in the first century after the Conquest it was the commonest male name of all, and not only among the Normans. In the later Middle Ages it was overtaken by ▷John, but continued to run second to that name until the 20th century, when the picture became more fragmented.

SHORT FORMS: Will, ▷Bill.

PET FORMS: Willy, Willie, Billy.

COGNATES: Irish: Uilliam. Scottish Gaelic: Uilleam. Welsh: Gwilym. German: Wilhelm. Dutch: Willem. Scandinavian: Vilhelm. French: Guillaume. Spanish: Guilermo. Catalan: Guillem. Portuguese: Guilherme. Italian: Guglielmo. Czech: Vilém. Slovenian: Viljem. Hungarian: Vilmos. Lithuanian: Vilhelmas. Latvian: Vilhelms.

Willis ♂ Transferred use of the surname, which is a derivative of ▷William.

Willoughby ♂ Transferred use of the surname, in origin a local name from any of various places in northern England so called from Old English *welig* 'willow' + Old Norse *býr* 'settlement'.

Willow ♀ From the name of the tree (Old English *welig*), noted for its grace and the pliancy of its wood.

Willy ♂ Pet form of ▷William.

Wilma ♀ Contracted form of ▷Wilhelmina, which has retained rather more currency (especially in America) than the full form of the name.

Wilmer ♂ From an Old English personal name, derived from *wil* 'will, desire' + *mær* 'famous'. This died out in the Middle Ages, but gave rise to a surname before it did so. The modern given name is probably a transferred use of that surname, perhaps adopted in particular as a masculine form of ▷Wilma.

Wilmette ♀ Mainly U.S.: recent coinage, elaborated from ▷Wilma by means of the productive ending *-ette* (originally a French feminine diminutive suffix).

VARIANT: Wilmetta.

Wilmot ♂, ♀ Transferred use of the surname, which is derived from a medieval pet form (with the Old French diminutive suffix -*ot*) of ▷William.

Wilson ♂ Transferred use of the surname, in origin a patronymic from ▷Will. Use as a given name in the United States was inspired by President (Thomas) Woodrow Wilson (1856–1924); compare the similar adoption as a given name of ▷Woodrow.

Win ♂, ♀ Short form of ▷Winifred or ▷Winfred.

Windsor ♂ Transferred use of the surname, which is derived from a place in Berkshire, originally named in Old English as *Windels-ōra* 'landing place with a windlass'. It is the site of a castle that is in regular use as a residence of the royal family. Use as a given name dates from the mid-19th century and was reinforced by its adoption in 1917 as the surname of the British royal family (from their residence at Windsor). It was felt necessary to replace the German name *Wettin*, which had been introduced to Britain by Queen Victoria's husband Albert, in deference to anti-German feeling during the First World War.

Winfred ♂, ♀ Revival of the Old English name *Wynnfrith*, from *wynn* 'joy' + *frith* 'peace'.

Winifred ♀ Anglicized form of the Welsh female personal name Gwenfrewi (see appendix). The form of the name has been altered by association with ▷Winfred and has been in general use among English speakers since the 16th century.

SHORT FORM: Win.

PET FORM: Winnie.

Winnie ♀, occasionally ♂ Pet form of ▷Winifred, ▷Winfred, and also of ▷Winston. As a girl's name it is occasionally used independently.

Winona ♀ Mainly North American: from a Sioux girl's name, said to be reserved normally for a first-born daughter. The American film star Winona Ryder (b. 1971 as Winona Horowitz) was named after her place of birth, Winona, Minnesota.

Winston ♂ Although there was an Old English personal name, *Wynnstan*, from *wynn* 'joy' + *stān* 'stone', which would have had this form if it had survived, the modern given name is a transferred use of the surname, a local name from *Winston* in Gloucestershire. Use as a given name originated in the Churchill family: the first Winston Churchill (b. 1620) was baptized with the surname of his mother's family. The name has continued in the family ever since, and has been widely adopted in honour of the statesman Winston Spencer Churchill (1874–1965).

Winthrop ♂ Mainly U.S.: from the surname of a leading American pioneering family. John Winthrop (1588–1649) was governor of Massachusetts Bay Colony from 1629, and played a major role in shaping the political institutions of New England. His son (1606–76) and grandson (1638–1707), who bore the same name, were also colonial governors. Their family probably came originally from one of the places in England called *Winthorpe* (named in Old English as the 'village of Wynna').

Winton ♂ Transferred use of the surname, in origin a local name from any of the various places so called. One in Cumbria gets its name from Old English *winn* 'pasture' + *tūn* 'enclosure, settlement'; another in the same county is from *wiðig* 'willow' + *tūn*; the one in North Yorkshire is from the Old English personal name *Wina* + *tūn*.

Wolf ♂ From the name of the animal (Old English *wolf*), in part a transferred use of the surname which originated as a nickname from this word, or an adoption of a German short form of any of the various compound

W

names (such as **Wolfgang** and **Wolfram**; see German appendix) with this first element.

Wolfe ♂ Transferred use of the surname (see ▷Wolf), sometimes used as a first name in honour of the Irish rebel Theobald Wolfe Tone (see ▷Tone) or the English General James Wolfe (1727–59), who died at the Battle of Quebec.

Woodrow ♂ Transferred use of the surname, in origin a local name for someone who lived in a row of houses by a wood. Use as a given name was inspired by the American president (Thomas) Woodrow Wilson (1856–1924).

Woody ♂ Pet form of ▷Woodrow, now also used as an independent given name. It has been borne by the American folk singer Woody (Woodrow Wilson) Guthrie (1912–67) and the 1940s band leader Woody (Woodrow Charles) Herman (1913–87). The American film director and humorist Woody Allen was born Allen Stewart Konigsberg in 1935; he adopted the name Woody in honour of Woody Guthrie.

Worth ♂ Transferred use of the surname, in origin a local name from any of the very numerous places named with the Old English word *worð* 'enclosure' (used especially of a subsidiary settlement dependent on a main village). Use as a given name has probably been inspired in part by the modern English vocabulary word referring to high personal merit (Old English *weorth*).

Wyatt ♂ Mainly North American: transferred use of the surname, derived from a medieval given name representing a Norman French alteration of the Old English personal name *Wīgheard*, from *wīg* 'war' + *heard* 'hardy, brave, strong'.

Wyndham ♂ Transferred use of the surname, which is derived from a contracted form of the name of *Wymondham* in Norfolk, originally named in Old English as the 'homestead of Wigmund'. John Wyndham was the pseudonym of the British science-fiction writer John Wyndham Parkes Lucas Beynon Harris (1903–69), creator of *The Midwich Cuckoos*.

Wynne ♂, ♀ Probably a transferred use of the surname, which is derived from the Old and Middle English personal name *Wine* 'friend'. See also Wyn (of which this is an elaborated form) in Welsh appendix.
VARIANT: **Wynn**.

Wystan ♂ From an Old English personal name derived from *wīg* 'battle' + *stān* 'stone'. St Wistan was a 9th-century prince of Mercia, murdered by his nephew Bertulf. The modern given name is rare, being best known as that of the poet Wystan Hugh Auden (1907–73).

W

Xx

Xander ♂ Shortened form of ▷Alexander, also used as an independent given name. It is pronounced, like other names beginning with X-, as though spelled with Z-.

Xanthe ♀ From the feminine form of the Greek adjective *xanthos* 'yellow, bright'. The name was borne by various minor figures in classical mythology and is occasionally chosen by parents in search of an unusual given name for a daughter.

Xavier ♂ From the surname of the Spanish soldier–saint Francis Xavier (1506–52), one of the founding members of the Society of Jesus (the Jesuits). He was born on the ancestral estate at Xavier (now Javier) in Navarre, which in the early Middle Ages was an independent Basque kingdom. *Xavier* probably represents a Hispanicized form of the Basque place name *Etcheberria* 'the new house'. (Spanish *x* was pronounced in the Middle Ages as 'sh', now closer to 'h'.) The given name is used almost exclusively by Roman Catholics.

Xaviera ♀ Name created as a feminine form of ▷Xavier.

Xena ♀ Apparently from Greek *xena* (feminine form) 'stranger, foreigner' (compare ▷Xenia). It has recently become familiar because of the popularity of the television show featuring Xena, the warrior princess.

Xenia ♀ Comparatively rare given name, coined from the Greek vocabulary word *xenia* 'hospitality', a derivative of *xenos* 'stranger, foreigner'.

Y y

Yael ♀ Jewish: from a Hebrew word denoting a female wild goat. The name is borne in the Bible by a Kenite woman who killed Sisera, the Canaanite general and an enemy of the Israelites, by hammering a tent peg through his temples while he was asleep (Judges 4:17–22). It has remained extremely popular among Jews to the present day, but has achieved little currency among non-Jews.

VARIANT: Jael.

Yakov ♂ Jewish: the modern Hebrew form of ▷Jacob (also the form of the name in Russian).

VARIANT: Yaakov.

PET FORM: Yankel (Yiddish).

Yale ♂ Transferred use of the Welsh surname, derived from the place name *Iâl*, meaning 'fertile or arable upland'. In the United States this may be bestowed with reference to the university in New Haven, Connecticut, which was named after Elihu Yale (1649–1721), an early benefactor, of Welsh ancestry.

Yarrow ♀ From the name of a plant, *Achillea millefolium* (Middle English *yarrowe*, from Old English *gearwe*), used in traditional medicine.

Yasmin ♀ Variant of ▷Jasmine, representing a 'learned' re-creation of the Persian and Arabic form. It has been popular in Britain since the 1990s. It is a Muslim as well as a Christian name.

Yehiel ♂ Jewish: Hebrew name, meaning 'God lives', borne in the Bible by an early Levite appointed to play the psaltery in sacred processions (1 Chronicles 15:20). In the Authorized Version the name is transliterated *Jehiel*. It is a popular modern Hebrew name.

Yehudi ♂ Jewish: modern Hebrew name, originally an ethnic byname meaning 'Jew'. It was borne, for example, by the violinist Yehudi Menuhin (1916–99).

Yelena ♀ Russian form of ▷Helen, occasionally used in the English-speaking world.

Yentl ♀ Jewish: Yiddish name, apparently from the French affectionate nickname *Gentille* 'kind, nice'.

Yetta ♀ Jewish: of uncertain origin, possibly a variant of ▷Etta originating in dialects of Yiddish subject to Slavic inflence, or else a derivative of *Yehudit* (the modern Hebrew form of ▷Judith) or ▷Esther.

Yigael ♂ Jewish: traditional Hebrew name of uncertain derivation, probably meaning 'he shall be redeemed'.

Yitzhak ♂ Jewish: modern Hebrew form of ▷Isaac.

Yola ♀ Short form of ▷Yolanda.

Yolanda ♀ Of uncertain origin. It is found in Old French as Yolande, of which this is a Latinate form. It may be ultimately of Germanic origin, but if so it has been altered beyond recognition. It is also sometimes identified with the name of St *Jolenta* (d. 1298), daughter of the king of Hungary.

VARIANT: Yolande.

Yoram ♂ Jewish: Hebrew name, meaning 'Yahweh is high', borne in the Bible by an evil king of Israel.

Yorick ♂ The name of the (defunct) court jester in Shakespeare's *Hamlet*. This is a respelling of *Jorck*, a Danish form of ▷George.

y

York ♂ Transferred use of the surname, which originated as a local name from the city in north-eastern England. The place name was originally *Eburacon*, a derivative of a Welsh word meaning 'yew'. The Anglo-Saxon settlers changed this to Old English *Eoforwīc* 'boar farm', which in Old Norse became *Iorvík* or *Iork*.

Yosef ♂ Jewish: the modern Hebrew form of ▷Joseph; also Muslim, a variant transliteration of the Arabic form of the same name (see Yūsuf in Arabic appendix).

Ysanne ♀ Pronounced 'iz-**ann**'; recent coinage, a blend of the first syllable of ▷Yseult + the given name ▷Anne.

Yseult ♀ Medieval French form of ▷Isolde, still occasionally used as a given name in the English-speaking world.

Yuan ♂ Manx form of ▷John.

Yuri ♂ The usual Russian form of ▷George, also used occasionally in the English-speaking world.

Yusuf ♂ Arabic form of ▷Joseph.

Yves ♂ French: from a Germanic personal name representing a short form of various compound names containing the element *iv* 'yew'. The final *-s* is the mark of the Old French nominative case. The name was introduced to Britain from France at the time of the Norman Conquest. See also ▷Ivo.

Yvette ♀ French feminine diminutive form of ▷Yves, now also established in the English-speaking world.

Yvonne ♀ French feminine diminutive form of ▷Yves (or simply a feminine form based on the Old French oblique case *Yvon*; compare ▷Ivon), now also widely used in the English-speaking world.

y

Zz

Zach ♂ Short form of ▷Zachary, also used as an independent given name.

Zachary ♂ English vernacular form of the New Testament Greek name *Zacharias*, a form of Hebrew ▷Zechariah 'God has remembered'. This was the name of the father of John the Baptist, who underwent a temporary period of dumbness for his lack of faith (Luke 1), and of a more obscure figure, Zacharias son of Barachias, who was slain 'between the temple and the altar' (Matthew 23:35; Luke 11:51). In the United States it is familiar as the name of a 19th-century president, Zachary Taylor. Since the 1990s the name has been remarkably popular in the English-speaking world, especially in the United States.

VARIANTS: Zacharias, Zachariah, ▷Zechariah; Zakari(y)a (also a common transcription of the Arabic form).

SHORT FORM: Zach.

Zack ♂ Short form of ▷Zachary or ▷Isaac, now frequently bestowed as an independent given name.

VARIANTS: Zak, Zac.

Zadok ♂ Jewish: Hebrew name meaning 'just' or 'righteous'. It was borne in the Bible by one of the chief priests of King David, who later anointed Solomon king of Israel (1 Kings 1:39), and it has been used ever since, no doubt partly because of its auspicious meaning.

Zane ♂ Transferred use of a surname of uncertain origin. It came to prominence as the given name of the American writer Zane Grey (1872–1939), a descendant of the Ebenezer Zane who founded *Zaneville* in Ohio.

Zanna ♀ Modern coinage, apparently a shortened form of ▷Susanna.

Zara ♀ Of uncertain origin. It is sometimes said to be of Arabic origin, from *zahr* 'flower', but is more probably a respelling of ▷Sara. It was given by Princess Anne and Mark Phillips to their second child (b. 1981), which aroused considerable comment at the time as it was a departure from the traditional patterns of royal nomenclature.

Zaylie ♀ Of uncertain origin, perhaps a respelling of the rare French name *Zélie*, an altered form of *Célie*, the French version of ▷Celia.

Zeb ♂ Short form of ▷Zebedee and ▷Zebulun, now occasionally used as an independent given name.

Zebadiah ♂ See ▷Zebedee.

Zebedee ♂ Name borne in the New Testament by the father of the apostles James and John, who was with his sons mending fishing nets when they were called by Christ (Matthew 4:21; Mark 1:20). This is from a Greek form of the Hebrew name that appears in the Old Testament as Zebadiah or *Zabdi* 'gift of Jehovah'.

Zebulun ♂ Biblical name, borne by the sixth son of Leah and Jacob. The name may mean 'exaltation', although Leah derives it from another meaning of the Hebrew root *zabal*, namely 'to dwell': 'now will my husband dwell with me, because I have born him six sons' (Genesis 30:20). It appears in the New Testament (Matthew 4:13) in the form Zabulon.

VARIANT: Zebulon.

Zechariah ♂ Name (meaning 'God has remembered' in Hebrew) of several figures in the Bible, most notably one of the twelve 'minor' prophets, author of the book that bears his name. It was

z

also the name of an earlier prophet, who was stoned by the people because of his preaching (2 Chronicles 24:20–23), and the last Israelite king of the race of Jehu, who was overthrown by Shallum the son of Jabesh (2 Kings 15:8–10). It is one of a number of Old Testament names that has enjoyed a modest revival in recent years. See also ▷Zachary.

Zed ♂ Mainly U.S.: short form of Zedekiah, which means 'justice of Yahweh' in Hebrew. It is borne in the Bible by three characters.

Zeev ♂ Jewish: Hebrew name meaning 'wolf'. It has become popular as a translation of European names with this meaning. The wolf is traditionally associated with the tribe of *Binyamin* or ▷Benjamin, because in his dying blessing the patriarch Jacob said 'Benjamin shall ravin as a wolf' (Genesis 49:27).

Zeke ♂ Mainly U.S.: short form of ▷Ezekiel, occasionally used independently.

Zelah ♀ Biblical name (meaning 'side' in Hebrew), borne by one of the fourteen cities of the tribe of Benjamin (Joshua 18:28). It is far from clear why it should have come to be used, albeit rarely, as a girl's given name in the English-speaking world. It may simply be a variant of ▷Zillah under the influence of the place name. However, for evidence that biblical place names did yield English given names, compare ▷Ebenezer.

Zelda ♀ Modern name of uncertain origin, possibly a short form of ▷Griselda. It came to prominence in the 1920s as the name of the wife of the American writer F. Scott Fitzgerald (1896–1940).

Zelig ♂ Jewish: variant of ▷Selig.

Zelma ♀ Modern coinage, an altered form of ▷Selma.

Zena ♀ Of uncertain origin, probably a respelling of ▷Zina or of ▷Xena. See also Scottish appendix.

Zenith ♀ From the vocabulary word referring to the highest point in the heavens, directly above the observer, and figuratively also to the greatest development of perfection. The word came into English in the Middle Ages, via French and Spanish, from Arabic *samt* 'way, path' (taken from the phrase *samt ar-rās* 'overhead path'). This has sometimes been used as a first name by parents who wish their daughter to 'reach the heights'.

Zeno ♂ From the classical Greek name *Zēnōn*, a short form of any of several names beginning with *Zēn-*, the stem form of the name of Zeus, king of the gods, for example *Zēnodōros* 'gift of Zeus'. Zeno was the name of two major Greek philosophers and a Christian Eastern Roman emperor (d. 491). Zeno of Elea (*c*.490–430 BC) was an original thinker who challenged common-sense notions like motion and number with sophisticated logical arguments. Zeno of Citium (*c*.334–262 BC) was the founder of the Stoics.

Zenobia ♀ Classical Greek name: feminine form of *Zēnobios*, a personal name composed of the elements *Zēn-* (see ▷Zeno) + *bios* 'life'. This was the name of a queen of Palmyra (*fl.* AD 267–272), who expanded her empire in the eastern Mediterranean and Asia Minor, but eventually came into conflict with Rome and was deposed by Aurelian. She was noted for her beauty and intelligence, but was also ruthless: she appears to have had her husband and his eldest son murdered.

Zephaniah ♂ Biblical name, meaning 'hidden by God' in Hebrew, borne by one of the minor prophets, author of the book of the Bible that bears his name. Its occasional use in Britain may be influenced by the poet Benjamin Zephaniah, who was born in Jamaica in 1958.

Z

SMALL FORM: **Zeph.**

Zephyrine ♀ From French *Zéphyrine*, an elaborated name derived from Latin *Zephyrus*, Greek *Zephyros* 'west wind'. St Zephyrinus was pope 199–217, but there is no equivalent female saint, so it is rather surprising that this name should have survived only in a female form.

Zeta ♀ Of uncertain origin, probably a variant spelling of ▷Zita. It also coincides in form with the name of the letter of the Greek alphabet equivalent to English *z* (but not the last letter of the Greek alphabet). In popular culture it is associated with the Welsh-born actress Catherine Zeta Jones (b. 1969).

Zillah ♀ Biblical name (from a Hebrew word meaning 'shade'), borne by one of the two wives of Lamech (Genesis 4:19). The name was taken up in the first place by the Puritans, and again by fundamentalist Christian groups in the 19th century, partly because Zillah is only the third woman to be mentioned by name in the Bible, and her name was therefore prominent to readers of the Book of Genesis.

Zina ♀ Russian short form of Zinaida (from Greek *Zēnais*, a derivative of the name of the god *Zeus*), the name of an obscure saint venerated in the Eastern Church. It is also a Russian short form of the rarer given name Zinovia (from Greek *Zēnobia*, a compound of *Zeus* + *bios* 'life'). Its adoption as a given name in the English-speaking world probably owes something to its resemblance to the popular girl's name ▷Tina. See Russian appendix.

Zinnia ♀ From the name of a genus of plants with brightly coloured flowers, originally native to Mexico and now widely cultivated. The botanical name is derived from the surname of the German botanist J.G. Zinn (1727–59).

Zipporah ♀ Biblical name borne by the wife of Moses and mother of Gershom and Eliezer (Exodus 18:2–4). It is the female form of the rare Hebrew male name *Zippor* meaning 'bird'. It now occurs mainly as a Jewish name, although it enjoyed wider currency during the 18th and 19th centuries.

Zita ♀ From the name of a 13th-century saint from Lucca in Tuscany, who led an uneventful life as a domestic servant; she was canonized in 1696, and is regarded as the patroness of domestic servants. Her name was probably a nickname from the medieval Tuscan dialect word *zit(t)a* 'girl', although efforts have been made to link it with Greek *zētein* 'to seek'.

Zoë ♀ From a Greek name meaning 'life'. This was already in use in Rome towards the end of the classical period (at first as an affectionate nickname), and was popular with the early Christians, who bestowed it with reference to their hopes of eternal life. It was borne by martyrs of the 2nd and 3rd centuries, but was taken up as an English given name only in the 19th century. It has been consistently popular in Britian since the 1970s.
VARIANT: **Zoe.**

Zola ♀ Apparently a late 20th-century creation, formed from the first syllable of ▷Zoë with the ending *-la*, common in girls' names. It coincides in form with the surname of the French novelist Émile Zola (1840–1902), who was of Italian descent, but it is unlikely that he had any influence on the use of the name.

Zula ♀ Modern coinage derived from the tribal name of the Zulus. The Zulu people of Southern Africa formed a powerful warrior nation under their leader Chaka in the 19th century, and controlled an extensive empire. In 1838, under the leadership of their ruler Dingaan, they ambushed and slaughtered a group of some five hundred Boers. Not surprisingly, this given name is chosen mainly by Black people proud of their African origins.

z

Zuleika ♀ Of unknown etymolgy. In Islamic and Renaissance Jewish tradition, *Zuleika* is the name of Potiphar's wife (not actually named in the Bible itself), who attempted to seduce Joseph and, when she failed, turned Potiphar against him (Genesis 39:7–20). In Max Beerbohm's satirical novel *Zuleika Dobson* (1911), the heroine is a fatally attractive young women who feels that she can only love a man who is indifferent to her. As a result, several of her admirers are driven to suicide.

Appendix 1:
Arabic Names

Note The names in this supplement, though of Arabic origin, have spread throughout the Muslim world. There are many local variations.

Aa

ʿAbbās ♂ 'Austere'. Abbās ibn ʿAbd-al-Muṭṭalib (c.566–652) was the Prophet's uncle and ancestor of the Abbasid caliphs, who ruled the Islamic world between 750 and 1258.

Abd-al-ʿĀṭi ♂ 'Servant of the Giver' (i.e. Allāh).

Abd-al-ʿAzīz ♂ 'Servant of the Mighty' (i.e. Allāh).

Abd-al-Fattāḥ ♂ 'Servant of the Opener' (i.e. Allāh as opener of the gates of wealth).

Abd-al-Hādi ♂ 'Servant of the Guider' (i.e. Allāh).

Abd-al-Ḥakīm ♂ 'Servant of the Wise' (i.e. Allāh).

Abd-al-Ḥalīm ♂ 'Servant of the Patient' (i.e. Allāh).

Abd-al-Ḥamīd ♂ 'Servant of the Praiseworthy' (i.e. Allāh).

Abd-al-Jawād ♂ 'Servant of the Magnanimous' (i.e. Allāh).

Abd-al-Karīm ♂ 'Servant of the Generous' (i.e. Allāh).

Abd-Allāh ♂ 'Servant of Allāh'. This was the name of the Prophet's father, who, however, died before Muḥammad was born.

Abd-al-Laṭīf ♂ 'Servant of the Kind' (i.e. Allāh).

Abd-al-Malik ♂ 'Servant of the King' (i.e. Allāh).

Abd-al-Muʿṭi ♂ 'Servant of the Giver' (i.e. Allāh).

Abd-al-Qādir ♂ 'Servant of the Capable' (i.e. Allāh).

Abd-al-Raḥīm, Abder-Raḥīm ♂ 'Servant of the Compassionate' (i.e. Allāh).

Abd-al-Raḥmān, Abder-Raḥmān ♂ 'Servant of the Merciful' (i.e. Allāh).

Abd-al-Rāziq, Abd-al-Razzāq, Abder-Razzāʾ ♂ 'Servant of the Provider' (i.e. Allāh).

Abd-al-Salām, Abdes-Salām ♂ 'Servant of the Peaceable' (i.e. Allāh).

Abd-al-Wahhāb ♂ 'Servant of the Giver' (i.e. Allāh).

Abid ♂ 'Worshipper'.

ʿAbīr ♀ 'Fragrance'.

ʿAbla ♀ 'Woman with a full figure'.

Ādil ♂ 'Just, fair'.

ʿAdnān ♂ Origin uncertain: possibly meaning 'settler'. The ʿAdnāniyūn were Arabs living in the north part of the Arabian Peninsula.

Afāf ♀ 'Chastity, decorum'.

Aḥlām ♀ 'Dream, vision of perfection'.

Aḥmad ♂ 'Highly commendable'.

Āʾisha ♀ 'Alive, thriving'; name of Muḥammad's third and favourite wife.

ʿAlāʾ ♂ 'Excellence, supremacy'.

ʿAli ♂ 'Sublime'; name of a cousin of the Prophet, who married his daughter Fāṭima and in 656 became the fourth rightly guided caliph. His sons ▸Hasan and ▸Husayn are regarded by Shiites as Muḥammad's true successors.
FEMININE FORM: ʿAliyya.

Amal ♀, ♂ 'Hope, expectation'.

Amāni ♀ 'Desires, aspirations'.

Amīn ♂ 'Honest, trustworthy'.

Amīna ♀ 'Peaceful, secure'; name of the Prophet's mother.

Amīr ♂ 'Prince, ruler'.
FEMININE FORM: Amīra.

ʿĀmir ♂ 'Prosperous'.

Amjad, Amgad ♂ 'Glorious'.

ʿAmmār ♂ 'Long-lived'; name of one of the earliest converts to Islam, renowned for his piety despite much persecution.

Anwar ♂ 'Clear, bright'.

Asʿad ♂ 'Happy, fortunate'.

Ashraf ♂ 'Honourable, distinguished'.

ʿĀṣim ♂ 'Protector, guardian'.

Asmāʾ ♀ 'Prestige'; name of a woman who helped Muḥammad and her father, Abu-Bakr, to escape from Mecca in 622, when their opponents were planning to murder them.

ʿĀṭif ♂ 'Compassionate, sympathetic'.

ʿAwāṭif ♀ 'Affections, tender feelings'.

ʿAyda ♀ 'Benefit, advantage'.

Ayman ♂ 'Blessed, prosperous'; name of Muḥammad's nurse.

ʿAzīz ♂ 'Invincible' or 'cherished'.
FEMININE FORM: ʿAzīza.

ʿAzza ♀ Probably from a word meaning 'pride' or 'power'.

Bb

Badr ♂, ♀ 'Full moon'. See also ▶Budūr.

Bahāʾ ♂ 'Splendour, glory'.

Bahīja, Bahīga ♀ 'Joyous, delightful'.

Bahiyya ♀ 'Beautiful, radiant'.

Bahjat, Bahgat ♂ 'Joy, delight'.

Bakr ♂ 'Young camel'. Abu-Bakr al-Ṣiddīq (573–634) was the Prophet's successor and the first rightly guided caliph (632–4).

Bāsim ♂ 'Smiling'.

Basma ♀ 'A smile'.

Bilil ♂ 'Moist': words denoting water, which is scarce in the desert, have positive associations in Arabic.

Budūr ♀ Plural of *badr* 'full moon', from *badara* 'to come up unexpectedly, take by surprise'. *Badr-al-Budūr* is a complimentary expression meaning roughly 'beauty of beauties'.

Buthayna, Busayna ♀ Diminutive of *bathua* 'flat fertile land'.

Dd

Dawūd ♂ Biblical. See David in main dictionary.

Dīma ♀ 'Torrential rain'. The word has positive connotations in Arabic.

Ḍiyāʾ ♂ 'Brightness'.

Duʿāʾ ♀ 'Prayer'.

Ḍuḥa ♀ 'Morning'.

Ff

Fādi ♂ 'Redeemer, saviour'; an attribute of Jesus Christ.
FEMININE FORM: Fadia.

Fāḍil ♂ 'Virtuous, generous, distinguished'.
ALSO: Fadle.

Fāḍila ♀ 'Moral excellence, virtue'.

Fahd ♂ 'Panther' or 'leopard'; name of the king of Saudi Arabia from 1982.

Fahīm ♂ 'Person of profound understanding'.

Fakhr-al-Dīn, Fakhr-ud-Dīn ♂ 'Glory of religion'.

Fakhri ♂ 'Meritorious, glorious'.
FEMININE FORM: Fakhriyya.

Faraj ♂ 'Remedy (for worries or grief)'.

Farīd ♂ 'Unique, unrivalled'.
FEMININE FORM: Farīda (also meaning 'gem').

Farūq ♂ Literally 'distinguisher', i.e. one who can distinguish right from wrong and truth from falsehood. *Al-Farūq* was a byname of ʿUmar ibn-al-Khaṭṭāb, second rightly guided caliph (634–44), known for his uncompromising execution of justice.

Fatḥi ♂ Probably from *fatiḥ* 'releaser' or 'conqueror'. FEMININE FORM: **Fatḥiyya**.

Fāṭima ♀ 'Abstainer (from forbidden things)', i.e. chaste; also 'weaner', i.e. one who cares for her children. This was the name of the Prophet's favourite daughter, wife of 'Ali ibn-Abi-Ṭālib, fourth rightly guided caliph, and mother of ►Ḥasan and ►Ḥusayn.

Fawzi ♂ From *fawz* 'triumph, victory, accomplishment'. FEMININE FORM: **Fawziyya**.

Fāyiz ♂ 'Victor, winner'. FEMININE FORM: **Fayza**.

Fayrūz ♀ 'Turquoise' (the precious stone); of Persian origin.

Fayṣal, Feisal ♂ 'Judge', literally 'separator' (i.e. between right and wrong).

Fiḍḍa, Fiẓẓa ♀ 'Silver'.

Fihr ♂ Ancient name of uncertain origin, apparently from a word denoting a type of stone pestle used for pounding the ingredients of medicines.

Fikri ♂ 'Intellectual, meditative'. FEMININE FORM: **Fikriyya**.

Firdos ♂ 'Paradise'.

Firoz ♂ 'Victorious' or 'successful'.

Fu'ād ♂ 'Heart'.

Gg

(see also J.)

Ghāda ♀ 'Graceful young woman'.

Ghadīr ♀ 'Brook, stream'.

Ghālib ♂ 'Conqueror, victor'.

Ghassān ♂ 'Prime of youth'.

Ghayth ♂ 'Rain'; a word with favourable connotations in a desert climate.

Ghufrān ♀ 'Forgiveness'.

Hh

Ḥabīb ♂ 'Beloved'. FEMININE FORM: **Ḥabība**.

Hādi ♂ **1** 'Guide, leader' (in particular, a spiritual guide or leader). **2** 'Calm, quiet, peaceable'. FEMININE FORM: **Hadya**.

Hadīl ♀ 'Cooing of doves'.

Ḥāfiẓ ♂ 'Custodian, guardian'. *Al-Ḥāfiẓ* was an honorific term denoting someone who knew the Qur'an by heart. FEMININE FORM: **Ḥafẓa**.

Haidar ♂ 'Lion'. *Haidar Allāh* 'Lion of Allāh' was an epithet of 'Ali, son-in-law of the Prophet Muḥammad and fourth rightly guided caliph.

Hājar, Hāgar ♀ Ancient name of uncertain origin. Hājar was the Egyptian concubine of ►Ibrāhīm (Abraham),

mother of Ismā'īl (Ishmael), from whom Arabs believe they are descended.

Ḥakīm ♂ 'Wise, judicious'.

Hāla ♀ Ancient name meaning 'halo (around the moon)'.

Ḥamdi ♂ 'Pertaining to praise and gratitude' (in particular for Allāh's favours).

Ḥāmid ♂ 'Thankful, praising' (i.e. praising Allāh).

Ḥamza ♂ Ancient name, probably meaning 'steadfast'.

Hanā' ♀ 'Bliss, happiness, well-being'.

Ḥanān ♀ 'Tenderness, affection'.

Hāni ♂ 'Happy'. FEMININE FORM: **Haniyya**.

Ḥārith ♂ 'Provider, breadwinner'. *Al-Ḥārith* is also an epithet of the lion.

Hārūn ♂ Biblical. See Aaron in main dictionary; the name of a famous caliph, Hārūn al-Rashīd (*c.*764–809).

Ḥasan ♂ 'Good, beautiful'. Shiites regard Ḥasan and his brother ►Ḥusayn as the legitimate successors of Muḥammad.

Hāshim ♂ Literally 'crusher', i.e. one who breaks bread; a byname of the great-grandfather of the Prophet, who provided food at the Ka'ba temple. Muslims are sometimes referred to as 'Hashemites' because they are regarded as the descendants of Hāshim.

Hāsim ♂ 'Decisive'. The ability to make a swift and decisive distinction between right and wrong is a quality greatly prized among Muslims.

Hātim ♂ 'Decisive, determined'. Hātim ibn-'Abd-Allāh (d. 605) was famous for his generosity.

Hayfā' ♀ 'Slender, delicate'.

Haytham ♂ 'Young eagle'.

Hiba ♀ 'Gift, grant'.

Hikmat ♂, ♀ 'Wisdom'.

Hind ♀ Ancient name of unknown origin. It was borne by one of the Prophet's wives, renowned for her beauty.

Hishām ♂ Literally 'crushing' but with the transferred meaning 'having a generous nature', by association with the crushing and distribution of bread. See ▶Hāshim.

Huda ♀ 'Right guidance'.

Husām ♂ 'Sword'.

Husayn ♂ Diminutive of *hasan* 'good, beautiful, exquisite'. Al-Husayn (*c.*626–680) was the grandson of the Prophet, whose supporters emerged after his death as the Shiite party.

Husni ♂ 'Excellence'.

I i

Ibrāhīm ♂ Arabic form of Abraham (see main dictionary), the biblical patriarch and father of Ismā'īl and Ishāq (Ishmael and Isaac), founding fathers of the Arabic and Jewish peoples respectively.

Ibtisām ♀ 'Smiling'.

Idrīs ♂ Name of a man mentioned twice in the Qur'an, described as 'a true man, a prophet' and 'of the righteous'. It was also the name of the founder of the first Shiite dynasty (788–974).

Ihāb ♂, ♀ 'Gift'.

Ihsān ♂, ♀ 'Charity, benefaction'.

Imām ♂ 'Leader'. For Sunnis this can denote any pious Muslim who leads prayers in a mosque, but for Shiites it refers specifically to the descendants of 'Ali and Fātima, whom they regard as the only true successors of Muhammad.

Imān ♀ 'Faith, belief'.

In'ām ♀ 'Benefaction, bestowal'.

Isām ♂ 'Strap (implying protection), pledge, security'. *Isām al-Dīn* is a title meaning 'protector of religion'.

Ismā'īl ♂ Name of the son of ▶Ibrāhīm

(Abraham) by Hājar, his Egyptian concubine. Arabs believe that they are descended from Ismā'īl, while the Jews are descended from Isaac, the son of Abraham by Sarah. The Ismaili sect of Shiites believe that on the death of the imam Ja'far al-Sidīq in 765 the Divine Spirit passed to his son Ismā'īl rather than to his other son Mūsa.

'Ismat ♂, ♀ 'Sinlessness' or 'infallibility'.

Isrā' ♀ 'Night journey', with reference to the story of Muhammad's night journey to Jerusalem, which recounts how he visited the mosque and the temple and met Jesus and Moses before returning to Mecca the same night.

I'tidāl ♀ 'Temperance, moderation'.

'Izz-al-Dīn, 'Izz-ed-Dīn ♂ 'Power (or glory) of religion'.

J j

Jābir, Gābir ♂ 'Comforter, restorer, one who assists in time of need'.

Jabr, Gabr ♂ 'Consolation, assistance in time of need'.

Ja'far, Ga'far ♂ 'Small river, stream'. Ja'far ibn-Abi-Tālib (d. 629) died heroically at the Battle of Mota (629), holding aloft the Muslim banner proclaiming 'Paradise!'

Jalāl, Galāl ♂ 'Greatness, glory'.

Jalīla, Galīla ♀ 'Honourable, exalted'.

Jamāl, Gamāl ♂, in some places also ♀ 'Good looks, beauty'.

Jamīl, Gamīl ♂ 'Handsome, graceful'. FEMININE FORM: Jamīla.

Jāthibiyya, Gāzibiyya ♀ 'Attractiveness, charm'.

Jawāhir, Gawāhir ♀ 'Jewels'.

Jawdat, Gawdat ♂ 'Goodness, excellence'.

Jinān ♂, ♀ 'Gardens, paradise'.

Jūda, Gūda ♂ 'Goodness, excellence'.

Kk

Kamāl ♂ 'Perfection'.

Kāmil ♂ 'Perfect'.

Karam ♂, ♀ 'Generosity, magnanimity'.

Karīm ♂ 'Noble, generous'. FEMININE FORM: Karīma.

Khadīja, Khadīga ♀ Ancient name, originally a byname meaning 'premature child'. Khadīja bint-Khuwaylid (d. 619) was the Prophet's first wife and mother of all his children.

Khālid ♂ 'Undying, eternal'. Khālid ibn-al-Walīd (d. 642) was the military strategist principally responsible for the spread of Islam by force in its early days.

Khalīfa ♂ 'Caliph', literally 'successor'.

Khalīl ♂ 'Bosom friend'.

Khayrat ♂ 'Good deed'.

Khayri ♂ 'Charitable, benevolent'. FEMININE FORM: Khayriyya.

Ll

Lamyā' ♀ 'Possessing brown lips'.

Lawāḥiz ♀ 'Shy glances'.

Layla ♀ 'Wine' or 'intoxication'; name of the beloved of the poet Qays ibn-al-Mulawwaḥ (d. 688).

Līna ♀ From a word denoting a type of palm tree.

Lubna ♀ 'Storax', a tree with a sweet honey-like sap, used for making incense and perfume and still popular in most Arab countries.

Lujayn ♀ 'Silver'.

Mm

Madīḥa ♀ 'Praise, commendation'.

Maha ♀ 'Oryx' (a species of antelope found in Arabia and North Africa). Oryxs are admired for their large, beautiful eyes.

Maḥāsin ♀ 'Charms, good qualities'.

Māhir ♂ 'Skilful, proficient'.

Maḥmūd ♂ 'Praiseworthy, commendable'.

Majdi, Magdi ♂ 'Praiseworthy'. FEMININE FORM: Magda.

Mājid ♂ 'Glorious, illustrious'. FEMININE FORM: Mājida.

Makram ♂ 'Generous, noble, magnanimous'.

Malak ♀ 'Angel'.

Mamdūḥ ♂ 'Praised, commended'.

Ma'mūn ♂ 'Reliable, trustworthy'.

Manāl ♂, ♀ 'Attainment' or 'acquisition'.

Manār ♂, ♀ 'Lighthouse, beacon'.

Manṣūr ♂ 'Victorious, triumphant'.

Marwa ♀ From a word denoting both a fragrant plant and a type of shiny pebble.

Maryam ♀ Biblical. See Miriam and Mary in main dictionary.

Mas'ūd ♂ 'Lucky'.

Maysa ♀ Perhaps from *mayyas* 'to walk with a graceful, proud gait'.

Māzin ♂ Of uncertain origin; possibly from *muzn* 'rain clouds'.

Midḥat ♂
'Commendation, eulogy'.

Mubārak ♂ 'Blessed, fortunate'.

Muḥammad ♂
'Praiseworthy, possessing fine qualities'. The most popular male Muslim name, bestowed in honour of Muḥammad ibn-'Abd-Allāh ibn-'Abd-al-Muṭṭalib (570–632) of Mecca, the Prophet of Islam.

Muḥayya ♀ 'Face, countenance' (i.e. beautiful face).

Muḥsin ♂ 'Charitable, beneficent'.
FEMININE FORM: Muḥsina.

Mujtaba ♂ 'Chosen', a byname of the Prophet Muḥammad.

Mukhtār ♂ 'Preferred'.

Muna ♀ 'Hope' or 'object of desire'.

Mun'im ♂ 'Benefactor, donor'.

Munīr ♂ 'Luminous, bright, shining'.
FEMININE FORM: Munīra.

Mus'ad ♂ 'Lucky, favoured by fortune'.

Muṣṭafa ♂ 'Pure' or 'chosen'. Al-Muṣṭafa 'the Chosen One' is an epithet of Muḥammad. For Arabic-speaking Christians it is an epithet of St Paul. Muṣṭafa Kamāl (1881–1938) was the founder of modern Turkey (president from 1922), known in Turkish as

Atatürk 'father of the Turks'.

Mu'taṣim ♂ 'Adhering to (God)' or 'seeking refuge in (God)'.

Mu'tazz ♂ 'Proud, powerful'.

Nn

Nabīl ♂ 'Noble, high-born, honourable'.
FEMININE FORM: Nabīla.

Nada ♀ 'Morning dew'; also 'generosity'.

Nadīm ♂ 'Drinking companion, confidant'.

Nādir ♂ 'Rare, precious'.
FEMININE FORM: Nād(i)ra.

Nadiyya ♀ 'Moist with dew'; in a hot, dry climate, morning dew is highly valued. There has been some influence from the Russian name Nadia (see main dictionary).

Nāhid ♀ From a word denoting a young girl with swelling breasts.

Nahla ♀ 'Drink of water, thirst-quenching draught'.

Nā'il ♂ 'One who attains his desires, winner'.
FEMININE FORM: Nā'ila.

Na'īm ♂ 'Contented, tranquil, happy'.
FEMININE FORM: Na'īma.

Najāḥ, Nagāḥ ♀
'Success, progress'.

Najāt, Nagāt ♀
'Salvation, redemption'.

Nāji, Nāgi ♂ 'Saved, rescued'.

Najīb, Nagīb ♂ 'Noble, well-born, distinguished, high-minded'.
FEMININE FORMS: Najība, Nagība.

Najlā', Naglā' ♀ 'Having large and beautiful eyes'.

Najwa, Nagwa ♀
'Intimate confidential conversation'.

Nāṣir ♂ 'Helper, supporter'.

Naṣr ♂ 'Victory, triumph'.

Nasrīn ♀ 1 From Persian: 'wild rose'. 2 Arabic: denoting the constellation of the Eagle and the Lyre.

Nawāl ♀ 'Gift, benefit'.

Nibāl ♀ 'Arrows'.

Nihād ♀ Of uncertain origin; perhaps from a word meaning both 'high ground' and 'female breasts'.

Nihāl ♀ 'Those whose thirst is quenched'.

Ni'mat ♀ 'Boon, favour, blessing'.

Nizār ♂ Of uncertain origin; possibly from a word meaning 'little one'.

Nuha ♀ 'Mind, intellect'.

Nūr ♀, ♂ 'Light'.

Nura ♀ Of uncertain origin, perhaps a variant of ▶Nūr, although there is also an Arabic word *nura* meaning 'feature, characteristic'.

Qq

Qāsim ♂ 'One who divides or distributes (money or food)'.

Quṣay ♂ Ancient name of uncertain origin; perhaps from a word meaning 'distant, remote'. Quṣay ibn-Fihr (*fl.* 420) of the Quraish tribe was the great-great-great-grandfather of the Prophet.

Rr

Rabāb ♀ From a word denoting a stringed musical instrument resembling the fiddle.

Raʿd ♂ 'Thunder'.

Raḍwa ♀ Name of a district of Mecca, the birthplace of the Prophet.

Raḍwān ♂ 'Pleasure, contentment'.

Raʾfat ♂ 'Mercy, compassion'.

Rafīq ♂ Meaning either 'comrade, friend' or 'kind, gentle'.

Raghīd ♂ 'Carefree, enjoyable'.
FEMININE FORM: **Raghda**.

Rajāʾ, Ragāʾ ♀ 'Hope, anticipation'.

Rajab, Ragab ♂ Seventh month of the Muslim calendar.

Rājya, Rāgya ♀ 'Hopeful'.

Ramaḍān ♂ Ninth month of the Muslim calendar, 'the hot month'. During Ramadan Muslims fast from dawn until sunset.

Rana ♀ 'Beautiful object'.

Randa ♀ From a word denoting a sweet-smelling tree that grows in the desert.

Ranya ♀ 'Looking or gazing at (the beloved)'.

Rashād ♂ 'Good sense' or 'good guidance' (especially in religious matters).

Rāshid, Rashīd ♂ 'Rightly guided'.
FEMININE FORM: **Rāshida**.

Raʾūf ♂ 'Merciful, compassionate'.

Rāwiya ♀ 'Narrator, reciter, transmitter' (especially of classical Arabic poetry).

Riaz ♂ 'Meadows, gardens'; in some countries denoting meadows where horses were broken in.

Riḍa ♂, ♀ 'Contentment, approval' (by Allāh).

Rīm ♀ 'White antelope'.

Ruqayya ♀ 'Ascent, progress', or 'spell, charm'; the name of one of Muhammad's daughters.

Rushdi ♂ 'Sensible conduct, emotional maturity'.

Ss

Ṣabāḥ ♀ 'Morning'.

Ṣābir, Ṣabri ♂ 'Patient, persevering'.
FEMININE FORM: **Ṣabriyya**.

Saʿd ♂ 'Good luck, fortune'. Saʿd ibn-Abi-Waqqāṣ was a cousin of the Prophet, who led the Muslims to victory in the Battle of Qadisiyya (637). In 639 he founded Kufa, the holy city of Shiites.

Ṣafāʾ ♀, ♂ 'Purity, sincerity'.

Safdar ♂ 'One who breaks ranks', suggesting an impetuous but brave soldier.

Ṣafiyya ♀ 'Confidante, bosom friend'.

Ṣafwat ♂ 'Choicest, best'.

Sahar ♀ 'Early morning, dawn'.

Saʿīd ♂ 'Happy, lucky'.

Ṣakhr ♂ 'Solid rock'.

Ṣalāḥ ♂ 'Goodness, righteousness'. *Salah-ud-Din* (Saladdin) means 'righteousness of religion'.

Salāma ♂ 'Safety, well-being'.

Ṣāliḥ ♂ 'Virtuous, devout'.
FEMININE FORM: **Ṣālḥa**.

Salīm, Sālim ♂ 'Safe, unharmed'.
FEMININE FORM: **Salma**.

Salwa ♀ 'Consolation, solace'.

Sāmi ♂ 'Elevated, sublime'.
FEMININE FORM: **Samya**.

Samīḥ ♂ 'Tolerant, magnanimous'.
FEMININE FORM: **Samīḥa**.

Samīr ♂ 'Companion in night talk'.
FEMININE FORMS: **Samar, Samīra**.

Sanā' ♀ 'Brilliance, radiance'.

Saniyya ♀ 'Brilliant, radiant, resplendent'.

Sāra ♀ Biblical. See Sarah in main dictionary.

Sarāb ♀ 'Mirage'.

Sawsan ♀ 'Lily of the valley'.

Sayyid ♂ 'Master, lord'.

Sha'bān ♂ Eighth month of the Muslim calender.

Shabbir ♂ Biblical, name of a son of Aaron.

Shādi ♂, **Shādya** ♀ 'Singer'.

Shafīq ♂ 'Compassionate'.
FEMININE FORM: **Shafīqa**.

Shahīra ♀ 'Famous'.

Shakīl ♂ 'Handsome'.

Shākir ♂ 'Thankful, grateful'.

Shamīm ♀, ♂ 'Fragrance, perfume'.

Sharīf ♂ 'Eminent, honourable'.
FEMININE FORM: **Sharifa**.

Shatha ♀ 'Fragrance, perfume'.

Shukri ♂ 'Giving thanks'.
FEMININE FORM: **Shukriyya**.

Sihām ♀ 'Arrows'.

Su'ād ♀ Of unknown origin.

Suha ♀ 'Star'.

Suhād, Suhair ♀ 'Sleeplessness'.

Suhayl ♂ Arabic name of the bright star Canopus.

Suleimān, Sulaymān ♂ Biblical. See Solomon in main dictionary.

Sultan ♂ 'Ruler, king, emperor'.
FEMININE FORM: **Sultana**.

Surayya ♀ Variant of ▶Thurayya.

Tt

Taghrīd ♀ 'Bird song'.

Ṭāha ♂ From the Arabic letters ṭa and ha, the opening letters of the twentieth sura in the Qur'an.

Ṭāhir ♂ 'Pure, virtuous'.

Taḥiyya ♀ 'Greeting, salutation'.

Ṭalāl ♂ 'Dew' or 'fine rain'.

Tāmir ♂ 'Rich in dates'.

Taqi ♂ 'Piety, fear of God'. Muhammad Taqi (811–835) was the ninth Shiite imam.

Ṭāriq ♂ 'One who knocks at the door at night, nocturnal visitor'; also 'morning star'.

Ṭarūb ♀ 'Enraptured'.

Tawfīq ♂ 'Good fortune, prosperity'.

Thanā' ♀ 'Praise, commendation'.

Thheiba ♀ 'Gold bar'.

Thurayya, Surayya ♀ 'The Pleiades'.

Uu

'Umar, Omar
'Flourishing'. 'Umar ibn-al-Khaṭṭāb was the second rightly guided caliph (634–44), a man noted for his justice, administrative ability, and the simplicity of his lifestyle.

'Umayma ♀ 'Little mother'.

'Um-Kalthūm ♀ 'Mother of one with plump cheeks'; name of one of the Prophet's daughters.

'Umniya ♀ 'Wish, desire'.

'Uthmān, 'Usmān ♂ 'Bustard' (the bird). 'Uthmān ibn-'Affān was the third rightly guided caliph (644–56), noted for his generosity and loyalty.

Ww

Wafā' ♀ 'Loyalty, fidelity'.

Wahīb ♂ 'Donor, generous giver'.
FEMININE FORM: Wahība.

Wā'il ♂ 'One who reverts' (i.e. to Allāh).

Wajīh ♂ 'Distinguished, notable'.

Walīd ♂ 'Newborn baby'. Al-Walīd ibn-'Abd-al-Malik (d. 715) was the Umayyad caliph (705–15) whose armies conquered Spain and attempted to capture Constantinople.

Wasīm ♂ 'Handsome, good-looking'.

Widād ♀ 'Affection, friendship'.

Yy

Yaḥya ♂ Biblical. See John in main dictionary.

Ya'qūb ♂ Biblical. See Jacob in main dictionary.

Yasīn ♂ From the Arabic letters *ya* and *sīn*, the opening letters of the thirty-sixth sura of the Qur'an.

Yāsir, Yusri ♂ 'Rich, well off'.
FEMININE FORM: Yusriyya.

Yasmīn ♀ 'Jasmine'.

Yūnis ♂ Biblical. See Jonah in main dictionary.

Yusra ♀ 'Prosperity, affluence, good fortune'.

Yūsuf ♂ Biblical. See Joseph in main dictionary.

Zz

Zāhir ♂ 'Shining, radiant'.

Zahra ♀ 'Shining', also 'flower'.

Zakariyya ♂ Biblical. See Zachary in main dictionary.

Zaki ♂ 'Pure, virtuous'.
FEMININE FORM: Zakiyya.

Zamir ♂ 'Thought'.

Zayd ♂ Ancient name, possibly meaning 'increase'. It was borne by one of Muhammad's earliest converts and most loyal supporters.

Zaynab, Zeinab ♀ From the name of a beautiful, sweet-smelling plant. This was the name of the Prophet's daughter, two of his wives, and his granddaughter. The latter brought Islam to Egypt.

Ziyād ♂ 'Growth'.

Zubaida ♀ 'Marigold'.

Zuhayr ♂ Diminutive of *zahr* 'flowers'.

Zulēkha ♀ Biblical: name of Potiphar's wife, who conceived a passion for Joseph. See Zuleika in main dictionary.

Appendix 2:
Chinese Names

Note Personal names in Chinese culture are very different from their English counterparts. They consist of one or two characters. In theory they can be freely chosen from the 60,000 or so characters which make up the Chinese lexicon, but in practice this is not the case, as some characters are more often chosen as names, and certain characters are more commonly associated with one or the other of the sexes. Names are often descriptive, for example *Dong*, a male name meaning 'winter', chosen partly for ornamental reasons, but often also indicating a connection with that season. A name may also represent qualities which the giver of the name, typically the grandparents or an elder in the family, hopes the bearer of the name will develop, for example *Fuhua* 'fortune, flourishing'. Female names of this sort often relate to beauty, flowers, fragrances, kindness, or intelligence, while male names often tend to the traditional male virtues of strength, benevolence, sharpness, uprightness, and honesty.

Aa

Ai ♀ 'Loving'.

Aiguo ♂ 'Love country', i.e. 'patriotic'.

Bb

Bai ♂ 'White'. Li Bai (701–762) was a famous Tang poet. This name is also pronounced 'Bo'.

Baozhai ♀ 'Precious hairpin'.

Bingwen ♂ 'Bright and cultivated'.

Biyu ♀ 'Jasper', a reddish-brown semiprecious stone, a type of quartz.

Bo ♂ 'Waves'. See also ▸Bai.

Bohai ♂ 'Elder brother sea'. *Bo* is used to refer to the eldest of a group of brothers.

Bojing ♂ 'Win admiration'.

Bolin ♂ 'Elder brother rain'. For the interpretation of *Bo* see ▸Bohai. *Lin* denotes a continuous downpour of rain lasting several days.

Boqin ♂ 'Win respect'.

Cc

Changchang ♀ 'Flourishing'. The reduplication of *Chang* makes the name more intimate and familiar.

Changming ♂ 'Forever bright'.

Changpu ♂ 'Forever simple'.

Changying ♀ 'Flourishing and lustrous'.

Chao ♂ 'Surpassing'.

Chaoxiang ♂ 'Expecting fortune'.

Cheng ♂ 'Accomplished'.

Chenglei ♂ 'Become great'.

Chenguang ♀ 'Morning light'.

Chongan ♂ 'Second brother peace'. For the interpretation of *Chong* see ▸Chonglin.

Chongkun ♂ 'Second brother Kunlun mountain'. For the interpretation of *Chong* see ▸Chonglin. *Kun* is short for *Kunlun*, the name of a mountain range extending across Qinghai, Tibet, and Xinjiang.

Chonglin ♂ 'Second brother unicorn'. *Chong* refers to the second brother in a family, while *lin* denotes a mythical beast similar to a unicorn.

Chuanli ♂ 'Transmitting propriety'.

Chunhua ♀ 'Spring flower' or 'spring flourishing'.

Chuntao ♀ 'Spring peach'.

Cuifen ♀ 'Emerald fragrance'.

Dd

Da ♂ 'Attainment'.

Daiyu ♀ 'Black jade'. See ▸Huidai.

Dandan ♀ 'Cinnabar' or 'cinnabar red'. Cinnabar is associated with loyalty and sincerity. The reduplication of *Dan* makes it more intimate and familiar.

Delun ♂ 'Virtuous order'.

Deming ♂ 'Virtue bright'.

Dingxiang ♂ 'Stability and fortune'.

Dong ♂ 1 'East'. 2 'Winter'.

Donghai ♂ 'Eastern sea'.

Dongmei ♀ 'Winter plum'.

Duyi ♂ 'Independent wholeness'.

Ee

Ehuang ♀ 'Beauty August'. In Chinese mythology this is the name of the twin sister of ▸Nuying.

Enlai ♂ 'Favour coming'. This was the given name of Premier Zhou Enlai (1899–1976).

Ff

Fa ♂ 'Setting off'.

Fang 1 ♂ 'Upright and honest'. 2 ♀ 'Fragrance'.

Fenfang ♀ 'Fragrant and aromatic'.

Feng ♂ 1 'Sharp blade'. 2 'Wind'.

Fengge ♂ 'Phoenix pavilion'.

Fu ♂ 'Wealthy'.

Fuhua ♀ 'Fortune flourishing'.

Gg

Gang ♂ 'Strength'.

Geming ♂ 'Revolution', a popular name after the founding of the People's Republic of China in 1949.

Gen ♂ 'Root'.

Guang ♂ 'Light'.

Guangli ♂ 'Making propriety bright'.

Gui ♂ 'Honoured' or 'noble'.

Guiren ♂ 'Valuing benevolence'.

Guoliang ♂ 'May the country be kind'.

Guowei ♂ 'State preserving' or perhaps 'May the state be preserved'.

Guozhi ♂ 'The state is ordered' or 'May the state be ordered'.

Hh

Hai ♂ 'Sea'.

He ♂ 'River'; specifically, the Yellow River.

Heng ♂ 'Eternal'.

Hong 1 ♀ 'Red', the auspicious colour of weddings, also of the Communist Party. 2 ♂ 'Wild swan'. 3 ♂ 'Great'.

Honghui ♂ 'Great splendour'.

Hongqi ♂ 'Red flag'.

Hualing ♀ 'Flourishing fu-ling'. Fu-ling (*Poris cocos*) is a herb used in Chinese medicine.

Huan ♀, ♂ 'Happiness'.

Hui ♂ 'Splendour'.

Huian ♀ 'Kind peace'.

Huidai ♀ 'Wise blacking'. Dai is a dark pigment, which was used by women in times past to paint their eyebrows.

Huifang ♀ 'Kind and fragrant'.

Huifen ♀ 'Wise fragrance'.

Huiliang ♀ 'Kind and good'.

Huiling ♀ 'Wise jade tinkling'. See ▸Ling 2.

Huiqing ♀ 'Kind and affectionate'.

Huizhong ♀ 'Wise loyalty'.

Huojin ♂ 'Fire metal'.

Jj

Jia ♀ 'Beautiful'.

Jian ♂ 'Healthy'.

Jiang ♂ 'River'; specifically the Yangtze.

Jianguo ♂ 'Building the country'; a common patriotic name in mainland China.

Jianjun ♂ 'Building the army'.

Jianyu ♂ 'Building the universe'.

Jiao ♀ 'Lovely' or 'dainty'.

Jiayi ♀ 'Household fitting' !

Jiaying ♀ 'Household flourishing'.

Jie ♀ 'Cleanliness'.

Jing 1 ♂ 'Capital'; used for a man born in the capital city. 2 ♀ 'Stillness'. 3 ♀ 'Luxuriance'.

Jingfei ♀ 'Still fragrance'.

Jingguo ♂ 'Administering the state'.

Jinghua ♀ 'Situation splendid'.

Jinhai ♂ 'Golden sea'.

Jinjing ♂ 'Gold mirror'.

Ju ♀ 'Chrysanthemum'.

Juan ♀ 'Graciousness'.

Junjie ♂ 'Handsome and outstanding'.

Kk

Kang ♂ 'Well-being'.

Ll

Lan ♀ 'Orchid'.

Lanfen ♀ 'Orchid fragrance'.

Lanying ♀ 'Indigo lustrousness'.

Lei ♂ 'Thunder'.

Li 1 ♂ 'Profit' or 'sharp'. 2 ♀, ♂ 'Upright'.

Liang ♂ 'Bright'.

Lifen ♀ 'Beautiful fragrance'.

Lihua ♀ 1 'Beautiful and flourishing'. 2 'Beautiful China'.

Lijuan ♀ 'Beautiful and graceful'.

Liling ♀ 'Beautiful jade tinkle'. See ▶Ling 2.

Lin ♀ 'Beautiful jade'. See ▶Ling 2.

Ling 1 ♀, ♂ 'Understanding' or 'compassion'. 2 ♀ 'Tinkle', in particular the tinkling sound of pieces of jade hanging in the wind. For the significance of jade in Chinese culture, see ▶Yu 1.

Liqin ♀ 'Beautiful zither'.

Liqiu ♀ 'Beautiful autumn'.

Liu ♀, ♂ 'Flowing'.

Liwei ♂ 'Profit and greatness'.

Longwei ♂ 'Dragon greatness'.

Luli ♀ 'Dewy jasmine'.

Mm

Mei ♀ 'Plum'. One of the three so-called 'friends of winter' (*dong sanyou*): plum (*mei*), pine (*song*), and bamboo (*zhu*), which stay green throughout the winter. It is also a symbol of endurance.

Meifen ♀ 'Plum fragrance'.

Meifeng ♀ 'Beautiful wind'.

Meihui ♀ 'Beautiful wisdom'.

Meili ♀ 'Beautiful'.

Meilin ♀ 'Plum jade'.

Meirong ♀ 'Beautiful countenance'.

Meixiang ♀ 'Plum fragrance'.

Meixiu ♀ 'Beautiful grace'.

Mengyao ♂ Meng is the surname of the Chinese philosopher Mencius (372–289 BC), founder of the idealist wing of Confucianism, holding that man's nature is inherently good. Yao is the name of a mythical sage emperor. This name is one of aspiration, implying the wish: 'May the child be as wise and good as Mencius and Yao.'

Mingli ♂ 'Bright propriety' or 'making propriety bright'.

Mingxia ♀ 'Bright glow'. *Xia* is the rosy glow seen through the clouds at dawn and dusk.

Mingyu ♀ 'Bright jade'. See ▶Yu 1.

Mingzhu ♀ 'Bright pearl'.

Minsheng ♂ 'Voice of the people'.

Minzhe ♂ 'Sensitive and wise'.

Nn

Nianzu ♂ 'Thinking of ancestors'.

Ning ♀ 'Tranquillity'.

Ninghong ♀ 'Tranquil red'; or conceivably 'rather be red'. See ▶Hong 1.

Niu ♀ 'Girl'.

Nuo ♀ 'Graceful'.

Nuying ♀ 'Female flower'. In Chinese mythology this is the name of the twin sister of ▶Ehuang, daughters of the mythical sage king Yao, and both were wives to Yao's successor in wise kingship, Shun.

Pp

Peijing ♀ 'Admiring luxuriance'.

Peizhi ♀ 'Admiring iris'. See ▶Xiaozhi.

Peng ♂ 'Roc', a legendary bird. This is the given name of the Chinese premier Li Peng (b. 1928).

Pengfei ♂ 'Flight of the roc'. See ▶Peng.

Ping ♂ 'Stable'.

Qq

Qi 1 ♂ 'Wondrous' or 'enlightenment'. 2 ♀ 'Fine jade'.

Qianfan ♂ 'Thousand sails'.

Qiang 1 ♀ 'Rose'. 2 ♂ 'Strong'.

Qiao ♀ 'Skilful'.

Qiaohui ♀ 'Skilful and wise'.

Qiaolian ♀ 'Skilful always'.

Qing ♀ 'Dark blue'.

Qingge ♀ 'Clear pavilion'.

Qingling ♀ 'Celebration of understanding'.

Qingshan ♂ 'Celebrating goodness'.

Qingsheng ♂ 'Celebrating birth'.

Qingzhao ♀ 'Clear understanding' or 'clear illumination'. This was the given name of China's greatest woman poet, Li Qingzhao (1084–c.1151).

Qiqiang ♂ 'Enlightenment and strength'.

Qiu ♀, ♂ 'Autumn'; given to a child born in that season.

Qiuyue ♀ 'Autumn moon'.

Quan ♂ 'Spring' (of water) as in 'hot spring'.

Rr

Renshu ♂ 'Benevolent forbearance'.

Renxiang ♀ 'Benevolent fragrance'.

Rong ♀, ♂ 'Martial'. This is the name of Zhang Rong (Jung Chang; b. 1952), author of *Wild Swans*. Before 1949, it was almost exclusively a male name.

Rou ♀ 'Gentle' or 'mild'.

Ru ♂ 'Scholar', specifically a Confucian scholar.

Ruiling ♀ 'Auspicious jade tinkling'. See ▶Ling 2.

Ruolan ♀ 'Like an orchid'.

Ruomei ♀ 'Like a plum'. See ▶Mei.

Ss

Shan 1 ♂ 'Mountain'. A symbol of greatness, achievement, and longevity. See ▶Shoushan. 2 ♀ 'Elegant bearing'.

Shanyuan ♂ 'Mountain source'.

Shaoqing ♀ 'Young blue'.

Shen ♂ 1 'Cautious'. 2 'Deep'.

Shi ♂ 'Horizontal front bar on a cart or carriage'. This was the given name of Su Shi, literary giant of the Song dynasty (1037–1101).

Shihong ♀ 'The world is red' or conceivably 'Let the world be red'.

Shining ♂ 'World at peace' or 'Let the world be at peace'.

Shirong ♂ 'Scholarly honour'.

Shoushan ♂ 'Longevity mountain'. There are at least six Chinese mountains with this name. Two lie in Fujian province, another in Hubei province, a fourth in Shanxi province, a fifth in Zhejiang province, and a sixth in Jilin province.

Shu ♀ 'Fair'.

Shuang ♀ 1 'Bright' or 'clear'. 2 'Frank' or 'open-hearted'.

Shuchun ♀ 'Fair purity'.

Shun ♀ 'Smooth'.

Shunyuan ♂ 'Follow to the source'.

Siyu ♂ 'Thinking of the world'.

Song ♀ 'Pine tree'. See ▶Mei.

Suyin ♀ 'Plain or unadorned sound', a classical expression referring to news, as in news of a person. This is the given name of the 20th-century writer Han Suyin, author of *A Many-Splendoured Thing* and *My House Has Two Doors*.

Tt

Tao ♂ 'Great waves'.

Tengfei ♂ 'Soaring high'.

Ting ♀ 'Graceful'.

Tingfeng ♂ 'Thunderbolt peak' (perhaps a place name).

Tingguang ♂ 'Courtyard bright'. see ▶Yaoting.

Tingzhe ♂ 'May the court be wise'.

Ww

Wei ♂ 'Impressive might'.

Wei ♂ 'Greatness'.

Weici ♀ 'Preserving love'. *Ci* 'love' is used of motherly love in particular.

Weimin ♂ 'Bring greatness to the people'.

Weisheng ♂ 'Greatness is born'.

Weiyuan ♂ 'Preserving depth'.

Weizhe ♂ 'Great sage' or 'greatness and sagacity'.

Wen ♀ 'Refinement'.

Wencheng ♂ 'Refinement accomplished'.

Wenling ♀ 'Refined jade tinkling'; see ▶Ling 2.

Wenqian ♀ 'Refined madder'. Madder is a type of herb whose red roots are used in the making of dyes.

Wenyan ♂ 'Refined, virtuous, and talented'.

Wuzhou ♂ 'Five continents'.

Xx

Xia ♀ 'Rosy clouds'. see ▶Mingxia.

Xiang 1 ♂ 'Circling in the air'. 2 ♀ 'Fragrant'.

Xianliang ♂ 'Worthy brightness'. Personal name of Zhang Xianliang (b. 1936), author of *Half of Man is Woman*.

Xiaobo ♂ 'Little wrestler'.

Xiaodan ♀, ♂ 'Little dawn'.

Xiaofan ♀ 'Little ordinary'.

Xiaofan ♀ 'Dawn ordinary'.

Xiaohui ♀ 'Little wisdom'.

Xiaojian ♀, ♂ 'Little healthy'.

Xiaojing ♀ 'Morning luxuriance'.

Xiaoli ♀ 'Morning jasmine'.

Xiaolian ♀ 'Little lotus'.

Xiaoling ♀ 'Morning tinkle'. See ▶Ling 2.

Xiaoqing ♀ 'Little blue'.

Xiaosheng ♀, ♂ 'Little birth'.

Xiaosi ♂ 'Filial thoughts'.

Xiaotong ♀ 'Morning redness'. See ▶Hong 1.

Xiaowen ♀ 'Morning cloud colouring'.

Xiaozhi ♀ 'Little iris'. *Zhi* denotes an iris, a symbol of noble character, true friendship, or beautiful surroundings. It is also a fungus with a purplish stalk, which will keep for a long time and indicates long life and prosperity.

Xifeng ♀ 'Western phoenix'.

Xin ♂ 'New'.

Xing ♂ 'Arising'.

Xingjuan ♀ 'Propagating grace'.

Xiu ♀ 'Grace'.

Xiu ♂ 'Cultivated'.

Xiulan ♀ 'Graceful orchid'.

Xiurong ♀ 'Elegant countenance'.

Xiuying ♀ 'Graceful flower'.

Xue ♂ 'Studious'.

Xue ♀ 'Snow', symbol of whiteness, purity, and beauty in a woman.

Xueman ♀ 'Snowy grace'. See ▶Xue.

Xueqin ♂ 'Snow-white celery'. This is the given name of China's greatest novelist, Cao Xueqin (1715–1764), author of *A Dream of Red Mansions*.

Xueyou ♂ 'Studious and friendly'.

Yy

Ya ♀ 'Grace'.

Yan ♀ 'Swallow'.

Yan ♀ 'Gorgeous'.

Yang ♂ 'Model' or 'pattern'.

Yanlin ♀; also ♂ 'Swallow forest'. *Yan* 'swallow' is also an old word for Beijing, so the name may also mean 'Beijing forest', denoting a person born in Beijing.

Yanmei ♀ 'Swallow plum' or 'Beijing plum'. See ▶Yanlin and ▶Mei.

Yanyu ♀ 'Swallow jade' or 'Beijing jade'. See ▶Yanlin for 'swallow' and ▶Yu 1 for 'jade'.

Yaochuan ♂ 'Honouring the river'. *Chuan* is sometimes a shortened form of *Sichuan* (a province of west central China).

Yaoting ♂ 'Honouring the courtyard', courtyard perhaps implying 'family'.

Yaozu ♂ 'Honouring the ancestors'.

Ye ♂ 'Bright'.

Yi ♂ 'Firm and resolute'.

Ying ♀ 1 'Clever'; a word which originally meant 'grain husk'. 2 'Eagle'.

Yingjie ♂ 'Heroic and brave'.

Yingpei ♂ 'Should admire'.

Yingtai ♀ 'Flower terrace'.

Yong ♂ 'Brave'.

Yongliang ♂ 'Forever bright'.

Yongnian ♂ 'Eternal years'.

Yongrui ♂ 'Forever lucky'.

Yongzheng ♂ 'Forever upright'.

You ♂ 'Friend'.

Yu ♀ 1 'Jade'. Jade is a symbol of purity, longevity, or immortality, also of feminine beauty. 2 'Rain'.

Yuan ♀ 'Shining peace'.

Yuanjun ♂ 'Master of Yuan river'. The Yuan is a river in Hunan, provincial birthplace of Chairman Mao.

Yubi ♀ 'Jade emerald'.

Yue ♀ 'Moon'.

Yuming ♀ 'Jade brightness'. For the significance of jade, see ▶Yu 1.

Yun ♀ 'Cloud'.

Yunru ♀ 'Charming seeming'.

Yunxu ♂ 'Cloudy emptiness'.

Yusheng ♀, ♂ 'Jade birth'.

Zz

Zedong ♂ 'East of the marsh'. This was the given name of Chairman Mao Zedong (1893–1976).

Zemin ♂ 'Favour to the people'. This is the given name of the president of China since 1993, Jiang Zemin (b. 1926).

Zengguang ♂ 'Increasing brightness'.

Zhaohui ♀ 'Clear wisdom'.

Zhen ♂ 'Shake' or 'greatly astonished'.

Zhengsheng ♂ 'May the government rise'.

Zhengzhong ♂ 'Upright and loyal'.

Zhenzhen ♀ 'Precious'. The reduplication of *Zhen* makes it more intimate and familiar.

Zhilan ♀ 'Iris orchid'. See ▶Xiaozhi for the significance of *zhi* 'iris'.

Zhiqiang ♂ 'The will is strong' or 'May your will be strong'.

Zhong ♂ 'Loyal' or 'steadfast'.

Zhu ♀ 'Bamboo'. See ▶Mei.

Zian ♂ 'Self peace'.

Zihao ♂ 'Son heroic'.

Zixin ♂ 'Self confidence'.

Zongmeng ♂ 'Take Mencius as a model'. See ▶Mengyao.

Zongying ♀ 'Taking heroes as a model' or conceivably 'taking flowers as a model', as *ying* denotes either flowers or heroes.

Appendix 3:
French Names

Aa

Achille ♂ From Greek *Achilleus*, hero of Homer's Iliad, also the name of one or two minor saints.

Adam ♂ Biblical. See main dictionary.

Adélaïde ♀ Germanic. See Adelaide in main dictionary, Adelheid in German appendix.

Adelard ♂ Germanic: from *adel* 'noble' + *hard* 'strong, hardy'.

Adèle ♀ Short form of ▶Adélaïde.

Adeline ♀ Pet form of ▶Adèle.

Adolphe ♂ Germanic. See Adolf in German appendix.

Adrien ♂ From Latin. See Adrian in main dictionary.
FEMININE FORM: Adrienne.

Agathe ♀ From Greek. See Agatha in main dictionary.

Agnès ♀ From Greek. See Agnes in main dictionary.

Aimée ♀ 'Beloved'; see Aimée and Amy in main dictionary.

Alain ♂ Breton form of *Alan*, now common in all parts of France. See Alan in main dictionary.

Albert ♂ Germanic. See main dictionary.

Alette ♀ Pet form of ▶Adèle.

Alexandre ♂ From Greek. See Alexander in main dictionary.

Alfred ♂ From English. See main dictionary.

Alice ♀ See main dictionary.

Aline ♀ Reduced form of ▶Adeline.

Alison ♀ See main dictionary.

Alphonse ♂ From Spanish Alfonso (see Spanish appendix).
FEMININE PET FORM: Alphonsine.

Ambroise ♂ From Late Latin *Ambrosius*. See Ambrose in main dictionary.
ALSO: Ambrois, Ambroix.

Amédée ♂ From Late Latin *Amadeus* 'love God', translating German *Gottlieb*; a royal name in the house of Savoy.

Amélie ♂ See main dictionary.

Anatole ♂ From Greek *Anatolē* 'sunrise'.

André ♂ New Testament. See Andrew in main dictionary.
FEMININE FORM: Andrée.

Ange ♀ From Latin *Angela* 'angel'.

Angeline ♀ Feminine derivative of Greek *Angelos* 'messenger (of God)'.

Angélique ♀ From Latin *Angelica* 'of the angels'; see Angela in main dictionary.

Anne ♀ Biblical. See main dictionary.

Annette ♀ Pet form of ▶Anne.

Antoine ♂ From Latin. See Anthony in main dictionary.

Antoinette ♀ Feminine pet form of ▶Antoine.

Apollinaire ♂ From Italian Apollinare. See Italian appendix.

Apolline ♀ From Greek *Apollōneia*. See Apollonia in main dictionary.

Arianne ♀ See Ariadne in main dictionary.

Aristide ♂ From Greek *Aristides*, from *aristos* 'best'; name of a 5th-century BC Athenian statesman noted for his incorruptibility; also the name of an early Christian apologist.

Arlette ♀ Of uncertain origin. See main dictionary.

Armand ♂ From Germanic. See Hermann in German appendix.

Armelle ♀ Breton. Feminine form of *Armel*, from Celtic *art* 'stone' +

mael 'chief'; name of a 6th-century saint.

Arnaud ♂ Germanic. See Arnold in main dictionary.

Arthur ♂ Celtic. See main dictionary.

Athanase ♂ From Greek. See Athanasius in main dictionary.

Aubry ♂ Germanic. See Aubrey in main dictionary.

Auguste ♂ From Latin. See Augustus in main dictionary.

Augustine ♂ Feminine pet form of ▶Auguste. See main dictionary.

Aurèle ♂ From Latin *Aurelius*, name of the philosopher-emperor Marcus Aurelius (121–180 AD).
FEMININE FORM: **Aurélie**.

Aurore ♀ From Latin. See Aurora in main dictionary.

Bb

Baptiste ♂ Religious name commemorating John the Baptist; often in the combination Jean-Baptiste.

Barbara ♀ Greek: 'foreign woman'. See main dictionary.

Barnabé ♂ New Testament. See Barnabas in main dictionary.

Barthélemy ♂ New Testament. See

Bartholomew in main dictionary.

Basil ♂ From Greek. See main dictionary.

Bastien ♂ Short form of ▶Sébastien.

Baudouin ♂ Germanic. See Baldwin in main dictionary.

Béatrice ♀ From Latin. See Beatrix in main dictionary.

Benjamin ♂ Bibical. See main dictionary.

Benoît ♂ From Latin. See Benedict in main dictionary.
FEMININE FORM: **Benoîte**.

Bérénice ♀ From Greek. See Berenice in main dictionary.

Bernadette ♀ Feminine of ▶Bernard. See main dictionary.

Bernard ♂ Germanic. See main dictionary.

Bernice ♀ Contracted form of ▶Bérénice.

Berthe ♀ Germanic. See Bertha in main dictionary.

Bertrand ♂ Germanic. See main dictionary.

Blaise ♂ From Latin. See main dictionary.

Blanche ♀ Literally 'white', i.e. 'pure'; also a nickname meaning 'blonde'. See main dictionary.

Brice ♂ Probably Gaulish, meaning 'speckled'. See ▶Bryce in main dictionary.

Brigitte ♀ From Irish *Brighid*, name of a patron saint of Ireland (English Bridget; see main dictionary), or from the Swedish form *Birgit*, name of the patron saint of Sweden.
ALSO: **Brigette**.

Cc

Camille ♂, ♀ From Latin *Camillus*. See Camilla in main dictionary.

Carole ♀ Feminine derivative of Latin *Carolus*. See Charles in main dictionary.

Caroline ♀ Feminine derivative of Latin *Carolus*. See Charles in main dictionary.

Catherine ♀ From Greek. See Katherine in main dictionary.

Cécile ♀ From Latin. See Cecilia in main dictionary.

Céleste ♀ From Latin *Caelestis* 'heavenly'.
PET FORM: **Célestine**.

Célie ♀ From Latin. See Celia in main dictionary.

Céline ♀ Apparently from Latin *Caelina*, a feminine form of *Caelinus*, derivative of *Caelius*, but possibly a short form of ▶Marcel(l)ine.

Césaire ♂ From the Late Latin personal name *Caesarius*; name of a 6th-century saint, a bishop of Arles.

César ♂ From Latin. See Caesar in main dictionary.

Chantal ♀ Name originally adopted in honour of Ste Jeanne-Françoise, Baronne de Chantal (1572–1641), co-founder of the Order of Visitation. See main dictionary.

Charisse ♀ From Greek *kharis* 'grace'. See Charis in main dictionary.

Charles ♂ Germanic. See main dictionary.

Charline ♀ Feminine pet form of ►Charles.

Charlotte ♀ Feminine pet form of ►Charles. See main dictionary. ALSO: **Charlette**.

Christelle ♀ Altered form of ►Christine, derived by replacement of the feminine diminutive suffix *-ine* with the equally feminine suffix *-elle*.

Christine ♀ From Christina. See main dictionary.

Christophe ♂ From Greek. See Christopher in main dictionary.

Claire ♀ From Latin. See Clara in main dictionary.

Claude ♂, ♀ From Latin. See main dictionary.

Claudette ♀ Feminine pet form of ►Claude.

Claudine ♀ Feminine pet form of ►Claude.

Clément ♂ From Late Latin. See Clement in main dictionary.

Clémentine ♀ Feminine pet form of ►Clément.

Clothilde ♀ Germanic: from *hlōd* 'famous' + *hild* 'battle'; name of the queen of the Franks (474–545) who was chiefly responsible for their conversion to Christianity.

Clovis ♂ Germanic. See main dictionary. Clovis (*c*.466–511) was the founder of the medieval Frankish kingdom, a precursor of modern France.

Colette ♀ Short form of ►Nicolette. ALSO: **Collette**.

Colombe ♂, ♀ From Late Latin *Columba* 'dove', representing Gaelic Callum (see main dictionary).

Constance ♀ From Late Latin. See main dictionary.

Constant ♂ From Late Latin. See main dictionary.

Constantin ♂ From Late Latin. See Constantine in main dictionary.

Corin ♂ From Latin *Quirinus*. See main dictionary.

Corinne ♀ From Greek. See Corinna in main dictionary.

Corneille ♂ Vernacular form of Cornelius. See main dictionary.

Cyrille ♂ From Greek. See Cyril in main dictionary.

Dd

Damien ♂ From Greek. See Damian in main dictionary.

Daniel ♂ Biblical. See main dictionary. FEMININE FORMS: **Danièle**, **Danielle**.

David ♂ Biblical. See main dictionary.

Delphine ♀ From Latin. See main dictionary.

Denis ♂ From Greek; name of a patron saint of Paris. See Dennis in main dictionary. FEMININE FORM: **Denise**.

Desirée ♀ From Latin *Desiderata* 'longed for'. MASCULINE FORM: **Desiré**.

Diane ♀ From Latin. See Diana in main dictionary.

Didier ♂ From Late Latin *Desiderius*, derivative of *desiderium* 'longing'; the name of an early bishop of Langres and 7th-century bishops of Auxerre, Cahors, and Vienne, all of whom are subjects of local cults.

Dieudonné ♂ Medieval given name, from Old French *Dieu* 'God' + *donné* 'given'.

Dion ♂ See main dictionary.

Dominique ♂, ♀ From Late Latin. See Dominic and Dominique in main dictionary.

Donat ♂ From Late Latin *Donatus* 'given (by God)'.

Donatien ♂ From Late Latin *Donatianus*, a derivative of *Donatus* 'given (by God)'.

Ee

Edgar ♂ From English. See main dictionary. ALSO: **Edgard**.

Edmond ♂ From English. See Edmund in main dictionary.

Édouard ♂ From English. See Edward in main dictionary.

Edwige ♀ Germanic. See Hedwig in German appendix.

Eléonore ♀ From Old Provençal. See Eleanor in main dictionary.

Éliane ♀ From Late Latin *Aelianus* (feminine form *Aeliana*). See Liane in main dictionary.

Elisabeth ♀ New Testament. See Elizabeth in main dictionary.

Élise ♀ Short form of ▶Elisabeth.

Élodie ♀ Germanic (Visigothic). See Elodia in Spanish appendix.

Eloi ♀ From the Latin name *Eligius*, a derivative of *eligere* 'to choose'. St Eligius (588–660) was a bishop of Noyon who evangelized the districts around Antwerp, Ghent, and Courtrai.

Éloise ♀ Probably Germanic in origin; the name of the wife of the 12th-century Parisian philosopher Pierre Abélard. The story of their love is famous: after they married secretly, Éloise's uncle had Pierre castrated; he became a monk and she a nun, but they continued to write to each other and were eventually buried side by side.
ALSO: **Héloïse**.

Émilie ♀ From Latin. See Emily in main dictionary. MASCULINE FORM: **Émile**.

Émilien ♂ From the Latin family name *Aemilianus*, a derivative of *Aemilius* (see Emily in main dictionary).

Ermenegilde ♂ Germanic (Visigothic). See Hermengildo in Spanish appendix.

Ernest ♂ Germanic. See main dictionary.

Esmé ♂ From Latin *Aestimatus* 'esteemed, highly valued'. FEMININE FORM: **Esmée**.

Étienne ♂ From Greek. See Stephen in main dictionary.

Étiennette ♀ Feminine form of ▶Étienne, with the diminutive suffix *-ette*.

Eugène ♂ From Greek. See Eugene in main dictionary. FEMININE FORM: **Eugénie**.

Eulalie ♀ From Late Greek. See Eulalia in main dictionary.

Euphémie ♀ From Latin. See Euphemia in main dictionary.

Eustache ♂ From Late Greek. See Eustace in main dictionary.

Eutrope ♂ From Late Greek *Eutropios*, from *eu* 'well, good' + *tropos* 'manner', or possibly from classical Greek *eutropos* 'versatile'. It was the name of various minor early saints.

Évariste ♂ From Late Greek *Euarestos*, from *eu* 'well, good' + *areskein* 'to please, satisfy'.

Eve ♀ Biblical. See main dictionary.

Eveline ♀ Pet form of ▶Eve, or French form of English Evelyn (see main dictionary).

Evette ♀ Pet form of ▶Eve. See also ▶Yvette.

Evrard ♂ Germanic. See Everard in main dictionary.

Ff

Fabien ♂ From Latin. See Fabian in main dictionary. FEMININE FORM: **Fabienne**.

Fabrice ♂ From the Latin family name *Fabricius*, probably of Etruscan origin.

Félix ♂ From Latin. See Felix in main dictionary.

Ferdinand ♂ From Spanish. See main dictionary. ALSO: **Fernand**.

Firmin ♂ From Late Latin *Firminus*, a derivative of *firmus* 'firm, steadfast'; the name of the first and third bishops of Amiens (2nd and 3rd centuries); the third bishop of Gévaudon; a 5th-century bishop of Metz; and 6th-century bishops of Viviers, Uzès, and Verdun.

Flavie ♀ From Latin. See Flavia in main dictionary.

Flavien ♂ From Latin *Flavianus*, a derivative of *Flavius* 'yellow-haired'.

Florence ♀ From Latin. See main dictionary.
MASCULINE FORM: **Florent**.

Francine ♀ Pet form of ►Françoise.

François ♂ Medieval name meaning 'French'. See Francis in main dictionary. Its popularity in France has been greatly influenced by Italian *Francesco* and the fame of St Francis of Assisi.

Françoise ♀ Feminine form of ►François.

Frédéric ♂ From German. See Friedrich in German appendix and Frederick in main dictionary.
FEMININE FORM: **Frédérique**.

Gg

Gabriel ♂ Biblical. See main dictionary.
FEMININE FORMS: **Gabrièle**, **Gabrielle**.

Gaétan ♂ From Italian Gaetano; see Italian appendix.

Gaspard ♂ According to tradition, the name of one of the three Magi. See Caspar in main dictionary.

Gaston ♂ Of uncertain origin; a traditional name in aristocratic families of Languedoc, so perhaps an altered form of Gascon, denoting someone from Gascony in Languedoc.

Gauthier ♂ Germanic. See Walter in main dictionary.
ALSO: **Gauthier**.

Geneviève ♀ Name of the patron saint of Paris. See Genevieve in main dictionary.

Geoffroi ♂ Germanic. See Geoffrey in main dictionary.

Georges ♂ From Greek. See George in main dictionary.

Georgette, Georgine ♀ Feminine pet forms of ►Georges.

Gérald ♂ Germanic. See Gerald in main dictionary.

Gérard ♂ Germanic. See Gerard in main dictionary.

Géraud ♂ Germanic. See Gerald in main dictionary.

Germain ♂ From Late Latin *Germanus* 'brother'.

Germaine ♀ Feminine form of ►Germain; Germaine Cousin (c.1579–1601) was a saint from Provençal, canonized in 1867. See also main dictionary.

Gervais ♂ Origin uncertain. See Gervaise in main dictionary.

Ghislaine ♀ Old French: oblique case of ►Giselle, in a spelling that suggests Dutch or Flemish influence.

Gigi ♀ Pet form of ►Giselle.

Gilbert ♂ Germanic. See main dictionary.

Gilles ♂ From Latin *Aegidus*, Old French *Gide*. See Giles in main dictionary.

Ginette ♀ Pet form of Gina; see Italian appendix and main dictionary.

Giselle ♀ Germanic (Frankish): from *gisil* 'pledge'. See main dictionary.
ALSO: **Gisèle**.

Godelieve ♀ From a Germanic personal name composed of *god* 'god' or *gōd* 'good' + *liob* 'dear'. St *Godleva* or *Godliva* (Latinized forms of the name) was murdered in the 11th century by her husband, Bertulf of Ghistelles; she has a cult in Flanders and the name is still in use there.

Gonzague ♂ From the name of St Aloysius Gonzaga (1568–91), a Jesuit of noble birth, who died at the age of twenty-three while tending victims of the plague. He is regarded as a special patron of young people.

Gratien ♂ From Latin *Gratianus*, a derivative of *Gratius*, from *gratus* 'pleasing'. St Gratian was the first bishop of Tours.

Grégoire ♂ From Late Greek. See Gregory in main dictionary.

Guillaume ♂ Germanic. See William in main dictionary.

Gustave ♂ From Scandinavian **Gustaf**. See **Gustav** in Scandinavian appendix.

Guy ♂ Germanic. See main dictionary.

Hh

Hector ♂ Classical. See main dictionary.

Hélène ♀ From Greek. See Helen in main dictionary.

Héloïse ♀ Variant of ▶Éloise.

Henri ♂ Germanic. See Henry in main dictionary.

Henriette ♀ Feminine pet form of ▶Henri.

Herbert ♂ Germanic. See main dictionary.

Hercule ♂ From Latin Hercules. See main dictionary.

Hervé ♂ Originally Breton. See Harvey in main dictionary.

Hilaire ♂ From Latin. See Hilary in main dictionary.

Hippolyte ♂ From Greek *Hippolytos*, composed of *hippos* 'horse' + *lyein* 'to loose, free'; name of several early saints.

Honore ♀ From Latin *Honoria*, a derivative of *honor* 'honour'.

Honoré ♂ From Late Latin *Honoratus* 'honoured'.

Honorine ♀ From Late Latin *Honorina*, a derivative of *Honoria*. See ▶Honore.
PET FORM: **Norine.**

Horace ♀ From Latin. See main dictionary.

Hortense ♀ From Latin. See main dictionary.

Hubert ♂ Germanic. See main dictionary.

Hugues ♂ Germanic. Hugues Capet (?938–96) was ruler of France (987–96) and founder of the Capetian dynasty. See Hugh in main dictionary.

Huguette ♀ Feminine pet form of ▶Hugues.
ALSO: **Huette.**

Humbert ♂ Germanic. See main dictionary.

Ii

Ignace ♂ From Latin. See Ignatius in main dictionary.

Irène ♀ From Greek. See Irene in main dictionary.

Iréné ♂ From Latin *Irenaeus*, from Greek *Eirēnaios* 'peaceable'. St Iréné (*c*.125–202), a Church Father, was an early bishop of Lyons.

Isabel ♀ From Spanish. See main dictionary.
ALSO: **Isabelle.**

Isaïe ♂ Biblical. See Isaiah in main dictionary.

Isidore ♂ From Greek *Isidōros*. See main dictionary.

Jj

Jacinthe ♀ From Greek. See ▶Hyacinth in main dictionary.

Jacqueline ♀ Feminine diminutive of ▶Jacques.

Jacques ♂ From Latin *Jacobus*. See James and Jacob in main dictionary.

Jean ♂ From New Testament Greek *Iōannēs*. See John in main dictionary.

Jeanne ♀ Feminine form of ▶Jean.

Jeanette ♀ Pet form of ▶Jeanne.
ALSO: **Jeannette.**

Jeannine ♀ Pet form of ▶Jeanne.

Jérôme ♂ From New Testament Greek *Hieronymos*. See Jerome in main dictionary.

Joachim ♂ Biblical. See main dictionary.
ALSO: **Joaquin**.

Joël ♂ Biblical. See Joel in main dictionary.
FEMININE FORM: **Joëlle**.

Josée ♀ Feminine form of ▶Joseph, at one time commonly used in the combination Marie-Josée, commemorating both parents of Jesus.

Joseph ♂ Biblical. See main dictionary.
FEMININE FORM: **Josèphe**.

Joséphine ♀ Feminine pet form of ▶Joseph.

Josette ♀ Pet form of ▶Joséphine.

Josiane ♀ Elaborated form of ▶Josée.

Jourdain ♂ See Jordan in main dictionary.

Jules ♂ From Latin. See Julius in main dictionary.

Julie ♀ From Latin. See Julia in main dictionary.

Julien ♀ From Late Latin *Julianus*. See Julian in main dictionary.
FEMININE FORM: **Julienne**.

Juliette ♀ Pet form of ▶Julie.

Just ♂ From Latin. See ▶Justus in main dictionary.
ALSO: **Juste**.

Justin ♂ From Latin. See main dictionary.
FEMININE FORM: **Justine**.

L|

Lambert ♂ Germanic. See main dictionary.

Laure ♀ From Latin. See Laura in main dictionary.
PET FORM: **Laurette**.

Laurence ♀ Feminine form of ▶Laurent.

Laurent ♂ From Latin. See Laurence in main dictionary.

Lazare ♂ Biblical. See Lazarus in main dictionary.

Léa ♀ Biblical. See Leah in main dictionary.

Léandre ♂ From Greek via Latin. See Leander in main dictionary.

Léger ♂ Germanic. See Luitger in German appendix.
ALSO: **Leodegar** (learned form).

Léon ♂ From Late Latin. See Leon in main dictionary.
FEMININE FORM: **Léonne**.

Léonard ♂ Germanic. See Leonard in main dictionary.

Léonce ♂ From Italian Leonzio; see Italian appendix. Sts Leontius the Elder (d. *c*.541) and Leontius the Younger (*c*.510–*c*.565) were successive bishops of Bordeaux.

Léonie ♀ From Latin *Leonia*, feminine form of *Leonius*, derived from *leo* 'lion'.

Léonore ♀ Short form of ▶Eléonore. See Leonora in main dictionary.

Léontine ♀ From Italian Leontina (see Italian appendix).

Léopold ♂ Germanic. See Leopold in main dictionary.

Liane ♀ Short form of ▶Éliane.
ALSO: **Lianne**.

Lisette ♀ Pet form of *Lise*, itself a shortened form of ▶Elisabeth.

Louis ♂ Germanic (Frankish): from *hlōd* 'fame' + *wīg* 'war'; the name of sixteen kings of France before the Revolution. See also main dictionary.
FEMININE FORM: **Louise**.

Luc ♂ From New Testament Greek. See Luke in main dictionary.

Lucie ♀ From Latin. See Lucy in main dictionary. This has now largely replaced the older French form Luce.

Lucien ♂ From Latin *Lucianus*, a derivative of the Roman given name *Lucius*, which is probably derived from *lux* 'light'.
FEMININE FORM: **Lucienne**.

Lucille ♀ From Latin Lucilla; see main dictionary.

Lucinde ♀ See Lucinda in main dictionary.

Lydie ♀ From Greek. See Lydia in main dictionary.

Mm

Macaire ♂ From the Late Greek name *Makarios* 'blessed'.

Madeleine ♀ New Testament. See main dictionary.

Magali ♀ Of Provençal origin: possibly a form of Margaret (see main dictionary).
ALSO: **Magalie**.

Manon ♀ Pet form of ▶Marie.

Marc ♂ From Latin *Marcus*. See **Mark** in main dictionary.

Marcel ♂ From Latin *Marcellus*, a pet form of Marcus (see main dictionary). It owes its popularity in France to a 3rd-century missionary of this name, martyred at Bourges.
FEMININE FORM: **Marcelle**.

Marcellin ♂ From Latin *Marcellinus*, a double diminutive of Marcus (see main dictionary).

Marcelline ♀ Female form of ▶Marcellin.
ALSO: **Marceline**.

Margot ♀ Pet form of ▶Marguerite.

Marguerite ♀ From Greek. See Margaret and Marguerite in main dictionary.

Marianne ♀ Blend of ▶Marie and ▶Anne, used as the name of the female figure symbolizing the French Republic.

Marie ♀ From Latin. See Maria and Mary in main dictionary.

Marie-Ange ♀ French equivalent of Spanish *Maria de los Angeles* 'Mary of the angels'.

Marie-France ♀ Name coined in the 19th century as invoking the protection of the Virgin Mary as the special guardian of France.

Marielle ♀ Pet form of ▶Marie.

Mariette ♀ Pet form of ▶Marie.

Marius ♂ Latin. See main dictionary.

Marjolaine ♀ From the French name of the herb marjoram.

Marthe ♀ New Testament. See Martha in main dictionary.

Martin ♂ From Latin. See main dictionary.
FEMININE FORM: **Martine**.

Maryvonne ♀ Combination of ▶Marie and ▶Yvonne.

Mathilde ♀ Germanic. See Matilda in main dictionary.
ALSO: **Matilde**.

Mathieu ♂ New Testament. See Matthew in main dictionary.

Maurice ♂ From Late Latin. See main dictionary.

Maxime ♂ From Latin *maximus* 'greatest'.

Mélanie ♀ From Greek. See Melanie in main dictionary.

Michel ♂ Biblical. See Michael in main dictionary.

FEMININE FORMS: **Michèle**, **Michelle**.

Micheline ♀ Pet form of ▶Michèle.

Mirabelle ♀ French coinage from Latin *mirabilis* 'wonderful'. See main dictionary.

Mireille ♀ From Provençal *Mireio*, probably a derivative of Provençal *mirar* 'to admire'. See also main dictionary.

Monique ♀ From Latin. See Monica in main dictionary.

Moïse ♂ Biblical; common as a Jewish name. See Moses in main dictionary.

Myriam ♀ Usual French form of Miriam; see main dictionary.

Nn

Nadia ♀ From Russian. See main dictionary.

Nadine ♀ French elaboration of ▶Nadia. See main dictionary.

Narcisse ♂ From Greek *Narkissos*. See Narcissus in main dictionary.

Natalie ♀ From Russian. See main dictionary.
ALSO: **Nathalie**.

Nazaire ♂ From the Late Latin Christian name *Nazarius* 'of Nazareth'; borne by several early saints.

Nicodème ♂ From Greek. See Nicodemus in main dictionary.

Nicolas ♂ From Late Greek. See Nicholas in main dictionary.

Nicole ♀ Feminine form of ►Nicolas.

Nicolette ♀ Pet form of ►Nicole.

Nina ♀ From Russian. See main dictionary.

Ninette ♀ Pet form of ►Nina.

Ninon ♀ Pet form of ►Anne or ►Nina.

Noë ♂ Bibilical. See Noah in main dictionary.

Noël ♂ From Latin *natalis* (*dies*) 'birthday' (i.e. the birthday of Christ, i.e. Christmas). FEMININE FORMS: Noëlle, Noelle.

Noémie ♀ Biblical. See Naomi in main dictionary.

Norine ♀ Pet form of ►Honorine.

Oo

Odette ♀ French feminine form of the Germanic male name *Oda* (from a word meaning 'prosperity fortune'), with the diminutive suffix -*ette*.

Odile ♀ From the medieval Germanic name *Odila*, a derivative of *od* meaning 'prosperity, wealth'; borne by a 8th-century saint who founded a

Benedictine convent at what is now Odilienburg in Alsace; she is the patron saint of Alsace.

Olivier ♂ Germanic. See Oliver in main dictionary.

Olympe ♀ From Greek *Olympia* 'woman of Olympus' (in classical mythology, the home of the gods).

Oriane ♀ See Oriana in main dictionary.

Ottilie ♀ French derivative of the medieval Germanic given name *Odila* (see ►Odile).

Ottoline ♀ Pet form of ►Ottilie. See main dictionary.

Pp

Pascal ♂ From Late Latin *Paschalis* 'relating to Easter'. ALSO: Paschal. FEMININE FORM: Pascale.

Patrice ♂ Medieval French form of Latin *Patricius* and *Patricia*, now used only as a boy's name.

Patrick ♂ See main dictionary. The name is popular in France, partly due to the influx of persecuted Catholics from Ireland during the 18th century.

Paul ♂ From Latin. See main dictionary. FEMININE FORM: Paule.

Paulette ♀ Feminine pet form of ►Paul, with the diminutive suffix -*ette*.

Pauline ♀ From Latin *Paulina*. See main dictionary.

Pélagie ♀ From Greek *Pelagia*, feminine form of *Pelagios* (Latin *Pelagius*), a derivative of Greek *pelagos* 'open sea'.

Philippe ♂ From Greek. See Philip in main dictionary.

Philippine ♂ Feminine pet form of ►Philippe.

Pierette ♀ Feminine form of ►Pierre, with the diminutive suffix -*ette*.

Pierre ♂ From New Testament Greek. See Peter in main dictionary.

Prosper ♂ From Latin *Prosperus* 'fortunate, prosperous'.

Qq

Quentin ♂ From Latin. See main dictionary.

Rr

Rachel ♀ Biblical. See main dictionary. ALSO: Rachelle.

Rainier ♂ Germanic. See Rayner in main dictionary.

Raoul ♂ Germanic. See Ralph in main dictionary. ALSO: Raul.

Raphael ♂ Biblical. See main dictionary.

Raymond ♂ Germanic.
See main dictionary.
FEMININE FORM:
Raymonde.

Rébecca ♀ Biblical.
See Rebecca in main
dictionary.

Régine ♀ From Latin.
See Regina in main
dictionary.

Régis ♂ From an Old
Provençal word
meaning 'ruler'; name
given in honour of
St Jean-François Régis
(d. 1640) of Narbonne,
who strove to reform
prostitutes.

Reine ♀ From the French
word corresponding to
Latin *regina* 'queen'.
Compare ▶Régine.

Rémy ♂ From Latin
Remigius, a derivative of
remex 'oarsman' or
'steersman'. This was the
name of a 6th-century
bishop of Rheims who
converted and baptized
Clovis, king of the Franks.
ALSO: Rémi.

René ♂ From Late
Latin *Renatus* 'reborn',
a popular name
among early Christians
celebrating spiritual
rebirth in Christ.
FEMININE FORM: Renée.

Reynaud ♂ Germanic.
See Reynold in main
dictionary.

Richard ♂ Germanic.
See main dictionary.

Robert ♂ Germanic.
See main dictionary.

Roch ♂ From Italian
Rocco; see Italian
appendix.

Rodolphe ♂ Germanic.
See Rudolf in main
dictionary and German
appendix.

Roger ♂ Germanic.
See main dictionary.

Roland ♂ Germanic.
See main dictionary.
ALSO: Rolland.

Romain ♂ From Late
Latin. See Roman in
main dictionary.
FEMININE FORM: Romaine.

Rosaire ♀ Roman
Catholic name meaning
'rosary'.

Rosalie ♀ From Latin.
See main dictionary.

Rose ♀ See main
dictionary.

Roxane ♀ From
Greek. See main
dictionary.
ALSO: Roxanne.

Ss

Sabine ♀ From Latin.
See Sabina in main
dictionary.

Sacha ♂ From
Russian. See main
dictionary and Sasha in
Russian appendix.

Salomé ♀ From Greek.
See Salome in main
dictionary.

Salomon ♂ Biblical.
See Solomon in main
dictionary.

Samuel ♂ Biblical. See
main dictionary.

Sébastien ♂ From
Latin. See Sebastian in
main dictionary.
FEMININE FORM: Sébastienne.

Serge ♂ From Latin
Sergius. See Sergei in
Russian appendix.

Séverine ♀ From a
feminine derivative
of the Latin family
name *Severinus*, a
derivative of *Severus*
'stern, severe'.
MASCULINE FORM: Séverin.

Simon ♂ Biblical. See
main dictionary.
FEMININE FORM: Simone.

Solange ♀ From the
Late Latin name
Sollemnia, a derivative
of *sollemnis* 'solemn'.
St Solange was a 9th-
century martyr of
Bourges.

Sophie ♀ From Greek.
See main dictionary.

Stéphane ♂ Learned
variant of ▶Étienne.

Stéphanie ♀ From
Latin. See Stephanie in
main dictionary.

Suzanne ♀ Biblical. See
Susanna and Susan in
main dictionary.
ALSO: Susanne.

Suzette ♀ Pet form of
▶Suzanne.

Sybille ♀ From Greek.
See Sybil in main
dictionary.

Sylvain ♂ From Italian Silvano (see Italian appendix).

Sylvie ♀ From Latin. See Silvia in main dictionary.

T t

Télésphore ♂ From Greek. See Telesforo in Italian appendix.

Théodore ♂ From Greek. See Theodore in main dictionary.

Théophile ♂ New Testament. See Theophilus in main dictionary.

Thérèse ♀ From Spanish. See Theresa in main dictionary.

Thibault ♂ From Germanic. See Theobald in main dictionary.

Thierry ♂ From Germanic *Theodoric*, composed of elements meaning 'people' and 'rule'. Compare Terry in main dictionary.

Thomas ♂ New Testament. See main dictionary.

Timothée ♂ From New Testament Greek. See Timothy in main dictionary.

Toussaint ♂ Chosen by parents who wish to invoke the blessing and protection of 'all the saints' (*tous les saints*); often given to a boy born on the feast of All Saints.

Tristan ♂ Celtic. See main dictionary.

V v

Valentin ♂ From Latin. See Valentine in main dictionary.

Valère ♂ From Latin *Valerius*, which is probably a derivative of *valere* 'to be healthy'. There are several early saints of this name who have connections with France, in particular a Roman missionary martyred at Soissons in 287. It has now largely been superseded by ▸Valéry.

Valérie ♀ From Latin *Valeria*. See Valerie in main dictionary.

Valéry ♂ Masculine form of ▸Valérie, which has absorbed an older name of Germanic origin composed of elements meaning 'foreign power'.

Véronique ♀ From Latin. See Veronica in main dictionary.

Victoire ♀ French form of English Victoria. See main dictionary.
PET FORM: **Victorine**.

Victor ♂ From Late Latin. See main dictionary.

Vincent ♂ From Latin. See main dictionary.

Violette ♀ From the name of the flower and the colour. See Violet in main dictionary.

Virginie ♀ From Latin. See Virginia in main dictionary.

Vivien ♂ From Latin. See main dictionary.

Vivienne ♀ Feminine form of ▸Vivien.

X x

Xavier ♂ See main dictionary.

Y y

Yolande ♀ Of uncertain origin. See main dictionary.

Yves ♂ From a short form of a Germanic compound name containing the element *iv*- 'yew'. St Yve was an 11th-century bishop of Chartres.
ALSO: **Yvon**.

Yvette ♀ Feminine pet form of ▸Yves.

Yvonne ♀ Feminine derivative of ▸Yves. See main dictionary.

Z z

Zélie ♀ Apparently an altered form of ▸Célie.

Zéphyrine ♀ See Zephyrine in main dictionary.

German Names

Aa

Achim ♂ Short form of
▶Joachim.
ALSO: **Akim**.

Adalbert ♂ Germanic:
older form of ▶Albrecht.
ALSO: **Adalbrecht,
Adelbrecht**.

Adam ♂ Biblical. See
main dictionary.

Adelheid ♀ Germanic:
from *adal* 'noble' + *heid*
'sort, kind'. See also
Adelaide in main
dictionary.

Adeltraud ♀ Germanic:
from *adal* 'noble' + *þrūþ*
'strength'.

Adolf ♂ Germanic:
from *Adelwolf*, a
compound of *adal* 'noble'
+ *wolf* 'wolf'.

Aegidus ♂ Latin, from
Greek. See Giles in main
dictionary.
ALSO: **Ägid**.

Agathe ♀ From Greek.
See Agatha in main
dictionary.

Agnes ♀ Latin, from
Greek. See main
dictionary.

Agnethe ♀ From Latin
Agnetis, genitive form of
▶Agnes.

Albrecht ♂ Germanic:
from *adal* 'noble' + *berht*
'bright'.

Aleida ♀ Form of
▶Adelheid, influenced by
the North German form
▶Aleit.

Aleit ♀ North German
contracted form of
▶Adelheid.

Alexander ♂ From
Greek. See main
dictionary.

Alexia ♀ Feminine of
▶Alexis.

Alexis ♂ From Greek.
See main dictionary.

Alfred ♂ From
English. See main
dictionary.

Alke ♀ North German
form of ▶Adelheid.

Alois ♂ = Latin *Aloysius*,
probably from Germanic
Alwisi 'all wise'.

Aloisa ♀ Feminine of
▶Alois.
ALSO: **Aloisia**.

Amalia ♀ Latinized
form of the Germanic
name *Amal* 'work'.

Andrea ♀ Feminine of
▶Andreas.

Andreas ♂ From Latin
and Greek. See Andrew
in main dictionary.
ALSO: **Andries** (North
German).

Angelika ♀ From Latin.
See Angelica in main
dictionary.

Anke ♀ North German
pet form of ▶Anne.

Anne ♀ Biblical.
See Anne in main
dictionary.
ALSO: **Anna**.

Anneliese ♀ Blend of
▶Anne and ▶Liese.

Anton ♂ From Latin.
See Anthony in main
dictionary.

Antonia ♀ Feminine
form of ▶Anton.

Apollonia ♀ Latin, from
Greek. See main
dictionary.

Armin ♂ Latin *Arminius*,
name of a Germanic
military leader who
defeated the Romans in
AD 9. Etymologically, the
name is probably
identical with ▶Hermann.

Arno ♂ Germanic:
originally a short form of
names beginning with
arn 'eagle', for example
▶Arnold and ▶Arnulf.

Arnold ♂ Germanic. See
main dictionary.
ALSO: **Arnd(t)** (contracted
form).

Arnulf ♂ Germanic:
from *arn* 'eagle' + *wulf*
'wolf'.

August ♂ From Latin.
See Augustus in main
dictionary.

Augustin ♂ From Latin.
See Augustine in main
dictionary.

Aurel ♂ Latin. From the
Roman family name
Aurelius, a derivative of
aureus 'golden'.

Bb

Baldur ♂ From Old
Norse *Baldr*, name of a
god, son of Odin.

Balthasar ♂ See main dictionary.

Balzer ♂ Vernacular form of ►Balthasar.

Baptist ♂ See main dictionary.

Barbara ♀ Greek. See main dictionary.

Barnabas ♂ New Testament. See main dictionary.

Barthold ♂ North German form of ►Berthold.

Bartholomäus ♂ New Testament. See Bartholomew in main dictionary.

Beat ♂ Swiss: from Latin *Beatus* 'blessed', name of the apostle of Switzerland; pronounced as two syllables.

Beate ♀ Feminine of ►Beat.

Beatrix ♀ Latin. See main dictionary.

Benedikt ♂ From Church Latin *benedictus* 'blessed'. See Benedict in main dictionary.
FEMININE FORM: **Benedicta**.

Benjamin ♂ Biblical. See main dictionary.

Benno ♂ Pet form of ►Bernhard, later associated with Latin *Benedictus* (see Benedict in main dictionary). St Benno (1010–1106) was a bishop of Meissen; he is the patron saint of Munich.

Bernhard ♂ Germanic: from *ber(n)* 'bear' + *hard* 'strong, hardy'. See Bernard in main dictionary.
ALSO: **Bernd**.

Berta ♀ Germanic: from *berht* 'bright' or 'famous'. See Bertha in main dictionary.

Berthold ♂ Germanic: *berht* 'bright' + *hold* 'splendid'; alteration of earlier *Bertwald*, from *berht* + *wald* 'rule, power'.
ALSO: **Barthold** (North German).

Bettina ♀ Pet form of ►Elisabeth.

Birgitta ♀ Variant of ►Brigitta.
ALSO: **Birgit**.

Bodo ♂ Germanic: from *bod* 'messenger, tidings'.

Bonifaz ♂ From Late Latin. See ►Boniface in main dictionary.

Börries ♂ North German, from the Late Latin personal name *Liborius*, possibly an altered form of *Liberius* (a derivative of *liber* 'free'), or of Celtic origin. The relics of St Liborius, a 4th-century bishop of Le Mans, were taken to Paderborn in the 9th century.

Brigitta ♀ From Irish *Brighid*. See Bridget in main dictionary.

Brünhild ♀ Germanic: from *brun* 'armour' + *hild* battle', name of a Valkyrie.
ALSO: **Brünhilde**.

Bruno ♂ Germanic: from *brun* 'brown'. See main dictionary.

Burkhard ♂ Germanic: from *burg* 'protection' + *hard* 'strong, hardy'; the name of an 8th-century saint, the first bishop of Würzburg.

Cc

Cäcilie ♀ From Latin *Caecilia*, patron saint of music. See Cecilia in main dictionary.
ALSO: **Cäcilia**.

Cajetan ♂ Variant spelling of ►Kajetan.

Carl ♂ Variant spelling of ►Karl.
FEMININE FORM: **Carla**.

Carsten ♂ North German form of ►Christian.

Charlotte ♀ Feminine of ►Karl; see main dictionary. Sophie Charlotte was the name of the wife of Friedrich I of Prussia.
ALSO: **Karlotte**.

Christa ♀ Pet form of ►Christiane.

Christhard ♂ Hybrid religious name based on the name *Christ* (see ►Christian) + the Germanic name element *hard* 'hardy, brave'.

Christian ♂ From Latin: 'follower of Christ'. See main dictionary.

Christiane ♀ Feminine of ►Christian.

Christoph ♂ Variant spelling of ►Kristof.

Clara ♀ Latin. See main dictionary.

Claudia ♀ From the Latin family name *Claudius*. See main dictionary.

Claus ♂ Variant spelling of ►Klaus.

Conrad ♂ Variant spelling of ►Konrad.

Constantin ♂ Variant spelling of ►Konstantin.

Constanze ♀ Variant spelling of ►Konstanze.

Cordula ♀ Probably from Late Latin. See main dictionary.

Corinna ♀ From Greek. See main dictionary.

Cornelia ♀ Feminine of ►Cornelius.

Cornelius ♂ Latin, a Roman family name. See main dictionary.

Corona ♀ From a Late Latin name meaning 'crown'; name of a minor saint martyred in Syria in the 2nd century, who was venerated in Bavaria, Austria, and Bohemia in the Middle Ages.

Cosima ♀ Feminine of ►Cosimo.

Cosimo ♂ From Greek *kosmios* 'orderly, well-formed'.

Crescentia ♀ South German: original Latin form of ►Kreszenz.

Curt ♂ Variant spelling of ►Kurt.

Dd

Dagmar ♀ See Scandinavian appendix.

Daniel ♂ Biblical: 'God is my judge'. See main dictionary.

Detlev ♂ North German: from *þeud* 'people' + *leib* 'relic, inheritance'. The standard German form *Dietleib* is rarer.
ALSO: **Detlef**.

Dieter ♂ Germanic: from *þeud* 'people' + *heri* 'army'.

Dietfried ♂ Germanic: from *þeud* 'people' + *frid* 'peace'.

Dietlind ♀ Germanic: from *þeud* 'people' + *lind* 'tender, soft'.
ALSO: **Dietlinde**.

Dietmar ♂ Germanic: from *þeud* 'people' + *māri* 'famous'; as *Theodemar(us)* the name of two 12th-century saints: a missionary to the Wends and an archbishop of Salzburg.

Dietrich ♂ Germanic: from *þeud* 'people' + *rīc* 'power'. See **Terry** in main dictionary.
ALSO: **Diederick** (North German).

Dietwald ♂ Germanic: from *þeud* 'people' + *wald* 'rule, power'.

Doris ♀ From Greek. See main dictionary.

Dorothea ♀ Latinate form of a post-classical Greek name. See main dictionary.

Ee

Ebba ♀ Germanic: short form of various names formed with *eber* 'boar'.

Ebbo ♂ Germanic: short form of various names formed with *eber* 'boar'.

Eberhard ♂ Germanic: from *eber* 'boar' + *hard* 'strong, hardy'.
ALSO: **Evert** (North German).

Eckhard ♂ Germanic: from *agi* 'edge, point (of a sword)' + *hard* 'strong, hardy'.
ALSO: **Eckehard; Eggert** (North German).

Edda ♀ Pet form of any of several old German names beginning with *Ed-*. The Elder and Younger *Eddas* are also the names of two influential Old Icelandic books of Norse myths and poems.

Edeltraud ♀ Germanic: later form of ►Adeltraud.
ALSO: **Edeltrud**.

Edith ♀ English. See main dictionary.

Eggert ♂ North German form of ►Eckhard.

Egmont ♂ Germanic: from *agi* 'edge, point (of a sword)' + *mund* 'protection'. Name of a libertarian hero of an opera by Beethoven.
ALSO: **Egmunt**.

Egon ♂ Short form of various Germanic names formed with *Egin-* or *Egil-*, from *agi(l)* 'edge, point (of a sword)'. St Egon or Egino (d. 1122) was abbot of the monastery of Ulric and Afra in Augsburg.

Ehrenfried ♂ Germanic: from *ēre* 'honour' + *frid* 'peace' or, earlier, *Arnfried*, from *arn* 'eagle' + *fried*.

Ehrenreich ♂ 17th-century coinage: a compound of elements meaning 'honour' and 'rich'.

Ehrentraud ♀ Germanic: from *ēre* 'honour' + *þrūþ* 'strength' or, earlier, *Arntraut*, from *arn* 'eagle' + *þrūþ*.

Eleanore ♀ From French or English. See Eleanor in main dictionary.

Elfriede ♀ Germanic: from *adal* 'noble' + *frid* 'peace', but compare English Elfreda in main dictionary.

Elisabeth ♀ Biblical. See Elizabeth in main dictionary.

Elke ♀ North German: reduced pet form of ▸Adelheid.

Ella ♀ Short form of ▸Elisabeth, Germanic names beginning with *El-*, or ▸Gabriella (see ▸Gabriele).

Elmar ♂ Germanic: from *agi(n)* 'point, edge (of a sword)' + *mar* 'fame'.

Else ♀ Pet form of ▸Elisabeth.

Emil ♂ German form of French Émile; see French appendix.

Emilie ♀ From Latin *Aemilia*. See ▸Emily in main dictionary.

Emma ♀ Germanic. See main dictionary.

Emmerich ♂ Germanic: from earlier *Heimerich*, a compound of *heim* 'home' + *rīc* 'power'.

Engelbert ♂ Germanic: from *engel* (representing *Ingal*, from *Ing*, the name of a Germanic god), *Angel* 'Angle', or *engel* 'angel' + *berht* 'bright'.
ALSO: Engelbrecht.

Erdmann ♂ 17th-century form of ▸Hartmann, altered by association with modern German *Erde* 'earth'.

Erdmut ♂ 17th-century altered form of ▸Hartmut. Compare ▸Erdmann.
ALSO: Erdmuth.

Erdmute ♀ Feminine form of ▸Erdmut.
ALSO: Erdmuthe.

Erhard ♂ Germanic: from *ēra* 'honour' + *hard* 'strong, hardy'; name of a 7th-century saint, allegedly of Irish origin, who served as a missionary bishop in the Regensburg area of Bavaria.

Erich ♂ Nordic. See Eric in main dictionary.

Erika ♀ See Scandinavian appendix.

Ermengard ♀ Germanic: from *erm(en)* 'whole, entire' + *gard* 'enclosure'.
ALSO: Ermgard, Irm(en)gard, Irmingard.

Ermenhilde ♀ Germanic: from *erm(en)* 'whole, entire' + *hild* 'battle'.
ALSO: Ermenhild, Irmhild(e).

Ermentrud ♀ Germanic: from *erm(en)* 'whole, entire' + *þrūþ* 'strength'.
ALSO: Ermentraud, Irmentr(a)ud.

Erna ♀ Reduced form of ▸Ernesta.

Ernesta ♀ Feminine of ▸Ernst.

Ernst ♂ Germanic: from *ern(e)st* 'serious business, fight to the death'.

Erwin ♂ Germanic: from *ēra* 'honour' + *wini* 'friend'.
ALSO: Irwin.

Eugen ♂ From Greek *Eugenios* 'well-born'. See Eugene in main dictionary.

Eva ♀ Biblical. See Eve in main dictionary.

Evert ♂ North German form of ▸Eberhard.

Ewald ♂ Germanic: from *Ewawalt*, a compound of *ēo* 'law' + *wald* 'rule, power'; borne in the 7th century by a pair of brothers ('Ewald the Fair' and 'Ewald the Dark'), originally from Northumbria, who evangelized north Germany and Frisia.

Ff

Felicie ♀ Latinate feminine form of Felix (see main dictionary), of medieval origin.

Ferdinand ♂
Traditional name among the Habsburgs, of Visigothic (Spanish) origin: see main dictionary.

Fester ♂ North German: variant of ▸Vester.

Flora ♀ Latin. See main dictionary.

Florenz ♂ From the Latin name *Florentius*, a derivative of *florens* 'blossoming, flourishing'.

Florian ♂ From Latin *Florianus* 'flowery'. St Florian is the patron saint of Upper Austria and of Poland.

Folker ♂ Variant spelling of ▸Volker.

Frank ♂ Germanic: byname meaning 'free', 'trustworthy', or 'Frankish'. See main dictionary.

Franz ♂ German form of Italian Francesco. See Italian appendix, and see Francis in main dictionary.

Franziska ♀ Feminine form of ▸Franz.

Frauke ♀ North German: originally a byname (representing a diminutive formation from *Frau* 'lady'). It has been used as a pet form of ▸ Veronika, because of the similarity in sound, and is now also used as an independent given name.

Frederik ♂ North German form of ▸Friedrich.

Frederika ♀ Feminine form of ▸Frederik.

Friede ♀ Short form of names beginning with *Fried* 'peace'.
ALSO: **Frieda**.

Friedelinde ♀ Germanic: from *frid* 'peace' + *lind* 'tender, soft'.

Friedemann ♂ Germanic: from *frid* 'peace' + *man* 'man'.

Friederike ♀ Feminine form of ▸Friedrich.

Friedhelm ♂ Germanic: from *frid* 'peace' + *helm* 'helmet, protection'.

Friedrich ♂ Germanic: from *frid* 'peace' + *rīc* 'power'; a royal and imperial name from an early date.
ALSO: **Friederich**.

Fritz ♂ Pet form of ▸Friedrich.

Fürchtegott ♂
Protestant name meaning 'fear God', intended as a translation of Greek *Timotheos*; see Timothy in main dictionary.

Gg

Gabriel ♂ Biblical. See main dictionary.

Gabriele ♀ Feminine of ▸Gabriel.
ALSO: **Gabriel(l)a**.

Gebhard ♂ Germanic: from *geb, gib* 'gift' + *hard* 'strong, hardy'. St Gebhard was a 10th-century bishop of Constance who founded the abbey of Petershausen.
ALSO: **Gebbert** (North German).

Geert ♂. North German form of ▸Gerhard.

Georg ♂ From Greek. See George in main dictionary.

Gerd ♂ Reduced form of ▸Gerhard.

Gerde ♀ Reduced form of ▸Gertrud.
ALSO: **Gerda**.

Gereon ♂ Apparently from Greek *gerōn* 'old man'; the name of a saint martyred in Cologne at the beginning of the 4th century.

Gerhard ♂ Germanic: from *gēr, gār* 'spear' + *hard* 'strong, hardy'.

Gerlach ♂ Germanic: from *gēr, gār* 'spear' + *lach* 'sport'. St Gerlach was a hermit who lived near Valkenburg in the 12th century.

Gerlinde ♀ Germanic: from *gēr, gār* 'spear' + *lind* 'soft, tender'. St Gerlinde lived in the 8th century; she was a member of the royal family of Alsace, sister of St Ottilie.
ALSO: **Gerlind**.

Gernot ♂ Germanic: from *gēr, gār* 'spear' + *nōt* 'need'.

Gert ♂ North German reduced form of ▸Gerhard.
ALSO: **Geert**.

Gertrud ♀ Germanic: from *gēr*, *gār* 'spear' + *prūþ* 'strength'; the name of two famous 13th-century nuns of the Cistercian Abbey of Helfta near Eisleben, whose spiritual writings had a great influence.
ALSO: Gertraud; Gertraut (by association with *traut* 'dear, beloved').

Gertrun ♀ Germanic: from *gēr*, *gār* 'spear' + *rūn* 'rune' or 'magic'.

Gervas ♂ Possibly Germanic. See Gervaise in main dictionary.

Gisela ♀ Germanic: from *gisil* 'pledge' or 'scion'. See Giselle in main dictionary.

Gottfried ♂ Germanic: from *god*, *got* 'god' + *frid* 'peace'; borne by the 13th-century poet Gottfried von Strassburg.

Gotthard ♂ Germanic: from *god*, *got* 'god' + *hard* 'strong, hardy'. St Gotthard was an 11th-century bishop of Hildesheim in Bavaria.

Gotthelf ♂ Religious name dating from the 17th century, a compound of *Gott* 'God' + the verbal stem *helf*, *hilf* 'help'.
ALSO: Gotthilf, Helfgott.

Gotthold ♂ Religious name, dating from the 17th century, composed of *Gott* 'God' + *hold* 'lovely'; variant by folk etymology of the older Germanic name *Gottwald* ('god' + 'rule, power').

Gottlieb ♂ Protestant coinage, meaning 'love God'; translation of Greek *Theophilos* (see Theophilus in main dictionary).

Gottlob ♂ Protestant coinage, meaning 'praise God'; one of the names that became popular in the 17th and 18th centuries with the rise of the Pietist movement.

Gottschalk ♂ Religious name, dating from the early Middle Ages; a compound of *god*, *got* 'God' + *scalc* 'servant'. St Gotteschalk (d. 1066) was a Wendish prince who was married to a grand-niece of King Canute of England. An earlier Gotteschalk (d. *c.*868) preached total predestination.

Götz ♂ Reduced form of ▶Gottfried.

Gratia ♀ From Latin *gratia*. See Grace in main dictionary.

Grete ♀ Short form of ▶Margarete.

Griet ♀ North German short form of Margriet, now used independently.

Gudrun ♀ Nordic. See main dictionary.

Gunther ♂ Germanic: from *gund* 'strife' + *heri* 'army'; name of a tragic hero in the *Nibelungenlied* and in Wagner's Ring cycle.
ALSO: Gunter, Günt(h)er.

Hh

Hagen ♂ **1** Germanic: short form of various compound names formed with *hag* 'stockade, enclosure'. **2** Altered form of Nordic Håkon. See Scandinavian appendix.

Hanne ♀ Short form of ▶Johanna.
ALSO: Hanna.

Hannelore ♀ Blend of ▶Hanne and ▶Eleanore.

Hans ♂ Pet form of ▶Johannes.
SOUTH GERMAN DOUBLE DIMINUTIVE: Hansel.

Hansine ♀ Feminine form of ▶Hans.

Harald ♂ Germanic: from earlier *Harwald*, composed of *heri*, *hari* 'army' + *wald* 'power, rule'. See also Harold in main dictionary.

Hartmann ♂ Germanic: from *hard* 'strong, hardy' + *man* 'man'. The Blessed Hartmann (d. 1164) enjoyed a cult in Austria. Hartmann von Aue (*c.*1170–*c.*1220) was an influential writer of chivalric romances.

Hartmut ♂ Germanic: from *hard* 'strong, hardy' + *muot* 'spirit'.

Hartwig ♂ Germanic: 'staunch in battle'. The Blessed Hartwig was archbishop of Salzburg 991–1023.

Hartwin ♂ Germanic: from *hard* 'strong, hardy' + *wini* 'friend'.

Hedda ♀ Nordic pet form of ▸Hedwig.

Hedwig ♀ Germanic: from *hadu* 'contention' + *wīg* 'war'.

Heidi ♀ Southern German pet form of ▸Adelheid.

Heike ♀ North German feminine pet form of ▸Heinrich.

Heilwig ♂ Germanic: from *heil* 'whole, safe' + *wīg* 'war'.

Heimo ♂ Pet form of any of various old Germanic names formed with *Heim* 'home'.

Heinrich ♂ Germanic: from *heim* 'home' + *rīc* 'power'. See Henry in main dictionary.

Heinz ♂ Pet form of ▸Heinrich.

Helene ♀ From Greek. See Helen in main dictionary. ALSO: **Helena.**

Helfgott ♂ Reversed form of ▸Gotthelf.

Helga ♀ Nordic. See Scandinavian appendix.

Helge ♂ Nordic. See Scandinavian appendix.

Helger ♂ Germanic: from a first element meaning either 'holy' or 'prosperous' + *gēr, gār* 'spear'.

Helme ♀ Feminine short form of names ending in *-helm*, e.g. ▸Friedhelm, ▸Wilhelm. ALSO: **Helma.**

Helmfried ♂ Germanic: from *helm* 'helmet, protection' + *frid* 'peace'. ALSO: **Helmfrid, Helfried.**

Helmina ♀ Short form of ▸Wilhelmina. ALSO: **Helmine.**

Helmut ♂ Germanic: from *heil* 'wholeness' or *helm* 'helmet, protection' + *muot* 'spirit'. ALSO: **Helmuth.**

Henk ♂ North German reduced form of ▸Heinrich.

Henrik ♂ North German form of ▸Heinrich. FEMININE FORM: **Henrike.**

Herbert ♂ Germanic: from *heri* 'army' + *berht* 'bright, famous'. ALSO: **Heribert** (older form).

Hermann ♂ Germanic: from *heri* 'army' + *man* 'man'.

Hermine ♀ 19th-century coinage as a feminine form of ▸Hermann.

Hertha ♀ From a misreading of Latin *Nertha*, name of a fertility goddess mentioned by Tacitus.

Hieronymus ♂ Latin form of Greek *Hieronymos* (see Jerome in main dictionary), still used in Germany, especially in Catholic Bavaria and the Rhineland.

Hilde ♀ Short form of Germanic names formed with *hild* 'battle'. ALSO: **Hilda.**

Hildebrand ♂ Germanic: from *hild*

'battle' + *brand* '(flaming) sword', borne by a saint (*c.*1020–85) who became pope under the name of Gregory VII.

Hildebrecht ♂ Germanic: from *hild* 'battle' + *berht* 'bright'. ALSO: **Hildebert.**

Hildegard ♀ Germanic: from *hild* 'battle' + *gard* 'enclosure'; name of the second wife of Charlemagne and of the mystic Hildegard of Bingen (1098–1179).

Hildegund ♀ Germanic: from *hild* 'battle' + *gund* 'strife'. ALSO: **Hildegunde.**

Hiltraud ♀ Germanic: from *hild* 'battle' + *þrūþ* 'strength'. St Hiltrude (d. *c.*790) was a Benedictine nun who lived as a recluse near Liesses. ALSO: **Hiltrud.**

Hinrich ♂ North German form of ▸Heinrich.

Holger ♂ Nordic. See Scandinavian appendix.

Horst ♂ Altered form, first recorded in the 15th century, of the Old Saxon name *Horsa* 'horse'.

Hubert ♂ Germanic: from *hug* 'heart, mind' + *berht* 'bright, famous'. See also main dictionary. ALSO: **Hugbert, Huppert, Hupprecht.**

Hugo ♂ Germanic: from *hug* 'heart, mind, spirit'.

Humbert ♂ Germanic: from *hun* 'bear-cub, warrior' + *berht* 'bright, famous'.

I i

Ignaz ♂ Vernacular form of Latin Ignatius. See main dictionary.

Ilse ♀ Pet form of ▸Elisabeth.
ALSO: Ilsa.

Imke ♀ North German pet form of Imma (an assimilated byform of ▸Irma), also used as an independent given name in northern Germany.

Immanuel ♂ Biblical. See Emmanuel in main dictionary.

Inge ♀ Pet form of ▸Ingeborg or ▸Ingetraud.
ALSO: Inga.

Ingeborg ♀ Nordic. See Scandinavian appendix.

Ingemar ♂ Nordic. See Scandinavian appendix.

Ingetraud ♀ Blend of ▸Ingeborg and names ending in *-traud*, such as ▸Adeltraud.

Ingrid ♀ Nordic. See Scandinavian appendix.

Irene ♀ Greek. See main dictionary.

Iris ♀ Greek. See main dictionary.

Irma ♀ Short form of any of the feminine names formed with *Irmen-* 'totality, all'. See also names beginning ▸Ermen-.

Irmengard ♀ Variant of ▸Ermengard.
ALSO: Irmgard, Irmingard.

Irmentrud ♀ Variant of ▸Ermentrud.
ALSO: Irmentraud.

Irwin ♂ Variant of ▸Erwin.

Isidor ♂ Greek. See Isidore in main dictionary.

Isolde ♀ Celtic. See main dictionary.

Izaak ♂ Biblical. See Isaac in main dictionary.

J j

Jakob ♂ Biblical. See Jacob and James in main dictionary.

Jan ♂ North German and Slavic reduced form of ▸Johannes.

Jeremias ♂ Biblical. See Jeremiah in main dictionary.

Jetta ♀ Short form of *Marietta*, diminutive of ▸Maria.

Joachim ♂ Biblical. See main dictionary.
ALSO: Jochim, Jochem, Jochen.

Jobst ♂ North German form of *Jodocus*, Latinized form of the Breton name *Iodoc*, meaning 'lord', altered under the influence of the biblical name Job (see main dictionary).

Johann ♂ Vernacular form of ▸Johannes.

Johanna ♀ Feminine form of ▸Johannes.

Johannes ♂ Latin. See John in main dictionary.

Jolanda ♀ German form of French and English Yolande; see main dictionary.

Jonas ♂ Biblical. See Jonah and Jonas in main dictionary.

Jordan ♂ Crusader name. See main dictionary.

Jörg ♂ Dialectal (Alemannic and Swabian) form of ▸Georg.

Josef ♂ Biblical. See Joseph in main dictionary.

Josefa ♀ Feminine form of ▸Josef.

Judith ♀ Biblical. See main dictionary.

Jürgen ♂ North German form of ▸Georg.

Justus ♂ Latin: 'fair, just'.

Jutte ♀ Pet form of ▸Judith, also used as an independent given name.
ALSO: Jutta.

K k

Kai ♂ Nordic. See main dictionary.

Kajetan ♂ From Latin *Caietanus* 'man from Caieta' (see **Gaetano** in Italian appendix); sometimes adopted by Roman Catholics in honour of Cardinal

Gaetano, an opponent of Martin Luther, not to be confused with his contemporary, St Gaetano of Naples.
ALSO: **Kayetan**.

Kamil ♂ From Latin *Camillus*, of unknown origin. St Camillus (1550–1614) was the founder of an order of monks who nursed the sick.

Kamilla ♀ Feminine form of ▶Kamil. See Camilla in main dictionary.

Karl ♂ Germanic: from *karl* '(free)man', an ancient royal and imperial name. See Charles in main dictionary.
FEMININE FORM: **Karla**.

Karlmann ♂ Germanic: elaborated form of ▶Karl. The Blessed Carloman (707–55) was a member of the Frankish royal family, being the eldest son of Charles Martel, brother of Pepin the Short, and uncle of Charlemagne.

Karlotte ♀ Variant of ▶Charlotte.

Karoline ♀ Vernacular form of Latin *Carolina*, a feminine derivative of *Carolus* (see Charles in main dictionary).

Karsten ♂ North German form of ▶Christian.

Kaspar ♂ See Caspar in main dictionary.

Katharina ♀ From Greek. See Katherine in main dictionary.

Käthe ♀ Pet form of ▶Katharina.

Katja ♀ Pet form of ▶Katharina.

Kinge ♀ Pet form of ▶Kunigunde.
VARIANT: **Kinga**.

Klara ♀ Variant spelling of ▶Clara.

Klaus ♂ Reduced form of ▶Nikolaus.

Klemens ♂ From Latin. See Clement in main dictionary.

Konrad ♂ Germanic: from *kuon* 'bold' + *rad* 'counsel'.

Konstantin ♂ From Late Latin *Constantinus*, a derivative of *Constans* 'steadfast'; the name of the first Christian Roman emperor (?288–337).

Konstanze ♀ From Late Latin *Constantia*. See Constance in main dictionary.

Korbinian ♂ Name bestowed in honour of a Frankish saint (?670–770), who evangelized Bavaria. His name appears to be an adjectival form of Latin *corvus* 'raven' (from the Late Latin variant *corbus*), possibly representing a translation of the Germanic personal name *Hraban*.

Kreszenz ♀ Vernacular form of Late Latin

Crescentia, feminine form of the male name *Crescens* 'growing, flourishing', used originally as a name of good omen.

Kriemhild ♀ Germanic: from *grim* 'mask' + *hild* 'battle'. In the *Nibelungenlied* this is the name of the sister of Gunther; she marries Siegfried, and later takes vengeance on her brother for her husband's murder.
ALSO: **Kriemhilde**.

Kristof ♂ From Greek. See Christopher in main dictionary.
ALSO: **Christoph**.

Kunigunde ♀ Germanic: from *kuoni* 'brave' + *gund* 'strife'. St Cunegund (d. 1039) was the wife of the Holy Roman Emperor Henry II, with whom she is said to have lived in 'conjugal virginity'.

Kurt ♂ Pet form of ▶Konrad, also used independently.

L

Ladislaus ♂ Latinized form of the Slavic name *Vladislav*, from *volod* 'rule' + *slav* 'glory'.

Lambert ♂ Germanic: from *land* 'land' + *beorht* 'shining, famous'.
ALSO: **Lamprecht**; **Lammert** (North German).

Laurenz ♂ From Latin. See Laurence in main dictionary.
ALSO: **Lorenz**.

Leberecht ♂ Protestant name meaning 'live right'.

Lena ♀ Short form of *Magdalena* (see ►Magdalene) or *Helena* (see ►Helene), also used as an independent given name.

Lene ♀ Short form of ►Helene or ►Magdalene, also used as an independent given name.

Leni ♀ Pet form of ►Lena and ►Lene.

Lenz ♂ Reduced form of ►Laurenz.

Leo ♂ Latin. See main dictionary.
ALSO: **Leon**.

Leodegar ♂ Learned form (influenced by Latin *leo* 'lion') of ►Luitger.

Leon ♂ Derivative of ►Leo, from the oblique case.

Leona ♀ Latinate feminine form of ►Leon.

Leonhard ♂ Blend of Latin *Leo(n)*- and Germanic *hard* 'strong, hardy'.

Leonore ♀ Short form of ►Eleanore.
ALSO: **Leonora**.

Lienhard ♂ South German variant of ►Leonhard.

Liese ♀ Pet form of ►Elisabeth.

Lieselotte ♀ 19th-century coinage: a blend of ►Liese and ►Lotte.
ALSO: **Liselotte**.

Lili ♀ Pet form of ►Elisabeth.
ALSO: **Lilli**.

Lilo ♀ Pet form of ►Lieselotte.

Lisa ♀ Pet form of ►Elisabeth.

Lora ♀ Vernacular feminine form of the Late Latin male name *Laurus* 'laurel'. See Laura in main dictionary.

Lore ♀ Much reduced form of ►Eleanore. Occasionally, a variant of ►Lora.

Lorenz ♂ Variant of ►Laurenz.

Lothar ♂ Germanic: from *hlud* 'fame' + *hari* 'army'; a Frankish royal name.

Lotte ♀ Short form of ►Charlotte.

Lottelore ♀ Compound of ►Lotte and ►Lore.

Ludger ♂ North German form of ►Luitger. St Ludger (*c.*744–809) was a Frisian who became a missionary in Westphalia and later first bishop of Münster, where he founded a monastery that gave the place its name.

Ludovica ♀ Latinate feminine form of ►Ludwig.

Ludwig ♂ Germanic: from *hlud* 'fame' + *wīg* 'war'; an ancient royal and imperial name. See Louis in main dictionary.

Luise ♀ Feminine form of French *Louis*. See Louise in main dicitonary.

Luitgard ♂ Germanic: from *liut* 'people' + *gard* 'protection'.

Luitger ♂ Germanic: from *liut* 'people' + *gēr*, *gār* 'spear'.
ALSO: ►**Leodegar**, ►**Ludger**.

Luither ♂ Germanic: from *liut* 'people' + *heri* 'army'.

Luitpold ♂ Germanic: from *liut* 'people' + *bald* 'bold'. See Leopold in main dictionary. This form is now little used except in a few particular families in which its use is traditional. It was associated particularly with the royal house of Bavaria.

Lukas ♂ Greek. See Luke in main dictionary.

Lulu ♀ Pet form of ►Luise.

Lutz ♂ Pet form of ►Ludwig.

M m

Magda ♀ Short form of ►Magdalene.

Magdalene ♀ New Testament: byname of Mary Magdalene. See Madeleine in main dictionary.
ALSO: **Magdalena**.

Maja ♀ **1** Pet form of ►Maria. **2** From Latin *Maia* (see Maya in main dictionary).

Manfred ♂ Germanic: from *man* 'man' + *fred* 'peace'.
ALSO: Manfried.

Margarete ♀ Latin, from Greek. See Margaret in main dictionary.
ALSO: Margarethe, Margaret(h)a.

Maria ♀ New Testament. See main dictionary.

Marian ♂ From Latin *Marianus*, a derivative of ►Marius. In the Christian era it has found favour as a name for devotees of the Virgin Mary (see ►Maria).

Marianne ♀ Blend of ►Maria and ►Anne.

Marius ♂ Latin. See main dictionary.

Markus ♂ Latin. See Marcus in main dictionary.

Marlene ♀ Blend of ►Maria and ►Magdalena.

Marthe ♀ New Testament. See Martha in main dictionary.
ALSO: Marte, Mart(h)a.

Martin ♂ From Latin. See main dictionary.

Mathilde ♀ Germanic: from *maht*, *meht* 'might' + *hild* 'battle'.
ALSO: Mechtild(e).

Matthäus ♂ From Latin *Matthaeus*; variant of ►Matthias.

Matthias ♂ New Testament. See Matthew in main dictionary.

Max ♂ Short form of ►Maximilian.

Maximilian ♂ From Latin. See main dictionary.

Maxine ♀ Feminine form of ►Max.

Mechthild ♀ Variant of ►Mathilde.

Meinhard ♂ Germanic: from *magin* 'strength' + *hard* 'strong, hardy'.

Meinrad ♂ Germanic: from *magin* 'strength' + *rād* 'counsel'.

Melchior ♂ See main dictionary.

Mercedes ♀ Spanish. See main dictionary and Spanish appendix.

Michael ♂ Biblical. See main dictionary.

Mirjam ♀ Biblical. See Miriam in main dictionary.

Mitzi ♀ South German pet form of ►Maria.

Monika ♀ Of uncertain origin. See Monica in main dictionary.

Moritz ♂ From Latin. See Maurice in main dictionary.

Nn

Nathan ♂ Biblical. See main dictionary.

Nepomuk ♂ Czech: 'from Pomuk', byname of St John Nepomuk (1350–93), patron saint of Bohemia.

Nikolaus ♂ Greek. See Nicholas in main dictionary.

Norbert ♂ Germanic: from *nord* 'north' + *berht* 'bright'.

Notger ♂ Germanic: from *nōt* 'need' + *gēr* 'spear'. The Blessed Notker Balbulus ('the Stammerer') was a Benedictine monk at the abbey of St Gall in Switzerland in the 10th century; he wrote a biography of Charlemagne.
ALSO: Notker.

Oo

Olaf ♂ Nordic. See Scandinavian appendix.

Olof ♂ North German reduced form of ►Ottwolf, influenced by ►Olaf.

Oskar ♂ See Oscar in main dictionary and Irish appendix.

Oswald ♂ See main dictionary.

Oswin ♂ See main dictionary.

Otmar ♂ Germanic: from *od*, *ot* 'riches' + *mar* 'fame'; the name of an 8th-century saint who refounded the monastery of St Gall in Switzerland.
ALSO: Ott(o)mar.

Ottilie ♀ Germanic: from the medieval given name *Odila*, a derivative of *od*, *ot* 'riches'.

Otto ♂ Short form of any of the Germanic male names formed with *ot-* 'riches'; a royal and imperial name from an early date.

Ottokar ♂ Germanic: from *ot*, *od* 'riches' + *wacar* 'watchful'; as *Odovacar*, name of the king of the Goths who controlled Italy 476–93 and also of two 13th-century kings of Bohemia.

Ottwolf ♂ Germanic: from *ot*, *od* 'riches' + *wulf* 'wolf'.
ALSO: **Otwolf**.

Pp

Pancraz ♂ From Greek. See Pancras in main dictionary.

Parzifal ♂ See Percival in main dictionary.

Paul ♂ From the Roman family name *Paulus*. See main dictionary.
ALSO: **Paulus** (Latin form).

Paula ♀ Feminine form of ▶Paul.

Peter ♂ From Greek. See main dictionary.

Petra ♀ Feminine form of ▶Peter.

Petrus ♂ Latin form of ▶Peter.

Philipp ♂ From Greek. See Philip in main dictionary.

Philippa ♀ Latinate feminine form of ▶Philip.

Philippina ♀ Latinate pet form of ▶Philippa.

Philo ♂ From the Late Greek personal name *Philōn*, a derivative of *phil-* 'love'.

Philomena ♀ Latin feminine form of Greek *Philomenēs*. See main dictionary.

Phyllis ♀ Greek. See main dictionary.

Pia ♀ Latin. See Italian appendix.

Pirmin ♂ Apparently an altered form of Firmin (see French appendix); name of an 8th-century saint who founded numerous Benedictine monasteries.

Rr

Rachel ♀ Biblical. See main dictionary.

Radegund ♀ Germanic: from *rād* 'counsel' + *gund* 'strife'.
ALSO: **Radegunde**.

Rafael ♂ German spelling of Raphael (see main dictionary), name of one of the archangels.

Raimund ♂ Germanic: from *ragin* 'advice' + *mund* 'protector'. See Raymond in main dictionary.

ALSO: **Rei(n)mund**.

Raimunde ♀ Feminine form of ▶Raimund.

Rainer ♂ Variant of ▶Reiner.

Randolf ♂ Germanic: from *rand* 'rim (of a shield)' + *wulf* 'wolf'.
ALSO: **Randulf**.

Rebekka ♀ Biblical. See Rebecca in main dictionary.

Reimund ♂ Variant of ▶Raimund.

Reineke ♂ North German pet form of any of the Germanic male names formed with *rein* 'counsel'.

Reiner ♂ Germanic: from earlier *Reinher*, composed of *ragin* 'advice' + *heri* 'army'.

Reinhard ♂ Germanic: from *ragin* 'advice' + *hard* 'strong, hardy'.

Reinhold ♂ Germanic: ostensibly a compound of *ragin* 'advice' + *hold* 'splendid', but actually a variant of earlier ▶Reinwald.

Reinmar ♂ Germanic: from *ragin* 'advice' + *mar* 'fame'.

Reinmund ♂ Variant of ▶Raimund.

Reinwald ♂ Germanic: from *ragin* 'advice' + *wald* 'power'.

Renata ♀ Feminine form of the Late Latin name *Renatus* 'reborn'.
ALSO: **Renate** (vernacular form).

Resi ♀ Pet form of
▸Therese.

Ria ♀ Short form of
▸Maria.

Ricarda ♀ Latinate
feminine form
of ▸Richard.

Richard ♂ Germanic:
'power' + 'strong'. See
main dictionary.
ALSO: Ri(c)kert (North
German).

Rike ♀ Short form of
▸Ulrike or ▸Friederike.

Robert ♂ Germanic:
'fame' + 'bright'. See
main dictionary.

Rodolf ♂ Variant of
▸Rudolf.

Roland ♂ Germanic:
'fame' + 'land'. See main
dictionary.

Rolf ♂ Germanic:
contracted form of the
old personal name
Hrōdwulf; see ▸Rudolf.

Romy ♀ Pet form of
▸Rosemarie, made
famous by the Austrian
film actress Romy
Schneider (1938–82).

Rosa ♀ See Rose in main
dictionary.

Rosamunde ♀
Germanic: from *hros*
'horse' + *mund*
'protection'.

Röschen ♀ Pet form of
▸Rosa, ▸Rosemarie, or
▸Rosamunde.

Rosemarie ♀ Blend of
▸Rosa and ▸Maria.

Roswithe ♀ Germanic:
from *hrōd* 'fame' + *swinþ*
'strength'; name of a

10th-century nun,
Roswitha of
Gandersheim, who wrote
Latin verse and plays in
the manner of Terence.
VARIANT: Roswitha
(Latinate form).

Rötger ♂ North
German form of
▸Rüdiger.

Rudi ♂ Pet form of
▸Rudolf.

Rüdiger ♂ Germanic:
from *hrōd* 'fame' + *gēr*
'spear'. This is the name
of a hero in the
Nibelungenlied. See Roger
in main dictionary.
ALSO: Rötger (North
German).

Rudolf ♂ Germanic:
from *Hrōdwulf*, a
compound of *hrōd* 'fame'
+ *wulf* 'wolf'.
ALSO: Rodolf.

Rupert ♂ North
German form of ▸Robert.
See Rupert in main
dictionary.

Ruprecht ♂ Variant of
▸Rupert.

Ruth ♀ Biblical. See
main dictionary.
ALSO: Rut.

Ss

Sabine ♀ From Latin.
See Sabina in main
dictionary.

Sascha ♂, ♀ German
spelling of Sasha, Russian
pet form of ▸Alexander
and Alexandra (see main
dictionary).

Sebastian ♂ From Latin.
See main dictionary.

Sepp ♂ Short form of
Josep, variant of ▸Josef.

Siegbert ♂ Germanic:
from *sige* 'victory' + *berht*
'bright, famous'.

Siegfried ♂ Germanic:
from *sige* 'victory' + *frid*
'peace'.

Sieghard ♂ Germanic:
from *sige* 'victory' + *hard*
'strong, hardy'.

Sieghilde ♀ Germanic:
from *sige* 'victory' + *hild*
'battle'.
ALSO: Sieghild.

Sieglinde ♀ Germanic:
from *sige* 'victory' + *lind*
'tender'.
ALSO: Siedlind(e).

Siegmund ♂ Germanic:
from *sige* 'victory' + *mund*
'protection'.
ALSO: Sigmund.

Siegrun ♀ Germanic:
from *sige* 'victory' + *rūn*
'rune' or 'magic'.
ALSO: Sigrun.

Siegward ♂ Germanic:
from *sige* 'victory' + *ward*
'protector'.

Siemen ♂ North
German form of ▸Simon.

Sigi ♂, ♀ Pet form of
▸Siegfried, ▸Siegmund,
▸Sieglinde, ▸Sigrid, etc.
ALSO: Siggi.

Sigismund ♂ Variant of
▸Siegmund.

Sigiswald ♂ Variant of
▸Siegwald.

Sigmund ♂ Variant of
▸Siegmund.

Sigrid ♀ Nordic. See
Scandinavian appendix.

Sigurd ♂ Nordic form of ▸Siegward. See Scandinavian appendix.

Silke ♀ North German pet form of ▸Cäcilie.

Silvester ♂ Latin: 'of the woods'. See main dictionary.

Simon ♂ New Testament. See main dictionary.

Simone ♀ Feminine form of ▸Simon.

Sissy ♀ South German pet form of ▸Elisabeth.

Sofie ♀ From Greek. See Sophia in main dictionary.
ALSO: **Sofia; Sophie.**

Sonje ♀ German spelling of the Russian name Sonya (see Russian appendix).
ALSO: **Sonja.**

Stefan ♂ From Greek. See Stephen in main dictionary.
ALSO: **Stephan.**

Stefanie ♀ Feminine form of ▸Stefan.
ALSO: **Stephanie.**

Steffen ♀ North German form of ▸Stefan.

Steffi ♀ Pet form of ▸Stefanie.

Stoffel ♂ Pet form of ▸Kristof.

Susann ♀ Vernacular form of ▸Susanna.
ALSO: **Susanne.**

Susanna ♀ New Testament. See main dictionary.

Susi ♀ Pet form of ▸Susann, etc.

Swanhild ♀ North German: from an Old Saxon female personal name composed of *swan* 'swan' + *hild* 'battle'.
ALSO: **Swanhilda, Swanhilde.**

Tt

Tabea ♀ Pet form of ▸Tabitha.

Tabitha ♀ New Testament. See main dictionary.

Tanja ♀ German spelling of the Russian name Tanya (see Russian appendix).

Teres(i)a ♀ Variant of ▸Theres(i)a.

Theda ♀ Latinate pet form of any of several names formed with *diet-* 'people', e.g. ▸Dietlind.

Theodor ♂ From Greek. See Theodore in main dictionary.

Theresa ♀ Name traditionally associated with the Habsburg family. See Theresa in main dictionary.
ALSO: **T(h)eresia, T(h)erese.**

Thomas ♂ New Testament. See main dictionary.

Till ♂ North German: from a medieval pet form of ▸Dietrich and other Germanic personal names with the same first element, *þeud* 'people'.

Timo ♂ Pet form of obsolete *Timotheus*, Latin form of Greek *Timotheos* 'honour God'. See Timothy in main dictionary.

Tönjes ♂ North German: short form of *Antonius* (see Anthony in main dictionary).

Traude ♀ Pet form of *Gertraud* (see ▸Gertrud), ▸Waltraud, etc.
ALSO: **Traute.**

Traugott ♂ Protestant name meaning 'trust in God'.

Trude ♀ Pet form of ▸Gertrud, also of ▸Ermentrud and other names ending with the same element.
ALSO: **Trudi.**

Trudeliese ♀ Combination of the names ▸Trude and ▸Liese.

Uu

Udo ♂ Germanic: from *uod(al)* 'riches'; probably originally a short form of the various compound names formed with this element.

Ulf ♂ Nordic. See Scandinavian appendix.

Ulla ♀ Pet form of ▸Ulrike.

Ulrich ♂ Germanic: from *uodal* 'riches' + *ric* 'power'; the name of two major German saints, Ulrich of Augsburg (d. 973) and Ulrich of Cluny (c.1018–93), and the

Blessed Ulrich of Einsiedeln in Switzerland (d. *c.*980).

Ulrike ♀ Feminine form of ▸Ulrich.
ALSO: Ulrika.

Urban ♂ From Latin. See main dictionary.

Urs ♂ Swiss: from Latin *Ursus* 'bear'.

Ursula ♀ Latin: diminutive of *ursa* '(she-)bear'; the name of a 4th-century saint martyred at Cologne. See also main dictionary.

Uschi ♀ Pet form of ▸Ursula.

Ute ♀ From earlier *Uda*, a Germanic name meaning 'heritage'; name of the mother of Kriemhild in the *Nibelungenlied*.

Utz ♂ Pet form of ▸Ulrich.

Uwe ♂ North German: from a Nordic name meaning either 'blade' or 'awe'.

Vv

Valentin ♂ From Latin. See Valentine in main dictionary.

Veit ♂ From Germanic *Wido* (see Guy in main dictionary), but confused with Latin *Vitus* (from *Vita* 'life'); name of an early child martyr in Sicily.

Vester ♂ Short form of ▸Silvester.

Velten ♂ South German form of ▸Valentin.

Veronika ♀ From Latin. See Veronica in main dictionary.

Viktor ♂ From Latin. See Victor in main dictionary.

Viktoria ♀ From Latin. See Victoria in main dictionary.

Vinzenz ♂ From Latin. See Vincent in main dictionary.

Volkard ♂ Variant of ▸Volkhard.

Volker ♂ Germanic: from earlier *Volkher*, composed of *folk* 'people' + *heri* 'army'.

Volkhard ♂ Germanic: from *folk* 'people' + *hard* 'strong, hardy'.

Volkmar ♂ Germanic: from *folk* 'people' + *mar* 'famous'.

Vroni ♀ Pet form of ▸Veronika.

Ww

Walburg ♀ Germanic: from *wald* 'rule' + *burg* 'stronghold'. St Walburg (d. ?779) was of Anglo-Saxon origin, and the original form of her name was *Wealdburh* or *Wealburh*. She became abbess of Heidenheim and her relics are preserved at Eichstatt.
ALSO: Walburga.

Waldemar ♂ Germanic: from *wald* 'rule' + *mar* 'fame'.

ALSO: Woldemar.

Waldo ♂ Short form of any of several old Germanic personal names formed with *wald* 'rule'.

Walther ♂ Germanic: from *wald* 'rule' + *heri* 'army'; name of the famous medieval minnesinger Walther von der Vogelweide (*c.*1170–*c.*1230).
ALSO: Walter; Wolter (North German).

Waltraud ♀ Germanic: *wald* 'rule' + *prūp* 'strength'; the name of a saint who founded a convent at the place that grew to be the town of Mons in Belgium.
ALSO: Waltrud(e).

Wendel ♂ Germanic: from the folk name for a Wend, a member of a Slavic people living in the area between the Elbe and the Oder, who were overrun by Germanic migrants in the 12th century. St Wendel was a 6th- or 7th-century shepherd and confessor, who is venerated especially at Sanktwendel on the River Nahe.

Wendelin ♀ Feminine form of ▸Wendel.

Wenzel ♂ German equivalent of Wenceslas, of Slavic origin; see main dictionary.

Werner ♂ Germanic: from the tribal name *Warin* + *heri* 'army'.
ALSO: Wernher.

Werther ♂ Probably from *wert* 'worthy' + *heri* 'army'; the name of the hero of a novel by Goethe.
ALSO: **Werter**.

Wetzel ♂ From a medieval pet form of ▶Werner, now sometimes used as an independent given name.

Wieland ♂ Germanic: from *wīg* 'war' + *land* 'territory'; borne in Germanic legend by Wieland the Smith, the king of the elves.

Wilfried ♂ Germanic: from *wil* 'will' + *frid* 'peace'.

Wilhelm ♂ Germanic: from *wil* 'will' + *helm* 'helmet'; an ancient royal name. See also William in main dictionary.

Wilhelmina ♀ Feminine form of ▶Wilhelm.
ALSO: **Wilhemine**.

Willi ♂ Pet form of ▶Wilhelm.

Willibald ♂ Germanic: from *wil* 'will' + *bald* 'bold, brave'. St Willibald (*c*.700–*c*.786) was of Anglo-Saxon origin, and aided his cousin Boniface in evangelical missions in Germany.

Willibrand ♂ Germanic: from *wil* 'will' + *brand* '(flaming) sword'.

Wilma ♀ Reduced form of ▶Wilhelmina.

Wim ♂ Reduced form of ▶Wilhelm.

Winfried ♂ Germanic: from *wini* 'friend' + *frid* 'peace'.

Winfriede ♀ Feminine form of ▶Winfried.

Witold ♂ Germanic: from *wīda* 'wide' or *witu* 'wood' + *wald* 'ruler'.

Woldemar ♂ Variant of ▶Waldemar.

Wolf ♂ Short form of any of several Germanic names formed with *wolf* 'wolf', especially ▶Wolfgang.

Wolfgang ♂ Germanic: from *wolf* 'wolf' + *gang* 'going'.

Wolfger ♂ Germanic: from *wolf* 'wolf' + *gēr* 'spear'.

Wolfram ♂ Germanic: from *wolf* 'wolf' + *hramn* 'raven'. The name was borne in the Middle Ages by the poet Wolfram von Eschenbach (*c*.1170–*c*.1220).

Wolter ♂ North German form of ▶Walther.

X

Xaver ♂ Roman Catholic name. See Xavier in main dictionary.

Xaveria ♀ Feminine form of ▶Xaver.

Z

Ziska ♀ Short form of ▶Franziska.

Zissi ♀ Pet form of ▶Franziska.

Indian Names

Note The names in this supplement are borne mainly by Hindus; also in some cases by Jains, Buddhists, Parsees, and Sikhs. India has a large population of Muslims, who bear names that are mostly of Arabic origin. For an explanation of Muslim names of Arabic origin, see Appendix 1. Muslim names of Persian and other origin are included here.

Aa

Ajit ♂ Sanskrit: 'invincible'.

Amitabh ♂ Sanskrit: 'of unmeasured splendour', one of the five aspects of Buddha in Mahayana Buddhism.

Amrit ♂, ♀ Sanskrit: 'immortal, ambrosia', a byname of Shiva and Vishnu.

Anand ♂ Sanskrit: 'happiness, bliss-consciousness', a byname of Shiva; also a Buddhist and Jain divine attribute.
FEMININE FORM: **Ananda**.

Anil ♂ Sanskrit: 'air, wind', one of the commonest names of the wind god Vayu, charioteer of Indra.
FEMININE FORM: **Anila**.

Anuradha ♀ Sanskrit: probably meaning 'stream of oblations', the name of one of the 28 asterisms at the heart of Hindu astrology.

Arjun ♂ Sanskrit: 'white' (the colour of dawn, lightning, milk, and silver), the name of the noblest of the five Pandava princes in the Mahabharata, who received Krishna's divine oration called the *Bhagavad Gita*.

Arun ♂ Sanskrit: 'reddish-brown', the colour of dawn, gold, and rubies, and personification of the dawn, the charioteer of the sun.
FEMININE FORM: **Aruna**.

Arvind ♂ Sanskrit: 'lotus'.

Asha ♀ Sanskrit: 'hope'.

Ashish ♂ Probably Sanskrit: 'prayer' or 'blessing'.

Ashok ♂ Sanskrit: 'not causing or feeling sorrow', the name of a common Indian tree. Emperor Asoka ruled *c*.269–232 BC over most of the subcontinent, from Afghanistan to Sri Lanka; he converted to Buddhism after a particularly bloody military campaign, and marked this by erecting thousands of inscribed pillars.

Bb

Babar ♂ Muslim name, from Turkish: 'lion', the byname of Zahir ud-Din Muhammad (*c*.1482–1530), first of the Mogul rulers in India.

Bala ♂, ♀ Sanskrit: 'young', often used in compound epithets of Krishna.

Baldev ♂ Sanskrit: 'god of strength', name of the elder brother of Krishna, described as wine-loving and irascible. The name is especially favoured by Sikhs.

Balu ♂ Pet form of ▶Bala.

Bano ♀ Muslim name, from Persian: 'lady, princess, bride'.

Bharat ♂ Sanskrit: 'being maintained', an epithet of Agni, the god of fire; also the name of a legendary emperor, ancestor of both the warring parties in the Mahabharata, and of Rama's loyal younger brother and regent in the Ramayana. Bharat was adopted as the official name of India at independence.
FEMININE FORM: **Bharati**.

Bhaskar ♂ Sanskrit: 'bright light', denoting the sun; also the name of ancient India's most famous mathematician and astrologer.

Bibi ♀ Muslim name, from Persian: 'lady of the house'.

Bishen ♂ North Indian variant of ▶Vishnu,

especially common among Sikhs.

Cc

Chandan ♂ Sanskrit: 'sandalwood', with reference especially to the paste made from sandalwood, used in Hindu ceremonies to anoint images of deities and to make an auspicious mark on the forehead of participants.

Chandra ♂, ♀ Sanskrit: 'moon'. Though the moon is always regarded as a male deity in Hinduism, it is also popular as a female name.

Chandrakant ♂ Sanskrit: 'moonstone', also 'white water-lily', literally 'beloved of the moon'.

Chandrakanta ♀ The feminine form of ▶Chandrakant, regarded as the wife of the moon and therefore used to denote night.

Dd

Damayanti ♀ Sanskrit: 'subduing (men)', i.e. by beauty or personality. In classical legend Damayanti is the name of a beautiful princess who is courted by Prince Nala, and by her intelligence distinguishes him from his rival suitors, four gods masquerading as him.

Damodar ♂ Sanskrit: 'having a rope round his belly', an epithet of Krishna based on the legend in which, as a child, he stole butter and broke pots of milk and curds in his foster-mother's house. She tied him to a large vessel by means of a rope round his waist to prevent him getting up to more mischief.
FEMININE FORM: **Damodari**.

Dayaram ♂ Sanskrit: 'compassionate as Rama'.

Deb ♂ Variant of ▶Dev.

Deo ♂ Variant of ▶Dev.

Dev ♂ Sanskrit: 'god', often referring in particular to Indra; also a term of address for kings, equivalent to 'Your Majesty'.

Devdan ♂ Sanskrit: 'gift of the gods'.

Devdas ♂ Sanskrit: 'servant of the gods'.

Devi ♀ Feminine form of ▶Dev; referring especially to the wife of Shiva.

Dilip ♂ Of uncertain etymology, probably Sanskrit: 'protector of Delhi', the name of various legendary kings.

Dinesh ♂ Sanskrit: 'lord of the day' (i.e. the sun).

Dipak ♂ Sanskrit: 'little lamp' or 'like a lamp'; an epithet of Kama, the god of love.

Durga ♀ Sanskrit: 'inaccessible', an epithet of the wife of Shiva, because of her propensity for prolonged meditation. Durga represents her terrifying form, reflecting her anger when disturbed.

Gg

Ganesh ♂ Sanskrit: 'lord of the hosts', a title of the god Shiva and the name of his eldest son, who has the head of an elephant and the body of a short fat imp with a huge belly.

Gauri ♀ Sanskrit: 'white', a byname of Shiva's previously dark-skinned wife who, after being teased by Shiva, acquired a brilliant white complexion through meditation in the Himalayas.

Gautam ♂ Sanskrit: 'descendant of Gotam', a name of the historical Buddha and of a major Jain saint, therefore especially favoured by Buddhists and Jains.

Gita ♀ Sanskrit: literally 'song', probably in the sense 'one whose praises are sung'.

Gobind ♂ Variant of ▶Govind, the name of one of the ten Sikh gurus, therefore especially popular among Sikhs.

Gopal ♂ Sanskrit: 'cowherd', also used to mean 'king', the earth being regarded fancifully as the milch-cow of the gods. It is a byname of

Krishna in the Mahabharata and among his cult worshippers.

Gotam ♂ Sanskrit: 'the best ox', name of an ancient Hindu sage. In Indian literature cattle are a symbol of wealth. The name was borne by the chief disciple of Mahavira, hence is popular among Jains.

Govind ♂ Sanskrit: 'cow finder', originally an epithet of the god Indra, but now most strongly associated with Krishna.

Gowri ♀ Variant of ►Gauri.

Gulzar ♂ Muslim name, from Persian: 'rose garden'.

Hh

Hari ♂ Sanskrit: byname of Vishnu or Krishna, from a word denoting a colour variously interpreted as brown, yellow, or green, and used particularly to describe the horses of Indra. It is also used as a noun with various meanings ('lion', 'sun', 'monkey', or 'wind').

Harinder ♂ Compound of ►Hari and ►Indra, favoured especially by Sikhs as suggesting the warrior attributes of the two great gods.

Harish ♂ Sanskrit: 'lord of the monkeys', used since medieval times as a byname of Vishnu.

Ii

Inderjit ♂, ♀ Sanskrit: 'conqueror of Indra', name of the son of the demon king Ravana in the Ramayana. Because of its martial connotations it is popular among Sikhs.

Inderpal ♂ Sanskrit: 'protector of Indra' or perhaps 'Indra's bodyguard', popular among Sikhs because of its martial connotations.

Indira ♀ Sanskrit: a byname of Lakshmi, the wife of Vishnu. It is said to mean 'beauty' or 'splendour'.

Indra ♂ Etymology uncertain; probably from a Sanskrit compound meaning 'possessing drops (of rain)'. Indra is the name of the god of the sky and lord of the rain, who conquers the demons of darkness by using his thunderbolt. Indra is now found mainly in compound names such as ►Inderjit and ►Jaswinder.

Jj

Jagannath ♂ Sanskrit: 'lord of the world', a byname of Vishnu, and especially the name of his image in the great temple of Puri.

Jagdish ♂ Sanskrit: 'ruler of the world', applied to the gods Brahma, Vishnu, and Shiva.

Jagjit ♂ Sanskrit: 'conqueror of the world', a popular name among Sikhs.

Jahangir ♂ Muslim name, from Persian: 'holder of the world'. It was the regnal name of the Mogul emperor Nur ud-Din Muhammad (1569–1627).

Jai ♂ Variant of ►Jay.

Jamshed ♂ Name borne chiefly by Parsis and Muslims. Jamshed was a legendary king of ancient Persia, the founder of Persepolis.

Janaki ♀ Sanskrit: meaning uncertain. It is an epithet of Sita, daughter of King Janaka and the wife of Rama.

Janmuhammad ♂ Muslim name, from Persian: 'breath (i.e. life) of Muhammad'.

Jaswinder ♀ Sikh name, from Sanskrit: 'Indra of the thunderbolt'.

Javed ♂ Muslim name, from Persian: 'eternal'.

Jay ♂ Sanskrit: 'victory'.

Jaya ♀ Feminine form of ►Jay; an epithet of Durga, the wife of Shiva. Also the name of a Buddhist goddess.

Jayakrishna ♂ Sanskrit: 'victorious Krishna'.

Jayant ♂ Sanskrit: 'victorious', name of the son of Indra.

Jayanti ♀ Feminine form of ▸Jayant; an epithet of Durga, the wife of Shiva; also the name of Indra's daughter.

Jayashankar ♂ Sanskrit: 'victorious Shiva'.

Jayashree ♀ Sanskrit: a byname of the goddess Lakshmi, wife of Vishnu, meaning 'goddess of victory'.

Jaywant ♂ Sanskrit: 'possessing victory', a popular name among Sikhs because of its martial connotations.

Jitender, Jitinder ♂ Variants of ▸Jitendra, especially common among Sikhs.

Jitendra ♂ Sanskrit: 'having conquered Indra' (i.e. so powerful as to have conquered even the god Indra), or a misunderstanding of Sanskrit *jitendriya* 'having one's senses under control', a central aim of yoga and meditation.

Jyoti ♀ Sanskrit: 'light', often used as a symbol of heaven, intelligence, and liberation.

Kk

Kailash ♂, ♀ Sanskrit: the name of a mountain in the Himalayas, the site of Shiva's paradise and abode of Kubera, the god of wealth.

Kalidas ♂ Sanskrit: 'servant of Kali' (literally 'the black one', name of Shiva's wife in her fierce form).

Kalpana ♀ Sanskrit: 'fantasy' or 'ornament'.

Kalyan ♂ Sanskrit: 'beautiful' or 'auspicious'. FEMININE FORM: Kalyani.

Kamal ♂ **1** Sanskrit: 'pink', also a name for the lotus. **2** Muslim name: see Arabic appendix.

Kamala ♀ Feminine form of ▸Kamal 1; a byname of the goddess Lakshmi, wife of Vishnu.

Kannan ♂ South Indian variant of ▸Krishna.

Kanta ♀ Sanskrit: 'desired; beautiful'.

Kanti ♀ Sanskrit: 'beauty', especially with reference to the shining beauty of the moon or a lovely woman.

Kapil ♂ Sanskrit: probably meaning 'monkey-coloured' or 'reddish brown'; the name of an ancient Hindu sage.

Karan ♂ Sanskrit: 'ear', name of a mighty warrior king of Anga (Bengal) in the Mahabharata. He is the son of Surya, the sun god, and (unbeknownst to them) the half-brother of the Pandava princes, against whom he fights.

Kasi ♂ Sanskrit: 'shining'; a name of Varanasi (Benares), most sacred Hindu city on the Ganges.

Kausalya ♀ Sanskrit: 'belonging to the Kosala people'; the name of the grandmother of both sets of princes who fight in the Mahabharata war; also the name of the mother of Rama in the Ramayana.

Khurshid ♂ Muslim name, from Persian: 'sun'.

Khwaja ♂ Muslim name, from Persian: 'master'.

Kiran ♂ Sanskrit: 'ray of light', especially 'sunbeam' or 'moonbeam'.

Kishen ♂ North Indian variant of ▸Krishna.

Kishore ♂ Sanskrit: 'colt' or 'young boy'. FEMININE FORM: Kishori ('filly').

Kistna ♂ Central Indian variant of ▸Krishna.

Krishna ♂ Sanskrit: literally 'black, dark'; the name of a legendary hero, later elevated to divinity and usually regarded an incarnation of Vishnu.

Kumar ♂ Sanskrit: 'boy, son; prince'; a byname of the beautiful youth Skanda, son of Shiva.

Kumari ♀ Sanskrit: feminine form of ▸Kumar, meaning 'daughter; princess'; an epithet of Shiva's wife.

L

Lakshman ♂ Sanskrit: 'having auspicious

marks', name of the half-brother and faithful companion of Rama in the Ramayana, regarded as a partial incarnation of Vishnu.

Lakshmi ♀ Sanskrit: 'sign, lucky omen'; name of the goddess of beauty, good fortune, and wealth, wife of Vishnu.

Lal ♂ **1** Sanskrit: a term of endearment, 'darling boy'. **2** Prakrit: 'king'.

Lalita ♀ Sanskrit: 'playful; amorous'; name of one of the cowherdesses who were the amorous playmates of the adolescent Krishna.

Lata ♀ Sanskrit: 'tendril' or 'creeper', often used in metaphors describing the slender curvature of eyebrows, arms, hair, swords, lightning, and women's bodies.

Laxman ♂ Modern variant of ▶Lakshman.

Leela ♀ Sanskrit: 'play; amorous sport'.

Liaqat ♂ Muslim name, from Persian: 'dignity; merit; ability; good judgement'.

Lila ♀ Variant of ▶Leela.

Mm

Madhav ♂ Sanskrit: a byname of Krishna, meaning 'descendant of ▶Madhu'.
FEMININE FORM: Madhavi (a byname of the goddess Lakshmi).

Madhu ♀ Sanskrit: 'sweet, honey'; also 'springtime'. This was the name of a legendary king, one of whose descendants was the god Krishna.

Madhukar ♂ Sanskrit: 'honey-maker', i.e. 'bee'.

Madhur ♀ Sanskrit: 'sweet'.

Mahavir ♂ Sanskrit: 'great hero'; the name of the founder of Jainism.

Mahendra ♂ Sanskrit: 'great Indra', a byname of Vishnu in the Ramayana and of Shiva in Tantric texts; also the name of Emperor Asoka's brother, the first great Buddhist missionary.

Mahesh ♂ Sanskrit: 'great ruler', a byname of Shiva; also the name of a Buddhist deity.

Mahinder ♂ North Indian variant of ▶Mahendra.

Malati ♀ Sanskrit name of the jasmine plant, whose flowers open in the evening.

Mani ♂, occasionally ♀ Sanskrit: 'jewel'; also used to denote the phallus. The name carries magical or mystical connotations. It is often used as a short form of Subrahmanya, son of Shiva and brother of Ganesh.

Meena ♀ Sanskrit: 'fish; Pisces'; name of the daughter of the goddess

of the dawn, and of the wife of the ancient sage Kasyapa. Often a short form of Meenakshi ('having eyes shaped like a fish'), the name of a princess of Madurai, now its patron goddess and commonly identified with Durga, the wife of Shiva.

Mehjibin ♀ Muslim name, from Persian: 'with temples like the moon', suggesting a woman with a beautiful face.

Mirza ♂ Muslim name, from Persian: 'prince', an honorific title introduced into the subcontinent by the Moguls.

Mohan ♂ Sanskrit: 'enchanting', a byname of Shiva and of one of the five arrows of Kama, the god of love. It is also an epithet of Krishna, who beguiles the cowherdesses and enchants his devotees.
FEMININE FORM: Mohana.

Mohinder ♂ North Indian variant of ▶Mahendra.

Mohini ♀ Sanskrit: 'enchanting woman', a name of Vishnu, from the myth in which he disguises himself as a beautiful woman in order to distract Shiva from a dangerously deep meditation.

Mukesh ♂ Sanskrit: of uncertain origin, probably from an epithet of Shiva, 'conqueror of the wild boar demon Muka'.

Murali ♂ Sanskrit: 'flute', with reference to various compound epithets of Krishna, especially **Muralidhara** 'bearer of the flute'.

Nn

Nagendra ♂ Sanskrit: 'mighty serpent' or 'mighty elephant' (literally 'a (veritable) Indra among serpents/ elephants').

Nanda ♂ Sanskrit: 'joy; son'; name of the foster-father of Krishna, also a byname of Vishnu. In Buddhist texts it is the name of the step-brother of Buddha. Associated with prodigious wealth as the name of a historical dynasty of kings.

Narain ♂ North Indian variant of ▸Narayan.

Narayan ♂ Sanskrit: literally 'path of man', i.e. 'son of man'; a byname of Brahma, god of creation, and of Vishnu.

Narendra ♂ Sanskrit: 'an Indra among men', i.e. 'mighty man, king'; also 'doctor', associated with cures and charms against snake-bite.

Naresh ♂ Sanskrit: 'ruler of men'.

Narottam ♂ Sanskrit: 'best of men'; popular especially among Jains.

Nataraj ♂ Sanskrit: 'lord of the dance', a byname of Shiva.

Naveed ♂ Muslim name, from Persian: 'glad tidings' or 'wedding invitation'.

Niaz ♂ Muslim name, from Persian: 'prayer; gift or offering'.

Pp

Padma ♂, ♀ Sanskrit: 'lotus', symbolizing the *cakras* or centres of psychic energy in the human body; the female name is a byname of the goddess Lakshmi.

Padmavati ♀ Sanskrit: 'full of lotuses' or 'lotus-like'.

Padmini ♀ Sanskrit: 'full of lotuses' or 'lotus pond'.

Parvaiz ♂ Muslim name, from Persian: 'victorious' or 'fortunate'.

Parvati ♀ Sanskrit: 'daughter of the mountain', a byname of Shiva's wife.

Parvin ♀ Muslim name, from Persian, denoting the Pleiades.

Pitambar ♂ Sanskrit: 'wearing yellow garments', an epithet of Vishnu or Krishna. Yellow (saffron) clothes are traditionally worn by Hindus for worship and for pilgrimage.

Prabhakar ♂ Sanskrit: 'light maker', a byname of Shiva. In medieval times, the name of a Hindu philosopher.

Prabhu ♂ Sanskrit: 'mighty, king'; an epithet of Surya, the sun god, and of Agni, god of fire.

Prabodh ♂ Sanskrit: 'awakening', also 'the blooming of flowers'; frequently used in religious and philosophical texts as a metaphor for the awakening of consciousness.

Pradeep ♂ Sanskrit: 'light, lantern; glory'.

Prakash ♂ Sanskrit: 'light; famous'.

Pramod ♂ Sanskrit: 'joy, pleasure'.

Pran ♂ Sanskrit: 'breath, life-force'.

Prasad ♂ Sanskrit: 'brightness'; also 'the grace of God', denoting especially the offerings made to a deity and then distributed to the worshippers.

Pratap ♂ Sanskrit: 'heat', also 'splendour, majesty, power', applied to kings and warriors.

Pratibha ♀ Sanskrit: 'light; image', also 'intelligence', 'audacity', or 'imagination'.

Pravin ♂ Sanskrit: 'skilful'.

Prem ♂ Sanskrit: 'love, affection'.
FEMININE FORM: **Prema**.

Premlata ♀ Sanskrit: denoting a kind of small creeping plant, sometimes used as a metaphor for love.

Priya ♀ Sanskrit: 'beloved'.

Purnima ♀ Sanskrit: 'day (or night) of the full moon'.

Purushottam ♂ Sanskrit: 'highest of beings', a byname of Vishnu or Krishna. It is the term for a deified teacher in the Jain religion, hence a popular name among Jains.

Rr

Radha ♀ Sanskrit: 'success'; the name of the favourite consort of Krishna.

Raghav ♂ Sanskrit: 'descendant of Raghu', an epithet of Rama.

Raghu ♂ Sanskrit: 'swift', name of an ancestor of Rama.

Raj ♂ Sanskrit: 'king', applied to various gods, for example Varuna, Aditya, Indra, and Yama. It is a name of Yudhisthira, the eldest Pandava prince in the Mahabharata.

Rajani ♀ Sanskrit: 'the dark one, night'; a byname of Durga, the wife of Shiva.

Rajanikant ♂ Sanskrit: 'beloved of the night', an epithet of the moon.

Rajendra ♂ Sanskrit: 'an Indra among kings', hence 'mighty king, emperor'.

Rajesh ♂ Sanskrit: 'ruler of kings, emperor'.

Rajiv ♂ Sanskrit: 'striped', the name of a species of fish and of the blue lotus.

Rajkumar ♂ Sanskrit: 'king's son, prince'.
FEMININE FORM: **Rajkumari**.

Rajni ♀ Either a contracted form of ▶Rajani or from a Sanskrit word meaning 'queen'.

Rajnish ♂ Sanskrit: 'ruler of the night', i.e. the moon.

Raju ♂ Variant of ▶Raj or abbreviation of any of various compound names with *Raja-* as first element.

Rakesh ♂ Sanskrit: 'ruler of the day of the full moon', a byname of Shiva.

Ram ♂ North Indian variant of ▶Rama.

Rama ♂ Sanskrit: 'pleasing'. Three famous bearers of the name are known: Parasurama 'Rama of the axe', the sixth incarnation of Vishnu; Balarama 'the strong Rama', elder brother of Krishna and eighth incarnation of Vishnu; and above all

Ramachandra, seventh incarnation of Vishnu, whose story is told in the Ramayana.

Ramakrishna ♂ Compound name from ▶Rama and ▶Krishna.

Ramesh ♂ Sanskrit: from 'rest, repose, night', a byname of Lakshmi + 'lord', hence meaning 'lord of Lakshmi', a byname of Vishnu.

Rameshwar ♂ Sanskrit: synonymous with ▶Ramesh; or ▶Rama + 'lord', i.e. 'lord Rama'.

Ramgopal ♂ Compound name from ▶Ram and ▶Gopal, synonymous with ▶Ramakrishna, *gopal* being originally an epithet of Krishna.

Ramnarayan ♂ Compound name from ▶Ram and ▶Narayan.

Ramnath ♂ Sanskrit: 'Lord Rama'.

Ramu ♂ Variant of ▶Ram or ▶Rama, or pet form of any of the many compound names formed with *Ram-* or *Rama-*.

Ranjit ♂ Sanskrit: 'coloured, painted', also meaning 'charmed' or 'delighted'. This name was borne by Ranjit Singh (1780–1839), founder of the Sikh kingdom in the Punjab.

Ratan ♂ Prakrit: 'jewel'.

Rati ♀ Sanskrit: 'repose'; 'pleasure', especially

'sexual pleasure', hence often personified as the wife of Kama, god of love.

Ratilal ♂ Prakrit: 'lord of pleasure', an epithet of Kama, the god of love.

Ravi ♂ Sanskrit: 'sun', name of the sun god.

Ravindra ♂ Sanskrit: 'mightiest of suns' (literally 'an Indra among suns').

Rohan ♂ Sanskrit: 'ascending', also used to mean 'healing' or 'medicine'.

Roshan ♂, ♀ Muslim name, from Persian: 'shining, splendid'. It is used in Urdu to mean 'famous'.

Roshanara ♀ Muslim name, from Persian: 'light of the assembly', suggesting a woman whose beauty attracts everyone.

Rukmini ♀ Sanskrit: 'adorned with gold'; name of a character in the Mahabharata who becomes the secret lover of Krishna.

Rupchand ♂ Sanskrit: 'as beautiful as the moon'.

Rupinder ♀ Sanskrit: 'superlatively beautiful'; literally 'an Indra of beauty'. The name is especially popular among Sikhs.

Ss

Sachdev ♂ Sanskrit: 'truth of god', i.e. 'of impeccable honesty'.

Samant ♂ Sanskrit: 'universal; whole'.

Sandhya ♀ Sanskrit: 'junction' or 'twilight', used to denote the rituals performed three times daily by the twice-born Hindu castes; personified in the Epics and Puranas as a daughter of the god Brahma.

Sanjay ♂ Sanskrit: 'triumphant'; name of the main narrator of the daily battles in the Mahabharata.

Sanjeev ♂ Sanskrit: 'reviving'.

Sankar ♂ Variant of ▶Shankar.

Sarala ♀ Sanskrit: 'straight, honest'; also denotes the pine tree.

Saraswati ♀ Sanskrit: 'having or possessing waters'; the name of a river (sometimes identified with the Indus) deified as a goddess; also the name of Brahma's wife, goddess of education, arts, and sciences.

Sardar ♂ Mainly Muslim, from Persian: 'head man; nobleman'. It was adopted as an honorific title by the Sikhs.
ALSO: Sirdar.

Sarfraz ♂ Muslim name, from Persian: 'holding one's head up high'.

Saroja ♀ Sanskrit: 'born in a lake', also 'lotus'.

Sarojini ♀ Sanskrit: 'having lotuses', 'lotus-pond'.

Satish ♂ Sanskrit: 'lord of Sati' (reality, truth); a byname of the goddess Durga.

Savitri ♀ Sanskrit: 'belonging to Savitr' (the sun god); the name of the main prayer in Hindu ceremonies, personified as the wife or daughter of the sun or of Brahma. In legend, she is the faithful wife who rescues her husband from Yama (Death, king of the underworld).

Sekar ♂ Sanskrit: 'peak, crest', also 'the best'. Common as an abbreviated form of compound names such as Chandrasekhar 'moon-crested', an epithet of the god Shiva.

Seth ♂ Of uncertain origin, possibly from Sanskrit *setu* 'bridge' or *sveta* 'white'.

Shah ♂ Muslim name, from Persian: 'king, emperor'. The name is especially associated with Sufi mystics.

Shahjahan ♂ Muslim name, from Persian: 'king of the world', name of the Mogul emperor (1592–1666) for whom the Taj Mahal in Agra was built.

Shahnawaz ♂ Muslim name, from Persian: 'cherisher of kings'.

Shahnaz ♀ Muslim name, from Persian: 'glory of kings'.

Shahzad ♂ Muslim name, from Persian: 'prince'.

Shakti ♀ Sanskrit: 'power', in particular the power of a deity, personified as his wife; especially a byname of Shiva's wife.

Shakuntala ♀ Sanskrit: the name of the heroine of a drama by Kalidasa. Her name is said to derive from the name of a type of bird, because she was abandoned in a forest soon after birth and reared by birds. She was the beloved of King Dushyanta, and their son Bharat was the founder of a race of kings.

Shamshad ♂, ♀ Muslim name, from Persian: 'box tree'. It suggests a woman who is tall, slender, and graceful.

Shankar ♂ Sanskrit: 'conferrer of welfare', a euphemistic epithet of the god Rudra (Shiva). It is the name of one of the most famous Hindu philosophers (8th–9th century AD).

Shanta ♀ Sanskrit: 'calmed', referring especially to spiritual calmness acquired through yoga or meditation.

Shanti ♀ Sanskrit: 'tranquillity', usually associated with yoga or meditation.

Sharada ♀ Sanskrit: 'autumnal; mature'; a byname of Durga, wife of Shiva.

Sharma ♂ Sanskrit: 'protection, refuge'; later 'joy' or 'comfort'; traditionally a name favoured by Brahmins (priests).

Sharmila ♀ Hindi: 'modest', from Sanskrit, 'protection', an epithet of Draupadi, shared wife of the Pandava princes in the Mahabharata, from the episode in which her sari miraculously grows longer and continues to cover her body, although it is being unwound and pulled off her by a shameless Kaurava prince.

Shashi ♂ Sanskrit: literally 'having a hare', an epithet of the moon (the visible features of the moon being interpreted as resembling a hare). It is often found as the first element in compound names such as Shashikant 'beloved of the moon' and Sashichand 'the hare-marked moon'.

Sheela ♀ Sanskrit: 'good character; piety'; in Buddhism one of the six perfections to be striven for.

Sher ♂ Muslim name, from Persian: 'lion'; Sher Shah (1486–1545) was Mogul emperor from 1540 to 1545.

Shirin ♀ Muslim name, from Persian: 'sweet, charming'; name of the daughter of the Byzantine emperor Maurice (c.539–602), celebrated in Persian and Turkish romances as the beloved of the lowly Farhad, whose royal rival Khusrao deceitfully brings about his death.

Shiva ♂ Sanskrit: 'benign; auspicious'; originally a euphemistic epithet of the terrifying god of destruction, Rudra. Shiva is one of the most important of the Hindu gods, associated in particular with asceticism, generative power, and the dance of cosmic destruction.

Shobha ♀ Sanskrit: 'brilliance; beauty'.

Shobhana ♀ Sanskrit: 'brilliant; beautiful'.

Shripati ♂ Sanskrit: 'husband of Sri, goddess of fortune' or 'lord of fortune'; a byname of Vishnu or Krishna.

Shyam ♂ Sanskrit: 'black; dark; beautiful', a byname of Krishna.

Shyama ♀ Feminine form of ▸Shyam, also meaning 'night'; a byname of Durga, the wife of Shiva. It is also the name of a Jain goddess.

Siddhartha ♂ Sanskrit: 'one who has accomplished his goal'; an epithet of the Buddha.

Sita ♀ Sanskrit: 'furrow', personified as the goddess of agriculture and the harvest; the name of the wife of Rama, identified with the goddess Lakshmi, and a symbol of all the wifely virtues: purity, tenderness, and fidelity.

Sitaram ♂ Compound name from ▸Sita and ▸Rama, meaning 'Rama whose wife was Sita', also denoting godhead as the union of male and female.

Sneh ♀ Sanskrit: 'viscous, oil', also 'affection, tenderness'.

Sri ♀ Sanskrit: 'light; beauty; prosperity', also 'rank, power, royal majesty', a byname of the goddesses Lakshmi and Saraswati. Also widely used as an honorific title.

Sridhar ♂ Sanskrit: 'bearing or possessing Sri (the goddess Lakshmi)', an epithet of the god Vishnu.

Srikant ♂ Sanskrit: **1** 'Having a beautiful throat', an epithet of Shiva, from the myth in which he saves the universe by swallowing the poison that threatens to engulf it, his throat turning blue in the process. **2** 'The beloved of Sri', an epithet of Vishnu.

Srinivas ♂ Sanskrit: 'the abode of the goddess Sri', an epithet of Vishnu.

Sriram ♂ Sanskrit: 'Lord Rama'; also used as a salutation by Rama devotees.

Subhash ♂ Sanskrit: literally '(of) good speech', hence 'eloquent'.

Sudhir ♂ Sanskrit: literally 'good firmness', hence 'wise; resolute'.

Sujata ♀ Sanskrit: 'of noble birth' or 'of an excellent nature'.

Suman ♂ Sanskrit: 'well-disposed, cheerful'; also 'wise'.

Sumanjit ♂ Sanskrit: 'the conqueror of the demon Sumana'.

Sumantra ♂ Sanskrit: '(giver of) good advice'; an archetypal name for a minister in classical and later texts.

Sumati ♀ Sanskrit: 'good mind', also denoting 'benevolence' or 'prayer'; originally a masculine name but now exclusively feminine. In legend, it is the name of the wife of King Sagara, who bore 60,000 sons.

Sundar, Sunder ♂ Sanskrit: 'beautiful'; often the first element in compound names such as Sundararaja and Sunder Ram.

Sunil ♂ Sanskrit: 'very dark blue'; also said to denote the pomegranate tree or the flax plant.

Sunita ♀ Sanskrit: **1** Probably meaning 'of good conduct'. **2** 'Giving good guidance, righteous'. Originally a masculine name, now exclusively feminine.

Suniti ♀ Sanskrit: 'of good conduct'; the name of the mother of the pole star Dhruva.

Surendra, Surinder ♂ Sanskrit: 'the mightiest of gods', an epithet of various gods, but especially of Indra. The form Surinder is especially common among Sikhs.

Suresh ♂ Sanskrit: 'ruler of the gods', sometimes the name of a distinct god, but more commonly an epithet of Indra, Shiva, or Vishnu.

Surjit ♂ Sanskrit: 'one who has conquered the gods'.

Surya ♂ Sanskrit: 'sun', the name of the sun god in his physical form, ruler of the sky, said to be the father of the twins Yama and Yami, primal man and woman.

Sushil ♂ Sanskrit: 'well-disposed' or 'good-tempered'.

Sushila ♀ Feminine form of ▸Sushil; the name of a wife of Krishna, or a female attendant of Krishna's mistress Radha.

Swapan ♂ Sanskrit: 'sleep, dream'.

Swaran ♂ Sanskrit: 'beautiful in colour; golden'.

T t

Tara ♂ Sanskrit:
1 Probably meaning 'carrying' or 'saviour', an epithet of Rudra, and of Vishnu. **2** 'Shining'.

Tara ♀ Sanskrit: 'star' or 'asterism', a byname of Durga, especially in her meditative and magical guise; also the name of the wife of Brhaspati, preceptor of the gods, and mother of Budha (the Indian equivalent of the god Mercury); in Mahayana Buddhism, the name of the wife of Buddha, and of a Buddhist goddess; in Jain texts, the name of a female deity.

Tarun ♂ Sanskrit: 'young, tender', used especially of the newly risen sun and of young plants; also 'tenderness of feelings' or 'affection'.

Tulsi ♂ Sanskrit: denoting the holy basil plant, regarded as sacred to Vishnu, and personified as a goddess.

U u

Uma ♀ Sanskrit: denoting the flax plant or turmeric; the name of a goddess who mediates between Brahma and the other gods, identified with the goddess Vac, the personification of speech; also a byname of Parvati, wife of Shiva.

Umashankar ♂ Sanskrit: compound name meaning either 'Shankar whose wife is Uma', (i.e. Shiva), or 'Uma and Shankar', referring to the godhead as the union of male and female.

Usha ♀ Sanskrit: 'dawn', personified as the daughter of heaven, the sister of the solar gods and of night, the wife of the god Rudra; said to be very beautiful, the friend of men, the bringer of wealth, and always young although she makes men grow old.

Uttam ♂ Sanskrit: 'highest; furthest; last; best'.

V v

Vasant ♂ Sanskrit: denoting the spring season, often personified and regarded as the friend or attendant of Kama, the god of love.
FEMININE FORM: **Vasanta**.

Vasu ♂ Sanskrit: 'bright; beneficent; excellent', an epithet of various gods, including Indra, Agni, and Vishnu; also the name of one of the seven great ancient sages, authors of the Rig-Veda; often used as an abbreviation of Vasudeva, a name of Vishnu and of the father of Krishna.

Venkat ♂ Sanskrit: the name of a sacred peak near Madras, dedicated to the god Vishnu, and a major Hindu pilgrimage centre.

Vijay ♂ Sanskrit: 'victory'; also 'booty'; an epithet of Arjuna.
FEMININE FORM: **Vijaya** (a byname of Durga, wife of Shiva).

Vijayalakshmi ♀ Sanskrit: a particular form of Lakshmi regarded as the goddess of victory.

Vijayashree ♀ Another name for ▶Vijayalakshmi.

Vikram ♂ Sanskrit: 'stride, pace', also 'heroism' or 'strength'; a byname of Vishnu, probably derived from his earlier epithet *trivikrama* 'thrice stepping', from the myth in which he encompasses the three worlds in three steps; also the name of a historical king of Ujjain, said to have driven the Scythian invaders out of India, and possibly the founder of the Vikrama era, which began in 58 BC.

Vimal ♂ Sanskrit: 'stainless, pure', a name especially frequent in Buddhist literature.

Vimala ♀ Sanskrit: feminine form of ▶Vimal; the name of various minor goddesses, and occasionally a byname of Durga, Shiva's wife.

Vinay ♂ Sanskrit: originally meaning

'leading asunder', but later usually 'guidance', training, education', sometimes personified as a son of Kriya (religious ritual) or of Lajja (modesty); a key term in Buddhist texts, meaning 'conduct appropriate to monks', the title of one of the three main sections of the Buddhist canon.

Vinayak ♂ Sanskrit: 'one who leads asunder', originally the name of a class of demons that cause despondency, failure, and madness, and are loosely connected with Rudra, god of destruction; later, a name of the elephant-headed god Ganesh, son of Shiva.

Vinod ♂ Sanskrit: 'driving away', hence 'diversion, sport, pleasure'.

Vishnu ♂ Sanskrit: the name of a secondary god in the Rig-Veda, who joins Indra in slaying the demon Vrtra and drinking the divine Soma juice. Vishnu is a personification of the sun, striding the heavens in three paces. In the Epics, Vishnu becomes a supreme god and Shiva's rival. Myths of his incarnations proliferate, now usually limited to ten, including Rama of the Ramayana, Krishna, Buddha, and Kalki (who is yet to come).

Vishwanath ♂ Sanskrit: 'lord of all', a byname of Shiva.

Y y

Yadav ♂ Sanskrit: 'descendant of Yadu', an epithet of Krishna.

Yashpal ♂ Sanskrit: 'protector of splendour'.

Z z

Zaibunissa ♀ Muslim name, from Persian: 'woman of beauty'; the name of the eldest child (1673–1702) of the Mogul emperor Aurangzeb.

Zarina ♀ Muslim name, from Persian: 'golden'.

Appendix 6:
Irish Names

Aa

Abbán ♂ From a diminutive of *abb* 'abbot'. It was borne by a 6th-century Irish saint, the son of Cormac of Leinster.

Ádhamh ♂ Gaelic equivalent of Adam. See main dictionary.

Ádhamhnán ♂ Traditionally said to be a diminutive form of ▶Ádhamh, but equally possibly a diminutive of *adomnae* 'great fear', i.e. 'little horror'. It was borne by a 7th-century saint, abbot of Iona and biographer of St Columba.

Áed ♂ Traditional spelling of ▶Aodh.

Áedán ♂ Traditional spelling of ▶Aodhán.

Aengus ♂ Usual Irish form of Angus. See main dictionary.

Aibhilín ♀ Variant spelling of ▶Eibhlín, sometimes Anglicized as Evelyn (see main dictionary).

Aidan ♂ Anglicized form of ▶Áedán. See also main dictionary.

Aignéis ♀ From Greek. See Agnes in main dictionary.

Ailbhe ♂, ♀ Traditional name, probably from Old Irish *albho* 'white'; borne in Irish legend by a female warrior of the Fianna.

Ailill ♂ Traditional name meaning 'elf'; borne by several characters in Irish mythology.

Ailín ♀ Irish equivalent of Alan. See main dictionary.

Ailish ♀ Irish equivalent of Alice. See main dictionary.
ALSO: **Ailís**.

Aindréas ♂ Irish equivalent of Andrew. See main dictionary.
ALSO: **Aindriú**.

Áine ♀ Traditional name, originally meaning 'brightness' or 'radiance'; the name of the queen of the fairies in Celtic mythology, also used as an Irish equivalent of *Anne*, to which it is unrelated.

Aingeal ♀ From the vocabulary word *aingeal* 'angel'.

Aisling ♀ Modern coinage: from *aisling* 'dream, vision'.
ALSO: **Aislin(n)**.

Aithne ♀ Variant of ▶Eithne.

Alaois ♂ Irish equivalent of Aloysius. See main dictionary.

Alastar ♂ Irish equivalent of Alexander. See main dictionary.

Alastríona ♀ Feminine form of ▶Alastar.

Alby ♂ Anglicized form of ▶Ailbhe.

Amhlaoibh ♂ Irish form of Olaf. See Scandinavian appendix.

Anéislis ♂ Traditional: originally a byname meaning 'careful, thoughtful'. It has been Anglicized as both ▶Stanislas and Standish.

Anluan ♂ Traditional name of uncertain origin: possibly composed of an intensive prefix + an element meaning 'hound' or 'warrior'. It has been Anglicized as Alphonse (see main dictionary), to which it is, however, unrelated.

Anraí ♂ Irish equivalent of Henry. See main dictionary.

Aodh ♂ Modern form of *Áed*, meaning 'fire'; the name of the Celtic sun god and a common personal name from earliest times.

Aodhán ♂ Modern form of an ancient Gaelic name, Ádhán, a pet form of *Áed* (see ▶Aodh).

Aogán ♂ Earlier *Aodhagán*, a double diminutive of ▶Aodh.

Aoibhe ♀ Irish equivalent of Eve (see main dictionary). Compare ▶Aoife, ▶Éabha.

Aoibheann ♀
Traditional name
meaning 'beautiful'.
ALSO: **Aoibhinn**.

Aoife ♀ Probably a
derivative of *aoibh*
'beauty' (compare
►Aoibheann), but it has
also been associated
with *Esuvia*, a Gaulish
goddess. It was borne by
several different
heroines in ancient Irish
legend, and in historical
times by a daughter of
King Dermot of Leinster,
who married Richard
de Clare, Earl of
Pembroke, leader of
the Anglo-Norman
incursion into Ireland
of 1169. It has
sometimes been
Anglicized as *Eva*.

Ardal ♂ Traditional
name from *ard* 'high'
(or possibly *art* 'bear') +
gal 'valour'.
ALSO: **Ardghal**.

Art ♂ Traditional name
meaning 'bear', also
'champion'; borne in
Irish legend by Art
Óenfer ('Art the Lonely'),
a son of Conn
Cétchathach ('Conn of
the Hundred Battles'),
who overcomes a series
of dangers and
challenges in order to
win his bride,
Delbchaem.

Ashling ♀ Anglicized
form of ►Aisling.

Assumpta ♀ From
Latin: Marian name
commemorating the
assumption of the
Virgin Mary into
heaven.

Attracta ♀ Latinized
version (as if from
attractus 'attracted,
drawn') of the Gaelic
name *Athracht*.
St Athract or Attracta
was a contemporary
of St Patrick, who lived
as a recluse in Sligo.

Auliffe ♂ Anglicized
form of ►Amhlaoibh.

Bb

Baibín ♀ Pet form of
►Báirbre.

Báirbre ♀ From Greek.
See Barbara in main
dictionary.

Barra ♂ From Old
Irish *Bairre*, a short
form of ►Fionnbarr.

Barry ♂ Anglicized form
of ►Barra.

Bearach ♂ Traditional
name from *biorach*
'sharp'.

Bearnard ♂ Irish
equivalent of Bernard.
See main dictionary.

Bedelia ♀ Variant of
►Brighid. See Bridget in
main dictionary.

Béibhinn ♀ Traditional
name meaning 'white
lady' or 'fair lady'.
ALSO: **Bébhinn**, **Bébhionn**,
Bébinn.

Bernadette ♀ French.
See main dictionary.

Berneen ♀ Pet form of
►Bernadette.

Bláithín ♀ From a
diminutive of *blath*
'flower'.

Blanid ♀ Anglicized
form of ►Bláthnat.

Bláthnat ♀ Traditional
name from a diminutive
of *blath* 'flower'.
ALSO: **Blánaid**.

Breandán ♂ Modern
Gaelic form (based on
the medieval Latin
form *Brendanus*) of the
old Irish personal name
Bréanainn, derived from
a Celtic word meaning
'prince'. See also
Brendan in main
dictionary.

Breda ♀ Anglicized
form of ►Bríd.
ALSO: **Breeda**.

Bree ♀ Anglicized form
of ►Brighe.

Brendan ♂ Anglicized
form of ►Breandán.

Brian ♂ Perhaps from
an Old Celtic word
meaning 'high' or
'noble'. See also main
dictionary.

Briartach ♂ Variant
form of ►Muiriartach,
common particularly in
Connacht.

Bríd ♀ Modern
contracted form of
►Brighid.
ALSO: **Bride** (Anglicized
form).

Brídín ♀ Pet form of
►Bríd.

Bríghe ♀ Contracted
form of Brighid.
ALSO: **Bree**, **Brie**
(Anglicized forms).

Brighid ♀ Traditional
name meaning 'the
exalted one'. See Bridget
in main dictionary.

ALSO: Brigid, Brigit, Bridget (Anglicized forms).

Brógán ♂ Traditional name: probably from a diminutive of *bróg* 'shoe'.

Brónach ♀ Traditional name meaning 'sorrowful'.

Bronagh ♀ Anglicized form of ▶Brónach.

Cc

Cahal ♂ Variant of ▶Cathal.

Cahan ♂ Variant of ▶Cathán.

Cainneach ♂ Traditional: originally a byname meaning 'handsome'; borne by a large number of early saints, most notably the 6th-century founder of the town of Kilkenny (Gaelic *Cill Chainnigh*). ALSO: Kenny (Anglicized form).

Cairbre ♂ Traditional name meaning 'charioteer'; borne in legend by a 3rd-century High King of Ireland, who was killed in battle fighting against the Fianna. ALSO: Carbrey, Carbry (Anglicized forms).

Cáit ♀ Short form of ▶Caitlín, ▶Caitrín, or ▶Caitríona.

Caitlín ♀ From Greek. See ▶Katherine in main dictionary. ALSO: Kathleen (Anglicized form), Katelyn (modern Anglicized elaboration).

Caitrín ♀ From Greek. See Katherine in main dictionary.

Caitríona ♀ From Greek. See Katherine in main dictionary. ALSO: Catriona (Anglicized form).

Cal ♂ Ulster variant of ▶Cathal.

Calbhach ♂ Traditional name meaning 'bald'.

Callum ♂ Scottish Gaelic form of ▶Colm, now widely used in Ireland and throughout the English-speaking world. ALSO: Calum.

Calvagh ♂ Anglicized form of ▶Calbhach.

Canice ♂ Anglicized form (from the Latinized form *Canicius*) of ▶Cainneach.

Caoilfhionn ♀ From *caol* 'slender' + *fionn* 'white'. ALSO: Caoilainn; Keelin (Anglicized form).

Caoimhe ♀ From a vocabulary word meaning 'gentleness, loveliness, grace'. ALSO: Keeva (Anglicized form).

Caoimhín ♂ Traditional: originally a byname representing a diminutive of *caomh* 'comely; beloved'; borne by a 7th-century saint who is one of the patrons of Dublin. ALSO: Kevin (Anglicized form).

Caolán ♂ Traditional: originally a byname

representing a diminutive of Irish *caol* 'slender'. ALSO: Kelan (Anglicized form).

Caolite ♂ Of uncertain derivation; this was the name of the legendary hero Caoilte Mac Rónáin, famous as a swift runner.

Carbry ♂ Anglicized form of ▶Cairbre. ALSO: Carbrey.

Carroll ♂ Anglicized form of ▶Cearbhall.

Cathair ♂ Traditional name from the Old Celtic words *cath* 'battle' + *vir* 'man'.

Cathal ♂ Traditional name from the Old Celtic words *cath* 'battle' + *val* 'rule'.

Cathán ♂ Traditional name from a diminutive of *cath* 'battle'.

Cathaoir ♂ Variant of ▶Cathair.

Catraoine ♀ Irish equivalent of Katherine (see main dictionary), less common than ▶Caitríona, ▶Caitrín, and ▶Caitlín.

Ceallach ♂ Traditional name said to mean 'bright-headed', or possibly 'strife', but it could equally well be from *ceall*, genitive plural of *cill* 'monastery, church'. See also Kelly in main dictionary.

Cearbhall ♂ Traditional name, perhaps from *cearbh* 'hacking'.

Cian ♂ Traditional name meaning 'ancient'; borne by a son-in-law of Brian Boru, who played a leading role in the battle of Clontarf (1014).
ALSO: **Kean(e)**, **Kian** (Anglicized forms).

Ciannait ♀ Modern coinage: feminine form of ▶Cian.

Ciara ♀ Modern coinage: feminine form of ▶Ciarán.

Ciarán ♂ Traditional: originally a byname, a diminutive form of *ciar* 'black'. It was borne by two Irish saints: a hermit of the 5th century, and the founder of the monastery at Clonmacnoise (d. 547).
ALSO: **Kieran** (Anglicized form).

Cillian ♂ Traditional: originally a byname from a diminutive of *ceallach* 'strife', or possibly from *ceall* 'monastery, church'. It was borne by various early Irish saints, including the 7th-century author of a 'Life of St Bridget', and missionaries to Artois and Franconia.
ALSO: **Kil(l)ian** (Anglicized forms).

Cinnéidigh ♂ Traditional name from *ceann* 'head' + *éidigh* 'ugly'.
ALSO: **Kennedy** (Anglicized form).

Clíodhna ♀ Traditional name of unknown origin; borne in Irish legend by one of three beautiful daughters of the poet Libra.

Clíona ♀ Modern coinage: reduced form of ▶Clíodhna.
ALSO: **Cliona** (Anglicized form).

Clodagh ♀ Of recent origin: apparently an arbitrary adoption of the name of the river in Tipperary. See also main dictionary.

Cnochúr ♂ Modern Gaelic form of ▶Conchobhar.

Colm ♂ Traditional Irish form of the Late Latin personal name *Columba* 'dove'. See **Callum** in main dictionary.
ALSO: **Colum**.

Colmán ♂ From Late Latin *Columbanus*, a derivative of *Columba* (see ▶Colm). It was borne by a number of early saints, including Colmán of Armagh, a 5th-century disciple of St Patrick. St Colmán or *Columban* (*c.*540–615), founder of the monastery at Bobbio, Italy, became something of a cult figure in central Europe.
ALSO: **Colman** (Anglicized form).

Comhghall ♂ Traditional name from *comh* 'together, joint' + *gall* 'pledge, hostage'.
ALSO: **Comgall**; **Cowall** (Anglicized form).

Comhghán ♂ From *comh* 'together, joint' + *gan-, gen-* 'born', originally probably a byname referring to a twin. The name was borne by an 8th-century

Irish prince who lived as a monk in Scotland.
ALSO: **Comgan** (Anglicized form).

Conall ♂ Traditional name, a compound of Old Celtic words meaning 'wolf' and 'strong'. See also main dictionary.

Conán ♂ From a diminutive of *cú* 'hound' or 'wolf'; in Irish legend, Conán was a foul-mouthed and abusive member of the Fianna, the band of followers of the legendary hero Finn mac Cumhaill (Finn MacCool). After undergoing many trials and tribulations, Conán was awarded the 'fourteen best women in the Land of Promise' as compensation for his troubles. See also **Conan** in main dictionary.

Concepta ♀ Latinate Marian name referring to the Immaculate Conception.

Conchobhar ♂ Traditional name, probably meaning 'lover of hounds'; borne by a legendary king of Ulster who lived at the time of Christ.
ALSO: **Con(n)or** (Anglicized forms); **Cnochúr** (modern Gaelic form).

Conlaodh ♂ Traditional name, probably from *connla* 'pure, chaste; sensible' + the personal name ▶Aodh. St Conlaodh or Conláed, a contemporary of St Brighid, was the first bishop of Kildare.

Conley ♂ Anglicized form of ▶Conlaodh.

Conn ♂ Traditional name from *conn* 'chief, leader'; now also used as a short form of Conor (see ▶Conchobhar).

Conor ♂ Anglicized form of ▶Conchobhar.

Conroy ♂ Transferred use of the surname, an Anglicized form of either *Ó Conraoi* 'descendant of *Cú Raoi*' ('hound of the plain') or *Ó Conaire* 'descendant of *Conaire*' ('keeper of the hound').

Cormac ♂ Traditional: unexplained. Cormac Ó Cuilleannáin, a 10th-century king and bishop, was the author of a dictionary of the Irish language. See also main dictionary.

Críostóir ♂ From Greek. See Christopher in main dictionary.

Crístíona ♀ From Latin. See Christina in main dictionary.

Crónán ♂ Traditional: originally a byname from a diminutive of *crón* 'swarthy'.
ALSO: **Cronan, Cronin** (Anglicized forms).

Cuán ♂ Traditional: originally a byname from a diminutive of *cú* 'hound'.

Cuimín ♂ Traditional: originally a byname from a diminutive of *cam* 'bent, crooked'.
ALSO: **Comyn**.

Dd

Dáire ♂ From a vocabulary word meaning 'fertile'; the name of an ancient Irish fertility god associated with a bull cult. See also ▶Darragh.

Dáireann ♀ Of uncertain origin: Irish *der Fhinn* 'daughter of Finn' has been suggested. It is probably the source of the English name Doreen, which is one of its Anglicized forms.
ALSO: **Doirind**.

Dáirine ♀ Feminine diminutive form of ▶Dáire.
ALSO: **Darina** (Anglicized form).

Daithí ♂ Traditional: possibly meaning 'swift'.

Damhnait ♀ Feminine diminutive, meaning 'fawn', of *damh* 'stag'; a 6th-century saint founded a convent in Co. Monaghan. See also Dymphna in main dictionary.
ALSO: **Davnat** (Anglicized form).

Dara ♂ Short form of ▶Mac Dara 'son of oak'.

Darina ♀ Anglicized form of ▶Dáirine.

Darragh ♂ Popularly associated with the vocabulary word *dair* 'oak', genitive *darach*. It also functions as an Anglicized form of ▶Dáire.
ALSO: **Daragh, Dara(ch)**.

Davnat ♀ Anglicized form of ▶Damhnait.

Deaglán ♂ Traditional: of uncertain derivation. It was borne by a 5th-century bishop of Ardmore, a disciple of St Colmán.

Deasún ♂ Irish form of Desmond. See main dictionary.

Declan ♂ Anglicized form of ▶Deaglán.

Deirbhile ♀ From *der* 'daughter' + *file* 'poet'. This name has absorbed the ancient Irish name *Dearbháil* 'daughter of Fál', Fál being a poetic name for Ireland.
ALSO: **Dervila** (Anglicized form).

Deirdre ♀ Traditional name of uncertain derivation; it was borne by a tragic heroine of Celtic legend. See main dictionary.

Delma ♀ Short form of ▶Fidelma.

Dermot ♂ Anglicized form of Diarmaid.

Derval ♀ Anglicized form of *Dearbháil*; see ▶Deirbhile.

Dervila ♀ Anglicized form of ▶Deirbhile.
ALSO: **Dervla**.

Devnet ♀ Anglicized form of ▶Damhnait.

Diarmaid ♂ Earlier *Diarm(u)it*, of uncertain derivation; perhaps from *dí* 'without' + *airmit* 'injunction' or *airmait* 'envy'. See also Dermot in main dictionary.
ALSO: **Diarmait, Diarmuid; Dermot** (Anglicized form).

Dimity ♀ Possibly originally a feminine equivalent of ▶Diarmaid which later fell together with the vocabulary word for a light cotton fabric. See main dictionary.

Donagh ♂ Anglicized form of ▶Donnchadh.

Dónal ♂ Earlier Domhnall, from Old Celtic *dubno* 'world' + *val* 'rule'.
ALSO: Donal(l) (Anglicized spellings).

Donla ♀ Modern spelling of a traditional name composed of *dunn* 'brown' + *flaith* 'lady', revived in this form in the 20th century.

Donn ♂ Ancient byname meaning either 'brown' or 'chief, noble', in use from the earliest times until the 19th century.
ALSO: Don.

Donncha ♂ Modern spelling of ▶Donnchadh.

Donnchadh ♂ Compound of *donn* 'brown' + *chadh* 'chief, noble'. See also Duncan in main dictionary.
ALSO: Donncha; Donagh, Donough (Anglicized forms).

Donough ♂ Anglicized form of ▶Donnchadh.

Donovan ♂ Transferred use of the surname, Anglicized form of Ó Donndubháin 'descendant of Donndubhán', a personal name from *donn* 'brown-haired man' or 'chieftain' + *dubh* 'black,

dark' + the diminutive suffix -*án*.

Doran ♂ Transferred use of the surname, Irish Ó Deoradháin 'descendant of *Deoradhán*', a byname from a diminutive of *deoradh* 'pilgrim; stranger, exile'.

Dorean ♀ Anglicized form of ▶Dáireann or the variant Doirind.

Doyle ♂ Transferred use of the surname, Anglicized form of Ó Dubhghaill 'descendant of *Dubhghall*', from *dubh* 'black, dark' + *gall* 'stranger'. See main dictionary.

Duald ♂ Anglicized form of ▶Dubhaltach.
ALSO: Dualta.

Duane ♂ Anglicized form of ▶Dubhán.

Dubhaltach ♂ Probably from a byname from *dubh-fholtach* 'black-haired'.
ALSO: Duald, Dualta (Anglicized forms).

Dubhán ♂ Originally a byname, from a diminutive of *dubh* 'dark, black'. In modern use it may be derived from the surname Ó Dubháin 'descendant of Dubhán'.
ALSO: Duane; Dwa(y)ne, Dwain (Anglicized forms).

Dubhdara ♂ Compound of *dubh* 'black' + *dara* 'oak'.

Dwyer ♂ Transferred use of the surname, Anglicized form of Ó Dubhuidhir 'descendant of

Duíbhuidhir', a personal name composed of *dubh* 'dark, black' + *odhar* 'sallow, tawny' (or possibly *eidhir* 'sense, wisdom').

Dymphna ♀ The name of a medieval Flemish saint, who according to legend was an Irish girl. Her name has been identified, rightly or wrongly, with ▶Damhnait. See also main dictionary.
ALSO: Dympna.

Ee

Éabha ♀ Irish form of Eve. See main dictionary.

Éadaoin ♀ Modern form of ▶Étaín.
ALSO: Eadan.

Eadbhárd ♂ Irish equivalent of Edward. See main dictionary.

Éamon ♂ Irish equivalent of Edmund (see main dictionary). Éamon de Valera (1882–1973) was president of Ireland 1959–73.
ALSO: Éaman(n); Eamon(n) (Anglicized forms).

Éanna ♂ From a derivative of *éan* 'bird'.

Earnán ♂ Possibly a derivative of *iarn* 'iron'.
ALSO: Ernan (Anglicized form).

Eavan ♀ Anglicized form of ▶Aoibheann.

Edan ♂ Variant of ▶Aidan. St Edan was an Irish disciple of David of

Wales, who later became bishop of Ferns.

Egan ♂ Anglicized form of ▸Aogán or a transferred use of the surname, which has the same origin.

Éibhear ♂ Origin unknown; it was borne in Irish legend by the son of Míl, leader of the Gaelic race that first conquered Ireland.

Éibhleann ♀ Said to be a derivative of Old Irish *óiph* 'radiance, beauty'.
ALSO: **Éibhliu; Evlin** (Anglicized form).

Eibhlín ♀ Irish form of Norman French Aveline, of Germanic origin. See main dictionary.
ALSO: **Ailbhilín, Eilín; Eileen** (Anglicized form).

Eileen ♀ Anglicized form of ▸Eibhlín; *bh* is normally pronounced as 'v' in Gaelic, but is sometimes silent, hence this form.

Eilín ♀ Variant of ▸Eibhlín.

Eilis ♀ Irish equivalent of Elizabeth. See main dictionary.

Eimear ♀ Variant of ▸Émer.

Éimhín ♂ Traditional name, possibly meaning 'speedy, prompt'; borne by an Irish saint, probably of the 6th century, who was abbot and bishop of Ros-mic-Truin in Leinster.

Einrí ♂ Irish equivalent of Henry. See main dictionary.

Éirinn ♀ From the dative case of *Éire* 'Ireland'.
ALSO: **Erin** (Anglicized form).

Eistir ♀ Irish equivalent of Esther. See main dictionary.

Eithne ♀ Traditional name, apparently from *eithne* 'kernel', which was used as a term of praise in bardic poetry. St Eithne was a daughter of King Laoghaire and one of St Patrick's first converts.
ALSO: **Edna, Ena, Et(h)na, Ethenia** (Anglicized forms).

Elwyn ♂ Of uncertain origin. It was borne by a 6th-century Irish saint. See Welsh appendix.

Émer ♀ Traditional name of uncertain derivation; the name of Cú Chulainn's beloved, a woman of many talents who was blessed with beauty, wisdom, and chastity. It was revived as a given name in the 20th century.
ALSO: **Eimear, Eimer; Emer** (Anglicized form).

Ena ♀ Anglicized form of ▸Eithne. See also main dictionary.

Enda ♂ Anglicized form of ▸Éanna.

Eóghan ♂ Traditional name, supposedly derived from *iúr* 'yew' and meaning 'born of yew'. It was borne in Irish legend by one of the two sons of Niall of the Nine Hostages.

Eoin ♂ Irish equivalent of John. See main dictionary.

Erin ♀ Anglicized form of ▸Éirinn. See also main dictionary.

Ernan ♂ Anglicized form of ▸Earnán.

Étaín ♀ Traditional Gaelic name, sometimes identified as that of the ancient Celtic sun goddess, said to be derived from *ét* 'jealousy'.

Ethenia ♀ Anglicized form of ▸Eithne.

Ethna ♀ Anglicized form of ▸Eithne.
ALSO: **Ethne, Etna**.

Ewan ♂ The usual Anglicized form in Scotland and Northern Ireland of ▸Eóghan.

Eunan ♂ Anglicized form of ▸Ádhamhnán.

Evlin ♀ Anglicized form of ▸Éibhleann.

Ff

Fachtna ♂ Traditional name of uncertain derivation, possibly meaning 'hostile'. It has sometimes been Latinized as **Festus** (see main dictionary), to which, however, it is not related.

Fáelán ♂ Variant of ▸Faolán.

Faoiltiarna ♀ Traditional name, from *faol* 'wolf' + *tighearna* 'lord'.

ALSO: **Whiltierna** (Anglicized form).

Faolán ♂ Traditional name from *faol* 'wolf' + the diminutive suffix *-án*.
ALSO: **Fillan, Foillan** (Anglicized forms).

Fardoragh ♂ Anglicized form of ▸Feardorcha.

Farry ♂ Anglicized form of ▸Fearadhach.

Fearadhach ♂ From a vocabulary word meaning 'manly' or 'masculine', a derivative of *fear* 'man'.
ALSO: **Farry, Ferdie** (Anglicized forms).

Fearchar ♂ From Irish *fear* 'man' + *char* 'dear'.

Feardorcha ♂ From Irish *fear* 'man' + *dorcha* 'dark'.

Fearghal ♂ From Irish *fear* 'man' + *gal* 'valour'; the name of an 8th-century king of Ireland, Fearghal mac Máeldúin, who was famous for his murderous exploits.
ALSO: **Fergal** (Anglicized form).

Fearghas ♂ From Irish *fear* 'man' + *gus* 'vigour'; the name of a shadowy hero in Irish mythology, also of the grandfather of St Columba.
ALSO: **Fergus** (Anglicized form).

Fedelma ♀ Latinized form of ▸Feidhelm.

Feichín ♂ Originally a byname representing a diminutive of Gaelic *fiach* 'raven'. It has sometimes been Latinized as **Festus**

(see main dictionary), to which, however, it is not related.

Feidhelm ♀ Traditional name of unknown derivation; borne in Irish legend by a female warrior renowned for her beauty, a daughter of Conchobhar mac Nessa, and also by one of St Patrick's first converts, a daughter of King Laoghaire and sister of St Eithne.
ALSO: **Fedelma, Fidelma** (Latinized forms).

Feidhlimidh ♂ Traditional name, said to mean 'eternally virtuous'.
ALSO: **Felim, Phelim** (Anglicized forms); **Fidelminus** (Latinized form).

Feoras ♂ Irish equivalent of **Piers**. See main dictionary.

Ferdie ♂ Anglicized form of ▸Fearadhach.

Fergal ♂ Anglicized form of ▸Fearghal.

Fergus ♂ Anglicized form of ▸Fearghas.

Ferris ♂ Anglicized spelling of the vocative case, *Phiarais*, of ▸Piaras.

Festus ♂ Latinized form of ▸Fachtna and ▸Feichín. See also main dictionary.

Fiachna ♂ Traditional name derived from *fiach* meaning both 'raven' and 'hunt'.

Fiachra ♂ Traditional name derived from *fiach* meaning both 'raven'

and 'hunt' + *rí* 'king'. It was borne by an Irish saint and missionary in France (d. 670 at Meaux).

Fidelma ♀ Latinized form of ▸Feidhelm.
ALSO: **Fedelma**.

Fidelminus ♂ Latinized form of ▸Feidhlimidh; see also ▸Phelim.

Fillan ♂ Anglicized form of ▸Faolán.

Fina ♀ Anglicized form of ▸Fíona.

Finbar ♂ Anglicized form of ▸Fionnbarr.
ALSO: **Finbarr, Finnbar(r)**.

Fínín ♂ Modern form of the Old Irish name *Fingín*, composed of elements meaning 'wine' and 'born'.

Finn ♂ Traditional name meaning 'white, fair'. See also Finn in main dictionary.
ALSO: **Fionn** (modern form).

Finnén ♂ Orginally a byname from a diminutive of Old Irish *finn* 'white, fair'; borne by two 6th-century Irish bishops.
ALSO: **Fionnán; Finnian, Finian** (Anglicized forms).

Finola ♀ Anglicized form of ▸Fionnuala.
ALSO: **Fionola, Finuala**.

Fintan ♂ Anglicized form of ▸Fiontan.

Fíona ♀ Traditional name meaning 'vine'. In origin this name has no connection with the Scottish name *Fiona*, which, however, is often now used as an Anglicized form of it.

Fionn ♂ Variant of ►Finn.

Fionnán ♂ Variant of ►Finnén.

Fionnbarr ♂
Traditional name from *fionn* 'white, fair' + *barr* 'head'; the name of at least three early Irish saints, including the first bishop of Cork (6th century).
ALSO: **Fionnbharr**.

Fionnuala ♀ Modern form of Fionnguala, a traditional name from *fionn* 'white, fair' + *guala* 'shoulder'.
ALSO: **Finuala, Fi(o)nola** (Anglicized forms).

Fiontan ♂ From Old Irish *finn* 'white, fair' + *tine* 'fire'.
ALSO: **Fintan** (Anglicized form).

Flaithrí ♂ Traditional name from *flaith* 'prince' + *rí* 'king'. In Irish legend, at the time of Cormac, a man named Flaithri contrived to test four pieces of advice given to him by his father, Fitheal, on his deathbed. He proved the wisdom of the advice, but almost forfeited his life in doing so.
ALSO: **Florry, Flurry** (Anglicized forms).

Flann ♂ Traditional name from a nickname meaning 'red, ruddy'.

Flannán ♂ Traditional name from a diminutive of *flann* 'red, ruddy'.
ALSO: **Flannan** (Anglicized spelling).

Florry ♂ Anglicized form of ►Flaithrí.
ALSO: **Flurry**.

Foillan ♂ Anglicized form of ►Faolán.

Gg

Gallchobhar ♂
Traditional name from *gall* 'strange, foreign' + *cabhair* 'help, support'.

Garbhán ♂ Traditional name from a diminutive of *garbh* 'rough; cruel'; borne by five Irish saints, including a 7th-century abbot who appears to have given his name to Dungarvan.

Gearóid ♂ From Old French *Geraud*. See Gerald in main dictionary.

Gobbán ♂ Traditional name from *gobha* 'smith'; in Irish legend Gobbán was a master craftsman who could fashion a sword or spear with just three blows of his hammer.

Gobnat ♀ Traditional name, feminine of ►Gobbán. St Gobnat was the foundress of the monastery at Ballyvourney, Co. Cork, at a place where she encountered nine white deer.

ALSO: **Gobnait**.

Gofraidh ♂ From Old French *Godefroy*. See Godfrey in main dictionary.
ALSO: **Goffraid**.

Gormlaith ♀
Traditional name, a compound of *gorm* 'illustrious, splendid' + *flaith* 'lady; princess'. This name was borne by the wife of Brian Boru and mother of Sitric, King of Dublin (d. 1030).

Gráinne ♀ Origin uncertain, possibly connected with *grán* 'grain', as the name of an ancient corn goddess. In Irish legend Gráinne was the daughter of King Cormac.
ALSO: **Grania** (Latinized form), **Granya** (Anglicized form).

Guaire ♂ Traditional name of uncertain origin, said to be from a word meaning 'noble' or 'proud'.

Hh

Heber ♂ Anglicized form of ►Éibhear. See also main dictionary.

Ii

Iarlaithe ♂ Traditional name from *ior* (of uncertain meaning) + *flaith* 'prince, leader'; St Iarlaithe was a 5th-century saint,

the patron of the diocese of Tuam in Co. Galway.
ALSO: Jarlath (Anglicized form).

Íde ♀ Origin uncertain: possibly connected with Old Irish *ítu* 'thirst'. It was borne by a 6th-century saint who founded a convent in Limerick.

Iobhar ♂ Irish equivalent of Ivor. See main dictionary.

Irial ♂ Origin uncertain. It was borne by a son of the Ulster hero Conall Cearnach.

Ita ♀ Anglicized form of ▸Íde.

Jj

Jarlath ♂ Anglicized form of ▸Iarlaithe.

Juno ♀ Anglicized form of ▸Úna, assimilated to the name of the Roman goddess Juno, consort of Jupiter.

Kk

Katelyn ♀ Modern Anglicized form of ▸Caitlín.

Kathleen ♀ Traditional Anglicized form of ▸Caitlín.

Keane ♂ Anglicized form of ▸Cian.
ALSO: Kean.

Keelin ♀ Anglicized form of ▸Caoilfhionn.

Keeva ♀ Anglicized form of ▸Caoimhe.

Kelan ♂ Anglicized form of ▸Caolán.

Kelly ♀, ♂ Originally an Anglicized form of the male name ▸Ceallach, now widely used as a girl's name. See also main dictionary.

Kenny ♂ Anglicized form of ▸Cainneach.

Kevin ♂ Anglicized form of ▸Caoimhín. See also main dictionary.

Kian ♂ Anglicized form of ▸Cian.

Kieran ♂ Anglicized form of ▸Ciarán.

Killian ♂ Anglicized form of ▸Cillian.
ALSO: Kilian.

Ll

Labhrás ♂ From Latin *Laurentius*. See Laurence in main dictionary.

Lachtna ♂ Traditional: from a byname meaning 'milk-coloured'; borne, according to tradition, by the great-great-grandfather of the legendary king, Brian Boru.

Laoghaire ♂ Said to be from Irish, meaning 'calf herd'. It was borne by several early Irish saints, princes, and kings, including the High King of Ireland at the time of St Patrick (5th century).
ALSO: Leary (Anglicized form).

Laoise ♀ Pronounced 'lee-sha', of uncertain origin; possibly identical with the old Gaelic name *Luigsech* 'radiance', a derivative of *Lug*, name of the goddess of light.

Laoiseach ♂ Traditional name, originally an ethnic name for someone from the region of *Laois* (the modern county of Leix). It has been Anglicized as Louis and Lewis (see main dictionary).

Lasairíona ♂ Traditional name from *lasair* 'flame' + *fíon* 'wine'.
ALSO: Lassarina, Lasrina (Anglicized forms).

Laughlin ♂ Anglicized form of ▸Lochlainn.

Léan ♀ Irish equivalent of Helen. See main dictionary

Leannán ♂ Traditional name meaning 'darling, sweetheart', also used to denote a fairy lover. This was a common medieval given name, which has enjoyed a revival in recent times.
ALSO: Lennan (Anglicized form).

Leary ♂ Anglicized form of ▸Laoghaire. It is found as a surname, also in the form *O'Leary*, and the modern given name may be a transferred use of the surname.

Líadan ♀ Probably a derivative of *liath* 'grey'. In Irish legend, Líadan

forsook her lover Cuirithir in order to enter a nunnery; both of them died of grief.
ALSO: **Liadan** (Anglicized form).

Liam ♂ Short form of ▸**Uilliam**, now a popular independent given name. See also in main dictionary.

Life ♀ Traditional name, borne, according to legend, by a figure who gave her name to the River Liffey.

Lochlainn ♂ Said to refer originally to a migrant from Norway, the 'land of the lochs' (compare **Lachlan** in Scottish appendix).
ALSO: **Laughlin**, **Loughlin** (Anglicized forms).

Lomán ♂ Traditional: originally a byname representing a diminutive of *lomm* 'bare'; borne by various early Irish saints, including a nephew of St Patrick who became first bishop of Trim in Meath in the early 5th century.
ALSO: **Loman** (Anglicized form).

Lonán ♂ Traditional: originally a byname representing a diminutive of *lon* 'blackbird'; borne by several minor early Irish saints.
ALSO: **Lonan** (Anglicized form).

Lorcán ♂ Traditional name from a diminutive of *lorc* 'fierce'; borne by St Lorcán Ó Tuathail

(1128–80), archbishop of Dublin, known in English as Laurence O'Toole.
ALSO: **Lorcan** (Anglicized form).

Loughlin ♂ Anglicized form of ▸**Lochlainn**.

Lughaidh ♂ Traditional name, a derivative of the divine name *Lugh* 'brightness' (see Lleu in Welsh appendix). It has been Anglicized as Lewie, Lewis, and Louis (see main dictionary).

Luíseach ♀ Traditional name, a feminine derivative of the divine name *Lugh* (see Lleu in Welsh appendix). It has been Anglicized as Lucy (see main dictionary).

Mm

Mac Dara ♂ Traditional name meaning 'son of oak'; the name of the patron saint of a parish in Connemara in which is situated Mac Dara's island, goal of an annual pilgrimage on 16 July.

Maeve ♀ Anglicized form of ▸**Meadhbh**.

Maghnus ♂ Irish form of **Magnus** (see main dictionary).
ALSO: **Mánus; Manus** (Anglicized form).

Mahon ♂ Anglicized form of ▸**Mathúin**.

Maidie ♀ Apparently a pet form of English *maid* 'young woman' (Old English *mæg(den)*),

originally used as an affectionate nickname.

Mainchín ♂ Traditional name from a diminutive of *manach* 'monk', originally used as a byname.
ALSO: **Mannix** (Anglicized form).

Máire ♀ From Old French *Marie*. See Mary in main dictionary.
ALSO: **Moira** (Anglicized form).

Mairéad ♀ Irish equivalent of Margaret (see main dictionary), pronounced '**my**-raid' (in Munster) or 'ma-**raid**' (in Connacht).

Mairenn ♀ Traditional name, said to be derived from Gaelic *muir* 'sea' + *fhionn* 'fair'.
ALSO: **Muireann**.

Máirín ♀ Pet form of ▸**Máire**.
ALSO: **Maureen, Maurene, Maurine** (Anglicized forms).

Mairtin ♂ From Latin *Martinus*. See Martin in main dictionary.

Malachy ♂ Traditional name. See Malachi in main dictionary.

Mannix ♂ Anglicized form of ▸**Mainchín**.

Mánus ♂ Variant of ▸**Maghnus**.

Maoilíosa originally ♂, now also ♀ Traditional name meaning 'devotee of Jesus'. It has been Anglicized as

Melissa (see main dictionary).

Maolra ♂ Modern spelling, common particularly in the west of Ireland, of earlier *Maoil-Mhuire* 'devotee of Mary'. It has been Anglicized as Myles (see main dictionary).

Mathúin ♂ Modern name meaning 'bear', a simplified form of the earlier *Mathghamhain*, borne by a brother of Brian Boru, High King of Ireland in the early 11th century.
ALSO: **Mahon** (Anglicized form).

Maura ♀ See main dictionary.

Maureen ♀ Anglicized form of ▶Máirín.
ALSO: **Maurene, Maurine.**

Mave ♀ Anglicized form of ▶Meadhbh.

Meadhbh ♀ Ancient name (earlier *Medb*) meaning 'intoxicating', 'she who makes drunk'; borne by the Queen of Connacht in the Irish epic *Táin Bó Cuailnge*. In this, Meadhbh leads a raid on Ulster in order to seize the Brown Bull of Cooley, but she is repulsed single-handed by the hero Cú Chulainn. Shakespeare's Queen Mab, 'the fairy's midwife' (*Romeo and Juliet* I. iv. 53), owes her name, if nothing else, to the legendary Queen of Connacht.

ALSO: **Maeve, Mave, Meave** (Anglicized forms).

Mel ♂ Traditional; borne by a medieval saint who founded the monastery at Ardagh. See also main dictionary.

Moira ♀ Anglicized form of ▶Máire.

Móirín ♀ Pet form of ▶Mór.
ALSO: **Moreen** (Anglicized form).

Mona ♀ Anglicized form of ▶Muadhnait.

Mór ♀ Traditional name from *mór* 'large, great'. This was the commonest of all girls' names in late medieval Ireland, and has continued in use in both Ireland and Scotland to the present day.

Moreen ♀ Anglicized form of ▶Móirín, now to a large extent confused with ▶Maureen.

Morna ♀ Anglicized form of ▶Muirne.

Mortimer ♂ Of Norman origin (see main dictionary), used as an Anglicized form of ▶Muiriartach.

Muadhnait ♀ From a feminine diminutive of *muadh* 'noble'.
ALSO: **Mona** (Anglicized form).

Muireann ♀ Traditional name, pronounced '**mwir**-an', apparently from *muir* 'sea' + *fionn* 'white, fair'. There has been considerable

confusion with ▶Maureen and ▶Moreen.
ALSO: **Muirinn.**

Muirgheal ♀ Traditional name, apparently from Old Celtic words meaning 'sea' + 'bright'.

Muirgheas ♂ Traditional name, a compound of *muir* 'sea' + *gus* 'choice'. It has been Anglicized as Maurice to which, however, it is unrelated (see main dictionary).

Muiriartach ♂ Modern form of earlier *Muicheachtach*, originally a byname meaning 'seaman, mariner'. It has been Anglicized as Mortimer (see main dictionary).
ALSO: **Briartach.**

Muiris ♂ Irish equivalent of Maurice (see main dictionary); also a contracted form of ▶Muirgheas.

Muirne ♀ Traditional name, originally a byname meaning 'beloved'.
ALSO: **Myrna, Morna** (Anglicized forms).

Murchadh ♂ Traditional name from *muir* 'sea' + *cadh* 'battle'.
ALSO: **Murrough** (Anglicized form).

Murty ♂ Pet form of ▶Muiriartach.

Myles ♂ Anglicized form of ▶Maolra.

Myrna ♀ Anglicized form of ▶Muirne.

N n

Naoise ♂ Traditional name of uncertain origin; borne, according to legend, by the lover of Deirdre, who was pursued and murdered by Conchobhar, King of Ulster. Thereupon, Deirdre died of a broken heart.

Naomh ♀ Recent coinage, from a word meaning 'holy' or 'saint'.

Nápla ♀ Derived in the early Middle Ages from Anglo-Norman *Anable, Anaple* (see Annabel in main dictionary).

Neil ♂ Anglicized form of ▸Niall.
ALSO: **Neal**.

Nessa ♀ Traditional name of unknown origin; borne by a character in *Táin Bó Cuailgne* (the Cattle Raid of Cooley), the mother of Conchobhar.
ALSO: **Neas(s)a, Ness**.

Neve ♀ Anglicized form of ▸Niamh.

Niall ♂ Traditional name of disputed derivation; it may mean 'cloud', 'passionate', or perhaps 'champion'. See also main dictionary.
ALSO: **Neil, Neal(e)** (Anglicized forms).

Niamh ♀ Traditional name from a vocabulary word meaning 'brightness' or 'beauty'. It was borne in Irish mythology by the daughter of the sea god, who fell in love with the youthful Oisín, son of Finn mac Cumhaill (Finn MacCool), and carried him off over the sea to the land of perpetual youth, Tír na nÓg, where there is no sadness, no ageing, and no death. See also main dictionary.
ALSO: **Neve** (Anglicized form).

Ninian ♂ See main dictionary.

Nioclás ♂ Irish equivalent of Nicholas. See main dictionary.

Nóirín ♀ Diminutive of ▸Nóra.
ALSO: **Noreen, Norene, Norine** (Anglicized forms).

Nola ♀ Anglicized short form of ▸Fionnuala, now also used as a feminine form of ▸Nolan.

Nolan ♂ Transferred use of the surname, Irish *Ó Nualláin* 'descendant of *Nuallán*', an ancient personal name, originally a byname representing a diminutive of *nuall* 'chariot-fighter, champion'.

Nóra ♀ Possibly a derivative of ▸Fionnuala, due to confusion of *l* and *r* (compare Molly in main dictionary), but more probably an ancient borrowing into Irish of Latin Honora (see main dictionary).

Noreen ♀ Anglicized form of ▸Nóirín.

Nuala ♀ Short form of ▸Fionnuala, now in general use as an independent given name.
ALSO: ▸Nola (Anglicized form).

O o

Odharnait ♀ See ▸Orna.

Odhrán ♂ Traditional name, originally a byname representing a diminutive of *odhar* 'dun, sallow'; borne by various early saints, notably a 6th-century abbot of Meath who accompanied Columba to Scotland and is said to have been buried alive by the latter as a foundation sacrifice.
ALSO: **Oran** (Anglicized form); see also Oren in main dictionary.

Oisín ♂ Pronounced 'oh-sheen', from a diminutive of *os* 'stag', borne in Irish mythology by the son of the hero Finn mac Cumhaill (Finn MacCool), who was carried off by Niamh to Tír na nÓg, the land of perpetual youth. The name was resuscitated in the 18th century and has enjoyed considerable popularity in recent times, both inside Ireland and beyond. See also Osian in main dictionary.
ALSO: **Os(s)ian, Osheen** (Anglicized forms).

Onóra ♀ Irish equivalent of Honora (see

main dictionary). See also ▶Nóra.

ALSO: **Onora** (Anglicized form).

Oona ♀ Anglicized form of ▶Úna.

ALSO: **Oonagh**.

Oran ♂ Anglicized form of ▶Odhrán.

Órla ♀ From an earlier form, *Ór(fh)laith*, composed of *ór* 'gold' + *flaith* 'lady, princess'. This is now among the most popular traditional girls' names in Ireland.

ALSO: **Orla** (Anglicized form).

Orna ♀ Anglicized form of Odharnait, a feminine diminutive form of *odhar* 'dun, sallow' (compare ▶Odhrán). The loss of the final consonant is due to the influence of ▶Órla.

Oscar ♂ Apparently from Irish *os* 'deer' + *cara* 'friend'. See also in main dictionary.

Osheen ♂ Anglicized form of ▶Oisín.

Osian ♂ Anglicized form of ▶Oisín.

ALSO: **Ossian**.

Pp

Paddy ♂ Pet form of ▶Pádraig.

Pádraig ♂ Irish equivalent of ▶Patrick.

ALSO: **Páraic**.

Páidín ♂ Pet form of ▶Pádraig.

ALSO: **Paudeen** (Anglicized form).

Páraic ♂ Variant of ▶Pádraig, current in Connacht.

Parthalán ♂ Origin uncertain; possibly from Latin *Bartholomaeus* (see Bartholomew in main dictionary). It was borne, according to Celtic legend, by an early invader of Ireland, the first to come to those shores after the biblical Flood. It has often been Anglicized as Bartholomew, and also as Barclay and Berkley (see main dictionary).

ALSO: **Párt(h)lán, Partnán**.

Patrick ♂ From Latin *Patricius* ('patrician'), the name of the apostle and patron saint of Ireland (*c*.389–461) as recorded in his Latin autobiography, which, however, may represent some lost Celtic (British) name. See also main dictionary.

Paudeen ♀ Anglicized form of ▶Páidín.

Peadar ♂ From Greek. See Peter in main dictionary.

Pearce ♂ Transferred use of the English surname (see main dictionary); popular among Irish nationalists since the rising of 1916, led by the writer and educationist Patrick Henry Pearce, who was executed by the British.

Pegeen ♀ Anglicized form of ▶Peigín.

Peig ♀ Irish equivalent of Peg. See main dictionary.

Peigín ♀ Diminutive of ▶Peig.

ALSO: **Pegeen** (Anglicized form).

Perais ♂ Irish equivalent of ▶Pearce. See also ▶Piaras.

Phelim ♂ Anglicized form of ▶Feidhlimidh. St Phelim or Fidelminus was a 6th-century disciple of St Columba.

Piaras ♂ Derived in the Middle Ages from Anglo-Norman Piers (see main dictionary). Piaras Feiritéar (1600–53) was a Kerry chieftain and poet. Since the 20th century *Piaras* has been used as a Gaelic equivalent of Pearce (see main dictionary).

Pierce ♀ Variant of Piers, in use in Ireland from the time of the Norman Conquest up to the present day. See also main dictionary.

Porick ♂ Anglicized spelling of ▶Pádraig, representing a common pronunciation of that name.

Proinséas ♀ Irish equivalent of Frances. See main dictionary.

Proinsias ♂ Irish equivalent of Francis. See main dictionary.

Rr

Raghnailt ♀ Gaelicized form of Norse Ragnhild,

composed of *regin* 'advice, decision' (also, 'the gods') + *hildr* 'battle'. This was a very common woman's given name in medieval Ireland, often rendered in Latin documents as Regina (see main dictionary).

Raghnall ♂ Gaelicized form of the Old Norse personal name *Rögnvaldr*, composed of *regin* 'advice, decision' + *valdr* 'ruler'.
ALSO: Raonull; Rannal (Anglicized form).

Ráichéal ♂ Biblical. See Rachel in main dictionary.

Rathnait ♀ From a feminine diminutive form of *rath* 'grace; prosperity'.
ALSO: Ronit (Anglicized form).

Rearden ♂ Anglicized form of ▸Ríordán.

Rian ♂ Ancient personal name, probably a derivative of *rí* 'king'.

Rina ♀ Anglicized form of ▸Ríonach. See also main dictionary.

Ríona ♀ Simplified form of ▸Ríonach, also used as a short form of ▸Caitríona.

Ríonach ♀ Traditional name meaning 'royal' or 'queenly'.
ALSO: Ríoghnach; Ríona (simplified form); Rinach, Rina (Anglicized forms); Regina (Latinized form; see also main dictionary).

Ríordán ♂ Later form of *Ríoghbhardán*, from *ríogh* 'king' + *bardán*, a diminutive of *bard* 'poet'. Modern use of the given name is influenced by the surname O'Riordan, derived from the Irish personal name.
ALSO: Riordan, Rearden (Anglicized forms).

Ristéard ♂ Irish equivalent of Richard. See main dictionary.

Robhartach ♂ Old Irish name meaning 'wielder of prosperity'.

Roibéard ♂ Irish equivalent of Robert. See main dictionary.

Róisín ♀ Pet form of ▸Rós.
ALSO: Rosheen (Anglicized form).

Rónán ♂ Traditional name, from a diminutive of *rón* 'seal' (the animal). The name is recorded as being borne by various early Celtic saints, but there has been much confusion in the transmission of their names and most of them are also reliably named as *Ruadhán* (see Rowan in main dictionary). The most famous is a 5th-century Irish saint who was consecrated as a bishop by St Patrick and subsequently worked as a missionary in Cornwall and Brittany.
ALSO: Ronan (Anglicized form).

Ronit ♀ Anglicized form of ▸Rathnait.

Rory ♂ Anglicized form of ▸Ruaidhrí.

Rós ♀ Irish equivalent of Rose. See main dictionary.

Rosheen ♀ Anglicized form of ▸Róisín.

Ruaidhrí ♂ Traditional name from *ruadh* 'red' + *rí* 'king'.
ALSO: Ruarí; Rory (Anglicized form).

Ryan ♂, ♀ From the Irish surname *Ó Riain* 'descendant of ▸Rian'. See also main dictionary.

S s

Sabia ♀ Latinized form of ▸Sadhbh, in use during the Middle Ages and occasionally in the present day.

Sadhbh ♀ Traditional name, pronounced 'syve', from an obsolete Irish word meaning 'sweet'. In Irish legend, Sadhbh, daughter of Conn Cétchathach (Conn of the Hundred Battles), was considered 'the best woman in Ireland who ever lay with a man'. It was a common girl's name during the Middle Ages and has been revived in modern times. It has been Anglicized as Sabina and Sally (see main dictionary).
ALSO: Sive (Anglicized form).

Saoirse ♀ Modern name, pronounced 'seersha', from the Irish word meaning 'freedom'.

Séaghdha ♂
Traditional name,
perhaps meaning 'hawk-
like' or 'fine, goodly'.

Séamas ♂ Modern
Irish equivalent
(pronounced '**shay**-mus')
of ▶James. See main
dictionary.

Séamus ♂ Earlier form
of ▶Séamas, which is also
used without the accent
as a partially Anglicized
form of the name.

Seán ♂ Derived in the
early Middle Ages via
Anglo-Norman *Jehan* from
Latin *Johannes*. See John
and Sean in main
dictionary.
ALSO: Sean, Shaun, Shawn,
Sha(y)ne (Anglicized
forms).

Seanach ♀ From *sean*
'old, venerable'.

Seanán ♂ Traditional
name, pronounced
'**shan**-nan', from a
diminutive of *sean* 'old,
venerable'.
ALSO: Senan.

Séarlait ♀ Irish
equivalent of Charlotte.
See main dictionary.

Séarlas ♂ Irish
equivalent of Charles. See
main dictionary.

Séimí ♂ Irish equivalent
of the Scottish male
name Jamie (see main
dictionary), in use in
Northern Ireland.

Seoirse ♂ Irish
equivalent of George. See
main dictionary.

Seonac ♂ Biblical. See
Jonathan in main
dictionary.

Seosaimhín ♀ Irish
equivalent of Josephine.
See main dictionary.

Seosamh ♂ Biblical.
See Joseph in main
dictionary.

Seumas ♂ Older
spelling of ▶Séamas.
ALSO: Seumus.

Shamus ♂ Anglicized
spelling of ▶Séamus or
▶Séamas, now used fairly
infrequently.

Shane ♂, occasionally ♀
Anglicized form of
▶Seán, representing a
Northern Irish
pronunciation of the
name.

Shaun ♂, ♀ Anglicized
spelling of ▶Seán.

Sheena ♀ Anglicized
spelling of ▶Síne.

Shevaun ♀ Anglicized
form of ▶Siobhán.

Sibéal ♀ Irish
equivalent of Isabel (see
main dictionary), derived
in the early Middle Ages
from the Anglo-Norman
name.

Síle ♀ Pronounced
'**shee**-la'; derived in the
early Middle Ages from
Anglo-Norman *Cecíle*.
See Cecily in main
dictionary.
ALSO: Sheila, Sheelah,
She(e)lagh, Shayla, Shilla
(Anglicized forms).

Síne ♀ Pronounced
'**shee**-na'; from Anglo-
Norman *Jeanne*. See Jane
in main dictionary.
ALSO: Sheena (Anglicized
form).

Sinéad ♀ Pronounced
'shin-**aid**'; from French
Jeanette. See Janet in
main dictionary.

Siobhán ♀ Pronounced
'shiv-**awn**' or '**shoo**-an';
from Anglo-Norman
Jehanne. See Joan in main
dictionary.
ALSO: Shevaun, Chevonne
(Anglicized forms).

Siothrún ♂ Irish
equivalent of Geoffrey.
See main dictionary.

Sirideán ♂ Origin
uncertain; possibly
connected with *sirim* 'to
seek'.

Sive ♀ Anglicized form
of ▶Sadhbh.

Somhairle ♂ Gaelicized
form of the Old Norse
personal name *Sumarliðr*,
probably originally a
byname meaning
'summer traveller'. See
also Somerled in Scottish
appendix.
ALSO: Sorley (Anglicized
form).

Sorcha ♀ From a Celtic
word meaning
'brightness'. In Ireland,
owing to a slight
similarity in its
pronunciation ('**sorr**-
kha'), it has long been
considered a Gaelic form
of Sarah (see main
dictionary), and has been
Anglicized as *Sarah* and
Sally.

Stanislas ♂ Latinized
form of an old Slavonic
personal name composed
of *stan* 'government' +
slav 'glory', used in
Ireland as an Anglicized
form of ▶Anéislis.

Stiofán ♂ Irish equivalent of Stephen. See main dictionary.

T t

Tadhg ♂ Traditional name, pronounced 'tyg', originally a byname meaning 'poet' or 'philosopher'; a very common given name throughout the Middle Ages. It is sometimes Anglicized as Tim (see main dictionary).

Talulla ♀ Anglicized form of ▸Tuilelaith.

Tárlach ♂ Modern reduced form of ▸Toirdhealbhach, pronounced 'tor-lakh'.

Teague ♂ Anglicized form of ▸Tadhg.
ALSO: Teigue.

Tighearnach ♂ Derivative of *tighearna* 'lord'. This was the name of a 6th-century saint who served as abbot of Clones and later as bishop of Clogher.

Tighearnán ♂ From a diminutive of *tighearna* 'lord'.

Tim ♂ Short form of Timothy (see main dictionary), sometimes used as an Anglicized form of ▸Tadhg.

Tiobóid ♂ Derived in the early Middle Ages from Anglo-Norman *Thebaud*. See Theobald in main dictionary.

Toal ♂ Anglicized form of ▸Tuathal.

Toirdhealbhach ♂ Traditional name, apparently from a byname meaning 'instigator', from *toirdhealbh* 'prompting'. It was the name of a High King of Ireland who died in 1156.
ALSO: Tárlach, Traolach; Turlough (Anglicized form).

Tomás ♂ Irish equivalent of Thomas. See main dictionary.

Tone ♂ Name used in Ireland in honour of Theobald Wolfe Tone, leader of the rebellion against English rule in 1798. His surname is of English origin: see main dictionary.

Traolach ♂ Dialectal form of ▸Toirdhealbhach.

Treasa ♀ Traditional name, said to be from *tréan* 'strength, intensity'. It is now more often used as the Irish equivalent of Theresa. See main dictionary.

Tríona ♀ Short form of ▸Caitríona.

Tuathal ♂ Traditional name meaning 'ruler of a tribe'.
ALSO: Toal (Anglicized form).

Tuilelaith ♀ Traditional name, pronounced 'til-a-la', from words meaning 'abundance' and 'lady' or 'princess'; borne by at least two Irish saints of the 8th and 9th centuries.

ALSO: Talulla(h), Tallulah (Anglicized forms; see main dictionary).

Turlough ♂ Anglicized form of ▸Toirdhealbhach.

U u

Uilleac ♂ Probably from Old Norse *Hugleikr* (from *hugr* 'heart, mind, spirit' + *leikr* 'play, sport'). Alternatively, it may be a diminutive of a short form of ▸Uilliam.
ALSO: Uilleag; Ulick (Anglicized form).

Uilliam ♂ Irish equivalent of William. See main dictionary.

Uinseann ♂ Irish equivalent of Vincent. See main dictionary.

Ulick ♂ Anglicized form of ▸Uilleac.

Ultán ♂ From a diminutive of the ethnic name *Ultach* 'Ulsterman'.

Úna ♀ Traditional name of uncertain derivation. It is identical in form with the vocabulary word *úna* 'hunger, famine', but is more likely to be derived from *uan* 'lamb'. See also Una in main dictionary.
ALSO: Una, Oona, Oonagh (Anglicized forms); Juno.

W w

Whiltierna ♀ Anglicized form of ▸Faoiltiarna.

Aa

Abbondio ♂ From Late Latin *Abundius*, from *abundans* 'abundant'; name of a 5th-century bishop of Como.

Achilleo ♂ From Greek *Akhilleus*, hero of Homer's *Iliad*, also the name of one or two minor saints.

Adalgisa ♀ Germanic: from *adal* 'noble' + *gisil* 'pledge'.

Adamo ♂ Biblical. See Adam in main dictionary.

Addolorata ♀ From a title of the Virgin Mary, *Madonna Addolorata* 'Our Lady of Sorrows'.

Adriano ♂ From Latin. See Adrian in main dictionary.
FEMININE FORM: **Adriana**.

Agata ♀ From Greek. See Agatha in main dictionary.

Agnese ♀ From Greek. See Agnes in main dictionary.

Agostino ♂ From Latin. See Augustine in main dictionary.

Alba ♀ From the feminine form of Latin *albus* 'white' or from Germanic *alb* 'elf'.

Alberto ♂ Germanic. See Albert in main dictionary and Albrecht in German appendix.

Aldo ♂ Germanic: ultimately from *adal* 'noble'.

Alessandro ♂ From Greek. See Alexander in main dictionary.
FEMININE FORM: **Alessandra**.

Alessio ♂ From Latin *Alexius*. See Alexis in main dictionary.
FEMININE FORM: **Alessia**.

Alfio ♂ Sicilian name of uncertain origin, borne in honour of a saint martyred in 251 under the Emperor Decius, together with his brothers Philadelphus and Cyrinus.

Alfredo ♂ From English. See Alfred in main dictionary.

Allegra ♀ From the feminine form of *allegro* 'happy, jaunty'. See main dictionary.

Amato ♂ From the Latin name *Amatus* 'beloved'; borne by two notable saints: the first abbot of Remiremont (*c*.597–*c*.630) and the tenth bishop of Sion (d. *c*.690).

Ambrogio ♂ From Late Greek *Ambrosios* 'immortal'. See Ambrose in main dictionary.

Amedeo ♂ From the medieval Latin name *Amadeus* 'love God'; a traditional name in the royal house of Savoy.

Amerigo ♂ An early byform of ►Enrico, sometimes used among Italian Americans in honour of the explorer Amerigo Vespucci, after whom the continent of America was named.

Amilcare ♂ From the name of the Carthaginian general Hamilcar Barca, father of Hannibal. The name is Phoenician and means 'friend of (the god) Melkar'.

Anacleto ♂ From the Late Latin personal name *Anacletus*, Greek *Anaklētos* 'invoked'; the name of the third pope.

Anastasio ♂ From Greek *Anastasios*, a derivative of *anastasis* 'resurrection'.
FEMININE FORM: **Anastasia**.

Andrea ♂ From Greek. See Andrew in main dictionary.

Angela ♀ From Latin. See main dictionary.

Angelo ♂ From Greek *angelos* 'messenger (of God)'.

Aniceto ♂ From Greek *Anikētos* 'unconquered' or 'unconquerable'.

Aniella ♀ Feminine form of ►Aniello.

Aniello ♂ Vernacular derivative of Church

Latin *Agnellus* 'little lamb', name of one of the patron saints of Naples.

Anna ♀ New Testament. See Anne in main dictionary.

Annibale ♂ From Phoenician *hann* 'grace, favour' + the name of the god *Baal* 'lord'; the name of the Carthaginian general Hannibal (247–182 BC), who led an army from Spain into Italy and wreaked havoc on the Romans for 15 years before eventually being defeated by Scipio in 202 BC.

Annunziata ♀ Religious name commemorating the Annunciation to the Virgin Mary of the forthcoming birth of Christ.

Anselmo ♂ Germanic: from 'divinity' + 'helmet'. St Anselm of Piedmont was Archbishop of Canterbury in the late 11th and early 12th centuries. See Anselm in main dictionary.

Antioco ♂ From Greek *Antiochos*, composed of *anti* 'against' + *ekhein* 'to have', i.e. 'to hold out against'; the name of a saint martyred in Sardinia in *c*.110.

Antonio ♂ From Latin. See Anthony in main dictionary.
FEMININE FORM: Antonia.

Apollinare ♂ Derivative of *Apollo*, the name of the Greek sun god. The name is characteristic of Romagna, especially Ravenna. St Apollinaris was a 1st-century bishop martyred under Vespasian.

Arduino ♂ Germanic: 'staunch' + 'friend'. See Hartwin in German appendix.

Arianna ♀ From classical mythology. See Ariadne in main dictionary.

Arnaldo ♂ Germanic. See Arnold in main dictionary.

Arrigo ♂ Vernacular form of the more learned ▶Enrico.

Arturo ♂ Celtic. See Arthur in main dictionary.

Asdrubale ♂ From Phoenician *asru* 'aid' + the divine name *Baal* 'lord'; the name of the Carthaginian general Hasdrubal Barca (d. *c*.207 BC), brother of Hannibal (see ▶Annibale).

Assunta ♀ Marian name, from a title of the Virgin Mary, *Maria Assunta*, referring to her assumption into heaven.

Attilio ♂ From the Latin family name *Attilius*, of Etruscan origin.

Augusto ♂ From Latin. See Augustus in main dictionary.

Aurelio ♂ From Latin *Aurelius*, name of the philosopher-emperor Marcus Aurelius (121–180 AD).
FEMININE FORM: Aurelia.

Bb

Baldassare ♂ See Balthasar in main dictionary.

Bartolomeo ♂ New Testament. See Bartholomew in main dictionary.
ALSO: Bartolommeo.

Battista ♂ Religious name commemorating John the Baptist.

Beatrice ♀ Italian form of Beatrix (see main dictionary), famous as the name of Dante's beloved.

Bella ♀ Short form of ▶Isabella.

Benedetto ♂ From Latin. See Benedict in main dictionary.
FEMININE FORM: Benedetta.

Benigno ♂ From Late Latin *Benignus* 'kind', a name borne by several early saints.

Benvenuto ♂ Literally 'welcome', from a medieval given name; the name of the Renaissance metalworker, sculptor, and writer Benvenuto Cellini (1500–71).

Beppe ♂ Italian: pet form of ▶Giuseppe.
ALSO: Beppo.

Berenice ♀ From Greek. See main dictionary.

Bernadetta ♀ Feminine pet form of Bernard (see main dictionary).

Bernardo ♂ Germanic. See Bernard in main dictionary.

Bettina ♀ Contracted elaboration of *Benedetta* (see ▶Benedetto).

Biagio ♂ From Latin *Blasius*. See Blaise in main dictionary.
ALSO: **Biaggio**.

Bianca ♀ From the vocabulary word *bianca* 'white' (i.e. pure). See Blanche in main dictionary.

Bionda ♀ From *bionda* meaning 'blonde', originally a nickname for a woman with fair hair.

Bona ♀ Feminine form of the Late Latin name *Bonus* 'good'; a traditional name in the royal house of Savoy, also borne by a Pisan saint (d. 1207).

Bonaventura ♂ Medieval vernacular personal name, from *b(u)ona* 'good' + *ventura* 'luck, fortune'.

Bonifacio ♂ From the Late Latin name *Bonifatius* 'good fate'; borne by several early saints.

Bonito ♂ From the Latin personal name *Bonitus*, a derivative of *bonitas* 'goodness'.

FEMININE FORM: **Bonita**.

Brigida ♀ From Irish Brighid (see Irish appendix and Bridget in main dictionary) or from its Swedish derivative Birgit (see Scandinavian appendix).

Brizio ♂ From *Brictius*, an ancient name probably of Gaulish origin, from a word meaning 'speckled'. It is the name of a patron saint of Umbria. The name is also a short form of ▶Fabrizio.

Bruno ♂ Germanic: 'brown'. See main dictionary.

Cc

Callisto ♂ From Greek *kallistos* 'best, most fair', the name of several early saints, including a 3rd-century pope.

Calogero ♂ From Greek *kalos* 'good' + *gēras* 'old age'. St Calogerus the Anchorite (d. *c*.486) lived near Grigenti in Sicily, and the name is typical of Sicily and southern Italy.

Camillo ♂ From the Roman family name *Camillus*. St Camillo de Lellis (1550–1614) founded the nursing order of the Ministers of the Sick.
FEMININE FORM: **Camilla**.

Carlo ♂ Italian form of Latin *Carolus*. See Charles in main dictionary.
FEMININE FORM: **Carla**.

Carlotta ♀ Feminine pet form of ▶Carlo. See Charlotte in main dictionary.

Carmela ♀ Religious name from a Marian title; see Carmel in main dictionary.

Carmine ♂ Masculine form of ▶Carmela, influenced by Latin *carminis*, genitive of *carmen* 'song'.

Carolina ♀ Feminine pet form of ▶Carlo.

Caterina ♀ Italian equivalent of Katherine. See main dictionary.

Cecilia ♀ From Latin. See main dictionary.

Celia ♀ From Latin *Caelia*. See main dictionary.

Celso ♂ From the Latin family name *Celsus*, originally a nickname meaning 'tall, lofty'. It was borne by various minor early Roman saints.

Cesare ♂ From Caesar (see main dictionary), name of the first imperial Roman family.

Chiara ♀ From Latin. See Clare in main dictionary. The name was borne by several saints, notably Santa Chiara di Assisi, an associate of Francis of Assisi and founder of the order of nuns known as the Poor Clares.

Cinzia ♀ From Greek. See **Cynthia** in main dictionary.

Cipriano ♂ From Latin *Cyprianus* 'man from Cyprus'.

Ciriaco ♂ From Latin *Cyriacus*, from Greek *Kyriakos*, a derivative of *kyrios* 'lord', borne by a large number of minor saints of the early centuries AD.

Ciro ♂ From Greek. See **Cyrus** in main dictionary.

Clara ♀ From Latin. See **Clara** and **Clare** in main dictionary.

Claudio ♂ From Latin *Claudius*. See **Claude** in main dictionary.
FEMININE FORM: **Claudia**.

Clelia ♀ From Latin *Cloelia*, the name of a semi-mythological heroine of early Roman history.

Clemente ♂ From Latin. See **Clement** in main dictionary.

Cleto ♂ Short form of ▸**Anacleto**.

Columbano ♂ From the Late Latin name *Columbanus*, a derivative of *Columba* 'dove'. See **Colmán** in Irish appendix.

Columbina ♀ Pet form of *Colomba* 'dove', the name of Harlequin's sweetheart in the tradition of the *commedia dell'arte*.

Concetta ♀ Marian name referring to a

title of the Virgin Mary, *Maria Concetta*, alluding to the Immaculate Conception.

Consilia ♀ Religious name referring to a Marian title meaning 'Mary of Good Counsel'.

Consolata ♀ Religious name referring to the Marian title *Maria Consolata* 'Mary of Solace'.

Corrado ♂ Germanic. This was a common name in several of the Italian royal houses during the Middle Ages. See **Conrad** in main dictionary.

Cosima ♀ Feminine form of ▸**Cosmo**.

Cosmo ♂ From the Greek name *Kosmas*, a short form of various names containing the word *kosmos* 'order, beauty'.
ALSO: **Cosimo**.

Cristina ♀ From Latin. See **Christina** in main dictionary.

Cristoforo ♂ From Greek. See **Christopher** in main dictionary.

Dd

Dalmazio ♂ From the Late Latin personal name *Dalmatius* 'person from Dalmatia'; borne by an early bishop of Pavia who was martyred in AD 304.

Damiano ♂ From Greek. See **Damian** in main dictionary.

Daniele ♂ Biblical. See **Daniel** in main dictionary.

Dante ♂ Medieval personal name representing a contracted form of *Durante* 'steadfast'. Nowadays it is bestowed in honour of the poet Dante Alighieri (1265–1321).

Dario ♂ From Greek *Dareios*. See **Darius** in main dictionary.
FEMININE FORM: **Daria**.

Davide ♂ Biblical. See **David** in main dictionary.

Delfina ♀ From Latin *Delphina* 'woman from Delphi'.

Demetrio ♂ From Greek *Dēmētrios*. See **Demetrius** in main dictionary.

Desiderio ♂ Italian form of Latin *Desiderius*, derivative of *desiderium* 'longing'.

Dino ♂ Short form of names with this ending, such as Bernardino, a pet form of ▸**Bernardo**.

Domenico ♂ Late Latin *Dominicus*. See **Dominic** in main dictionary.

Domitilla ♀ Feminine pet form of the Roman family name *Domitius*, borne by a 2nd-century saint who was a member of the Roman imperial family.

Donatella ♀ Feminine pet form of ▸Donato.

Donato ♂ Late Latin *Donatus* 'given (by God)'; borne by over twenty early saints, including a bishop of Arezzo in Tuscany who was beheaded under Julian the Apostate.

Ee

Edda ♀ Nordic. See ▸Hedda in Scandinavian appendix.

Edmondo ♂ From English. See Edmund in main dictionary.

Edoardo ♂ From English. See Edward in main dictionary.

Edvige ♀ Germanic. See Hedwig in German appendix.

Efisio ♂ Sardinian name, from Latin *Ephesius*, denoting someone from the Greek city of Ephesus. It is borne in honour of a martyr allegedly put to death in 303 at Cagliari.

Egidio ♂ From Greek *Aigidios*. See Giles in main dictionary.

Elda ♀ Apparently an altered form of Hilda (see main dictionary), not in use before the 20th century.

Elena ♀ From Greek *Hēlēnē*. See Helen in main dictionary.

Eleonora ♀ From Old French. See Eleanor in main dictionary.

Elettra ♀ From Greek *ēlektōr* 'brilliant'. The name of a heroine in classical mythology (in English Electra) who, with her brother Orestes, avenges the murder of her father Agamemnon by her mother and stepfather.

Eliana ♀ From Late Latin. See Éliane in French appendix.

Eligio ♂ From Latin *Eligius* 'chosen'.

Elisabetta ♀ New Testament. See Elizabeth in main dictionary.

Eliseo ♂ Bibilical. See Elisha in main dictionary.

Elmo ♂ Originally probably Germanic, from *helm* 'helmet, protection'. Later used as a pet form of Erasmus (see main dictionary).

Elpidio ♂ From the Late Latin name *Elpidius*, Greek *Elpidios*, a derivative of Greek *elpis* (genitive *elpidos*) 'hope'. Among various early saints so named was a 4th-century hermit who spent twenty-five years in a cave in Cappadocia. Relics believed to be his were kept in the Middle Ages at Sant'Elpidio in the marches of Ancona, and the name was most

commonly used in that region.

Emanuele ♂ Biblical. See Emmanuel in main dictionary.

Emidio ♂ Of uncertain origin; it is bestowed in honour of St *Emidius* or *Emygdius* (d. *c*.303), the patron saint of Ascoli Piceno.

Emilio ♂ From the Latin family name *Aemilius* (probably from *aemulus* 'rival').
FEMININE FORM: Emilia.

Ennio ♂ From the Latin family name *Ennius*.

Enrico ♂ Germanic: equivalent of German Heinrich (see German appendix) and English Henry (see main dictionary).

Enzo ♂ Probably originally a short form of given names such as ▸Lorenzo or ▸Vincenzo, or perhaps an Italianized version of German Heinz (see German appendix).

Ercole ♂ Italian derivative of *Hercules*, Latin name of the Greek hero *Hēraklēs*, who was noted for his exceptional physical strength.

Ermanno ♂ Italian form of German Hermann (see German appendix), apparently introduced from Germany relatively recently.

Ermenegildo ♂ Italian equivalent of **Hermengildo** (see Spanish appendix).

Ermete ♂ From Greek *Hermēs*, name of the Greek messenger god. This was borne as a personal name by several early Christians.

Ernesto ♂ Germanic. See **Ernest** in main dictionary.

Ettore ♂ From Greek. See **Hector** in main dictionary.

Eufemia ♀ From Greek. See **Euphemia** in main dictionary.

Eugenio ♂ From Greek. See **Eugene** in main dictionary.
FEMININE FORM: **Eugenia**.

Eulalia ♀ From Greek. See main dictionary.

Eusebio ♂ From Late Greek *Eusebios* 'pious, reverent'; the name of numerous early saints, including a 4th-century bishop of Bologna.

Eustachio ♂ From Late Greek. See **Eustace** in main dictionary.

Eva ♀ Biblical. See **Eve** in main dictionary.

Evaristo ♂ From the Late Greek personal name *Euarestos* from *eu* 'well, good' + *areskein* 'to please, satisfy'.

Ezio ♂ From the Late Latin personal name *Aetius*, a conflation of the Roman family name *Aetius* with *Aëtios*, a Late Greek name derived from *a(i)etos* 'eagle'.

Ezzo ♂ Possibly Germanic, from *adal* 'noble'.

Ff

Fabiano ♂ From Late Latin. See **Fabian** in main dictionary.

Fabio ♂ From the Roman family name *Fabius*. Members of this family were prominent in republican Rome. The name was also used among the early Christians: St Fabius (d. 300) was a Roman soldier beheaded at Caesarea in Mauretania under the Emperor Diocletian.
FEMININE FORM: **Fabia**.

Fabiola ♀ Feminine pet form of ▶Fabio.

Fabrizio ♂ From the Roman family name *Fabricius*, probably of Etruscan origin. Gaius Fabricius Luscinus (d. 250 BC) was a Roman statesman noted for his incorruptibility.

Fania ♀ Short form of ▶Stefania.

Fedele ♂ Italian form of Fidel (see Spanish appendix).

Federico ♂ Germanic. See **Frederick** in main dictionary. The name was introduced to Sicily by the Normans, where it was borne by the son of the Norman Queen Constance and the German Emperor Henry VI. At the age of three, in 1197, Federico became King of Sicily; he later went on to become King of the Germans and Holy Roman Emperor. He was a patron of the arts and sciences, and in 1224 founded the University of Naples.

Felice ♂ From the Roman family name *Felix* 'lucky'. See **Felix** in main dictionary.

Feliciano ♂ From Latin *Felicianus*, a derivative of Felix (see main dictionary), borne by a number of early saints, notably a 3rd-century bishop of Foligno in Umbria.

Felicita ♀ From the Late Latin personal name *Felicitas* 'good fortune'. See **Felicity** in main dictionary.

Ferdinando ♂ From Spanish. See **Ferdinand** in main dictionary.

Ferruccio ♂ From a medieval pet form of the byname *Ferro* 'iron'.

Fiamma ♀ Recent coinage meaning 'flame, fire'.

Fiammetta ♀ Pet form of ▶Fiamma.

Filiberto ♂ Germanic: from *fil* 'much' + *berht* 'bright'. A traditional name in the royal house of Savoy.

Filippo ♂ From Greek. See Philip in main dictionary.

Fiorella ♀ Recent coinage, a pet form from *fiore* 'flower'.

Fiorenzo ♂ From Latin *Florentius*, a derivative of *florens* 'blossoming, flourishing'.

Firmino ♂ From the Late Latin personal name *Firminus*, from *firmus* 'steadfast'.

Flavio ♂ From the old Roman family name *Flavius* (from *flavus* 'yellow(-haired)'). FEMININE FORM: **Flavia**.

Fortunato ♂ From the Late Latin personal name *Fortunatus* 'fortunate'. FEMININE FORM: **Fortunata**.

Franca ♀ Feminine form of ▶Franco.

Francesco ♂ Originally a vocabulary word meaning 'French' or 'Frenchman', from Late Latin *Franciscus*. Its popularity as a given name has been much influenced by St Francis of Assisi. See Francis in main dictionary. FEMININE FORM: **Francesca** (see main dictionary).

Franco ♂ Contracted form of ▶Francesco.

Fulgenzio ♂ From Latin *Fulgentius*, a derivative of *fulgens* 'shining'.

Fulvia ♀ From the feminine form of the old Roman family name *Fulvius*, from Latin *fulvus* 'dusky, tawny'. See main dictionary.

Gg

Gabriele ♂ Biblical. See Gabriel in main dictionary. FEMININE FORM: **Gabriella** (see main dictionary).

Gaetano ♂ From Latin *Caietanus*, originally an ethnic name for someone from Caieta, a town in Latium (now *Gaeta*); the name of a Neapolitan saint and religious reformer (*c.*1480–1547).

Gaspare ♂ See Caspar in main dictionary. ALSO: **Gasparo**.

Gavino ♂ Sardinian, probably from Late Latin *Gabinus* 'man from Gabium', a city in Latium. St Gabinus was martyred at Torres in Sardinia *c.*130.

Gemma ♀ From a medieval Italian nickname meaning 'jewel'. See main dictionary.

Gennaro ♂ From Latin *Januarius* 'January' (from the divine name *Janus*, god of beginnings). This was borne by several saints, including a bishop of Benevento beheaded at Pozzuoli in 304, the patron saint of Naples.

Genoveffa ♀ From French *Geneviève*. See Genevieve in main dictionary. ALSO: **Ginevra**.

Gerardo ♂ Germanic. See Gerard in main dictionary.

Geronimo ♂ Learned form of ▶Girolamo.

Gervasio ♂ Norman. See Gervaise in main dictionary.

Gesualdo ♂ From a medieval personal name of Germanic origin, probably composed of *gisil* 'pledge' + *wald* 'rule'. It has been influenced in form by association with *Gesù* 'Jesus'.

Giachetta ♀ Feminine pet form of ▶Giacomo.

Giacobbe ♂ Biblical. See Jacob in main dictionary.

Giacomo ♂ New Testament. See James in main dictionary.

Giambattista ♂ Contracted form of *Giovanni Battista* 'John the Baptist'.

Giampaolo ♂ Contracted form of ▶Giovanni + ▶Paolo.

Gianmaria ♂ Contracted form of ▶Giovanni + ▶Maria.

Gianni ♂ Contracted form of ▶Giovanni. FEMININE FORM: **Gianna**.

Gilda ♀ Germanic: feminine short form of names containing the element *gild* 'sacrifice'.

Ginevra ♀ Variant of ▶Genoveffa.

Gino ♂ Short form of any of the many given names ending in -*gino*, e.g. *Giorgino*, pet form of ►Giorgio, and *Luigino*, pet form of ►Luigi.
FEMININE FORM: Gina.

Gioacchino ♂ Biblical. See Joachim in main dictionary.
ALSO: Gioachino.

Gioconda ♀ From the vocabulary word meaning 'happy, jovial' (from Latin *jucunda*). St Jucunda (d. 466) was a virgin of Reggio in Aemilia, associated with St Prosper.

Giordano ♂ Biblical, name of the river Jordan. See Jordan in main dictionary.

Giorgio ♂ From Greek. See George in main dictionary.

Giosuè ♂ Biblical. See Joshua in main dictionary.

Giovanni ♀ From Latin. See John in main dictionary.
FEMININE FORM: Giovanna.

Giraldo ♂ Germanic. See Gerald in main dictionary.

Girolamo ♂ Biblical. See Jerome in main dictionary.

Giulietta ♀ Pet form of *Giulia*; see ►Giulio.

Giulio ♂ From the old Roman family name Julius (see main dictionary).
FEMININE FORM: Giulia.

Giuseppe ♂ Biblical. See Joseph in main dictionary.

Giuseppina ♀ Feminine pet form of ►Giuseppe.

Goffredo ♂ Germanic (Lombard). See Geoffrey in main dictionary.

Grazia ♀ From Latin. See Grace in main dictionary.

Graziano ♂ From the Latin name *Gratianus*, a derivative of *gratus* 'pleasing, lovely'.

Graziella ♀ Pet form of ►Grazia.

Gregorio ♂ From Greek. See Gregory in main dictionary.

Gualtiero ♂ Germanic. See Walter in main dictionary.

Guglielmo ♂ Germanic. See William in main dictionary.

Guido ♂ From Old French. See Guy in main dictionary.

Ii

Ignazio ♂ From Late Latin *Ignatius*, a personal name derived from the old Roman family name *Egnatius*, possibly of Etruscan origin. See Ignatius in main dictionary.

Ilario ♂ From Late Latin *Hilarius*, from *hilaris* 'cheerful'. See Hilary in main dictionary.

Imelda ♀ Germanic: apparently from *irm(en)*, *erm(en)* 'whole' + *hild* 'battle'.

Immacolata ♀ Marian name meaning 'without taint', referring to the doctrine of the Immaculate Conception.

Innocenzo ♂ From Late Latin *Innocentius*, from *innocens* 'harmless, non-violent', name of several saints and popes.

Ippolito ♂ From the Greek name *Hippolytos* 'horse free', borne by several early saints.

Isabella ♀ Italian form of Spanish Isabel (see main dictionary).

Isaia ♂ Biblical. See Isaiah in main dictionary.

Italo ♂ From Latin *Italus*, in mythology the name of the father of Romulus and Remus, founders of Rome.
FEMININE FORM: Itala.

Jj

Jolanda ♀ Possibly Germanic (see Yolanda in main dictionary); traditional name in the royal house of Savoy, revived in Italy in 1901, when it was given by King Victor Emmanuel III to his first child.

Julitta ♀ Probably a Late Latin form of Judith (see main dictionary).

Ll

Ladislao ♂ From a Latinate form of an Old Slavic name; see Ladislas in main dictionary.

Laura ♀ Feminine form of the Late Latin male name *Laurus* 'laurel'; name of Petrarch's beloved. See main dictionary.
MASCULINE FORM: **Lauro.**

Lazzaro ♂ New Testament. See Lazarus in main dictionary.

Leandro ♂ From Greek. See Leander in main dictionary.

Leonardo ♂ Germanic. See main dictionary.

Leone ♂ From Late Latin. See Leo in main dictionary.

Leontina ♀ Feminine derivative of *Leontius*; see ▶Leonzio.

Leonzio ♂ From the Late Latin personal name *Leontius*, a derivative of *Leo* 'lion'.

Leopoldo ♂ Germanic. See Leopold in main dictionary.

Letizia ♀ From Latin *Laetitia* 'happiness'.

Lia ♀ Probably a short form of ▶Rosalia.

Licio ♂ From Late Latin *Lycius* 'man from *Lycia*' (a region of Asia Minor). The name was borne principally by slaves, some of whom may have come from this region.

Liduina ♀ Germanic: from *Lidwina*, composed of *liut* 'people' + *win* 'friend'.

Lodovico ♂ Learned form of ▶Luigi. See Ludovic in main dictionary.

Loredana ♀ Invented by Luciano Zoccoli for the heroine of his novel *L'amore de Loredana* (1908).

Lorenzo ♂ From Latin *Laurentius* 'man from Laurentum'. See Laurence in main dictionary.

Luana ♀ Made-up name of a character in King Vidor's 1932 film *The Bird of Paradise*; the film achieved considerable popularity in Italy under the title *Luana, la vergine sacra*.

Luca ♂ From Greek. See Luke in main dictionary.

Lucia ♀ Feminine form of ▶Lucio. See also main dictionary.

Luciano ♂ From Latin *Lucianus*, a derivative of the Roman personal name *Lucius*, itself probably derived from *lux* 'light'.
FEMININE FORM: **Luciana.**

Lucio ♂ From *Lucius*, a Roman personal name, probably derived from Latin *lux* 'light'.

Lucrezia ♀ From a feminine form of the Roman family name *Lucretius*. See Lucretia in main dictionary.

Luigi ♂ Germanic. See Louis in main dictionary.

Mm

Macario ♂ From Greek *Makarios* 'blessed'; borne by numerous early saints.

Maddalena ♀ New Testament. See Madeleine in main dictionary.

Mafalda ♀ Germanic name, bestowed by King Victor Emmanuel III of Italy on a daughter of his in 1902. See Matilda in main dictionary.

Manfredo ♂ Germanic name, borne by a 13th-century king of Sicily. See Manfred in main dictionary.

Manlio ♂ From Latin *Manlius*, name of a Roman family famous for its republican virtues.

Marcellino ♂ Pet form of ▶Marcello.
FEMININE FORM: **Marcellina.**

Marcello ♂ From the Latin name *Marcellus*. See Marcel in main dictionary.
FEMININE FORM: **Marcella.**

Marco ♂ From Latin *Marcus*. See Mark in main dictionary.

Margherita ♀ From Greek. See Margaret in main dictionary.

Maria ♀ New Testament. See Mary in main dictionary.

Mariano ♂ From Latin *Marianus*, a derivative of Marius (see main dictionary), taken in the early Christian era to be an adjective from ►Maria, and associated with the cult of the Virgin Mary.
FEMININE FORM: **Mariana**.

Mariella ♀ Pet form of ►Maria.

Marietta ♀ Pet form of ►Maria.

Marina ♀ From Latin. See main dictionary.

Mario ♂ From the Roman family name Marius (see main dictionary), but in modern times generally taken as a masculine equivalent of ►Maria.

Marisa ♀ Elaboration of ►Maria.

Marta ♀ New Testament. See Martha in main dictionary.

Martino ♂ From Latin *Martinus*. See Martin in main dictionary.
FEMININE FORM: **Martina** (see main dictionary).

Maso ♂ Short form of ►Tommaso.

Massimo ♂ From Latin *maximus* 'greatest'.

Matteo ♂ From Hebrew. See Matthew in main dictionary.
ALSO: **Mattia**.

Maurizio ♂ From Late Latin *Mauricius*. See Maurice in main dictionary.

Mauro ♂ From Latin *Maurus* 'Moor', i.e. 'swarthy'; the name of one of the earliest followers of St Benedict.
FEMININE FORM: **Maura**.

Medardo ♂ Germanic: from a personal name formed with an unidentified first element + *hard* 'hardy, strong'.

Melchiorre ♂ Traditionally, the name of one of the three Magi. See Melchior in main dictionary.

Michele ♂ Biblical. See Michael in main dictionary.

Michelangelo ♂ From ►Michele + *angelo* 'angel', famous as the name of the Florentine painter, sculptor, and architect Michelangelo Buonarotti (1475–1564).

Mirabella ♀ From Latin *mirabĭlis* 'wondrous, lovely'.

Mirella ♀ Italian form of French Mireille (see main dictionary).

Modesto ♂ From the Late Latin personal name *Modestus* 'restrained'.
FEMININE FORM: **Modesta**.

Nn

Naldo ♂ Short form of various given names with this ending, e.g. ►Rinaldo.

Narciso ♂ From Greek. See Narcissus in main dictionary.

Natanaele ♂ New Testament. See Nathaniel in main dictionary.

Nazario ♂ From the Late Latin name *Nazarius* 'of Nazareth', borne by several saints, notably one martyred with Celsus at Milan in the 1st century.

Nerina ♀ Possibly a feminine diminutive of ►Nero or of ►Nerio, or alternatively a Latinized form of Greek *Nērĭnē*, from the name of the sea god *Nēreus*.

Nerio ♂ From Greek *Nēreus*, name of a sea god. This was the name in the 1st century of a Roman soldier who was baptized by St Paul and exiled with Sts Achilleus and Flavia.

Nero ♂ Tuscan name, a short form of ►Raniero.

Nestore ♂ From the Greek personal name *Nestōr*. In Homer's Iliad Nestor, King of Pylos, is one of the leaders of the Greeks at Troy. The name was borne by several early Christian martyrs.

Nico ♂ Short form of ►Nicola or *Nicolò*, or, more rarely, of ►Nicomedo or ►Nicostrato.

Nicodemo ♂ From Greek. See Nicodemus in main dictionary.

Nicola ♂ From Greek. See Nicholas in main dictionary.
ALSO: **Nic(c)olò**.

Nicomedo ♂ From Greek *Nikomēdēs*, from *nike* 'victory' + *mēdesthai* 'to ponder, scheme'. St Nicomedes was a Roman priest martyred during the 1st century.

Nicostrato ♂ From Greek *Nikostratos*, from *nikē* 'victory' + *stratos* 'army'. St Nicostratos was the leader of a group of Roman soldiers martyred in Palestine under the Emperor Diocletian (*c*.303).

Nino ♂ Short form of *Giannino*, a pet form of ▶Gianni.

Noemi ♀ Biblical. See Naomi in main dictionary.

Nolasco ♂ Name adopted in honour of St Peter Nolasco (*c*.1189–1258), who founded the order of Our Lady of Ransom with the purpose of obtaining the release of Christians captured by the Moors during the Crusades.

Norma ♀ Apparently coined by Felice Romani in his libretto for Bellini's opera of this name. See main dictionary.

Nunzia ♀ Short form of ▶Annunziata.
MASCULINE FORM: **Nunzio.**

O o

Orazio ♂ From *Horatius*, an old Roman family name, probably of Etruscan origin.

Orfeo ♂ From Greek *Orpheus*, borne in classical mythology by a Thracian musician who descends into the Underworld in search of his dead wife, Eurydice. His name is of uncertain origin, and it seems likely that the legend originally concerned a pre-Greek divinity of the natural world.

Orlando ♂ Germanic. See Roland in main dictionary.

Ornella ♀ Name of a character in Gabriele d'Annunzio's *Figlia de Iorio* (1904), probably taken from the Tuscan dialect word *ornello* 'flowering ash tree'.

Ornetta ♀ Altered form of ▶Ornella.

Ottavio ♀ From the Latin personal name Octavius (see main dictionary).
FEMININE FORM: **Ottavia.**

P p

Palmiro ♂ From the vocabulary word *palmiere* 'pilgrim' (specifically, one who had brought back a palm from the Holy Land).

Pancrazio ♂ From Greek *pankratios* 'all-powerful'; borne by a 1st-century saint stoned to death in Sicily.

Paolo ♂ From Latin. See Paul in main dictionary.
FEMININE FORM: **Paola.**

Pasquale ♂ From Late Latin *Paschalis* 'relating to Easter'.

Patrizio ♂ Italian form of English and Irish Patrick (see main dictionary), name of the apostle and patron saint of Ireland.
FEMININE FORM: **Patrizia.**

Pellegrino ♂ From Latin. See Peregrine in main dictionary.

Perla ♀ From the vocabulary word meaning 'pearl'.

Pia ♀ From the feminine form of Latin *pius* 'pious'.
MASCULINE FORM: **Pio.**

Pierluigi ♂ Compound name from *Piero* (see ▶Pietro) and ▶Luigi.

Pietro ♂ From Greek. See Peter in main dictionary.
ALSO: **Piero.**
FEMININE FORM: **Piera.**

Pino ♂ Short form of any of various diminutive given names such as *Filippino* (from ▶Filippo) and *Giuseppino* (from ▶Giuseppe).

Placido ♂ From the Late Latin name *Placidus* 'untroubled'; the name of several minor saints.

Pompeo ♂ From the Roman family name *Pompeius*, of uncertain origin.

Ponzio ♂ From Latin *Pontius*, a family name of uncertain origin.

Porfirio ♂ From the Greek name *Porphyrios* (Late Latin *Porphyrius*), from Greek *porphyra* 'purple dye'; the name of some half-dozen early saints.

Primo ♂ From the Late Latin name *Primus* 'first'; the name of four minor early saints.

Prospero ♂ From Latin. See Prosper in main dictionary.

Prudenzio ♂ From the Late Latin name *Prudentius*, from *prudens* 'prudent'.

Qq

Quirino ♂ From Latin. See Corin in main dictionary.

Rr

Rachele ♀ Biblical. See Rachel in main dictionary.

Raffaele ♂ Italian form of Raphael, name of one of the archangels (see main dictionary).
ALSO: **Raffaello**.
FEMININE FORM: **Raffaella**.

Raimondo ♂ Germanic. See Raymond in main dictionary.
FEMININE FORM: **Raimonda**.

Raniero ♂ Germanic. See Rayner in main dictionary.

Raul ♂ From Norman French. See Ralph in main dictionary.

Remigio ♂ From the Latin name *Remigius*, from *remex* (genitive *remigis*) 'oarsman'.

Remo ♂ From *Remus*, the name, according to ancient Roman tradition, of the brother of Romulus, co-founder with him of the city of Rome.

Renato ♂ From the Late Latin name *Renatus* 'reborn', popular among early Christians as a name celebrating spiritual rebirth in Christ.
FEMININE FORM: **Renata**.

Riccardo ♂ Germanic. See Richard in main dictionary.

Rinaldo ♂ Germanic. See Reynold in main dictionary.

Roberto ♂ Germanic. See Robert in main dictionary.

Rocco ♂ Germanic: from *hrok* 'rest'; name of a 14th-century French saint who tended plague victims in northern Italy.

Rodolfo ♂ Italian form of Rudolf. See main dictionary.

Romano ♂ From the Late Latin personal name *Romanus* 'Roman'; the name of numerous early saints.

Romeo ♂ Medieval religious name

meaning 'pilgrim to Rome', from Latin *Roma* 'Rome'.

Romilda ♀ Germanic: from *hrōm* 'fame' + *hild* 'battle'.

Romolo ♂ From the Latin name *Romulus*, borne by the legendary founder of Rome.

Rosa ♀ Italian form of English Rose (see main dictionary).

Rosalba ♀ Ornamental name from Latin *rosa* 'rose' + *alba* 'white'.

Rosalia ♀ From Latin. See Rosalie in main dictionary.

Rosangela ♀ Compound name from ►Rosa and ►Angela.

Rosetta ♀ Pet form of ►Rosa.

Rufino ♂ From Latin *Rufinus*, a derivative of *Rufus* 'red-haired'.
ALSO: **Ruffino**.

Ruggiero ♂ Germanic. See Roger in main dictionary.
ALSO: **Ruggero**.

Rut ♀ Biblical. See Ruth in main dictionary.

Ss

Salvatore ♂ Religious name borne in honour of Christ the Saviour, from Late Latin *salvator* 'saviour'.

Sandro ♂ Short form of ►Alessandro.

Sansone ♂ Biblical. See Samson in main dictionary.

Saturnino ♂ Derivative of Latin *Saturnus*, name of the Roman god of agriculture and vegetation.

Saverio ♂ Italian form of Spanish Xavier (see main dictionary).

Scevola ♂ From Latin *Scaevola*, a derivative of *scaevus* 'left-handed'; the name of a Roman semi-legendary hero of the 6th century BC, Gaius Mucius Scaevola.

Sebastiano ♂ From Latin. See Sebastian in main dictionary.

Serafino ♂ Masculine form of Seraphina. See main dictionary.

Sergio ♂ From the old Roman family name *Sergius*, which is probably of Etruscan origin.

Sesto ♂ From Latin *Sextus* 'sixth'.
ALSO: Sisto.

Severiano ♂ From Latin *Severianus*, a derivative of *Severus*. See ▶Severo.

Severino ♂ From the Latin family name *Severinus*, a derivative of *Severus*. See ▶Severo.

Severo ♂ From the Roman family name *Severus* 'stern, severe'.

Silvano ♂ From Latin *Silvanus*, from *silva* 'wood'.

FEMININE FORM: Silvana.

Silvestro ♂ From Latin. See Silvester in main dictionary.

Silvia ♀ Ancient Latin name. See main dictionary.
MASCULINE FORM: Silvio.

Stefania ♀ Feminine form of ▶Stefano. See also Stephanie in main dictionary.

Stefano ♀ From Greek. See Stephen in main dictionary.

Tt

Taddeo ♂ New Testament. See Thaddeus in main dictionary.

Tammaro ♂ Germanic: from *thank* 'thought' + *mār*, *mēr* 'fame'. St Tammarus was a priest from Africa who landed in southern Italy in the 5th century, after being cast adrift by the Arian Vandals.

Tancredo ♂ Germanic: from *thank* 'thought' + *rād* 'counsel'.

Telesforo ♂ From Greek *Telesphoros*, derived from *telos* 'end, completion' + *pherein* 'to bring, bear'; borne by an early pope, a Calabrian Greek by origin, who was martyred under Hadrian in 136.

Teodoro ♂ From Greek. See Theodore in main dictionary.
FEMININE FORM: Teodora.

Teodosio ♂ From Greek *Theodosios*, from *theos* 'god' + *dōsis* 'giving'.

Teofilo ♂ New Testament. See Theophilus in main dictionary.

Teresa ♀ Of uncertain origin. See Theresa in main dictionary.

Timoteo ♂ From Greek. See Timothy in main dictionary.

Tito ♂ From Latin *Titus*, an old Roman given name, of unknown origin. See Titus in main dictionary.

Tiziano ♂ From Latin *Titianus*, a derivative of *Titus* (see ▶Tito); bestowed in honour of the medieval painter Tiziano Vecellio (1490–1576), known in English as Titian.

Tommaso ♂ New Testament. See Thomas in main dictionary.

Tonio ♂ Short form of ▶Antonio.

Tullio ♂ From the Roman family name *Tullius*, borne by the orator Marcus Tullius Cicero (106–43 BC).

Uu

Ugo ♂ Italian form of English Hugh. See main dictionary.

Ulisse ♂ Italian form of Ulysses. See main dictionary.

Umberto ♂ Germanic. See Humbert in main dictionary. The former Italian royal family is descended from the Blessed Umberto of Savoy (1136–88).

Vv

Valentino ♂ From Latin. See Valentine in main dictionary.
FEMININE FORM: **Valentina**.

Vasco ♂ From Spanish. See Spanish appendix.

Venceslao ♂ From a Latinized form of an Old Slavic name; see Wenceslas in main dictionary.

Vigilio ♂ From Latin *Vigilius*, probably a derivative of *vigil* 'watchful'. St Vigilius, bishop of Trent (d. 405), was stoned to death for overturning a statue of Saturn.

Vincente ♂ From Latin. See Vincent in main dictionary.
ALSO: **Vincenzo** (from the elaborated form *Vincentius*).

Viola ♀ From Latin. See main dictionary.

Violetta ♀ From Late Latin. See Violet in main dictionary.

Virgilio ♂ From Latin. See Virgil in main dictionary.

Virginia ♀ From Latin. See main dictionary.

Vitale ♂ From the Late Latin name *Vitalis* 'lively; life-affirming', derivative of *vita* 'life'. There are more than a dozen early saints bearing this name, including Vitalis of Milan, the father of Gervasius and Protasius.

Vittore ♂ From Late Latin. See Victor in main dictionary.

Vittorio ♂ From Latin *Victorius*, a derivative of *Victor* 'conqueror'.
FEMININE FORM: **Vittoria**.

Zz

Zita ♀ Probably from the medieval Tuscan dialect word *zit(t)a* 'girl'; the name of a 13th-century saint from Lucca in Tuscany, the patroness of domestic servants. See also main dictionary.

Appendix 8:
Japanese Names

Notes: Most Japanese personal names are written using combinations of one, two, or three Chinese characters. In English transcription, many names may have dozens of possible meanings, because several different Japanese characters can have the same pronunciation. Also, a single character can have more than one pronunciation and meaning. Often, characters are used phonetically to 'spell' a name, with no regard to meaning, and puns are common. Only the one or two most common meanings can be given here. From the mid 20th century onwards, female names tended to have the suffix *-ko* ('child'). Recently, that suffix has begun to disappear again, as people mimic the naming habits of popular entertainers. Female names of western origin are becoming popular, usually written in the *kana* syllabary instead of Chinese characters.

Aa

Aika ♀ 'Love song'.

Aiko ♀ 'Loving or beloved child'.

Akemi ♀ 'Bright beauty'.

Aki ♂, ♀ 'Autumn'; 'bright'; also short for any name beginning with *Aki-*.

Akihiko ♂ 'Bright or shining prince'.

Akihiro ♂ 'Shining abroad'; 'bright scholar'.

Akiko ♀ 'Bright child'; 'child (born in) autumn'.

Akio ♂ 'Bright man'.

Akira ♂, ♀ 'Clear'; 'bright'; 'dawn'.

Anna ♀ Japanese adoption of the name. See main dictionary.

Arisu ♀ Japanese version of the name Alice. See main dictionary.

Asami ♀ 'Morning beauty'.

Atsuko ♀ 'Warm child'; 'industrious child'.

Atsushi ♂ 'Cordial'; 'industrious'.

Ayako ♀ 'Literary or scholarly child'.

Ayumi ♀ 'Stroll'.

Azumi ♀ 'Safe residence'.

Bb

Bunko ♀ 'Literary or scholarly child'.

Cc

Chiasa ♀ 'One thousand mornings'.

Chie ♀ 'Wisdom'; 'thousand blessings'.

Chieko ♀ 'Wise child'; 'thousand blessings child'.

Chiharu ♀ 'One thousand springs'.

Chisato ♂ 'Sagacious'.

Dd

Daisuke ♂ 'Great helper'.

Ee

Eiji ♂ 'Splendid ruler'; 'excellent second (son)'.

Eiko ♀ 'Splendid child'; 'long-lived child'.

Emi ♀ 'Smile'.

Emiko ♀ 'Smiling child'.

Eri ♀ 'Blessed prize'.

Erika ♀ Japanese version of the name Erica (see main dictionary). This name is usually written in *kana*, although it is sometimes also written with characters meaning 'blessed prize increasing'.

Etsuko ♀ 'Joyful child'.

Ff

Fuji ♀ 'Wisteria'. Resemblance to the name of Mount Fuji is mostly coincidental, but in some cases both meanings could be intended.

Fumiko ♀ 'Child of treasured beauty'; 'literary or scholarly child'.

Fumio ♂ 'Literary or scholarly man'.

Hh

Hajime ♂ 'Beginning'.

Hanako ♀ 'Flower child'.

Haruki ♀ 'Springtime tree'.

Haruko ♀ 'Springtime child'.

Harumi ♀ 'Springtime beauty'.

Haruo ♂ 'Springtime man'.

Hideaki ♂ 'Splendid brightness'; 'shining excellence'.

Hideki ♂ 'Splendid opportunity'. The most famous bearer was Tōjō Hideki (1884–1948), prime minister during the Second World War.

Hideko ♀ 'Splendid child'.

Hideo ♂ 'Splendid man'.

Hiro ♂, ♀ 'Widespread'; 'broad'; also short for any name beginning with *Hiro-*.

Hiroaki ♂ 'Widespread brightness'.

Hiroki ♂ 'Abundant joy'; 'abundant strength'.

Hiroko ♀ 'Generous child'; 'prosperous child'.

Hiromi ♂, ♀ 'Wide-seeing'; 'widespread beauty'.

Hiroshi ♂ 'Abundant'; 'widespread'.

Hiroyuki ♂ 'Widespread happiness'.

Hisako ♀ 'Long-lived child'.

Hisao ♂ 'Long-lived man'.

Hisashi ♂ 'Long-lived'.

Hitomi ♀ 'Pupil' (of the eye), given to girls with especially beautiful eyes.

Hitoshi ♂ 'Level'; 'even (tempered)'.

Ii

Ichirō ♂ 'First son'.

Isamu ♂ 'Courageous'; 'warrior'.

Isao ♂ 'Merit'; 'honour'.

Iwao ♂ 'Stone man'.

Jj

Jirō ♂ 'Second son'.

Jun ♂, ♀ 'Obedient'; as a female name, possibly referring to the English name June (see main dictionary).

Jun'ichi ♂ 'Obedience first'; 'purity first'.

Junko ♀ 'Obedient child'; 'pure child'.

Kk

Kaori ♀ 'Fragrance'.

Kaoru ♀ 'Fragrance'.

Katsumi ♀ 'Victorious beauty'.

Kayo ♀ 'Beautiful generation'; 'increasing generation'.

Kazue ♀ 'First blessing'; 'harmonious branch'.

Kazuhiko ♂ 'Harmonious prince'; 'first prince'.

Kazuhiro ♂ 'Harmony widespread'.

Kazuko ♀ 'Harmonious child'.

Kazumi ♀ 'Harmonious beauty'.

Kazuo ♂ 'Harmonious man'.

Kei ♀ 'Respectful'; also possibly a Japanese version of the English name Kay (see main dictionary).

Keiichi ♂ 'Respectful first (son)'.

Keiji ♂ 'Respectful second (son)'.

Keiko ♀ 'Blessed child'; 'respectful child'.

Ken'ichi ♂ 'First builder'; 'govern first'.

Kenji ♂ 'Intelligent ruler'.

Kiku ♀ 'Chrysanthemum'.

Kimi ♀ Short for any name beginning with *Kimi-*.

Kimiko ♀ 'Ruling child'; 'dear child'; 'beautiful history child'.

Kiyoko ♀ 'Pure child'.

Kiyomi ♀ 'Pure beauty'.

Kiyoshi ♂ 'Pure'; 'saintly'. A famous bearer was the actor Atsumi Kiyoshi (1929–96), but the name was popular before he became well known.

Kōichi ♂ 'Widespread first (son)'; 'shining first (son)'.

Kōji ♂ 'Filial ruler'; 'happy second (son)'.

Kumiko ♀ 'Long-lived, beautiful child'.

Kunio ♂ 'Countryman'.

Kyōko ♀ 'Child of the capital city'.

Mm

Madoka ♂, ♀ 'Tranquil'.

Maiko ♀ 'Dancing child'.

Maki ♀ 'True record'; 'true tree'.

Makoto ♂ 'True'.

Mamoru ♂ 'Protect'.

Mana ♀ 'True'.

Manabu ♂ 'Studious'.

Mari ♀ Japanese version of the English name Mary. See main dictionary.

Maria ♀ Japanese version of the name Maria. See main dictionary.

Mariko ♀ 'True reason child'.

Masa ♂, ♀ Short for any name beginning with *Masa-*.

Masaaki ♂ 'Correct brightness'.

Masahiko ♂ 'Correct prince'.

Masahiro ♂ 'Govern widely'.

Masaki ♂ 'Elegant tree'; 'correct record'.

Masako ♀ 'Governing child'; 'correct child'. The most famous bearer of the name was Hōjō Masako (1157–1225), wife of the Shōgun Minamoto Yoritomo, who ruled Japan from behind the scenes after her husband's death.

Masami ♀ 'Elegant beauty'; 'correct beauty'.

Masanori ♂ 'Correct principles'; 'prosperous government'.

Masao ♂ 'Correct man'.

Masaru ♂ 'Victorious'; 'intelligent'.

Masashi ♂ 'Correct'; 'splendid official'.

Masato ♂ 'Elegant man'; 'correct man'.

Masayoshi ♂ 'Govern righteously'; 'shining goodness'.

Masayuki ♂ 'Correct happiness'.

Masumi ♀ 'True purity'; 'increasing beauty'.

Mayumi ♀ 'True intent beauty'; 'true bow' (as in archery).

Megumi ♀ 'Blessing'.

Michi ♂, ♀ 'Pathway'.

Michiko ♀ 'Child on the (correct) path'; 'thousand beauties child'.

Michio ♂ 'Man on the (correct) path'.

Midori ♀ 'Verdant'.

Mieko ♀ 'Beautiful blessing child'.

Miho ♀ 'Beautiful bay'. The Miho pine grove in Shimizu City is famous for its view of Mount Fuji.

Mika ♀ 'Beautiful fragrance'.

Miki ♀ 'Three trees'; 'beautiful tree'.

Mikio ♂ 'Tree trunk man'; implying one who will have many descendants.

Minori ♂, ♀ 'Beautiful harbour'; 'village of beautiful fields'.

Minoru ♂ 'Ear of grain'; 'fruitful'.

Mitsuko ♀ 'Shining child'; 'child full (of blessings)'.

Mitsuo ♂ 'Shining man'; 'third male (son)'.

Mitsuru ♂ 'Full'; 'growing'.

Miwa ♀ 'Three rings'; 'beautiful harmony'.

Mount Miwa is a sacred hill in Nara Prefecture.

Miyoko ♀ 'Beautiful generation child'; 'child (of the) third generation'.

Miyuki ♀ 'Happiness'; 'beautiful happiness'.

Momo ♀ 'Peach'.

Momoe ♀ 'Hundred blessings'; 'hundred rivers'; popularized in the 1970s as the name of the singer Yamaguchi Momoe (b. 1959).

Nn

Nana ♀ 'Seven'; often given to girls born on the seventh day of the seventh month.

Nao ♂, ♀ 'Honest'; also short for any name beginning with *Nao-*.

Naoki ♀ 'Honest tree'; 'honest joy'.

Naoko ♀ 'Honest child'.

Natsuko ♀ 'Summer child'.

Natsumi ♀ 'Summer beauty'.

Noboru ♂ 'Climb, ascend'; 'virtuous'.

Nobuko ♀ 'Faithful child'.

Nobuo ♂ 'Faithful man'.

Nobuyuki ♂ 'Faithful happiness'.

Nori ♂, ♀ Short for any name beginning with *Nori-*.

Noriko ♀ 'Child of principles'.

Norio ♂ 'Man of principles'.

Oo

Osamu ♂ 'Ruler'.

Rr

Reiko ♀ 'Courteous child'; 'beautiful child'.

Rie ♀ 'Valued blessing'.

Rika ♀ 'Valued fragrance'.

Rina ♀ Japanese version of the English name Lena. See main dictionary.

Risa ♀ Japanese version of the English name Lisa. See main dictionary.

Ryōko ♀ 'Good child'.

Ss

Saburō ♂ 'Third son'.

Sachiko ♀ 'Happy child'.

Sadao ♂ 'Decisive man'.

Sakiko ♀ 'Earlier child' (given in the hope of more children); 'blossoming child'.

Sara ♀ Japanese version of the English name Sara(h). See main dictionary.

Sari ♀ Japanese version of the English name Sally. See main dictionary.

Satoru ♂ 'Enlightened'; from the Japanese word for *nirvana*.

Satoshi ♂ 'Wise'; 'quick-witted'; 'clear (thinking)'.

Seiichi ♂ 'Admonishing first (son)'; 'pure first (son)'.

Seiji ♂ 'Admonishing second (son)'; 'pure second (son)'.

Setsuko ♀ 'Temperate child'.

Shig ♂, ♀ Short for any name beginning with *Shige-*.

Shigeko ♀ 'Luxuriant child'.

Shigeo ♂ 'Luxuriant man'.

Shigeru ♂ 'Luxuriant'; 'excellent'.

Shin'ichi ♂ 'Faithful first (son)'.

Shinji ♂ 'Faithful second (son)'.

Shiori ♀ 'Bookmark'; 'guide'.

Shirō ♂ 'Fourth son'.

Shizuko ♀ 'Quiet child'.

Shōichi ♂ 'Prosperous first (son)'; 'correct first (son)'.

Shōji ♂ 'Shining second (son)'; 'correct second (son)'.

Shūichi ♂ 'Governing first (son)'; 'excellent first (son)'.

Shūji ♂ 'Governing second (son)'; 'excellent second (son)'.

Sumiko ♀ 'Clear (thinking) child'; 'pure child'.

Susumu ♂ 'Progressing'.

T t

Tadao ♂ 'Loyal man'.

Tadashi ♂ 'Correct'; 'loyal'; 'righteous'.

Takahiro ♂ 'Abundantly filial'; 'widespread nobility'.

Takako ♀ 'Filial child'; 'noble child'; 'high child'.

Takao ♂ 'Filial man'; 'noble man'; 'high man'.

Takashi ♂ 'Praiseworthy'; 'filial official'.

Takayuki ♂ 'Noble'; 'filial happiness'.

Takeo ♂ 'Warrior'.

Takeshi ♂ 'Warrior'; 'fierce'.

Tamotsu ♂ 'Protect'; 'complete'.

Tarō ♂ 'Great son'; name given only to a first son.

Tatsuo ♂ 'Dragon man'; the dragon is believed to be wise and long-lived.

Tatsuya ♂ 'Become dragon' (and possess its virtues).

Teruko ♀ 'Shining child'.

Teruo ♂ 'Shining man'.

Tetsuo ♂ 'Clear (thinking) man'; 'iron man'.

Tetsuya ♂ 'Clear evening'; 'become iron'.

Tomiko ♀ 'Treasured child'; 'treasured beauty child'.

Tomio ♂ 'Treasured man'.

Tomoko ♀ 'Friendly child'; 'wise child'.

Tōru ♂ 'Wayfarer'; 'penetrating (mind)'.

Toshi ♂, ♀ 'Alert': not usually used by itself, but often as a short form for names beginning with Toshi-.

Toshiaki ♂ 'Ripe brightness'; 'alert and bright'.

Toshiko ♀ 'Alert child'; 'valued child'; 'child of (many) years'.

Toshio ♂ 'Alert man'; 'valued man'; 'man of genius'.

Toshiyuki ♂ 'Alert and happy'.

Tsuneo ♂ 'Common man'.

Tsutomu ♂ 'Worker'.

Tsuyoshi ♂ 'Strong'.

Y y

Yasuhiro ♂ 'Abundant honesty'; 'widespread peace'.

Yasuko ♀ 'Honest child'; 'peaceful child'.

Yasuo ♂ 'Honest man'; 'peaceful man'.

Yasushi ♂ 'Honest'; 'peaceful'.

Yayoi ♀ 'Spring'; from a traditional name for the third lunar month, corresponding approximately to April. This is also the name of a district in Tokyo where important prehistoric archaeological artefacts from the period c.300 BC–AD 300 were first discovered.

Yōichi ♂ 'Masculine first (son)'.

Yōko ♀ 'Positive child'; 'ocean child'.

Yoshi ♂, ♀ 'Good'; also short for any name beginning with Yoshi-.

Yoshiaki ♂ 'Righteous glory'; 'shining luck'.

Yoshie ♀ 'Fragrant branch'; 'good bay'.

Yoshihiro ♂ 'Widespread goodness'.

Yoshikazu ♂ 'Righteous first (son)'; 'good and harmonious'.

Yoshiko ♀ 'Good child'; 'fragrant child'; 'noble child'.

Yoshinori ♂ 'Noble virtue'; 'righteous principles'.

Yoshio ♂ 'Good man'.

Yoshito ♂ 'Good man'; 'lucky man'.

Yoshiyuki ♂ 'Righteous happiness'.

Yūichi ♂ 'Courageous first (son)'; 'friendly first (son)'.

Yūji ♂ 'Second male'; 'courageous second (son)'.

Yuka ♀ 'Fragrant'; 'friendly blossom'.

Yuki ♂, ♀ 'Happiness'; 'snow'; also short for any name beginning with *Yuki-*.

Yukiko ♀ 'Happy child'.

Yukio ♂ 'Happy man'.

Yūko ♀ 'Helpful or superior child'.

Yumi ♀ 'Bow' (as in archery); 'helpful beauty'; also short for any name beginning with *Yumi-*.

Yumiko ♀ 'Helpful, beautiful child'.

Yūna ♀ Possibly a Japanese version of the Irish name Una. See main dictionary.

Yuri ♀ 'Lily'.

Yuriko ♀ 'Prized child'; 'lily child'.

Yutaka ♂ 'Abundant'; 'prosperous'.

Aa

Afanasi ♂ From Greek *Athanasios*. See Athanasius in main dictionary.

Agafya ♀ From Greek *Agapia*, a derivative of *agapē* 'love'.

Agata ♀ From Greek. See Agatha in main dictionary.

Aglaia ♀ From Greek, probably related to Aegle; see main dictionary.

Agnessa ♀ From Greek. See Agnes in main dictionary.

Agrafena ♀ From Latin *Agrippina*, from an old Roman family name of uncertain (probably Etruscan) origin.

Akilina ♂ From Latin *Aquilina* 'eagle-like'. St Aquilina is revered in the Orthodox Church as a young virgin martyr beheaded in Syria at the end of the 3rd century.

Akim ♂ From Hebrew: 'established by God'. See Joachim in main dictionary.
ALSO: Yakim.

Aleksandr ♂ From Greek. See Alexander in main dictionary.

Aleksandra ♀ Feminine form of ▶Aleksandr.

Aleksei ♂ From Greek. See Alexis in main dictionary.

Anastasia ♀ From Greek. See main dictionary.

Anatoli ♂ From Greek *anatolē* 'sunrise'; St Anatolius was bishop of Constantinople from 449 to 458.

Andrei ♂ From Greek. See Andrew in main dictionary.

Anfisa ♀ From Greek *Anthousa*, a derivative of *anthos* 'flower'; St Anthousa was a 9th-century abbess who lived near Constantinople.

Anisim ♂ From Greek *Onēsimos* 'useful'.
ALSO: Onisim.

Anna ♀ From Hebrew: 'God has favoured me'. See Anne in main dictionary.

Antip ♂ From Greek *Antipas*, a short form of *Antipatēr* (from *anti-* 'like' + *patēr* 'father'); the name of the first bishop of Pergamum (Book of Revelation 2:13), who is greatly revered in the Orthodox Church.

Anton ♂ From Latin *Antonius*. See Anthony in main dictionary.

Apollinaria ♀ From Latin. See main dictionary.

Arina ♀ Variant of ▶Irina.

Arkadi ♂ From Greek *Arkadios* 'man from Arcadia'; St Arkadios was

a 4th-century missionary bishop venerated in the Eastern Church.

Arkhip ♂ From Greek *Arkhippos*, composed of *arkhē* 'beginning' or 'rule' + *hippos* 'horse'. St Arkhippos was one of the earliest Christians, twice mentioned by St Paul in his epistles (Colossians 4:17; Philemon 2).

Arseni ♂ From Greek *Arsēnios* 'virile'.

Artemi ♂ From Late Greek *Artemios* 'devotee of Artemis'.
ALSO: Artyom.

Avdotya ♀ From Greek *Eudokia* (a compound of *eu* 'well, good' + *dokein* 'to seem').

Averki ♂ From the Greek name *Aberkios*, of uncertain origin; borne by a 2nd-century bishop of Hieropolis in Phrygia, who is revered as a saint in the Orthodox Church.

Avgust ♂ From Latin. See Augustus in main dictionary.

Bb

Boleslav ♂ Slavic: from *bole* 'large' + *slav* 'glory'.

Boris ♂ Probably from a Tartar nickname meaning 'small'. Saints

Boris and Gleb were sons of Prince Vladimir, first Christian ruler of Kiev in the 10th-century.

Dd

Daniil ♂ Biblical. See Daniel in main dictionary.

Darya ♀ Greek, from a feminine form of a Persian royal name apparently meaning 'good ruler'.

Demid ♂ From Greek *Diomēdēs* 'counsel of Zeus'. St Diomedes was born at Tarsus in Cilicia and martyred at Nicaea in Bithynia under the emperor Diocletian.

Demyan ♂ From Greek *Damianos*. See Damian in main dictionary.

Denis ♂ From Greek *Dionysios*. See Dennis in main dictionary.

Dmitri ♂ From Greek *Dēmētrios* 'devotee of Demeter'. See Demetrius in main dictionary.

Dorofei ♂ From Greek *Dōrotheos* (from *dōron* 'gift' + *theos* 'god'); name borne by various early saints much venerated in the Eastern Church, including a 4th-century bishop of Tyre and the abbots Dorotheus the Archimandrite (7th century) and Dorotheus the Younger (11th century).

Dosifei ♂ From Greek *Dōsitheos*, from *dōsis* 'giving' + *theos* 'god'. St Dositheus (d. *c*.530) was a monk of Gaza who is much venerated in the Eastern Church.

Ff

Faddei ♂ New Testament. See Thaddeus in main dictionary.

Fedora ♀ From Greek. See Theodora in main dictionary.
ALSO: **Feodora**.

Fedosi ♂ From Greek *Theodosios*, composed of *theos* 'god' + *dōsis* 'giving'. Compare ▶Dosifei.
ALSO: **Feodosi**.

Fedot ♂ From Greek *Theodotos*, composed of *theos* 'God' + *dotos* 'given'.

Feofil ♂ From Greek. See Theophilus in main dictionary.

Ferapont ♂ From the Greek name *Therapōn* 'servant; worshipper'.

Filat ♂ Contracted form of *Feofilakt*, from Greek *Theophylaktos*, composed of *theos* 'god' + *phylassein* 'to guard, protect'.

Firs ♂ From Greek *Thyrsos*. See Tirso in Spanish appendix.

Florenti ♂ From Latin *Florentius*, a derivative of *florens* 'blossoming, flourishing'.

Foka ♂ From Greek *Phōcas*, denoting someone from the ancient city of Phocaea in Asia Minor. The stress is on the second syllable.

Foma ♂ New Testament. See Thomas in main dictionary. The stress is on the second syllable.

Fyodr ♂ From Greek *Theodōros*. See Theodore in main dictionary.

Gg

Galina ♀ Probably from Greek *galēnē* 'calm'.

Gennadi ♂ Probably from a short form of Greek names such as *Diogenēs* 'born of Zeus' and *Hermogenēs* 'born of Hermes'; the name of a saint long venerated in the Eastern Church.

Georgi ♂ From Greek *Georgios*. See George in main dictionary.
ALSO: **Yuri, Yegor**.

Gerasim ♂ From Greek *Gerasimos*, from *geras*, meaning either 'old man' or 'honoured'; borne by a 5th-century saint venerated in the Eastern Church; he lived as a hermit in the Holy Land.

Gleb ♂ From Old Norse *Gudleifr*, composed of *guð* 'god' + *leifr* 'life'. Saints Boris and Gleb were sons of Prince Vladimir, first Christian ruler of Kiev in the 10th century.

Grigori ♂ From Greek *Grēgorios* 'watchful'. See Gregory in main dictionary.

Ii

Ignati ♂ From Latin Ignatius. See main dictionary.

Igor ♂ From Old Norse *Yherr* (see Ivor in main dictionary), one of the names taken to Russia by Scandinavian settlers in the 9th century.

Illari ♂ From Latin *Hilarius*, derivative of *hilaris* 'cheerful'. Compare ▶Illarion.

Illarion ♂ From Greek *Hilarion* 'cheerful'.

Ilya ♂ From Greek *Elias*, the name used in the New Testament for the prophet *Elijah* 'Yahweh is God'.

Innokenti ♂ From Latin *Innocentius* 'innocent'; the name of various early saints venerated in the Eastern Church, including the leader of a group of martyrs killed at Sirmium, now Mitrovica, in the Balkans.

Iosif ♂ Biblical. See Joseph in main dictionary.
ALSO: **Osip**.

Ipati ♂ From Greek *Hypatios*, derivative of *hypatos* 'highest'; the name of several early saints venerated in the Eastern Church, notably a bishop of Ganyra in Paphlagonia who played a prominent part at the Council of Nicaea.

Ira ♀ Pet form of ▶Irina.

Irina ♀ From Greek *Eirēnē* 'peace'. See Irene in main dictionary.
ALSO: **Arina**.

Irinei ♂ From Greek *Eirēnaios*, derivative of *eirēnē* 'peace'; the name of several early saints venerated in the Eastern Church.

Ivan ♂ From Hebrew: 'God is gracious'. See John in main dictionary.

Kk

Kapiton ♂ From Late Latin *Capito*, originally a nickname meaning 'big-headed'; the name of a missionary who preached in the Crimea and south Russia in the 4th century.

Karp ♂ From Greek *Karpos* 'fruit'; the name of an early Christian mentioned in St Paul's epistle to Timothy.

Katerina ♀ Popular form of ▶Yekaterina.

Katya ♀ Pet form of ▶Yekaterina.

Kirill ♂ From Greek *Kyrillos* 'of the Lord'; name of the saint who brought Christianity to Russia in the 9th century. See Cyril in main dictionary.

Klara ♀ From Latin *Clara* 'bright, famous'. See Clare in main dictionary.

Klavdia ♀ From the feminine form of the Latin family name *Claudius*. See Claudia in main dictionary.

Kliment ♂ From Latin *Clemens* 'merciful'. See Clement in main dictionary.

Kolya ♂ Pet form of ▶Nikolai.

Kondrati ♂ From Latin *Quadratus*, a byname meaning 'square', i.e. 'stout'. This was the name of the writer of the first known apologia for Christianity, addressed to the emperor Hadrian.

Konstantin ♂ From Latin *Constantinus* 'steadfast', the name of the first Christian Roman emperor (?288–337).

Ll

Lana ♀ Short form of ▶Svetlana.

Lara ♀ Pet form of ▶Larissa.

Larissa ♀ From Greek, of uncertain meaning (perhaps from the name of a town in Thessaly). This was the name of an early Christian martyr venerated in the Eastern Church.

Lavrenti ♂ From Latin *Laurentius* 'man from Laurentum'. See Laurence in main dictionary.

Lena ♀ Short form of ▶Yelena.

Leonid ♂ From Greek *Leōnidas*, the name of a Spartan hero who was named after his grandfather *Leōn* 'lion'. Later the name was borne by two early saints venerated in the Eastern Church.

Leonti ♂ From Greek *Leonteios* 'lion-like'.

Lev ♂ From Russian *lev* 'lion', hence a vernacular equivalent of Leo (see main dictionary).

Luka ♂ From Greek *Loukas*. See Luke in main dictionary.

Lyuba ♀ Pet form of ▶Lyubov.

Lyubov ♀ From the Russian vocabulary word meaning 'love'; vernacular equivalent of ▶Agafya.

Lyuda ♀ Pet form of ▶Lyudmila.

Lyudmila ♀ Slavic: from *lud* 'people, tribe' (a borrowing from Germanic *liut*) + *mil* 'grace, favour'. This was the name of the grandmother of St Wenceslas of Bohemia.

Mm

Makari ♂ From Greek *Makarios*, derivative of *makaros* 'blessed'.

Maksim ♂ Variant transliteration of ▶Maxim.

Margarita ♀ From Greek *Margarites*. See ▶Margaret in main dictionary.

Marina ♀ Latin. See main dictionary.

Marta ♀ From Aramaic: 'lady'. See Martha in main dictionary.

Marya ♀ From Hebrew. See Maria and Mary in main dictionary.

Masha ♀ Pet form of ▶Marya.

Matrona ♀ From Late Latin *Matrona* 'lady'; the name of various early saints martyred for their faith.

Matvei ♂ From Hebrew: 'gift of God'. See Matthew in main dictionary.

Mavra ♀ From Latin *Maura* 'swarthy'.

Mavriki ♂ From Latin. See Maurice in main dictionary.

Maxim ♂ From Latin *Maximus* 'greatest'. See main dictionary.

Mefodi ♂ From Greek *Methodios*, from *meta* 'with' + *hodos* 'road, path'; the name of the 9th-century evangelist who first translated the Bible into Slavonic.

Melor ♂ Name devised during the Communist era, from the initial letters of the words *Marx*, *Engels*, *Lenin*, *October*, *Revolution*.

Mikhail ♂ From Hebrew: 'Who is like God?' See Michael in main dictionary.

Misha ♂ Pet form of ▶Mikhail.

Mitrofan ♂ From Greek *Mētrophanēs* 'appearance of the Mother' (i.e. Mary, Mother of God); borne by the first bishop of Byzantium.

Mitya ♂ Pet form of ▶Dmitri.

Modest ♂ From Latin *Modestus*, originally a byname meaning 'unassuming'.

Mstislav ♂ Slavic: from *mshcha* 'vengeance' + *slav* 'glory'.

Nn

Nadezhda ♀ From the Russian vocabulary word meaning 'hope'.

Nadya ♀ Pet form of ▶Nadezhda.

Nastasia ♀ Short form of ▶Anastasia.

Natalya ♀ From Late Latin *Natalia*: 'associated with birth', i.e. the birth of Christ at Christmas or the concept of Christian rebirth.

Natasha ♀ Pet form of ▶Natalya.

Naum ♂ From Hebrew 'comforter'. See Nahum in main dictionary.

Nikifor ♂ From Greek *Nikēphoros* 'bringer of victory'.

Nikita ♂ From Greek *Anikētos* 'unconquered'; the name of an early pope (*c*.152–160) who is particularly honoured in the Eastern Church.

Nikodim ♂ From Greek *Nikodēmos*. See Nicodemus in main dictionary.

Nikolai ♂ From Greek *Nikolaos*. See Nicholas in main dictionary.

Nina ♀ In origin a short form of *Antonina*, but now usually used as an independent name.

Ninel ♀ Coinage of the Communist era, representing *Lenin* spelled backwards.

Oo

Oktyabrina ♀ Coinage adopted in the Soviet period, in commemoration of the October Revolution of 1917, which brought the Bolsheviks to power.

Oleg ♂ From Old Norse *Helgi* 'prosperous'. This was the name of a Scandinavian leader (d. 912) who established the city of Kiev; since he was not a Christian, the name has never been sanctioned by the Russian Orthodox Church.

Olga ♀ Feminine of ▶Oleg. See also main dictionary.

Onisim ♂ Variant of ▶Anisim.

Osip ♂ Variant of ▶Iosif.

Pp

Pankrati ♂ From Greek *Pankratios*, from an epithet meaning 'all-powerful'. See Pancras in main dictionary.

Pavel ♂ From Latin. See Paul in main dictionary.

Pelageya ♀ From Greek *Pelagia*, a derivative of *pelagos* 'open sea, ocean'.

Petya ♂ Pet form of ▶Pyotr.

Pimen ♂ From Greek *Poimēn* 'shepherd'; borne by a 5th-century hermit who lived in the Egyptian desert; he is a saint still greatly venerated in the Eastern Church.

Praskovya ♀ From Greek *Paraskeuē* 'Friday', literally 'preparation' (i.e. Friday as the day of preparation for Easter); the name of a 1st-century saint who is venerated in the Eastern Church.

Prokhor ♂ From Greek *Prokhōros*, derived from *pro* 'before, ahead' + *khorein* 'to sing, dance', originally a name given to the leader of a troupe of singers or dancers.

Prokopi ♂ From Greek *Prokopios*, a derivative of *prokopē* 'successful'. ALSO: **Prokofi** (vernacular form).

Pyotr ♂ From Greek *Petros* 'rock'. See Peter in main dictionary.

Rr

Raisa ♀ Slavic: 'paradise'.

Rodion ♂ From Greek: short form of *Hērodion* 'devotee of Hera'. The name Herodion was borne by a kinsman of St Paul mentioned in the New Testament (Romans 16:11); according to post-biblical tradition he became bishop of Patras and met a martyr's death.

Roman ♂ From Latin *Romanus* 'Roman'. This was the baptismal name of St Boris.

Rostislav ♂ Slavic: from *rosts* 'usurp, arrogate' + *slav* 'glory'.

Rurik ♂ From Old Norse *Hrodrik* 'fame rule' (see Roderick in main dictionary); the name of a Scandinavian leader who established the city of Novgorod in the 9th-century.

Ss

Sasha ♂ Pet form of ▶Aleksandr.

Sava ♂ From Late Greek *Sab(b)as*, a derivative of Hebrew *saba* 'old man'. Two early saints of this name are venerated in the Eastern Church: the first was martyred *c*.372

near Tirgovist in Romania; the second (439–532) was a Cappadocian, regarded as one of the founders of Eastern monasticism.

Semyon ♂ From Hebrew: 'hearkening'. See Simon in main dictionary.

Serafima ♀ From Hebrew *seraphim* 'burning ones'. See Seraphina in main dictonary.

Serezha ♂ Pet form of ▶Sergei.

Sergei ♂ From Latin *Sergius*, an old Roman family name of uncertain origin. St Sergei of Radonezh (1314–92) is one of the most popular of all Russian saints.

Sevastyan ♂ From Greek *Sebastianos* 'man from Sebasta'. See Sebastian in main dictionary.

Shura ♂, ♀ Short form of *Sashura*, itself an elaborated version of ▶Sasha; found occasionally as a female name, ultimately from ▶Alexandra.

Slava ♂, ♀ Short form of many Slavic names containing the element *slav* 'glory'.

Sofya ♀ From Greek *Sophia* 'wisdom'. See Sophia in main dictionary.

Sonya ♀ Pet form of ▶Sofya.

Spiridion ♂ From Late Greek, a diminutive formation from Latin *spiritus* 'soul'; borne by a bishop of Tremithus in Cyprus who was persecuted under the Emperor Diocletian, but survived to play a major role in the Council of Nicaea (AD 325).

Stanislav ♂ Slavic: from *stan* 'government' + *slav* 'glory'.

Stepan ♂ From Greek *Stephanos* 'crown'. See Stephen in main dictionary.

Sveta ♀ Pet form of ▶Svetlana.

Svetlana ♀ Slavic: 'light', adopted as a vernacular equivalent of the Greek name *Phōtinē*, which was borne by a saint martyred at Rome in the 1st century; in the Eastern Church she has been identified with the 'Samaritan woman' mentioned in St John's gospel, chapter 4.

Svyatoslav ♂ Slavic: from *svyanto* 'bright, holy' + *slav* 'glory'.

Tt

Tamara ♀ Probably from Hebrew *Tamar*. See main dictionary.

Tanya ♀ Pet form of ▶Tatyana.

Taras ♂ From Greek *Tarasios* 'man from Tarentum' (a town in southern Italy); St Tarasius, a 9th-century bishop of Constantinople, is venerated in the Orthodox Church.

Tatyana ♀ From Latin: from an old Roman family name, *Tatianus*, of uncertain (apparently Sabine) origin. See Tatiana in main dictionary

Tikhon ♂ From Greek *Tychōn* 'hitting the mark'.

Timofei ♂ From Greek *Timotheos* 'honour God'. See Timothy in main dictionary.

Trofim ♂ From Greek *Trophimos* 'nutritious, fruitful'; borne by half a dozen early Christian saints martyred under the emperors Probus and Diocletian and much venerated in the Eastern Church.

Vv

Vadim ♂ Of uncertain origin, perhaps a contracted form of ▶Vladimir.

Valentin ♂ From Latin *Valentinus* 'flourishing'. See Valentine in main dictionary.

Valentina ♀ Feminine form of ▶Valentin.

Valeri ♂ From Latin *Valerius* 'healthy'.

Vanya ♂ Pet form of ▶Ivan.

Varfolomei ♂ New Testament. See Bartholomew in main dictionary.

Varvara ♀ From Greek *Barbara* 'foreign woman'. See Barbara in main dictionary.
PET FORM: **Varya.**

Vasili ♂ From Greek *Basilios* 'royal'. See Basil in main dictionary.

Vera ♀ Slavic: 'faith'. See main dictionary.

Viktor ♂ From Latin *Victor* 'conqueror'. See Victor in main dictionary.

Vissarion ♂ From Greek *Bessarion*, of uncertain origin; the name of a 2nd-century saint who lived as a hermit in the Egyptian desert, and is still greatly venerated in the Orthodox Church.

Vitali ♂ From Latin *Vitalis*, a derivative of *vita* 'life'.

Vladilen ♂ Name constructed from that of the founder of the Soviet state, Vladimir Ilyich Lenin (1870–1924).

Vladimir ♂ Slavonic: from *volod* 'rule' + *meri* 'great, famous'; the name of the ruler of Kiev who brought Russia into the Christian Church.

Vladislav ♂ Slavic: from *volod* 'rule' + *slav* 'glory'.

Vlas ♂ From the Latin name *Blasius*, probably from *blaesus* 'lisping'. See Blaise in main dictionary.
ALSO: **Vlasi** (learned form).

Volodya ♂ Pet form of ▶Vladimir.

Vsevolod ♂ Slavic: from *vse* 'all' + *volod* 'rule', coined as a vernacular equivalent of Greek *Pankratios*.

Vyacheslav ♂ Slavic: from *ventie* 'more, greater' + *slav* 'glory'. The Czech and Polish version of this name is familiar in the Latinized form Wenceslas (see main dictionary).

Yy

Yakim ♂ Variant of ▶Akim.

Yakov ♂ From Hebrew: 'supplanter'. See Jacob in main dictionary.

Yaroslav ♂ Slavic: from *jaro* 'spring' + *slav* 'glory'.

Yefim ♂ From Greek *Euphēmios*, from *eu* 'well, good' + *phēnai* 'to speak'.

Yefrem ♂ From Hebrew *Ephraim* 'fruitful'.

Yegor ♂ Variant of ▶Georgi.

Yekaterina ♀ From Greek *Aikaterinē*. See Katherine in main dictionary.

Yelena ♀ From Greek *Hēlēnē*. See Helen in main dictionary.

Yelisaveta ♀ From Hebrew: 'God is my oath'. See Elizabeth in main dictionary.

Yermolai ♂ From Greek *Hermolaos*, from *Hermēs* (the name of the messenger god) + *lāos* 'people, tribe'. St Hermolaos (d. *c.*300) was martyred in Nicomedia.

Yevgeni ♂ From Greek *Eugenios*. See Eugene in main dictionary.

Yevgenia ♀ Feminine form of ▶Yevgeni.

Yura ♂ Pet form of ▶Yuri.

Yuri ♂ Variant of ▶Georgi.

Zz

Zina ♀ Pet form of ▶Zinaida or ▶Zinovia.

Zinaida ♀ From Greek *Zēnais* 'descended from Zeus'; at least two saints of this name are revered in the Orthodox Church as 1st-century martyrs.

Zinovia ♀ From Greek *Zēnobia* 'life of Zeus'; a St Zenobia was martyred in Asia Minor, together with her brother Zenobios, probably at the beginning of the 3rd century.

Appendix 10:
Scandinavian Names

Aa

Abelone ♀ Danish form of **Apollonia** (see main dictionary).

Agata ♀ From Greek. See Agatha in main dictionary.
ALSO: **Agda** (Swedish); Ågot (Norwegian).

Agnes ♀ From Greek: 'pure, holy'. See main dictionary.

Agnethe ♀ Vernacular form of ►Agnes.
ALSO: **Agnete**.

Ågot ♀ Norwegian variant of ►Agata.

Åke ♂ Of recent origin. Possibly from a Germanic element *ano* 'ancestor'. It has been linked to the Latin name *Achatius* 'agate'.
ALSO: **Åge** (Danish and Norwegian).

Alexander ♂ From Greek: 'defender of men'. See main dictionary.

Alexandra ♀ Feminine form of ►Alexander. See main dictionary.

Algot ♂ From the Old Norse personal name *Alfgautr*, from *alfr* 'elf' + *Gautr* 'Goth'.

Ambjörn ♂ Swedish variant of ►Arnbjörn.
NORWEGIAN SPELLING: Ambjørn.

Åmund ♂ Norwegian: from the Old Norse personal name *Agmundr*, from *ag* 'awe, fear', also 'edge' + *mundr* 'protector'.

Anders ♂ Vernacular form of ►Andreas.

Andreas ♂ Greek. See Andrew in main dictionary.
FEMININE FORM: **Andrea**.

Anna ♀ Biblical. See Anne in main dictionary.
ALSO: **Anne**.

Anneli ♀ Shortened form of the originally German name Anneliese (see German appendix).

Annfrid ♀ Norwegian: from the Old Norse personal name *Arnfríðr*, based on *arn* 'eagle' + *fríðr* 'fair, beautiful'.

Annika ♀ Swedish pet form of ►Anna, apparently derived from the Low German name *Anniken*.

Anton ♂ From the old Roman family name *Antonius*. See Anthony in main dictionary.

Are ♂ From Old Norse *Ari*, originally a byname meaning 'eagle', or else a short form of any of the compound names with this first element.

Arnbjörn ♂ Swedish: from an Old Norse personal name from *arn* 'eagle' + *björn* 'bear'.
ALSO: **Ambjörn**
NORWEGIAN: Arnbjørn.

Arne ♂ Short form of various Old Norse names formed with *arn* 'eagle', e.g. ►Arnbjörn, *Arnfinn*, and *Arnsten*. It is now also used as a given name in its own right.

Arvid ♂ From an Old Norse personal name from *arn* 'eagle' + *viðr* 'wood, tree'.

Åsa ♀ Short form of various Old Norse personal names formed with *áss* 'god'.
ALSO: **Åse** (Norwegian and Danish).

Aslög ♀ Swedish: from an Old Norse personal name from *áss* 'god' + *laug* 'consecrated'.
ALSO: **Åslög**. NORWEGIAN: Åslaug; NORWEGIAN AND DANISH: Aslaug.

Åsmund ♂ From the Old Norse personal name *Ásmundr*, from *áss* 'god' + *mundr* 'protector'.

Asta ♀ Short form of ►Astrid, or a variant of ►Åsta.

Åsta ♀ From the Old Norse personal name *Ásta*, from *ást* 'love'.

Astrid ♀ From Old Norse *áss* 'god' + *fríðr* 'fair, beautiful'.

Aurora ♀ From Latin *aurora* 'dawn', popular in Norway especially.

Axel ♂ Danish form of ►Absalom (see main dictionary), also used in Sweden and Norway.

Bb

Balder ♂ From the name of an Old Norse god, meaning 'prince' or 'ruler'. According to Norse mythology, this was the name of a son of Odin by his wife Frigg, and in some stories Balder was the god of light. His mother persuaded everything in the world to swear an oath not to harm him, but she overlooked the mistletoe. The evil and cunning god Loki persuaded the blind god Hoder to aim a dart made of mistletoe at Balder, and it killed him. He is sometimes taken as a personification of doomed purity and beauty.

Barbro ♀ Swedish and Norwegian equivalent of Barbara (see main dictionary).

Bendik ♂ Norwegian: from Latin *benedictus* 'blessed'. See Benedict in main dictionary.

Bengt ♂ Swedish equivalent of ▸Bendik.

Benjamin ♂ Biblical. See main dictionary.

Berit ♀ Contracted variant of ▸Birgit.

Bernt ♂ Scandinavian equivalent of Bernard. See main dictionary.

Bertil ♂ Either from a Germanic pet form of Berthold (see German appendix) or a Danish form of the same name.

ALSO: Bertel.

Birger ♂ From Old Norse: apparently an agent derivative of *biarga* 'to help'. Earlier forms of the name are *Birghir* and *Byrghir*. It has been in use from the Viking period to the present day, and it may in some cases have been chosen as a masculine form of ▸Birgit.
ALSO: ▸Börje (Swedish).

Birgit ♀ Borrowing of the Irish name *Brighid* (see ▸Bridget in main dictionary). This name owes its enormous popularity in Scandinavia, especially in Sweden, to St Birgitta (1304–73), patron saint of Sweden. She was a noblewoman who bore her husband eight children. After his death, she founded an order of nuns, the 'Bridgettines' or Order of the Most Holy Saviour. She also went to Rome, where she attempted to reform religious life.
ALSO: Berit, Britt, Brit(t)a; Birgitta. DANISH: Birgitte, Birt(h)e.

Birre ♂ Swedish pet form of ▸Birger.

Björn ♂ Swedish: from an Old Norse byname meaning 'bear'. It is also a short form of compound names such as ▸Arnbjörn and ▸Torbjörn.
NORWEGIAN AND DANISH: Bjørn, Bjarne.

Bo ♂ Swedish and Danish: originally a byname for a householder, derived from Old Norse *búa* 'to dwell, have a household'.

Bodil ♀ From an Old Norse personal name from *bót* 'remedy, compensation' + *hildr* 'battle'.
ALSO: Botilda (Latinized); Bothild (Swedish).

Borghild ♀ Mainly Norwegian: from an Old Norse personal name from *borg* 'fortification' + *hildr* 'battle'.

Börje ♂ Swedish variant of ▸Birger, first found in the 16th century.
DANISH AND NORWEGIAN: Børge, Børre.

Bosse ♂ Swedish pet form of ▸Bo.

Bothild ♀ Swedish variant of ▸Bodil.

Botilda ♀ Latinized form of ▸Bodil.

Britt ♀ Contracted form of ▸Birgit.

Broder ♂ Swedish and Danish: from Old Norse *bróðir* 'brother' (formerly a name bestowed on a younger son).
ALSO: Bror.

Cc

Carl ♂ Variant of ▸Karl.

Charlotte ♀ French. See main dictionary.
ALSO: Charlotta.

Christer ♂ Swedish variant of ▸Kristian.

Dd

Dag ♂ From Old Norse *dagr* 'day'.

Dagmar ♀ From the Slavic (male) name *Dragomir*, from *dorog* 'dear' + *meri* 'great' (later taken as the medieval and modern word *mir* 'peace'), reinterpreted as Old Danish *dag* 'day' + *mār* 'maid'. This was the name of a Czech princess (d. 1212), who became queen of Denmark under the official name Margarethe.

Dagny ♀ From an Old Norse personal name derived from *dag* 'day' + *ný* 'new'.
ALSO: **Dagna, Dagne**.

Daniel ♀ Biblical: 'God is my judge'. See main dictionary.

Disa ♀ Old Norse short form of various female personal names containing the final element *dís* 'goddess', e.g. ▶Hjördis, ▶Tordis.

Dorete ♀ Danish equivalent of **Dorothea**. See main dictionary.

Ee

Edvard ♂ Scandinavian form of English Edward. See main dictionary.

Egil ♂ From the Old Norse personal name *Egill*, a diminutive of *ag, eg* 'edge, point'.

Eilif ♂ Norwegian: from an Old Norse personal name from *ei* 'always, ever' or *einn* 'one, alone' + *lífr* 'alive'.

Einar ♂ From an Old Norse personal name from *einn* 'one, alone' + *herr* 'army, warrior'.

Eirik ♂ From the Old Norse personal name *Eirikr*, a compound of *ei* 'ever, always' (or *einn* 'one, alone') + *ríkr* 'ruler'.
ALSO: **Erik**.

Elias ♂ Biblical. See main dictionary.

Elisabet ♀ New Testament: 'God is my oath'. See **Elisabeth** in main dictionary.

Elise ♀ Short form of ▶Elisabet.
ALSO: **Elisa**.

Elof ♂ Swedish: from an Old Norse personal name based on *ei* 'ever, always' or *einn* 'one, alone' + *láfr* 'descendant, heir'.
ALSO: **Elov**.

Emil ♂ From French Émile (see main dictionary).
FEMININE FORM: **Emilie** (see **Emily** in main dictionary).

Erik ♂ Later variant of ▶Eirik, now in frequent use, especially in Sweden.

Erika ♀ Modern female form of ▶Erik.

Erland ♂ From an Old Norse personal name, originally a byname from *örlendr* 'foreigner, stranger'.

Esbjörn ♂ Swedish: from an Old Norse personal name from *áss* 'god' + *björn* 'bear'.
NORWEGIAN: **Esbjørn, Asbjørn**. DANISH: **Esben**.

Ester ♀ Biblical. See **Esther** in main dictionary.

Eyolf ♂ Norwegian: based on Old Norse *anja* 'luck, gift' + *(w)olf* 'wolf'. It became famous as the name of the hero of Ibsen's play *Little Eyolf* (1894) and has been in regular use ever since.

Ff

Filip ♂ From Greek *Philippos* ('love' + 'horses'). See **Philip** in main dictionary.

Finn ♂ From the Old Norse personal name *Finnr*, ethnic byname for a Finn.

Folke ♂ From the Old Norse personal name *Folki*, based on *folk* 'people, tribe' (for example in *Folkvarðr* 'people' + 'guard', which has given rise to the modern forms **Folkvar** and **Falkor**).

Frederik ♂ Danish and Norwegian variant of ▶Fredrik.

Fredrik ♂ Germanic: 'peace' + 'ruler', borne by two 18th-century kings of Sweden: Fredrik I (1720–51) and Adolf Fredrik (1751–71). See **Frederick** in main dictionary.

Freja ♀ Swedish: from an Old Norse word meaning 'lady', the name of the goddess of love in Scandinavian mythology.
NORWEGIAN: Frøya, Freia, Freyja.

Fridtjof ♂ From an Old Norse personal name, from *friðr* 'peace' + *þjófr* 'thief'. The Norwegian explorer Fridtjof Nansen (1861–1930) also served as the League of Nations' high commissioner for refugees and was responsible for the issuing of 'Nansen' passports to stateless persons after the First World War.
ALSO: Fritjof, Fri(d)tjov.

Frode ♂ Danish and Norwegian: from the Old Norse personal name *Fróði*, originally a byname from *fróðr* 'knowing, well-informed'. It was revived *c*.1930.

Frøya ♀ Norwegian: see ▶Freja.

Gg

Gerd ♀ Probably connected with the Old Norse word *garðr* 'enclosure, stronghold'. It was borne in Old Norse mythology by a beautiful goddess who was the wife of Frey; originally a goddess of fertility.
ALSO: Gärd (Swedish).

Gerda ♀ Weak form of ▶Gerd.

Gillis ♂ From Late Latin. Danish and Swedish equivalent of Giles. See main dictionary.

Gislög ♀ Swedish: from an Old Norse personal name based on *gisil* 'hostage' + *laug* 'consecrated'.
NORWEGIAN: Gislaug.

Gitte ♀ Danish: short form of Birgitte (see ▶Birgit).

Gjord ♂ Swedish: reduced form of an (unattested) Old Norse personal name from *guð* 'god' + *friðr* 'peace', or of the German cognate Gottfried (see German appendix).
NORWEGIAN: Gyrd, Jul.

Göran ♂ Swedish variant of ▶Örjan.

Gösta ♂ Swedish: vernacular form of ▶Gustav.

Greger ♂ Scandinavian equivalent of Gregory. See main dictionary.
ALSO: Gregers (Danish and Norwegian).

Gro ♀ From an Old Norse personal name, possibly derived from Norse *gróa* 'to grow', or possibly related to the Celtic element *gruach* 'woman'.

Gudrun ♀ From an Old Norse personal name from *guð* 'god' + *rún* 'rune, secret lore'. It was revived in the second part of the 19th century.

Gull ♀ Pet form of the various women's names of Old Norse origin derived from *guð* 'god' or

gull 'gold'. It is often found in Swedish compound names such as *Gull-Britt*, *Gull-Lis*, and *Gull-Maj*.

Gunder ♂ Danish variant of ▶Gunnar.

Gunilla ♀ Swedish: Latinized form of ▶Gunnhild, in use from the 16th century to the present day. It was particularly popular in Sweden during the 1940s.

Gunn ♀ Short form of the various women's names of Old Norse origin with the first element *gunnr* 'strife', e.g. ▶Gunnborg, ▶Gunnhild, and ▶Gunnvor.
ALSO: Gun.

Gunnar ♂ Scandinavian equivalent of Gunther (see German appendix). The name is of West Germanic, not Old Norse, origin but has been used in Scandinavia since the time of the sagas at least.
ALSO: Gunder (Danish).

Gunnborg ♀ From an Old Norse personal name based on *gunnr* 'strife' + *borg* 'fortification'.
ALSO: Gunborg.

Gunne ♂, ♀ From Old Norse *Gunni*, a short form of ▶Gunnar and other (rarer) male names formed with *gunnr* 'strife', such as Gunnbjörn (+ 'bear') and Gunnleif (+ 'descendant'). In Norway it is occasionally used as a female name, from Old Norse *Gunna*, a short form of the various female names containing this same element.

Gunnhild ♀ From an Old Norse personal name from *gunnr* 'strife' + *hildr* 'battle'. The name has been in common use since the Viking period.
ALSO: **Gunhild**.

Gunnvor ♀ From an Old Norse personal name from *gunnr* 'strife' + *vor* 'cautious'.
ALSO: **Gunvor**; **Gunver** (chiefly Danish).

Guro ♀ Norwegian: pet form of ▶Gudrun.

Gustav ♂ Most probably from an Old Norse personal name from *Gautr* 'Goth' + *stafr* 'staff'. It has been borne by several kings of Sweden, beginning with Gustav Vasa (?1496–1560), who was elected king in 1523 after freeing Sweden from Danish rule.
ALSO: **Gustavus** (Latinized); **Gustaf**, **Gösta** (Swedish).

Gyrd ♂ Norwegian: see ▶Gjord.

Hh

Hagen ♂ Danish form of ▶Håkon.

Håkon ♂ Norwegian: from the Old Norse personal name *Hákon*, from *há* 'horse' or 'high' + *konr* 'son, descendant'; borne by

Haakon VII of Norway (1872–1957), and by Crown Prince Haakon Magnus (b. 1973).
SWEDISH: **Håkan**. DANISH: **Hakon**, **Hagen**.

Halfdan ♂ From an Old Norse personal name, originally a byname for someone who was part Danish (from Old Norse *hálfr* 'half' + *Danr* 'Dane').
ALSO: **Halvdan**.

Halldor ♂ From an Old Norse personal name from *hallr* 'rock' + *þórr* name of the god of thunder.

Halle ♂ Short form of names formed with *Hall-*, e.g. ▶Halldor, ▶Hallstein.

Hallstein ♂ Mainly Norwegian: from an Old Norse personal name from *hallr* 'rock' + *steinn* 'stone'.
ALSO: **Halstein**. SWEDISH: ▶Hal(l)sten.

Halvard ♂ From an Old Norse personal name from *hallr* 'rock' + *varðr* 'guardian, defender'.
ALSO: **Halvor**; **Hallvard**, **Hallvor** (Norwegian); **Halvar** (Swedish).

Halvdan ♂ Variant of ▶Halfdan.

Hanna ♀ Either the biblical name (see Hannah in main dictionary) or a short form of ▶Johanna.
ALSO: **Hanne**.

Harald ♂ From the Old Norse personal name *Haraldr*, meaning 'army

leader', cognate with English Harold (see main dictionary).

Härlief ♂ Variant of ▶Herleif.

Håvard ♂ Norwegian: from the Old Norse personal name *Hávarðr* 'high' + 'protector'.

Hedda ♀ Pet form of ▶Hedvig; the name of the heroine of Henrik Ibsen's play *Hedda Gabler* (1890).

Hedvig ♀ Scandinavian equivalent of Hedwig 'battle strife' (see German appendix), borne by the young girl who is the central character in Henrik Ibsen's play *The Wild Duck* (1886).

Helene ♀ From Greek *Hēlēnē*. See Helen in main dictionary.

Helga ♀ Feminine form of ▶Helge.
ALSO: **Hella**.

Helge ♂ From an early medieval personal name, a derivative of *heilagr* 'prosperous'. The popularity of the name greatly increased with the subsequent change in meaning of the vocabulary word to 'blessed, holy'.
ALSO: **Helje** (Danish).

Hemming ♂ Probably a derivative of Old Norse *hamr* 'shape', and thus a byname for a 'shape changer', i.e. a werewolf.
ALSO: **Heming**.

Hendrik ♂ Variant of ▶Henrik.

Henning ♂ Danish: derivative (originally patronymic in form) of a short form of ▸Henrik and also of ▸Johannes.

Henrik ♂ Scandinavian equivalent of Henry (see main dictionary and Heinrich in German appendix), especially common in Denmark.

Herleif ♂ From an Old Norse personal name from *herr* 'army' + *leifr* 'heir, descendant'.
ALSO: Härlief, Herlof, Herluf, Herleiv.

Hillevi ♀ Mainly Danish: reworking of German Heilwig 'safe war'. See German appendix.

Hjalmar ♂ From an Old Norse personal name from *hjálmr* 'helmet, protection' + *herr* 'army, warrior'.

Hjördis ♀ From an Old Norse personal name from *hjǫrr* 'sword' + *dís* 'goddess'.

Hogge ♂ Pet form of ▸Holger.

Holger ♂ From an Old Norse personal name from *hólmr* 'island' + *geirr* 'spear'. It was borne by one of Charlemagne's generals, known in English as 'Ogier the Dane'.

Hulda ♀ 18th-century derivation of *huld* 'sweet, lovable'.

Ii

Ib ♂ Danish: probably a contracted form of Jep,

vernacular form of ▸Jacob (see main dictionary).

Ingeborg ♀ From an Old Norse personal name from the name of the fertility god *Ing* + *borg* 'fortification'.

Ingegerd ♀ From an Old Norse personal name from the name of the fertility god *Ing* + *garðr* 'enclosure, stronghold'.
ALSO: Ingegärd (Swedish).

Ingemar ♂ From an Old Norse personal name from the name of the fertility god *Ing* + *mærr* 'famous'.
ALSO: Ingmar.

Inger ♀ Variant of ▸Ingegerd and ▸Ingrid, attested from the 16th-century.

Ingrid ♀ From an Old Norse personal name from the name of the fertility god *Ing* + *fríðr* 'beautiful'.

Ingvar ♂ From an Old Norse personal name from the name of the fertility god *Ing(w)-* + *arr* 'warrior'.
ALSO: Yngvar.

Isak ♂ Biblical: 'hireling'. See Isaac in main dictionary.

Ivar ♂ From an Old Norse personal name from *ýr* 'yew, bow' + *herr* 'army, warrior'.
ALSO: Iver (Danish).

Jj

Jakob ♂ Biblical. See Jacob in main dictionary.

Jan ♂ Contracted form of ▸Johan.

Jannike ♀ Probably a derivative of French *Jeannique*, a diminutive of Jeanne (see French appendix), or a pet form of local forms of ▸Johanna.

Jens ♂ Mainly Danish: variant of ▸Johan.
SWEDISH: Jöns.

Jensine ♀ Danish and Norwegian: feminine form of ▸Jens.

Jerker ♂ Swedish: dialect form of ▸Erik, formerly found mainly in the Uppland region.
ALSO: Jerk.

Joakim ♂ Biblical: 'established by God'. See Joachim in main dictionary.
ALSO: Jokum (Norwegian and Danish).

Johan ♂ Vernacular form of ▸Johannes.
ALSO: Jan; Jens (Norwegian and Danish); Jöns, Jon.

Johanna ♀ Latinate feminine form of ▸Johan.
ALSO: Jonna (Danish).

Johanne ♀ Danish and Norwegian feminine form of ▸Johan.

Johannes ♂ New Testament: 'God is gracious'. See John in main dictionary.

Jokum ♂ Danish variant of ▸Joakim.

Jon ♂ Contracted form of ▸Johan.

Jonas ♂ See main dictionary.

Jonna ♂ Danish: contracted form of ▶Johanna.

Jöran ♂ Variant of ▶Örjan also Jörn.

Jørgen ♂ Danish equivalent of ▶George, though possibly via a Latinate elaboration *Georgianus*, rather than directly from *Georgius*. This is a common name throughout Scandinavia. ALSO: **Jørn**.

Josef ♂ Biblical: '(God) shall add (another son)'. See Josef in main dictionary.

Josefa ♀ Feminine form of ▶Josef. (see Joseph in main dictionary).

Jul ♂ Norwegian form of ▶Gjord.

Kk

Kai ♂ Mainly Danish: popular name of uncertain origin. A connection with the Old Norse word *kaða* 'hen', or the Roman name *Caius* (see Cayo in Spanish appendix) has been suggested. ALSO: **Kaj**.

Kåre ♂ From the Old Norse personal name *Kári*, originally a byname meaning 'curly-haired'.

Karen ♀ Danish equivalent of Katherine. See main dictionary.

Kari ♀ Norwegian equivalent of Katherine. See main dictionary.

Karin ♀ Swedish and Norwegian equivalent of Katherine. See main dictionary.

Karita ♀ From the Late Latin name *Caritas* 'charity'. See Charity in main dictionary.

Karl ♂ Germanic: 'free man'; the name of numerous kings of Sweden. See Charles in main dictionary and Karl in German appendix. ALSO: **Carl**.

Karla ♀ Feminine form of ▶Karl.

Karolina ♀ From Latin. See Caroline in main dictionary.

Kaspar ♂ The usual Scandinavian form of Caspar. See main dictionary.

Katarina ♀ Scandinavian equivalent of Katherine. See main dictionary.

Keld ♂ Danish form of ▶Kjell.

Kerstin ♀ Variant of ▶Kristine.

Ketil ♂ Variant of ▶Kjetil.

Kirsten ♀ Danish and Norwegian variant of ▶Kristine.

Kjell ♂ Norwegian and Swedish: contracted form of ▶Kjetil. DANISH: **K(j)eld**.

Kjetil ♂ Mainly Norwegian: modern

form of Kettil, from the Old Norse name *Ketill*, a short form of various compound names formed with *ketill* 'kettle, sacrificial cauldron', e.g. *Thorketill* (see ▶Torkel), *Arnketill*. ALSO: **Ketil**.

Klemens ♂ From Late Latin *Clemens* 'merciful'. See Clement in main dictionary.

Knud ♂ Danish form of ▶Knut.

Knut ♂ Norwegian and Swedish: from Old Norse *Knútr* 'knot', originally a byname given to a short, squat man. King Knut (d. 1035) ruled over Denmark, Norway, and England in the 11th century; he is known in English as *Canute*. His great-nephew Knut (d. 1086) was another king of Denmark; he was murdered by opponents of the laws enforcing payment of tithes to the Church and was canonized as a martyr. His nephew, also Knut (d. 1131), was Duke of Schleswig and is also venerated as a martyr, although for what reason is not clear.

Konstantin ♂ From Late Latin *Constantinus*. See Constantine in main dictionary.

Kristen ♂ Danish and Norwegian variant of ▶Kristian.

Kristian ♂ From Latin. See Christian in main dictionary.

Kristina ♀ From a feminine form of Latin *Christianus* (see **Christina** in main dictionary). Queen Kristina of Sweden (1626–89) succeeded her father Gustavus Adolphus in 1632. Growing to adulthood, she presided over a glittering court, but in 1654 she abdicated, left Sweden dressed as a man, converted to Roman Catholicism, and lived for most of the rest of her life in Rome.

Kristine ♀ Variant of ▶Kristina.
ALSO: **Kerstin; Kirsten** (Danish and Norwegian).

Kristoffer ♂ From Greek. See ▶Christopher in main dictionary.

L|

Lars ♂ Scandinavian equivalent of **Laurence** (see main dictionary); one of the most perennially popular names in Sweden and Denmark.

Leif ♂ From Old Norse *Leifr*, a short form of various compound names containing the second element *leifr* 'heir, descendant'.

Leiv ♂ Norwegian variant of ▶Leif. Leiv Eiriksson was a Norse navigator who, in around 1000, discovered the New World.

Lennart ♂ Scandinavian equivalent

of **Leonard**. See main dictionary.

Linnéa ♀ Swedish: popular given name first bestowed in honour of the Swedish botanist Carl von *Linné* (1707–78; Latinized as *Linnaeus*). He gave his name to the now internationally recognized *Linnaean* system of taxonomic classification, and to a type of flower known as *Linnaea*.

Lis ♀ Much reduced form of ▶Elisabet, first used in the early years of the 20th century and frequently found as the second element of compound names such as *Anne-Lis*, *Ing-Lis*, and *Maj-Lis*.

Liv ♀ From an Old Norse personal name identical in form with the vocabulary word *hlíf* 'defence, protection'. In modern use it is often associated with Norwegian *liv* 'life', and is sometimes taken as a short form of ▶Elisabet.

Lone ♀ Danish: short form of ▶Abelone and *Magdelone* (see **Magdalen** in main dictionary), now very commonly used as an independent name.

Lovisa ♀ Scandinavian equivalent of **Louisa** (see main dictionary), used mainly in Sweden.
ALSO: **Lovise** (Norwegian and Danish).

Ludvig ♂ See **Ludwig** in German appendix.

Mm

Mads ♂ Danish and Norwegian equivalent of **Matthew**. See main dictionary.

Magnus ♂ Latin. See main dictionary.

Mai ♀ Pet form of ▶Maria and ▶Margit, now also used as an independent given name and as an element of compound names such as *Mai-Britt*, *Mai-Lis*, *Anne-Mai*, and *Britt-Mai*.

Malvina ♀ See main dictionary.

Måns ♂ Swedish vernacular form of ▶Magnus.

Marcus ♂ Latin. See main dictionary.

Margareta ♀ From the Latin form of Greek *Margarítēs*. See **Margaret** in main dictionary.
ALSO: **Margaretha; Margrethe.**

Margit ♀ Vernacular form of ▶Margareta.

Maria ♀ New Testament. See main dictionary.
ALSO: **Marie.**

Marit ♀ Norwegian and Swedish: vernacular form of ▶Margareta.

Marna ♀ Swedish: contracted form of ▶Marina. See main dictionary.

Märta ♀ Danish: contracted form of *Märeta*, an obsolete variant of ▶Merete. The name is also popular in Sweden.

Martha ♀ New Testament. See main dictionary.
ALSO: **Marta, Mart(h)e**.

Mårten ♂ Swedish equivalent of Martin. See main dictionary.

Mathias ♂ Danish and Norwegian: learned doublet of ▶Mads.
ALSO: **Mathies**.

Matilda ♀ Mainly Swedish. See main dictionary.
ALSO: **Mathilda** (mainly Swedish), **Mat(h)ilde** (mainly Danish).

Mats ♂ Norwegian and Swedish equivalent of Matthew. See main dictionary.

Mattias ♂ Danish and Norwegian common variant spelling of ▶Mathias.

Maurits ♂ From Late Latin *Mauricius*. See Maurice in main dictionary.

Merete ♀ Danish: vernacular form of ▶Margareta.
ALSO: **Mereta, Mette**.

Meta ♀ Swedish and Danish: pet form of ▶Margareta. It was very popular in the 19th and early 20th centuries, but is now perceived as old-fashioned.

Mia ♀ Swedish and Danish: pet form of ▶Maria.

Mikael ♂ Biblical. See ▶Michael in main dictionary.
ALSO: **Mikal; Mikkel** (Norwegian and Danish).

Mogens ♂ Danish vernacular form of ▶Magnus.

Monika ♀ See Monica in main dictionary.

Morten ♂ Norwegian and Danish equivalent of Martin. See main dictionary.

Nn

Nanna ♀ From an Old Norse personal name, *Nanna*, a derivative of *nanþ* 'daring'.

Nanne ♂ Swedish: originally a short form of the Old Norse personal name *Nannulf*, based on *nanþ* 'daring' + *ulfr* 'wolf'. Nowadays it is used as a pet form of ▶Anders.

Niels ♂ Danish vernacular form of ▶Niklas.

Niklas ♂ Scandinavian learned equivalent of Nicholas. See main dictionary.

Nils ♂ Norwegian and Swedish vernacular form of ▶Niklas.
ALSO: **Nels** (S. Swedish).

Nilsine ♀ Feminine form of ▶Nils.

Njord ♂ The name of a minor Norse deity, of

uncertain derivation; it is recorded in the form *Nerthus* by the Roman historian Tacitus in the 1st century AD. It was revived as a given name in the early 19th-century.

Oo

Odd ♂ From an Old Norse personal name, originally perhaps a byname, derived from *oddr* 'point (of a weapon)'. Occasionally in modern use it may also be a short form of compound names with this as the first element, such as **Oddbjørn** (+ 'bear').

Ola ♂ Norwegian variant of ▶Olaf, also widely used in southwest Sweden.

Olaf ♂ From an Old Norse personal name, *Óláfr*, derived from *anu* 'ancestor' + *leifr* 'heir, descendant'. St Olaf, King of Norway (995–1030), encouraged the adoption of Christianity in his kingdom. In modern times it was borne by King Olav of Norway (1903–1991).
ALSO: **Olav** (Norwegian and Danish); **Ole, Oluf** (Danish); ▶Olof, Olov (Swedish); **Ola** (Norwegian and Swedish); **Olaus, Olai** (Latinized forms).

Olof ♂ Swedish form of ▶Olaf. St Olof, King of Sweden (d. *c.*950) was murdered by his rebellious heathen subjects for refusing to sacrifice to idols.

Örjan ♂ From *Jurian*, a Scandinavian equivalent of **George** (see main dictionary).

Oskar ♂ Scandinavian form of Irish **Oscar** (see main dictionary); the name of two 19th-century kings of Sweden.

Ove ♂ Originally a Danish vernacular form of *Aghi*, a short form of the various names of Old Norse origin containing the element *ag* 'edge (of a weapon)' or 'awe, terror'.

Pp

Pål ♂ Swedish and Norwegian: from Old Norse *Páll*, from Latin *Paulus* (see **Paul** in main dictionary); in use as a given name in Norway since *c*.1100.
ALSO: **Påvel** (Swedish).
DANISH: **Poul**.

Pär ♂ Swedish vernacular form of ▶**Peter**.

Påvel ♂ Swedish variant of ▶**Pål**.

Pella ♀ Swedish: much contracted form of ▶**Pernilla**.

Pelle ♂ Swedish: pet form of ▶**Per**.

Per ♂ Danish and Norwegian vernacular form of ▶**Peter**.

Pernilla ♀ Swedish: contracted form of Latin *Petronilla*. See **Petronel** in main dictionary.
DANISH: **Pernille**.

Peter ♂ From Greek. See main dictionary.
ALSO: **Petter**.

Poul ♂ Danish equivalent of **Paul**. See main dictionary.

Preben ♂ Danish: from medieval Danish *Pridbjørn*, a reworking (influenced by ▶**Bjørn** 'bear') of Slavic *Pritbor* (from *prid* 'foremost' + *bor* 'battle').

Rr

Ragna ♀ From the Old Norse personal name *Ragna*, a short form of the various female compound names formed with *regin* 'advice, decision' (also, 'the gods'), for example ▶**Ragnhild**. The name, used in the Viking period, was revived in the late 19th century. In modern use it is usually taken as a feminine form of ▶**Ragnar**.

Ragnar ♂ From an Old Norse personal name cognate with **Rayner**. See main dictionary.
ALSO: **Regner** (Danish).

Ragnborg ♀ From an Old Norse personal name from *regin* 'advice, decision' (also, 'the gods') + *borg* 'fortification'.
ALSO: **Ramborg** (Swedish).

Ragnhild ♀ From an Old Norse personal name from *regin* 'advice,

decision' (also, 'the gods') + *hildr* 'battle'.
ALSO: **Ragnild**.

Ragnvald ♂ From the Old Norse personal name *Rögnvaldr*, from *regin* 'advice, decision' (also, 'the gods') + *valdr* 'ruler'. Compare **Ronald** in main dictionary.

Rakel ♀ Biblical. See **Rachel** in main dictionary.

Ramborg ♀ Swedish variant of ▶**Ragnborg**.

Regner ♂ The usual Danish form of ▶**Ragnar**.

Reine ♂ Swedish short form of the (originally German) given names ▶**Reinhard** and ▶**Reinhold**.

Reinhard ♂ German name used in Sweden. See German appendix.

Reinhold ♂ German name used in Sweden. See German appendix.

Rigborg ♀ Danish: from an Old High German personal name from *rīc* 'power' + *burg* 'fortification'.

Rigmor ♀ Danish: from an Old High German personal name from *rīc* 'power' + *muot* 'spirit, courage' (the latter replaced by Scandinavian *mār* 'maid').

Rikard ♂ Germanic. See **Richard** in main dictionary.
ALSO: **Rikhard**.

Roald ♂ Norwegian: from Old Norse *hróðr* 'fame' + *valdr* 'ruler'.

Roar ♂ Germanic. See Roger in main dictionary.

Robert ♂ Germanic. See main dictionary.

Rosmarie ♀ Scandinavian equivalent of Rosemary. See main dictionary.

Ruben ♂ Biblical: 'behold, a son'. See Reuben in main dictionary.

Runa ♀ From Old Norse *Rúna*, a short form of various female compound names formed with *rún* 'rune, secret lore'.

Rune ♂ From Old Norse *Rúni*, a short form of various male compound names formed with *rún* 'rune, secret lore', for example *Rúnólfr*. It has been very popular since the 20th century.

Rut ♀ Biblical. See Ruth in main dictionary. ALSO: **Rutt**.

Ss

Sander ♀ Short form of ►Alexander, now popular as an independent given name, especially in Norway.

Sanna ♀ Short form of ►Susanna, perhaps influenced by the word *sann* 'true'.

Sara ♀ Biblical. See Sarah in main dictionary.

Sassa ♀ Swedish: pet form of both ►Astrid and ►Sara.

Sebastian ♂ From Latin *Sebastianus*. See main dictionary.

Sigbjörn ♂ Swedish: from an Old Norse personal name from *sigr* 'victory' + *björn* 'bear'. NORWEGIAN: **Sigbjørn**.

Sigmund ♂ From an Old Norse personal name from *sigr* 'victory' + *mund* 'protector'.

Signy ♀ From an Old Norse personal name from *sigr* 'victory' + *ný* 'new'. ALSO: **Signi, Signe**.

Sigrid ♀ From an Old Norse personal name from *sigr* 'victory' + *friðr* 'beautiful'.

Sigrun ♀ From an Old Norse personal name from *sigr* 'victory' + *'rún* 'secret lore'.

Sigurd ♂ From an Old Norse personal name from *sigr* 'victory' + *vöðr* 'guardian'.

Silje ♀ Danish and Norwegian form of *Silja*, Finnish equivalent of Cecilia. See main dictionary.

Simon ♂ New Testament. See main dictionary. ALSO: **Simen** (Norwegian).

Siri ♀ Norwegian: reduced form of ►Sigrid.

Sissel ♀ Scandinavian (mainly Norwegian)

equivalent of Cicely (see main dictionary).

Siv ♀ From Old Norse, originally a byname meaning 'bride, wife'; in mythology the name of Thor's golden-haired wife.

Sixten ♀ Swedish: from an Old Norse personal name from *sigr* 'victory' + *steinn* 'stone'.

Sjur ♂ Norwegian: reduced form of ►Sigurd. ALSO: **Sjurd**.

Sofia ♀ Norwegian and Swedish variant spelling of ►Sophia. ALSO: **Sofie**.

Solveig ♀ Norwegian: from an Old Norse personal name derived from *salr* 'house' + *veig* 'strength'. SWEDISH: **Solvig**; DANISH: **Solvej**.

Sondre ♂ Norwegian: from the Old Norse personal name *Sindri* (of uncertain derivation and meaning), borne in Norse mythology by a dwarf who, with his brother Brokk, crafted various treasures with magical properties.

Sophia ♀ Greek: 'wisdom'. See main dictionary.

Sören ♂ Danish and Norwegian derivative of *Severinus* (see Severino in Spanish appendix).

Stefan ♂ From Greek *stephanos* 'garland,

crown'. See ▶Stephen in main dictionary.
ALSO: **Staffan** (Swedish); **Steffen** (Norwegian).

Stein ♂ Norwegian: from a short form of an Old Norse personal name formed with *steinn* 'stone'.
SWEDISH: **Sten**; DANISH: **Ste(e)n**.

Stian ♂ From the Old Norse personal name *Stígandr*, originally a byname meaning 'wanderer'. As a modern name, it is taken as a short form of ▶Kristian.

Stig ♂ From the Old Norse personal name *Stígr*, a short form of *Stígandr* (see ▶Stian).

Sture ♂ Swedish: from a medieval byname from *stura* 'to be wilful or independent-minded'.

Sunniva ♀ Latinized form of the Old English personal name *Sunngifu*, from *sunne* 'sun' + *gifu* 'gift'. According to legend, this was the name of an Irish princess (died AD 900), who fled from Ireland to escape marriage to a pagan. She hid in a cave on the island of Selje in Western Norway, where she became entombed; she was later revered as a saint and a church was built on the site. See also ▶Synnøve.

Susanna ♀ New Testament: 'lily'. See main dictionary.

Svanhild ♀ Mainly Norwegian: from an Old

Saxon personal name composed of *swan* 'swan' + *hild* 'battle'.

Svea ♀ Swedish: patriotic name formed in the 19th century from the former name of Sweden, *Svearike* (now *Sverige*).

Sven ♂ Swedish: from the Old Norse byname *Sveinn* 'boy, lad'.
NORWEGIAN: **Svein**; DANISH: **Svend**.

Sverre ♂ Norwegian: from the Old Norse personal name *Sverrir*, originally apparently a byname from *sverra* 'to spin or swirl about'.

Sylvia ♀ See Silvia in main dictionary.

Synnøve ♀ Norwegian vernacular form of ▶Sunniva.
ALSO: **Synneva**, **Synnøv**, **Synne**. SWEDISH: **Synnöve**.

Tt

Tage ♂ Danish: from Old Danish *Taki*, originally a byname meaning 'guarantor' or 'receiver' (from *taka* 'to take').

Tekla ♀ From Greek *Theokleia*. See Thecla in main dictionary.

Teodor ♂ Norwegian and Swedish equivalent of Theodore. See main dictionary.

Terje ♂ Variant of *Torgeir*; see ▶Torger.

Thomas ♂ New Testament. See main dictionary.

ALSO: **Tomas**.

Thorkel ♂ Norwegian and Swedish: variant spelling of ▶Torkel.

Thorstein(n) ♂ Older forms of ▶Torsten.

Thorwald ♂ (Older) variant spelling of ▶Torvald.

Tilde ♀ Short form of *Mathilde*; see ▶Matilda.
ALSO: **Tilda** (Swedish).

Tobias ♂ Biblical: 'God is good'. See main dictionary.

Tor ♂ Originally the name of the god of thunder in Norse mythology, Thor (Old Norse *Þórr*). It was not used as a personal name during the Middle Ages. The modern name is either a late 18th-century revival of the god's name or else a vernacular development of ▶Tord.
ALSO: **Thor** (chiefly Danish).

Torbjörn ♂ Swedish: from an Old Norse personal name, from *Þórr* (see ▶Tor) + *björn* 'bear'.
NORWEGIAN: **Torbjørn**; DANISH: **T(h)orbjørn**, **Torbe(r)n**.

Torborg ♀ From an Old Norse personal name, from *Þórr* (see ▶Tor) + *borg* 'fortification'.
ALSO: **Thorborg**; **Torbjørg** (Norwegian).

Tord ♂ Reduced form of Old Norse *Þorfriðr*, from

þórr (see ▶Tor) + friðr 'peace'.

Tordis ♀ From an Old Norse personal name from þórr (see ▶Tor) + dís 'goddess'.

Tore ♂ From the Old Norse personal name þórir (perhaps from þórr; see ▶Tor) + verr 'man'. As early as the Viking period, however, þóri was used as a short form of all compound names beginning with þórr.
ALSO: **Ture** (Swedish).

Torger ♂ Norwegian: from an Old Norse personal name based on the name of the god þórr (Thor) + geirr 'spear'.
ALSO: **Torgeir, Terje**.

Torkel ♂ Norwegian and Swedish: from a contracted form of the Old Norse personal name þorketill, from þórr (see ▶Tor) + ketill 'kettle, helmet'.
ALSO: **Torkil, Thorkel; Torkjell** (Norwegian).
DANISH: **Torkil(d)**.

Torolf ♂ From an Old Norse personal name from þórr (see ▶Tor) + úlfr 'wolf'.
ALSO: **Torulf; Torolv** (Norwegian).

Torsten ♂ Swedish and Danish: from an Old Norse personal name, from þórr (see ▶Tor) + steinn 'stone'.
ALSO: **Thorstein(n)** (older forms). NORWEGIAN: **Torstein**.

Torvald ♂ From an Old Norse personal name from þórr (see

▶Tor) + Old Norse valdr 'ruler'.
ALSO: **Thorwald**.

Tova ♀ From the Old Norse personal name Tófa, a short form of þorfriðr (see ▶Turid).
ALSO: **Tove** (Danish), **Tuva** (Norwegian).

Tove ♀ Mainly Danish variant of ▶Tova.

Trond ♂ Norwegian: from an Old Norse byname for someone from Trøndelag in central Norway.
ALSO: **Tron**.

Tryggve ♂ Mainly Norwegian: from an Old Norse personal name, originally a byname from the adjective tryggr 'true, trusty'.
ALSO: **Trygve**.

Ture ♂ Swedish variant of ▶Tore.

Turid ♀ Norwegian: from an Old Norse personal name from þórr (see ▶Tor) + friðr 'beautiful'.

Tuva ♀ Mainly Norwegian variant of ▶Tova.
ALSO: **Tuve**.

Uu

Uffe ♂ Danish variant of ▶Ulf.

Ulf ♂ Danish and Swedish: from Old Norse Úlfr 'wolf'. See **Wolf** in main dictionary.
ALSO: **Uffe** (Danish).
NORWEGIAN: **Ulv**.

Ulrik ♂ From German. See Ulrich in German appendix.

Ulrika ♀ Feminine form of ▶Ulrik.

Ulv ♂ Norwegian spelling of ▶Ulf.

Vv

Valdemar ♂ Danish and Swedish derivative of Vladimir. See Russian appendix.
ALSO: **Waldemar**.

Valentin ♂ Swedish and Danish vernacular form of Latin Valentinus. See Valentine in main dictionary.

Valter ♂ Variant spelling of ▶Walter.

Veronika ♀ From Latin. See Veronica in main dictionary.

Vidkun ♂ Norwegian: from an Old Norse personal name from víðr 'wide' + kunnr 'wise, experienced', now rarely used, as it was borne by Vidkun Quisling (1887–1945), the Norwegian collaborator with the Nazis.

Vigdis ♀ Mainly Norwegian: from an Old Norse personal name from víg 'war' + dís 'goddess'.

Viggo ♂ Latinized form of the Old Danish personal name Vigge, a short form of various compound names beginning with *víg* 'war'.

Viktor ♂ Latin: 'conqueror'. See Victor in main dictionary.

Viktoria ♀ Scandinavian equivalent of Victoria. See main dictionary.

Vilfred ♂ Scandinavian equivalent of Wilfrid. See main dictionary.

Vilhelm ♂ Scandinavian form of William (see main dictionary), from Old Norse *Vilhjalmr*. The name was borrowed from English *c.*1100.

Vincent ♂ Swedish and Danish. See main dictionary.

Ww

Waldemar ♂ Variant spelling of ▶Valdemar.

Walter ♂ From German: 'rule' + 'army'. See main dictionary.

Yy

Yngvar ♂ Variant of ▶Ingvar.

Appendix 11:
Scottish Names

Aa

Adaidh ♂ Gaelic spelling of ▸Adie.

Àdhamh ♂ Scottish Gaelic equivalent of Adam. See main dictionary.

Adie ♂ Pet form of Adam (see main dictionary) or, less commonly, of ▸Aidan.

Aidan ♂ Anglicized spelling of the ancient Gaelic name Áedán, a pet form of Áed (see ▸Aodh). See also main dictionary. ALSO: **Aedan, Edan.**

Ailbeart ♂ Scottish Gaelic equivalent of Albert. See main dictionary.

Ailean ♂ Scottish Gaelic equivalent of Alan. See main dictionary.

Aileen ♀ Mainly Scottish variant spelling of Eileen. See main dictionary.

Ailie ♀ Pet form of ▸Aileen or an Anglicized spelling of ▸Eilidh.

Ailig ♂ See ▸Alick.

Ailpein ♂ Traditional name, which has been borne in the Highlands from the time of the earliest historical records; it has no obvious Gaelic etymology, and is therefore often taken to be of Pictish origin.

Ailsa ♀ Modern name taken from the name of the rocky islet *Ailsa Craig*, which is from Old Norse *Alfsigesey* 'island of *Alfsigr*' (a personal name derived from *alf* 'elf, supernatural being' + *sigi* 'victory'). Use as a given name has been influenced by ▸Ealasaid.

Aindrea ♂ Scottish Gaelic equivalent of Andrew. See main dictionary.

Alasdair ♂ Scottish Gaelic equivalent of Alexander. See main dictionary. ALSO: **Alistair, Allaster** (Anglicized forms).

Alec ♂ Short form of Alexander. See main dictionary.

Alexina ♀ Elaborated form of Alex (see main dictionary), used in the Highlands as an unambiguously female name.

Alick ♂ Variant of ▸Alec, now sometimes used as a given name in its own right. In the Highlands the form *Ellic* was also formerly in use; the Gaelic form is Ailig.

Alickina ♀ Feminine form of ▸Alick, used in the Highlands.

Alistair ♂ Anglicized form of ▸Alasdair.

Allaster ♂ Anglicized form of ▸Alasdair, borne, for example, by a minstrel in Sir Walter Scott's *Rob Roy*

(1818), which ensured its 19th-century popularity.

Alpin ♂ Anglicized form of ▸Ailpein. ALSO: **Alpine.**

Amhladh ♀ Scottish Gaelic form of Olaf. See Scandinavian appendix. ALSO: **Amhlaidh; Aulay** (Anglicized form).

Angie ♂ Pet form of ▸Angus, pronounced 'an-ghee', representing Gaelic Angaidh.

Angus ♂ Anglicized form of ▸Aonghas.

Anndra ♂ Scottish Gaelic equivalent of Andrew. See main dictionary.

Aodh ♂ Modern form of the Old Irish name *Áed*, meaning 'fire'; the name of the Celtic sun god and a common personal name from the earliest times.

Aoife ♀ Probably a derivative of Gaelic *aoibh* 'beauty', but it has also been associated with *Esuvia*, a Gaulish goddess.

Aonghas ♂ Pronounced 'een-yis'; from Celtic words meaning 'one' and 'choice'. This is the name of an ancient Celtic god, and is first recorded as a personal name in Adomnan's 'Life of St Columba', where it occurs in the form *Oinogus(s)ius* as the name

of a man for whom the saint prophesied a long life and a peaceful death. This is also almost certainly the name of the 8th-century Pictish king variously recorded as *Onnust* and *Hungus*.
ALSO: Aonghus; Angus (Anglicized form).

Arailt ♂ Scottish Gaelic equivalent of Harold. See main dictionary.

Archibald ♂ Of Norman French origin, from a Germanic (Frankish) personal name derived from *ercan* 'genuine' + *bald* 'bold, brave'. It has long been associated with Scotland, where it is in regular use as the English equivalent of Gaelic *Gilleasbaig* (see ▶Gillespie).
VARIANT: Archibold.

Archie ♂ Pet form of ▶Archibald, adopted as an independent given name from the 19th century.

Arran ♂ Modern name, apparently taken from the name of the Isle of Arran off the west coast of Scotland.

Artair ♂ Scottish Gaelic equivalent of Arthur. See main dictionary.

Atholl ♂, ♀ Transferred use of the place name denoting a district of Perthshire, thought to derive its name from Gaelic *ath Fodla* 'new Ireland'.

Aulay ♂ Anglicized form of *Amhla(i)dh*; see ▶Amhladh.

Bb

Baldie ♂ Pet form of ▶Archibald.

Bean ♂ Anglicized form of ▶Beathan.

Bearnard ♂ Scottish Gaelic equivalent of Bernard. See main dictionary.

Bearnas ♀ Scottish Gaelic equivalent of Berenice (see main dictionary), often considered a feminine equivalent of ▶Bearnard.

Beathag ♀ Feminine form of ▶Beathan.

Beathan ♂ Traditional: derivative of Gaelic *beatha* 'life'; sometimes Anglicized as Benjamin (see main dictionary).

Beileag ♀ Pet form of ▶Iseabail.

Beistean ♂ Pet form of *Gille Easbaig*. See ▶Gillespie.

Beitidh ♀ Scottish Gaelic equivalent of Betty. See main dictionary.

Beitiris ♀ Scottish Gaelic equivalent of Beatrice. See main dictionary.

Benneit ♂ Scottish Gaelic equivalent of Benedict. See main dictionary.

Bhàtair ♂ Scottish Gaelic equivalent of Walter. See main dictionary.
ALSO: Bhaltair.

Bhictoria ♀ Scottish Gaelic equivalent of Victoria. See main dictionary.

Blair ♂ Transferred use of the surname, in origin a local name from any of various places named with Gaelic *blàr* 'plain, field'. See also main dictionary.

Cc

Cairistine ♀ Variant of ▶Cairistiona.

Cairistiòna ♀ Scottish Gaelic equivalent of Christine. See main dictionary.

Càitir ♀ Misanalysis of ▶Caitriona as *Caitir Fhiona*, the second element taken as meaning 'of wine'. It has sometimes been Anglicized as Clarissa (see main dictionary), to which it is, however, not related.

Caitriona ♀ Scottish Gaelic equivalent of Katherine. See main dictionary.
ALSO: Catrìona; Catriona (Anglicized form).

Calaminag ♀ Feminine form of ▶Calum.

Calum ♂ Scottish Gaelic form of the Late Latin personal name *Columba* 'dove'. See also Callum in main dictionary.
FEMININE FORMS: Calaminag, Calumina.

Cameron ♂, ♀ Transferred use of the

surname, which in the Highlands is derived from Gaelic *cam sròn* 'crooked nose', and in the Lowlands is apparently an assimilated form of a Norman baronial name derived from Cambernon in Normandy. It is very popular as a boy's name, and now also occurs as a girl's name. See also main dictionary.

Campbell ♂ Transferred use of the surname derived from Gaelic *cam beul* 'crooked mouth'. It is borne by one of the great Highland clans, whose head is the Duke of Argyll.

Ceit ♀ Scottish Gaelic equivalent of Kate. See main dictionary.

Chirsty ♀ Usual spelling in the Highlands of ▶Kirsty.

Ciorstaidh ♀ Scottish Gaelic form of ▶Kirsty. ALSO: Ciorstag.

Cliamain ♂ Scottish Gaelic equivalent of Clement. See main dictionary.

Coinneach ♂ Traditional: originally a byname meaning 'handsome, comely'. See also Kenneth in main dictionary.

Conall ♂ Traditional: compound of Old Celtic words meaning 'wolf' and 'strong'. See also main dictionary.

Cormag ♂ Traditional name of uncertain origin.

Craig ♂ Originally a nickname from Gaelic *creag* 'rock', or in some cases a transferred use of the surname derived as a local name from this word. See also main dictionary.

Creighton ♂ Transferred use of the Scottish surname, in origin a local name from *Crichton* in Midlothian (from Gaelic *crìoch* 'border, boundary' + Middle English *tune* 'settlement').

Crìsdean ♂ From *Criosd* 'Christ', used as an equivalent of Christopher or Christian (see main dictionary).

Cuddy ♂ Lowland Scottish: pet form of Cuthbert. See main dictionary.

Cuithbeart ♂ Scottish Gaelic equivalent of Cuthbert. See main dictionary.

Curstaidh ♀ Scottish Gaelic form of ▶Kirsty. ALSO: Curstag.

Dd

Dàibhidh ♂ Scottish Gaelic equivalent of David. See main dictionary.

Darragh ♂ Name popularly associated with Scottish Gaelic *darach* 'oak'.

Deòiridh ♀ From the Gaelic vocabulary word meaning 'pilgrim'; sometimes Anglicized as Dorcas (see main dictionary), to which it is unrelated.

Deònaid ♀ Dialectal variant of ▶Seònaid.

Deòrsa ♂ Scottish Gaelic equivalent of George. See main dictionary.

Dermid ♂ Anglicized form of ▶Diarmad.

Devorgilla ♀ Anglicized form of ▶Diorbhail, earlier *Diorbhorguil*.

Diarmad ♂ Scottish Gaelic form of Irish Diarmaid, which is possibly from *dí* 'without' + *airmit* 'injunction' or *airmait* 'envy'. See also Dermot in main dictionary. ALSO: Diarmid, Dermid (Anglicized forms).

Diorbhail ♀ Scottish Gaelic: apparently meaning 'true testimony'. It has frequently been Anglicized as Dorothy (see main dictionary), to which it is unrelated, and also as ▶Devorgilla.

Dolina ♀ Latinate formation based on the Scottish Gaelic name Dolag, a feminine diminutive of ▶Donald.

Domhnall ♂ Scottish Gaelic: from Old Celtic *dubno* 'world' + *val* 'rule'.

See also Donald in main dictionary.

Donald ♂ Anglicized form of ▶Domhnall.

Donella ♀ Feminine equivalent of ▶Donald.

Donnchadh ♂ Scottish Gaelic: compound of Old Celtic *donn* 'brown' + *chadh* 'chief' or 'noble'.
ALSO: Duncan (Anglicized form).

Dougal ♂ Anglicized form of ▶Dubhghall.
ALSO: Dugal(d).

Douglas ♂ Transferred use of the surname, in origin a local name from a place in the Southern Uplands named with Gaelic *dubh* 'black' + *glas* 'stream'. This was the stronghold of what became one of the most powerful families in Scotland, the earls of Douglas and of Angus, notorious in earlier times as Border reivers. See also main dictionary.

Dubhghall ♂ Scottish Gaelic: from *dubh* 'black, dark' + *gall* 'stranger'. This was a byname applied to Danes, in contrast to the fairer Norwegians and Icelanders (compare ▶Fionnghall).
ALSO: Dùghall; Dougal, Dugal(d) (Anglicized forms)

Duff ♂ Originally a nickname, from Gaelic *dubh* 'black', i.e. 'dark-haired one'. In modern use it is in part a transferred use of the surname *Duff*, derived from the nickname.

Dugald ♂ Anglicized form of ▶Dubhghall. The final -*d* is due to a mishearing of the Gaelic form, in which the final -*ll* sounds like -*ld* to English ears.

Duncan ♂ Anglicized form of ▶Donnchadh. See also main dictionary.

Ee

Eairdsidh ♂ Scottish Gaelic equivalent of ▶Archie.
ALSO: Eairrsidh.

Ealasaid ♀ Scottish Gaelic equivalent of Elizabeth. See main dictionary.

Eanraig ♂ Scottish Gaelic equivalent of Henry. See main dictionary.

Edan ♂ Variant of ▶Aidan.

Edmé ♀ Scottish variant of ▶Esmé (see main dictionary). The change of -*s*- to -*d*- may have been due to the influence of the coexisting names ▶Esmond and ▶Edmund. In spite of its accent, it is not found as a French name.

Efric ♀ Anglicized form of ▶Oighrig.

Eideard ♂ Scottish Gaelic equivalent of Edward. See main dictionary.

Eilidh ♀ Modern Gaelic coinage on the basis of English Ellie.
ALSO: Ailie (Anglicized form).

Eimhir ♀ Scottish Gaelic form of the Irish name Émer (see Irish appendix), familiar through the 'Poems to Eimhir' of Sorley MacLean (1911–96).

Eiric ♀ Variant of ▶Oighrig.

Eithrig ♀ Variant of ▶Oighrig.

Ellair ♂ From a byname, *Ceallair*, referring to someone who was a butler or steward in a monastery (Latin *cellarius*, a derivative of *cella* 'storeroom, cellar'). The initial *C*- was lost through elision in the common patronymic surname *Mac Ceallair*.
ALSO: Ellar (Anglicized form).

Elsie ♀ Originally a simplified form of *Elspie*, a pet form of ▶Elspeth. See also main dictionary.

Elspeth ♀ Scottish contracted form of Elizabeth. See main dictionary.

Eóghan ♂ Traditional name, pronounced 'yew-en' or 'yo-wen'; supposedly derived from Gaelic *iúr* 'yew' and meaning 'born of yew'.
ALSO: Euan, Ewan, Evan (Anglicized forms).

Eòin ♂ Scottish Gaelic equivalent of John. See main dictionary.

Euan ♂ Anglicized form of ▸Eóghan.

Eubh ♀ Scottish Gaelic equivalent of Eve. See main dictionary.

Eumann ♂ Scottish Gaelic equivalent of Edmund. See main dictionary.

Euna ♀ Anglicized form of ▸Ùna.

Eunan ♂ Anglicized form of Ádhamhnán, traditionally said to be a diminutive of ▸ Àdhamh but probably a diminutive of *adomnae* 'great fear', i.e. 'little horror'.

Evan ♂ Anglicized form ▸Eóghan. See also main dictionary.

Evander ♂ Classical name used in the Scottish Highlands as an Anglicized form of ▸Iomhar. This form is peculiar to the MacIver family, apparently coined to differentiate it from the surname. See also main dictionary.

Ewan ♂ Anglicized form of ▸Eóghan.

Ff

Farquhar ♂ Anglicized form of ▸Fearchar. In modern use as a given name it may also be a transferred use of the

surname derived from this name.

Fearchar ♂ Traditional: from Gaelic *fear* 'man' + *char* 'dear, loving'.

Fearghas ♂ Traditional: from Gaelic *fear* 'man' + *gus* 'vigour'.
ALSO: **Fergus** (Anglicized form).

Fenella ♀ Anglicized form of ▸Fionnuala.

Fergus ♂ Anglicized form of ▸Fearghas.

Fife ♂ Transferred use of the surname, originally a local name for someone from the Kingdom (now region) of Fife, which is said to get its name from the legendary Pictish hero *Fib*, one of the seven sons of Cruithne.
ALSO: **Fyfe**.

Filib ♂ Scottish Gaelic equivalent of Philip. See main dictionary.

Fillan ♂ Anglicized form of Gaelic Faolán (see Irish appendix). St Fillan was an early medieval missionary to Scotland.

Findlay ♂ Variant spelling of ▸Finlay.

Finella ♀ Anglicized form of ▸Fionnuala.

Fingal ♂ Anglicized form of ▸Fionnghall.
ALSO: **Fingall**.

Finlay ♂ Anglicized form of ▸Fionnlagh or a transferred use of the surname derived from this name.
ALSO: **Findlay, Finley**.

Finola ♀ Anglicized form of ▸Fionnuala.

Fiona ♀ Latinate derivative of the Gaelic word *fionn* 'white, fair', first used by James Macpherson (1736–96). See also in main dictionary.

Fionnghall ♂ Traditional: from Gaelic *fionn* 'white, fair' + *gall* 'stranger', originally a byname applied to Norse settlers (compare ▸Dubhghall).
ALSO: **Fingal(l)** (Anglicized forms).

Fionnlagh ♂ Traditional: from Gaelic *fionn* 'white, fair' + *laogh* 'warrior, hero', reinforced apparently by an Old Norse personal name composed of *finn* 'Finn' + *leikr* 'battle; hero'.
ALSO: **Fin(d)lay, Finley**. (Anglicized forms).

Fionnuala ♀ Modern Gaelic form of the traditional name *Fionnguala*, from *fionn* 'white, fair' + *guala* 'shoulder'.
ALSO: **Fenella, Finella, Finola** (Anglicized forms).

Fraser ♂ Transferred use of the surname borne by a leading Scottish family. It appears to be Norman in origin, the earliest forms recorded being *de Frisselle* and *de Fresel(iere)*, but these do not correspond with any place name in France and may in fact represent a Gaelic name corrupted

beyond recognition by an Anglo-Norman scribe.
ALSO: Frazer, Frazier.

Freya ♀ Of Old Norse origin: as *Freya* or *Fröja*, borne by the goddess of love in Scandinavian mythology, and probably derived from a word related to Old High German *frouwa* 'lady, mistress'. It has long been a traditional name in Shetland, and is now more widely popular.

Fyfe ♂ Variant spelling of ▶Fife.

Gg

Gillanders ♂ Anglicized form of Gaelic *Gille Ainndreis* or *Gille Anndrais* 'servant of St Andrew' (see **Andrew** in main dictionary).

Gilleonan ♂ Anglicized form of Gaelic *Gille Ádhamhnain* 'servant of St Adomnan' (see ▶Eunan).

Gillespie ♂ Anglicized form of Gaelic *Gille Easbaig* 'bishop's servant'. Gille Easbaig Cambeul was the founder of Clan Campbell.

Gillies ♂ Anglicized form of Gaelic *Gille Ìosa* 'servant of Jesus'.

Gormlaith ♀ Traditional: from Gaelic *gorm* 'illustrious, splendid' + *flaith* 'lady, princess'.

Gregor ♂ Scottish form of Gregory (see main dictionary); in part an Anglicized form of Gaelic ▶Griogair, which gave rise to the Highland surname *MacGregor*.

Griogair ♂ Gaelic derivative of Norman French *Grégoire*. See **Gregory** in main dictionary.

Hh

Hamish ♂ Anglicized spelling of the vocative case, *Sheumais*, of ▶Seumas.

Hùisdean ♂ Variant of ▶Ùisdean.

Ii

Iagan ♂ Modern spelling of *Aodhagán*, a diminutive form of ▶Aodh.

Iain ♂ Gaelic spelling of ▶Ian.

Ian ♂ Scottish form of John (see main dictionary), also used extensively in the wider English-speaking world.

Innes ♂ Anglicized form of ▶Aonghas (based on the pronunciation), or a transferred use of the surname derived from this name or as a local name from the barony of Innes in Moray, named with Gaelic *inis* 'island, piece of land'.

Íomhar ♂ Scottish Gaelic equivalent of Ivor. See main dictionary.

Iona ♀ Modern coinage from the name of the tiny sacred island in the Hebrides, off the west coast of Mull. Its name is said to be the result of a misreading of Latin *Ioua*, representing its Gaelic name *Ì*, from Old Norse *ey* 'island'. See also in main dictionary.

Isbel ♀ Contracted form of Isabel (see main dictionary).

Iseabail ♀ Scottish Gaelic equivalent of Isabel (see main dictionary).
ALSO: Ishbel (Anglicized form, based on the Gaelic pronunciation).

Isla ♀ Modern: popular 20th-century coinage, from the name of the Hebridean island of Islay.

Jj

Jock ♂ Scottish variant of Jack (see main dictionary), sometimes used as an archetypal nickname for a Scotsman.

Johan ♂, ♀ Older Scottish spelling of Joan (see main dictionary), which was traditionally pronounced as two syllables.

Kk

Keith ♂ Transferred use of the Scottish surname, originally a local name from lands so called in East Lothian, probably from a Celtic (Brythonic) word meaning 'wood'. See also main dictionary.

Kenneth ♂ Anglicized form of *Cinaed*, originally most probably a personal name meaning 'born of fire', and *Cainnech*, a byname meaning 'handsome'. See also main dictionary.

Kester ♂ Medieval Scottish form of ▶Christopher (see main dictionary), occasionally revived as a modern given name.

Kina ♀ Highland short form of ▶Alickina.

Kirstie ♀ Variant of ▶Kirsty.

Kirstin ♀ Scottish vernacular form of Christine. See main dictionary.

Kirsty ♀ Pet form of ▶Kirstin, now also a popular independent given name.
ALSO: Kirsti(e); Chirsty (the usual spelling in the Scottish Highlands).
GAELIC FORMS: Ciorstaidh, Ciorstag, Curstaidh, Curstag.

Kyle ♂ Modern: from a topographic term denoting a narrow strait or channel, from Gaelic *caol* 'narrow'; in part a transferred use of the surname, a local name from the region in Ayrshire named with this

word. See also main dictionary.

L l

Labhrainn ♂ Scottish Gaelic equivalent of Laurence. See main dictionary.

Lachina ♂ Highland feminine form of ▶Lachlan.

Lachlan ♂ Earlier *Lochlann*, said to refer originally to a migrant from Norway, the 'land of the lochs'.
ALSO: Lachlann.

Leagsaidh ♀ Scottish Gaelic equivalent of Lexie. See main dictionary.

Lexine ♀ Elaboration of Lexie (see main dictionary), with the addition of the feminine diminutive suffix *-ine*.

Liùsaidh ♀ Scottish Gaelic equivalent of Louisa or Lucy (see main dictionary).

Logan ♂, ♀ Transferred use of the Scottish surname, in origin a local name from a place so called in Ayrshire.

Luthais ♂ Scottish Gaelic equivalent of Louis. See main dictionary.

Lyall ♂ Transferred use of the Scottish surname, which is probably derived from the Old Norse personal name *Liulfr*, composed of an

unexplained first element + Old Norse *úlfr* 'wolf'. See also ▶Lyle.

Lyle ♂ Transferred use of the mainly Scottish surname, in origin a local name for someone who came 'from the island' (Anglo-Norman *de l'isle*), in many cases an area of higher, dry ground in a marsh or fen, rather than in a sea or river. There may have been some confusion with ▶Lyall.

M m

Magaidh ♀ Scottish Gaelic equivalent of Maggie. See main dictionary.

Magnus ♂ Originally a Latin byname meaning 'great', used as a given name by the Scandinavians and imported to Scotland and Ireland during the Middle Ages. See also main dictionary.
ALSO: Mànas (Gaelic form).

Màili ♀ Variant of ▶Màiri.

Mairead ♀ Scottish Gaelic equivalent of Margaret. See main dictionary.
ALSO: Maighread.

Màiri ♀ Scottish Gaelic equivalent of Mary. See main dictionary.
ALSO: Màili.

Maisie ♀ Pet form derived from ▶Mairead, with the Scottish and northern English diminutive suffix -*ie*.

Malcolm ♂ Anglicized form of the medieval Gaelic name *Mael Coluim* 'devotee of St Columba' (meaning 'dove' in Latin). See also main dictionary.

Malvina ♀ Creation of the Scottish antiquarian poet James Macpherson (1736–96), who published works allegedly translated from the ancient Gaelic bard Ossian. It is based on Gaelic *mala mhìn* 'smooth brow'. See also main dictionary.

Mànas ♂ Scottish Gaelic equivalent of ▶Magnus.

Maoilios ♂ Scottish Gaelic name meaning 'devotee of Jesus'. It has been Anglicized as Myles, to which it is unrelated (see Miles in main dictionary).

Marsaili ♀ Scottish Gaelic equivalent of Margery and Marcella (see main dictionary).

Maretta ♀ Anglicized form of ▶Mairead. ALSO: ▶Marietta (see main dictionary).

Mina ♀ Highland short form of ▶Calumina and ▶Normina, also used independently.

Moirean ♂ Derivative of *Moire*, the name of the Virgin Mary.

Mór ♀ Originally a byname from the vocabulary word *mór* 'large, great'. It has

sometimes been Anglicized as Sarah (see main dictionary), to which it is unrelated.

Mórag ♀ Pet form of Mór, now also used as an independent given name. ALSO: Morag (Anglicized form).

Moray ♂ Variant of ▶Murray, and the more usual spelling of the place name from which the surname is derived.

Morna ♀ Anglicized form of Scottish Gaelic *Muirne*, originally a byname meaning 'beloved'; borne by Fingal's mother in the Ossianic poems of James Macpherson (compare ▶Malvina).

Morven ♀ The name of Fingal's kingdom in the Ossianic poems of James Macpherson; in reality a district in north Argyll, on the west coast of Scotland, properly *Morvern*, known in Gaelic as *a' Mhorbhairne* 'the big gap'. *Morven* could alternatively be held to represent Gaelic *mór bheinn* 'big peak'.

Muir ♂ Transferred use of the surname, in origin a local name from a Scottish dialect variant of Middle English *more* 'moor, fen'.

Muireall ♀ Traditional name, apparently from Old Celtic words meaning 'sea' + 'bright'. ALSO: Muriel (Anglicized form; see main dictionary).

Munga ♂ Scottish Gaelic equivalent of ▶Mungo.

Mungo ♂ Of uncertain derivation. It is recorded as the byname of St Kentigern, the 6th-century apostle of south-west Scotland and north-west England. Having been glossed in Latin by his biographer as *carissimus amicus* 'dearest friend', the name (in its Brythonic form *Munghu*) was taken to represent later Welsh *fy nghi* 'my dog', i.e. 'my pet'. ALSO: Munga (Gaelic form).

Murchadh ♂ Modern Gaelic form of the traditional name *Muireadhach*; see ▶Murdo.

Murdag ♀ Feminine form of ▶Murdo. ALSO: Murdann, Murdina.

Murdo ♂ Anglicized spelling of *Muireadhach*, meaning 'lord', but said to be a derivative of *muir* 'sea'. ALSO: Murdoch.

Murray ♂ Either a transferred use of the Scottish surname, in origin a local name from the region now called Moray, or an Anglicized form of *Muireach*, a contracted form of *Muireadhach* (see ▶Murdo). ALSO: Moray.

Myles ♂ Anglicized form of ▶Maoilios.

Myra ♀ English name (see main dictionary) used occasionally in the

Highlands as an Anglicized form of ▶Mairead, being almost identical in pronunciation with it, though unrelated.

Nn

Naughton ♂ Anglicized form of the Gaelic name *Neachdann*, a derivative of *necht* 'pure'.

Neacal ♂ Scottish Gaelic equivalent of Nicholas. See main dictionary.

Neil ♂ Anglicized form of ▶Niall.
ALSO: **Neal(e)**.

Netta ♀ In Gaelic-speaking areas, a feminine form of ▶Neil, but see also main dictionary.

Niall ♂ Gaelic: of disputed derivation; it may mean 'cloud', 'passionate', or perhaps 'champion'. See also main dictionary.
ALSO: **Neil, Neal(e)** (Anglicized forms).

Niallghus ♂ Compound of ▶Niall + Gaelic *gus* 'strength'.

Ninian ♂ Of uncertain origin. It was the name of a 5th-century British saint who was responsible for evangelizing the northern Britons and the Picts and was used in his honour in Scotland until at least the 16th century. His name first appears in the Latinized form *Ninianus* in the 8th century; this seems to be identical to the *Nynnyaw* recorded in the *Mabinogi*.

Niven ♂ Anglicized form of the Gaelic name *Naoimhean* or **Gille Naomh**, a borrowing of Irish *Gille na Naomh* 'servant of the saint'.

Normina ♀ Highland feminine form of Norman (see main dictionary).

Oo

Oighrig ♀ Scottish Gaelic: apparently from an earlier name, *Aithbhreac*, meaning 'new speckled one'. It has commonly been Anglicized as **Erica, Effie, Euphemia**, and (formerly) also as **Africa** (see these in main dictionary), though related to none of them.
ALSO: **Eithrig, Eiric; Efric** (Anglicized form).

Ossian ♂ Anglicized form of Irish *Oisín*, Scottish Gaelic *Oisein*, originally a byname representing a diminutive of *os* 'stag'. It was coined by James Macpherson, author of the 'Ossianic' poems. See also **Oisín** in Irish appendix and **Osian** in main dictionary.

Pp

Pàdraig ♂ Scottish Gaelic equivalent of Patrick; also of **Peter**, the form **Peadar** being reserved for the saint.
ALSO: **Pàra, Pàdair** (dialectal forms).

Pàidean ♂ Pet form of ▶Pàdraig.

Pàrlan ♂ Scottish Gaelic form of Parthalán, which is of uncertain origin (see Irish appendix).

Peigi ♀ Scottish Gaelic equivalent of Peggy. See main dictionary.

Rr

Rabbie ♂ Pet form of ▶Robert, from the short form *Rab, Rob*, now often associated with the poet Robert Burns (1759–96).

Raghnaid ♀ Gaelicized form of Norse Ragnhild, from *regin* 'advice, decision' (also, 'the gods') + *hildr* 'battle'.

Raghnall ♂ Gaelicized borrowing of Old Norse *Rögnvaldr*, a compound of *regin* 'advice, decision' (also, 'the gods') + *valdr* 'ruler'.
ALSO: **Ronald, Ranald, Randal** (Anglicized forms).

Raibeart ♂ Scottish Gaelic equivalent of Robert. See main dictionary.

Ran ♂ Short form of the various names beginning with this syllable, for example, ▶Ranald and ▶Ranulf.

Ranald ♂ Anglicized form of ▶Raghnall.

Ranulf ♂ From an Old Norse personal name, *Reginulfr* (a compound of *regin* 'advice, decision' + *úlfr* 'wolf'), introduced into Scotland and northern England by Scandinavian settlers in the early Middle Ages.

Reid ♂ Transferred use of the Scottish and northern English surname, in origin a nickname for someone with red hair or a ruddy complexion (from Old English *rēad* 'red'; compare **Read** in main dictionary).

Reith ♂ Transferred use of the Scottish surname, pronounced 'reeth', of uncertain derivation.

Rhona ♀ Modern, apparently originating *c.*1870, but of uncertain derivation; probably it was devised as a feminine form of ▸Ronald (as evidenced by the alternative spelling, Rona) or it may have been taken from the name of the Hebridean island (compare ▸Ailsa, ▸Iona, ▸Isla).

Roderick ♂ English name of Germanic origin (see main dictionary), used as an Anglicized form of ▸Ruairidh, to which it is unrelated.

Rory ♂ Anglicized form of ▸Ruairidh.

Ross ♂ Either directly from Gaelic *ros*

'headland' or a transferred use of the Scottish surname.

Roy ♂ Anglicized spelling of a Gaelic nickname, *Ruadh* 'red'.

Ruairidh ♂ Traditional: pronounced '**rue**-er-ee', meaning 'red-haired' or 'fiery'.
ALSO: Ruaraidh; Rory, Roderick (Anglicized forms).

Ruiseart ♂ Scottish Gaelic equivalent of Richard. See main dictionary.

S<small>s</small>

Sachairi ♂ Scottish Gaelic equivalent of Zachary. See main dictionary.

Sandaidh ♂ Gaelic form of ▸Sandy.

Sandy ♂, ♀ Pet form of Alexander or Alexandra (see these in main dictionary).

Saundra ♀ Scottish variant of Sandra (see main dictionary), reflecting the same development in pronunciation as is shown by surnames such as *Saunders* and *Saunderson*, originally from short forms of ▸Alexander.

Sawney ♂ Variant of ▸Sandy, resulting from a pronunciation which is also reflected in the surname *Saunders*. Use of the name declined after

the 18th century, influenced no doubt by the use of *Sawney* as a term for a simpleton.

Scott ♂ Originally a byname for a member of the Gaelic-speaking people who came to Scotland from Ireland, but in modern use a transferred use of the surname derived from the byname.

Seaghdh ♂ Traditional name, perhaps meaning 'hawk-like' or 'fine, goodly'. It has been Anglicized as Shaw and Seth, to which, however, it is unrelated.

Seathan ♂ Scottish Gaelic: from Old French *Je(h)an*. See John in main dictionary.

Senga ♀ Popularly supposed to represent Agnes (see main dictionary) spelled backwards (which it undeniably does), but more likely from Gaelic *seang* 'slender'.

Seocan ♂ Scottish Gaelic pet form of ▸Jock.

Seonag ♀ Scottish Gaelic equivalent of Joan. See main dictionary.
ALSO: **Shona** (Anglicized).

Seònaid ♀ Scottish Gaelic equivalent of Janet (see main dictionary), pronounced 'shaw-natch'.
ALSO: **Shona** (Anglicized); Seona (semi-Anglicized).

Seòras ♂ Scottish Gaelic equivalent of

George. See main
dictionary.
ALSO: **Seòrsa, Deòrsa.**

Seòsaidh ♂ Scottish
Gaelic equivalent of
Joseph. See main
dictionary.

Seumas ♂ Scottish
Gaelic equivalent of
James (see main
dictionary), pronounced
'**shay**-mas'.

Sgàire ♂ Traditional
name, probably a
borrowing of the Old
Norse byname *Skári* 'sea-
mew'. It has sometimes
been Anglicized as
Zachary (see main
dictionary).

Shaw ♂ Anglicized form
of ▸Seaghdh.

Sheena ♀ Anglicized
spelling of ▸Sìne.

Sholto ♂ Apparently an
Anglicized form of Gaelic
Sìoltach, originally a
byname meaning
'sower', i.e. 'fruitful' or
'seed-bearing'. This name
is traditional in the
Douglas family.

Shona ♀ Anglicized
spelling of ▸Seonag or
▸Seònaid. See also main
dictionary.

Sinclair ♂ Transferred
use of the Scottish
surname, in origin a
Norman baronial name
from a manor in
northern France called
Saint-Clair, probably
Saint-Clair-sur-Elle in La
Manche. See also main
dictionary.

Sìne ♀ Scottish Gaelic
equivalent of Jane. See
main dictionary.

ALSO: **Sheena** (Anglicized
spelling).

Siubhan ♀ Scottish
Gaelic: from the Old
French disyllabic name
Jehanne (see Jean in main
dictionary). This name is
usually Anglicized as
Judith. See main
dictionary.

Siùsan ♀ Scottish Gaelic
equivalent of Susan. See
main dictionary.
ALSO: **Siùsaidh.**

Skye ♀ Elaborated
spelling of Sky (see main
dictionary), influenced
by the name of the island
of *Skye* in the Hebrides,
which is of Gaelic origin.

Somerled ♂ From the
Old Norse personal name
Sumarliðr, probably
originally a byname
meaning 'summer
traveller'. This is a
Highland name, borne by
the founder of the
powerful and widespread
Clan Macdonald, Lords of
the Isles from the 12th to
the 15th century, and it is
still occasionally bestowed
on members of Clan
Macdonald and its septs.
ALSO: **Summerlad.**

Somhairle ♂ Gaelic
form of ▸Somerled.
ALSO: **Sorley** (Anglicized
form).

Sorcha ♀ Gaelic:
pronounced '**sorr**-kha';
from a Celtic word
meaning 'brightness'. In
Scotland it has been
translated as Clara (see
main dictionary).

Sorley ♂ Pronounced
'**sorr**-lee'; Anglicized

form of the Highland
name ▸Somhairle.

Steaphan ♂ Scottish
Gaelic equivalent of
Stephen. See main
dictionary.

Stewart ♂ See ▸Stuart.

Stineag ♀ Pet form of
▸Cairistìona.

Stuart ♂ From the
French version of the
surname *Stewart*,
introduced to Scotland in
the 16th-century by Mary
Stuart, Queen of Scots,
who was brought up in
France. The surname
originated as an English
occupational or status
name for someone who
served as a *steward* in a
manor or royal
household.
ALSO: **Stewart.**

Summerlad ♂ Variant
spelling of ▸Somerled,
being taken by folk
etymology as derived
from the words *summer*
and *lad*.

Tt

Tadhg ♂ Traditional:
pronounced 'tyg',
originally a Gaelic
byname meaning 'poet'
or 'philosopher'. It has
been Anglicized as Tim
(see main dictionary), to
which it is unrelated.
ALSO: **Tad, Teague, Teigue**
(Anglicized forms).

Tam ♂ Scottish short
form of Thomas. See
main dictionary.

Tasgall ♂ Traditional
name, originally a

borrowing of the Old Norse personal name *Ásketill* (*ás* 'god' + *ketill* 'sacrificial cauldron'). It is in use among the MacAskills in the Isle of Berneray, whose surname derives from a patronymic form of the same name.
ALSO: **Taskill** (Anglicized form).

Teàrlach ♂ Modern reduced form (pronounced 'tchar-lakh') of the ancient Gaelic name Toirdhealbhach, apparently from a byname meaning 'instigator', from *toirdhealbh* 'prompting'.

Teàrlag ♀ Feminine form of ▶Teàrlach.

Teasag ♀ Scottish Gaelic equivalent of Jessie. See main dictionary.

Tiobaid ♂ Scottish Gaelic equivalent of Theobald. See main dictionary.

Tòmas ♂ Scottish Gaelic equivalent of Thomas. See main dictionary.

Torcall ♂ Traditional name, originally a borrowing into Gaelic of the Old Norse personal name Þorketill, from Þorr (Thor, name of the god of thunder) + *ketill* '(sacrificial) cauldron'.
ALSO: **Torquil** (Anglicized form).

Tormod ♂ Traditional name, originally a borrowing into Gaelic of the Old Norse personal name Þórmóðr, from Þorr (Thor, name of the god of thunder) + Old Norse *móðr* 'mind, courage'.

Uu

Ualan ♂ Scottish Gaelic equivalent of the male name Valentine. See main dictionary.
ALSO: **Uailean**.

Uarraig ♂ Traditional name composed of Gaelic *uall* 'pride' + *garg* 'fierce'. It has been Anglicized as Kennedy (see main dictionary) apparently because it was a common given name in kindreds with that surname.

Uilleam ♂ Scottish Gaelic equivalent of William. See main dictionary.

Ùisdean ♂ Traditional name, originally a borrowing of the Old Norse personal name *Eysteinn*, from *ei, ey* 'always, forever' + *steinn* 'stone'. It has been Anglicized as Hugh; see main dictionary.
ALSO: **Hùisdean**.

Ùna ♀ Scottish Gaelic form of Irish Úna, which is of uncertain derivation. It is identical in form with Irish *úna* 'hunger, famine', but is more likely to be derived from *uan* 'lamb'. See also Una in main dictionary.
ALSO: **Euna** (Anglicized form).

z

Zena ♀ Highland short form of ▶Alexina.

Spanish Names

Note: Many Spanish girls' names are derived from terms used in various aspects of the cult of the Virgin Mary. As a result many common female names, e.g. *Pilar* and *Rosario*, are based on words that have masculine grammatical gender.

Aa

Adán ♂ Biblical. See Adam in main dictionary.

Adolfo ♂ Germanic. See Adolf in German appendix.

Adrián ♂ From Latin. See Adrian in main dictionary.
FEMININE FORM: **Adriana**.

Águeda ♀ From Greek. See Agatha in main dictionary.

Agustín ♂ From Latin. See Augustine in main dictionary.
FEMININE FORM: **Agustína**.

Aitor ♂ Basque: name of the legendary founder of the Basque people.

Alberto ♂ Germanic. See Albert in main dictionary and Albrecht in German appendix.

Alejandro ♂ From Greek. See Alexander in main dictionary.
FEMININE FORM: **Alejandra**.

Alejo ♂ From Latin. See Alexis in main dictionary.

Alfonso ♂ Visigothic: probably a compound of *adal* 'noble' + *funs* 'ready'; a traditional royal name.
ALSO: **Alonso**.

Alfredo ♂ From English. See Alfred in main dictionary.

Alicia ♀ Spanish form of Alice (see main dictionary).

Alirio ♂ Of uncertain origin; perhaps from a popular form of Latin *Hilarius* (see Hilary in main dictionary) or *Hilarion* (see Illarion in Russian appendix). A saint variously known as *Allyre* or *Illidius* was a 4th-century bishop of Clermont: his name may be connected with this one.

Alonso ♂ Variant of ▸Alfonso.
ALSO: **Alonzo**.

Álvaro ♂ Visigothic: of uncertain etymology.

Amado ♂ From the Latin name *Amatus* 'beloved'. See Amato in Italian appendix.

Amador ♂ From Latin *Amator* 'lover'; borne by a 9th-century Cordoban priest who was executed by the Moors for his Christian faith.

Amancio ♂ From Latin *Amantius* 'loving'; borne by several minor early saints, but there has been much confusion in the sources with the name *Amandus* 'lovable'.

Ambrosio ♂ From Late Greek. See Ambrose in main dictionary.

Amparo ♀ Marian name meaning 'protection', with reference to the role of the Virgin Mary in protecting Christians.

Ana ♀ From Hebrew. See Anne in main dictionary.

Anacleto ♂ From the Late Latin personal name *Anacletus*, Greek *Anaklētos* 'invoked'.

Andrés ♂ From New Testament Greek. See Andrew in main dictionary.
FEMININE FORM: **Andrea**.

Ángel ♂ From Greek *Angelos* 'messenger (of God)'.

Ángela ♀ From Latin. See Angela in main dictionary.

Ángeles ♀ Marian name honouring *Nuestra Señora de los Ángeles* 'Our Lady of the Angels'.

Angelita ♀ Pet form of ▸Ángela.

Angosto ♀ Mainly Galician: Marian name honouring *Nuestra Señora de Angosto* 'Our Lady of Angosto'. Angosto is a place in the province of Álava where the Virgin is supposed to have appeared in a vision.

Angustias ♀ Marian name honouring *Nuestra Señora de las Angustias*, from *angustias* 'sufferings'.

Aniceto ♂ From Greek *Anikētos* 'unconquered' or 'unconquerable'; the name of a 2nd-century pope of Syrian origin.

Anita ♀ Pet form of ▶Ana.

Antonio ♂ From Latin. See Anthony in main dictionary.
FEMININE FORM: **Antonia**.

Anunciación ♀ Marian name commemorating the Annunciation to the Virgin Mary of the forthcoming birth of Christ.
ALSO: **Anunciata**.

Aparición ♀ Religious name, referring to Christ's appearance to the apostles after the Resurrection.

Aquiles ♂ From Greek *Achilleus*, name of the hero of Homer's Iliad, also the name of one or two minor saints. See Achilles in main dictionary.

Araceli ♀ Mainly Latin American: apparently a modern coinage from Latin *ara* 'altar' + *c(o)eli* 'of the sky'.

Arantxa ♀ Pet form of the Basque name *Aránzazu*, derived from

a place name meaning 'thorn bush'.

Armando ♂ Germanic. See Hermann in German supplement.

Arnaldo ♂ Germanic. See Arnold in main dictionary.

Arsenio ♂ From Greek *Arsenios* 'virile'.

Arturo ♂ Celtic. See Arthur in main dictionary.

Asunción ♀ Marian name commemorating the assumption of the Virgin Mary into heaven.

Augusto ♂ From Latin. See Augustus in main dictionary.

Aurelio ♂ From Latin. See Italian appendix.

Auxilio ♀ Religious name meaning 'help', referring to the feast of *Maria Auxiliadora* 'Mary the Helper' celebrated on 24 May.

Azucena ♀ Marian name meaning 'madonna lily' (from Arabic *as-susana*). Adopted as a personal name because the flower is used as a symbol of the Virgin Mary.

Bb

Baldomero ♂ Germanic (Frankish): from a personal name, composed of the elements *bald* 'bold,

brave' + *mari, meri* 'famous'; borne by a 7th-century saint from Lyons, patron of locksmiths.

Baltasar ♂ See Balthasar in main dictionary.

Barbara ♀ Greek: 'foreign woman'. See main dictionary.

Bartolomé ♂ New Testament. See Bartholomew in main dictionary.

Bautista ♂ Religious name commemorating John the Baptist.

Beatriz ♀ From Latin. See Beatrix in main dictionary.

Begoña ♀ Marian name honouring *Nuestra Señora de Begoña*, the Virgin Mary as patron saint of Bilbao.

Belén ♀ Religious name, Spanish form of *Bethlehem*.

Beltrán ♂ Germanic. See Bertram in main dictionary.
ALSO: **Bertran**.

Benigno ♂ From Late Latin *Benignus* 'kind'; the name of the 3rd-century martyr to whom Dijon cathedral is dedicated and of a 5th-century disciple of St Patrick.

Benito ♂ From Latin. See Benedict in main dictionary.
FEMININE FORM: **Benita**.

Bernabé ♂ New Testament. See Barnabas in main dictionary.

Bernardo ♂ Germanic. See Bernard in main dictionary.
FEMININE FORM: **Bernarda**.

Berta ♀ Germanic. See Bertha in main dictionary.

Bertan ♂ Variant of ▶Beltrán.

Blanca ♀ From *blanca* 'white' (i.e. pure). See Blanche in main dictionary.

Blas ♂ From Latin. See Blaise in main dictionary.

Bonifacio ♂ From Late Latin. See Boniface in main dictionary.

Brígida ♀ From Irish Brighid (see Irish appendix and Bridget in main dictionary), or from the Swedish form, *Birgit*.

Bruno ♂ Germanic. See main dictionary.

Cc

Calisto ♂ From Greek. See Callisto in Italian appendix.

Camilo ♂ From the Roman family name *Camillus*.
FEMININE FORM: **Camila**.

Candelaria ♀ Marian name, referring to Candlemas, the festival commemorating the purification of the Virgin Mary and the presentation of Christ in the temple.

Caridad ♀ From *caridad* 'charity'.

Carlos ♂ Spanish form of Latin *Carolus*. See Charles in main dictionary.
FEMININE FORM: **Carlota**.

Carmel ♀ Marian name honouring *Nuestra Señora de Carmel* 'Our Lady of Carmel'. Carmel is a mountain in the Holy Land populated from an early date by Christian hermits, who were later organized into the Carmelite order of monks.
ALSO: **Carmela**.
MASCULINE FORM: **Carmelo**.

Carmen ♀ Alteration of ▶Carmel under the influence of the word *carmen* 'song'.

Casilda ♀ Origin uncertain; the name of an 11th-century saint born in Toledo, who was probably of Moorish descent. She lived as an anchorite nun in the province of Burgos, and is particularly venerated in Burgos and Toledo.

Catalina ♀ See Katherine in main dictionary.

Cayetano ♂ From Italian Gaetano. See Italian appendix.

Cayo ♂ From the Latin personal name *Caius*; borne by numerous saints of the early Christian period.

Cebrián ♂ From Latin. See Cipriano in Italian appendix.

Cecilia ♀ From Latin. See main dictionary.
MASCULINE FORM: **Cecilio**.

Celso ♂ From Latin. See Italian appendix.

Cesar ♂ From the Latin family name *Caesar*. See Caesar in main dictionary.

Ciriaco ♂ From Latin *Cyriacus*, from Greek *Kyriakos*, a derivative of *kyrios* 'lord', borne by a large number of minor saints of the early centuries AD.

Clara ♀ From Latin. See Clare in main dictionary.

Clarisa ♀ From Latin. See Clarice in main dictionary.

Claudio ♂ From Latin. See Claude in main dictionary.
FEMININE FORM: **Claudia**.

Clemente ♂ From Latin. See Clement in main dictionary.

Cleto ♂ Short form of ▶Anacleto.

Concepción ♀ Marian name commemorating the Immaculate Conception of the Virgin Mary.

Conchita ♀ Pet form of ▶Concepción.
ALSO: **Concha**.

Conseja ♀ Marian name honouring *Nuestra Señora del Buen Consejo* 'Our Lady of Good Counsel'.

Consuelo ♀ Marian name honouring

Nuestra Señora del Consuelo 'Our Lady of Solace'.

Corazón ♀ Religious name meaning 'heart', referring to the Sacred Heart of Jesus.

Cristina ♀ From Latin. See **Christina** in main dictionary.

Cristo ♂ Short form of ▶Cristobál.

Cristobál ♂ From Greek. See **Christopher** in main dictionary.

Cruz ♀ Religious name meaning 'cross', referring to the agony of Mary at the foot of the Cross.

Cugat ♂ Catalan, a name of Carthaginian origin (Latin *Cucuphas*) and unknown derivation.

Curro ♂ Pet form of ▶Francisco.

Dd

Dalmacio ♂ From Latin. See **Dalmazio** in Italian appendix.

Damaso ♂ From Greek *damān* 'tame, subdue'; borne in honour of a 4th-century pope.

Damián ♂ From Greek. See **Damian** in main dictionary.

Daniel ♂ Biblical. See main dictionary.
FEMININE FORM: **Daniela**.

David ♂ Biblical. See main dictionary.

Delfina ♀ From Latin. See **Delphine** in main dictionary.

Demetrio ♂ From Greek *Dēmētrios* 'devotee of Demeter'. See **Demetrius** in main dictionary.

Desiderio ♂ From Late Latin *Desiderius*, a derivative of *desiderium* 'longing'.

Diana ♀ From Latin. See main dictionary.

Diego ♂ Origin uncertain; perhaps from ▶Santiago or from a native Iberian name found in Latin as *Didacus*.

Digna ♀ From the Late Latin name *Digna* 'worthy'; borne by a martyr beheaded in Spain during the 9th century.

Dolores ♀ Marian name honouring *Nuestra Señora de los Dolores* 'Our Lady of Sorrows', a reference to the Seven Sorrows of the Virgin in Christian belief.

Domingo ♂ From Late Latin. See **Dominic** in main dictionary.
FEMININE FORM: **Dominga**.

Donato ♂ From Latin *Donatus* 'given (by God)'; the name of over twenty early saints.

Ee

Edmundo ♂ From English. See **Edmund** in main dictionary.

Eduardo ♂ From English. See **Edward** in main dictionary.

Efraín ♂ Biblical. See **Ephraim** in main dictionary.

Eladio ♂ From Late Greek *Helladios* 'from Greece'.

Elena ♀ From Greek. See **Helen** in main dictionary.

Eliana ♀ From Late Latin. See **Éliane** in French appendix.

Eliseo ♂ Biblical. See **Elisha** in main dictionary.

Elodia ♀ Latinized form of a Visigothic name composed of *ali* 'other, foreign' + *od* 'wealth'; the name of a 9th-century saint, martyred at Huesca together with her sister Nuncilo, at the behest of their Islamic stepfather.

Eloy ♂ From Latin *Eligius*, a derivative of *eligere* 'to choose'.
ALSO: **Eligio** (see Italian appendix).

Elpidio ♂ From Greek. See Italian appendix.

Elvira ♀ Germanic (Visigothic): probably a compound of *ali* 'other, foreign' + *wēr* 'true'.

Emeterio ♂ From Latin *Emeterius* or *Hemiterius*, of uncertain (probably Greek) origin. St Hemiterius was martyred at Calahorra in Spain in the 4th century.

Emilio ♂ From the Latin family name *Aemilius* (probably from *aemulus* 'rival').
FEMININE FORM: **Emilia**.

Encarnacíon ♀
Religious name
commemorating the
festival of the
Incarnation (Spanish
encarnación, from Late
Latin *incarnatio*, a
derivative of *caro* flesh),
celebrated on Christmas
Day.

Engracia ♀ From the
Latin name *Encratis* or
Encratia, derived from
Greek *'enkratēs* 'in
control, temperate'
but influenced by
Latin *gratia* 'grace'.
St Encratia (d. *c.*304)
was martyred at
Saragossa under
Diocletian.

Enrique ♂ From
German Heinrich (see
German appendix) or
English Henry (see main
dictionary).
FEMININE FORM: **Enriqueta**.

Ermengildo ♂ Variant
of ▸Hermengildo.

Ernesto ♂ From
German Ernst (see
German appendix) or
English Ernest (see main
dictionary).

Esperanza ♀ From Late
Latin *Sperantia* meaning
'hope'.

Estéban ♂ From Greek.
See Stephen in main
dictionary.
FEMININE FORM: **Estefanía**.

Estrella ♀ From Latin.
See Stella in main
dictionary.

Eufemia ♀ From Greek.
See Euphemia in main
dictionary.

Eugenio ♂ From Greek.
See Eugene in main
dictionary.
FEMININE FORM: **Eugenia**.

Eulalia ♀ From Late
Greek (see main
dictionary); the name of
two famous Spanish
martyrs, Eulalia of
Barcelona (d. 304) and
Eulalia of Mérida (d. 364),
who may possibly be
identical.
ALSO: **Olalla**.

Eusebio ♂ From the
Late Greek name *Eusebios*,
from *eusebēs* 'pious,
reverent'; the name of
numerous early saints,
including a friend of St
Jerome traditionally
regarded as the founder
of the abbey of
Guadalupe in Spain.

Eustaquio ♂ From Late
Greek. See Eustace in
main dictionary.

Eutropio ♂ From the
Late Greek name
Eutropios, from *eu* 'well,
good' + *tropos* 'manner',
or possibly from classical
Greek *eutropos* 'versatile'.
It was the name of
various minor early
saints.

Eva ♀ Biblical. See Eve in
main dictionary.

Evaristo ♂ From Late
Greek *Euarestos*, from *eu*
'well, good' + *areskein* 'to
please, satisfy'; borne by
an early pope, said to
have been martyred
under the Roman
emperor Hadrian in
about 107.

Evita ♀ Pet form of ▸Eva.

Ff

Fabián ♂ From Late
Latin. See Fabian in main
dictionary.

Fabio ♂ From Latin
Fabius, name of a Roman
family whose members
were prominent in
republican Rome.

Fabricio ♂ From Latin.
See Fabrizio in Italian
appendix.

Federico ♂ From
German Friedrich (see
German appendix) or
English Frederick (see
main dictionary).

Feliciano ♂ From
Latin *Felicius*, derivative
of Felix 'happy,
fortunate' (see main
dictionary).

Felicidad ♀ From Latin.
See Felicity in main
dictionary.

Felipe ♂ From Greek.
See Philip in main
dictionary.

Fermin ♂ From Late
Latin *Firminus*. See
▸Firmin in French
appendix.

Fernando ♂ A modern
form of the old Spanish
name *Ferdinando*, which
is of Germanic
(Visigothic) origin, from
farð 'journey' (or possibly
an altered form of *frið*
'peace') + *nand* 'ready,
prepared'. The name was
hereditary in the royal
families of Spain from an
early date. It was borne
by Ferdinand I (d. 1065) of
Castile and Leon, who
conducted successful

campaigns against the Moors, and by his descendant Ferdinand V (1452–1516), who finally expelled the Moors from Spain altogether; he also gave financial backing to Columbus. Through the marriage in 1496 of his daughter Joan the Mad of Castile to the Habsburg Archduke Philip, the name Ferdinand also became hereditary in the Austrian imperial family. Their younger son, Ferdinand (1503–64), acquired the succession to the kingdoms of Hungary and Bohemia by marriage in 1521, and became Holy Roman Emperor in 1558. See Ferdinand in main dictionary.
ALSO: Hernando, Fernán, Hernán.

Fidel ♂ From Late Latin *Fidelis* 'faithful', borne by St Fidelis (d. *c*.570), bishop of Mérida. The name is now chiefly associated with the Cuban leader Fidel Castro (b. 1927).

Florencio ♂ From Latin *Florentius*, a derivative of *florens* 'blossoming'.

Fortunato ♂ From Late Latin *Fortunatus* 'fortunate', a derivative of *fortuna* 'fortune, fate'; the name of numerous early saints.
FEMININE FORM: **Fortunata**.

Francisco ♂ Spanish form of Italian *Francesco*. See Francis in main dictionary.
FEMININE FORM: **Francisca**.

Fulgencio ♂ From the Latin name *Fulgentius*, a derivative of *fulgens* 'shining'; the name of a 7th-century Spanish saint, brother of Isidore of Seville.

Gg

Gabino ♂ Spanish form of Italian Gavino. See Italian appendix.

Gabriel ♂ Biblical. See main dictionary.
FEMININE FORM: **Gabriela**.

Gaspar ♂ See Caspar in main dictionary.

Gerardo ♂ Germanic. See Gerard in main dictionary.

German ♂ From the Late Latin name *Germanus* 'brother', sometimes used with the meaning 'brother in God'.

Gertrudis ♀ Germanic. See Gertrude in main dictionary.

Gervasio ♂ Norman. See Gervaise in main dictionary.

Gil ♂ From Latin *Aegidus*. See Gilles in French appendix and Giles in main dictionary.

Gilberto ♂ Germanic. See Gilbert in main dictionary.

Gloria ♀ From Latin. See main dictionary.

Godofredo ♂ Germanic. See Geoffrey in main dictionary.

Goito ♂ Variant of ▶Goyo.

Gonzalo ♂ Visigothic: from a personal name formed with *gund* 'battle, strife'.

Gracia ♀ From Latin. See Grace in main dictionary.

Graciano ♂ From Latin *Gratianus*. See Gratien in French appendix.

Graciela ♀ Pet form of ▶Gracia.

Gregorio ♂ From Greek. See Gregory in main dictionary.

Guadalupe ♀ Marian name from a place (named from Arabic *wādī al-lubb* 'river of the wolf') in Cáceres, the site of a convent with a famous image of the Virgin.

Gualtiero ♂ Germanic. See Walter in main dictionary.

Guillermo ♂ From German *Wilhelm* or English William (see main dictionary).

Gumersindo ♂ Visigothic: from a personal name composed of *guma* 'man' + *sind* 'path'.
FEMININE FORM: **Gumersinda**.

Gustavo ♂ From Scandinavian Gustav. See Scandinavian appendix.

Hh

Hector ♂ From Greek. See main dictionary.

Herlinda ♀ From a Germanic personal name composed of *heri, hari* 'army' + *lind* 'weak, tender'.

Hermengildo ♂ Visigothic: from a personal name composed of *ermen, irmen* 'whole, entire' + *gild* 'sacrifice'. St Hermenigild (d. 585) was a son of the Visigothic king Leovigild; he is considered a martyr, though the reasons for the revolt against his father which led to his death were at least as much political as religious.
ALSO: **Ermengildo**.

Hernán ♂ Variant of ▶Fernando.

Hernando ♂ Variant of ▶Fernando.

Hilario ♂ From Latin. See Hilary in main dictionary.

Hipolito ♂ From Greek *Hippolytos*. See Hippolyte in French supplement.

Hugo ♂ See main dictionary.

Humberto ♂ See Humbert in main dictionary and Umberto in Italian appendix.

Ignacio ♂ From Latin. See Ignatius in main dictionary.

Imelda ♀ Germanic (Visigothic): from a personal name

composed of *irm(en), erm(en)* 'whole, entire' + *hild* 'battle'.

Indalecio ♂ From the Latin name *Indaletius*, of unknown origin.

Inés ♀ From Greek. See Agnes in main dictionary.

Inmaculada ♀ Marian name meaning 'without taint', referring to the doctrine of the Immaculate Conception.

Inocencio ♂ From Late Latin *Innocentius*, a derivative of *innocens* 'innocent'; name of several early saints.

Isabel ♀ Of Spanish origin: a much altered version of Elizabeth (see main dictionary).

Isaura ♀ From the Late Latin personal name *Isaura*, originally an ethnic byname denoting a woman from *Isauria* in Asia Minor.

Isidro ♂ From Greek. See Isidore in main dictionary.
ALSO: **Isidoro**.

Jj

Jacinto ♂ From Greek *Hyakinthos*; the name of several early saints. See also the English girl's name Hyacinth in main dictionary.

Jaime ♂ New Testament. See James in main dictionary.

Javier ♂ Another spelling in Spanish of Xavier (see main dictionary).

Jenaro ♂ From Latin *Januarius*. See Gennaro in Italian appendix.

Jerónimo ♂ From Greek. See Jerome in main dictionary.

Jesús ♂ Religious name bestowed as a token of Christian faith. *Jesus* 'saviour' is an Aramaic form of the earlier Hebrew name Joshua (see main dictionary).

Joaquin ♂ Biblical. See Joachim in main dictionary.

Jorge ♂ From Greek. See George in main dictionary.

José ♂ Biblical. See Joseph in main dictionary.
FEMININE FORM: **Josefa**.

Juan ♂ New Testament. See John in main dictionary.
FEMININE FORM: **Juana**.

Juanita ♀ Feminine pet form of ▶Juan.
MASCULINE FORM: **Juanito**.

Julián ♂ From Late Latin. See Julian in main dictionary.

Julio ♂ From Latin. See Julius in main dictionary.
FEMININE FORM: **Julia**.

L│

Laura ♀ From Latin. See main dictionary.

Leandro ♂ From Greek. See Leander in main dictionary.

Leocadia ♀ Latinate derivative of Greek *leukas* (genitive *leukados*), poetic feminine form of *leukos* 'bright, clear'. St Leocadia (d. *c*.303) was a virgin martyr of Toledo.
MASCULINE FORM: Leocadio.

León ♂ From Late Latin. See Leo in main dictionary.

Leonardo ♂ Germanic. See Leonard in main dictionary.

Leoncio ♂ Spanish form of Italian Leonzio. See Italian appendix.

Leopoldo ♂ Germanic. See Leopold in main dictionary.

Leticia ♀ From the Latin personal name *Laetitia*; see Lettice in main dictionary.

Licerio ♂ From the Late Latin personal name *Lycerius*, a derivative of either Greek *lykē* 'light' or *lykos* 'wolf'. St Licerius was born in Lérida, and became bishop of Conserans in France (506–*c*.548).

Ligia ♀ Apparently a shortened form of *Eligia*, the feminine form of *Eligio* (see ▸Eloy).

Lola ♀ Nursery form of ▸Dolores.

Lope ♂ From the Late Latin name *Lupus* 'wolf', probably adopted as a calque of the Germanic name ▸Wolf (see main dictionary).

Lorena ♀ Spanish equivalent of Lauren (see main dictionary).

Lorenzo ♂ From Latin. See Laurence in main dictionary.

Lourdes ♀ Religious name, from the place in southern France where a young girl had visions of the Virgin Mary in 1858. ALSO: Lurdes.

Lucía ♀ From Latin. See Lucy in main dictionary.

Luciano ♂ From Latin. See Italian appendix. FEMININE FORM: Luciana.

Lucio ♂ From Latin Lucius; see main dictionary.

Luis ♂ Germanic. See Louis in main dictionary. FEMININE FORM: Luisa.

Lurdes ♀ Variant of ▸Lourdes.

Luz ♀ Marian name honouring *Nuestra Señora de la Luz* 'Our Lady of Light' (Spanish *luz*, from Latin *lux*).

Luzdivina ♀ Apparently derived from *Lidwina*, a feminine form of the Germanic name *Lidwin*, composed of *liut* 'people, race' + *win* 'friend', but altered by popular etymology to mean 'divine light' (compare ▸Luz and Italian Liduina).

Mm

Mabel ♀ Contracted form of *María Isabel* (compare ▸Maribel).

Macario ♀ From Greek *Makarios*, from *makaros* 'blessed'.

Magdalena ♀ New Testament. See Madeleine in main dictionary.

Manuel ♂ Biblical. See Emmanuel in main dictionary. FEMININE FORM: Manuela.

Marcelino ♂ From Latin *Marcellinus*, a double diminutive of Marcus. FEMININE FORM: Marcelina.

Marcelo ♂ From Latin *Marcellus*. See Marcel in main dictionary. FEMININE FORM: Marcela.

Marco ♂ From Latin. See Mark in main dictionary. ALSO: Marcos.

Margarita ♀ From Greek. See Margaret in main dictionary.

María ♀ Biblical. See Maria and Mary in main dictionary. Also used as a male name in combinations such as José María.

María José ♀ Compound of ▸María and ▸José, religous name bestowed in honour of Mary and Joseph.

Mariano ♂ From the Roman family name *Marianus*. See Italian appendix. FEMININE FORM: Mariana.

Maribel ♀ Contracted form of *María Isabel*.

Marieta ♀ Pet form of ▸María.

Marina ♀ From Latin. See main dictionary.

Mario ♂ From the Roman family name Marius (see main dictionary), but in modern times generally taken as a masculine equivalent of ▸María.

Marisol ♀ Compound name from ▸María and ▸Sol.

Marta ♀ New Testament. See Martha in main dictionary.

Martín ♂ From Latin *Martinus*. See Martin in main dictionary. FEMININE FORM: **Martina**.

Martirio ♀ Religious name alluding to the spiritual quality of martyrdom (Spanish *martirio*).

Mateo ♂ New Testament. See Matthew in main dictionary.

Matilde ♀ Germanic. See Matilda in main dictionary.

Mauricio ♂ From Late Latin. See Maurice in main dictionary.

Mauro ♂ From Latin. See Italian appendix. FEMININE FORM: **Maura**.

Máximo ♂ From Latin *maximus* 'greatest'.

Medardo ♂ From a Germanic personal name formed with an unidentified first element + *hard* 'hardy, strong'.

Mercedes ♀ Marian name honouring *Nuestra Señora de las Mercedes* 'Our Lady of Mercies'.

Miguel ♂ Biblical. See Michael in main dictionary.

Milagros ♀ Marian name honouring *Nuestra Señora de los Milagros* 'Our Lady of Miracles'.

Modesto ♂ From the Late Latin name *Modestus* 'restrained'. FEMININE FORM: **Modesta**.

Montserrat ♀ Marian name from a Catalan title of the Virgin Mary, *Nuestra Señora del Montserrat*, referring to the Benedictine monastery on Mt Montserrat near Barcelona.

Nn

Narciso ♂ From Greek. See Narcissus in main dictionary.

Natividad ♀ Religious name meaning 'nativity' (from Late Latin *nativitās*, a derivative of *nasci* 'to be born'), referring to the festival of the Nativity of the Virgin Mary, celebrated on 5 September.

Nazaret ♀ Religious name, referring to Christ's native village, *Nazareth*.

Nazario ♂ Religious name, from the Late Latin name *Nazarius*, a

derivative of *Nazareth* (compare ▸Nazaret).

Nicanor ♂ From Late Greek *Nikanēr*, composed of the elements *nikē* 'victory' + *anēr* 'man' (genitive *andros*).

Nicasio ♂ From Late Greek *Nikasios* 'victorious'. St Nicasius was a bishop of Rheims who was martyred either by the Vandals in 407 or by the Huns in 451.

Nicodemo ♂ New Testament. See Nicodemus in main dictionary.

Nicolás ♂ From Greek. See Nicholas in main dictionary. ALSO: **Nicolao**.

Nicolasa ♀ Feminine form of ▸Nicolás.

Nieves ♀ Marian name honouring *Nuestra Señora de las Nieves* 'Our Lady of the Snows', referring to a miracle alleged to have taken place in the 4th century, when Mary caused it to snow in Rome during August.

Oo

Octavio ♂ From Latin. See Octavius in main dictionary.

Ofelia ♀ See Ophelia in main dictionary.

Olalla ♀ Vernacular form of ▸Eulalia.

Onofre ♂ From an Egyptian saint's name, said to mean 'he who opens the good'.

Oscar ♂ From Gaelic. See main dictionary.

Osvaldo ♂ From English. See **Oswald** in main dictionary.

Pp

Pablo ♂ From Latin *Paulus*. See **Paul** in main dictionary.

Paco ♂ Pet form of ▸**Francisco**.

Paloma ♀ From Latin *palumba* 'dove'.

Pascual ♂ From Late Latin *Paschalis* 'of or relating to Easter'. FEMININE FORM: **Pascuala**.

Patricio ♂ Spanish form of English and Irish **Patrick** (see main dictionary). FEMININE FORM: **Patricia**.

Paulino ♂ Pet form of *Paulus*. See ▸**Pablo**. FEMININE FORM: **Paulina**.

Paz ♀ Marian name honouring *Nuestra Señora de la Paz* 'Our Lady of Peace'.

Pedro ♂ From Greek. See **Peter** in main dictionary.

Pelayo ♂ From the Greek name *Pelagios* (Latin *Pelagius*), a derivative of Greek *pelagos* 'open sea'; borne by a 10th-century saint who was martyred at the hands of the Moors in Cordoba.

Pepe ♂ Pet form of ▸**José**. ALSO: **Pepito**.

Perico ♂ Pet form of ▸**Pedro**, derived from the archaic variant *Pero*.

Perla ♀ From *perla* 'pearl'.

Piedad ♀ Religious name meaning 'piety', from Latin *pietas*. The Virgin Mary is honoured under the title *Nuestra Señora de la Piedad* on 5 November.

Pilar ♀ Marian name honouring *Nuestra Señora del Pilar* 'Our Lady of the Pillar', referring to an alleged appearance of the Virgin standing on a pillar to St James the Greater at Saragossa.

Pio ♂ From Latin *pius* 'pious, respectful'.

Placido ♂ From the Late Latin name *Placidus*, meaning 'untroubled'.

Poncio ♂ From Latin *Pontius*, originally a family name of uncertain origin.

Porfirio ♂ From the Greek name *Porphyrios* (Late Latin *Porphyrius*), from Greek *porphyra* 'purple dye'; the name of some half-dozen early saints.

Presentación ♀ Religious name referring to the feast of the Presentation (Spanish *presentación*), commemorating the presentation of the Virgin Mary in the temple at Jerusalem after the birth of Christ; celebrated on 21 November.

Primitivo ♂ From the Late Latin name *Primitivus* 'earliest', a derivative of *primus* 'first'; borne by various early martyrs, most notably one born at León in Spain and beheaded *c.*300 together with his companion St Facundus.

Primo ♂ From the Late Latin name *Primus* 'first', borne by four minor early saints.

Prospero ♂ From Latin. See **Prosper** in main dictionary.

Prudencio ♂ From the Late Latin name *Prudentius* (a derivative of *prudens* 'prudent'), borne by two Spanish saints: one, who lived in the 8th century, became bishop of Tarazona in Aragon; the second (d. 861), originally called Galindo, moved to France to escape the Moors, eventually becoming bishop of Troyes.

Purificación ♀ Marian name, bestowed in honour of the feast of the Purification (Spanish *purificación*), in which the infant Jesus was presented to God at the temple and his mother was purged of the uncleanliness associated with childbirth.

Qq

Quirce ♂ From Latin *Quiricus*; the name of a three-year-old boy martyred at Tarsus in 304 together with his mother Julitta.

Rr

Rafael ♂ Biblical; Spanish form of **Raphael** (see main dictionary), name of one of the archangels.

Rafaela ♀ Feminine form of ▸**Rafael**.

Raimundo ♂ Germanic. See **Raymond** in main dictionary.
FEMININE FORM: **Raimunda**.

Rainerio ♂ Germanic. See **Rayner** in main dictionary.

Ramiro ♂ Visigothic: probably composed of *ragin* 'advice' + *māri*, *mēri* 'famous'.

Ramón ♂ Germanic: variant of ▸**Raimundo**. See **Raymond** in main dictionary.
FEMININE FORM: **Ramona**.

Raquel ♀ Biblical. See main dictionary.

Raúl ♂ Germanic. See **Ralph** in main dictionary.

Rebeca ♀ Biblical. See **Rebecca** in main dictionary.

Refugio ♀ Religious name referring to the Marian title, *Nuestra Señora de Refugio* 'Our Lady of Refuge'.

Reinaldo ♂ Germanic. See **Reynold** in main dictionary.

Remedios ♀ Marian name honouring *Nuestra Señora de los Remedios* 'Our Lady of Remedies', with reference to her promise to relieve the sufferings of those who pray to her.

Remigio ♂ From the Latin name *Remigius*, from *remex* (genitive *remigis*) 'oarsman'.

Renato ♂ From Late Latin *Renatus* 'reborn', used by early Christians as a baptismal name.
FEMININE FORM: **Renata**.

Ricardo ♂ Germanic. See **Richard** in main dictionary.

Rigoberto ♂ From a Germanic name composed of the elements *rīc* 'power' + *berht* 'bright, shining, famous'.

Roberto ♂ Germanic. See **Robert** in main dictionary.

Rocío ♀ Marian name honouring *Nuestra Señora de la Rocío* 'Our Lady of the Dew'. Dew is associated in Roman Catholic hagiography with tears shed by the Virgin Mary for the wickedness of the world.

Rodolfo ♂ Spanish form of **Rudolf** (see main dictionary).

Rodrigo ♂ Visigothic: composed of the elements *hrōd* 'fame' + *rīc* 'power'. It was the name of the last king of the Visigoths, defeated by the Moors in 711.

Rogelio ♂ From Late Latin *Rogelius* (or *Rogellus*), a name of uncertain derivation. Sts Rogellus and Servus-Dei were martyred at Cordoba under the Moors in 852.

Rogerio ♂ Germanic. See **Roger** in main dictionary.

Roldán ♂ Germanic. See **Roland** in main dictionary.

Román ♂ From Late Latin *Romanus* 'Roman'.

Roque ♂ From Germanic. See **Rocco** in Italian appendix.

Rosa ♀ Spanish equivalent of English Rose (see main dictionary).

Rosario ♀ Marian name honouring *Nuestra Señora del Rosario* 'Our Lady of the Rosary'.

Rosendo ♂ Visigothic: from *hrōd* 'fame' + *sinps* 'path'. St Rudesind or Rosendo (907–77) was born in Galicia and served as bishop of Mondoñedo.

Rosita ♀ Pet form of ▸**Rosa**.

Rubén ♂ Biblical. See **Reuben** in main dictionary.

Rufino ♂ From Latin *Rufinus*, a derivative of *Rufus* 'red-haired'.

Rut ♀ Biblical. See **Ruth** in main dictionary.

Ruy ♂ Pet form of ▶Rodrigo. This form was common in the Middle Ages, being borne, for example, by El Cid, Ruy Diaz de Vivar (?1043–99).

Ss

Sabina ♀ From Latin. See main dictionary.
MASCULINE FORM: **Sabino**.

Salud ♀ Religious name referring to the Marian title *Nuestra Señora de la Salud* 'Our Lady of Salvation'.

Salvador ♂ Religious name borne in honour of Christ the Saviour, from Late Latin *salvator* 'saviour'.

Sancho ♂ Of uncertain origin, perhaps from Latin *sanctus* 'holy'. It will always be associated with Sancho Panza, Don Quixote's companion.

Sandalio ♂ From Latin *Sandal(i)us*, possibly representing a Latinized form of a Germanic (Visigothic) name composed of *sand* 'true' + *ulf* 'wolf'. A saint of this name was martyred at Cordoba by the Moors in *c*.855.

Santiago ♂ Literally 'Saint James': *Iago* is an obsolete Spanish form of the biblical name *Jacobus* (see **Jacob** and **James** in main dictionary). The disciple St James the Greater, brother of John the Baptist, is the patron saint of Spain.

Santos ♂ Religious name meaning 'saints', a name chosen to invoke the protection of all the saints.

Saturnino ♂ From Latin *Saturninus*, a derivative of *Saturnus*, the name of the Roman god of agriculture and vegetation.

Sebastián ♂ From Latin. See **Sebastian** in main dictionary.

Sergio ♂ From Latin *Sergius*. See **Sergei** in Russian appendix.

Seve ♂ Pet form of ▶Severiano and ▶Severino.

Severiano ♂ From Latin *Severianus*, a derivative of *Severus* (see ▶Severo).

Severino ♂ From Latin *Severinus*, a derivative of *Severus* (see ▶Severo).

Severo ♂ From the Roman family name *Severus* 'stern, severe'.

Silvestre ♂ From Latin. See **Silvester** in main dictionary.

Silvia ♀ Ancient Latin name; also the name of the mother of Gregory the Great. See main dictionary.
MASCULINE FORM: **Silvio**.

Simón ♂ New Testament. See **Simon** in main dictionary.

Socorro ♀ Marian name honouring *Nuestra Señora del Socorro* 'Our Lady of Perpetual Succour'.

Sofía ♀ From Greek. See **Sophia** in main dictionary.

Sol ♀, ♂ From the vocabulary word *sol* 'sun' (Latin *sol*). This was a common given name in the Middle Ages, being borne, for example, by one of the daughters of El Cid, and it is still in use today; in part it may now be taken as a short form of ▶Soledad.

Soledad ♀ Marian name honouring *Nuestra Señora de Soledad* 'Our Lady of Solitude'.

Susana ♀ From Hebrew. See **Susanna** in main dictionary.

Tt

Tadeo ♂ New Testament. See **Thaddeus** in main dictionary.

Telesforo ♂ From Greek *Telesphoros* derived from *telos* 'end, completion' + *pherein* 'to bring, bear'.

Teodoro ♂ From Greek. See **Theodore** in main dictionary.
FEMININE FORM: **Teodora**.

Teodosio ♂ From Greek *Theodosios*, composed *theos* 'god'

+ *dōsis* 'giving'; the name of several early saints, notably Theodosius the Cenobiarch (423–529), a Cappadocian who founded several monasteries in Palestine.

Teofilo ♂ New Testament. See Theophilus in main dictionary.

Teresa ♀ See Theresa in main dictionary.

Timoteo ♂ From New Testament Greek. See Timothy in main dictionary.

Tirso ♂ From the Greek name *Thyrsos* (from the word, possibly of Oriental origin, denoting a vine-decked staff carried by devotees of the god Dionysus). The relics of St Thyrsos, martyred at Apollonia in Phrygia in *c.*251, were brought to Spain in the early Middle Ages.

Tito ♂ From Latin. See Titus in main dictionary.

Tomás ♂ New Testament. See Thomas in main dictionary.

Toribio ♂ From Latin *Turibius*, probably a Latinized form of an indigenous Iberian name; borne by a 5th-century bishop of Astorga and by the 6th-century founder of the abbey of Liébana in Asturias.

Trinidad ♀ Religious name taken in honour of the Holy Trinity (Spanish *trinidad*).

Uu

Ulises ♂ Spanish form of Ulysses (see main dictionary).

Vv

Valentín ♂ From Latin. See Valentine in main dictionary.
FEMININE FORM: **Valentina**.

Vasco ♂ Contracted form of the medieval Spanish personal name *Velasco* or *Belasco*, from which is derived the surname *Velásquez*. The modern name has the same form as the Spanish adjective *vasco* 'Basque'.

Vicente ♂ From Latin. See Vincent in main dictionary.

Victor ♂ From Late Latin. See main dictionary.

Victoria ♀ From Latin. See main dictionary.

Vidal ♂ From Latin. See Vitale in Italian appendix. Also used by Sephardic Jews as a translation of the Hebrew name *Hayyim* 'life'.

Violeta ♀ From Late Latin. See Violet in main dictionary.

Virgilio ♂ From Latin. See Virgil in main dictionary.

Virginia ♀ From Latin. See main dictionary.

Virtudes ♀ Religious name given as a reference to the Seven Christian Virtues (Spanish *virtudes* 'virtues').

Visitación ♀ Religious name recalling the visit (Spanish *visitación*) by the Virgin Mary to her cousin Elizabeth, mother of John the Baptist (Luke 1:39–56), an event commemorated in the Catholic Church with a feast on 2 July.

Xx

Xavier ♂ See main dictionary.

Welsh Names

Aa

Aeddan ♂ Welsh equivalent of Aidan. See main dictionary.

Aeron ♀ Probably a derivative of Welsh *aer* 'battle'; borne in Celtic mythology by the goddess of battle, known in a Latinized form as *Agrona*. Modern use may have been influenced by the word *aeron* 'fruit, berries'.

Aeronwen ♀ From ►Aeron + (*g*)*wen* 'white, fair; blessed, holy'.

Aeronwy ♀ Extended form of ►Aeron using a suffix of ancient origin and uncertain derivation.

Afanen ♀ Modern: from *afanen* 'raspberry'.

Afon ♀, ♂ Modern: from *afon* 'river'.

Aled ♂ Modern name meaning 'child'.

Aledwen ♀ Modern feminine form of ►Aled formed with -*wen*, a common ending of female names in Welsh.

Alis ♀ Welsh equivalent of Alice. See main dictionary.
ALSO: **Alys**.

Alun ♂ Traditional name, indirectly related to Alan (see main dictionary), of which it is now generally taken to be the Welsh equivalent.

Andras ♂ Welsh equivalent of Andrew. See main dictionary.

Aneirin ♂ Traditional: possibly from a lost Old Welsh word cognate with Irish *nár* 'noble; modest'. The original form of the name was **Neirin**; the initial *A*- was added in the 13th century. See also Aneurin in main dictionary.

Angharad ♀ From the Old Celtic intensive prefix *an*- + *cār* 'love' + the noun suffix -*ad*. This was the name of the mother of the 12th-century chronicler Giraldus Cambrensis ('Gerald the Welshman'). In the *Mabinogi*, Angharad Golden Hand at first rejects Peredur's suit, but later falls in love with him when he comes back as the unknown Mute Knight. The name has been strongly revived in Wales since the 1940s, borne, for example, by the actress Angharad Rees (b. 1949).

Anwen ♀ From the Old Celtic intensive prefix *an*- + (*g*)*wen* 'fair; blessed'.
ALSO: **Annwen**.

Annwyl ♀ From *annwyl* 'beloved'.
ALSO: **Anwyl**.

Aranrhod ♀ Apparently a compound of Old Celtic elements meaning 'huge, round, humped' + 'wheel'. See also ►Arianrhod.

Arianrhod ♀ Altered form of ►Aranrhod, influenced by modern Welsh *arian* 'silver' + *rhod* 'wheel'.

Arianwen ♀ From *arian* 'silver' + (*g*)*wen*, feminine of *gwyn* 'white, fair; blessed, holy'.

Arwel ♂ 'Wept over'.

Awstin ♂ Welsh equivalent of Austin. See main dictionary.

Bb

Berwyn ♂ From an ancient Welsh personal name composed of *barr* 'head' + (*g*)*wyn* 'white, fair'.

Bethan ♀ Pet form of Beth (see main dictionary), now widely used in the English-speaking world.

Betrys ♀ Welsh spelling of Beatrice. See main dictionary.

Bleddyn ♂ Traditional: from an ancient byname from *blaidd* 'wolf' + the diminutive suffix -*yn*. *Blaidd* was often used in medieval Welsh as a term for a hero.

Blodeyn ♀ Traditional name meaning 'flower'.
ALSO: **Blodyn**.

Blodwedd ♀ Name borne by a character in

the *Mabinogi*. She was conjured up out of flowers as a bride for Lleu Llaw Gyffes, and was originally called *Blodeuedd*, a derivative of *blawd* 'flowers'. After she had treacherously had her husband killed, she was transformed into an owl, and her name was changed to *Blodeuwedd* 'flower face', an allusion to the markings round the eyes of the owl.

Blodwen ♀ Traditional: from *blawd* 'flowers' + (*g*)*wen* 'white', feminine of *gwyn* 'white, fair; blessed, holy'.
ALSO: **Blodwyn**.

Braith ♀, ♂ From a vocabulary word meaning 'speckled'.

Bran ♂ Traditional: from *brân* 'raven'; borne in Welsh and Irish mythology by Bran the Blessed, a giant-sized god, the son of the sea god Mannannan Mac Lir.

Branwen ♀ Traditional: apparently from *brân* 'raven' + (*g*)*wen*, feminine of *gwyn* 'white, fair; blessed, holy', but more probably a variant of ▶Bronwen.
ALSO: **Brangwen**.

Briallen ♀ Modern coinage from the vocabulary word meaning 'primrose'.

Bronwen ♀ From *bron* 'breast' + (*g*)*wen*, feminine of *gwyn* 'white, fair; blessed, holy'.
ALSO: **Bronwyn**.

Brychan ♂ Traditional: from an Old Welsh byname meaning 'speckled'; the name of a legendary Welsh figure who was the father of ten sons and twenty-four daughters, many of whom came to be venerated as saints.

Bryn ♂ 20th-century coinage from *bryn* 'hill'; also a short form of ▶Brynmor.
ALSO: **Brynn**.

Brynmor ♂ 20th-century coinage from a place in Gwynedd named with *bryn* 'hill' + *mawr* 'large'.

Cc

Cadell ♂ Traditional: from *cad* 'battle' + the diminutive suffix *-el*.

Cadfael ♂ Traditional: from *cad* 'battle' + *mael* 'prince'. The detective monk Brother Cadfael features in a series of novels by Ellis Peters.

Cadfan ♂ Traditional: from *cad* 'battle' + *ban* 'peak'.

Cadoc ♂ Traditional: from a derivative of *cad* 'battle'; borne by a 6th-century Welsh saint, a missioner and the founder of Nant Carfan (later Llancarfan) monastery.

Cadogan ♂ Anglicized form of ▶Cadwgan. It was revived in the 19th century, perhaps in part as a transferred use of the surname.

Cadwaladr ♂ Ancient Celtic name composed of *cad* 'battle' + *gwaladr* 'leader', commonly given to the sons of kings and princes. St Cadwaladr was killed while maintaining a stronghold against the invading Saxons in the 7th century.
ALSO: **Cadwalader** (Anglicized form).

Cadwgan ♂ Traditional: from Old Welsh *cad* 'battle' + *gwogawn* 'glory, distinction', or 'honour'; the name of several Welsh princes in the early Middle Ages and of two characters mentioned in the *Mabinogi*.
ALSO: **Cadwgawn**; **Cadogan** (Anglicized form).

Caerwyn ♂ Altered form of ▶Carwyn, influenced by the many Welsh place names with the first element *caer* 'fort'.

Caradoc ♂ Respelling of *Caradog*, an ancient Celtic name apparently derived from the root *câr* 'love'. This name was borne by a British chieftain of the 1st century AD in the Latinized form *Caractacus*, son of Cunobelinos.

Caron ♀ From *caru* 'to love'.

Carwyn ♂ Modern: compound of *câr* 'love' + (*g*)*wyn* 'white, fair; blessed, holy'.

Carys ♀ Modern: from *câr* 'love' + the ending -*ys*, derived by analogy with names such as ▶Gladys. ALSO: **Cerys**.

Catrin ♀ Welsh equivalent of Katherine. See main dictionary.

Ceinwen ♀ Traditional: from *cain* 'fair, lovely' + (*g*)*wen* 'white, fair; blessed, holy'; borne by a 5th-century saint, daughter of the chieftain Brychan.

Celyn ♂ From the vocabulary word meaning 'holly'.

Cenydd ♂ Welsh equivalent of Kenneth. See main dictionary.

Ceri ♀, ♂ Of uncertain origin: as a girl's name it is probably a short form of ▶Ceridwen.

Ceridwen ♀ Apparently derived from *cerdd* 'poetry' + (*g*)*wen*, feminine form of *gwyn* 'white, fair; blessed, holy'. In Celtic folklore it is the name of the goddess of poetic inspiration and the mother of the 6th-century Welsh hero Taliesin. ALSO: **Cerridwyn**.

Cerys ♀ Variant of ▶Carys.

Cledwyn ♂ Traditional: apparently derived from *caled* 'hard, rough' + (*g*)*wyn* 'white, fair; blessed, holy'.

Colwyn ♂ Modern: adoption of the Daffyd place name.

Crystin ♀ Welsh equivalent of Christine. See main dictionary.

Cynddelw ♂ Traditional: perhaps from an Old Celtic element meaning 'high, exalted' + Welsh *delw* 'image, statue'.

Cystenian ♂ Welsh equivalent of Constantine. See main dictionary.

Dd

Dafydd ♂ Welsh equivalent of David (see main dictionary). In widespread use during the Middle Ages, it was later largely replaced by the English form, but since the late 19th century it has come into its own again.

Dai ♂ Now used as a pet form of David (see main dictionary), but originally of distinct origin, probably from an Old Celtic word *dei* 'to shine'. See also ▶Dewi.

Deiniol ♂ Usually regarded as the Welsh form of Daniel (see main dictionary), but the name is ancient in Wales and possibly of Celtic origin.

Delwyn ♀ Modern: composed of *del* 'pretty, neat' + (*g*)*wyn* 'white, fair; blessed, holy'.

Delyth ♀ Modern: composed of *del*

'pretty, neat' + the ending -*yth*, formed on the analogy of names such as ▶Gwenyth.

Dewi ♂ A Welsh equivalent (earlier *Dewydd*) of ▶David (see main dictionary), traditionally associated with the patron saint of Wales. See also ▶Dai.

Dilwen ♀ Modern: from *dil*- (see ▶Dilys) + (*g*)*wen*, feminine form of *gwyn* 'white, fair; blessed, holy'.

Dilwyn ♂ Modern: composed of *dil* (see ▶Dilys) + (*g*)*wyn* 'white, fair; blessed, holy'.

Dilys ♀ Modern: from *dilys* 'genuine, true; steadfast'. ALSO: **Dylis, Dyllis**.

Disgleirio ♀, ♂ Modern: related to *disglair* 'bright, glittering'.

Drystan ♂ Variant of ▶Trystan. Drystan son of Tallwch is briefly mentioned in the *Mabinogi* as one of King Arthur's advisers.

Dylan ♂ Of uncertain origin, probably connected with a Celtic word meaning 'sea'; in the *Mabinogi* it is the name of the miraculously born son of Arianrhod, who became a minor divinity of the sea. See also main dictionary.

Dylis ♀ Variant spelling of ▶Dilys.

Ee

Eiddwen ♀ Modern: apparently derived from *eiddun* 'desirous; fond' + the feminine names suffix (g)*wen*, from *gwyn* 'white, fair; blessed, holy'.

Eiluned ♀ Variant of ▶Eluned.

Eilwen ♀ Possibly from *ael* 'brow' + (g)*wen*, feminine of *gwyn* 'white, fair; blessed, holy'.

Einion ♂ Traditional: originally a byname meaning 'anvil'.

Einwys ♂ Pet form of ▶Einion.

Eira ♀ Modern: from *eira* 'snow'.

Eirian ♀ Modern: from the vocabulary word meaning 'beautiful, bright' or 'silver'.

Eirlys ♀ Modern: from the vocabulary word meaning 'snowdrop'.

Eirwen ♀ Modern: from *eira* 'snow' + (g)*wen*, feminine form of *gwyn* 'white, fair; blessed, holy'.

Elen ♀ Welsh equivalent of Helen (see main dictionary). It is identical with the Welsh vocabulary word *elen* 'nymph', but this is unlikely to be the origin. ALSO: Elin.

Eleri ♀ Ancient name of uncertain origin. *Eleri* is also a Welsh river name, probably derived from *alar* 'surfeit', but it is not clear whether there is a connection between the personal name and the river name.

Elin ♀ Variant of ▶Elen.

Elisud ♂ Traditional: from *elus* 'kind, benevolent'.
ALSO: Ellis (Anglicized form; see main dictionary).

Eluned ♀ Apparently a revival of the older Welsh name Luned, or *Lunet*. *Lunete* is the form of the name used by the French writer Chrétien de Troyes.
ALSO: Eiluned.

Elwyn ♂ Of uncertain origin. In the modern Welsh name the influence of the word (g)*wyn* 'white, fair; blessed, holy' is apparent. However, this is also one of the forms used for the name of a 6th-century Irish saint; it may be no more than a variant of Alan (see main dictionary).

Emlyn ♂ Of uncertain origin, possibly from Latin *Aemilianus* (a derivative of the old Roman family name *Aemilius*, which is probably from *aemulus* 'rival'). Alternatively, it may have a Celtic origin; there are Breton and Irish saints recorded as *Aemilianus*, which may be a Latinized form of a lost Celtic name.

Emrys ♂ Welsh equivalent of Ambrose (see main dictionary),

commonly used in families of Welsh origin since the early 20th-century.

Emyr ♂ Traditional: originally a byname meaning 'ruler, king, lord'.

Enfys ♀ Modern: from *enfys* 'rainbow'.

Enid ♀ Of uncertain derivation. See main dictionary.

Ercwlff ♀ Welsh equivalent of Hercules. See main dictionary.

Esyllt ♀ Traditional name, probably meaning 'of fair aspect'; the Welsh equivalent of Isolde (see main dictionary).

Evan ♂ Anglicized form of ▶Iefan. See also main dictionary.

Ff

Ffion ♀ Welsh form of Fiona (see main dictionary). The spelling *ff-* is used in Welsh to represent the sound *f* rather than the *v* indicated by a single *f-*.

Ffraid ♀ Welsh equivalent of Bridget. See main dictionary.

Folant ♂ Welsh equivalent of Valentine. See main dictionary.

Gg

Gaenor ♀ Apparently a form of Gaynor (see main dictionary) adapted to Welsh orthography. It also may have been influenced by the name of the saint commemorated at Llangeinwyr in Glamorgan, known popularly as *Llangeinor*. Her name is derived from Welsh *cain* 'beautiful' + (*g*)*wyry*(*f*) 'maiden'.

Gareth ♂ Of uncertain derivation. See main dictionary.

Geraint ♂ From a British name that first appears in a Greek inscription in the form *Gerontios*, possibly influenced by the Greek vocabulary word *gerōn* (genitive *gerontos*) 'old man'. In recent years the name has become very popular in Wales.

Gerallt ♂ Welsh equivalent of Gerald. See main dictionary.

Gethin ♂ Traditional: from a lenited adjectival form of the byname *Cethin* 'dusky, swarthy'.
ALSO: **Gethen**.

Gladys ♀ From the Old Welsh name ▶Gwladus, of uncertain derivation.

Glaw ♂, ♀ Modern: from *glaw* 'rain'.

Glenda ♀ Modern: composed of *glân* 'clean, pure, holy' + *da* 'good'.

Glendower ♂ Anglicized form of ▶Glyndwr.

Glenys ♀ Modern: from *glân* 'pure, holy' + the

ending *-ys* by analogy with names such as ▶Dilys and ▶Gladys.
ALSO: **Glynis**.

Glyn ♂ Modern: from the Welsh place name element *glyn* 'valley'.
ALSO: **Glynn**.

Glyndwr ♂ Adopted in the 20th century in honour of the medieval Welsh patriot Owain Glyndŵr (*c*.1359–1416; known in English as Owen Glendower). In his case it was a byname referring to the fact that he came from a place named with Welsh *glyn* 'valley' + *dŵr* 'water'.
ALSO: **Glendower** (Anglicized form).

Glynis ♀ Variant of ▶Glenys.

Goronwy ♂ Traditional name of uncertain derivation, borne in the *Mabinogi* by Goronwy the Staunch, Lord of Penllyn. He became the lover of the flower-maiden Blodeuedd and murdered her husband Lleu Llaw Gyffes, but Lleu was later restored to life and definitively dispatched Goronwy.
ALSO: **Gronw**.

Griff ♂ Informal short form of ▶Griffith.

Griffin ♂ From a medieval Latinized form, *Griffinus*, of ▶Griffith.

Griffith ♂ Anglicized form of ▶Gruffudd.

Grigor ♂ Welsh equivalent of Gregory. See main dictionary.

Gronw ♂ Variant of ▶Goronwy.

Gruffudd ♂ From Old Welsh *Grip(p)iud*, from an unexplained first element + a second element meaning 'lord, prince'. Gruffydd ap Llewelyn (d. 1063) was one of the most able rulers of Wales in the Middle Ages, scoring notable victories over the English until he was eventually defeated by King Harold in 1063.
ALSO: **Gruffud, Griffudd**; **Griffith** (Anglicized form).

Grwn ♂ Modern name meaning 'ridge'.

Guto ♂ Pet form of ▶Gruffudd.
ALSO: **Gutun, Gutyn**.

Gwalchmai ♂ Traditional: from *gwalch* 'hawk' + *mai* 'plain'. In the *Mabinogi*, Gwalchmai (or *Gwalchmei*) is the name of one of King Arthur's nine captains, 'the most distinguished for his fighting ability and his noble bearing'.

Gwallter ♂ Welsh equivalent of Walter. See main dictionary.

Gwatcyn ♂ Welsh equivalent of Watkin. See main dictionary.

Gwawr ♀ Modern: from *gwawr* 'dawn'.

Gwen ♀ Short form of ▶Gwendolen or

▶Gwenllian, or an independent name from *gwen*, the feminine form of *gwyn* 'white, fair; blessed, holy'. It was borne by a 5th-century saint, aunt of St David and mother of the minor saints Cybi and Cadfan.

Gwenda ♀ Modern: from *gwen*, the feminine form of *gwyn* 'white, fair; blessed, holy' (see ▶Gwen) + *da* 'good'.

Gwendolen ♀ Traditional: from *gwen*, the feminine form of *gwyn* 'white, fair; blessed, holy' (see ▶Gwen) + *dolen* 'ring; bow'. See also main dictionary.

Gweneth ♀ Variant of ▶Gwyneth.

Gwenfrewi ♀ Traditional: from *gwen*, the feminine form of *gwyn* 'white, fair; blessed, holy' (see ▶Gwen) + *frewi* 'reconciliation'. This was borne by a 7th-century Welsh saint around whom a large body of legends grew up.

Gwenhwyfar ♀ Traditional: from *gwen*, the feminine form of *gwyn* 'white, fair; blessed, holy' + *hwyfar* 'smooth, soft'. See also Jennifer, Guinevere in main dictionary.

Gwenllian ♀ Traditional: from *gwen*, the feminine form of *gwyn* 'white, fair; blessed, holy' (see ▶Gwen) + *lliant* 'flood, flow' (probably in the transferred sense 'foamy'

or 'white', referring to a pale complexion).

Gwenyth ♀ Variant of ▶Gwyneth; alternatively, possibly based on *gwenith* 'wheat', a word used in poetry to mean 'the favourite' or 'the pick of the bunch'.

Gwerful ♀ Traditional name composed of *gwair* 'bend, ring, circle' + the mutated form of *mul* 'shy, modest'.
ALSO: **Gweirful, Gwerfyl**.

Gwilym ♂ Welsh equivalent of William (see main dictionary), in use since the Middle Ages.
ALSO: **Gwilim, Gwillym**.

Gwladus ♀ Old form of ▶Gladys, of uncertain derivation.
ALSO: **Gwladys**.

Gwydyr ♂ Variant of ▶Gwythyr.

Gwyn ♂ Originally a byname from Welsh *gwyn* 'white, fair; blessed, holy'. See also ▶Wyn.
ALSO: **Gwynn**.

Gwynedd ♂ Taken from a region of medieval North Wales (now resurrected as the name of a composite county in Wales).

Gwyneira ♀ Compound of *gwyn* 'white, fair; blessed, holy' + *eira* 'snow'.

Gwyneth ♀ Altered form of ▶Gwynedd, used as a girl's name.
ALSO: **Gwynneth, Gweneth, Gwenyth**.

Gwynfor ♂ Modern: coined in the 20th century from *gwyn* 'white, fair; blessed, holy' + the mutated form of *mawr* 'great, large' (found in this form in a number of place names).

Gwythyr ♂ Traditional: derived in Roman times from the Latin name Victor (see main dictionary). A character with this name appears in the *Mabinogi*.
ALSO: **Gwydyr**.

Hh

Haul ♂ Modern: from *haul* 'sun'.

Heddwyn ♂ Modern: from *hedd* 'peace' + (g)*wyn* 'white, fair; blessed, holy'. Use as a given name was popularized by the fame of the bard Hedd Wyn (Ellis Humphrey Evans), who posthumously won the bardic chair at the National Eisteddfod in 1917, having been killed in the First World War.

Hefin ♂ Modern: from a derivative of *ha(f)* 'summer'.

Hefina ♀ Feminine form of ▶Hefin.

Heilyn ♂ Traditional: originally an occupational byname for a steward or wine-pourer, from the stem of the verb *heilio* 'to prepare; wait on' + the diminutive suffix *-yn*. The name is borne in the *Mabinogi* by two characters: Heilyn the son of Gwynn the Old, and Heilyn the Red, son of Cadgwawn.

Heledd ♀ Traditional name of uncertain derivation; borne by a semi-legendary princess of the 7th-century, in whose name a lament for her brother's death was composed in the 9th-century.
ALSO: **Hyledd**.

Heulog ♀, ♂ Modern: from *heulog* 'sunny'.

Heulwen ♀ Modern: from *heulwen* 'sunshine'.

Hopcyn ♂ Welsh spelling of Hopkin. See main dictionary.

Howell ♂ Anglicized form of ▶Hywel or a transferred use of the surname derived from that name.

Huw ♂ Welsh equivalent of Hugh. See main dictionary.

Hyledd ♀ Variant of ▶Heledd.

Hywel ♂ Traditional: originally a byname from a vocabulary word meaning 'eminent, conspicuous'; it was common in the Middle Ages and was revived in the 20th-century.
ALSO: **Hywell**; **Howell** (Anglicized form).

I i

Iago ♂ Welsh equivalent of Jacob. See main dictionary.

Ianto ♂ Pet form of *Ifan*; see ▶Ieuan.

Idris ♂ Traditional: from *iud* 'lord' + *rīs* 'ardent; impulsive'. It was common in the Middle Ages and earlier, and has been strongly revived since the late 19th-century.

Idwal ♂ Traditional: from *iud* 'lord, master' + (*g*)*wal* 'wall, rampart'.

Iefan ♂ Later form of ▶Ieuan.

Iestyn ♂ Welsh equivalent of Justin. See main dictionary.

Ieuan ♂ From Latin *Iohannes*. See John in main dictionary.
ALSO: **Iefan**, **Ifan** (later forms).

Ifor ♂ Traditional name of uncertain derivation; sometimes Anglicized as ▶Ivor, but there is no connection in origin between the two names.

Ilar ♂ Welsh equivalent of Hilary. See main dictionary.

Illtud ♂ Traditional: from *il*, *el* 'multitude' + *tud* 'land; people'; borne by a famous Welsh saint (d. *c.*505) who founded the abbey of Llantwit (originally *Llan-Illtud* 'church of Illtud').
ALSO: **Illtyd** (modern spelling).

Ioan ♂ Welsh equivalent of John. See main dictionary.

Iolo ♂ Pet form of ▶Iorwerth.

Iolyn ♂ Pet form of ▶Iorwerth.

Iorwerth ♂ Traditional: from *iōr* 'lord' + a mutated form of *berth* 'handsome'; borne in the *Mabinogi* by the jealous brother of Madawg, son of Maredudd. *Iorwerth* came to be regarded as a Welsh equivalent of Edward, but it has no actual connection with that name.
ALSO: **Yorath** (Anglicized form).

Islwyn ♂ Modern: from the name of a mountain in the county of Gwent, named with Welsh *is* 'below' + *llwyn* 'grove'.

Ithel ♂ Traditional: compound of *iud* 'lord, prince' + *hael* 'generous'; borne in the *Mabinogi* by the son of Llarian.

L l

Lleu ♂ Traditional name meaning 'bright, shining'; akin to the name of the Celtic god known in Old Irish as *Lugh*, Gaulish *Lugus*. It was borne in the *Mabinogi* by Lleu Llaw Gyffes ('Lleu Skilful Hand'), the son of Aranrhod, and has been revived in modern times.

Lleulu ♀ Welsh equivalent of Lucia. See main dictionary.

Llew ♂ Traditional name meaning 'lion'; also used as a short form of ▶Llewelyn.

Llewella ♀ Modern:
feminine form of
▸Llewelyn.

Llewelyn ♂ Traditional:
altered form (influenced
by *llew* 'lion') of *Llywelyn*,
an ancient name of
uncertain derivation. It
probably goes back to the
Old Celtic name
Lugobelinos, the first
element of which is *Lugu-*
(the name of a god; see
▸Lleu); the second is a
name-forming element
found also in names such
as *Cunobelinus* (*Cymbeline*).
The name was borne by
Llewelyn ap Iorwerth
(1173–1240) and his
grandson Llewelyn ap
Gruffydd (d. 1282),
Welsh princes who for
a time united their
countrymen in
North Wales and led
opposition to the power
of the Norman barons
in South Wales and
the Marches.
ALSO: **Llewellyn**,
Llywel(l)yn.

Lloyd ♂ Transferred use
of the Welsh surname,
originally a nickname
meaning 'grey(-haired)'
(Welsh *llwyd*).

Llywarch ♂ Traditional,
now only occasionally
used: compound of the
god's name *Lugu-* (see
▸Lleu) + Old Celtic *marcos*
'horse'.

Llywelyn ♂ See
▸Llewelyn.

Lowri ♀ Welsh
equivalent of Laura. See
main dictionary.

Luned ♀ See ▸Eluned.

Lyn ♂ Short form of
▸Llewelyn. See also Lynn
in main dictionary.

Mm

Mabon ♂ 20th-century
revival of an Old Welsh
personal name derived
from Old Celtic *mab*
'son'. This seems to have
been originally the name
of a divinity; it is also
borne by a character in
the tale of Culhwch and
Olwen.

Macsen ♂ Welsh
equivalent of Maxim. See
main dictionary.

Madoc ♂. Traditional
name, possibly having
the sense 'fortunate' or
alternatively from Celtic
aodh 'fire'.
ALSO: **Madog**.

Mair ♀ From Latin
Maria via Old Welsh *Meir*.
See **Mary** in main
dictionary.

Mairwen ♀ Compound
of ▸Mair + (*g*)*wen*,
feminine form of (*g*)*wyn*
'white, fair; blessed,
holy'.

Maldwyn ♂ Welsh
form of ▸Baldwin. See
main dictionary.

Mallt ♀ Welsh
equivalent of Maud (see
main dictionary), a
common name in the
Middle Ages.

Mared ♀ Simplified
form of ▸Marged.

Marged ♀ Welsh
equivalent of Margaret.
See main dictionary.

ALSO: **Mared** (simplified
form).

Mari ♀ Welsh
equivalent of Mary;
compare ▸Mair.

Megan ♀ Pet form of
Margaret. See main
dictionary.

Meical ♂ Welsh
equivalent of ▸Michael.

Meilyr ♂ Traditional:
from an Old Celtic name,
Maglorīx, derived from
maglos 'chief' + *rīx* 'ruler'.

Meinir ♀ Modern:
compound of *main* 'thin,
slender' + *hir* 'long'.

Meinwen ♀ Modern:
compound of *main*
'slender' + (*g*)*wen*,
feminine form of *gwyn*
'white, fair; blessed,
holy'.

Meirion ♂ Traditional:
derived in the Roman
period from Latin
Marianus (a derivative of
Marius; see main
dictionary).
ALSO: **Merrion**.

Meiriona ♀ Modern:
feminine form of
▸Meirion.

Meirionwen ♀ Modern
feminine elaborated
form of ▸Meirion.

Meredith ♀, ♂ From
the Old Welsh male
personal name *Maredudd*,
later *Mereudd*, from an
unexplained first
element + *iudd* 'lord'. See
also main dictionary.

Mererid ♀ Welsh
equivalent of Margaret
(see main dictionary).

See also ▶Mared and ▶Marged.

Merfyn ♂ Traditional: from Old Welsh *mer*, probably meaning 'marrow' + *myn* 'eminent'; borne by a shadowy 9th-century Welsh king.
ALSO: **Mervin, Mervyn** (Anglicized forms).

Merlin ♂ English form of ▶Myrddin. See also main dictionary.

Merrion ♂ Variant of ▶Meirion.

Meurig ♂ From Latin *Mauricius* via Old Welsh *Mouric*. See Maurice in main dictionary.
ALSO: **Meuric**.

Mihangel ♂ Older Welsh equivalent of Michael (see main dictionary), representing a contraction of the phrase 'Michael the Archangel'.

Morcant ♂ Traditional: composed of an unexplained first element + a second representing the Old Celtic element *cant* 'circle; completion'.
ALSO: **Morgan** (Anglicized form; see main dictionary).

Morwenna ♀ From an Old Celtic personal name derived from an element akin to Welsh *morwyn* 'maiden'. It was revived in Wales in the mid 20th century.
ALSO: **Morwen**.

Mostyn ♂ From the name of a place in Clwyd, on the Dee estuary, which in fact derives its name from Old English (*mos* 'moss' + *tūn* 'enclosure, settlement') rather than Welsh.

Myfanwy ♀ Compound of the Welsh affectionate prefix *my-* + *banwy*, a variant form of *banw*, akin to *benyw* or *menyw* 'woman'.

Myrddin ♂ Traditional: apparently composed of Old Celtic elements meaning 'sea' and 'hill' or 'fort'.
ALSO: **Merlin** (Anglicized form).

Nn

Neirin ♂ See ▶Aneirin.

Nerys ♀ Modern: perhaps intended to be from Welsh *nêr* 'lord', with the suffix *-ys* by analogy with other girls' names such as ▶Dilys and ▶Gladys.

Nesta ♀ Latinized version of *Nest*, a Welsh pet form of Agnes (see main dictionary); the name of the grandmother of the 12th-century chronicler Giraldus Cambrensis ('Gerald the Welshman').

Nia ♀ Welsh form of the Irish name Niamh (see Irish appendix).

Nye ♂ Pet form of ▶Aneirin.

Oo

Olwen ♀ From *ôl* 'footprint, track' + (*g*)*wen*, feminine form of *gwyn* 'white, fair; blessed, holy'; in Welsh legend the name of a character who had the magical property of causing flowers to spring up behind her wherever she went.
ALSO: **Olwin, Olwyn**.

Owain ♂ Perhaps derived in the Roman period from the Latin name *Eugenius* (see Eugene in main dictionary); alternatively, possibly from an Old Celtic name meaning 'born of Esos'. Esos (or Aesos) was a Celtic god known to have been the subject of a cult in ancient Gaul.

Owen ♂ Modern form of ▶Owain or a transferred use of the surname derived from the personal name. See also main dictionary.

Owena ♀ Modern: feminine form of ▶Owen.

Pp

Paderau ♀, ♂ Modern: from *paderau* 'beads, rosary'.

Padrig ♂ Welsh equivalent of Patrick. See main dictionary.

Pedr ♂ Welsh equivalent of Peter. See main dictionary.

Pryderi ♂ Traditional name meaning 'caring for' (later 'anxiety'). It is borne in the *Mabinogi* by Pryderi, son of Pwyll, who makes several appearances in the narrative.

Rr

Reece ♂ Anglicized spelling of ▸Rhys, in some cases representing a transferred use of the surname.
ALSO: **Rees(e)**.

Rhamantus ♀ Modern: from *rhamantus* 'romantic'.

Rheanna ♀ Altered form of ▸Rhiannon, influenced by the spelling of *Deanna*.

Rheinallt ♂ Welsh equivalent of Reynold. See main dictionary.

Rhian ♀ Modern: 'maiden', but also taken as a short form of ▸Rhiannon.
ALSO: **Rian, Rhianu**.

Rhiannon ♀ Probably from the Old Celtic title *Rigantona* 'great queen'; borne in Celtic mythology by a minor deity associated with the moon, and in the *Mabinogi* by a daughter of Hyfeidd the Old. It was not used as a given name before the 20th century.
ALSO: **Rhianon, Riannon**.

Rhianu ♀ Variant of ▸Rhian.

Rhisiart ♂ Welsh equivalent of Richard. See main dictionary.

Rhodri ♂ Traditional: from *rhod* 'wheel' + *rhi* 'ruler'; the name of a 9th-century Welsh king.

ALSO: **Rhodrhi**.

Rhonwen ♀ Traditional: either from *rhon* 'lance' + (*g*)*wen*, feminine form of *gwyn* 'white, fair; blessed, holy', or from *rhawn* 'hair' + (*g*)*wen*. It was used by medieval Welsh poets as a form of Rowena (see main dictionary), regarded as the progenitrix of the English nation, and is now fairly common in Wales.

Rhosyn ♀ Modern: from *rhosyn* 'rose'.

Rhydderch ♂ Recent revival of a traditional name meaning 'reddish-brown', which gave rise to the surname *Prothero(e)* (from *ap Rhydderch* 'son of Rhydderch'). Though unrelated, it is commonly Anglicized as Roderick (see main dictionary).

Rhys ♂ Traditional name meaning 'ardour'; borne in the Middle Ages by various rulers in south-west Wales, including Rhys ap Tewdur (d. 1093) and Rhys ap Gruffudd (1132–97).
ALSO: **Reece, Rees** (Anglicized forms).

Rolant ♂ Welsh equivalent of Roland. See main dictionary.

Ss

Sawyl ♂ Welsh equivalent of Samuel (see main dictionary), a

reduced version of earlier *Safwyl*.

Seissylt ♂ Apparently a Brittonic or Old Welsh form of the Latin name *Sextilius*, from *Sextus* 'sixth'. See also Cecil in main dictionary.

Seren ♀ Modern: from *seren* 'star'.

Shanee ♀ Anglicized form of ▸Siani.

Siân ♀ From Anglo-Norman *Jeanne*. See Jane in main dictionary.

Siani ♀ Pet form of ▸Siân.

Siarl ♂ Welsh equivalent of Charles. See main dictionary.

Sieffre ♂ Welsh equivalent of Geoffrey. See main dictionary.

Siencyn ♂ Welsh form of Jenkin. See main dictionary.

Siôn ♂ From Anglo-Norman *Jean*. See John in main dictionary.

Sioned ♀ Welsh equivalent of Janet. See in main dictionary.

Siôr ♂ Welsh equivalent of George. See main dictionary.

Siors ♂ Welsh equivalent of George. See main dictionary.
ALSO: **Siorus, Siorys**.

Siwan ♀ Welsh equivalent of Joan. See main dictionary.

Steffan ♂ Welsh equivalent of Stephen. See main dictionary.

Tt

Taffy ♂ Pet form of ▶Dafydd.

Talfryn ♂ Modern: originally a local name, from Welsh *tal* 'high; end of ' + a mutated form of *bryn* 'hill'.

Taliesin ♂ Pronounced 'tahl-**yes**-in', from *tâl* 'brow' + *iesin* 'shining'; the name of a legendary 6th-century Welsh poet. It has been revived in recent times.

Tegan ♀ Modern: based on *teg* 'lovely'.

Tegwen ♀ Modern: from *teg* 'lovely' + (g)*wen*, feminine form of *gwyn* 'white, fair; blessed, holy'.

Teleri ♀ Extension of the name ▶Eleri, with the addition of the honorific prefix *ty-* 'your'; Teleri, daughter of Peul, is mentioned in the *Mabinogi*.

Tirion ♀ Modern: from the vocabulary word meaning 'kind, gentle'.

Tiwlip ♀ Modern: from the vocabulary word meaning 'tulip'.

Tomos ♂ Welsh equivalent of Thomas. See main dictionary.

Trahaearn ♂ Traditional: composed of the intensive prefix *tra-* + *haearn* 'iron'.
ALSO: **Traherne** (Anglicized form).

Trefor ♂ Transferred use of the surname, derived in turn from a place name composed of *tref* 'settlement' + *fŏr*, mutated form of *mawr* 'large'.
ALSO: **Trevor** (Anglicized form).

Trystan Welsh variant spelling of Tristan. See main dictionary.

Tudur ♂ Traditional: from the Old Celtic form *Teutorix*, composed of elements meaning 'people, tribe' and 'ruler, king'. It has been described as a Welsh form of *Theodore*, but there is no connection between them, though it is ultimately akin to the Germanic name *Theodoric* (see **Terry** in main dictionary).
ALSO: **Tudyr** (an earlier spelling); **Tudor** (Anglicized spelling).

Uu

Urien ♂ Possibly derived from Old Celtic *ŏrbo* 'privileged' + *gen* 'birth'; borne by a character in the *Mabinogi*, Urien of Rheged, who is probably identical with the historical figure Urien who fought against the

Northumbrians in the 6th-century.

Vv

Vaughan ♂ Transferred use of the surname, in origin a nickname from the mutated form (*fychan* in Welsh orthography) of the Welsh adjective *bychan* 'small'.
ALSO: **Vaughn**.

Ww

Wmffre ♂ Welsh equivalent of Humphrey. See main dictionary.

Wyn ♂ Traditional: originally a byname from (g)*wyn* 'white, fair; blessed, holy'; the name is found in this form from the early Middle Ages.
ALSO: **Wynne** (see also main dictionary).

Wynfor ♂ Variant of ▶Gwynfor.

Yy

Ynyr ♂ Traditional: pronounced '**inn**-eer', probably from the Latin name *Honorius* (a derivative of *honor* 'renown').

Yorath ♂ Anglicized form of ▶Iorwerth or, in some cases, a transferred use of the surname derived from it.

Appendix 14:
Unisex Names

Adina	Cameron	Erin	Jess	Lesley	Patsy	Shea
Ainsley	Carey	Esmé	Jesse	Leslie	Phil	Shelby
Alex	Casey	Evelyn	Jessie	Lexie	Pip	Shelley
Alexis	Casy	Finlay	Jo	Lexis	Rafferty	Sheridan
Alfa	Cassidy	France	Jocelyn	Lexy	Randy	Sidney
Ali	Charley	Frankie	Jody	Lindsay	Raven	Silver
Alpha	Charlie	Freddie	Jordan	Logan	Reagan	Simcha
Angel	Chris	Gabriel	Jos	Loren	Regan	Simran
Ariel	Christian	Gaby	Joss	Lou	René	Sky
Armani	Christie	Gene	Jude	Lynden	Ricky	Skylar
Ashley	Christy	Georgie	Jules	Macey	Riley	Slaney
Ashton	Clem	Germaine	Kacey	Mackenzie	Rio	Sly
Atholl	Clemmie	Gerry	Kay	Maddison	Robbie	Stacey
Aubrey	Cody	Ginger	Kelly	Madison	Robin	Stevie
Avery	Comfort	Glenn	Kelsey	Mallory	Roni	Storm
Bailey	Courtney	Harley	Kendall	Mandy	Ronnie	Sydney
Beau	Cyrille	Harper	Kennedy	Marty	Rowan	Tate
Billie	Dale	Hilary	Kerry	Maxie	Rusty	Taylor
Billy	Dana	Izzy	Kim	Mel	Ryan	Teagan
Blair	Darcy	Jackie	Kimberley	Meredith	Sam	Teddy
Blaise	Devin	Jacky	Kiran	Morgan	Sammy	Tempest
Bobbie	Devon	Jada	Kit	Nicky	Sandy	Tierney
Bobby	Drew	Jaime	Kris	Nico	Sasha	Tracy
Brady	Dusty	Jamie	Kristen	Nikita	Shae	Tyler
Brodie	Eden	Jan	Kristian	Noël	Shannon	Valentine
Brogan	Effie	Jay	Larry	Ophrah	Sharman	Vivian
Brooke	Elisha	Jaye	Laurie	Paris	Shaun	Wilmot
Brooklyn	Ellis	Jean	Lee	Pat	Shawn	Winfred
Brynn	Ennis	Jerry	Leigh	Patrice	Shay	Wynne

Appendix 15:
Most Popular Names in England and Wales 2003

(Data supplied by Office for National Statistics)

Girls Rank	Name	Rank in 1998	Boys Rank	Name	Rank in 1998
1	Emily	2	1	Jack	1
2	Ellie	22	2	Joshua	5
3	Chloe	1	3	Thomas	2
4	Jessica	4	4	James	3
5	Sophie	5	5	Daniel	4
6	Megan	3	6	Oliver	20
7	Lucy	10	7	Benjamin	16
8	Olivia	16	8	Samuel	7
9	Charlotte	6	9	William	14
10	Hannah	7	10	Joseph	9
11	Katie	13	11	Harry	15
12	Ella	38	12	Matthew	6
13	Grace	36	13	Lewis	18
14	Mia	77	14	Luke	13
15	Amy	11	15	Ethan	47
=15	Holly	27	16	George	17
17	Lauren	8	17	Adam	21
18	Emma	15	18	Alfie	75
19	Molly	23	19	Callum	8
20	Abigail	21	20	Alexander	19
21	Caitlin	28	21	Ryan	12
22	Amelia	48	22	Mohammed	34
23	Bethany	14	23	Cameron	29
24	Lily	62	24	Connor	11
25	Rebecca	9	25	Charlie	33
26	Georgia	12	26	Ben	28
27	Leah	40	27	Jacob	27
28	Millie	66	28	Dylan	46
29	Eleanor	19	29	Liam	23
30	Jasmine	47	30	Nathan	25
31	Daisy	63	31	Jake	22
32	Elizabeth	30	32	Jamie	35
33	Alice	25	=32	Owen	43
34	Courtney	17	34	Max	50
35	Shannon	18	35	Tyler	61
36	Erin	79	36	Harvey	90
37	Isabella	89	37	Kieran	25
38	Abbie	52	38	Michael	24
39	Anna	41	39	Kyle	38
=39	Amber	31	40	Brandon	36
41	Freya	98	42	Louis	51
42	Isabelle	90	43	Aaron	30
43	Poppy	99	44	Bradley	31
44	Paige	32	45	Edward	43
45	Phoebe	43	=45	Reece	42
46	Sarah	18	47	Harrison	72
47	Isabel	96	48	Charles	40
48	Rachel	29	49	David	39
49	Aimee	67	50	Archie	below 100
50	Ruby	below 100			

Appendix 16:
Most Popular Names in Scotland 2004

(*Data supplied by General Register Office for Scotland*)

Boys			Girls		
Rank	**Name**	**Rank in 1998**	**Rank**	**Name**	**Rank in 1998**
1	Lewis	4	1	Emma	4
2	Jack	2	2	Sophie	11
3	James	6	3	Ellie	below 50
4	Cameron	5	4	Amy	4
5	Ryan	below 50	5	Chloe	5
6	Liam	15	6	Katie	17
7	Jamie	21	7	Erin	14
8	Ben	39	8	Emily	19
9	Kyle	19	9	Lucy	16
10	Callum	10	10	Hannah	10
11	Matthew	14	11	Rebecca	3
12	Daniel	12	12	Rachel	7
13	Connor	7	13	Abbie	48
14	Adam	26	14	Lauren	8
15	Dylan	22	15	Megan	below 50
16	Andrew	8	16=	Aimee	43
17=	Aidan	41	16=	Olivia	below 50
17=	Ross	3	18	Caitlin	6
19	Scott	9	19	Leah	below 50
20	Nathan	30	20	Niamh	47
21	Thomas	27	21	Sarah	13
22	Kieran	17	22	Jessica	33
23	Alexander	28	23	Holly	23
24	Aaron	32	24=	Eilidh	22
25	Joshua	46	24=	Anna	36
26	David	13	26	Molly	below 50
27	Finlay	below 50	27=	Nicole	12
28	Michael	16	27=	Zoe	37
29	Logan	below 50	29	Mia	below 50
30=	Luke	below 50	30	Isla	below 50
30=	Josh	below 50	31	Morgan	25
32	Aiden	below 50	32	Keira	below 50
33	William	38	33	Abigail	below 50
34=	Euan	33	34	Cara	below 50
34=	Sam	below 50	35	Shannon	9
36	Sean	20	36	Abby	below 50
37=	John	23	37	Eve	below 50
37=	Ethan	below 50	38	Charlotte	45
39	Samuel	below 50	39	Brooke	below 50
40=	Christopher	24	40	Grace	below 50
40=	Joseph	40	41	Louise	21
42	Fraser	34	42	Millie	below 50
43	Robert	31	43	Megan	below 50
44	Robbie	45	44	Kirsty	18
45	Jay	below 50	45=	Amber	below 50
46	Calum	25	45=	Beth	below 50
47=	Benjamin	below 50	47	Taylor	below 50
47=	Owen	below 50	48	Jodie	below 50
49	Craig	18	49	Eva	below 50
50	Mark	29	50	Jenna	below 50

Appendix 17:
Most Popular Names in the Republic of Ireland 2004

(Data from the Central Statistics Office Ireland)

Boys			Girls		
Rank	**Name**	**Rank in 1998**	**Rank**	**Name**	**Rank in 1998**
1	Sean	2	1	Emma	5
2	Jack	3	2	Sarah	3
3	Adam	5	3	Aoife	4
4	Conor	1	4	Ciara	2
5	James	4	5	Katie	13
6	Daniel	10	6	Sophie	17
7	Michael	9	7	Rachel	7
8	Cian	12	8	Chloe	1
9	David	8	9	Amy	12
10	Dylan	7	10	Leah	27
11	Luke	15	11	Niamh	6
12	Ryan	16	12	Caoimhe	24
13	Aaron	6	13	Hannah	18
14	Thomas	17	14	Ella	94
15=	Darragh	28	15	Lauren	10
15=	Eoin	20	16	Megan	8
17	Joshua	52	17=	Kate	22
18	Ben	48	17=	Rebecca	9
19	Patrick	17	19	Jessica	19
20	Oisín	37	20	Emily	25

Appendix 18:
Most Popular Names in the United States 2003

(Data from the Department of Social Security)

Boys		**Girls**	
Rank	**Name**	**Rank**	**Name**
1	Jacob	1	Emily
2	Michael	2	Emma
3	Joshua	3	Madison
4	Matthew	4	Hannah
5	Andrew	5	Olivia
6	Joseph	6	Abigail
7	Ethan	7	Alexis
8	Daniel	8	Ashley
9	Christopher	9	Elizabeth
10	Anthony	10	Samantha
11	William	11	Isabella
12	Ryan	12	Sarah
13	Nicholas	13	Grace
14	David	14	Alyssa
15	Tyler	15	Lauren
16	Alexander	16	Kayla
17	John	17	Brianna
18	James	18	Jessica
19	Dylan	19	Taylor
20	Zachary	20	Sophia

Appendix 19:
Most Popular Names in Australia (New South Wales) 2003

(Data from the NSW Registry of Births, Deaths, and Marriages)

Boys		Girls	
Rank	**Name**	**Rank**	**Name**
1	Joshua	1	Emily
2	Jack	2	Jessica
3	Lachlan	3	Chloe
4	Thomas	4	Isabella
5	William	5	Sarah
6	Daniel	6	Emma
7	Benjamin	7	Georgia
8	Nicholas	8	Grace
9	Matthew	9	Ella
10	Samuel	10	Charlotte
11	Liam	11	Mia
12	Luke	12	Lily
13	Ryan	13	Zoe
14	Jayden	14	Jasmine
15	Jordan	15	Olivia
16	Alexander	16	Jade
17	Harrison	17	Holly
18	James	18	Caitlin
19	Michael	19	Amy
20	Ethan	20	Ruby

Appendix 20:
Most Popular Names in New Zealand 2003

(Data supplied by Statistics New Zealand)

Boys		**Girls**	
Rank	**Name**	**Rank**	**Name**
1	Joshua	1	Emma
2	Jack	2	Sophie
3	Benjamin	3	Ella
4	Samuel	4	Emily
5	Daniel	5	Jessica
6	Jacob	6	Hannah
7	Ethan	7	Olivia
8	James	8	Grace
9	Thomas	9	Charlotte
10	Matthew	10	Georgia
11	Liam	11	Sarah
12	William	12	Paige
13	Caleb	13	Isabella
14=	Luke	14	Caitlin
14=	Oliver	15	Lucy
16	Ryan	16	Holly
17	Jayden	17	Samantha
18	Cameron	18	Brooke
19	Connor	19	Kate
20	Logan	20	Lily

Appendix 21:
Most Popular Names in England and Wales 1954–2003

(Data from the Office for National Statistics)

Boys

Rank	1954	1964	1974	1984	1994	2003
1	David	David	Paul	Christopher	Thomas	Jack
2	John	Paul	Mark	James	James	Joshua
3	Stephen	Andrew	David	David	Jack	Thomas
4	Michael	Mark	Andrew	Daniel	Daniel	James
5	Peter	John	Richard	Michael	Matthew	Daniel
6	Robert	Michael	Christopher	Matthew	Ryan	Oliver
7	Paul	Stephen	James	Andrew	Joshua	Benjamin
8	Alan	Ian	Simon	Richard	Luke	Samuel
9	Christopher	Robert	Michael	Paul	Samuel	William
10	Richard	Richard	Matthew	Mark	Jordan	Joseph

Girls

Rank	1954	1964	1974	1984	1994	2003
1	Susan	Susan	Sarah	Sarah	Rebecca	Emily
2	Linda	Julie	Claire	Laura	Lauren	Ellie
3	Christine	Karen	Nicola	Gemma	Jessica	Chloe
4	Margaret	Jacqueline	Emma	Emma	Charlotte	Jessica
5	Janet	Deborah	Lisa	Rebecca	Hannah	Sophie
6	Patricia	Tracey	Joanne	Claire	Sophie	Megan
7	Carol	Jane	Michelle	Victoria	Amy	Lucy
8	Elizabeth	Helen	Helen	Samantha	Emily	Olivia
9	Mary	Diane	Samantha	Rachel	Laura	Charlotte
10	Anne	Sharon	Karen	Amy	Emma	Hannah

Appendix 22:
Most Popular Names in the United States 1954–2003

(Data from the Department of Social Security)

Boys

(Years 1954–1984 are based on 1% samples; 1994 and 2003 on 100% samples)

Rank	1954	1964	1974	1984	1994	2003
1	Robert	Michael	Michael	Michael	Michael	Jacob
2	Michael	John	Jason	Christopher	Christopher	Michael
3	John	David	Christopher	Matthew	Matthew	Joshua
4	James	Robert	David	Joshua	Joshua	Matthew
5	David	James	James	David	Tyler	Andrew
6	William	Mark	John	Daniel	Brandon	Joseph
7	Richard	William	Robert	James	Jacob	Ethan
8	Thomas	Richard	Brian	Robert	Daniel	Daniel
9	Mark	Thomas	William	John	Nicholas	Christopher
10	Gary	Joseph	Daniel	Ryan	Andrew	Anthony

Girls

(Years 1954–1984 are based on 1% samples; 1994 and 2003 on 100% samples)

Rank	1954	1964	1974	1984	1994	2003
1	Mary	Lisa	Jennifer	Jennifer	Jessica	Emily
2	Deborah	Mary	Amy	Jessica	Ashley	Emma
3	Linda	Maria	Michelle	Ashley	Emily	Madison
4	Debra	Susan	Angela	Amanda	Samantha	Hannah
5	Patricia =	Karen	Kimberly	Sarah	Sarah	Olivia
6	Susan =	Patricia	Heather	Stephanie	Taylor	Abigail
7	Barbara	Donna	Lisa	Nicole	Amanda	Alexis
8	Maria	Linda	Melissa	Elizabeth	Brittany	Ashley
9	Karen	Kimberly	Maria	Heather	Elizabeth	Elizabeth
10	Nancy	Elizabeth	Stephanie	Melissa	Megan	Samantha

Oxford Paperback Reference

The Concise Oxford Dictionary of Quotations
Edited by Elizabeth Knowles

Based on the highly acclaimed *Oxford Dictionary of Quotations*, this
paperback edition maintains its extensive coverage of literary and
historical quotations, and contains completely up-to-date material. A
fascinating read and an essential reference tool.

The Oxford Dictionary of Humorous Quotations
Edited by Ned Sherrin

From the sharply witty to the downright hilarious, this sparkling
collection will appeal to all senses of humour.

Quotations by Subject
Edited by Susan Ratcliffe

A collection of over 7,000 quotations, arranged thematically for easy
look-up. Covers an enormous range of nearly 600 themes from 'The
Internet' to 'Parliament'.

The Concise Oxford Dictionary of Phrase and Fable
Edited by Elizabeth Knowles

Provides a wealth of fascinating and informative detail for over 10,000
phrases and allusions used in English today. Find out about anything
from the 'Trojan horse' to 'ground zero'.

Oxford Paperback Reference

The Concise Oxford Dictionary of Art & Artists
Ian Chilvers

Based on the highly praised *Oxford Dictionary of Art*, over 2,500 up-to-date entries on painting, sculpture, and the graphic arts.

'the best and most inclusive single volume available, immensely useful and very well written'

Marina Vaizey, *Sunday Times*

The Concise Oxford Dictionary of Art Terms
Michael Clarke

Written by the Director of the National Gallery of Scotland, over 1,800 entries cover periods, styles, materials, techniques, and foreign terms.

A Dictionary of Architecture
James Stevens Curl

Over 5,000 entries and 250 illustrations cover all periods of Western architectural history.

'splendid ... you can't have a more concise, entertaining, and informative guide to the words of architecture'

Architectural Review

'excellent, and amazing value for money ... by far the best thing of its kind'

Professor David Walker

Oxford Paperback Reference

The Kings of Queens of Britain
John Cannon and Anne Hargreaves

A detailed, fully-illustrated history ranging from mythical and pre-conquest rulers to the present House of Windsor, featuring regional maps and genealogies.

A Dictionary of Dates
Cyril Leslie Beeching

Births and deaths of the famous, significant and unusual dates in history – this is an entertaining guide to each day of the year.

'a dipper's blissful paradise ... Every single day of the year, plus an index of birthdays and chronologies of scientific developments and world events.'

Observer

A Dictionary of British History
Edited by John Cannon

An invaluable source of information covering the history of Britain over the past two millennia. Over 3,600 entries written by more than 100 specialist contributors.

Review of the parent volume
'the range is impressive ... truly (almost) all of human life is here'
Kenneth Morgan, *Observer*

OXFORD

Oxford Paperback Reference

The Concise Oxford Dictionary of English Etymology
T. F. Hoad

A wealth of information about our language and its history, this
reference source provides over 17,000 entries on word origins.

'A model of its kind'

Daily Telegraph

A Dictionary of Euphemisms
R. W. Holder

This hugely entertaining collection draws together euphemisms from all
aspects of life: work, sexuality, age, money, and politics.

Review of the previous edition
'This ingenious collection is not only very funny but extremely
instructive too'

Iris Murdoch

The Oxford Dictionary of Slang
John Ayto

Containing over 10,000 words and phrases, this is the ideal reference for
those interested in the more quirky and unofficial words used in the
English language.

'hours of happy browsing for language lovers'

Observer

Oxford Paperback Reference

The Concise Oxford Companion to English Literature
Margaret Drabble and Jenny Stringer

Based on the best-selling *Oxford Companion to English Literature*, this is an indispensable guide to all aspects of English literature.

Review of the parent volume
'a magisterial and monumental achievement'

Literary Review

The Concise Oxford Companion to Irish Literature
Robert Welch

From the ogam alphabet developed in the 4th century to Roddy Doyle, this is a comprehensive guide to writers, works, topics, folklore, and historical and cultural events.

Review of the parent volume
'Heroic volume ... It surpasses previous exercises of similar nature in the richness of its detail and the ecumenism of its approach.'

Times Literary Supplement

A Dictionary of Shakespeare
Stanley Wells

Compiled by one of the best-known international authorities on the playwright's works, this dictionary offers up-to-date information on all aspects of Shakespeare, both in his own time and in later ages.

OXFORD

Oxford Paperback Reference

The Concise Oxford Dictionary of World Religions
Edited by John Bowker

Over 8,200 entries containing unrivalled coverage of all the major world religions, past and present.

'covers a vast range of topics ... is both comprehensive and reliable'
The Times

The Oxford Dictionary of Saints
David Farmer

From the famous to the obscure, over 1,400 saints are covered in this acclaimed dictionary.

'an essential reference work'
Daily Telegraph

The Concise Oxford Dictionary of the Christian Church
E. A. Livingstone

This indispensable guide contains over 5,000 entries and provides full coverage of theology, denominations, the church calendar, and the Bible.

'opens up the whole of Christian history, now with a wider vision than ever'

Robert Runcie, former Archbishop of Canterbury

OXFORD

More Art Reference from Oxford

The Grove Dictionary of Art

The 34 volumes of *The Grove Dictionary of Art* provide unrivalled coverage of the visual arts from Asia, Africa, the Americas, Europe, and the Pacific, from prehistory to the present day.

'succeeds in performing the most difficult of balancing acts, satisfying specialists while ... remaining accessible to the general reader'

The Times

The Grove Dictionary of Art – Online
www.groveart.com

This immense cultural resource is now available online. Updated regularly, it includes recent developments in the art world as well as the latest art scholarship.

'a mammoth one-stop site for art-related information'

Antiques Magazine

The Oxford History of Western Art
Edited by Martin Kemp

From Classical Greece to postmodernism, *The Oxford History of Western Art* is an authoritative and stimulating overview of the development of visual culture in the West over the last 2,700 years.

'here is a work that will permanently alter the face of art history ... a hugely ambitious project successfully achieved'

The Times

The Oxford Dictionary of Art
Edited by Ian Chilvers

The Oxford Dictionary of Art is an authoritative guide to the art of the western world, ranging across painting, sculpture, drawing, and the applied arts.

'the best and most inclusive single-volume available'

Marina Vaizey, *Sunday Times*

Oxford Paperback Reference

The Oxford Dictionary of Dance
Debra Craine and Judith Mackrell

Over 2,500 entries on everything from hip-hop to classical ballet, covering dancers, dance styles, choreographers and composers, techniques, companies, and productions.

'A must-have volume ... impressively thorough'

Margaret Reynolds, *The Times*

Who's Who in Opera
Joyce Bourne

Covering operas, operettas, roles, perfomances, and well-known personalities.

'a generally scrupulous and scholarly book'

Opera

The Concise Oxford Dictionary of Music
Michael Kennedy

The most comprehensive, authoritative, and up-to-date dictionary of music available in paperback.

'clearly the best around ... the dictionary that everyone should have'

Literary Review

More History titles from OUP

The Oxford History of the French Revolution
William Doyle

'A work of breath-taking range ... It is the fullest history to appear of the Revolutionary era, of the events preceding it and of its impact on a wider world. Masterfully written.'

Observer

The Twentieth Century World
William R. Keylor

The complete guide to world history during the last century.

Tudor England
John Guy

'Lucid, scholarly, remarkably accomplished ... an excellent overview.'

The Sunday Times

VISIT THE HIGHER EDUCATION HISTORY WEB SITE AT
www.oup.com/uk/best.textbooks/history

OXFORD